"The definitive book on rock and its origins in rhythm-and-blues."
—Henry Pleasants, *Saturday Review*

"The most exhaustive study yet of rock and roll and the music industry. . . . Few [rock books] can stand up to [Gillett's]. . . . It includes nearly everybody who was anybody, and is an invaluable reference. . . . It's really difficult to convey the breadth of this book. . . . Take your time, and have fun." —John Morthland, *Rolling Stone*

"The bible for rock writers and listeners alike . . . it is still the definitive history, exhaustive in its content and exhaustingly pleasurable to read." —*City Limits*

"This remains the best available rock history: the details and why they matter, in one volume. In the immortal words of Dobie Gray, 'the original is still the greatest.'" —Dave Marsh

"History has to begin somewhere, and the history of rock 'n' roll began with this fine book. It will be read for as long as people are interested in the subject." —Jon Landau, *The Phoenix*

"[Gillett] writes affectionately and often evocatively about songs and singers and he is politically alert without being politically bent—he doesn't confuse rock with revolution. He doesn't apologize for the subject, he doesn't jump on it, and he doesn't make any messianic claims for it. Best of all, the book is a reliable and carefully drawn map of an essentially uncharted territory."
—Michael Wood, *New Society*

"Both enthusiastic and exact, [this] is the best history of rock yet published." —*Time*

"An excellent, accurate and detailed account. . . . An invaluable guide not only to the music and the musicians of rock and roll but also to the record industry of the past quarter century."
—Philip Elwood, *San Francisco Examiner*

1945 **1950** **1955**

LEADBELLY
PETE SEEGER
HARRY BELAFONTE
KINGSTON TRIO
WOODY GUTHRIE
WEAVERS
PAUL ANKA
DION & BELMONTS
STAN FREBERG
ANDREW SISTERS
SPIKE JONES & HIS CITY SLICKERS
BOBBY DARIN
CONNIE FRANCIS
KAY STARR
BING CROSBY
FRANKIE LAINE
JOHNNIE RAY
CHORDETTES
PAT BOONE
BRENDA LEE
CHARLIE RICH
DON GIBSON
FRANK SINATRA
PEGGY LEE
GUY MITCHELL
PATTI PAGE
CREW CUTS
DIAMONDS
EVERLY BROTHERS
FREDDIE CANNON
JOHNNY HORTON
BILL MONROE & BLUEGRASS BOYS
ELLA MAE MORSE & FREDDIE SLACK
LES PAUL & MARY FORD
TENNESSEE ERNIE FORD
SANFORD CLARK
DUANE EDDY
JOHNNY & HURRICANES
CHET ATKINS
MARTY ROBBINS
JACK SCOTT
HANK THOMPSON
HANK SNOW
RED FOLEY
BUDDY HOLLY
CHAMPS
BOB WILLS & TEXAS PLAYBOYS
RICKY NELSON
JAN & DEAN
DELMORE BROTHERS
HANK WILLIAMS
MOON MULLICAN
BILL HALEY & HIS COMETS
GENE VINCENT & BLUE CAPS
EDDIE COCHRAN
RICHIE VALENS
BILL BLACK'S COMBO
JOHNNY CASH
IKE TURNER'S KINGS OF RHYTHM
HOWLIN' WOLF
JERRY LEE LEWIS
LITTLE JUNIOR PARKER
ELVIS PRESLEY
JOHN LEE HOOKER
CARL PERKINS
SONNY BOY WILLIAMSON
LITTLE WALTER
FREDDY FENDER
RONNIE HAWKINS & HAWKS
JIMMY REED
T BONE WALKER
LOWELL FULSON
MUDDY WATERS
B.B. KING
ELMORE JAMES
BO DIDDLEY
JOHNNY KIDD & PIRATES
JOHNNY 'GUITAR' WATSON
JOHNNY ACE
LOUIS JORDAN'S TYMPANY FIVE
EARL BOSTIC
CHUCK BERRY
CLIFF RICHARD
ROSCO GORDON
BOBBY BLAND
LITTLE WILLIE JOHN
EDDIE 'CLEANHEAD' VINSON
ROY BROWN
FATS DOMINO
LONNIE DONEGAN
LIONEL HAMPTON & HIS ORCHESTRA
LLOYD PRICE
EARL KING
HUEY SMITH & THE CLOWNS
CHRIS KENNER
JOE TURNER
WYNONIE HARRIS
GUITAR SLIM
SHIRLEY & LEE
PROFESSOR LONGHAIR
WILBERT HARRISON
BILL DOGGETT
TINY BRADSHAW
LUCKY MILLINDER ORCHESTRA
ROY MILTON
PERCY MAYFIELD
KING CURTIS
AMOS MILBURN
JAMES BROWN & FAMOUS FLAMES
JOE LIGGINS
RAY CHARLES
LITTLE RICHARD
BUDDY JOHNSON ORCHESTRA
IVORY JOE HUNTER
JOHNNY MOORE'S THREE BLAZERS
CHARLES BROWN
CHUCK WILLIS
DON & DEWEY
LARRY WILLIAMS
NAT KING COLE
RICHARD BERRY
PEREZ PRADO
JULIA LEE
NELLIE LUTCHER
JESSE BELVIN
ETTA JAMES
SAM COOKE
BROOK BENTON
ROY HAMILTON
BILLIE HOLIDAY
JOHNNY OTIS ORCHESTRA
DINAH WASHINGTON
LITTLE ESTHER
LaVERN BAKER
MICKEY & SYLVIA
JACKIE WILSON
JERRY BUTLER
RUTH BROWN
HANK BALLARD & MIDNIGHTERS
PLATTERS
CADILLACS
DRIFTERS
CLOVERS
COASTERS
INK SPOTS
RAVENS
ORIOLES
DOMINOES
DELLS
LITTLE ANTHONY & IMPERIALS
FIVE ROYALES
CLYDE McPHATTER & DRIFTERS
MOONGLOWS
FRANKIE LYMON & TEENAGERS
FLAMINGOS
CHANTELS
ROSETTA THARPE
ALEX BRADFORD
DIXIE HUMMINGBIRDS
SENSATIONAL NIGHTINGALES
ISLEY BROTHERS
CARAVANS
SWAN SILVERTONES
MAHALIA JACKSON
SOUL STIRRERS
JAMES CLEVELAND
PILGRIM TRAVELLERS
FIVE BLIND BOYS OF MISSISSIPPI

Careers of Influence

1960 1965 1970

FOUR SEASONS
PETER PAUL & MARY
BOB DYLAN
SIMON & GARFUNKEL
RASCALS
VELVET UNDERGROUND
CARLY SIMON
DON McLEAN
STEELY DAN
LOVIN SPOONFUL
TOMMY JAMES & SHONDELLS
JAMES TAYLOR
DR. HOOK & MEDICINE SHOW
DION
JOAN BAEZ
JERRY REED
GENE PITNEY
CAROLE KING
LITTLE EVA
NEIL DIAMOND
BOX TOPS
MERLE HAGGARD
DOLLY PARTON
THE BAND
JOE SOUTH
ALLMAN BROTHERS BAND
GEORGE JONES
CHIFFONS
LESLEY GORE
SIR DOUGLAS QUINTET
TAMMY WYNETTE
J.J.CALE
SHIRELLES
DIXIE CUPS
BOBBIE GENTRY
EAGLES
ROY ORBISON
SHANGRI-LAS
CREEDENCE CLEARWATER REVIVAL
LITTLE FEAT
JONI MITCHELL
BUFFALO SPRINGFIELD
RONETTES
BYRDS
MONKEES
RIGHTEOUS BROTHERS
CROSBY STILLS NASH & YOUNG
CRYSTALS
SONNY & CHER
TURTLES
DOORS
CANNED HEAT
NEIL YOUNG
PAUL REVERE & RAIDERS
MAMAS & PAPAS
MOTHERS OF INVENTION
DR JOHN
DEL SHANNON
TOM WAITS
CAPTAIN BEEFHEART & MAGIC BAND
RY COODER
MITCH RYDER & DETROIT WHEELS
BEACH BOYS
JEFFERSON AIRPLANE
GRATEFUL DEAD
JIMI HENDRIX EXPERIENCE
JANIS JOPLIN
VENTURES

WALKER BROTHERS
CREAM
JOHN MAYALL & BLUESBREAKERS
LED ZEPPELIN
ERIC CLAPTON
ADAM FAITH
DUSTY SPRINGFIELD
YARDBIRDS
FLEETWOOD MAC
WHO
THEM
PROCOL HARUM
SPRINGFIELDS
HOLLIES
DONOVAN
JEFF BECK
FREE
ROD STEWART
SEARCHERS
SPENCER DAVIS GROUP
TRAFFIC
SLADE
BEATLES
KINKS
VAN MORRISON
PINK FLOYD
AMEN CORNER
DAVE EDMUNDS
SMALL FACES
T.REX
SHADOWS
ANIMALS
MOODY BLUES
JOE COCKER
ROLLING STONES
DAVID BOWIE
MANFRED MANN
TROGGS
GEORGIE FAME & BLUE FLAMES

BIG YOUTH
PRINCE BUSTER
JIMMY CLIFF
SKATALITES
DESMOND DEKKER & ACES
U ROY
WAILERS
JOHNNY NASH
PIONEERS
MAYTALS
AARON NEVILLE
RANDY NEWMAN
SLIM HARPO
LEE DORSEY
IRMA THOMAS
ALLEN TOUSSAINT
METERS
HERB ALPERT
HUGH MASEKELA
DYKE & BLAZERS
SLY & FAMILY STONE
WAR
FREDDIE KING
ALBERT KING
BILL WITHERS
JOE SIMON
PERCY SLEDGE
CLARENCE CARTER
GLADYS KNIGHT & PIPS
JOE TEX
ARETHA FRANKLIN
BETTY WRIGHT
ARTHUR ALEXANDER
OTIS REDDING
CARLA THOMAS
BOOKER T. & M.G.s
WILSON PICKETT
ISAAC HAYES
JOHNNIE TAYLOR
AL GREEN
ANN PEEBLES
IKE & TINA TURNER
SAM & DAVE
CHUCK JACKSON
SOLOMON BURKE
DON COVAY
DIONNE WARWICK
KOOL & THE GANG
BEN E. KING
BABATUDE OLATUNJE
MONGO SANTAMARIA
RAY BARRETTO
DELFONICS
CHUBBY CHECKER
GARY US BONDS
PATTI LABELLE
O'JAYS
INTRUDERS
ARCHIE BELL & DRELLS
STYLISTICS
HAROLD MELVIN & BLUENOTES
SPINNERS
GENE CHANDLER
IMPRESSIONS
MAJOR LANCE
RAMSEY LEWIS TRIO
TYRONE DAVIS
EMOTIONS
CHI-LITES
CURTIS MAYFIELD
EARTH WIND & FIRE
MARY WELLS
BARBARA LEWIS
STEVIE WONDER
JUNIOR WALKER
DRAMATICS
OHIO PLAYERS
PARLIAMENT
MARVELETTES
MARVIN GAYE
DIANA ROSS & SUPREMES
EDWIN STARR
FUNKADELIC
SMOKEY ROBINSON & MIRACLES
MARTHA & VANDELLAS
JACKSON FIVE
FOUR TOPS
STAPLE SINGERS
TEMPTATIONS

PART I

THEY GOT WHAT THEY WANTED: ROCK 'N' ROLL, 1954-61

Library of Congress Cataloging in Publication Data

Gillett, Charlie.
The sound of the city: the rise of rock and roll / Charlie Gillett—2nd ed., newly illustrated and expanded.
p. cm.
"1st Da Capo Press ed."—Verso of t.p.
Originally published: Rev. & expanded ed. New York: Pantheon Books, c1984. With new introd., photo section, discography (p.), and bibliography (p.).
Includes index.
ISBN-10: 0-306-80683-5 ISBN-13: 978-0-306-80683-4
1. Rock music—United States—History and criticism. I. Title.
ML3534.G54 1996 95-49510
781.66'09—dc20 CIP
MN

First Da Capo Press edition 1996

This Da Capo Press paperback edition of *The Sound of the City* is an unabridged republication of the edition published in New York in 1983 with the addition of a new introduction, a new photo section, and a new section on Recommended records; a new bibliography has been substituted for the previous one. It is reprinted by arrangement with Souvenir Press Ltd., London.

Published by Da Capo Press, Inc.
A member of the Perseus Books Group

CONTENTS

I, too, hear America singing
But from where I stand
I can only hear Little Richard
and Fats Domino
But sometimes,
I hear Ray Charles
Drowning in his own tears
or Bird
Relaxin' at Camarillo
or Horace Silver, Doodling
Then I don't mind standing a little longer.

Julian Bond

INTRODUCTION TO THE DA CAPO EDITION

When the first edition of *The Sound of the City* was published in 1970, it felt as if the rock 'n' roll music of the mid-fifties was about to become just another dim memory from a bygone era. Perceived in its own time as the "teenage music" of its particular generation, over the next ten years rock 'n' roll had been buried ever deeper under several waves of music aimed at successive generations of teenagers, each championed as being better than anything and everything that had gone before.

It wasn't only the marketing men who wanted to move on and leave rock 'n' roll for dead. Most of the artists who were collectively classified as "rock 'n' rollers" were dismayed by a description which they suspected not only demeaned them, but also built in their own obsolescence—one generation's teenage idol was surely destined to be the next's has-been. Many couldn't move fast enough to claim some other territory—country music or nightclubs, Hollywood or Las Vegas. There were times during the late sixties when this writer's determination to identify, articulate and celebrate the "lasting qualities" of the new music of the mid-fifties felt as futile as trying to stop a steamroller with his bare hands.

But not long after the book came out, something strange began to happen: records from the fifties, which for ten years had been next-to-impossible to find, began to be played on the radio all over again. Over the next twenty-five years, the songs of Buddy Holly, Chuck Berry and the rest chalked up literally millions of radio plays, both in their original versions and in countless covers.

Meanwhile, the music of the sixties confounded most of the rules by hardly fading away at all in the years since. Where pop music had raced headlong, nonstop and breathless from the bland pop of the early fifties into the far-out underground explosions of the late sixties, during the seventies its pace slowed dramatically: the music of the past recovered its breath, caught up—and even moved ahead of the new stuff, continuing to sound as fresh, adventurous, and experimental as much of what followed.

This retroaction wasn't confined to the emergence of "gold" radio stations on the new FM wavelengths. Producers of TV ads, who had traditionally used custom-written music for their mentally-infectious "jingles," began during the seventies to put contemporary pop hits behind their hard-sell messages. In Britain, a handful of agencies made their reputations by choosing hip records in their campaigns for jeans, cars and beer, not only leading to revival hits for soul singers Marvin

Gaye, Ben E. King, and Percy Sledge, but shifting the electric blues of Muddy Waters and John Lee Hooker from "down-home" to "up-market."

In parallel, the film industry also began to target a new generation in the nostalgia market. As late as 1972, Peter Bogdanovitch used the pre-rock 'n' roll country and pop music of Hank Williams and Tony Bennett to represent the naive innocence of a small Texas town in *The Last Picture Show.* A year later, two film directors moved into the front line by powering their pictures with rock 'n' roll.

On the West Coast, writer-director George Lucas crammed almost forty well-established rock 'n' roll hits into *American Graffiti,* going far beyond any previous use of "found records" to hook the audience into his teen-dream scenario. Making ingenious use of a radio disc jockey played by real-life DJ Wolfman Jack, the film was an enormous success and launched the careers of actors Richard Dreyfuss and Ron Howard; in addition, the soundtrack double album topped the charts, featuring tracks which had been anthologized many times on "oldie-but-goodie" albums but never promoted beyond the collectors market.

In contrast to the popcorn, car-cruising, high-school-dance world of Lucas's *American Graffiti,* Martin Scorcese's *Mean Streets* used more obscure vocal group records alongside operatic arias to paint a darker and moodier picture, full of menace and near-psychotic behavior, in New York's Little Italy; despite compelling performances from newcomers Harvey Keitel and Robert de Niro, *Mean Streets* was not a box office hit, and there was no soundtrack album. But Scorcese's astute juxtaposition of records with the film's narrative was very influential on other directors (including Jonathan Demme, David Lynch, and Quentin Tarrantino), reinforcing the impact of *American Graffiti*'s commercial success and spurring Hollywood producers to pursue the potential of rock and pop soundtracks.

Since then, the film and music industries have moved ever closer, culminating in a succession of films with titles borrowed directly from hits of the fifties and sixties—*Pretty Woman, La Bamba, Stand By Me, Sea of Love.* So now, in the mid-nineties, the music of the mid-to-late-fifties seems no further away than it did in 1970, and in many ways seems closer. Songs which were once fondly-remembered secrets, shared among the people who happened to be teenagers at the time, are now just as familiar to people who weren't even born then.

On top of all that, the record industry has recycled its entire catalog in the new digital compact disc format. Now virtually every artist has a mass-marketed *Greatest Hits* collection (stretching a point for many one-hit and two-hit wonders); specialist boxed-set retrospectives not only present entire artist careers, but chronicle whole genres and record labels, packaging all those hard-to-find records with detailed sleeve notes which would have made researching this book a breeze had they been available at the time.

Among the mostly kind responses to the first edition of *Sound of the City,* several reviewers noted that it tailed off towards the end, as if the author either had not heard or did not like much of what was happening in the second half of the sixties. Neither was the case—I was simply too close to see and understand the patterns and connections. They had become easier to discern ten years later, when I made substantial revisions, particularly in the second half of the book, for the second edition which was first published in 1983 and is now made available again in the United States. In this edition, there is proper recognition for the generation of musicians born during the 1940s, whose impressionable years coincided with the impact of rock 'n' roll, and whose own creativity peaked during the mid-to-late sixties.

In looking for a "narrative thread" for the first edition, I honed in on what seemed to be the two principal roles in determining the quality of pop music records—artists and producers. These roles were "public" in the sense that they were listed on the sleeves and labels of records and in the *Billboard* charts, and were therefore readily available to the armchair and library researcher who wrote the first edition.

One of the book's main theses is that there were regional "patterns" of creativity in pop music. Many, if not most, of the interesting records made in the fifties and early-to-mid-sixties were recorded in a few regional studios, where the roles of artists, songwriters, producers and record label owners overlapped—where the artist or producer was also the songwriter, and/or where the producer was also the owner of the record label.

As I reviewed the events to be revised in the second edition, it became clear how important managers could be, particularly in Britain during the sixties, where all the major artists were managed by men with a sense of vision and purpose who were as important in directing their artists' energy as the producers in the recording studios. Having grasped their significance in Britain, I went back to acknowledge the contributions of some managers in the earlier period, notably the Nashville-based publisher-manager Wesley Rose, who took the Everly Brothers from Columbia to Archie Blayer's Cadence label, and Roy Orbison from RCA to Fred Foster at Monument. And for every manager who played a positive role, I could have found his opposite number, breaking up a successful label-artist relationship in pursuit of the promise of higher advances or royalties from another company. In 1959, when Atlantic's artists Ray Charles and Clyde McPhatter finally hit the pop top ten for the first time after six years with the label, both artists were persuaded by their managers to leave. Ray Charles went on to great success with ABC, and may never have regretted the move; but it was hard to see Irving Feld's logic in taking Clyde McPhatter to MGM and then to Mercury, away from the company which had nurtured him.

The unabashed bias of *The Sound of the City* is in favor of the independent record labels in their battles against the monolithic major companies—a bunch of little Davids against a few Goliaths. There's an inference that the little guys are the good guys, and not much sympathy for anyone who works for a major. In some ways, I was fortunate never to have actually met anybody from either side when I wrote the first edition, because if I had, I might not have been so sure that small was good and big was bad. Soon after the book came out, I spent time with three of the most famous major-label A&R men of the period, Milt Gabler (Decca), John Hammond and Mitch Miller (both at Columbia); considering how negatively I had portrayed the major labels, all three were remarkably hospitable to me, at pains to explain their point of view that a major company could not afford to tilt its A&R policy towards a youth market. Ironically, by the time I was talking to them, they had all been eased out of their positions, usurped by a younger generation of A&R men taking more or less the opposite view; I could only have sympathy for these semi-retired, middle-aged men, for whom music was the center of their lives—they had contributed so much to the reputations of companies whose receptionists now did not even know their names.

Meanwhile, journalists spoke to many of the artists who recorded for independent companies, and came back to report tales of fraud, deception, and unpaid royalties. There is always a danger in taking one period's attitudes and morality back in time, and inappropriately applying them to another era when they were not part of the general consciousness. Many of the men who formed independent labels had no sense of the artistic worth of what they or their musicians were doing—they were simply businessmen, buying a specified service for an agreed fee, in much the same way as they would employ a plumber or an accountant.

It was common practice to deny artists their entitlement as songwriters by buying their songs outright for twenty-five or fifty dollars, or simply by falsely claiming co-writing credits. There was no reason why the owners of independent record companies should not also act as publishers of the songs they released, which entitled them to retain fifty percent of the income from the songs they launched: they took financial risks in making the recordings, only a few of which recovered the further costs in manufacture, distribution and promotion.

But for many owners, who ploughed most of the company's income money back into the business, it was galling to see songwriters being entitled to personal income which the indie record men felt was mostly the result of their own entrepreneurial efforts; so some claimed all or part of the writer's fifty percent of songs which they had played no part in writing, composing, or arranging.

Sometimes, there was a nominal validity to the transactions: it was (and still is) technically legal to buy a song outright from a writer, for as little as twenty-five or fifty dollars, if the writer knowingly signed a contract of assignment in which he waived all rights to future earnings. In the forties and fifties, a song did not always carry the "weight" that is now attributed to it, in terms of being a "copyright"; in many cases the songs were made up in a few minutes at the start of the session or on the way to the studio, and the writer often felt that twenty-five dollars was fair payment for something that took so little effort. When the song did not even earn that much in royalties, the writer came out the winner.

On the West Coast in the fifties, Richard Berry was among several writers able to supply a song on demand at short notice, coming up with a few apt phrases over the standard chord changes for the offered price. But among his many songs which sank without trace was one which seven years later became one of the biggest songs of the era, "Louie Louie." The name "Richard Berry" was always credited as the writer, but having sold his interest outright for between fifty and seventy-five dollars (the figures vary in the reports), Berry himself received no income until more than twenty-five years after he wrote it, when attorneys on his behalf were able to establish that he had not been fully aware of his rights when making the original assignment.

In many cases, label owners credited themselves as writers, often using pseudonyms: at King Records in Cincinatti, owner Syd Nathan was "Lois Mann"; at Duke/Peacock, Don Robey put the name "Deadric Malone" under songs reputedly bought at twenty dollars a time from writers on the streets of Houston; at Modern/RPM in Los Angeles, the three Bihari brothers listed themselves as cowriters, adding "Josea," "Ling," or "Taub" to B.B. King's name—not until the late seventies did B.B.'s new manager retrieve B.B.'s share.

In New York, George Goldner used no alibis, simply adding his own name as cowriter alongside the actual writers; when he sold all his interests to Roulette's owner Maurice Levy to pay off gambling debts, "Goldner" was replaced by "Levy" in the writer credits for "Why Do Fools Fall in Love" and other songs. Maurice Levy gets mentioned only once in this book, which does scant justice to his influence on the industry; but it may fairly reflect his creative contribution. His company was one of the principal distributors in the New York area, with particular control over jukeboxes; his publishing company had several affiliate identities, while also representing the catalogs of others including the Chicago-based Chess family of labels; and he acted as personal manager not only for many artists, but also for disc jockeys, including Alan Freed.

Widely known to have gangster associations, Levy wielded inordinate influence on which records were installed in jukeboxes, got played on New York radio stations, and were distributed to stores throughout the Northeast. If the rest of the industry was dismayed by how many fingers he had in so many pies, or by the strongarm tactics with which he kept them there, they did nothing to show it; not until the early nineties did government investigators finally pin him down, take him to court, and have him jailed. Levy died in ignominious disgrace, but not before he had amassed a personal fortune and tainted the record business with sleazy tales of "cut-out" racketeering and payola associations.

Fortunately, there were several companies whose reputations have stood up to closer scrutiny, notably Specialty on the West Coast and Atlantic in New York, who both paid royalties at a time when it was not yet standard practice, and who never made "buy-outs" of songs from their writers. Atlantic owner Ahmet Ertegun's name appeared as writer of several hits by the Clovers, because he really did write them, along with several others—there's a fascinating rehearsal tape of Ahmet teaching Ray Charles the words of his song "Mess Around."

As more information comes to the surface, it is tempting to try to make this book more "definitive" by plugging the gaps and adjusting the balance of its judgments. But more facts could weigh the book down, and make it ever harder to sustain the narrative; no matter how many gaps are plugged, others remain and new ones appear. What bothers me more is that I sometimes slid too fast past records which I now wish I had given more space to, to point out their enduring qualities. At the time I consciously avoided too many superlatives, hoping to indicate the significance of some artists or records simply by mentioning them; the purpose of the book was to explain their context—how they related to other artists and records—rather than write a full-blown and definitive aesthetic critique. But the result can sometimes be frustrating—how could I have flitted so quickly through references to Little Willie John or Jimmy Reed, without pausing to comment on the magical, apparently eternal, appeal of their records, the effectiveness of their astonishingly "visual" lyrics, the irresistible effect of their voices?

But here it stands, a rough guide rather than the final word. The revised bibliography includes several strongly-recommended books which join up some more of the dots. In response to the editor's request, for the first time we have added photographs, and thanks to the cooperation of the collectors involved we have been able to include several rarely-seen pictures. With the advantage of hindsight, this would have been a good idea the first time around—better late than never. And now there is also a list of recommended records which are likely to remain in catalog for a year or two at least. I hope you will find them, and play them as you read!

CHARLIE GILLETT
London
November 1995

INTRODUCTION

DANCING IN THE STREET

Calling out, around the world,
Are you ready for a brand new beat?
(*Martha and the Vandellas*)

The city's sounds are brutal and oppressive, imposing themselves on anyone who comes into its streets. Many of its residents, committed by their jobs to live in the city, measure their freedom by the frequency and accessibility of departures from it.

But during the mid-fifties, in virtually every urban civilization in the world, adolescents staked out their freedom in the cities, inspired and reassured by the rock and roll beat. Rock and roll was perhaps the first form of popular culture to celebrate without reservation characteristics of city life that had been among the most criticized. In rock and roll, the strident, repetitive sounds of city life were, in effect, reproduced as melody and rhythm.

This book attempts to identify the circumstances that produced rock and roll and to examine what is existence meant to those who listened to it. A number of assumptions are made here which are not always granted to popular culture, the most important one being that audiences or creators can determine the content of a popular art communicated through the mass media. The businessmen who mediate between the audience and the creator can be forced by either to accept a new style. The rise of rock 'n' roll is proof.

With rock 'n' roll, major corporations with every financial advantage were out-manoeuvred by independent companies and labels who brought a new breed of artist into the pop mainstream–singers and musicians who wrote or chose their own material, whose emotional and rhythmic styles drew heavily from black gospel and blues music. The corporations took more than ten years to recover their positions, through artists with similar autonomy and styles.

The structure of the book is simple. It begins by examining the emergence of rock 'n' roll and why it was so successful, then discusses the music that inspired rock 'n' roll, and closes with an examination of the music that evolved from it. Historically, the book covers roughly thirty years of American popular music–and its recent transatlantic influences. To keep the history manageable, I have recounted it primarily in terms of hit records as determined by *Billboard*, one of the trade magazines read by people in the popular music industry who want to keep in touch with current events and trends. (The other magazines are *Variety*, which is oriented mainly to the film world, but has sections on radio/TV and music, and *Cash Box* and *Record World*, which have formats similar to *Billboard*'s.)

Billboard focuses on music, and has substantial sections organized around record production and sales, publishing, juke box distribution (called "coin machine operating" in the trade), and radio. As guides for retailers, disc jockeys, juke box operators, and others with similar interests, *Billboard* during the fifties published three general lists that documented the state of the national popular music industry: one covered the twenty records that had sold the most copies in the previous week (popularly known as the "the hit parade" or "the top twenty"), a second covered the records that had been played most by disc jockeys, and a third covered the records that had been played most often on juke boxes. In the period with which we are concerned, these lists were supplemented by lists covering the best-selling records in the big cities across the nation, and by lists giving similar information (on sales, air-play, and jukebox exposure) in the industry's two specialty markets, "rhythm and blues" and "country and western". From a comparison of the lists, it is possible to trace the development of rock 'n' roll out of the previously entrenched musical forms–and to see the defensive tactics of the major music publishers, record companies, and radio networks as they sought to resist it.

One of the intriguing results of the popularity of rock 'n' roll was that both the role and the number of successful black singers became more prominent. Whereas during the forties and early fifties there were rarely as many as three black singers simultaneously in the popular music hit parades; after 1956 at least one fourth of the best-selling records were by black singers. Before rock 'n' roll the black singers tended to sing in variations of the white crooning style; afterwards they usually sang in their own cultural idioms.

Did this change indicate any difference in the way adolescents in particular thought about Negroes compared to the way many older white Americans had felt? This book does not provide an answer to the idealist's question that was part of the original inspiration behind the desire to examine rock 'n' roll. But while interracial tension became more evident during the period when this book was being written, there also seemed to be increasing numbers of young white people who rejected traditional attitudes of superiority towards black people, some of them working politically with (or for) black people and others adopting black cultural styles.

Did the change in the role of black singers reflect or affect a more general social change in the acceptance of black culture? Fats Domino presented more of the black culture to white people than Nat "King" Cole had done; and Ray Charles presented even more than both of them (for a while, anyway). And as first rhythm and blues, then pop-gospel, and finally, soul, became nationally recognized styles, the civil rights movement shifted from boycott through demonstration to riot. Again, this book cannot provide the answers to the question, but it is worth observing that the recent history of popular music partially follows what the sociologist Talcott Parsons describes as the process by which a minority group achieves social acceptance.

The first stage is *exclusion*, when the minority group as a whole is denied the privileges enjoyed by the rest of society. The second stage is *assimilation*, when these privileges are granted to favoured members of the minority group but continue to be withheld from the rest. The favoured few are accepted on the condition that they break most of their contacts with their own group and adopt the standards of the established society. The final stage is *inclusion*, when the entire minority group is granted access to everything in the society, without having to yield its distinctive characteristics. (This model differs from the conventional idea of integration, in which the members of the minority group reduce their interaction with one another, and increase the frequency of their contacts with the larger society.)

From the time popular music had been recorded, there had never been complete exclusion of Negro music, but there had been two kinds of assimilation. One of these was to accept black singers who adopted styles that were specially developed for the white audience (and so had little relation to styles popular with the black audience). The other was to take a song or style from the black culture and reproduce it using a white singer.

According to Parsons, inclusion can only be achieved when the established society modifies its relationship with the minority group, adjusting its attitudes and mobilizing its institutions to accommodate the group. Throughout the late forties and early fifties, increasing numbers of white adolescents became interested in black "rhythm and blues" music. By 1956 this group had grown so large that its taste was reflected in the hit parades. The change in attitudes (as the Parsons model suggests) forced a change in institutions. The large radio stations, which at first had resisted the broadcasting of records by black singers by suggesting that the words of the songs were corrupting America's youth, were obliged to play the records or give up their audience to the smaller stations that did play the records. The major record companies, which had recorded black singers with white styles, or white singers with black songs, yielded to smaller independent companies that recorded black singers with their own songs and styles.

Perhaps the whole shift in American popular music has only marginal relevance to the social relationships between black and white Americans. The English rock singer Eric Burdon has commented on the fact that he knew a southern white girl who considered the black singer Otis Redding to be the best in the world and at the same time despised black people in general. But this paradox might not be what it seems: it is possible that while the girl echoed her parents' feelings about black people in general, she might be sympathetic towards some Negroes she had personal contact with. In any case, these matters must remain beyond the scope of a study of the music and meaning of rock 'n' roll.

The function of popular music has not received much notice from sociologists, who perversely have spent more time assessing the impact of television despite the fact that many people from the ages of ten to twenty-five are more heavily exposed to radio and records. For many people in this age group, popular music provides a sense of change, as records and styles replace each other in the instant history of the hit parades. At any time in this history, each listener has a few records that enrich his feelings, extend his sense of love or despair, and feed his fantasies or fire some real relationship. He switches on the radio and waits for this music, or buys the records and plans his own programme of moods.

Faced with a daunting network of interlocking tastes in which no two people share the same set of preferences and dislikes, the radio stations have to programme their records so that nobody has to wait too long before he hears what he likes, and nobody has to endure too many records he actively dislikes. The result is a patchwork quilt of sound and moods in which few records can be too uncompromising or obtrusive, and through which the range of predictable emotions of the audience–elation, despondency, relaxation, tension–can be cultivated in turn. Some listeners use the radio to reinforce the mood they already have, while others hope that the radio will create some mood out of their apathy, and still others wish that some song would destroy their present mood and instil another.

Traditionally, popular music has used three modes of expression–sentimental, melodramatic, and trivial-novelty. Although the majority of popular songs have nominally been about love, rarely have they attempted to confront either the emotional or the physical reality of love relationships: *love, adore, care, need, want* were used as substitutes for expressing feeling, with dramatic overstatement or narcissistic simplification. *Charms* was the universal descriptive term, which simultaneously invoked the loved one's physical attractiveness and his or her personality. Singers were not concerned with real relationships, and their songs did not seem to be located in any real physical context.

Only by determined resistance to this fare did the audience of the mid-fifties force the music industry to provide something else: rock 'n' roll. Drawn in varying proportions from the music of southern country singers and northern city singers, rock 'n' roll was an improbable cultural mixture that had magical effects on those who heard it, whether in the form of Chuck Berry chiding "Maybellene, why can't you be true", or Gene Vincent wailing in tortured delight "Well, Be-Bop-A-Lula, She's my Baby". Cars, streets, suede shoes, alleys, hotels, motels, freeways, juke boxes, stations, parties, and parents provided the context in which singers began to consider love that not only had physical aspects but also was not inevitably eternal. Absorbing this music without necessarily thinking much about it, the generations of popular music audiences since 1956 have formed quite different sensibilities from the preceding generations which were raised on sentiment and melodrama. Members of these preceding generations were in charge of most of the record companies, and tried hard to reinstate the music they preferred. Now, more than ten years later, these men are giving way in the record companies to younger people who were raised on rock 'n' roll and whose influence, in all likelihood, is responsible for the rapid acceptance of radically new styles by companies that once adamantly resisted the novelty of rock 'n' roll.

PART I

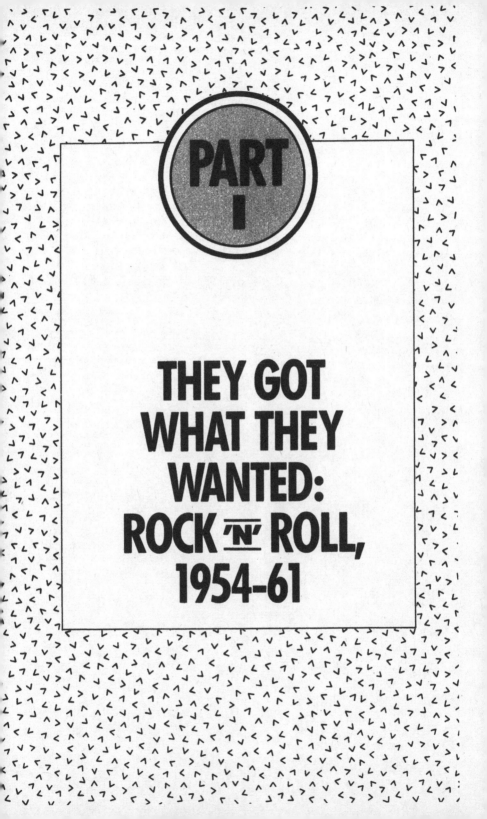

THEY GOT WHAT THEY WANTED: ROCK 'N' ROLL, 1954-61

1 THE SOUND BEGINS

In tracing the history of rock and roll, it is useful to distinguish *rock 'n' roll*–the particular kind of music to which the term was first applied–both from *rock and roll*–the music that has been classified as such since rock 'n' roll petered out around 1958–and from *rock*, which describes post-1964 derivations of rock 'n' roll.

It is surprisingly difficult to say when rock 'n' roll "started". The term had been in use in blues songs to describe lovemaking long before it came to signify a dance beat. By 1948 it was being used in a number of songs to suggest both lovemaking and dancing–in "Good Rockin' Tonight" (recorded by Roy Brown) and in "Rock All Night Long" (the Ravens, and many others). In 1951 Gunter Lee Carr recorded a straight dance song, "We're Gonna Rock", dropping the sexual implication, and a year later Alan Freed, the disc jockey who was to rise to fame on rock 'n' roll, named his radio show "Moondog's Rock and Roll Party". But as a kind of music, rock 'n' roll did not make its impact on the national popular music market until 1953, when "Crazy Man Crazy", a recording by Bill Haley and His Comets, became the first rock 'n' roll song to make the best-selling lists on *Billboard*'s national chart.

By the early fifties, the interrelated institutions of major music publishers, record companies, and radio networks, which between them constituted the effective source of power in the popular music industry, were all threatened by rock 'n' roll's writer performers and the businessmen who helped them find their audience.

I

Publishers had dominated the popular music industry since the years before music was recorded. Sales of sheet music to amateur and professional musicians were then the major source of revenue in the industry. The introduction of records did not immediately change this: the early inventors of sound recording were more interested in the spoken word than in music, and more in classical or serious music than in popular music. Thus, well into this century, live performances of songs were more important to the publishers than were the firms that recorded them.

In the early years of the century, the most important source of new live songs was vaudeville and music halls, and many publishers had their offices close to the 27th Street vaudeville theatres in Manhattan, an area that became known as "Tin Pan Alley". When stage musicals began replacing vaudeville in its role of introducing new songs, publishers began moving uptown. By the end of the 1930s "Tin Pan Alley" was the area in the forties and lower fifties close to Broadway.

The record companies took their cues from the publishers, and up to the end of the thirties the vast majority of recorded music were "show tunes", or sounded like show tunes. They ranged from the witty comments of Cole Porter on love and society, through the elegant ballads of Hoagy Carmichael and Lorenz Hart, to the nonsense novelties of numerous long-forgotten writers. Occasionally there were writers like George Gershwin, with aspirations to make popular music as complicated as classical music.

Towards the end of the thirties, Tin Pan Alley and its show tunes were challenged briefly and in an indirect way by the sudden trend to the orchestral "name" bands, whose "swing" music was a derivation of the Kansas City jazz style developed by various black bands in the late twenties and early thirties. So far as we can tell from record sales, the spirit of these bands brought a welcome change from the bland temper of the lighthearted show tunes. The record industry revived from a depression which had seen sales slump from $106,000,000 in 1921 to a little over 5 per cent of that, $6,000,000, in 1933. By 1939, with the big bands, the figures had recovered to $44,000,000.

Records by the bands dominated the best-selling lists from 1937 to 1941. During this period band recordings accounted for twenty-nine of the forty-three records that sold over a million copies each.[1] The publishing houses were affected because the repertoires of the swing bands consisted mainly of original material written by band members, or compositions by the black band leaders (Count Basie, Jay McShann, and others) whose musical style was often imitated, or familiar songs given new arrangements, and so the houses had a hard time introducing new songs.

But they came into demand again from 1942 to 1945, as the vocalists with the bands began to gain more prominence. The shift from the bandleader to the singer was begun by the bandleaders themselves, who competed with one another by featuring their increasingly famous singers. The strategy soon backfired. While Glenn Miller's reputation always exceeded that of his singer, Tex Beneke, Frank Sinatra in particular began to attract more attention than the bandleaders he sang with (who included Tommy Dorsey and Harry James). The singers, in any case, depended on the publishing houses for their songs.

Since 1912 songwriters and publishers had protected their interests through ASCAP–the American Society of Composers, Authors and Publishers–who licensed performance rights to broadcasting outlets, primarily radio; in 1941 an association of radio stations set up a rival licensing organisation, BMI–Broadcast Music Incorporated–who represented many previously ignored writers and publishers (hillbilly, race, ethnic and foreign) whose business boomed during an ASCAP boycott on radio broadcasts in 1941.

The band vocalists, having re-established the need for new songs, were supplied with novelty songs and sing-along ballads. Perhaps the appeal of this material lay in its ability to relieve wartime tension, but even after the end of the war these songs continued to proliferate, in the company of growing numbers of the kind of sentimental and melodramatic ballads that were still in sway ten years later.

The singers of this kind of material were all influenced to some extent by the creator of the modern ballad style, Bing Crosby, whose light tenor, in its flexibility, gentle humour, and easy charm, was ideally suited to the needs of Tin Pan Alley material. Crosby had begun his career in vaudeville, where he developed the technique of singing quickly and wittily. Then, as a vocalist with Paul Whiteman, he had learned the techniques of singing with a megaphone (necessary before the days of electrical amplification if the singer was to make himself heard above the orchestra). The megaphone produced a curious deadpan and emotionless manner of expression, which was to form the basis of the "crooning" style that developed after microphones and electrical amplification were introduced.

Two distinct kinds of crooning were developed, one the smooth, "soft", emotionally relaxed style of Perry Como, the other the more angular-toned, "hard", involved style of Frank Sinatra. The soft style was best suited to sing-along novelty songs and sentimental ballads, while the hard style was better for more melodramatic songs. But singers of either style were expected by their record companies to handle all kinds of songs.

Hardly any vocalists wrote their own material, and their "creativity" was measured in their ability to improvise phrasing and impart meaning on Tin Pan Alley songs. The leading virtuosos were Billie Holiday, dry and bitter; Ella Fitzgerald, sweet and warm; Louis Armstrong, and Fats Waller, both gruff-voiced and humorous. But most so-called jazz singers were crooners whose ambitions outran their imaginations.

The most original of the ex-band vocalists was the hard crooner

Frank Sinatra, who rejected the style of singing that encouraged the audience to sing along with him, and instead took risks with melodies, improvising his own timing of phrases by stretching some syllables and cutting others. The effect was a personal style that gave specific meaning even to songs that had been written as conventional "general" love songs.

Sinatra's style involved audiences in his singing–and in him–as no previous singer had done, and stimulated devotion comparable to that previously aroused only by film stars like Rudolph Valentino. The audiences willingly confused Sinatra's image with his private self, amplifying the character promoted by the singer's public relations staff and the press. Perhaps largely as a result of Sinatra's popularity, a singer's image became as important to his style and its effectiveness as the words of a song. Audiences expected singers to project themselves (or what was publicly known of their selves), and each listener wanted to feel as if the singer were singing to her (or for him, if the listener was male).

With this intense level of audience involvement in the singer's stage personality, the physical appearance of the singer became important. The conventional dark and handsome stereotype of the American romantic hero favoured the dark-complexioned singers of Italian descent who suddenly dominated the hit parades. Tony Martin, Al Martino, the Ames Brothers, the Four Aces, Dean Martin, Tony Bennett, Vic Damone, Sinatra, Como, and Frankie Laine were a few of the most successful, all of them helped at a crucial stage in their careers by night-club owners of Italian descent who were glad to feature them.

In terms of audience involvement, Frankie Laine, whose style was drawn from the western ballad style, from Al Jolson, and from Vaughn Monroe, inspired a following even more vociferous than Sinatra's with a series of unprecedented melodramatic epics of love and fury, including "That's My Desire" and "Jezebel". And in 1951, involvement rose to a new peak when another singer, for once not of Italian descent, inspired furores at airports, hotels, and backstage theatre doors–Johnnie Ray. In contrast to his predecessors, Ray lacked smoothness, precision of phrasing, or vocal control; instead, he introduced passionate involvement into his performance, allowing sighs, sobs, and gasps to become part of the sound relayed by the amplifiers. News of his style horrified observers across the Atlantic. The columnist Laurie Henshaw wrote in the British *Melody Maker* (February 9, 1952):

> Johnnie Ray, a 25-year-old Oregon-born vocalist, has jumped from the $90 to $2,000 bracket by hitting on the excruciating formula of virtually breaking into tears while singing a song.

> According to a U.S. report, "his stentorian sobbing sometimes so unhinges him that he has to rush offstage to compose himself". That this uninhibited and tasteless showmanship registers with American audiences is indicated that [sic], within eight weeks of issue, Johnnie's tearful version of "Little White Cloud That Cried" shot past the 1,000,000-sales mark.
>
> If an artist has to descend to this level to capture the masses, then the outlook for popular music is bleak indeed.

However bleak the future, the present was barren enough. Even Johnnie Ray was hardly as remarkable as the enthusiasm of his supporters, or the distaste of his decriers, would suggest. Only in comparison with the generally emotionless music of the times, to which Ray, like Laine, were exceptions, could the silly and sentimental "Cloud" have attracted anybody's interest.

II

Six major recording companies dominated the popular music market. All had their own distributing systems, which enabled them to ensure that each of their records would get to retailers in every regional market. Each of them had their own A&R staff–the Artist and Repertoire men who decided what singers to use and what records to issue. Independent record companies, in contrast, relied on a loose network of independent regional distributors, and had to persuade each one in turn to distribute their products. The independents specialized mainly in ethnic folk music and in rhythm and blues, and before 1953 they were of little significance in the popular-music market; of one hundred and sixty-three records that each sold over a million copies from 1946 to 1952, all but five were recorded by one of the six major companies.[2]

Of the major companies, two, Columbia and Victor, had survived from the early days of recording at the end of the last century. A third, Decca, had been founded as the American branch of British Decca in 1932, and like its rivals was based in New York. In 1942 the first major West Coast firm, Capitol, was established in Hollywood, and in 1946 the film corporation MGM set up a record-producing department, again in the film capital. In 1946 the Mercury Corporation was established in Chicago.

During the twenties, the big record companies had been challenged by a number of small independents, which had been particularly successful in the specialist markets of black music, especially the "race" market, as the Negro buyers of blues records were then classified. But the Great Crash at the end of the twenties undermined the independent companies, which either went bankrupt or were bought up by one of the majors.

By the end of the thirties, the major companies had a solid hold on the complete market for records, but during the war they yielded the specialist "race" and "new jazz" markets when forced to make economy cuts by the government ruling that customers must trade in an old record every time they bought a new one (so that the material could be melted down and used again). By the end of the war, a new generation of "indies" had established a firm hold on the "race" market, but the major labels had consolidated their grip on the "hillbilly" market, now becoming known as "country and western".

The term "country and western" was coined to escape the derogatory associations of "hillbilly", but the new phrase soon became as limiting as the one it had replaced. "Country" music was never literally played only by and for people who lived in rural areas, but represented that strain of pop music which presented "real" attitudes and situations in a "sincere" manner and with "traditional" musical accompaniment. Country music shared roots in gospel music with black music, and during the forties probably absorbed more elements of black music than were accepted into the mainstream pop of the time. Decca's "sacred" country singer Red Foley recorded gospel songs written in the thirties by the black composer Thomas Dorsey; Ernest Tubb, also with Decca, updated the white blues style of Jimmie Rodgers by introducing electrically-amplified guitar into what became known as a "honky tonk" style. For Columbia, both Roy Acuff and Bill Monroe showed black influences in their respective "Smokey Mountain" and "Blue Grass" styles, while the Delmore Brothers (for King, one of the few indie labels in the country market) and several others played what they called "hillbilly boogie". When Hank Williams emerged on the new MGM label in the late forties, he shook all these black-influenced country styles together, using as strong a beat as his recording supervisor Fred Rose would sanction.

As head of Acuff-Rose Music and A&R man for MGM's country division, Fred Rose was one of a coterie of businessmen who centralized the country and western industry in Nashville, Tennessee, a process which led to the virtual elimination of most of the "western" associations of the term "country and western", in particular the western swing of bands like Bob Wills and his Texas Playboys. As if hoping to deny the strain of black music implicit in most country styles, there was a virtual embargo on drums in Nashville recording sessions and, more relevant in this period, broadcasts on WSM's "Grand Ole Opry", the premier radio showcase for country music.

Radio was a more important outlet than records were for country music, and although the majority of country radio shows were at off-peak hours on low-wattage stations in small towns, they provided the framework for performers to develop their style, repertoire, and reputation which enabled the most determined to get exposure on one of the big five shows beamed across several states–"The Barn Dance" from WLS in Chicago, the "Midwestern Hayride" on WLW in Cincinnati, the "Big D Jamboree" on KRLD in Dallas, the "Louisiana Hayride" on KWKH in Shreveport, and the "Opry" on WSM. (The names of these shows recur in the life stories of every country artist, among which *Country Gentleman* by Chet Atkins is particularly well-told and evocative.)[3]

The influence of the "Opry" became increasingly apparent during the early fifties as firms based in Nashville outran rivals based elsewhere–talent booking agencies, publishers, recording studios, and the record companies themselves. Decca was the first company to set up a Nashville office, with Paul Cohen as head of A&R, and the other majors followed suit with Columbia appointing Don Law, Capitol setting up Ken Nelson, and RCA-Victor's Steve Sholes deputing Chet Atkins to oversee the Nashville office.

Most of the companies regarded "country and western" as a specialist music without pop appeal, but during the late forties and early fifties some of the pop A&R men began to exploit the BMI affiliation of most country publishers by recording pop covers of country songs; Mitch Miller was particularly adept, first at Mercury where he produced the enormous hit version of "Tennessee Waltz" by Patti Page, and then at Columbia where virtually every major artist on his roster had at least one million-selling version of a country song. This practice of covers benefitted the publishers, among whom the leaders were Nashville-based Acuff-Rose and two New York-based companies, Peer-Southern and Hill and Range; but most country artists were shut out of the pop charts, even the remarkable Hank Williams, whose songs proved universally adaptable. Among the few country artists who did occasionally cross over to the pop, most recorded for Capitol's West Coast A&R department, whose promotion team brought pop hits home as "novelty" records for Red Ingle and his Natural Seven, Tex Williams, Merle Travis, Tex Ritter, Hank Thompson and Tennessee Ernie Ford.

But still, for an audience that lived predominantly in cities and sought its entertainment in their centres, the music that came out of the radios and juke boxes was incongruous. And there was, as increasing numbers of people were coming to realize, a much more appropriate alternative–rhythm and blues–and here the main companies were far less successful in satisfying what at first seemed to be only another speciality audience.

III

According to a report on rhythm and blues in a special edition of *Billboard* (March, 1954), the "Negro market" did not exist in a national sense until the end of the Second World War. Until that time, so-called race records, produced primarily by independent companies, tended to be distributed within particular areas–the East Coast, the Midwest, the South, the Southwest, and the West Coast. In the sixties, these areas still constituted distinct markets in that there were particular singers whose sales depended mainly on the local audiences within them. But now it is relatively easy for a company to distribute records across the country if there is a demand, which is usually created by disc jockeys playing the records in different areas.*

During the ten years after the War, Los Angeles had the largest number of successful independent companies specializing in rhythm and blues. (On occasion, a few firms offered hillbilly or country and western catalogues.) The companies included Specialty, Aladdin, Modern, Swingtime, and Imperial. But across the country, similar types of record companies were established from humble beginnings in garages, store-rooms, and basements, with early distribution carried out by the owners from the trunks of their cars. King, in Cincinnati; Peacock, in Houston; Chess, in Chicago; Savoy, in Newark New Jersey; and Atlantic, in New York, were all founded between 1940 and 1950, a decade in which as many Negroes (one and a quarter million) left the South as had done so in the previous thirty years. By 1952 there were over one hundred independent companies in business (apart from many others which had failed to last), many of them specializing in rhythm and blues.†

In almost every respect, the sounds of rhythm and blues contradicted those of popular music. The vocal styles were harsh, the songs explicit, the dominant instruments–saxophone, piano, guitar, drums–were played loudly and with an emphatic dance rhythm, the

* *The man responsible for enabling greater mobility of distribution between regions was a Los Angeles distributor, Jack Gutshall, who established a national network in 1945.*

† *In a* Billboard *survey of the proliferation of independent companies (5 September, 1953), Bob Rolontz wrote: "there is a street in New York that is rarely visited by dealers, publishers, A & R men, and other distinguished members of the music fraternity. It has no plush restaurants, no uniformed elevator operators, and few Cadillacs. Pushcart peddlers still sell hot dogs and pop from their carts and on hot summer days no male wears a coat or tie. Yet it is, in a competitive sense, one of the most vital and stimulating avenues of the music business. The street is Tenth Avenue, and in the area bounded on the North by 56th Street and the South by 42nd Street are poured daily the hard work and boundless optimism of a score of indie labels, indie distributors, one-stops, and juke-box distributors. . . . Over the years, the Tenth Avenue independent companies have furnished the larger firms with personnel, ideas and records to cover."*

production of the records was crude. The prevailing emotion was excitement.

Only some Negro records were of this type, but they were played often enough on some radio programmes to encourage the listeners who found these programmes to stay tuned. The other records played were similar to the music already familiar in the white market. But as the white listeners began to understand the different conventions by which black audiences judged their music, they came to appreciate the differences between the sing-along way white singers handled ballads, and the personal way black groups handled them.

The early and fullest impression on the new white audience of these stations was made by the dance blues–whose singers included Amos Milburn, Roy Brown, Fats Domino, and Lloyd Price–which provided a rhythm and excitement not available in white popular music. At first the number of white people interested in this music was not enough to have much effect on the sales of popular music. This portion of the audience probably consisted at first of college and a few high school students who cultivated an "R & B cult" as most of their equivalents earlier (and even then) cultivated a jazz cult.

By a happy coincidence, we happen to have some observations of remarkable insight made by the sociologist David Riesman on the popular music audience in this period, which illuminate the character of the specialist audience. In an article, "Listening to Popular Music", Riesman noted that two groups could be identified: the majority audience, which accepted the range of choices offered by the music industry and made its selections from this range without considering anything outside it; and the minority audience, which he described with details that are relevant here.

> The minority group is small. It comprises the more active listeners, who are less interested in melody or tune than in arrangement or technical virtuosity. It has developed elaborate, even over-elaborate, standards of music listening; hence its music listening is combined with much animated discussion of technical points and perhaps occasional reference to trade journals such as *Metronome* and *Downbeat*. The group tends to dislike name bands, most vocalists (except Negro blues singers), and radio commercials.
>
> The rebelliousness of this minority group might be indicated in some of the following attitudes towards popular music: an insistence on rigorous standards of judgment and taste in a relativist culture; a preference for the uncommercialized, unadvertised small bands rather than name bands; the development of a private language and then a flight from it when the private language (the

same is true of other aspects of private style) is taken over by the majority group; a profound resentment of the commercialization of radio and musicians. Dissident attitudes towards competition and cooperation in our culture might be represented in feelings about improvisation and small "combos"; an appreciation for idiosyncrasy of performance goes together with a dislike of "star" performers and an insistence that the improvisation be a group-generated phenomenon.

There are still other ways in which the minority may use popular music to polarize itself from the majority group, and thereby from American popular culture generally: a sympathetic attitude or even preference for Negro musicians; an egalitarian attitude towards the roles, in love and work, of the two sexes; a more international outlook, with or without awareness, for example, of French interest in American jazz; an identification with disadvantaged groups, not only Negroes, from which jazz springs, with or without a romantic cult of proletarianism; a dislike of romantic pseudo-sexuality in music, even without any articulate awareness of being exploited; similarly a reaction against the stylized body image and limitations of physical self-expression which "sweet" music and its lyrics are felt as conveying; a feeling that music is too important to serve as a backdrop for dancing, small talk, studying, and the like; a diffuse resentment of the image of the teenager provided by the mass media.

To carry matters beyond this descriptive suggestion of majority and minority patterns, requires an analysis of the social structure in which the teenager finds himself. When he listens to music, even if no one else is around, he listens in a context of imaginary "others"–his listening is indeed often an effort to establish connection with them. In general what he perceives in the mass media is framed by his perception of the peer-groups to which he belongs. These groups not only rate the tunes but select for their members in more subtle ways what is to be "heard" in each tune. It is the pressure of conformity with the group that invites and compels the individual to have recourse to the media both in order to learn from them what the group expects and to identify with the group by sharing a common focus for attention and talk.[4]

Riesman's observation that no matter what the majority chooses, there will be a minority choosing something different explains how popular music continues to change, no matter how good–or bad–the dominant types of music are at any particular period. And because the minority audience defines itself as being radical within the music audience, its taste is likely to favour, consciously or unconsciously, music with some element of social comment or criticism in it.

During the early fifties, young people like those described by Riesman turned in increasing numbers to rhythm and blues music, and to the radio stations that broadcast it. If the first listeners were those with relatively sophisticated standards for judging music, those that came later included many whose taste was more instinctive, who liked the dance beat or the thrilling effect of a hard-blown saxophone, people who may have found the rough voices of the singers a bit quaint and appealing as novelties.

It was this second group of listeners who provided the inspiration and audience for Alan Freed, who, with Bill Haley, played a crucial role in popularizing rhythm and blues under the name "rock 'n' roll".

Alan Freed was a disc jockey on an evening quality music programme in Cleveland, Ohio, when he was invited, sometime in 1952, to visit a downtown record store by the owner, Leo Mintz. Mintz was intrigued by the musical taste of some of the white adolescents who bought records at his store, and Freed was amazed by it. He watched the excited reaction of the youths who danced energetically as they listened to music that Freed had previously considered alien to their culture–rhythm and blues. He recalled (in the British *New Musical Express*, September 23, 1956):

> I heard the tenor saxophones of Red Prysock and Big Al Sears. I heard the blues-singing, piano-playing Ivory Joe Hunter. I wondered. I wondered for about a week. Then I went to the station manager and talked him into permitting me to follow my classical programme with a rock 'n' roll party.

At Mintz's suggestion, Freed introduced a euphemism for rhythm and blues by calling his show "Moondog's Rock 'n' Roll Party", which started in June, 1951. By March, 1952 Freed was convinced he had enough listeners to justify promoting a concert featuring some of the artists whose records he had been playing. "Moondog's Coronation Ball" was to be staged at the Cleveland Arena, capacity 10,000; but according to firemen's estimates more than 21,000 people showed up, mostly black, causing such a panic that the show had to be called off (as reported in the *Cleveland Press*). Abandoning the idea of holding mammoth dances, Freed persevered with reserved-seat shows, and climaxed his career in Cleveland in August, 1953 with a bill that featured the Buddy Johnson Orchestra, Joe Turner, Fats Domino, the Moonglows, the Harptones, the Drifters, Ella Johnson, Dakota Staton, and Red Prysock.

Freed's success among white audiences with Negro music was widely reported in *Billboard*, and in 1954 he was signed by a New York station, WINS, which he quickly established as New York's leading popular music station. He continued to champion the original Negro performers of songs which were "covered"–recorded by someone else–for the white market by the major companies, and in interviews he accused other disc jockeys of prejudice when they preferred to play the cover versions.

Once the new audience became apparent, juke-box distributors began putting rock 'n' roll records in juke boxes, which then provided a new channel of communication for white record buyers who did not yet tune in to the Negro radio stations. At the same time, in response to the new demand for uptempo dance tunes with a black beat from audiences at dance halls, a number of white groups were incorporating rhythm-and-blues-type material into the repertoires. It was with such a song, "Crazy Man Crazy", recorded for the independent Essex, that Bill Haley and His Comets made their first hit parade appearance in 1953 and pushed rock 'n' roll up another rung of popular attention.

By the end of 1953, at which point the Negro market comprised only 5.7 per cent of the total American record sales market, a number of people in the music industry were beginning to realize the potential of Negro music and styles for at least a segment of the white market. Decca took a chance and considerably outpaced its rival major companies by contracting Haley from Essex. At his first session with Decca, he recorded "Rock Around the Clock" and "Shake, Rattle and Roll", which between them were to transform throughout the world the conception of what popular music could be.

Haley's records were not straight copies of any particular black style or record. The singer's voice was unmistakably white, and the repetitive choral chants were a familiar part of many "swing" bands. In these respects the music was similar to a style known as "western swing" (and in particular a group called Bob Wills and His Texas Playboys). But the novel feature of Haley's style, its rhythm, was drawn from black music, although in Haley the rhythm dominated the arrangements much more than it did in Negro records. With Haley, every other beat was heavily accented by the singers and all the instrumentalists at the expense of the relatively flexible rhythms and complex harmonies of dance music records cut for the black audience.

"Shake, Rattle and Roll" was in the top ten for twelve weeks from September, 1954; "Rock Around the Clock" was in the list for nineteen weeks, including eight at the top, from May, 1955. By the summer of 1955, roughly two years after Haley's "Crazy Man Crazy", with most of the majors still moving uncertainly, the demand for records with an insistent dance beat was sufficient for three independently manufactured records to reach the top ten in record sales–"Seventeen" by Boyd Bennett (King), "Ain't That a Shame" by Pat Boone (Dot), and "Maybellene" by Chuck Berry (Chess), the last recorded by a black singer.

IV

The growth of rock 'n' roll cannot be separated from the emergence, since the Second World War, of a new phenomenon: the adolescent or youth culture. Since the War, adolescents have made a greater show of enjoying themselves than they ever did before. Their impact has been particularly sharp because there were so few facilities that easily accommodated their new attitudes, interests, and increased wealth. Neither individual communities nor the mass communication industries anticipated the growth of adolescent culture, or responded quickly to it.

The initial reaction of society was generally disapproving, which served to reinforce whatever rebellious feelings existed among the adolescents, thereby contributing to an identity and a style which were fostered until, by the early fifties, adolescents really seemed to consider themselves a "new breed" of some kind. Among the creators of popular culture, this self-impression was fostered in particular by Hollywood, whose producers began to adjust their films to the realization that an increasing proportion of their audience were in their teens.

Apart from various films dealing with the general social life of adolescents (in family, school, and leisure situations), there were two pictures in the first half of the fifties that focused specifically on the generation conflicts of the time, *The Wild One* (1954) and *Rebel Without a Cause* (1955). With Marlon Brando and James Dean, respectively, these pictures provided figures with whom the new teenagers could identify, figures whose style of dress, speech, movement, facial expressions, and attitudes helped give shape and justification to unrealized feelings in the audience. The plot in both films was clumsy, artificial, and morally compromised, but the undercurrents of frustration and violence in each were sufficient to give the films credibility. The sullen defiance of Brando and the exploited integrity of Dean were simultaneously reflections of and models for large segments of the audience.

Cinema was at this time the epitome of "mass culture", drawing situations from the lives of its audience, ordering these situations to fit a dramatic plot, and then returning the packaged product to its source as entertainment. There was little real interchange between the producers and the customers; the customers, having no alternative source of films, could only choose from what was made available to them, and the producers measured their audience's taste almost entirely in terms of the way they spent money. The producers thus tended to put their own money into formulas that had already proved successful. New ideas were notoriously difficult to introduce into this arrangement.

Despite these rigidities, the film industry realized and responded to the needs of its audience faster than did the music industry. The film industry, for example, was prepared to accept Negro styles of speech into scripts much faster than ASCAP would allow these styles to infiltrate radio broadcasts: "Dig", "flip", "cat", "jive", "square", and the rest of be-bop talk all made their way on to the screen with apparently no strong opposition–although of course black people themselves weren't very often evident on the screen. So, while in the film the images and the script were telling a new story in new words, as in *The Wild One* and *Rebel Without a Cause*, the music on the sound track remained the big band music that the new young audience had already rejected. Their rejection became explicit in a third film, *Blackboard Jungle* (released in 1955, the same year as *Rebel Without a Cause*), which was a major factor in accelerating the popularity of rock 'n' roll.

Blackboard Jungle, adapted from the novel by Evan Hunter, was about a teacher's experience in a vocational high school in the Bronx. His students, of various national and racial origins, were near-delinquents whose threatened violence gave the plot most of its dramatic strength.

One of the main scenes in the novel, where the students came into open defiance and conflict with a teacher, described an attempt by a teacher to establish rapport with his class by playing records from his collection. He began with Bunny Berigan's "I Can't Get Started". The collective reaction of the class was: "So it's a guy singing. Does he stack up against Como? Where does he shine to Tony Bennett? Guys singing are a dime a dozen. . . . Ain't he got no stuff by The Hill-toppers?" The teacher tried again–Harry James, Will Bradley, Ray McKinley, Ella Mae Morse. The students grew more restless. "What the hell is this, a history lesson? Come on, let's have some music." Their impatience turned to violence, and they broke up the teacher's treasured collection, throwing the records across the classroom. The teacher broke down in tears.

The scene accurately expressed the dislocation between the cultures of two generations.

Hunter's book was published in 1954, and in the relatively short space of time between the date of publication and the release of the film late in 1955, the musical culture of the young had gone a step beyond the terms of the novel. In the film version (directed by Richard Brooks), it was the relentless rhythm of Bill Haley's "Rock Around the Clock" that emphasized the rejection of the relatively sophisticated "swing" of the jazz records played by the teacher. By late 1955, Tony Bennett and Perry Como were as obsolete as Bunny Berigan and Will Bradley, so far as the self-consciously youthful adolescents were concerned. The film version of *Blackboard Jungle* was a large success and a much discussed movie. What the presence in it of the music of Bill Haley, rather than of Tony Bennett and Perry Como, helped to establish in the minds of both adolescents and adults was the connection between rock 'n' roll and teenage rebellion.[5]

V

Both large segments of the general public and the music industry establishment looked upon the growing popularity of rock 'n' roll with uneasiness. There were three main grounds for mistrust and complaint: the rock 'n' roll songs had too much sexuality (or, if not that, vulgarity), that the attitudes in them seemed to defy authority, and that the singers either were Negroes or sounded like Negroes. This last change was a matter of most open concern in the South.

Some of the general attitudes towards rock 'n' roll were perhaps represented in the comments of the syndicated television critic John Crosby, who on most matters represented a civilized and sophisticated point of view. To Crosby, Elvis Presley, who was soon to begin his amazing rise to popularity, was an "unspeakably untalented and vulgar young entertainer". Crosby asked: "Where do you go from Elvis Presley, short of obscenity–which is against the law?"

The most extreme and bizarre expressions of antagonism towards rock 'n' roll tended to take place in the South. In April 1956, the *New York Times* reported several attempts by white southern church groups to have rock 'n' roll suppressed. The whole movement towards rock 'n' roll, the church groups revealed, was part of a plot by the NAACP to corrupt white southern youth.

A well-publicized outbreak of southern antagonism occurred in Birmingham, Alabama, where it was directed, ironically, at the non-rock 'n' roll singer, Nat "King" Cole. The incident was reported by Nat Hentoff as follows in the British music paper *New Musical Express* (April 13, 1956):

> One of the world's most talented and respected singing stars, Nat "King" Cole, was the victim of a vicious attack by a gang of six men at Birmingham (Alabama), during his performance at a concert on Tuesday.

His assailants rushed down the aisles during his second number and clambered over the footlights. They knocked Nat down with such force that he hit his head and back on the piano stool, and they then dragged him into the auditorium.

Police rushed from the wings and were just in time to prevent the singer from being badly beaten up. They arrested six men, one of whom is a director of the White Citizen's Council–a group which has been endeavouring to boycott "bop and Negro music" and are supporters of segregation of white and coloured people. The audience–numbering over 3,000–was all white.

In the music industry, the feelings of antagonism were mixed with and reinforced by economic considerations.

ASCAP, the association of the "establishment" publishers, maintained such a restrictive attitude on the use of their material that many smaller publishers, who handled most of the songs recorded by the independent companies, joined a rival organization, Broadcast Music Incorporated (BMI). ASCAP did everything it could to prevent the major radio networks from playing BMI material–which necessarily meant most rock 'n' roll songs. The association's greatest triumph was getting Johnnie Ray's "Such a Night" banned from the airwaves on the grounds of sexual suggestiveness.

Although Ray's version was for a major company, Columbia, the song was originally recorded for the independent Atlantic, by Clyde McPhatter and the Drifters early in 1954, and was registered with BMI. A typical "rhythm and blues" love song of the period, "Such a Night" recalled a recent evening's experience of the singer:

It was a night, ooh,
Ooh, what a night it was. . . .
The moon was bright,
Ooh how bright it was, . . .
Just the thought of her kiss
Sets me afire,
I reminisce,
And I'm filled with desire.

I gave my heart to her
In sweet surrender,
How well I remember,
I'll always remember. . . .
Came the dawn
And my heart and my love and the night were gone.
But I know I'll never forget
Her kiss in the moonlight,

Ooh, such a kiss,
Such a night.

McPhatter was so intense about the memory of the experience that the audience often found the performance funny. The singer slightly overdid the ecstasy, feigning innocence of the humour in the situation yet somehow also communicating the sense that he was aware of his own ridiculousness.

Because of the intensity of McPhatter's style, and the success of the record in the Negro market, the producer in charge of Johnnie Ray's repertoire at Columbia thought that the song would be suitable for Ray, who had not managed in three years to repeat the huge success in 1951 of "Cry". In contrast to McPhatter, Ray showed no awareness of the essential humour of "Such a Night", and recorded the song straight in his usual dramatic style. In April, 1954, soon after its release, the record appeared in *Billboard*'s list of the twenty records most played by disc jockeys. But during the next week, largely through the efforts of ASCAP, the radio networks agreed that the song was offensive to good taste, and the record was banned from the airwaves, which effectively ended its sales potential in the United States. Meanwhile, in the United Kingdom the record held second place in the best-seller list throughout the summer (kept from the top by Doris Day's "Secret Love").

Billy Rose, a senior member of ASCAP, was quoted in *Variety*: "Not only are most of the BMI songs junk, but in many cases they are obscene junk, pretty much on a level with dirty comic magazines."[6] In general and as usual, the case against accusations of obscenity is hard to argue for, since a listener's interpretation, different from one person to another, is the final arbiter. Many of the songs that Rose would have classified as obscene were enjoyed as funny records by the Negro audience.

Nonetheless, to combat the accusations, the composers of rock 'n' roll songs were obliged to amend words originally written for the Negro audience. One of the most popular records in the Negro market in 1954 was "Work With Me, Annie", by Hank Ballard and the Midnighters (Federal). Written by Ballard, the song made crude double use of the expression "work", as the singer implored:

Work With Me, Annie [four times]
Let's get it while the gitting is good.

The next lines were unambiguous:

Annie, please don't cheat,
Give me all my meat.

In this form the song was an easy target for critics of BMI's rhythm and blues songs, and a modified version, closely following the original's tune and arrangement, was recorded by Etta James as "Wallflower" (Modern). Written by the singer and Johnny Otis, the song provided the reply to "Henry" (Ballard) by challenging his ability to dance (and, by implication, his sexual prowess). The opening chant was changed to:

Roll with me, Henry [five times]
You better roll it while the rollin' is on.

In the last verse, the singer challenged Henry, while Henry–Richard Berry on the record–wailed his willingness to do as she asked:

Well, I ain't teasin' *talk to me baby*
You better stop your freezin' *all right, mama*
If you want romancin' *OK, sugar*
You better learn some dancin' *mm, mm*

Although the song was more respectable than "Work With Me, Annie", it still was not considered suitable for the general public–that is, the white audience. When Mercury recorded a version by Georgia Gibbs, the song was retitled "Dance With Me, Henry", and the opening lines were unequivocally about dancing:

Dance with me, Henry [four times]
Let's dance while the music rolls on.

Although the Gibbs version was spirited compared to most records made for the white market, it lost the sense of dialogue and communal feeling that the other versions had.

A similar destruction of feeling took place when Bill Haley transcribed "Shake, Rattle and Roll". The song was first recorded by Joe Turner for Atlantic, whose version was very popular in the Negro market in 1954. As written by Charles Calhoun, the song begins, in effect, in bed:

Get out of that bed,
And wash your hands. [twice]

Get into the kitchen,
Make some noise with the pots and pans.

Well you wear low dresses,
The sun comes shinin' through. [twice]

I can't believe my eyes,
That all of this belongs to you.

As transcribed by Haley the song begins more vaguely and more decorously:

Get out in that kitchen,
And rattle those pots and pans. [twice]

Roll my breakfast
'Cause I'm a hungry man.

You wear those dresses,
Your hair done up so nice. [twice]

You look so warm,
But your heart is cold as ice.

One verse of the Calhoun/Turner original is missing entirely from the Haley version:

I said over the hill,
And way down underneath. [twice]
You make me roll my eyes,
And then you make me grit my teeth.

Haley, commenting on the charges of obscenity, insisted:

> We steer completely clear of anything suggestive! We take a lot of care with lyrics because we don't want to offend anybody. The music is the main thing, and it's just as easy to write acceptable words.[7]

For a time, ASCAP was effective in encouraging radio stations to play their songs (invariably recorded by major companies) rather than BMI songs. But, particularly after Alan Freed moved from Cleveland to New York, in 1954, an increasing number of disc jockeys on stations oriented to white audiences began to feature independently recorded BMI songs. And as this opened up a previously inaccessible market to independent companies and their singers, some of the companies began to orient their records deliberately to the white audience.

Although Alan Freed did not, as he sometimes claimed, coin the expression "rock 'n' roll" or create a new music single-handed, he did play an incalculable role in developing the concept of an exciting music that could express the feelings of adolescence. When he first used the term "rock 'n' roll", he was applying it to music that already existed under another name, "rhythm and blues". But the change in name induced a change in the music itself. "Rhythm and blues" had meant music by black people for black people. "Rock 'n' roll" meant at first only that this music was being directed at white listeners, but then, as the people producing the music became conscious of their new audience, they changed the character of the music, so that "rock 'n' roll" came to describe–and be–something different from "rhythm and blues".

2

FIVE STYLES OF ROCK 'N' ROLL

In the years 1954 to 1956, there were five distinctive styles, developed almost completely independently of one another, that collectively became known as rock 'n' roll: northern band rock 'n' roll, whose most popular exemplar was Bill Haley; the New Orleans dance blues; Memphis country rock (also known as rockabilly); Chicago rhythm and blues; and vocal group rock 'n' roll. All five styles, and the variants associated with each of them, depended for their dance beat on contemporary Negro dance rhythms.

The styles gave expression to moods of their audience that hitherto had not been represented in popular music. Each style was developed in particular regions or locales and expressed personal responses to certain experiences in a way that would make sense to people with comparable experiences. This grass-roots character gave the styles of rock 'n' roll their collective identity, putting it in sharp contrast with established modes of popular music, which were conceived in terms of general ideas formulated in ways that made the finished product available for millions of people to accept.

I

Northern band rock 'n' roll, exemplified by Bill Haley and His Comets, was concerned mainly with expressing high-spirited feelings of togetherness. Haley had little of the romantic appeal familiar to the fans of Frankie Laine or Eddie Fisher. More quaint than good looking, Haley rested his appeal on his music, which he had been developing for ten years before the general audience discovered him in 1953. Haley's earliest records were in conventional country and western style; by 1947 he had begun experimenting with it. As he recalled in an interview much later: ". . . the style we played way back in 1947, 1948, and 1949 was a combination of country and western, Dixieland, and the old style rhythm and blues."[1]

The "old style rhythm and blues" he referred to was probably the roaring, riff-laden music of bands like Lionel Hampton's, itself a simplified descendant of the Kansas City jazz, committed to creating as much excitement as possible, with musicians playing solos on one or two notes, lying on their backs or climbing on pianos or basses, or playing their instruments above their heads in search of thrilling visual effects. Contrasting the enjoyment of the audiences at this kind of dance with the staid reaction of audiences where white dance bands played, Haley saw the chance for change. "We decided to try for a new style, mostly using stringed instruments but somehow managing to get the same effect as brass and reeds."[2]

> ... Around the early fifties the musical world was starved for something new ... the days of the solo vocalist and the big bands had gone. About the only thing in fact that was making any noise was progressive jazz, but this was just above the heads of the average listener ... I felt then that if I could take, say, a Dixieland tune and drop the first and third beats, and accentuate the second and fourth, and add a beat the listeners could clap to as well as dance this would be what they were after. From that the rest was easy ... take everyday sayings like "Crazy Man Crazy", "See You Later, Alligator", "Shake, Rattle and Roll", and apply what I have just said.[3]

It wasn't quite as easy as Haley suggested. Another group, Freddie Bell and the Bellboys, tried the same formula with "Giddy-Up a Ding Dong" (Mercury) but had much less success, despite being featured with Haley, the Platters, and Alan Freed in the film *Rock Around the Clock*. And in 1955 Haley's own Comets left him to form the Jodimars, who sang "Let's All Rock Together" (Capitol) in the prescribed fashion without impressing the customers. (Boyd Bennett's "Seventeen" did confirm, however, that in 1955 a record with little musical quality and banal lyrics could satisfy the popular audience; a singer called Big Moe chanted the words tonelessly, while the band played a rough beat. Bennett, a protégé of the Louisiana honky-tonk singer Moon Mullican, had no other hits.)

II

One of the first of Haley's successors in covering rhythm and blues material for white audiences was Pat Boone, whose first big hit "Ain't That a Shame" (Dot) remained in the top ten for fourteen weeks through the summer of 1955. Whereas Haley had developed his style of rock 'n' roll himself, Boone had been surprised and rather shocked when he had been asked to record the uptempo "Two Hearts, Two Kisses" as his first release for Dot, a southern independent company based in Gallatin, Tennessee. He had been accustomed to slow ballads, of the kind well established in the popular and country and western markets. With the rest of middle-class America, Boone regarded rhythm and blues material as being rather crude, musically and lyrically. Nonetheless, he went on to record "Ain't That a Shame", "Tutti Frutti", and a succession of cover versions of other rhythm and blues hits.

In contrast to Bill Haley, Boone was young and good looking and had a more expressive voice. But unlike Haley, he did not seem to be involved with the spirit of the musicians behind him, and he was important to rock 'n' roll only in the role he played bringing a little conservative respectability to the music's image. Although his early success delayed the mass public's awareness of real rock 'n' roll/rhythm and blues singers, it may also have indirectly generated interest in them. A few disc jockeys, for example, played the original versions of the Boone hits "Tutti Frutti" and "Ain't That a Shame", and when the original singers became better known, Boone retreated to the ballads he seemed from the start to have preferred to record.

"Ain't That a Shame" and "Tutti Frutti" were both originally recorded in the "New Orleans dance blues" style, by Fats Domino and Little Richard, respectively, and Boone's cover versions used instrumentation closely based on the New Orleans arrangements. In these records the rhythms were looser, less mechanical than in the northern band rock 'n' roll records, and the singers were more prominent. There was rarely any singing by the band, and the musicians accepted a supportive role.

Fats Domino, working with Dave Bartholomew, a local big-band leader and trumpeter, as his recording supervisor, co-writer, and session bandleader, helped to evolve the New Orleans dance blues through a remarkable series of records which began with "The Fat Man" (for Imperial), a big hit in the rhythm and blues market in 1949–50. At that time Domino sang in a high, exuberant tenor, and played piano with a distinctive boogie-influenced style that featured chords with both hands. The effervescent good humour of his fast records was eventually discovered by the popular music audience, which in 1956, after he had achieved many hits in the black market, raised "I'm In Love Again" into *Billboard*'s top ten. Domino's follow-up to "I'm In Love Again" was a slow version of the standard "Blueberry Hill", sung with impressive control and apparently no effort at all. Domino's curious "creole" accent immediately identified his records, and he maintained a long string of hits, including both infectiously happy songs and plaintive appeals.

A feature of virtually all Domino's records was a tenor-sax solo, taken usually about two-thirds of the way through, often by either Lee Allen or Herb Hardesty. These solos were probably shortened versions of the solos that would have been played at dances, and they matched the relaxed control of Domino's voice. Like his singing, the sax tone was melodic, economical, warm, and slightly rough.

Although Little Richard came from Georgia and did not record for the same company as Domino, he often played with the same musicians. But in contrast to Domino's cool style, Little Richard was intensely involved in everything he sang, exhilarating his audiences with a frantic, sometimes hysterical performance which was distinguished by pure-voiced swoops and whoops out of a raucous shouting style.

With Little Richard, the rock 'n' roll audience got the aggressive extrovert to enact their wilder fantasies, and his stage performance set precedents for anyone who followed him. Dressed in shimmering suits with long drape jackets and baggy pants, his hair grown long and slicked straight, white teeth and gold rings flashing in the spotlights, he stood up at, and sometimes on, the piano, hammering boogie chords as he screamed messages of celebration and self-centred pleasure. From "Long Tall Sally":

Well, Long Tall Sally,
She's built for speed,
She's got everything that uncle John needs.

From "Rip It Up":

Well, it's Saturday night
And I just got paid,
A fool about my money,
Don't try to save. . . .
Gonna rock it up,
Gonna rip it up,
Gonna shake it up,
Gonna ball it up,
Gonna rock it up,
And ball tonight.

Both songs became standards in the repertoire of almost every rock 'n' roll singer, for the spirit of Little Richard affected and influenced most singers who followed him. Compared to Domino, Little Richard, musically and stylistically speaking, was coarse, uncultured, and uncontrolled, in every way harder for the music establishment to take. Among the white rock 'n' roll singers, Elvis Presley was similarly outrageous as compared with his predecessors Bill Haley and Pat Boone.

III

Presley was the most commercially successful of a number of Memphis singers who evolved what they themselves called "country rock" and what others, record collectors and people in the industry, have called "rockabilly". Country rock was basically a Southern white version of 12-bar boogie blues, shouted with a minimum of subtlety by ex-hillbilly singers over an accompaniment featuring electric guitar, stand-up bass, and–from 1956–drums, still taboo in Nashville. The style evolved partly from the imaginative guidance of a Memphis radio station engineer, Sam Phillips, who entered the recording business by supervising sessions with local blues singers and leasing the masters to a number of independent companies (Chess in Chicago, owned by the Chess brothers, or Modern/RPM in Los Angeles, owned by the Bihari brothers). The success of some of these singers, notably B. B. King and Howlin' Wolf, encouraged Phillips to form his own label, Sun, and two of the singers he recorded for his own label, Little Junior Parker and Rufus Thomas, had hit records in the Negro market.

The Memphis blues singers used small bands which featured piano, guitar, and saxophone. No particular dominant style linked them all, but common to many of their records was a kind of intimate atmosphere created by the simple and cheap, but unorthodox, "tape delay echo" recording technique of Phillips. The singers invariably made their personal presence felt on the records, menacingly in Howlin' Wolf's case, impatiently in Junior Parker's. These recordings, and other more traditional blues, and rhythm and blues records issued by Sun, were known to a substantial number of white youths through the South, and presented a source of song material and stylistic inspiration that was in many ways more satisfactory than the orthodox country and western culture.

Jimmie Rodgers sang the "white blues" in the twenties but Elvis Presley was the first to make it work as pop music. According to the legend of his recording debut, his discovery by Sam Phillips was casual and lucky. Presley is said to have attracted the attention of Phillips when he used Sun's studios to cut a record for his mother's birthday present; Phillips encouraged him to make a record with proper accompaniment, and the two men were rewarded with a local hit from one of the sides, "That's All Right".

The story of Presley's discovery has the elements of romance, coincidence, and fate that legends need, and in fact seems to be true, but it is likely that if Phillips and Presley had not met, two other such people would soon have done what they did–merge rhythm and blues with country and western styles and material, and come up with a new style. In the panhandle of west Texas, in Arkansas, in north Louisiana, and in Memphis there were other singers whose cultural and musical experience were comparable to Presley's; indeed, some of them followed him into the Sun studios, while others tried studios in Nashville and Clovis, New Mexico.

It is difficult to assess how great a part Sam Phillips played in influencing his singers–among other things, by introducing them to blues records–and how much they already knew. Presley told one interviewer:

> I'd play [guitar] along with the radio or phonograph, and taught myself the chord positions. We were a religious family, going round together to sing at camp meetings and revivals, and I'd take my guitar with us when I could. I also dug the real low-down Mississippi singers, mostly Big Bill Broonzy and Big Boy Crudup, although they would scold me at home for listening to them.
>
> "Sinful music", the townsfolk in Memphis said it was. Which never bothered me, I guess.

In the same interview, Presley stressed the importance of Phillips:

> Mr. Phillips said he'd coach me if I'd come over to the studio as often as I could. It must have been a year and a half before he gave me an actual session. At last he let me try a western song–and it sounded terrible. But the second idea he had was the one that jelled.
>
> "You want to make some blues?" he suggested over the 'phone, knowing I'd always been a sucker for that kind of jive. He mentioned Big Boy Crudup's name and maybe others too. I don't remember.
>
> All I know is, I hung up and ran 15 blocks to Mr. Phillips' office before he'd gotten off the line–or so he tells me. We talked about the Crudup records I knew–"Cool Disposition", "Rock Me, Mama", "Hey Mama", "Everything's All Right", and others, but settled for "That's All Right", one of my top favourites. . . .[4]

What Presley achieved was certainly not "the same thing" as the men he copied. On "That's All Right" and "Mystery Train" (written and first recorded by Junior Parker for Sun), he evolved a personal version of this style, singing high and clear, breathless and impatient, varying his rhythmic emphasis with a confidence and inventiveness that were exceptional for a white singer. The sound suggested a young white man celebrating freedom, ready to do anything, go anywhere, pausing long enough for apologies and even regrets and recriminations, but then hustling on towards the new. He was best on fast songs, when his impatient singing matched the urgent rhythm from bass (Bill Black) and guitar (Scotty Moore). Each of his five Sun singles backed a blues song with a country and western song, most of them already familiar to the respective audiences; each sold better than its predecessor, and increasing numbers of people discovered Presley either through radio broadcasts or through his stage appearances.

But Presley did not reach the mass popular music audience with his Sun records, which sold mainly to audiences in the South and to the minority country and western audience elsewhere. Only after Presley's contract was bought by RCA-Victor did his records make the national top ten, and the songs on these records were not in a country rock style. At Victor, under the supervision of Chet Atkins, Presley's records featured vocal groups, heavily electrified guitars, and drums, all of which were considered alien by both country and western audiences and by the audience for country rock music. Responding to these unfamiliar intrusions in his accompaniment, Presley's voice became much more theatrical and self-conscious as he sought to contrive excitement and emotion which he had seemed to achieve on his Sun records without any evident forethought.

Presley's success for Sun, and later for RCA-Victor, encouraged Phillips to try other singers with comparable styles and material, and attracted to his studios young southerners with similar interests. Carl Perkins and Warren Smith from the Memphis area, Roy Orbison from west Texas, Johnny Cash, Conway Twitty, and Charlie Rich from Arkansas, and Jerry Lee Lewis from northern Louisiana brought songs, demonstration tapes, and their ambitions to Phillips, who switched almost completely from black singers to white singers once the latter became commercially successful.

Not all of the singers were as obviously influenced by blues styles as Presley was. Carl Perkins and Johnny Cash, for example, both sang in a much more predominantly country and western style. But, as with Bill Haley, the music and particularly the rhythms of all of them had the emphatic dance beat of rhythm and blues. "Rockabilly" effectively describes this style, which differed from the northern band rock 'n' roll of the Comets. Rockabilly has much looser rhythms, no saxophones, nor any chorus singing. Like the New Orleans dance blues singers, the rockabilly singers were much more personal–confiding, confessing–than Haley could ever be, and their performances seemed less calculated and less prepared. But unlike the lyrical, warm instrumentalists in the dance blues, the instrumentalists in rockabilly responded more violently to unpredictable inflections in the singer's voice, shifting into double-time for a few bars to blend with a sudden acceleration in the singer's tempo. Presley's "You're a Heartbreaker" (his third single for Sun) typifies the style, as does Carl Perkins's "Blue Suede Shoes". The latter was the first million-selling record in the rockabilly style, and brought a new dimension to popular music in its defiant pride for the individual's cultural choice. (For legal reasons the song unfortunately cannot be quoted here.)

Later, in 1956, Johnny Cash made *Billboard*'s top twenty with another Sun record, "I Walk the Line", much closer to conventional country and western music in both style and material, and in 1957 the Louisiana pianist-singer Jerry Lee Lewis, heavily influenced by Little Richard, had the first of several big hits with his boogie-based "Whole Lotta Shakin' Goin' On" (also for Sun). Rockabilly became a major part of American popular music, as much in its continuing inspiration for singers from outside the South as in the occasional commercial successes enjoyed by the rockabilly singers other than Presley.

IV

The nearest equivalent to rockabilly among black styles was the "Chicago rhythm and blues" style of Chuck Berry, perhaps the major figure of rock 'n' roll, and Bo Diddley. Many of the black singers who had recorded around Memphis before Presley (among them Howlin' Wolf, Elmore James, and James Cotton) moved to Chicago during the early fifties, where they helped Muddy Waters and others develop the Chicago bar blues style–loud, heavily amplified, shouted to a socking beat.

Chicago became the hot-bed for any black musician trying to make a living from the blues, many of whom hoped to work for Muddy Waters or Howlin' Wolf and to record for Chess or its subsidiary Checker. Muddy's harmonica player Little Walter gave Checker two of its biggest rhythm and blues hits in the early fifties with "My Babe" (1952) and "Juke" (1955), and the Chess label's big rhythm and blues hits of the period were by the soft-voiced club pianist, Willie Mabon: "I Don't Know" (1953) and "I'm Mad" (1954). In 1955 the company became one of the first rhythm and blues indies to break into the pop market with Chuck Berry and Bo Diddley, two guitar-playing singers who recorded with blues musicians but aimed their lyrics and dance rhythms at a younger audience.

"Maybellene" was a "formula" song, carefully constructed to meet the apparent taste of the recently emerged mass audience for rock 'n' roll. The song lived out the fast-car fantasy:

As I was motorvatin' over the hill,
I saw Maybellene in a Coupe-de-ville
Cadillac rollin' on the open road,
Tryin' to outrun my V-8 Ford.

Berry has since said that he conceived "Maybellene" as a country and western song which he originally called "Ida May". But disc jockeys

Alan Freed and Russ Fratto were "motivated" to play the record regularly–by being credited as part-authors–and the result was instant rock 'n' roll. The beat was much cruder than any Berry ever used again, echoing Bill Haley more than anyone else, and the shouted-back chorus lines were also derived from the Comets' style. Berry's clear enunciation probably enabled his record to "pass for white" on the radio stations that generally kept such stuff off the air.

The stations could not have made the same mistake with "Bo Diddley". Even worse, the rhythm was a bump-and-grind shuffle, which could not be rendered any the more innocent by such lines as: "Bo Diddley bought-a-baby a diamond ring . . .". The record hardly had the impact on radio stations that "Maybellene" had, but it ensured demand for Bo Diddley at high school dances.

Both singers had immeasurable influence on other rock 'n' roll singers and styles, Berry particularly as a songwriter and guitarist, Diddley as the interpreter of one of the most distinctive rhythms of rock and roll.*

V

"Vocal group rock 'n' roll" was the loosest of the five types of rock 'n' roll, bracketing the groups who sang mainly fast novelty songs together with those which specialized in slow ballads. Where the other four styles developed in reaction to the evolution of electrically-amplified guitars and to the emphatic back-beat from drummers, the vocal group style was almost a throw-back to earlier eras; almost, but not quite.

Most of the black vocal groups who emerged in this period were young, inexperienced, and amateur singers whose rehearsals were in improvised settings without the benefit of musicians to help with the arrangements. To compensate, each of the back-up singers had to evolve a part which was more concerned with rhythmic and percussive impact than with harmonic sophistication, and it was often the ingenious chants that attracted attention to their records.

But although the rehearsals may have been "acapella" (without instruments), most of the records were made with hastily convened back-up bands, often the bare minimum of guitar, bass, and drums, with sometimes a saxophone player in the solo break. The paradox for the supervising A&R man was that the less he interfered with a group's own arrangement, the better, although a few companies did

* *The syncopation of this rhythm almost certainly derives from an African drum rhythm, and one example of it was recorded in the Deep South in 1951, for Alan Lomax by Lonnie and Ed Young, whose "Oree", using this syncopation, was released on an album,* Roots of the Blues (*Atlantic*).

find sympathetic arrangers who learned to tidy up the groups' ideas without making them merely conventional. In New York, Atlantic benefited from Jesse Stone's coaching efforts with the Chords, whose "Sh-Boom" made the pop charts in 1954, while Al Silver of Herald Records sent both the Turbans ("When You Dance") and the Nutmegs ("Story Untold") to Leroy Kirkland for help with their arrangements. The most productive team in this period was George Goldner and Richard Barrett, who were respectively the supervisor and arranger at the session which produced "Why Do Fools Fall in Love" by the Teenagers featuring Frankie Lymon, issued on Goldner's Gee label at the end of 1955.

"Why Do Fools Fall in Love" was in many ways the definitive fast novelty vocal group record of the period, combining an unforgettable web of back-up noises with a classic teenage-lament lyric. Bass singer Sherman Garnes kicked the song off: "Ay, dum-da di-dum dah dum ..." and in came Frankie, wailing high in his little boy's cry: "Ooh-wah, oo-ooh wah-ah". And then, with the rest of the group weaving in and out, and saxman Jimmy Wright honking along with them, came the song itself, as simple as a nursery rhyme, and as effective, but sung with such heartfelt conviction that it sounded–like the group's name–teenage, not kindergarten.

The record made the top ten in the States, and then took off around the world, topping the charts in Britain where none of the previous black vocal group records had made any impact. But although the Teenagers had a couple more hits (which was better than most novelty-oriented vocal groups managed), they soon faded into the swamps of obscurity, and Frankie Lymon's life wasted away to an inevitable death from a drug overdose in 1968.

Of the other novelty groups who made their mark early, the Crows had no more success after their first hit, "Gee", made the pop charts on George Goldner's Rama label in 1954; that record was hardly more than a repetition of the title, chanted over a simple dance beat, and mainly served to prove that the teenage audience was starved of records with an emphatic off-beat. The Chords were next up, with "Sh-Boom", and down they went too, followed by the Charms from Cincinnatti, who lasted long enough to chalk up two hits, "Hearts of Stone" and "Ling Ting Tong", and then one more in 1956, "Ivory Tower", billed as Otis Williams and his Charms, all for DeLuxe Records. In 1955, the El-Dorados ("At My Front Door", Vee Jay), the Cadillacs ("Speedoo", Josie) and the Turbans took their turn on the wheel of fortune, and in 1956 another of George Goldner's groups, the Cleftones, made it with "Little Girl of Mine". Each record implanted itself in the minds of listeners, and several attracted cover versions at the time and revival versions since; but for most of the singers involved, it was back to day jobs at best, or hustling on the streets at worst. The term "novelty group" seemed to be a euphemism for one-hit wonder, and the one notable exception was the Coasters, who made their mark in 1957 with the Leiber-Stoller productions of "Young Blood" and "Searchin'", and sustained a career of hits until 1964.

For slow groups, career prospects were potentially much better, because they could hope to move into the supper-club and cabaret world where Las Vegas was the ultimate target. The paradox was, could a group meet the needs of that world and yet satisfy the criteria for play on the teen-oriented rock 'n' roll radio shows? Buck Ram, manager of the Platters and writer of several of their hits, proved that it could be done.

Although there were slow groups making the rhythm and blues charts from all areas of the States, the three which made most impact on the pop charts in rock 'n' roll's breakthrough period were all based in Los Angeles: the Penguins, the Teen Queens, and the Platters. Both the Penguins and the Teen Queens turned out to be one-hit wonders, but their records were typical of an on-going West Coast style which had previously surfaced on the rhythm and blues charts via "Dream Girl" by Jesse and Marvin (Specialty, 1953) and "Cherry Pie" by Marvin and Johnny (Modern, 1954). In both cases, the singers slurred and dragged their phrases to ludicrous extents in order to declare their heartfelt devotion, and this was the sound that the Penguins brought to the nation in "Earth Angel".

For the professionals in the industry, "Earth Angel" was seen as undeniable proof that the youth of the day had lost their marbles. Was the singer male or female? (Male: Cleveland Duncan.) Where was the song? "Earth angel (*thud*, from the drummer), earth angel (*thud*) (pause) will you be mine? (*thud*)". To compound the felony, the record featured the bane of all professional musicians, triplets, where the pianist just held a chord and hammered it three times on every beat; so simple, no self-respecting musician could bear to do it. But it made for hypnotic dancing, and was what worked. Dootone Records had its one and only hit, and encountered some of the attendant problems when Buck Ram moved in as manager of the group and took them off to Mercury Records along with his other protégés the Platters.

The Platters had been just one of the countless black vocal groups in Los Angeles, recording for Federal in all the current styles without ever establishing a distinct identity, but after their move to Mercury all the focus was put on to the voice of lead tenor Tony Williams. The first recording for the new label was of a song (written by Ram) which the group had already recorded for Federal with no success, "Only

You". This time around, the record went unnoticed again for three months before it began to get play, yet it came to represent a milestone in the era's music.

The back-up singers in the Platters never sounded as interesting as most of the other groups of the day, and in many ways the group's records could have been billed as by Tony Williams. He had a genuinely good voice, obviously influenced by gospel, and he threw in a kind of hiccup on the high notes which became his trademark. Swooping up to stratospheric heights, he declared the now familiar undying devotion in "Only You", and followed through with a better song (again written by Buck Ram), "The Great Pretender". Tailor-made to showcase the high-flying voice of Williams, this topped the American pop chart, and set the group up for a long career, achieving Ram's declared ambition to launch "the new Ink Spots". Later records veered away from the triplet, teen-ballad idiom of the first two hits, but that idiom became part of the basic rock 'n' roll heritage, for better or (quite often) for worse.

These five styles of rock 'n' roll covered most of the records which broke through to the pop charts from 1954 through 1956, and basically set up the "ingredients" which were mixed together in slightly varying combinations for the next thirty years by musicians, producers, and singers aiming at the "youth market". Bill Haley's brand of Northern Band rock 'n' roll was probably the least influential, being the end, rather than a beginning, of a tradition; sometimes derided for his old-fashioned image, Haley was in fact an astute bandleader who outlasted most of his contemporaries by accommodating the back-beat rhythm that was required of the new dance music.

The piano-and-saxophone orientation of New Orleans rock 'n' roll gradually lost favour during the sixties, when the majority of groups featured guitars as both lead and rhythm instruments, inspired equally by Memphis-style rockabilly and Chicago-style rhythm and blues. The gospel attack of Little Richard had incalculable influence, both directly and through the other gospel-styled singers who found more favour after he had crashed into public view. And many of the performers who synthesized these influences worked as groups, incorporating vocal harmonies which took off from the Teenagers and the other vocal groups. Between them, these styles provided the basis for all the major artists and producers of the sixties–obviously the Four Seasons, the Beach Boys, and the Motown groups in the States, and the Beatles and Rolling Stones in Britain, and less obviously but just as certainly, Bob Dylan and Sly Stone. In most cases, the second generation were able to make more from their records than the innovators had, in terms of money, fame, and prestige, as they reclaimed the music from the businessmen who tried to reproduce the effects of rock 'n' roll without risking the personal elements that had been fundamental in the first place.

3

HOW TO MAKE A ROCK 'N' ROLL RECORD

I

Around 1954 and 1955, when the first rock 'n' roll records started hitting the market, after having developed a reputation in the rhythm and blues market or perhaps having been deliberately promoted by an independent company specifically as "rock 'n' roll", the major companies varied in their initial reactions from attempts to co-opt the audience for a given record by making a "cover" version of it (a recording of the song by one of their own singers) on the pretence that the record and the demand did not exist. In general, the big companies had been so powerful that if they did not support a trend, it had no strong chance of gathering momentum. Disc jockeys on radio stations and network stations directed at the white audience usually obliged the major companies by playing their cover versions rather than the originals of the independents.

When Bill Haley's "Crazy Man Crazy" (for the independent Essex) entered the best-selling lists, the disc jockeys ignored it, and played a Mercury-label version of the song by Ralph Marterie–which did not make the best-selling lists. Similarly, although the Orioles' version of "Crying in the Chapel" (for the independent Jubilee) stayed several weeks on the best-selling lists and sold over a million copies, the disc jockeys did not play it often enough to put it on the list of the twenty most-played records; but they did play the other three best-selling versions, all recorded for major companies, enough times to get *them* on the lists. (They also played the version by Ella Fitzgerald on Decca, but it did not make the top twenty.)

During 1954 and 1955, black vocal groups and their companies sought to satisfy the tastes of the white record-buying audience by adapting as closely as they could the singing style that appealed to it. A number of such records that were successful were trivial novelty songs with catchy titles and meaningless or irrelevant words, some of which were noted in the last chapter: "Gee" by the Crows (Rama, 1954), "Sh-Boom" by the Chords (Cat, distributed by Atlantic, 1954), "Ling Ting Tong" and "Hearts of Stone" by the Charms (De

Luxe, 1954), "Ko Ko Mo" by Gene and Eunice (Combo, 1955), and "Tweedle-Dee" by LaVern Baker (Atlantic, 1955). All these songs sold quite well in the white market–and would probably have done better had it not been for cover versions by white singers which usually captured the majority of customers interested in the songs.

With the same aim, black singers also recorded sentimental songs far more often then ever before. The songs included "I Understand" and "Marie" by the Four Tunes (Jubilee), "Goodnight, Sweetheart, Goodnight" by the Spaniels (Vee Jay), "Sincerely" by the Moonglows (Chess), "Earth Angel" by the Penguins (Dootone), and "Pledging My Love" by Johnny Ace (Duke), all recorded in 1954. Like the novelty songs, most of these were covered by white singers for the major companies. The major exception was the records of the Four Tunes ("I Understand" and "Marie"), which so successfully imitated white styles that it was not evident that the people concerned were black. The other songs were covered by such singers as the Crew Cuts and Georgia Gibbs (Mercury), the Four Lads (Columbia), and the McGuire Sisters (Coral, a subsidiary of Decca). Whereas the black records were by groups who generally had developed an elaborate style, the white cover versions tended to be in the simple "sing-along" mode, emphasizing the melody with little concern for the more complicated feelings contained in the original versions by the black groups.

Until the end of 1954, the cover versions invariably outsold the originals. Whether this was because of the assistance of much greater exposure from disc jockeys and the easier distribution to the retailers in white areas available to the major companies is impossible to say with certainty. But it seemed that the major companies expected, or hoped, that the audience would be satisfied by having the "black" songs, and would not worry too much about not getting the black singers.

If the majors had hoped that they could accommodate the audience's taste for rock 'n' roll through their traditionally effective methods of more thorough promotion and faster distribution, they were foiled. The audience was determined to have the real thing, not a synthetic version of the original. Independent companies, sensing this desire, were eager to satisfy it. A group of disc jockeys helped to bring these two mutually dependent groups together, and to keep them in contact. Apart from Freed in New York, disc jockeys who significantly helped the original rhythm and blues versions of rock 'n' roll songs were Danny "Cat Man" Stiles, at WNJR, Newark, New Jersey; George "Hound Dog" Lorenz at WKBW, Buffalo, New York; "Symphony Sid" Torin and Ken Malden at WBMS, Boston; Hunter Hancock, Peter Potter, and "Spider" Webb on the West

Coast; Tommy "Dr. Jive" Smalls in New York; Al Benson in Chicago; Ken "Jack the Cat" Elliott and Clarence "Poppa Stoppa" in New Orleans; and Zenas "Big Daddy" Sears in Atlanta. And perhaps more important than any of them, three disc jockeys on WLAC out of Nashville, Gene Nobles, Hoss Allen, John "R" Richbourg. In the day-time, WLAC played country music for a white audience, but at night those three men took over to play rhythm and blues and, beamed out on the station's 50,000-watt clear channel, they were heard as far south as the Gulf of Mexico, way up north in Buffalo, New York, across the Caribbean in Jamaica, and as far west as the states at the foot of the Rockies. Most of the advertising on these WLAC rhythm and blues shows was directed to a black audience, but there were plenty of white kids writing in for the records being sold on mail order. And it was the same for the other more local stations: from a commercial point of view, the stations were regarded as "black", but from the audience's point of view, this was where the best music could be heard.

II

In 1955, the music industry started booming, beginning a climb in sales that kept going till 1959, by which time sales were almost treble what they had been in 1954. In this five-year period, they jumped from $213,000,000 in record sales to $603,000,000.[1] A large proportion of the increase in sales accrued to independent companies, who made their break into the market by providing assorted kinds of rock 'n' roll. The majors had cause to rue their casual attitude to the music.

There are no figures available that detail the precise sources and recipients of income from record sales, but some analysis can be made through a breakdown of *Billboard's* top ten lists in the period 1955 – 59.[2]

If rock 'n' roll as art and entertainment was the expression of a new generation, as a commercial product it was the dynamite that blew apart the structure of an industry. Until 1954, the majors had the market more or less under control, or so it seemed; and even in 1955, the majors had four fifths of the top ten hits. But during the years of hard fighting among the independents who constituted the rhythm and blues market, the companies that had survived had acquired ambitions for growth that were no longer restricted to a section of the music market. Then, once they realized the possibilities of rock 'n' roll, they were prepared to record almost anybody singing almost anything, and to put all their energy and money into promoting the records that seemed to stand a chance. The independents doubled their top ten hits from 1955 to 1956, then doubled them again in 1957.

The majors, for their part, despite a much greater turnover of hits–achieved through faster distribution to record stores, and more intensive exposure over the radio–didn't even maintain their absolute number of hits, and by the end of the decade had only a third of the records that made the top ten.

The vintage year for rock 'n' roll was 1956. Only nineteen rock 'n' roll records made the top ten that year, but they included many of the best records in that style. Singers and producers had distilled the best qualities from the various styles that interested them and produced strong, fresh sounds by mixing them together. They had not yet had time to do any kind of market research to discover what the audience liked, or any content analysis of other successful records to find the formula for success. Most of the singers and musicians had been singing and playing this way for years; now popular taste had suddenly caught up with them.

Although the majority of hit records in 1956 were comparable to the traditional pop music fare–several versions of "Canadian Sunset", "Moonglow/Theme from Picnic", and "True Love" were among the hits of the year–the spontaneous quality of the rock 'n' roll hits suggested that the industry's conception of music was likely to change in the next few years. Instead, within a remarkably short space of time, a cynical derision of performers' styles and a disregard for audience's tastes were re-established, having spread like some plague through many independent companies.

Commercially speaking, 1957 was the most promising year yet for independent companies and the most depressing one for the majors, but alongside the few rock 'n' roll records that compared with the best of the previous year were others that told of the shape of things to come, records whose sound was determined more by a producer's formula than by a singer's uninhibited spirit–"Butterfly" by Charlie Gracie (Cameo), "At the Hop" by Danny and the Juniors (ABC-Paramount), "Teddy Bear" and "Jailhouse Rock" by Elvis Presley (RCA-Victor).

The discovery that rock 'n' roll could, after all, be subjected to the traditional production techniques of the industry encouraged old-style producers to give the idiom another try. They had previously failed to absorb the music by covering the songs with established pop singers; but now they could establish their product's credibility by using unknown singers–who were emphatically described as "rock 'n' rollers"–to record new songs with appropriate lyrics and a steady rhythm.

Gradually, but thoroughly, the characteristics that had distinguished the rock 'n' roll of 1956 were eliminated: strong regional accents; self-composed songs; simple open musical arrangements, featuring a small number of instruments with an improvised solo by saxophone, guitar, or piano, worked out spontaneously in the studio. In their place, unlocalized voices, songs composed by people who didn't sing, written arrangements for large orchestras and choruses.

Not only did some of the majors take steps to knock the rough edges off rock 'n' roll, but so did most of the independents with ambitions to survive. Rock 'n' roll suffered, but the independents as a whole did not. The justification was in the sales, which kept climbing despite the elimination of the music's character, and in the demise of the few companies, Specialty and Sun, that refused to make their product more "sophisticated".

The implication was that people didn't want their music to be as brash, blatantly sexual, and spontaneous as the pure rock 'n' roll records were. But although the position was maintained through to 1963, the success in the United States around this time of British groups with similar qualities suggested that the audience still did prefer this kind of music, if it knew about its availability.

III

For a while, during 1956, rock 'n' roll had commercial appeal through its novelty and the controversy surrounding it: but in the long run, it was irritatingly loud, "unmusical" (in terms of conventional pop music standards), and suggestive. Radio stations began cutting down on the number of "wild" records they included on their play lists. Record companies either chose to accept the criteria unofficially set by the stations, or else hoped to reach the audience through other channels, particularly juke boxes, though there was less prestige in the industry in a juke-box hit–despite the fact that there were nearly half a million boxes across the country and they accounted for up to 40 per cent of record sales each year.

In general, rock 'n' roll was cultivated primarily by independents. Although two leading rock 'n' roll singers, Bill Haley and Elvis Presley, had their biggest success with majors, both had previously been with independents. The majors did not entirely ignore rock 'n' roll–most recorded at least a couple of authentic rock 'n' roll singers, and among their releases were some that are now acknowledged to be among the best records of all rock 'n' roll. But there does appear to have been a general feeling among the executives of the majors that rock 'n' roll was a rather shoddy music, associated with ill-educated southerners who were difficult to patronize–they looked a little too rough to be patted on the back, and too unsophisticated to get along with as equals. So although their commercial instincts told them to sign up at least one rock 'n' roll singer who could handle the style better than their crooners, the majors generally did not go much further than that.

The majors did not altogether ignore either black singers or white southern singers, but they preferred such singers if they appealed to audiences the companies already knew about and understood. Almost all the black singers contracted by major companies until 1958 were ballad singers whose voices could be adapted to sentimental, melodramatic, or novelty songs, which the white audience was believed to prefer. Since the black audience was relatively uninterested in such songs, the singers who chose to record for major companies usually had to cut themselves off from the black audience.

The white southern singers who recorded for major companies usually sang country and western music, whose audience was spread throughout the United States, and although it was not large in relation to the pop music audience, it was much more conservative and reliable in its taste than was the rhythm and blues audience. A major company that contracted a popular country and western singer could be fairly confident that the singer would still be needed by his audience five years later. In the rhythm and blues market, some singers maintained loyal audiences for twenty or more years, but only those who understood the music and the audience well could make any confident prediction which singers would be likely to stay popular. The major company executives were right if they guessed that the taste of the new rock 'n' roll audience would resemble the rhythm and blues pattern more closely than the country and western pattern, and chose to take a safe course by contracting only one or two singers and biding time till the fad faded.

The executives of the independents, in contrast, had every reason to promote rock 'n' roll, the more singers and records the better. Several of them already had the music in their catalogues, classified until now as rhythm and blues; for these it was easy enough to modify the arrangements, simplify the beat, and promote rhythm and blues as rock 'n' roll. Imperial with Fats Domino, King with Bill Doggett, and Aladdin with Shirley and Lee made the pop lists this way. Other executives welcomed new singers–and had the musical understanding to be able to recognize good ones. Still others saw the chance to break into the pop market, and although they had no greater sympathy for rock 'n' roll than the major company executives, they had far stronger motives to ensure the success of their records. This last group, in particular, had the least emotional loyalty to rock 'n' roll when radio stations began playing the music less often, and were the most ruthless in their treatment of the music in order to meet the changing standards.

The fortuitousness of Elvis Presley's discovery by Sam Phillips of

Sun records had made every record producer across the country a little more sympathetic to the hopeful young singers who asked if they could make a record, particularly if, like Presley, they came from Memphis. Presley's dark, heavy features, greasy black hair, and surly expression became elements of an image that producers everywhere sought or attempted to re-create.

In many cases, whether the singers they found had strong motivations for singing appeared to be irrelevant, or at least incidental. At one extreme was Paul Anka, scarcely into his teens and, according to his publicity, ambitious and bursting with feelings to share with the world; at the other, Fabiano Forte (known as Fabian), converted into a singer despite having no voice nor evident interest in singing. Between them was a range which included some singers who had been working in obscurity for several years and found in rock 'n' roll a lucky chance to reach a wider audience (Buddy Holly, Sonny James) and some who by inclination probably would have sought fame by being something other than a singer–a film star (Tab Hunter) or an athlete (Johnny Burnette).

By 1957, rock 'n' roll in general, and Elvis Presley in particular, had shown that once the range of catch-phrase novelty songs and suitable rhythm and blues hits had been exhausted, new kinds of songs became necessary. The songs needed a "beat", had to have a catchy chorus, and had to relate to adolescent life. Composers who had been writing show tunes and their equivalents could sometimes adapt to the new idiom, but most of the rock 'n' roll songs needed by the music industry were written by younger, or anyway different, people.

The conditions seemed to be present for a considerable change in the whole of the industry. But again, most of the serious challenges were diverted. Although adolescents had discovered a form of music that reflected their feelings about life in the city streets, juke joints, and dance halls, the music was also broadcast on the radio and television, and played on home record players. Programme planners, sifting through weekly batches of new releases, had to consider which records would satisfy the need for a beat without irritating parents. Anticipating this, songwriters, in turn, had to work in their teen-oriented messages without taking too great a stand against the adult world.

In 1957, a wide range of teen songs were popular, extending into a major genre of popular music songs with references to adolescence, the type of reference that had previously been made directly only occasionally, in such songs as "Goodnight, Sweetheart, Goodnight" (where the young boy has a hard time saying goodnight to his date), "Be-Bop-A-Lula", and "Blue Suede Shoes", and in such names of groups as the Teen Queens and the Teenagers.

The topics for discussion and comment in the new teen songs included preparing for a dance ("White Sport Coat") and getting there ("Short Fat Fanny", "Rock and Roll Music", "At the Hop"); declaring a particular kind of adolescent passion ("Young Love", "Butterfly", "Party Doll", "Peggy Sue", "Teenagers' Romance", "April Love", "Stood Up") and resenting adult derision of it ("Teenage Crush"); fearing parental discipline ("Wake Up, Little Susie") and expressing resentment against school ("School Day", "Waitin' in School"); and teenage slang ("Young Blood"). The singers sang less for themselves than for the people who listened, learned the words, and sang along. A new generation identified itself by the seriousness with which it regarded the feelings and experiences described in the songs.

"Young Love", recorded in million-selling versions by Sonny James for Capitol and Tab Hunter for Dot, was the first such song of 1957, and it nicely set the themes for the year:

Young love, first love/Is filled with true devotion;
Young love, our love/We share with deep emotion.

"Young Love" enabled the teenage listeners to reassure themselves that their emotions had unique, even eternal significance, and did it without imposing the message on people who might disagree.

"Teenage Crush", recorded soon afterwards by Tommy Sands (for Capitol), similarly preached to the converted without offending dissenters:

They call it a teenage crush,
They don't know how I feel;
They call it a teenage crush,
They can't believe this is real.

They've forgotten when they were young,
And the way they tried to be free;
All they say is, this young generation
Is just not the way that it used to be.

I know, I know my own heart,
But you say I'm trying to rush
Please don't try to keep us apart,
Don't call it a teenage crush.

Although the last lines of the lyric appeared to be addressing the adult generation, the appeal was rhetorical; the song was for young people to wallow in, and there was no aim to draw adult attention to it.

Sonny James, Tab Hunter, and Tommy Sands were among the first of the I-Owe-It-All-To-Elvis group of singers, who in their interviews vowed eternal gratitude to Presley for his influence and inspiration. Many of the singers had been professionals for some time before Presley started with Sun; few of them had direct stylistic connections with him. But in most cases, they would not have attracted much attention if Presley had not sung the way he did, looked the way he did, and sung the songs he did.

While some producers looked for singers with background and ability comparable to Presley's, those with the least patience came up with a number of alternatives, comparable to the kind of alternatives that had been presented to the people a few years earlier who had wanted rhythm and blues.

One source of singers was the infinite pool of aspiring crooners, which included singers not yet known for their preferred style and who therefore were available for presentation as "rock 'n' roll singers". Dot had proved it could be done with Pat Boone on "Tutti Frutti" and "Ain't That a Shame"; Coral, with Steve Lawrence, and Cadence, with Andy Williams, successfully offered cover versions of "Party Doll" and "Butterfly", respectively. This was comparable to a device more often employed by the majors–presenting an unknown country and western singer as a rock 'n' roller, as Capitol did with Sonny James and Tommy Sands, and Columbia with Marty Robbins ("White Sport Coat").

Film and television were both a useful source of people who already had large numbers of admirers. Tab Hunter, Sal Mineo (with "Start Movin'" for Epic), and Rick Nelson were the most successful of such media-derived performers in the early rock 'n' roll years; James Darren, Connie Stevens, and others made a similar move in the early sixties. Even a disc jockey, Jim Lowe, had a hit ("Green Door" for Dot).

Alongside these opportunists who jumped onto the teenage bandwagon were some genuine enthusiasts of rock 'n' roll, who understood its intentions and made contributions which compared with the best: in Clovis, New Mexico, Buddy Holly and his group the Crickets made some of the best rock 'n' roll records which dealt with love relationships; Eddie Cochran in Los Angeles and Jack Scott in Detroit came up with more formalized variants of the Memphis rockabilly style.

Meanwhile, some of the industry professionals who adapted to teenage tastes came up with such well-crafted records that their motives were irrelevant. In Nashville, Boudleaux and Felice Bryant wrote songs for the Everly Brothers which were unrivalled expressions of teen angst, while in New York the writers Jerry Leiber and Mike Stoller produced a series of records for the Coasters which may never be surpassed as economical frameworks for witty narrative cameos.

Realizing that teenage tastes were here to stay, the industry began to restructure itself to deal with them on a less arbitrary basis. Their key was to have A&R men who understood the new standards. Although the next two chapters discuss the majors and the indies as separate categories, increasingly the A&R men drew on the same pool of resources, serviced by producers who used the same session musicians, recording songs published by the same flock of independent companies, in studios which became noted for their ability to get that elusive "sound".

Where the orchestras and big bands of earlier pop styles had needed large rooms to capture their ambient sounds, now a more relevant criterion was an intimate atmosphere supervised by an engineer who would cope patiently with the sometimes amateur or eccentric performances coming onto their recording machines from behind the glass. Judicious use of echo, and ingenious editing of a master from the best bits of several different recordings, could make a silk purse out of a collection of sows' ears.

Among the adept engineers in New York were Tom Dowd (eventually contracted exclusively to Atlantic), Bobby Fein at Finesound, Al Weintraub at Bell Sound, and Irv Joel at A & R; on the West Coast, Bunny Robyn at Hollywood Studios and Bones Howe at Gold Star were the favourites for rock 'n' roll producers, all of them looking for the kind of effects that Sam Phillips had achieved at his own Sun studios in Memphis, and Cosimo Matassa had provided for the many producers who used his J & M Studio in New Orleans.

Feeding all this activity, a throng of publishers found a hungry market for any songs they could find with teen content. Hill and Range made an astute move in contributing to the "transfer fee" which brought Elvis Presley from Sun to RCA, acquiring the rights to the songs he had recorded for Sun and giving themselves the role of screening the songs he would record for RCA. The writers who were already signed to one of their companies had first shot, which helped the teams of Leiber and Stoller and Pomus and Shuman. Among the other publishers, Robert Mellin and Don Kirshner were outstanding. Mellin signed two particularly bright young writers, Paul Anka and Bobby Darin, and published early songs by the team of Neil Sedaka and Howie Greenfield before they signed to Kirshner.

Don Kirshner had been a co-writer and manager of Bobby Darin before he formed his own publishing company, Aldon, in partnership with Al Nevins. Long term contracts with Sedaka and Greenfield,

Carole King and Gerry Goffin, Barry Mann and Cynthia Weil, Jack Keller and several others enabled Kirshner to supply apparently endless streams of hits for Bobby Vee, Connie Francis, the Drifters, and whoever else asked for them; and everybody did ask.

4

THE MAJORS

Each of the major companies had a slightly different policy regarding rock 'n' roll, but until 1956 only Decca responded with real sympathy to the music by contracting a genuine rock 'n' roll singer–Bill Haley–and encouraging him to record in his preferred style. Given the general belief of the majors that rock 'n' roll was a fad which would soon disappear, their reluctance to get involved with it then stemmed partly from executive distaste for, or disinterest in, the music itself, and partly from the pattern of contracting practised by the majors.

The standard contract among the majors was for five years. This period enabled companies to spend some time in establishing a singer's reputation and to have sufficient time afterwards to earn the rewards when the singer became popular. In return for committing himself to a particular company, the singer normally was guaranteed a certain number of releases every year (although he could never insist that such releases be adequately promoted). This procedure of long-term contracts both relied on and tended to produce a system of gentle change in musical styles, as the majors recorded any kind of new song with the singers they already had, thus minimizing its new characteristics.

Singers who justified five-year contracts had to have wide, "all-round", long-term appeal. The quality they needed above all others to impress the A&R men of a major company was adaptability. Rock 'n' roll singers, who seemed to be flash-in-the-pan novelties with only one style, promised to be redundant before a couple of years were up.

Even before rock 'n' roll gave a name and an identity to the new music and market that emerged in the mid-fifties, the major companies had begun to make changes which in effect anticipated the emergence of a teenage sub-section of pop music. The evolution of the indie labels in the "rhythm and blues" market led to the creation of new distribution companies in each territory, and these distributors liaised with the local radio stations. The stores and radio shows which specialized in rhythm and blues had no regular contact with the major labels, and may even have boycotted them; Columbia and Victor were respectively associated with the network broadcasting companies CBS and NBC, and local radio stations might have preferred to play records on other labels. Partly to disguise their connections, some of the major companies formed subsidiary labels which could be distributed through the independent wholesalers.

Decca* was the best placed company to understand the appeal of rock 'n' roll as a result of the long-standing interest in black dance music of the company's founder, Jack Kapp. Under his direction Decca had signed up the majority of leading black acts including the dance-jazz big bands of Jay McShann, Lucky Millinder and Lionel Hampton, gospel singers Marie Knight and Rosetta Tharpe, vocal groups the Mills Brothers and the Ink Spots, and boogie combo leader Louis Jordan and his Tympany Five. These artists sold not only to black record buyers but through the pop market too, until the emergence of the indie distribution system made it harder for Decca to reach the black audience.

Jack Kapp's early death in 1949 forestalled his plans to adapt Decca to the changing times, and his brother Dave shuffled the A&R staff between Decca and its subsidiaries Coral and Brunswick in attempts to revitalize them. Milt Gabler made an inspired move in 1954 by signing Bill Haley and His Comets after the rock 'n' roll combo had scored one hit on the independent Essex label of Philadelphia. Milt was personally more proud of his work with Louis Jordan (and earlier with Billie Holiday on his own Commodore label), but he made his biggest dent in pop history by supervising the Haley sessions that

* DECCA. *Formed in 1934 as the American subsidiary of British Decca with Jack Kapp as President; bought from UK Decca in the mid-forties, and later taken over by MCA who dropped the Decca label in favour of the MCA label in the seventies. A&R staff in the fifties: Dave Kapp, Milt Gabler, Jimmy Hilliard, Bob Thiele, plus Paul Cohen and Owen Bradley (Nashville). Music Directors: Gordon Jenkins, Dick Jacobs.*
Black pop: Mills Brothers, Ink Spots, Al Hibbler, Ella Fitzgerald.
Rhythm and blues: Louis Jordan (till 1950), Buddy Johnson, Lionel Hampton, Lucky Millinder.
Gospel: Marie Knight, Sister Rosetta Tharpe.
Country and western: Red Foley, Ernest Tubb, Webb Pierce, Kitty Wells.
Rock 'n' roll: Bill Haley and His Comets.
Country pop: Bobby Helms, Brenda Lee.
Subsidiaries:

CORAL. *Formed 1949.*
Pop: McGuire Sisters, Teresa Brewer.
Rock 'n' Roll: Buddy Holly.

BRUNSWICK. *Revived 1957.*
Rock 'n' roll: The Crickets.
Rhythm and blues: Jackie Wilson.

LONDON. *Formed in 1948 as American division of UK Decca.*
Pop: Mantovani.

resulted in "Shake Rattle and Roll" and "Rock Around the Clock".

For the rest, Decca's records were mostly imitative (the McGuire Sisters and Teresa Brewer had several cover hits for Coral), or conservative (country crooner Bobby Helms had a couple of big pop hits with "Fraulein" and "My Special Angel" in 1957). Notable exceptions were Buddy Holly, the Crickets, and Brenda Lee, whose records matched the best that the indie labels could offer.

Brenda Lee's records were produced in Nashville by Owen Bradley, but she rarely made the country charts. Aged 15 when she recorded her first hit, "Sweet Nothin's", Brenda sang with an intriguing mixture of childish innocence and mature innuendo, evidently influenced more by rhythm and blues singers Ruth Brown and LaVern Baker than by any country singers. Her ballads were more conventional, but she maintained a sprinkling of lively, raunchy rockers in her remarkable run of 19 top twenty hits from 1959 through 1966. By contrast, Owen Bradley failed to bring the best out of Buddy Holly when he came from Texas to record for Decca in 1956, and seems to have missed the Johnny Burnette Trio as they trekked from their native Memphis in search of an audition. Surprisingly, Coral's New York office let them loose to record some of the most hard-edged, uninhibited rockers of the period, more or less unnoticed at the time but acclaimed since.

In 1957 A&R man Bob Thiele contracted to release masters produced in Clovis, New Mexico by Norman Petty of a local rock 'n' roll group the Crickets, putting the group's records out on Brunswick and lead singer Buddy Holly's records out on Coral. Brunswick also released records from 1957 by Jackie Wilson (formerly part of the vocal group, the Dominoes), who was to become one of the most consistent hit makers of the next fifteen years, performing material that ranged from pseudo-operatic melodramas, to more conventional ballads, to searing, gospel-styled dance songs.

Following Decca's contract with Bill Haley, no other major company made any significant move towards genuine rock 'n' roll performers until almost eighteen months later, when Mercury* contracted

* MERCURY. *Founded in 1946 in Chicago with Irving Green as President. Absorbed Majestic records in 1947. A&R staff included Mitch Miller (1948–50), Art Talmadge, Arnold Maxin, Bob Shad, Clyde Otis.*
Pop: Georgia Gibbs, Ralph Marterie, Xavier Cugat, Patti Page, Rusty Draper, the Crew Cuts, the Diamonds, Johnny Preston.
Rhythm and blues bands and combos: Buddy Johnson, Eddie Vinson, Sil Austin.
Rhythm and blues ballad singers: Dinah Washington, Sarah Vaughan, Brook Benton.
Vocal group: the Platters.
Rock 'n' Roll: Freddie Bell & the Bell Boys, The Big Bopper.
Swamp pop: Phil Phillips, Jivin' Gene.
Subsidiary:
SMASH. *Formed in 1961.*
Pop. Bruce Channel, Joe Barry.

the Penguins, a Los Angeles black vocal group whose "Earth Angel" (recorded for the independent Dootone) had provided material for Mercury's own Crew Cuts to cover. The Penguins were managed by Buck Ram, an experienced songwriter who negotiated a contract that obliged Mercury to sign up not only the Penguins but a second group, managed by Ram, the Platters. Although the Penguins made no more hits, the Platters produced more than any other group of the rock 'n' roll era.

Stylistically, the connections between the Platters and rock 'n' roll were thin; invariably the group's material was conventional pop music ballads, but in some records lead singer Tony Williams followed an improvised melody, distinguishing his sound from conventional pop music.

Earlier, Mercury had been the most thorough of all the majors in covering suitable rhythm and blues hits, a policy that effectively delayed the entry into the pop music market of several independents (in particular Atlantic, who had to sit back and watch while Mercury took cover versions of Atlantic's songs up the charts: "Sh-Boom", "Tweedle Dee", "Oh, What a Dream", and others).

But as cover versions by pop singers ceased to be acceptable to the audience, Mercury moved towards more authentic kinds of rock 'n' roll, following the northern band rock 'n' roll style of Bill Haley and His Comets with Freddie Bell and the Bell Boys, whose "Giddy-Up-A-Ding-Dong" was, in 1956, just too late to meet the demand for that kind of novelty song. Records made in the same year by Eddie Bond, a Memphis country rock singer, including "Rockin' Daddy" and "Boppin' Bonnie", seemed more likely to succeed, but despite the stylistic similarity to Carl Perkins, they received little attention.

In 1957 Mercury developed a more sophisticated method of covering rhythm and blues songs, with a version of "Little Darlin' " by the white Canadian group the Diamonds, who faithfully reproduced the entire sound–accent, intonation, arrangement–of the original version of the song by the Gladiolas on the independent Excello. This record established high-pitched wailing and shrill harmonies among the sounds that were acceptable to white record buyers, and eventually the members of the Gladiolas, renamed Maurice Williams and the Zodiacs, enjoyed their own success by topping the hit lists with "Stay" (Herald) in 1960. Meanwhile, Mercury continued a relatively adventurous policy of investigating new sounds and styles, particularly after Shelby Singleton joined the staff in the late fifties. Singleton was especially interested in southern styles, and recruited east Texas's Big Bopper, Johnny Preston, and Bruce Channel to the roster of Mercury and its Smash subsidiary, and acquired the rights to release various records that had sold well on independent lables in the South.

*

In contrast to the activity of Decca and Mercury, the initial reaction of RCA-Victor, Columbia and Capitol to rock 'n' roll was to hope it would go away. Victor and Columbia gave token recognition to the new idiom by announcing through the trade press in January, 1955, that they would record the novelty song, "Ko Ko Mo". This was probably the most extensively recorded rock 'n' roll song of that time. It was first recorded by Gene and Eunice for a small independent label, Combo, in 1954. A larger independent company, Aladdin, contracted Gene and Eunice and had them rerecord the song, and this version became a rhythm and blues hit. Featuring simple words (chiefly the title, followed by "I love you so"), sung to a jaunty rhythm and broken up by some lively sax playing, the song was covered by other rhythm and blues groups for Checker (the Flamingos) and Modern (Marvin and Johnny), whose owners presumably hoped to break into the pop market with the song. Such ambitions were foiled first by Mercury, who had the Crew Cuts do a version, and then by RCA-Victor and Columbia, who had Perry Como and Tony Bennett record their versions.

Bennett's sophisticated phrasing was uneasy with the rigid rhythm of the song, but Como's slicker version was more successful and became the most popular of all the "Ko Ko Mo" recordings, giving him and Victor their first rock 'n' roll hit. However, it became clear even to such pop music manufacturers as Hugo Winterhalter at Victor and Mitch Miller at Columbia that rock 'n' roll had its own particular idiom which needed talents different from those possessed by crooners. Miller at Columbia chose to ignore the music as best he could, but Victor's response was to go looking for somebody to do rock 'n' roll.

Towards the end of 1955, nine months after Como's "Ko Ko Mo", Victor* paid $30,000 to the independent company Sun–and gave Elvis Presley a Cadillac–for Presley's contract and rights to all his Sun

* RCA-VICTOR. *The Victor Talking Machine Company was formed in October 1901 by Emile Berliner and Eldridge Johnson, the pioneer inventors of mechanical recording and reproducing equipment. All six of the records estimated to have sold over a million copies in the United States prior to 1920 were issued on Victor, including two by Al Jolson and one by Caruso. In 1929 Victor was taken over by the Radio Corporation of America (RCA). A&R staff during the fifties: Charlie Green, Manie Sachs, Steve Sholes. Music director: Hugo Winterhalter. Head of Nashville division: Chet Atkins.*
Pop: Perry Como, Kay Starr, Lou Monte, Perez Prado, Harry Belafonte, Eartha Kitt, Neil Sedaka.
Country: Eddy Arnold, Hank Snow, Skeeter Davis, Don Gibson, Jim Reeves.
Rock 'n' Roll: Elvis Presley, Janis Martin.
Black pop: Jesse Belvin, Sam Cooke, the Isley Brothers.
Subsidiaries:

GROOVE. *Formed in 1953 under supervision of Bob Rolontz.*
Rhythm and blues: the Du-Droppers, Mickey and Sylvia, Piano Red.

X. *Formed in 1953 (renamed VIK in 1956).*
Pop: the Norman Petty Trio, Joe Valino.

material. The singer had been seen at a disc jockey's convention in Miami by Steve Sholes, RCA-Victor's A&R man in charge of music from the southern states. Sholes was impressed by the novelty of Presley's vocal style, his uninhibited movements on the stage, and the electrifying effect he had on the audience.

Compared to the money that record companies paid out to rock singers during the late nineteen-sixties (Columbia paid $300,000 to Johnny Winter in 1969), Victor's fee for Presley was nominal. But at the time it was huge, and the company committed itself to recouping the investment as fast as possible. To promote Presley's first RCA recording, "I Was the One"/"Heartbreak Hotel", the singer was booked for six weeks on Jackie Gleason's prime-time TV show.

The record coupled a modified country and western song with a modified blues song. Supplementing the bare instrumental accompaniments of slapped bass and rhythm guitar on typical Sun records, RCA introduced vocal group chorus and a much fuller orchestral sound, while still keeping the guitar prominent. "Heartbreak Hotel", an unremittingly gloomy chant of doom, proved to be the song that most affected the TV audience, and its sales quickly spread from the country and western market into first the pop market and then the rhythm and blues market. RCA had established that rock 'n' roll, theoretically a fusion of country and western, pop, and rhythm and blues, could in fact appeal simultaneously to audiences of all three kinds of music. Yet, like Decca, the company made little attempt to extend its success by contracting other good rock 'n' roll singers.

For eight years, from 1956 to 1963, the success of Elvis Presley preoccupied the music industry. In his first two years with RCA, Presley had the best-selling record in fifty-five of a hundred and four weeks, a domination that vastly exaggerated the quality of his records compared to others, but testified to the effective promotion from RCA and to the careful management of his career by Colonel Tom Parker, who tied Presley's career in music to an equally successful and valuable one in film.[1] And later, when it was not inevitable that every one of Presley's records would achieve the magic "Number One", they were still assured of sales of over a million copies throughout the world. Presley's voice had some quality that enabled people with a huge range of experiences, sensibilities, and interests to identify with him. Anxious to keep hold of an already interested audience, and extend Presley's appeal to an even wider public, RCA-Victor's producers gradually transformed the singer's style into a version of crooning, which had enabled Bing Crosby and Perry Como to keep large sales over a number of years.

Presley's vocal style became deeper, more self-conscious, and a tone of self-pity entered it. Instead of expressing the impatient determination to enjoy himself which had been the common mood on the Sun songs, he went through a succession of themes that he apparently was asked to interpret, which he did with commendable conviction and an increasingly mannered style. Of his 1956 releases, "Heartbreak Hotel" required the singer to be wracked by despair, which Presley seemed to be; with "Hound Dog", he became surly, derisive, tough; with "Don't Be Cruel", his voice became breathy, and the rhythm light; in "Love Me Tender", he became a ballad singer. Subsequent releases followed a similar pattern, and Presley's emotions were presented with accompaniments and emphasis that suggested they had epic significance. Occasionally, the records in 1956 and 1957 did not seem so contrived. "My Baby Left Me", probably previously recorded with Sun, sounded as if Presley was telling somebody in particular, rather than the world in general, of his predicament, and it had an undemonstrative urgency and excitement that later records tended to try for too obviously.

Following the success of "Hound Dog"/"Don't Be Cruel", RCA-Victor released seven singles simultaneously, almost all of which were cover versions of previous rhythm and blues hits, and some of which were probably recorded before the Victor contract, under the supervision of Sam Phillips, for intended release on Sun. "Blue Suede Shoes" made deliberate use of the rebellious potential in the song, which Carl Perkins, who originally recorded it, had tended to understate. "Trying to Get to You" was as close as Presley ever came to a blues song, which had excellent hard guitar playing behind Presley's suitably modest singing. "Lawdy, Miss Clawdy" (originally recorded as a rhythm and blues song by Lloyd Price) had a real desolation which made the artificiality of some later performances more obvious; the arrangement transposed the rhythm and blues song to rock 'n' roll without losing its plaintive appeal and gave it a good bouncy rhythm.

"Too Much" and "All Shook Up", Presley's first records of 1957, showed the style beginning to become contrived, as Presley dragged his vowels and punched every other beat harder than he needed to. But the songs for Presley's films *Loving You* and *Jailhouse Rock* were worse. Written by Leiber and Stoller, they allowed Presley to indulge his tendency to exaggerate the importance of his feelings and began his decline towards melodramatic popular songs, a decline that became "official" when he recorded "It's Now or Never" in a pseudo-operatic style in 1960.

The decline was in some ways the inevitable result of being uprooted from the culture that had produced his original style and of living in the limbo of Hollywood, Germany (during his army stint), and soft hotel rooms in between.

Occasionally, he was given a better song than his usual material, and it drew an improved performance from him. Such songs include "One Night" (previously recorded, with slightly different words, as "One Night of Sin" by Smiley Lewis) and "Mess of Blues". But essentially Presley was a pop music singer, more competent than most, with a mystique that retained a devoted audience. None of the singers who owed their original success to his were able to sustain their appeal for so long, or so consistently.

Apart from Presley, RCA-Victor achieved remarkably little success in the new market for teen music, and seemed content to reap the considerable benefits of acting as the main manufacturer of singles for many of the independent companies (including Dot). A fairly serious commitment was made to recording the "female answer to Elvis", Janis Martin, but although collectors have retrospectively cherished her energetic delivery of "Drugstore Rock 'n' Roll" and "Let's Elope", her records failed to impress teenagers at the time; made in Nashville, they sounded too tame for pop but too wild for country.

In an attempt to infiltrate the indie world, RCA formed the Groove and X subsidiaries in 1953, one aimed at the rhythm and blues market and the other covering all the bases but with a specific teen bias. Groove was modestly successful, with rhythm and blues hits by the old-fashioned boogie pianist Piano Red and the humorous vocal group the Du Droppers, and delivered one genuine classic: "Love is Strange" by Mickey and Sylvia. The duo comprised session guitarist Mickey Baker and 20-year old singer Sylvia Vanderpool, who delivered an intriguing, bantering vocal over a Caribbean-flavoured rhythm and made the top twenty in 1956; Baker's guitar break was probably the first real blues solo to reach so many people, and Sylvia's odd way of singing the word "baby" ("bay-ee-bee") infiltrated the whole of pop after Buddy Holly played around with a similar pronunciation.

By 1960, RCA had abandoned its subsidiaries and belatedly picked up a few "quality" artists with teen appeal for its main Victor label: Neil Sedaka, Jesse Belvin, Sam Cooke. But the phenomenal success of Elvis Presley tended to dwarf the success of other artists on the label, and RCA-Victor never achieved a satisfactory relationship with the artists, producers, and audience of teen music.

If Columbia* was in any way impressed by the income Presley was

* COLUMBIA. *Founded circa 1885. Musical Director and A&R chief during the fifties: Mitch Miller.*
Black ballad singer: Johnny Mathis.
Country and western: Gene Autry, Marty Robbins.
Rock 'n' roll: Sid King, Ronnie Self.
Pop: Doris Day, Guy Mitchell, Frankie Laine, Johnnie Ray, The Four Lads, Rosemary Clooney, Jo Stafford.

earning for his record company, or jealous of RCA's success, it gave little sign. There was one small hint that it did notice–Johnnie Ray's hit of 1956, "Just Walkin' in the Rain": the song was lifted from a Sun recording (by the Prisonaires). Otherwise, the company did its best to keep up the techniques that had been so effective during the early fifties, when Columbia had been the most successful of all the majors, with Frankie Laine, Guy Mitchell, Rosemary Clooney, Doris Day, Johnnie Ray, and Jo Stafford chasing each other up the charts, more or less in rotation. These singers were obliged to be adaptable. Guy Mitchell described how their records were planned:

> Before you begin to think of cutting a tune, you've got to find it. This takes anywhere from two days to two months. You may take time out every day to look over the material–may have to try a hundred new songs before you find one you like.
>
> At the same time your manager is doing the same thing–and so is the record company.
>
> You finally find the song you'd like to do and then the fun begins.
>
> "It's a good tune," your manager tells you. "But it's not your type." "It's okay," says the recording director. "Okay, but it won't sell. Not commercial."
>
> So you give up and look over the number your manager has selected. "It's great," you tell him. "But this is for Johnnie Ray, not for me."
>
> Then you look at the recording director's choice.
>
> "This is a song?" you ask him.
>
> "Maybe it doesn't look like anything now," he replies. "But wait till you hear the arrangement we can do on it. We can give it a real sound."
>
> "To me it sounds screwy from scratch, but who knows what makes a record a hit?[2]

As some kind of justification for failing to match RCA's success with an equivalent rock 'n' roll singer, Columbia's A&R head, Mitch Miller, could point to his remarkable success with Johnny Mathis, a young black singer with a "husky" voice similar to Nat "King"

Subsidiary labels:

EPIC
Black ballad singer: Roy Hamilton.

OKEH.
Rhythm and blues singers: The Treniers, Chuck Willis, Larry Darnell, Paul Gayten, Titus Turner, Big Maybelle, Annie Laurie, Chris Powell.
Rock 'n' roll singer: Screamin' Jay Hawkins.

Cole's who was one of the first singers to have albums that sold over a million copies. Columbia's country and western division did record some country rock late in 1955, including "Sag, Drag and Fall" by Sid King and the Five Strings, and in 1957 some harsh rasping songs by Ronnie Self. But the most enterprising records made were those made by the autonomous subsidiary OKeh.

OKeh had been one of the first independent "race" labels, recording various kinds of blues in the nineteen twenties. Its catalogue was acquired by Columbia during the depression, and was kept "alive" by the addition of rhythm and blues singers through the nineteen-fifties. Johnnie Ray's "Cry", which did exceptionally well in the rhythm and blues market in addition to its pop success, was issued on OKeh, and may even have been originally intended for the smaller market.

One of the most extraordinary records ever made was "I Put a Spell On You", the first rock 'n' roll record made for OKeh in 1956 by a former rhythm and blues singer, Jalacy Hawkins, who now called himself Screamin' Jay Hawkins. Reputedly in a drunken stupor, the singer ranted and raved through the parts of the song he could remember, while equally drunk musicians laid down a beat as best they could. The performance had a compelling atmosphere, although the grunts and groans that originally began the record were wiped off when radio stations objected to their outrageous implications.

The most immediate, successful major company response to Presley's Victor recordings was by Ken Nelson, the Nashville A&R man for Capitol,* who signed a group from Norfolk, Virginia, led by Gene Vincent whose first record for Capitol was a convincing recreation by Capitol engineers of the immediacy of country rock. Using what the technicians called "flutter echo" to distort Vincent's naturally gentle voice and allowing the accompanying musicians (the Blue Caps) to play with uncomplicated arrangements, the company achieved the desired effect. Lead guitarist Cliff Gallop produced a swirling, dipping sound that provided a hard background harmony to Vincent's impassioned vocal on both sides of his first single, "Be-Bop-A-Lula"/"Woman Love". Both songs used evocative images out of the blues tradition.

In "Be-Bop-A-Lula", Vincent cried:

* CAPITOL. *Founded by Glenn E. Wallichs, Buddy DeSylva, and Johnny Mercer in Los Angeles in 1942. Bought out by E.M.I. (UK), 1956. Music Directors: Les Baxter, Billy May, Nelson Riddle, A&R man: Ken Nelson, Voyle Gilmore, Dave Cavanagh, Dave Dexter, Jr.*
Black ballad singers: Nat "King" Cole, Julia Lee, Nellie Lutcher.
Country and western: Hank Thompson, Tennessee Ernie Ford, Ella Mae Morse, Merrill Moore, Ferlin Husky.
Black vocal group: The Five Keys.
Rock 'n' roll: Gene Vincent, Esquerita, Johnny Otis.

See the woman walkin' down the street.
She's the woman that's got that beat.

"Be-Bop-A-Lula"–Gene Vincent & Sheriff Tex Davis,
Copyright © 1956–Lowery Music Co., Inc., Atlanta. Ga. 30319

His high-pitched, emphatic voice was in some ways the definitive white rock 'n' roll singing style, matching Chuck Berry's among black singers. Vincent did not sound like either a country and western singer or a rhythm and blues singer, as so many other so-called rock 'n' roll singers did. Yet with remarkable quickness, he lost the powerful impact of the first record, first through much weaker songs, and then through attempts to modify his sound through the addition of background voices and the substitution of gentle rhythms for the fierce attack of "Be-Bop-A-Lula". (During the early fifties, the company had also made some records that featured a boogie piano rhythm behind a country and western vocal style–Tennessee Ernie's "Shotgun Boogie", and Ella Mae Morse's "Cow Cow Boogie"–but achieved no real fusion of styles in the sense of either's being modified to fit the conventions of the other.)

In addition to finding the most effective "answer" to Elvis Presley, Capitol was also the only company to find any kind of answer to the wildness of Little Richard, in an equally bizarre performer who called himself Esquerita. As "S. Q. Reeder" he had recorded "Green Door", an excellent rock 'n' roll song that was not done justice to in the hit version by Jim Lowe. For Capitol Esquerita cut a series of the most frantic rock 'n' roll records ever made. If a producer or arranger was deputed to the sessions, he must have been bound and gagged and put in a corner, for there was little sign that anyone responsible for the records had been concerned for their commercial potential. Several of Esquerita's eight records were roughly based on recent Little Richard hits, but only roughly. The singer had a lower register and narrower range than Richard, and virtually spoke the lyrics in a gruff, hoarse shout, occasionally breaking into a wavering falsetto. Few of the records sounded as if the band had ever played the songs before, and frequently most of the musicians took off on searing solos whose key and tempo were only vaguely connected to those of others in the band. Esquerita played piano with a speed and staccato attack that echoed Little Richard's style, but the overall sound here in some way conjured a chaotic symphony, as a succession of chords chased each other desperately up the keyboard. The violence that was normally only a promise (or threat) in rock 'n' roll was realized in Esquerita's sound. Yet even in these records the songs were still about conventional themes–being deprived of love ("I Need You"), being isolated from the enjoyment of a party ("Rockin' the

Joint"), and simply being ecstatic about a girl ("Batty over Hattie").

A more representative reflection of the prevailing attitudes towards rock 'n' roll at Capitol was expressed in a series of parody records released by Stan Freberg. Already well-known through various radio and TV shows, Freberg became the unofficial spokesman for the anti-rock 'n' roll lobby with spoof versions of early rock 'n' roll hits "Sh-Boom", "The Great Pretender" and "Heartbreak Hotel". Mocking the muffled voices, triplet piano parts and overloaded echoes, Freberg populated his records with bored musicians who did not know how to play badly enough and who refused not to swing. "The Banana Boat Song" was less bitter and funnier, but "The Old Payola Roll Blues" came near the bone in 1960, presenting a cynical producer who stopped a kid out in the street, congratulated him on having such a marketable name ("Clyde Ankle"), and provoked a satisfactory vocal performance out of him by judicious use of a sharp stick. The record is probably the best available document of how badly the industry establishment felt about rock 'n' roll and the men who made money from it. One man who might have been upset at the time was Johnny Otis.

One of the first to realize the potential of a travelling rhythm and blues show that featured several outstanding singers, Otis gradually changed the line-up and sound of his band to accommodate the shift to rock 'n' roll. Joining Capitol in 1957, he made the top twenty in 1958, with "The Johnny Otis Hand Jive", a novelty dance song that used the "Bo Diddley" rhythm. Singing in a clear tone with a plaintive edge to it, Otis made several ingenious, witty songs that had little musical originality but more spirit than most other so-called rock 'n' roll records of the time–"Crazy Country Hop", "Telephone Baby", "Three Girls Named Molly Doin' the Hully Gully", and "Mumblin' Mose". He also featured the strongly blues-tinged voice of Marie Adams on several records, including "Ma, He's Makin' Eyes at Me", which featured a screaming audience and was a big hit in Britain, and "The Light Shines in My Window", a fine ballad blues that rode well on a jaunty rock 'n' roll rhythm.

While Capitol seemed baffled by the tastes of the new teenage audience, the company was probably the most alert of the majors in recognizing and satisfying a slightly older, college-based audience who provided the Kingston Trio with a large and loyal album market after they surfaced in the pop market with the folk song "Tom Dooley" (top of the singles chart in 1958). The names of other Capitol acts made the college connection more obvious: the Four Freshmen perfected a slick, four-part jazz harmony style that influenced many vocal groups including two more of Capitol's college groups, the Four Preps and the Lettermen.

The Four Preps had sung behind Ricky Nelson before going with Capitol, but they never came close even to his softened version of rock 'n' roll, and settled for a pop sing-along approach under Voyle Gilmore's supervision. But "Big Man" was a good song (written by group members Bruce Belland and Glen Larson) enhanced by a majestic piano part from Lincoln Mayorga. Larson "graduated" from the group to become one of Hollywood's most successful film and television producers, and another member Ed Cobb became a writer and producer of several minor classics including Gloria Jones's "Tainted Love", the Standells' "Dirty Water", and Brenda Holloway's "Every Little Bit Hurts". Capitol belatedly and ironically catered for a young teenage audience to much better effect during the sixties with the Beach Boys and the Beatles.

MGM* came into the record market just after the Second World War finished, and seemed entrenched in a comfortable, inconspicuous position when rock 'n' roll came along to shake the scene up. The company showed little interest until a new A&R team was brought in with Arnold Maxim at the helm, whose adroit moves included signing Connie Francis as an artist and Jim Vienneau as a producer.

Connie Francis was from the same Italian-American background as most of the male teen idol types who moved into charts through TV shows and the picture-based fan magazines, and with help from a succession of Hollywood movies aimed at the same market she maintained a run of 22 top twenty hits in the six years from 1958 through 1963. Alongside tailor-made songs from Howie Greenfield (in collaboration with both Neil Sedaka and Jack Keller), Connie did several oldies in the new teen-beat genre that arranger Jack Hansen concocted, enabling Connie to reach the moms and dads as well as the kids. Almost buried in the corny arrangements were occasional glimpses of "rock 'n' roll" styled guitar breaks, and some of the songs were clever angles on teen romance: "My Heart Has a Mind of its Own", and "Lipstick on Your Collar".

Jim Vienneau was a new young producer based in Nashville when MGM took him on, and he specialized in devising epic arrangements

* MGM. *Formed in Hollywood in 1946 as a division of the film company. A&R staff: Frank Walker, Harry Meyerson; replaced circa 1956 by Arnold Maxin and Morty Craft; Nashville: Jim Vienneau. Music Director: Leroy Holmes.*
Country and western: Hank Williams.
Black pop: Billy Eckstine, Ivory Joe Hunter, Tommy Edwards.
Pop: Conway Twitty, Connie Francis.

Subsidiary:

CUB.

Black pop: Jimmy Jones, The Impalas.

for over-blown ballads of torment and distress. Roy Orbison later became the master of this kind of record, but he must have been impressed by the MGM hits by Conway Twitty and Mark Dinning. "Conway Twitty" was the name taken on by a would-be rocker from Arkansas called Harold Jenkins, who failed an audition at Sun and made a couple of obscure singles on Mercury before finding his feet–or rather, his voice–at MGM. Elvis Presley had just made number one with "Don't", in a breathy, extravagantly moody style, when Twitty recorded a mournful ballad called "It's Only Make Believe", and his gasping, end-of-the-world vocal seemed to bring an end to the era of innocence that had opened with "Young Love". Now the message was, we can't dupe them any more:

People see us everywhere
They think that you really care
But myself I can't deceive
I know it's only make believe

As his name hinted, there was a tongue-in-cheek slant to Twitty's performances, but after a few more years of making similar but less successful records he switched to straight country; after a period of obscurity he emerged with a series of hits on Decca/MCA which made him one of Nashville's most consistent hit-makers ever.

MGM's other hits of the fifties tended to be one-offs; the label's pop subsidiary Cub had a couple of hits by Jimmy Jones ("Handy Man" and "Good Timin'", arranged by Leroy Kirkland and Bob Mersey) and one by the Impalas ("Sorry (I Ran All the Way Home)" arranged by Ray Ellis), but the company probably had the greatest satisfaction from the enormous world-wide success of "It's All in the Game" by Tommy Edwards, a black singer in an old-fashioned Nat "King" Cole vein.

ABC* was the first major company to be formed in the middle of the rock 'n' roll era, and along with Mercury had the most open-minded and flexible approach to the teen market. A&R was shared between music directors Don Costa and Sid Feller, whose two "finds" were respectively Paul Anka and Lloyd Price, and apart from these direct signings the company made a regular habit of licensing

* ABC-PARAMOUNT. *Formed in Hollywood in 1955. President: Sam Clark. A&R and Music Directors: Don Costa, Sid Feller.*
Pop: Paul Anka.
Black pop: Lloyd Price, Ray Charles.
Rock 'n' roll: Danny and the Juniors.

Subsidiary:

APT
Vocal group: the Elegants.

finished masters or even released records from independent producers.

Paul Anka was, along with Bobby Darin, the most versatile of the singers who have been thrown into the "teen idol" category. A precocious fifteen-year old from Canada, Anka had already made an obscure single for Modern Records of Hollywood before joining ABC, where his first single "Diana" became a teen anthem that spent more than six months on the national charts. Where rock 'n' roll had seemed to be about self-assertion, Anka brought in the self-pity that was to become a feature of teen music from then on. Twelve more hits in the next four years mostly repeated the same mood, to greatest effect over the bullfighter beat of "Lonely Boy", before Anka switched to RCA-Victor and became an institution through cabaret, TV, Hollywood movies, and songs for other people including the English lyric for the all-time Las Vegas hit "My Way".

For a more authentic rock 'n' roll, ABC went to the independent producers: "Short Shorts" by the Royal Teens, "Black Slacks" by Joe Bennett and the Sparkletones, but best of all, "At The Hop" by Danny and the Juniors. A blatant copy of the triplets-and-boogie woogie approach of Jerry Lee Lewis, "At The Hop" did have a life and identity of its own through the dumb lyric and back-up noises, but the Philadelphia five-piece were never able to recapture such a combination of infectious words and dance beats.

Lloyd Price also came to ABC through a licensed record deal, when his "Just Because" on KRC attracted air-play. Already well known through his earlier rhythm and blues hit "Lawdy Miss Clawdy", Price was signed direct to ABC for future recordings, and proceeded to concoct with arranger Sid Feller a New York version of the New Orleans sound which Dave Bartholomew had organized to such effect for Fats Domino, Shirley and Lee, and for Lloyd himself five years before on "Lawdy Miss Clawdy".

Impressed by the success of this former rhythm and blues artist in the pop market, ABC scanned the rhythm and blues indies for another likely crossover candidate, and focussed in on Ray Charles. After a ten-year run of rhythm and blues hits, first with Swingtime and since 1953 with Atlantic, Ray had just broken through with his first big pop hit, "What'd I Say?" when his Atlantic contract expired in 1959. ABC stepped in with an offer which Atlantic could not match, improving Ray's artist royalty and adding the bonus of a producer royalty for supervising his own sessions; plus the concession that rights to his recordings would revert to him when he left the company.

In his autobiography, *Brother Ray*, Ray Charles insisted that the move to ABC did not change the approach to recording he had honed under the benevolent supervision of Ahmet Ertegun and Jerry Wexler at Atlantic: "the microphones didn't know what label they belonged to". With ABC's machine and assertive marketing behind him, Ray Charles became an institution, building on the "genius" tag that Atlantic had given him with concept albums including *Genius Hits The Road* which spawned the languorous, and now definitive, version of "Georgia On My Mind", *Genius + Soul = Jazz*, and most successful of all, *Modern Sounds in Country & Western Music* whose "I Can't Stop Loving You" was one of the biggest hits of the period.

During the heyday of rock 'n' roll from 1955 through 1959, just under half of the top ten hits (147 of 342) could be classified as rock 'n' roll, through their use of either an emphatic back-beat from the drummer or a vocal style with obvious rhythm and blues influences. Of those 147 rock 'n' roll hits, just under one third (46) were issued on major labels, compared to 101 on indie labels. Of the ten artists who had three or more hit records in the top ten, only Elvis Presley (with fifteen) and Lloyd Price (three) recorded for major companies.[3]

The general feeling of the major companies towards rock 'n' roll was probably expressed through their heavy promotion, during the last months of 1956 and on into 1957, of calypso music, which they believed–or anyway hoped–would be the new craze to replace rock 'n' roll. Victor did the best in this new style, with several hits by Harry Belafonte. (Columbia also had hits by Terry Gilkyson and the Easy Riders, and by the Tarriers.)

Given the way the major companies seemed to think and operate, calypso no doubt seemed to them a logical and clever answer to the dilemma of needing to divert their audience's attention from a product that the independent companies were best able to supply. Calypso was a black people's music, as jazz and rhythm and blues before it had been. Further, it had a Latin beat, which had always seemed to fit nicely into North American popular music. (Mambo had recently been successful in the United States and was even featured in *Rock Around the Clock*.) Best of all, there were enough novelty songs in calypso with no *sensual* implications for the companies to escape having to deal with the disturbing content of rhythm and blues. (Of course there were many calypso songs in existence that were far more suggestive than Hank Ballard's hits. But these could be–and were–ignored by Harry Belafonte.)

The calypso hits–"Banana Boat Song", "Mama Look-A-Boo-Boo", "Marianne"–were chiefly novelty songs with a lilting rhythm. Almost the only one with enduring quality was the charming "Love is Strange", recorded by Mickey and Sylvia for RCA's rhythm and blues market subsidiary, Groove.

But while rock 'n' roll continued to interest record buyers, despite major company indifference to it, calypso was never more than a fad, despite the enthusiasm with which the major labels promoted it. To the company's credit, in the early sixties RCA did sign up Sparrow, the leading calypsonian from Trinidad, but by then the impetus for the music had been lost, and Sparrow had to be content with the considerable achievement of selling out Madison Square Gardens every year without ever seeing his records in any American charts.

The mostly slow and unsympathetic response of the major companies to rock 'n' roll enabled independent companies to dictate the fate of the music. They brought it to life in 1953, force-fed it for five years, and left it for dead in 1958. Yet if they thought they could outlive the music which put them shoulder-to-shoulder with the majors, they were to discover that nothing was so easy; within five years, most of the indies had themselves followed rock 'n' roll to an early grave. Their story follows.

5

THE INDEPENDENTS

Rock 'n' roll expressed the spontaneous, personal response of singers to city environments. Considered objectively, it did not seem to contain any characteristic that should have made it impossible for major company studios to capture its essential qualities. Yet very few such studios did capture them, and most of those were the Nashville "outposts" of the companies, whose directors were allowed to produce relatively unsophisticated records for the local market. The overwhelming majority of both the best (musically and artistically) and the most successful (commercially) rock 'n' roll records were produced by independent companies.

By the mid-fifties, the independent labels had evolved a structure for reaching their audience which gave them as good a chance of having a hit with a new record as any of the majors. But the structure which had evolved to serve the pioneer rhythm and blues labels was just as accessible to a new company, and for eight years from 1956 through 1963 the American record business exploded with a profusion of labels. Among the most successful new companies were several formed by businessmen who shared the contemptuous attitude of some major label A&R men towards rock 'n' roll, whose producers had no background experience of the music from which rock 'n' roll drew and who simply handled it as a product like any previous form of popular music.

There was a strong tendency for the rock 'n' roll records made by companies with rhythm and blues experience to be considerably better than those made by companies with little or no such experience. The following discussion of the roles of the various companies in developing rock 'n' roll divides the companies accordingly and begins with the companies that formerly had recorded rhythm and blues.

I

The year 1954 was the one in which most rhythm and blues companies broadened the horizons of their market to include youthful white record buyers in the popular music market. Many of the companies had built themselves up from humble beginnings immediately after World War II, when garages served as recording studios and the boots of the owner's cars were the companies' only form of distribution. Unlike the majors, overlaid with conventional corporation structures of administration and decision-making, the independents relied almost entirely on the ingenuity of their owners, who functioned as their own talent scouts, producers, and distributors, as well as the makers of all policy decisions.

Many of the companies that were started after the end of the Second World War ceased to operate before rock 'n' roll was conceived. Even National, the most successful of all the independents between 1945 and 1950, folded in the early fifties–despite several hits by Dusty Fletcher and the Ravens and million-selling records by Billy Eckstine and Eileen Barton.

Of the companies that did survive, almost every one made some attempt to meet the taste for rock 'n' roll. In contrast to the majors, the independents often looked for singers with specific styles that would appeal to particular, often local, audiences. The independents had low overheads–office rental, a secretary, payment to the record manufacturer (many of the biggest plants were, ironically, owned by the majors, who thus earned money even from independent successes), and maybe a few gifts to certain disc jockeys in return for playing the record. To cover this, independents needed sales of a few thousands, in contrast to the tens of thousands a major had to sell to meet the high overheads incurred in a big organization. In the rhythm and blues market, and now with rock 'n' roll in the popular market, there were local audiences with particular tastes that the independents were ready to serve.

Of the various rock 'n' roll styles, country rock perhaps had the most localized audience, appealing particularly to white southern youth when it was not nationally accepted. Sun Records of Memphis, the company that introduced the style, continued to be the dominant source, but other southern-based companies (including Meteor, also in Memphis, and Excello, in Nashville) recorded the style, as did King in Cincinnati, Chess in Chicago, and Specialty in Los Angeles: all these companies recorded country rock only with southern singers, to whom the style was natural.

The New Orleans band rock 'n' roll, introduced by Fats Domino on Imperial, Shirley and Lee on Aladdin, and Little Richard on Specialty, continued to be recorded by these companies, and from 1955 by Ace Records–founded near New Orleans, in Jackson, Mississippi. One of the most universally acceptable rock 'n' roll styles, it was nevertheless surprisingly hard to either adapt or adopt successfully, and other companies could not convincingly reproduce the sound without New Orleans musicians and singers.

In Chicago, Chess continued to record the guitar rock 'n' roll of the inventive Chuck Berry and Bo Diddley, and while other companies all over the country made use of the "Bo Diddley" rhythm, nobody else could effectively use Chuck Berry's style.

Although companies in each region tended to concentrate particularly on styles with local associations, almost all of them recorded vocal groups during 1954 in an attempt to break into the national market. In New York, Philadelphia, Boston, Chicago, Detroit, Los Angeles, Baltimore, Pittsburgh, and the other big cities of the North, Midwest, and West, there were large audiences of young record buyers of various racial origins interested in the group sound (whose development as a rhythm and blues style is discussed in the section "Into the Cities"). Curiously, no important record companies were formed in Boston, Baltimore, or Pittsburgh, and until 1956, there were none of significance in Detroit or Philadelphia. But companies based in New York (Jubilee, Atlantic, Herald/Ember, and Rama), Chicago (Chess/Checker, Chance, and Vee Jay), Cincinnati (King/Federal/De Luxe), and Los Angeles (Aladdin, Modern, Specialty, and Imperial) served this audience with records in various group styles. Many records sold very well locally, and a few were accepted outside their own areas and became national hits.

i. Jubilee,* formed in 1948, had been the first to establish the possibility of reaching the white market with a black vocal group, when the Orioles' "Crying in the Chapel" made the pop music top twenty in 1953. In 1954 the company repeated its success with simple sing-along songs by the Four Tunes: "Marie" and "I Understand". The subsidiary Josie had hits with the fast scat harmonies and bragging attack of "Speedoo" by the Cadillacs (1956) and the Mexican-influenced rhythms of the timeless invitation "Do You Wanna Dance?" by Bobby Freeman (1958). Jubilee's last rock 'n' roll hit was "Poor Boy"/"Wail!" by the Royaltones, an unusually good instrumental that featured a screaming sax reminiscent of the rhythm and blues of almost ten years before.

Although Jubilee continued to have occasional hits in various styles, the company concentrated mainly on minority and specialist

* JUBILEE. *Founded in 1948, in New York by Jerry Blaine.*
Rhythm and blues singers: Edna McGriff.
Groups: The Orioles, the Four Tunes, the Cadillacs.
Rock 'n' Roll: Bobby Freeman, the Royaltones.

Subsidiary:

JOSIE.

markets outside the mainstream of popular music, including "party records". Showing neither great initiative nor undue commercialism, the company nevertheless made some exceptional records, particularly those of the Orioles. Its history contrasts with the flamboyance of Atlantic,* formed in the same years, 1948.

The staff of Atlantic (still an active company) has shown a flair for assessing performing styles and audience tastes that has been unmatched in the post-war history of popular music. Beginning with a roster of performers randomly collected from individuals without contracts, Atlantic–founded by Ahmet Ertegun and Herb Abramson, who together supervised the label's sessions through to 1953–picked up a succession of singers from various sources and with various styles. From the modest total of three records that made the rhythm and blues top ten in 1950, Atlantic steadily increased its share of the market through 1956, when the company had seventeen hits (of a total of eighty-one that made the top ten in that year).[1] Although some of these successes were achieved with singers who had already had hits with other labels–Ray Charles, Ivory Joe Hunter, and Chuck Willis–in each case the singer developed a distinctly new style with Atlantic. The other singers who made top records were either virtually unknown when Atlantic contracted them, or else had not yet had a major hit.

Most of the hits until 1956 were supervised by Ahmet Ertegun and from 1954 onward with Jerry Wexler's assistance. Several were aimed at the pop market, but during the first half of the fifties Atlantic did not have the resources to compete with the better distribution systems of the major companies who copied its records. Atlantic records by the Chords, LaVern Baker, Ruth Brown, and Joe Turner had modest pop success in 1954, but in each case were outsold by million-selling cover versions. Ertegun had discovered formulas to meet the taste of the growing rock 'n' roll audience, but apparently would not receive the reward. Ironically, the catchy song titles, nonsense choruses, and

* ATLANTIC. *Formed in 1948 in New York by Herb Abramson and Ahmet Ertegun.*
A&R: Jerry Wexler (from 1953), Nesuhi Ertegun (jazz, from 1954), Jerry Leiber and Mike Stoller (freelance, from 1956).
Rhythm and blues (male): Joe Turner, Ray Charles, Clyde McPhatter, Chuck Willis, Ivory Joe Hunter.
Rhythm and blues (female): LaVern Baker, Ruth Brown.
Groups: The Clovers, Drifters, Cardinals.
Subsidiary labels:

ATCO
Pop: Bobby Darin.
Rock 'n' roll group: the Coasters.
Rhythm and blues: Ben E. King.

CAT
Rhythm and blues group: the Chords.

lively rhythms with which he had hoped to draw the white audience's attention to his (unknown) singers were easily adopted by other producers. Atlantic was obliged to develop styles that were more personal and that relied less on the catchiness of the material.

One example was LaVern Baker, whose little-girl charm on "Tweedle Dee" (1954) and "Tra La La" (1956) was borrowed by Georgia Gibbs. On "Jim Dandy" (1957), Baker displayed a rougher, deeper voice that successfully evaded imitation and established her name in the pop market. Another example was Chuck Willis, who, with "C. C. Rider" in 1957, became one of the few singers with a genuine blues style to make the pop music top twelve as a rock 'n' roll singer.

"C. C. Rider" was a triumph of production technique for Jerry Wexler. The band, led by Jesse Stone, opened with marimba, while a girl group chanted gently in the background, "see . . . see . . . rider . . . see . . . see . . . rider . . .". Almost lost, far away in the background, Chuck Willis came in with an easy rocking, high-wailing vocal, taking Ma Rainey's song along a new melody, pausing a while for a beautifully restrained tenor solo from Gene Barge and then soaring back to finish the song. This was one of the best records of its time, not really rock 'n' roll or rhythm and blues but an inspired mood that drew from both styles and also from conventional popular music. Other records by Willis were good, but not comparable to "C. C. Rider", and his only other hit, "What Am I Living For?" was sweeter, a more obvious compromise with popular music's demands for a simple melody and an easily memorable chorus. Willis, variously acclaimed as "the king of the stroll" and "the sheik of the shake", was apparently a fine performer with a good feeling for the flamboyance required of certain kinds of rock 'n' roll singers, and dressed himself in the garb of the East, complete with turban. He died in 1958, near his home town, Atlanta, Georgia.

Atlantic continued to link aspects of traditional blues and rhythm and blues to conventional forms of popular music, making use of outstanding session men, among them the pianists and session leaders Jesse Stone, Howard Biggs, and Henry Van Walls, guitarist Mickey Baker, and sax men King Curtis and Sam Taylor. When the wave of rock 'n' roll swept white singers and several pop-oriented record companies into the rhythm and blues market in 1957, companies such as Atlantic were in the curious position of being edged out of their own market at the same time as they were expanding into the pop market themselves. Atlantic's response was to record straight rock 'n' roll by a local singer of Italian origin, Bobby Darin.

The band arrangements on Darin's rock 'n' roll records were

modelled roughly on the New Orleans style, but had a less relaxed feeling and seemed incongruous behind the contrived "drive" of Darin's voice. Whatever their failings, the records sold well enough–"Splish Splash" and "Queen of the Hop" (Atco, 1958) made the top ten in both pop and rhythm and blues markets. But although he could "pass" as a rock 'n' roll singer, this was not Bobby Darin's special strength. He was a versatile and capable singer-writer who could take a turn at virtually any current style of popular music, and over the next few years he went through most of them, one by one. In 1959 he got to number two on the chart with "Dream Lover", an exercise in writing a classy song using the very basic chord structure that the old guard of professional song crafters despised so much in the new teen ballads; a huge orchestra and vocal chorus backed up Darin's plea for his perfect partner.

Having conquered the teen market, Darin switched his attention to the grown-up world of cabaret clubs with a swinging (rather than rocking) version of "Mack the Knife", the hit song from the Weill and Brecht *Threepenny Opera*, which he sang as Frank Sinatra might have done it. Top of the chart for nine weeks towards the end of 1959, the record was far-and-away Atlantic's biggest record so far, and duly set Darin up for whatever kind of career he wanted. Continuing to update pre-rock-era standards with arrangements that probably appealed more to adults than teenagers, he returned to form in 1961 with a couple of witty pop songs recorded out in Los Angeles, where he had moved in pursuit of a film career. "Multiplication" had some funny lines, and "Things" in 1962 was even better, snappily sung over a mock-vaudeville accompaniment.

Never really committing himself to the teenagers who had bought his first records, Darin in effect sketched out the possibilities of a career for a new kind of artist, the singer-songwriter, and along with Paul Anka and Neil Sedaka he prepared the way for Paul Simon, Neil Diamond, and even Bob Dylan, who sang their own songs through the sixties.

Meanwhile Atco enjoyed a parallel series of hits by the Coasters, who were contracted by Atlantic in 1956, in a deal that involved not only the group but their songwriter/producers Jerry Leiber and Mike Stoller. Maintaining an independent status (which enabled them to write and produce for other companies), Leiber and Stoller contracted to write and produce material for the Coasters, and created one of the most entertaining series of hits associated with rock 'n' roll. The two men were among the few writers to put to advantage rock 'n' roll's restriction on verse forms–the fact that images needed to be specific, complete, preferably succinct. Accepting this limitation, Leiber and Stoller produced songs in which a part of life was described from a particular person's experience, and some conclusion, perhaps a moral, was drawn.

Leiber, who wrote the words, had grown up in an integrated section of Baltimore, and had an unusual flair for vernacular phrasing and language, which he used in most of the Coasters' hits. The writers had been working with the group–at that time called the Robins–in Los Angeles for a couple of years before they moved to Atlantic, and had some local and national rhythm and blues hits. But the first pop market hit was "Searchin'"/"Young Blood" in 1957, two good songs which were both widely imitated.

"Searchin'" had a pounding rhythm from an "alley" piano style–essentially two bass notes, played alternately on every second beat–and with a raw vocal from the group's baritone, Billy Guy, and suitably rough support from the rest of the group, was one of the greatest of all rock 'n' roll hits. The basic idea behind the song was traditional rhythm and blues–get a simple rhythm, and restrict improvisation to melody and phrasing. Here, Leiber's imagination served him well–the singer declared his determination to find his girl, if necessary by using the battery of detective techniques developed by Charlie Chan, Sam Spade, Bulldog Drummond. "And like that Northwest Mountie, you know I'll bring her in some day."* This was one of the first songs to introduce specific figures from American popular culture into its lyrics. After "Searchin'" they kept coming into other songs, and in the Olympics' "Western Movies" (1958), and the Hollywood Argyles' "Alley Oop" (1960), a similar piano figure was used as well.

"Young Blood", a view of street corner society that was the second–the 'B'-side of "Searchin'", introduced in its arrangement a technique that Leiber and Stoller subsequently used in most of the Coasters' songs, one of breaking up the rhythm by having the music stop and the bass singer speak a line in a deep, "fool" voice. While the device seemed to confirm every stereotype of the black man as indolent and stupid, it was consistent with the role taken by many black comedians who performed for black audiences, and the Coasters were at least as popular in the rhythm and blues market as in the pop market.

A number of the group's hits featured the stuttering "yakety" sax of King Curtis between chants and dragged-out cool talk by the group. "Yakety Yak" used King Curtis not only between lines but in a solo which was the definitive version of the style he developed–a few notes, given variation by different lengths of pauses between them, jumping in front of and behind the beat. Around this the group sang the best whining song of rock 'n' roll:

Take out the papers and the trash,
Or you don't get no spending cash;
If you don't scrub that kitchen floor,
You ain't gonna rock 'n' roll no more.
Yakety yak, don't talk back.

Just finish cleaning up your room,
Let's see that dust fly with that broom,
Get all that garbage out of sight,
Or you don't go out Friday night.
Yakety yak, don't talk back.

You just put on your coat and hat,
And walk yourself to the laundrymat,
And when you finish doing that,
Bring in the dog and put out the cat.
Yakety yak, don't talk back.

Don't you give me no dirty looks,
Your father's hip; he knows what cooks,
Just tell your hoodlum friend outside,
You ain't got time to take a ride.
Yakety yak, don't talk back.

The song brilliantly conveyed the cumulative sense of being put upon which the singers were asked to present, although the complaint was one that probably had little reality behind it–there were few among the people buying the record who had quite that load of dues to pay before being granted Friday evening play time.

Among the group's other hits, "Charlie Brown" (1958) and "Along Came Jones" (1959) weren't up to the standard of "Searchin'" and "Yakety Yak", but still were better than much contemporary music. "Poison Ivy" (1959) was the group's last big hit, a clever play with words rather than the type of situation comedy that the Coasters more often sang. "Little Egypt", recorded in 1962, though it was not a large hit, was on a par with their best records. With an appropriately low-down alley piano accompaniment, the group muttered and gasped in wondrous recollection of the song's heroine:

She did a triple somersault
And when she hit the ground,
She winked at the audience
And then she turned around.

She had a picture of a cowboy
Tattoed on her spine
Saying "Phoenix, Arizona,
Nineteen-forty-nine."

Having successfully made the transition from rhythm and blues to rock 'n' roll by bringing in new singers to substitute for now redundant performers, as well as adjusting others to the new idioms, Atlantic subsequently made equally impressive adjustments in order to present soul and British blues to meet the changing tastes of American youth. The other New York independents were much less adaptable, and few outlived rock 'n' roll.

Of the others, Herald/Ember* had the most hits and endured the longest, specializing particularly in group records, although many of the label's groups made only one hit each. Owner Al Silver either had an unusually good ear for group sounds, or else was particularly lucky, for in the Nutmegs, the Five Satins, the Turbans, and the Mello Kings he had four of the most admired vocal groups (the last of which consisted of Italians who succeeded remarkably well in achieving the "pure" sound of black groups). The Silhouettes were revolutionaries in disguise to judge by the scarcely intelligible lyric of their top ten hit "Get a Job" (1958): the lyric could easily have been fitted into the opening chapter of Richard Wright's novel *Native Son*. But first, before the words, came the opening chant, "sha-da-dada".[2] Once the rocking rhythm had been set by that, the singer began:

Every mornin' about this time,
She gets me out of my bed
A-cryin', "Get a job."
After breakfast, every day,
She throws the want ads right my way,
And never fails to say,
"Get a job."
And when I get the paper
I read it through and through
And my girl never fails to say

* HERALD/EMBER. *Formed ca. 1952, in New York, by Al Silver.*
Rhythm and blues: Joe Morris Orchestra, Faye Adams.
Groups: The Nutmegs, the Five Satins, the Turbans, the Mello Kings, the Silhouettes.
Duo: Charlie and Ray.

If there is any work for me.
Then I go back to the house,
I hear the woman's mouth,
Preachin' and a-cryin'
Tells me that I'm lyin'
'Bout a job
That I never could find.

It was one of the most extraordinary and compelling performances of rock 'n' roll, but did not stand out in the Herald/Ember catalogue quite so conspicuously as it might have done in most other rosters, since the label seemed to specialize in groups with unusual sounds. "Get a Job" no more than matched the strange chants of "I'll Remember" ("In the Still of the Night") by the Five Satins (1956) and the weird shrieks of "Stay" by Maurice Williams and the Zodiacs (1960), both discussed later in the book.

More conventional–and probably more closely supervised–group sounds were recorded on Rama* and a succession of later labels also owned by George Goldner. Whereas Herald/Ember had tended to record out-of-town groups, Goldner recruited from the streets of New York. With arranger Richard Barrett, Goldner was able to keep improving production techniques without destroying the quality of the group sound, and his hits on Gone and End (such as "Could This Be Magic?" by the Dubs, "Maybe" by the Chantels, and "I Only Have Eyes For You" by the Flamingos) were beautiful evocations of the innocence that his first groups had sought. Goldner's record by the Crows, "Gee" (1954), was sometimes described as the record that began the rock 'n' roll era because, unlike the earlier hit "Crying in the Chapel" by the Orioles, "Gee" was an original composition and had a quick dance rhythm. But "Gee" was not a hit until almost a year after Bill Haley's "Crazy Man Crazy".

Innumerable other former rhythm and blues companies in New York contributed to rock 'n' roll, invariably with vocal group re-

* RAMA. *Formed in New York in 1953 by George Goldner as a subsidiary of Tico, a company that specialized in Spanish music.*
Groups: the Crows, the Harptones, the Valentines.

Subsidiaries:

GEE. *Formed 1956.*
Groups: Frankie Lymon and the Teenagers, the Cleftones.

ROULETTE. *Formed in 1956. Sold to Hugo and Luigi, 1957. (See later note on Roulette.)*

GONE/END. *Formed in 1957. Producer: Alan Freed.*
Groups: the Dubs, the Chantels, the Flamingos, Little Anthony and the Imperials.

cords.* Because the style was so extensively recorded, there were more poor vocal group records than any other kind in rock 'n' roll.

Most companies, though, succeeded in making a few good records, notably Old Town with the Harptones' "Life is But a Dream" and Winley with the Jesters' "The Wind". Apollo and Savoy, despite outstanding rhythm and blues rosters, were among the few surviving important rhythm and blues independents that did not manage at least one big rock 'n' roll hit. The closest Savoy came was with a couple of Nappy Brown songs, including "Don't Be Angry" (covered by the Crew Cuts for Mercury, 1955) and "It Don't Hurt No More" (1957).

ii. Apart from New York's Atlantic Records, the company that suffered most from the practice of covering in the period 1954 – 1955 was King of Cincinnati.† Unlike the New York companies, King recorded virtually the entire range of rock 'n' roll styles, including

* *Other New York record companies.*

APOLLO. *Formed by Ike and Bess Berman ca. 1942.*
Gospel: Mahalia Jackson, Famous Georgia Peach, Dixie Humming Birds.
Rhythm and blues: Wynonie Harris, the Five Royales.
Group: the Larks.

SAVOY. *Formed in Newark, New Jersey, by Herman Lubinsky ca. 1942.*
A&R: Ralph Bass (from Black and White, 1948 to 1952), Fred Mendohlson (from 1953).
Gospel: the Selah Singers, James Cleveland, the Caravans, Alex Bradford.
Rhythm and blues: Big Maybelle, Nappy Brown, Varetta Dillard, Wilbert Harrison, Johnny Otis, Bonnie Davis, Little Esther, Big Jay McNeely, Paul Williams.
Groups: the Four Buddies, the Jive Bombers.

OLD TOWN. *Formed ca. 1955, by Hy Weiss.*
Rhythm and blues: Ruth McFadden.
Black ballad singer: Arthur Prysock.
Groups: Fiestas, Solitaires, Valentines, Harptones.
Rock 'n' roll: Robert and Johnny, Billy Bland.

BATON. *Formed ca. 1955, by Sol Rabinowitz.*
Groups: the Revileers, the Hearts, the Fidelitys.

WINLEY/WHIRLIN' DISC. *Formed ca. 1956, by Paul Winley.*
Groups: the Paragons, the Collegians, the Jesters, the Channels.

RED ROBIN/ROBIN. *Formed in 1953, by Bobby Robinson.*
Groups: Lewis Lymon and the Teen Chords, the Kodaks, the Scarlets.

MELBA. *Formed ca. 1955, by Morty Craft.*
Group: the Willows.

† KING. *Formed in Cincinnati, Ohio, by Sydney Nathan in 1945.*
Rhythm and blues (instrumental): Tiny Bradshaw, Lucky Millinder, Todd Rhodes, Bill Doggett, Big Jay McNeely, Sonny Thompson, Earl Bostic.
Vocal: Royal Brown, Synonie Harris, Bullmoose Jackson, Little Willie Littlefield, Eddie "Cleanhead" Vinson, Jimmy Witherspoon, Annie Laurie, Lula Reed.
Country and western: Moon Mullican, Cowboy Copas, Grandpa Jones, the Delmore Brothers, Hawkshaw Hawkins, Wayne Raney, Hank Penny, Jimmie Osborne, Clyde Moody.

northern band rock 'n' roll and Memphis country rock. Having fostered the rich instrumental sounds of jump combos and big bands, and having developed several styles of shouting blues, King (and its subsidiaries De Luxe, Federal, and Queen) made several important innovations in the early fifties that were major contributions to rock 'n' roll, first by having rhythm and blues singers record versions of country and western songs (usually material already recorded by one of King's country and western singers) and then by introducing various novelty songs in a rock 'n' roll style.

King was the only independent company to have equally strong rosters of rhythm and blues and country and western singers, and was geographically well placed to record singers who lived in the South or the Midwest, or who were on tour. The rhythm and blues versions of country and western songs, including Bullmoose Jackson's "Why Don't You Haul Off and Love Me" (covered from Wayne Raney) and Wynonie Harris's "Bloodshot Eyes" (covered from Hank Penny) were evidently not directed at the pop market. But this did not seem to concern King until 1954, when Otis Williams and the Charms recorded a series of commercial novelty songs for the subsidiary De Luxe and they invariably fared better on cover versions–"Hearts of Stone" by the Fontane Sisters, "Two Hearts, Two Kisses" by Pat Boone, "Ivory Tower" by Gale Storm (all for Dot), and "Gum Drop" by the Crew Cuts (for Mercury).

In contrast to almost all of the other groups that recorded novelty songs in an effort to reach the pop market, Otis Williams and the Charms were an exceptional group. Williams had both a flexible range that enabled him to reach as high as Tony Williams of the Platters without ever sounding melodramatic and a tone that was plaintive without being self-pitying. The arrangements on the records were much fuller than on most novelty group records, and featured tenor sax breaks which echoed the sound of earlier jump combos.

King's biggest rock 'n' roll success was Bill Doggett's "Honky Tonk", which stayed in the top ten for fourteen weeks in 1956. Riding on a jumpy organ rhythm set up by Doggett, the record featured a series of restrained staccato solos by tenor sax player Clifford Scott, linked by fast guitar chords from Billy Butler. The record's success confirmed the similarity in taste of at least some buyers of rock 'n' roll to that of the rhythm and blues audience of some years before and

---

Groups: the Royals, the Platters, the Midnighters, the Dominoes, the Five Royales, Otis Williams and the Charms.
Guitar blues: Albert King, Freddy King, Johnny "Guitar" Watson.
Gospel blues: Little Willie John, James Brown.
Rock 'n' roll: Hank Ballard, Mac Curtis, Hayden Thompson, Charlie Feathers, Lattie Moore, Bonnie Lou, Boyd Bennett and the Rockets, featuring Big Moe.

inspired several other similar instrumental hits, including Sil Austin's "Slow Walk" (Mercury, 1956), Bill Justis's "Raunchy" (Phillips International), and Ernie Freeman's "Jivin' Around" (Cash), both 1957.

Among King's most high-spirited records were those by Hank Ballard and the Midnighters, which were made in 1954 and effectively kept at a distance from the rock 'n' roll audience because of their impolite lyrics. By the time Ballard had adopted more acceptable material, rock 'n' roll had already begun to "cool" off, and the uninhibited nature of his singing was obsolete; he had to wait until 1960, when music had once more become loud and unsophisticated, in order to reach the mass audience. Meanwhile, his melodies and rhythm had been appropriated in "Dance With Me, Henry" and in Jesse Lee Turner's "Shake Baby Shake", one of several records that were based on Ballard's "Sexy Ways".

Except for the rough arrangement of "Seventeen" by Boyd Bennett and the Rockets, which made the top ten in 1955 (as did the Fontane Sisters with their cover version for Dot), King's country rock records had relatively little success, although Charlie Feathers in particular created a rich sound and a heavy rhythm.

Apart from King, the most important Midwest company recording rock 'n' roll was Chess in Chicago.* For several years the company concentrated quite narrowly on the market for bar blues in Chicago and the Mississippi Delta, but in 1954 it recorded the vocal groups the Moonglows and the Flamingos singing sentimental songs in a style that seemed suitable for the national white audience. Once again, the songs were covered (the Moonglows' "Sincerely" by the McGuire Sisters on Coral, the Flamingos' "I'll Be Home" by Pat Boone for Dot). But Chess received considerable help from disc jockey Alan Freed, who got into the action by being credited as co-writer of the Moonglows' "Sincerely" and Chuck Berry's "Maybellene" and on his radio shows helped to promote the records and the singers by

* CHESS. *Formed in 1947, in Chicago by Leonard and Phil Chess. Label first called Aristocrat; changed to Chess in 1949.*
Rhythm and blues: Muddy Waters, Howlin' Wolf, John Lee Hooker, Jimmy Rodgers, Willie Mabon, Gene Ammons, Eddie Boyd.
Groups: the Moonglows.
Rock 'n' roll: Chuck Berry, Bobby Charles, Johnnie and Joe, the Monotones.
Subsidiaries:

CHECKER. *Formed in 1953.*
Rhythm and blues: Little Walter, Lowell Fulson, Sonny Boy Williamson, Little Milton.
Groups: the Flamingos, the Tune Weavers.
Rock 'n' roll: Bo Diddley, Dale Hawkins.

ARGO. *Formed in 1956.*
Rock 'n' roll: Clarence "Frogman" Henry.

featuring them in the stage shows and films he organized.

While the records by the Moonglows and the Flamingos helped to establish the Chess and Checker labels in midwestern districts whose retailers had not previously stocked them, much more important contributions to the musical development of rock 'n' roll were made by the company through the records of Bo Diddley and Chuck Berry. While singers on almost every other label (except Sun and Specialty) made evident, and self-destructive, efforts to change their style in order to maintain their popularity with the hit making audience–or to make their records suitable for playing on pop music radio stations–Berry and Diddley continued to work within their own styles. Berry was able to do this and still please the audience *and* the radio station programmers until 1959, but Bo Diddley placed too much emphasis on dance rhythm to satisfy the programmers's need for "novelty". However, he was good for juke boxes and for live performances, and kept making records regularly as successive "new" sounds, including the twist, surf-music, and British rhythm and blues, kept obligingly close to the rhythm he introduced in "Bo Diddley" in 1955. His hits, though, were rare, only "You Pretty Thing" (1958) and "Say Man" (1959) making the top twenty.

If importance in popular music were measured in terms of imaginativeness, creativeness, wit, the ability to translate a variety of experiences and feelings into musical form, and long-term influence and reputation, Chuck Berry would be described as the major figure of rock 'n' roll. At the time of his greatest popularity, 1955–59, there were several other singers who had more hits, were more often copied, and commanded higher fees for personal performances. But Chuck Berry had the greatest long-term effect on his audience, shown in the immense influence his music had on the Beatles, Bob Dylan, the Rolling Stones, and other singers and musicians who began making records in the mid-sixties, having been part of the audience who listened to Chuck Berry through the late fifties.

Berry's first record, "Maybellene", made the top ten in 1955 but bore little similarity to anything else he produced. In most respects, the record was country rock, even though Berry's electric guitar and the drummer knocked out a much noisier beat than the unamplified instruments used at the time by Sun, which originated the style. Nevertheless the sound and Berry's flat whine showed little sign that the musicians were the same men who played on blues sessions at Chess, or that Berry preferred blues and jazz. But his next four singles, performed in a blues style and presenting in their themes some strong criticisms of aspects of American life, showed his interests much more obviously. Judges and courts in "Thirty Days", credit and car salesmen in "No Money Down", high culture in "Roll Over,

Beethoven", and all these plus more in "Too Much Monkey Business" were cause for complaint. Since these records were performed in a strong "blues" voice, the songs, with the exception of "Roll Over, Beethoven", which had brilliant rolling rhythm and a lyric that was particular to adolescents rather than a general one oriented to adults (as were the others), received relatively little attention from disc jockeys. But even "Roll Over, Beethoven", despite its graceful power, did not make the national top twenty best-selling records.

The basis of Berry's rhythm was an alternation of guitar chords comparable to the "alley" piano style of the Coaster's "Searchin'", but the effect was complicated by frequent lead guitar figures and by a piano that seemed to be played almost regardless of the melody taken by the singer and the rest of the musicians. Apart from a few vocal groups such as the Five Satins, few rock 'n' roll performers dared to challenge the conventions of harmony in this way, and part of the immediately recognizable sound of Berry's records was the interesting piano playing.

"School Day", in 1957, was the singer's first hit after "Maybellene", two years earlier. In it, Berry described events from the position of somebody standing close to them but not actually taking part in them (a position similar to his role in "Roll Over, Beethoven"). The song effectively captured the feeling of penned adolescence.

Soon as 3 o'clock rolls around,
You throw your burden down,
Close your books, get out of your seat,
Out of the classroom into the street,
Up to the corner and round the bend,
Right to the juke joint you go in.

Drop the coin right into the slot,
You've got to hear something that's really hot,
With the one you love you're makin' romance,
All day long you've been wanting to dance.

Despite the fact that it was a hit, the song was a little too long, and the rhythm insufficiently varied, to be numbered among Berry's best performances. "Rock and Roll Music" (1957), Sweet Little Sixteen" and "Johnny B. Goode" (1958) were more ingenious, with a faint suggestion of Latin-styled variation in the rhythms.

"Sweet Little Sixteen" presented the breathless world of a music-mad girl, using a traditional technique of American popular song writing of introducing several place names in the hope that residents of those places would identify with the theme of the song:

They're really rockin' in Boston,
In Pittsburg, Pa.,
Deep in the heart of Texas,
And round the Frisco bay,
All over St. Louis,
And down in New Orleans,
All the kids want to dance with
Sweet Little Sixteen.

Sweet Little Sixteen,
She's just got to have
About a half-a-million
Signed photographs;
Her wallet's filled with pictures,
She gets them one by one,
Becomes so excited,
Won't you look at her run!

Oh mommie, mommie,
Please may I go?
It's such a sight to see,
Somebody steal the show.
Oh daddy, daddy,
I beg of you,
Whisper to mommie,
It's all right with you.

Sweet Little Sixteen,
She's got the grown up blues,
Tight dresses and lipstick,
She's sporting high heel shoes,
Oh but tomorrow morning,
She'll have to change her trend,
And be sweet sixteen
And back in class again.

"Johnny B. Goode" was one of the finest songs that treated another traditional theme of American popular song (and culture): local country boy makes it in the big city. The opening guitar figure on that record has become one of the classic sounds of rock 'n' roll.

In other songs, Berry developed themes that were his own, and in

"Memphis, Tennessee" (1959), he even sang in the first person. The record was not a popular hit (its 'B' side, "Back in the U.S.A.", was a small hit), but was an example of rock 'n' roll at its best, with the musicians playing a modified version of the boogie rhythm developed on guitar by Jimmy Reed, while Berry created an unusual mood of tension through his restrained vocal, which tried to convey the singer's feelings about a six-year-old girl, whose relationship to the singer remained obscure:

Last time I saw Marie,
She was waving me good-bye,
With hurry-home tear on her cheek
That trickled from her eye:
Marie is only six years old
But information, please,
Try to put me through to her
In Memphis, Tennessee.

Apart from Chuck Berry and Bo Diddley, Chess/Checker recorded several other rock 'n' roll singers, almost always preferring southern singers to those who may have been more easily accessible in Chicago. The Louisiana singers Bobby Charles and Dale Hawkins were contracted, but Charles's promising "See You Later, Alligator" was successfully covered by Bill Haley and His Comets, and Hawkins's only hit was "Susie Q", an atmospheric country rock dance song that made the pop music top twenty in 1957. Chess/Checker also had rock 'n' roll hits with novelty songs by the Monotones ("Book of Love", 1958), by the black New Orleans singer Clarence "Frogman" Henry ("Ain't Got No Home", 1956), and with slow sentimental songs by the Tune Weavers ("Happy Happy Birthday, Baby", 1957) and Johnnie and Joe ("Over the Mountain", 1957).

If the styles of Chuck Berry and Bo Diddley were in any way representative of a more general response of black Chicago youth to life in the city, no other company was able to find others with similar styles. It seems that Berry and Diddley were in fact more or less unique, and that unlike the country rock singers of Memphis or the group singers of northern cities they had entirely personal reactions to their environment. The more common style among their contemporaries in Chicago was to adopt blues styles much closer to those of the bar blues singers. (Several examples are discussed later.)

But in contrast to the many New York labels that reached the popular music market with at least one rock 'n' roll record, most of the many small Chicago companies retained their obscurity. One company, Chance, formed by Art Sheridan, might have done well with rock 'n' roll, given its roster, but it folded in 1953. Two of the label's groups, the Flamingos and the Moonglows, moved to Chess, while a third, the Spaniels, along with Jimmy Reed, went to Vee Jay.*

Vee Jay's biggest rock 'n' roll hits were "Just Keep It Up" and "Hey Little Girl" (1958) by Dee Clark, a singer who was contracted by the company because of his ability to sound like either Little Richard or Clyde McPhatter. The novelty song "At My Front Door" by the El-Dorados (1953), the beautiful slow ballad "Oh What a Night" by the Dells (1956), and the mournful "For Your Precious Love" by Jerry Butler and the Impressions (1958) were among the other hits for the label, whose black owners Vivian ("Vee") Carter and Jimmy ("Jay") Bracken inspired other black entrepreneurs with visions of running their own labels–including Berry Gordy in Detroit. Vee Jay topped the pop chart in 1962 with the extraordinary "Duke of Earl" by Gene Chandler, and again with the Four Seasons and the Beatles, but the company's roster in the fifties was strongly rooted in authentic black idioms. As well as best-selling blues artists Jimmy Reed and John Lee Hooker were some major gospel groups including the Swan Silvertones (featuring the lyrical lead singer Claude Jeter) and the Staples Singers, whose leader Pop Staples evolved an influential bluesy guitar style and shared lead vocals with his deep-voiced daughter, Mavis.

iii. In contrast to most of the New York and Midwest companies, the independent companies on the West Coast less often recorded singers whose styles reflected events and feelings experienced near the locality of the record companies. Until 1957, most of the singers recorded by the West Coast independents were southerners, among them some who had been residents on the Coast since the war but also others who still lived in the South, particularly southern Louisiana and Texas.

Aladdin,† a very important rhythm and blues label and one of the

* VEE JAY. *Formed in 1953 in Chicago by Vivian Carter and James Bracken. Producers: Calvin Carter, Al Smith.*
Rhythm and blues: Jimmy Reed, John Lee Hooker, Rosco Gordon, Big Jay McNeely, Gene Allison.
Groups: the Spaniels, the El-Dorados, the Dells, the Magnificents, Jerry Butler and the Impressions.
Pop rhythm and blues: Dee Clark, Gene Chandler.

† ALADDIN. *Formed in 1945 in Los Angeles by Eddie and Leo Mesner. Producers: Maxwell Davis, Dave Bartholomew.*
Rhythm and blues: Amos Milburn, Charles Brown, Big Jay McNeely, Peppermint Harris, Lynn Hope, Lloyd Glenn, Floyd Dixon.
Group: the Five Keys.
Rock 'n' roll: Shirley and Lee, Thurston Harris.

first sources of rock 'n' roll (through Gene and Eunice's "Ko Ko Mo"), had only occasional success in the popular music market, chiefly through Shirley and Lee, and Thurston Harris. The label's most successful group, the Five Keys, was contracted by Capitol at the moment when it might have broken into the popular market, and Aladdin's other major rhythm and blues singers, Amos Milburn and Charles Brown, had no direct impact as rock 'n' roll singers.

The success of Shirley and Lee, with "Let the Good Times Roll" (which made the popular market's top twenty in 1956), was due partly to the dramatic arrangements (probably provided by Dave Bartholomew); a full two-note riff, played by a big band, conveyed a sense of excitement that other rock 'n' roll records promised but rarely achieved. Shirley's high little-girl voice contrasted with Lee's sad drawl in one of the most unusual duo records of the time.

Thurston Harris made the top ten in 1957 with the strange "Little Bitty Pretty One", a song (written, and first recorded, by Bobby Day) that consisted of a weird chant–"mm-mm-m-muh-muh-mm"–from a vocal group, the Sharps, while Harris repeated the line "Little bitty pretty one, won't you come with me?" An erratic syncopated rhythm was set up that was unusual in rock 'n' roll, and Harris was unable to repeat his success when handling more conventional rhythms.

Harris was the last success the label had, and the company folded during the late fifties, having lost the reliable audience for rhythm and blues and finding it impossible to support the high promotional costs needed for success in the national market.

Modern* seemed much more determined to succeed commercially than did Aladdin, but despite a few fairly successful hits in the period 1954 to 1956, the company did not consolidate its position. Modern was one of the few former rhythm and blues companies to make a practice of covering other rhythm and blues hits, presumably hoping to provide more commercial arrangements and reach the popular market.

Etta James's "Wallflower" came closest to achieving this aim, but

* MODERN. *Formed in 1945 in Los Angeles by Jules and Saul Bihari. Producers: Joe, Jules and Saul Bihari.*
Rhythm and blues: Floyd Dixon, Johnny Moore's Three Blazers, Roy Hawkins, Smokey Hogg, Lightnin' Hopkins, Jimmy McCracklin, Jimmy Witherspoon, Pee Wee Crayton, John Lee Hooker.
Groups: the Cadets, Marvin and Johnny.
Rock 'n' roll: Etta James, Jimmy Beasley, Joe Houston, Young Jessie.

Subsidiaries:

RPM. *Formed 1950.*
Rhythm and blues: B. B. King, Rosco Gordon, Johnny "Guitar" Watson, Jimmy Nelson.
Groups: the Jacks, the Teen Queens.

FLAIR. *Formed in 1953.*
Rhythm and blues: Elmore James.
Rock 'n' roll: Richard Berry and the Pharaohs, Shirley Gunter, the Flairs.

was foiled by Georgia Gibbs and "Dance With Me, Henry". Etta James was virtually the only female rock 'n' roll singer who regularly achieved exciting effects at fast tempos. Apart from "Wallflower", both "Good Rockin' Daddy" and "Most of All" were good dance songs, with a spirit that compared to Little Richard's performances.

Other good "raving" uptempo records produced by the company included tenor sax player Joe Houston's "Blow, Joe, Blow", Marvin and Johnny's "Tick Tock", and Young Jessie's "Mary Lou". But the biggest hits were the slow group song "Why Don't You Write Me?" (1955) by the Jacks, the novelty song "Stranded in the Jungle" (1956) by the Cadets (a group comprising the same personnel as the Jacks), the thinly arranged amateurishly sung "Eddie My Love" (1956) by the Teen Queens (who made the top twenty despite the similar success by the Fontane Sisters' cover), and the ballad "Goodnight, My Love" by Jesse Belvin. None of the singers were able to follow these successes with other hits, and Modern plus its group of companies virtually abandoned the chase for a hit and concentrated instead on producing budget-line LP's on their Crown label. The company went bankrupt, but the catalogue was revived on Kent, under similar management.

Modern's willingness to record anything that might sell contrasted with the much more selective and consistent policy of Specialty,* which was one of the two labels–the other was Sun–that committed themselves totally to rock 'n' roll. The label's most important rock 'n' roll discovery was Little Richard, whose output on Specialty retained a consistency that was unusual at a time when most producers introduced girl groups, strings, and assorted unsuitable instruments. The worst thing Little Richard had to contend with was songs such as "Baby Face" and "By the Light of the Silvery Moon" as songwriters exhausted their fund of expressions that could do justice to his exclamatory style.

Little Richard was one of very few singers who became more expressive with meaningless sounds and disconnected phrases and images than he was with properly constructed songs. Almost every other singer needed some solid idea from which he could improvise images, but Little Richard worked from almost nothing. "Rip It Up" was an exception, in that it did have a strong lyric, but "Good Golly, Miss Molly", "Lucille", and "Hey, Hey, Hey" were scarcely more elaborate than their titles.

* SPECIALTY. *Formed in 1945 in Hollywood by Art Rupe. Producers: Rupe, Robert "Bumps" Blackwell, J. W. Alexander, Johnny Vincent.*
Rhythm and blues: Roy Milton, Frankie Lee Sims, Percy Mayfield, Joe Liggins, Jimmy Liggins, Lloyd Price, Guitar Slim.
Gospel: the Pilgrim Travellers, the Soul Stirrers, Wynona Carr, Joe May.
Rock 'n' roll: Little Richard, Larry Williams, Jerry Byrne, Don and Dewey.

Specialty's president, Art Rupe, spent a lot of time searching for another singer to match the success of Little Richard, but did not even come as close as Capitol had with Esquerita. He did best with Larry Williams, whose flat tone gave a quite different atmosphere to his records as compared with the effervescence of Little Richard's. A hard, rather rigidly structured band accompanied Williams, whose best and most popular record, "Short Fat Fannie" (1957), was virtually a check list of the best recent rock 'n' roll hits, with a couple of more obscure rhythm and blues titles thrown in. The titles are emphasized here:

Tired of slippin' and a-slidin' *with* Long Tall Sally
Peekin' and a-hidin' duckin' back in the alley,
Don't wanna rip it up, *don't wanna* work with Annie,
I've got a brand new lover, her name is Short Fat Fannie.

One day when I was visitin' at Heartbreak Hotel,
That's where I met Fannie and she sure looked swell;
I told her that I love her, and that I'd never leave her,
She put her arms around me and she gave me fever.

She's my tutti frutti *and I love the child so,*
Tho' she watches me like a hound dog *everywhere I go,*
Whenever I'm around her I'm on my P's and Q's
She might step on my blue suede shoes.

Well at a honky tonk *party just the other night*
Fannie got jealous and she started a fight,
Because I was dancing with Mary Lou
I had to call Jim Dandy *to the rescue.*

These songs had variously been sung by Little Richard, Elvis Presley, the Midnighters, Little Willie John, Carl Perkins, Bill Doggett, Young Jessie, and LaVern Baker. There was also a reference to Fats Domino's "Blueberry Hill" in the last verse, not quoted here.

The world of rock 'n' roll, as Williams understood, was on its own now, separate from other events and with its own characters, relationships, and standards of behaviour. In it, people cared, but tended to behave aggressively, hiding their insecurity behind a tough front. It was a world that Specialty's rock 'n' roll singers reflected back at their audience better than the singers of any other company except Sun.

Through 1958, Rupe maintained an active recording programme, under the supervision of Sonny Bono in Los Angeles and Harold Battiste in New Orleans, which resulted in one or two late gems for rock 'n' roll fans. Don and Dewey made several exciting records in

Los Angeles, sounding intense on fast numbers like "Big Boy Pete" and "Farmer John" (both of which were picked up by several groups during the sixties), and delivering impassioned vocals on the ballad "Leavin' It Up to You", which carried on the celebrated Los Angeles duo tradition with a tougher beat and bluesier feel than usual.

Down in New Orleans, Harold Battiste cultivated a session group from the musicians who were not part of the Dave Bartholomew team, and although Battiste never came up with any hits to match the Little Richard sessions of a couple of years earlier, he did produce one undeniable classic, "Lights Out" by Jerry Byrne. The song was co-written by Seth David and Mac Rebennack, but although the latter was keen to be in the recording, Battiste trusted pianist Art Neville to keep up with the breath-taking pace set by drummer Charlie Williams. Jerry Byrne delivered the vocal with exactly the right dead-pan tone, but although the record lit up every room it was played in, its tempo may have been too frantic for the average dancer. For whatever reason, it was never any kind of hit; afterwards, people involved recollected that by then Art Rupe had grown tired of the dirty business of paying to get his records heard on the radio, and this was one that didn't get the necessary "promotional help". Subsequently, Specialty all but closed down, staying in business mainly to repackage its marvellous catalogue for the benefit of latecomers.

Imperial,* another Los Angeles company, was the only label that succeeded in carrying a singer from rhythm and blues through rock 'n' roll and its demise into the twist period, without drastically changing his style. Fats Domino was the singer, whose apparently eternal and universal appeal defies musical analysis. His records were simple, convincing, memorable, and danceable. While a steady rhythm pounded from his full-chorded piano playing, a band led and arranged by his producer Dave Bartholomew played easy riffs that emphasized the dance beat, and Domino sang a few phrases with a strong melody, in a deep Louisiana accent. After suffering one Pat Boone cover version ("Ain't That a Shame", 1955), Domino himself made the top ten in 1956 and was infrequently absent until the end of 1962. Juke joints, dances, and parties replaced one Domino record with the next when it came out a couple of months later. There seemed to be no suitable substitute for Domino's plaintive voice, or the haunting sax solos of Lee Allen and Herb Hardesty. Other people may have occasionally come up with something better, but Domino

* IMPERIAL. *Founded in 1947 in Los Angeles by Lew Chudd. Producer: Dave Bartholomew.*
Rhythm and blues: Jimmy McCracklin, T-Bone Walker, Smokey Hogg, Smiley Lewis, Fats Domino, the Spiders, Ernie Freeman.
Rock 'n' roll: Domino, Rick Nelson.

could be relied on: his records could be ordered without hearing them first. And there would be just enough variety for a semi-attentive audience to be able to tell that each one was different.

Occasionally Domino could sound as bad as the people who dared to try to achieve his sound–Domino's "Margie" (1958) was sung as clumsily as Bobby Darin could have done it. But "I'm Ready", recorded the same year, was a brilliant invitation to "rock 'n' roll all night", kept moving by clapping hands and a drummer whose hard, crisp beat jumped and rocked through every Domino record.

Imperial did not find any other black singer with adaptability comparable to Domino's. One singer with whom the company tried, Smiley Lewis, who had in some ways been a more expressive rhythm and blues singer, apparently could not make the adjustment to the disciplined routine required of a mass entertainer. But Imperial did find a white singer whose consistency matched Domino's–Rick Nelson.

At a time when record companies were looking desperately for a singer who could effect the desired compromise between the youth appeal of rock 'n' roll and the need not to irritate adults, Rick Nelson was playing "teen-age son" in a television soap opera, "Ozzie and Harriet". Verve Records, a West Coast independent, conceived the idea of recording Nelson doing rock 'n' roll, and had him cover Fats Domino's recent hit "I'm Walkin' ". Impressed with Nelson's success and style, Imperial bought his contract from Verve and promoted him as a "soft-rock" alternative to Elvis Presley. Although Nelson had a modest vocal range, and tended to speak rather than project his voice, he kept up with the rock 'n' roll beat more convincingly than most non-southern singers, and produced a pleasant series of hits. On the faster songs, the accompaniment featured the excellent country rock-styled guitar of James Burton (formerly a member of Dale Hawkins's group) and the drumming of Ritchie Frost. "Believe What You Say", written by the Burnette brothers, was Nelson's best rock 'n' roll song, although it could have done with a little more determination and conviction from the singer.

Although Imperial had virtually no hits apart from those by Domino and Nelson, these two performers kept the company going into the early sixties, when it was taken over by the rapidly expanding Liberty in 1963, after which it functioned as a general pop music label.

iv. During the late fifties, when innumerable labels offering assorted kinds of rock 'n' roll were formed on the West Coast without producing a single major figure, the label that had produced more major rock 'n' roll singers than any other, Sun, in Memphis, Tennessee, declined into insignificance.

Sun* was the only important rock 'n' roll company that produced virtually nothing else. Owner Sam Phillips had released just over thirty blues records when he first recorded Elvis Presley in 1954; from then on he recorded well over two hundred rock 'n' roll records, a handful of blues, and some country and western. The company's sales graph reflected the history of rock 'n' roll.

Perhaps better than any other producer in the country, Phillips understood the nature of rock 'n' roll. He helped singers to develop the style, giving them confidence to try rhythm patterns, vocal inflections, and song material that southern white adults normally disapproved. Ironically, the records that the young singers made still had to be directed at the country and western market, since they were too unsophisticated (in 1954 and 1955) for the white market, and since the rhythm and blues market was not yet used to accepting white singers. Consequently, many of the early "country rock" records still emphasized a country and western accent, and many of the records had straight country and western performances on their 'B' sides.

All of the first six country rock singers Phillips recorded were exceptional rock 'n' roll singers–Elvis Presley, Malcolm Yelvington, Carl Perkins, Johnny Cash, Charlie Feathers, and Warren Smith. Of these, Yelvington and Feathers were never widely known, and Smith had relatively minor success. Presley has already been discussed.

The distinctive characteristic of the country rock "Sun sound" was aggression, but curiously the target was enigmatically vague. The importance of the music, for the singers and for the audience, was that it effected a release of violent feelings, not that any particular group was attacked. The fact that country rock could be effectively performed only by southern whites suggested that this style was an expression of the white South that included among its assumptions a derision of black people and a distrustful dislike of people from the North. When the original form of country rock was revived in the late sixties, one of the most convincing uses made of it was Jerry Reed's furious "I'm from Dixie", in which the title's implications were suggested with raucous laughter. But although several singers, including Jerry Lee Lewis, proudly upheld traditional southern values,

* SUN. *Formed in 1953 in Memphis, Tennessee, by Sam Phillips. Producers: Phillips, Jack Clement, Bill Justis (musical arranger).*
Rhythm and blues: Little Junior Parker, Little Milton, Rufus Thomas, Jr., Billy "The Kid" Emerson.
Group: the Prisonaires.
Rock 'n' roll: Elvis Presley, Jerry Lee Lewis, Carl Perkins, Johnny Cash, Sonny Burgess, Billy Riley, Warren Smith, Malcolm Yelvington, Charlie Feathers, Roy Orbison.
Subsidiary:
PHILLIPS INTERNATIONAL. *Formed 1957.*
Rock 'n' roll: Bill Justis, Charlie Rich, Carl Mann, Jeb Stuart.

and did their best to express them in music (enjoying the irony that black people had contributed so much to the music), other singers with more gentle personalities and liberal views used the music not as an expression of their own character but as an escape from it, revelling in a confidence on stage that they did not have off stage.

Country rock was comparable to the vocal group style of rock 'n' roll–and unlike the band styles–in that it seemed to be a spontaneous, informal sound, created by a few friends who had no evident musical training but a determined spirit "that had to come out". Although some of Sun's songs, particularly the country and western 'B' sides, were about the familiar themes of dedicated love and desolation after its loss, its rock 'n' roll songs sometimes presented unconventional subjects. Some of these seemed like novelty songs planned to catch the mass audience–Warren Smith's "Ubangi Stomp", Billy Riley's "Flying Saucers Rock 'n' Roll", and Sonny Burgess's "Sadie's Back in Town". But others, such as Carl Perkins's "Dixie Fried", used the aggressive sound of rock 'n' roll to convey a violent mood of drinking and potential razor fights.

Perkins divided his few Sun records (he only made seven for the label) between these tough songs and simple country and western ballads in which his tone was indistinguishable from hundreds of Nashville singers. On the fast songs, which used an increasingly strong, deep boogie beat, Perkins sounded as if he was trying to get a rough, cracked tone similar to that of screamer sax players, letting his voice drag across several vowels. But the sound was too raucous for the popular music market, and Perkins faded into obscurity. A road crash that killed his brother–who had been in his group–set Perkins back in 1956, but during the early sixties his career revived a little with Columbia, which ironically showed belated interest in rock 'n' roll but was unable to produce anything by Perkins to compare with his Sun recordings.

After Perkins's "Blue Suede Shoes" had made the popular music top ten in 1956, the next Sun singer to reach the national audience was Johnny Cash, with "I Walk the Line" at the end of the year. Cash, from Arkansas, had a much deeper, slower voice than the other country rock singers, and did not have their flair for quick-witted improvisation of melody, harmony, and rhythm. With an unwavering commitment to loyalty, integrity, and a sense of predictable, inevitable routine, Cash sang with as much melodic flow as his exceptionally narrow vocal range could muster, to a beat provided by "The Tennessee Two" (bass guitar and drums) that was as simple and repetitive as any in popular music. "Cry, Cry, Cry", "Folsom Prison Blues", "I Walk the Line", and "Train of Love" all had extraordinary atmosphere, derived mainly from Cash's ability to be dramatically convincing.

Only "I Walk the Line" made the national top twenty, and in 1958 Sun added a vocal group chorus to Cash's records to add a more sophisticated effect. (Phillips, who liked the simple feeling of authentic country rock, handed over the supervision of these Cash-with-vocal-group sessions to Jack Clement). The records thus produced were Cash's biggest hits, secular sermons of great moral intensity and modest insight–"Ballad of the Teenage Queen", "Guess Things Happen That Way", "The Ways of a Woman in Love". Like Perkins, Cash also moved to Columbia, where he became one of the most successful country and western singers of the sixties.

Whereas other companies tended to be limited to one or two outstanding rock 'n' roll singers, Phillips kept finding more. Or rather, they kept finding him, for once the first records by Presley, Perkins, and Cash were heard, singers from the entire South, who had tried in vain to persuade country and western-oriented labels to record their blues-influenced style, now flocked to Memphis. The best was Jerry Lee Lewis.

Although he gave the impression of being as frantic and emotionally involved as Little Richard, Jerry Lee Lewis was one of the most controlled, self-conscious rock 'n' roll singers, and introduced a sophisticated technique of varying the emotional pitch of his fast songs, building to intense peaks and then slackening off, dropping his voice to a whisper and the beat to a gentle lapping rhythm, before starting up again into another climax. Because he also played piano in a hammering style and had a wild stage act, Lewis was often compared to Little Richard, but the tone of his voice was altogether different. Little Richard, and virtually every other rock 'n' roll singer, abandoned himself in his efforts to express his devotion, but in Lewis's voice there was almost always an edge of cynical detachment or even derision, as if he was suggesting how ridiculous the idea of total love was by exaggerating the styles of expressing it. This detachment enabled Lewis to pace his records, and control his audience at live performances, with a finesse few rock 'n' roll singers showed. He would have needed only Chuck Berry's flair for writing songs to be a comparably important figure.

Lacking the ability to supply himself with enough material, Lewis depended on the quality of what could be found, which was inevitably erratic. At his best–as in "Whole Lotta Shakin' Goin' On" (1957), "Breathless", "High School Confidential", and "Lewis Boogie" (1958)–Lewis epitomized the careless confidence that some people liked rock 'n' roll for. Although at times he used material and even stylistic inventions of Little Richard, Fats Domino, Chuck Berry, and

Elvis Presley, Lewis was a major figure in his own right. His success outlasted all of the other Sun singers, but by 1960 he was reduced to recording rock 'n' roll versions of pop-rhythm and blues hits ("What'd I Say?" "Money", "Save the Last Dance For Me") in order to attract an audience. When he left Sun in 1962 for a more lucrative contract with Mercury's subsidiary, Smash, Phillips lost interest in the label.

Apart from the hits of Perkins, Cash, and Lewis, Phillips also made the national market with the instrumental "Raunchy" by Bill Justis, the light "Mona Lisa" by Carl Mann, and the effectively sad "Lonely Weekends" by Charlie Rich, all on the Phillips International subsidiary. Charlie Rich, a pianist-composer-singer from Arkansas, was potentially as good a performer as Johnny Cash, but lacked the kind of relentless ambition needed to build himself a career. He wrote several simple, memorable ballads that were widely recorded by other people, but "Lonely Weekends" was his only hit for Phillips. The record was marred by a chanting chorus that Phillips included on most records after 1958.

Rich later had an anachronistic rock 'n' roll hit, when "Mohair Sam" (Smash) made the top thirty in 1965. Several other records he made for Smash at that time fulfilled the potential he had shown earlier, but by 1965 the audience was interested in other sounds.

There were several other Southern companies that contributed to rock 'n' roll.

Meteor* was formed as a Memphis "outpost" for the Los Angeles label Modern, and was managed by Lester Bihari, brother of the three who owned Modern. Meteor's most important performer was Elmore James, the bar blues singer-guitarist. But in 1956 it had three excellent country rock records, made by Wayne McGinnis, Charlie Feathers, and Junior Thompson; none, though, were distributed outside Memphis.

Excello* was one of the first blues labels to be established in

* METEOR. *Formed in 1952 in Memphis by Lester Bihari.*
Rhythm and blues: Elmore James, Rufus Thomas, Jr.
Rock 'n' roll: Wayne McGinnis, Junior Thompson, Charlie Feathers.

* EXCELLO. *Formed in 1953 in Nashville by Ernie Young as a subsidiary of the Nashboro gospel label. Producer: Jay Miller.*
Rhythm and blues: Lonnie Brooks, Lightnin' Slim, Slim Harpo, Lonesome Sundown, Arthur Gunter, Roscoe Shelton, Lonnie Brooks, the Gladiolas, the Marigolds.
Rock 'n' roll: Al Ferrier.

Subsidiary:

NASCO.
Group: the Crescendos.

Nashville. The label made an indirect contribution to rock 'n' roll in 1954, by having blues singer Arthur Gunter record an answer to Eddy Arnold's country and western record "I Wanna Play House with You", titled "Baby, Let's Play House". One of Elvis Presley's finest performances was his reinterpretation of the song on Sun, which closely followed Gunter's version.

Excello also recorded the country rock singer Johnny Jano, but did better with less obviously southern-styled vocal groups, the most successful of whom were the Crescendos, whose simple harmony ballad, "Oh Julie", made the top ten in 1958 (despite an RCA cover version by Sammy Salvo). The Crescendos' record achieved its success with relatively little promotion by the company, but owner Ernie Young later said that he lost $37,000 in promoting follow-ups by the group that did not sell.

Among the label's other groups, the Marigolds had a minor hit with "Rollin' Stone". The group consisted of four of the five members of the Prisonaires, a group Sam Phillips had recorded on Sun when they were still inmates at the Tennessee State Prison.

The contribution to rock 'n' roll of Duke/Peacock,* located in Houston, was Willie Mae Thornton's "Hound Dog" (1953), whose fierce humour and biting guitar (played by Pete "Guitar" Lewis), apart from providing the model for one of Elvis Presley's most successful records for Victor, anticipated the country rock style. But if there were singers who wanted to record rock 'n' roll in east Texas, owner Don Robey evidently was not much interested, for he concentrated instead on gospel and the gospel-tinged blues of Bobby Bland and Junior Parker.

The company's only hits in the rock 'n' roll era were "Pledging My Love" by Johnny Ace and "Tell Me Why" by Norman Fox and the Rob Roys, the first a gentle ballad whose simple charm was quite different from the novelty songs that at the time, 1954, tended to be the only way into the pop market for independently recorded black

* DUKE/PEACOCK. *Peacock formed in Houston by Don Robey in 1949. Producers/arrangers: Bill Harvey, Johnny Otis, Joe Scott, Johnny Board, J. W. Alexander.*
Rhythm and blues: Clarence "Gatemouth" Brown, Willie Mae "Big Mama" Thornton, Jimmy McCracklin.
Gospel: The Dixie Hummingbirds, the Five Blind Boys of Mississippi, the Bells of Joy, the Sensational Nightingales, Cleophus Robinson and the Spirit of Memphis.

Subsidiaries:

DUKE. *Formed in 1952, in Memphis by James Mattis. Taken over by Peacock in 1953. Rhythm and blues: Johnny Ace, Bobby Bland, Rosco Gordon, Earl Forrest, Junior Parker*

BLACK BEAT. *Formed ca. 1956.*
Group: Norman Fox and the Rob Roys.

singers, and the other a fast harmony song of little distinction that did quite well in 1957.

In contrast, Ace,* established by former Specialty producer Johnny Vincent in Jackson, Mississippi, produced several important rock 'n' roll records. The label's earliest releases were assorted blues, none of which were successful outside the local market, but in 1956, Vincent started recording a New Orleans rhythm and blues/rock 'n' roll band, Huey Smith and the Clowns. Featuring three vocalists apart from himself–Bobby Marchan, Junior Gordon, and Roland Stone–Smith developed a sound and rhythm that was quite distinct from Fats Domino's New Orleans style. Whereas Domino's records invariably had a jaunty, boogie-based rhythm, Smith's was closer to a shuffle, with all four beats given more or less equal emphasis as the same chord was repeated for several bars, followed by a shift into another, perhaps a third, and then back to the first. Most of the improvisation was concentrated in Smith's right-hand piano breaks, which were studded with honks from the band's saxes. It was a good sound to dance to, and Smith had several hits, including "Rockin' Pneumonia and the Boogie Woogie Flu" (1957) and "Don't You Just Know It" (1958), both of which featured Marchan as vocalist.

Smith's kind of rhythm became as pervasive in the South as did Fats Domino's and was borrowed directly for hits by Minit's Jessie Hill, Chris Kenner, and others. Meanwhile, Frankie Ford made the national top twenty with "Sea Cruise". Ford, a white singer who grew up in the black section of New Orleans, was exceptional with a band, able to sing at fast rhythms without emphasizing the dance beats and yet somehow implying which ones they were, confident and good natured in his tone.

Although Smith, the Clowns, and the singers Marchan and Ford had the greatest influence of the Ace performers, Jimmy Clanton had the biggest immediate impact. Effectively picking up the gentle ballad style of Johnny Ace, Clanton made the national top twenty with "Just a Dream", "Letter to an Angel", and "Ship on a Stormy Sea". But where Ace had some charm to buttress the sentimentality of his songs, Clanton seemed to be able to contribute nothing to distinguish himself from pop singers with more conventional home backgrounds in Brooklyn or Philadelphia. He was the South's first contribution to the softening of rock 'n' roll.

While Excello/Nashboro and Duke/Peacock thrived through their

* ACE. *Formed in 1955 in Jackson, Mississippi, by Johnny Vincent.*
Rhythm and blues: Earl King, Frankie Lee Sims.
Rock 'n' roll: Huey Smith and the Clowns, Frankie Ford, Bobby Marchan, Joe Tex, Jimmy Clanton.

gospel sales, and continued to serve the southern market for rhythm and blues of various kinds, Ace committed itself to the pop market through Vee Jay's distribution, and when Vee Jay went into bankruptcy, Ace went down with the sinking ship.

For independent companies, the struggle to survive never eased up. Plagued by competition from bootleggers who pirated copies of their hits, and always fighting to get their distributors to pay up, indie labels had to pay out for pressings, pay "consultancy fees" to disc jockeys, and the monthly overheads of a staff and their offices. Sometimes the wisest move was to license a likely hit to larger companies like Mercury, ABC, or Dot, who formed fruitful relationships with independent producers.

II

Studio recordings had in the past been supervised by record company staff, variously known as Head of A&R, Music Director, or House Producer. Most of the major companies employed such a person, and most of the pioneer indie label owners took on this role themselves, but from the mid-fifties onwards a new and key figure emerged: the freelance, Independent Producer.

Sometimes, the independent producer did everything from writing the songs to finding singers, financing the recordings, supervising the sessions and then leasing the tape to the record companies; Jerry Leiber and Mike Stoller worked their way into the industry as this kind of writer-producer, setting a precedent for Lee Hazelwood, Bob Crewe, Phil Spector and Bert Berns, who became major figures in the industry. A parallel type of producer had a more managerial role, supporting a self-sufficient artist in the studio and then representing the finished tapes to the record industry; Norman Petty was the pioneer for this kind of manager-producer, although he did also engineer the sessions, and contribute to arrangements on songs for his most famous protégé, Buddy Holly.

Norman Petty was based in Clovis, New Mexico, just across the border from North Texas, where Buddy Knox, Jimmy Bowen, Roy Orbison and Buddy Holly all grew up. Petty made cocktail-lounge trio records with his wife Vi playing organ, and used the income from a couple of hits to finance his own studio in Clovis. In 1956, local college boys Knox and Bowen brought their Rhythm Orchids group in to make a record to sell at their high-school hops; Petty had not yet figured out how to cope with the volume that rock 'n' roll drummers could make, and wound up using a cardboard box instead of a kit. Originally issued locally back-to-back on the same record, "Party Doll" by Knox and "I'm Stickin' With You" by Bowen were released separately on a new label in New York, Roulette, and they both sold a million copies.

By the time Buddy Holly came in to make some demos to send to New York, Norman Petty was alert to the possibilities of the new music; he recorded the drums properly, signed up the publishing rights, and took the results up to New York himself. Various companies turned down the tape, but Bob Thiele in Decca's A&R department at Coral and Brunswick took a chance and licensed "That'll Be The Day"/"I'm Looking for Someone to Love", to be released under the name of the Crickets.

Of all the Southern singers who came into pop music through rock 'n' roll, Buddy Holly seemed to have the widest vision, the keenest sense of what was possible in just over two minutes for a guitar-playing singer with a basic framework of guitar, bass, and drums embellished by backing voices and various keyboards. He was lucky to have in Jerry Allison a drummer who thought as freely as he did himself, who was happy to try out new patterns, play just on the tom-toms, or whatever fitted with the rhythm set by Holly's guitar and with the mood set by his voice.

Most of the records issued under the name of the Crickets were tough, almost vengeful songs, which Allison powered with loose but assertive cracks on his snare, inspired by the style of the drummers Earl Palmer and Cornelius Coleman on Fats Domino's records. Holly and Allison rehearsed at home, just guitar and drums, and a tape survives of their demo of Fats' "Blue Monday", which Holly introduced with the guitar figure that he later used to start "That'll Be The Day". At a time when rock 'n' roll was already losing the edge that had made it so exciting a year earlier, "That'll Be The Day" was abrasive and challenging, but it was also relaxed and melodic, and its words expressed an attitude that many of its listeners wished they could be brave enough to say out loud:

Well that'll be the day
When you say goodbye
Yes that'll be the day
When you make me cry
You say you're gonna leave me
You know it's a lie
Cause that'll be the day-ay
When I die.

Later songs by the Crickets continued the theme of warning the girl to mend her ways or else; "Oh Boy", "Maybe Baby", and "Think It

Over" defined a unique sound of jangling guitar against strong drums, with backing vocals filling in the spaces. But it was in the softer records which were released under Buddy Holly's own name that his personality and originality came across most strongly. On "Words of Love", he double-tracked his lead vocal, a technique which was still novel at the time, and on the next record, "Peggy Sue", he let his voice be as vulnerable and intimate as the microphone could make it. Where "That'll Be The Day" had been abrasive, "Peggy Sue" was tender; Holly strummed his guitar very fast, sixteenths, all on the down stroke, with the guitar close-miked to pick up the sound of the plectrum on the strings; Jerry Allison played just on the tom-toms. Nothing else, just Buddy playing around with the sound of a girl's name, repeated endlessly with slightly different phrasing and enunciation.

"Well ... All Right", "Heartbeat", and "Everyday" were perfect representations of innocent longing, attractive melodies framed by acoustic guitar and percussion, presented in Holly's odd, stylized way, with vowels stretched and bent. His peculiar pronunciation of "bay-beh" became his trademark, but he was liable to pick on any word and play around with how it could sound and what it could mean. Black singers had often made this approach the trick of their trade–Jimmy Reed, Clyde McPhatter, Fats Domino, and Mickey and Sylvia's "Love Is Strange" were all influences–but Buddy Holly made the technique standard for white singers too.

Norman Petty's role in Buddy Holly's records has become a topic of some controversy among pop chroniclers, many of whom have felt that by adding his name as co-writer to most of the songs he was overstating his involvement. Petty engineered the sessions, and contributed ideas towards arrangements which included bringing his wife Vi in to play keyboards (notably the rousing, robust piano solo in "Think It Over"). The producers who doubled as manager and publisher have often tended to be "disowned" later by the artists they helped, and in this case we'll never know: Buddy Holly was killed in a plane crash early in 1959, after just one session in New York with Dick Jacobs's orchestra, a pure-pop version of Paul Anka's "It Doesn't Matter Anymore" with pizzicato strings and an extravagantly mannered vocal. If anyone could have grappled with New York attitudes to pop and twisted them to his own advantage, surely it would have been Buddy Holly. Most people who tried to follow where he had led were smothered by their arrangements, although Adam Faith and his arranger John Barry in England did create an interesting variation in "What Do You Want"; back in Hollywood, Liberty producer Snuff Garrett processed the approach into a formula with Bobby Vee.

A few hundred miles north of Clovis, in Phoenix, Arizona, local disc jockey Lee Hazelwood began exploring ways to fuse country and blues, finding local singers and musicians to work on his songs. Guitarist Al Casey became the cornerstone of his sound, playing simple rhythmic riffs which Hazelwood routed through every kind of echo device he could think of. In 1956, Hazelwood and Casey "borrowed" the guitar riff from Howlin' Wolf's "Smokestack Lightnin'" for his own song "The Fool", which local country singer Sanford Clark intoned in a mournful, deadpan voice; Dot licensed the track and made the national top ten, but despite a series of inventive records for Dot and then Jamie, including "Run Boy Run" and "Son of a Gun", Clark never repeated the first success. Many of Hazelwood's songs had interesting story-lines and clever twists, but ironically his greatest success in the fifties was a series of instrumental records featuring guitarist Duane Eddy, who had five top-twenty hits for Jamie of Philadelphia, including "Rebel Rouser" (1958).

If Duane Eddy was any kind of guitar virtuoso, he displayed admirable restraint on his records, playing childishly simple melodies on the lower notes of the guitar, giving Hazelwood a sound to stretch, delay, and bounce around his tape recorders and echo chambers. This was the ultimate reduction of rock 'n' roll to its basic elements of a party atmosphere and emphatic dance beat, achieved with honking tenor sax (by Steve Douglas and Jim Horn) and handclaps, all wildly echoed. Phil Spector was so impressed, he went to watch Hazelwood in the studio to see what he did.

Through the rest of the fifties and all through the sixties, the trend towards independent producers accelerated, and by the seventies there were few companies left with "in-house" producers. But although the examples of Petty and Hazelwood showed that independent producers could function effectively away from the traditional centres of the music industry, still the tendency was for artists, writers, producers and musicians to congregate around Los Angeles and New York. Country music set up permanent headquarters in Nashville, but teen pop music seemed able only to set up temporary outposts in Philadelphia and Detroit while settling down to stay in Los Angeles.

III

There was no particular "Sound of Los Angeles" in the late fifties. What there was, was a "Los Angeles Attitude": there are no rules to this game; anything goes, the more ridiculous, the more likely to succeed. With no rules and no referee, anyone could play, and everyone did. Literally dozens of Los Angeles-based labels hit the national pop charts during the late fifties and early sixties, of which two–Dot and Liberty–were substantial rivals to the majors, and three more at least lasted long enough to look as if they were there to stay–Era/Dore, Keen/Del Fi, and Challenge.

The story of Dot* epitomized the history of pop music in the fifties. Randy Wood owned a record store and mail-order operation in the tiny town of Gallatin, Tennessee during the forties, and to stimulate orders for Randy's Records he took out some advertisements on the evening radio shows presented by Hoss Allen and Gene Nobles on WLAC-Radio in neighbouring Nashville. Wood was inundated with orders for the kind of records that Allen and Nobles played–boogie blues by Roy Milton, Amos Milburn and the rest–and the next step was to form a label to record local artists in this style. Although early Dot releases included the most popular local rhythm and blues combo, the Griffen Brothers featuring Margie Day and Tommy Brown, Wood very quickly shifted his attention to straight pop, and he was remarkably successful from 1952 onwards, with national hits by the Hilltoppers, Johnny Maddox, and the Fontane Sisters. Alert to the growing demand for rhythm and blues music from the white market, Wood was one of the prime movers in the "cover record" syndrome, assigning one likely rhythm and blues song after another to college-boy crooner Pat Boone.

By his own account, Boone was not particularly keen on the blunt and ungrammatical approach of some rhythm and blues songs, but he did his best and that turned out to be enough to smother the originals of "Ain't That a Shame" (by Fats Domino), "Tutti Frutti" (by Little Richard) and "At My Front Door" (by the El Dorados). Boone later drifted towards ballads, and as a kind of junior Bing Crosby or Perry Como had a very successful career which included several very effective teen anthems, notably "Don't Forbid Me" and "Love Letters in the Sand".

Among the oddities picked up by Dot was Nervous Norvus, the *nom de disque* for middle-aged truck driver Jimmy Drake, who made the top twenty in 1956 with "Transfusion", a cautionary tale about dangerous driving complete with macabre rhymes like "pass the claret, Barrett". On the B-side, "Dig" was a catalogue of the meanings which that word could have in current hip-talk. Both songs, and the peculiar follow-up "Ape Call" were in no particular idiom, apparently being recorded by one mike which was close to the singer's

* DOT. *Founded in 1951 in Gallatin, Tennessee by Randy Wood; moved in 1956 to Hollywood, California. Music Director: Billy Vaughn.*
Pop: The Hilltoppers, Fontane Sisters, Gale Storm, Pat Boone, Jim Lowe, Tab Hunter, Lawrence Welk, Nervous Norvus.
Rock 'n' roll: Sanford Clark, the Dell Vikings.
Sold in 1965 to Gulf-Western, when Randy Wood formed Ranwood.

mouth, but a long way from whoever was playing the fast-strummed guitar (could that have been a ukelele?) and regular bass drum beat.

In 1956 Randy Wood moved his record company out to Hollywood with former Hilltopper Billy Vaughn as music director. From a rock 'n' roll point of view, Dot only rarely became involved with genuine innovators, by picking up completed masters from independent producers, but the label's twenty-year span in the pop industry was impressive evidence of what a determined independent company could achieve.

Liberty* was also run by a Southerner, Al Bennett, a self-styled "farm-boy from Mississippi" who had been a sales and promotion man before being hired to run Liberty, formed by West Coast businessmen in 1955. Julie London's cool and classy "Cry Me a River" gave the label an early hit, and in 1956 the company signed Eddie Cochran. Originally from Oklahoma, Cochran took a while to evolve a style, but just as some of the rock 'n' roll pioneers began to lose their direction, he found his in 1958 with "Summertime Blues". The gruff vocal and staccato rhythm guitar were reminiscent of Presley's recent "Jailhouse Rock", but Cochran had a lyric and pose which captured the teenage bravado that James Dean had been going for in *East of Eden* and *Rebel Without a Cause*.

In America, Eddie was apparently out-of-time, virtually a one-hit wonder. But a tour of Britain with Gene Vincent in 1960 generated great excitement, not only with the fans but also with budding musicians like guitarist Jim Sullivan, who learned first-hand from Eddie some of the tricks of a rock 'n' roll guitarist's trade. Cochran was killed in a car crash on that tour, but his songs, including "C'mon Everybody" and "Somethin' Else", were thrown in with the gems from Chuck Berry and the Coasters to tell the teenage story, and his thick, aggressively rhythmic guitar sound became an import-

* LIBERTY. *Founded in 1955 in Hollywood with Al Bennett as vice president and head of A&R; Tommy "Snuff" Garrett head of A&R from 1959.*
Pop: Julie London, David Seville (and the Chipmunks), Patience and Prudence, Timi Yuro, Dick and Dee Dee.
Teen pop: Johnny Burnette, Bobby Vee.
Black pop: Billy Ward and The Dominoes, Gene McDaniels, the Rivingtons.
Rock 'n' roll: Eddie Cochran.

Distributed labels:

DOLTON (*formerly* DOLPHIN), *formed by Bob Reisdorf in Seattle.*
Pop: the Ventures, the Fleetwoods.

DEMON (*formed by Joe Green in Los Angeles*).
Rock 'n' roll: Jody Reynolds, the Olympics.

IMPERIAL (*bought from Lew Chudd in 1963*).
Pop: Cher, Jackie de Shannon, Johnny Rivers.
Rhythm and blues: Irma Thomas.

ant ingredient in the "heavy rock" sound that developed in Britain through the Kinks and the Who.

Cochran did most of his recording at the Gold Star studio in Hollywood, bouncing ideas off his manager and co-producer Jerry Capehart, and making effective use of drummer Earl Palmer. Black musicians played an important role in enabling Los Angeles producers and artists to evolve a credible version of rock 'n' roll, and as well as Palmer (who arranged and produced Thurston Harris's hit version of "Little Bitty Pretty One"), other important arranger-musicians included pianist Ernie Freeman, guitarist Rene Hall, tenor sax man Plas Johnson, and all-round utility men H. B. Barnum and Harold Battiste. These men formed the nucleus of the first-choice session group for any A&R man needing an authentic rock 'n' roll sound, and made crucial but often uncredited contributions to the majority of the West Coast hits of the period.

In 1958 Liberty Records appointed a teenage Texan ex-disc jockey, Tommy "Snuff" Garrett, to run their A&R department, and in short order he delivered million-sellers by Johnny Burnette, Bobby Vee, and Gene McDaniels. Taking many of his songs off the assembly-line from Don Kirshner's Brill Building office in New York, Garrett called in the sessionmen but kept their sound well back so the words could be easily heard. With almost 30 top twenty hits 1960–63, Garrett was one of the hottest producers of the period. Meanwhile, Al Bennett brought more hits to Liberty by taking on distribution for other independent labels including Dolton (the Fleetwoods and Ventures) and Demon (Jody Reynolds and the Olympics).

Among the other companies who benefited from the experienced black session arrangers, Keen* had one of the luckiest breaks any company could dream of. Across town at Specialty, house producer Bumps Blackwell and arranger Rene Hall organized a pop session for Sam Cooke, the golden-toned lead singer in the label's best-known gospel group, the Soul Stirrers. Knowing how touchy the gospel community was about sacred singers dealing in satanic secular music, Specialty's owner Art Rupe was furious to discover the session in progress, and angrily told them to finish it, take the tape away, and never come back. Blackwell duly found Bob Keene, who had no inhibitions about releasing a pop record by Sam Cooke; the reward

* KEEN. *Formed in 1957 in Hollywood by Bob Keene. A&R: "Bumps" Blackwell. Black pop: Sam Cooke, Johnny "Guitar" Watson.*

Subsidiaries:

DEL-FI.
Pachuko pop: Ritchie Valens, Chan Romero, Addrisi Brothers.

MUSTANG.
Tex-Mex pop: the Bobby Fuller Four.

was a double-sided number one: "You Send Me"/"Summertime".

Sam Cooke was one of the most expressive, technically-gifted, and versatile singers of the era, and "You Send Me" was virtually a vehicle for his voice: just a few words, which he floated, stretched, and repeated with endless variation, to create a mood of pure, utterly sincere devotion. Once at Keen, Cooke went into a fruitful partnership with budding song-writers Lou Adler and Herb Alpert, who helped to orient his songs to specific teenage situations: "Only Sixteen", and "Wonderful World". All three went their separate ways in 1960 when Cooke signed a lucrative contract with Hugo and Luigi at RCA.

Meanwhile, Bob Keene had launched a subsidiary label Del Fi, which specialized in recording singers from the local "pachukos", as the Mexicans in Los Angeles were known. Rene Hall supervised the arrangements for records by Ritchie Valens, already popular as a live artist at shows organized by Johnny Otis and other promoters. "C'Mon Let's Go" was a minor hit in 1958, and the double-sided "Donna"/"La Bamba" made the top three at the end of the year, but as Valens looked set to become the first Mexican-American pop star he was killed in the same plane crash as Buddy Holly. Del Fi offered Chan Romero ("Hippy Hippy Shake") as an alternative, but another Los Angeles writer-producer Jim Lee had better luck in 1962 with "Let's Dance" by Chris Montez on his own Monogram label, and cabaret-folk singer Trini Lopez surfaced a year later with "If I Had a Hammer" for Reprise, which led to a substantial career for him. Bob Keene had a couple of minor hits in the mid-sixties with the Bobby Fuller Four including "I Fought the Law" (Mustang, 1966), briefly reviving what had become known as the "Tex-Mex" sound of the Crickets.

Era* had topped the national pop chart in 1955 with "The Wayward Wind" by Gogi Grant, but managed the trick only twice more, with the novelty "Mr. Custer" by Larry Verne in 1962, and with "To Know Him is to Love Him" by the Teddy Bears on its subsidiary label, Dore. An ethereal declaration of self-denying submission, "To Know Him is to Love Him" seemed at the time to be just one more lucky accident, as the group failed to repeat its success, but although

* ERA. *Formed in Hollywood in 1955 by Herb Newman and Lew Bidell.*
Pop: Gogi Grant, Larry Verne, Ketty Lester.

Subsidiary:

DORE.
Teen pop: the Teddy Bears, Jan and Dean.

Distributed label:

GREGMARK, *owned by Lester Sill and Lee Hazelwood.*
Pop: the Paris Sisters.

its teenage producer took a while to recover his bearings, Phil Spector did come back with his own Philles label* to prove that it had been no fluke. Participants in the session recalled years later how long Spector had taken, how meticulously he had planned the tape-to-tape transfers to achieve the perfect balance of fragile innocence. Era and Dore subsequently picked up countless independently-produced masters, notably Lincoln Mayorga's majestic arrangement of "Love Letters" by Ketty Lester (top five in 1962).

The biggest hit on Challenge† was the instrumental "Tequila" by the Champs, a dramatic mesh of lilting riffs played on guitar (by Dave Burgess) and sax (Chuck Rio). Top of the chart for five weeks in 1958, it spawned a rash of all-instrumental records by session musicians who hoped their studio jams might metamorphose into hits. Challenge recorded all the members of the Champs as solo artists, and had a few more minor hits by the group, but another Los Angeles indie, Rendezvous,‡ got the best of the rest, notably "In the Mood" (credited to the Ernie Fields Orchestra, but actually made by the top Los Angeles session group of Rene Hall, Plas Johnson, and Earl Palmer) and "Nut Rocker" by B. Bumble and the Stingers (whose line-up could not have included all the people who have claimed an association with the record). Among the other instrumentalists, Sandy Nelson deserves a mention: he played drums on "To Know Him is to Love Him", and had his moment of glory as the featured name on "Teen Beat", a simple instrumental produced by Richard Podolor which made the top five in 1959 on Original Sound.§ Sandy switched to Imperial where he had another big hit with "Let There Be Drums", and he was at the session that resulted in "Alley Oop" by the Hollywood Argyles.

"Alley Oop" sounded like a Coasters record, made while Leiber and Stoller were taking a lunch-break; it had some of the same ingredients, including an alley piano style borrowed from

* PHILLES. *Founded in 1961 by Phil Spector and Lester Sill.*
Girl groups: the Crystals, Ronettes.
Pop rhythm and blues: the Righteous Brothers, Bob B. Soxx and the Blue Jeans, Darlene Love, Ike and Tina Turner.

† CHALLENGE. *Founded in Hollywood in 1956 by Joe Johnson and Gene Autry.*
Country pop: Jerry Wallace.
Pop: Jerry Fuller.
Rock 'n' roll: the Champs, Big Al Downing.

‡ RENDEZVOUS. *Founded in 1958 by Ron Pierce and Gordon Wolf.*
Rock 'n' roll: the Ernie Fields Orchestra, B. Bumble and the Singers.

§ ORIGINAL SOUND. *Founded in 1957 by Art Laboe.*
Instrumental rock 'n' roll: Sandy Nelson, Preston Epps.
Punk: Music Machine.

"Searchin'", and a lyric about a figure from current American pop culture; but there was a sloppiness that Leiber and Stoller would have tidied up. And no wonder, as Sandy Nelson ruefully recalled: all the participants were helplessly drunk on cider by the time they recorded the song, and vocalist Gary Paxton had to be held upright within range of the microphone as he read Dallas Frazier's lyric from the brown paper bag it had been written on. Chanting the chorus along with the rest of the gang, Nelson banged an empty bottle with an opener, and let out an unrehearsed yell at what felt to him like a timely moment. The resultant record had some claim to being the ultimate reduction of rock 'n' roll to a dumb, absurd, bad joke, but it had an undeniably hypnotic appeal. Against all the odds (which included competition from a cover version by Dante and the Evergreens, produced by Lou Adler for Larry Utall's Madison label), the Hollywood Argyles topped the national chart on Paxton's own Lute label. And in flat contradiction of the theory that lightning does not strike in the same place twice, Paxton repeated the trick two years later with "The Monster Mash" by Bobby "Boris" Pickett on his Garpax label; this novelty record was relatively sophisticated, with sound effects of creaking doors which had obviously been predetermined, and it also made the top of the national chart (1962).

Two other los Angeles indies, Class and Ebb, scored hits with vocalist Bobby Day, who recorded for countless labels under various guises during the late fifties and early sixties. Class* was owned by Leon Rene, who had been in the music business since the early thirties when he wrote several standards with his brother Otis, including "When It's Sleepy Time Down South" (which became Louis Armstrong's theme tune) and "When the Swallows Fly Back to Capistrano". During the forties, the brothers ran the pioneer indie rhythm and blues labels Exclusive and Excelsior, and seemed set to rival Specialty and Imperial, but got caught out as the format changed from 78s to microgroove 45s; they had invested in a pressing plant which could only make 78s, and they went out of business. So it was an impressive come-back for Leon when he wrote a *bona fide* rock 'n' roll song for Bobby Day, "Rockin' Robin", complete with a nursery level lyric and a sophisticated-but-relentless arrangement. Bobby had previously recorded his own "Little Bitty Pretty One" for Class, but lost out to a superior cover version for Aladdin by Thurston Harris and the Sharps; "Rockin' Robin" went to number two on the national chart in 1958, and "Over and Over" on the B-side (written by Bobby) was a minor hit in its own right, and became a number one hit itself seven years later for the Dave Clark Five.

* CLASS RECORDS. *Founded in 1956 by Leon Rene. A&R: Googie Rene. Rock 'n' roll: Bobby Day, Eugene Church.*

Meanwhile, Bobby doubled his money as lead singer for the Hollywood Flames, whose biggest hit was "Buzz Buzz Buzz" in 1957 for Ebb Records,* a label run by Art Rupe's ex-wife.

Amid all the chaos of these little labels in Los Angeles, in 1959 Warner Brothers Pictures launched a record division† which made some mileage out of the existing teen market for screen stars like Connie Stevens and Ed Byrnes, paid a huge transfer fee to Cadence Records to buy its contract with the Everly Brothers, and played an important role in the folk-rock movement by recording Peter, Paul and Mary.

The spirit of rock 'n' roll still generally eluded major label producers; the Everly Brothers retained it, and even improved their grip, but significantly they recorded at arms' length from the Warner Brothers offices. Away from the traditional recording centres, rock 'n' roll's elusive qualities could still sometimes be recaptured. The moments became harder to achieve, but every now and then something still happened, in Nashville, in Norfolk, Virginia, in Pittsburgh and Philadelphia, in Detroit and New York.

When rock 'n' roll cracked open the pop market for Southern white singers, for a couple of years (1956–58) it looked as if the margins between "pop" and "country" were being wiped out. Producers in Nashville organized their sessions with an ear to what had worked for Elvis Presley, and brought in electric guitars, boogie piano, harmonica, saxophone, and vocal groups to embellish their arrangements and give their records "teen appeal". And for a while, country stations played the records as enthusiastically as the pop stations: Elvis, the Everly Brothers, and Gene Vincent had country hits with their rock 'n' roll records, alongside the dual-market hits made by the Sun rockabillies in Memphis.

But in 1958, the country music establishment reasserted the segregation between pop and country which had prevailed before rock 'n' roll, and country radio virtually boycotted records which sounded as if they had been made with the pop market in mind. From then on, artists had to decide which way to go, country or pop,

* EBB RECORDS. *Formed in 1957 by Mrs. Art Rupe.*
Rock 'n' roll: the Hollywood Flames.
Rhythm and blues: Professor Longhair.

† WARNER BROTHERS. *Founded in 1959 in Hollywood, with Mike Maitland as head of A&R.*
Screen pop: Connie Stevens, Ed Byrnes, Tab Hunter.
Rock 'n' roll: the Everly Brothers.
Folk: Peter, Paul and Mary.

knowing that to choose one route would mean sacrificing the other.

For a Southern white singer, the pop market was always an elusive target, being more accessible to the artists and producers based near the main media centres, and most of the singers who had broken through eventually retreated to the more predictable and reliable country market. But they were not always allowed to make the switch overnight, and many had to endure a two- or three-year period of "paying their dues", criss-crossing the South with tours that took them into every country music club on the circuit, before radio programmers accepted them into the country fold.

Elvis Presley's career reflected the change in attitudes. His first 11 hits for RCA were all equally big country hits, through to "Hard Headed Woman" in June 1958; suddenly, country radio play dropped right off, and Elvis had no more records in the country top ten until 1971, when his straight country renditions of "I Really Don't Want to Know" and "There Goes My Everything" were finally, if grudgingly, accepted. The story was similar for the Everly Brothers, who had only one minor country hit after they joined Warner Brothers. Brenda Lee had no country hits at all during the period when she had 19 hits in the pop top twenty, Conway Twitty had no country hits until 1966, and Roy Orbison never did make the country charts. All of them recorded in Nashville, but that was not enough to qualify as "country".

From 1958, the world of country music virtually isolated itself from the world of pop, and most of the time it seemed that this was the way the major labels chose to keep it. Each of them appointed a Nashville-based A&R man to oversee their country music roster of artists, and little effort was made to push even the biggest country stars on to pop radio.

But while that division may have been reinforced by the major label policy makers, it was not always accepted by the artists, their managers, and most of all their publishers, who were anxious to reap the much larger rewards of pop success. The publisher who achieved the most impressive pop results from a Nashville base was Wesley Rose, who ran the Acuff-Rose music firm which had become a major country music institution as a result of the enormous success of Hank Williams, the protégé of Wesley's father, Fred Rose. Within a few years in the mid-fifties, Acuff-Rose recruited an outstanding roster of writers who all achieved substantial pop success: Marty Robbins, Don Gibson, Boudleaux and Felice Bryant, John D. Loudermilk, and Roy Orbison.

Marty Robbins' career typified the struggle encountered by a singer-writer who was branded by his label as "country". He joined Columbia before the rock 'n' roll "revolution", and was quick to adapt to teenage preferences for music with a back-beat; he covered Elvis Presley's version of "That's All Right", recorded Chuck Berry's "Maybellene", and then had his first number one country hit in 1956 with "Singing the Blues". Compared to most of his contemporaries, Marty did not have a particularly pronounced Southern twang to his singing voice, but it did not suit Columbia's master-plan to promote his record to the pop market; instead New York A&R chief Mitch Miller covered the song with Guy Mitchell, who had the biggest international hit of his career. Evidently determined to crack the system one way or another, Marty went back to covering rhythm and blues hits, but his "Long Tall Sally", missed all its targets, somehow lacking the sensuality that Elvis and Jerry Lee brought to their all-out rockers.

Back with the ballads, Marty Robbins suffered two more in-house cover versions, as Johnnie Ray trumped him with a pop hit of "You Don't Owe Me a Thing", and Guy Mitchell came back to steal the pop sales for "Knee Deep in the Blues". Finally Columbia relented, and in 1957 let Marty through to the pop market with no opposition to his "White Sport Coat (and a Pink Carnation)", which made the pop top three and stuck in the charts for six months. Vindicated at last, Marty Robbins became one of the few Nashville recording artists who survived the country radio boycott on pop hits after 1958, by developing a style which was more "western" than "country". Reminiscent in some ways of Frankie Laine, but without his overblown melodramatic delivery, Marty wrote a series of narrative ballads about life in the Texas/Mexico border country. Using Spanish guitar and other unconventional devices, Marty and his producer Don Law created a memorable series of classic story songs, among which "El Paso" topped both country and pop charts early in 1960, "Don't Worry" made the top five in 1961, and "Devil Woman" made the British top five in 1962. Among the singer-writers who owed obvious debts to his distinctive style were the Canadian folk singer Gordon Lightfoot, the New York singer-songwriter Neil Diamond, and the California-based country singer Merle Haggard.

Among the other writers signed to Acuff-Rose, Don Gibson had the satisfaction of seeing his songs accepted into the repertoire of countless international pop singers, but he never quite cracked that market himself. After a few fruitless years with MGM during the mid-fifties, when his "Sweet Dreams" began its reign as a country and pop standard through Faron Young's record for Capitol, Don joined RCA-Victor where A&R chief Chet Atkins made a concerted attempt to make pop hits with him. Their first effort together boded well: "Oh Lonesome Me" was recorded with an unusually heavy bass-drum beat (for a record made in Nashville), and made the pop top ten as well as topping the country chart; its B-side "I Can't Stop Loving You" became a standard for unrequited lovers. Gibson's sobbing voice was ideal for the weep-in-my-beer-songs he sang, but it was a bit too ponderous and heavy for teen-oriented pop radio. The Everly Brothers, by contrast, sounded exactly right.

The Everly Brothers joined Acuff-Rose in 1956, and made a couple of records for Columbia in the same kind of duo style that had been popular in the country market since the thirties, almost always sung by brothers: the Blue Sky Boys, the Monroe Brothers, the Delmore Brothers, and the Louvin Brothers all came from the Appalachian region, and featured a high voice set against a tenor. The style was regarded as a quaint novelty by pop professionals, and had never been consistently successful outside the country market; and even there it was regarded as a little old-fashioned by the mid-fifties. In 1957, Wesley Rose catalysed a breakthrough for his teenage protégés by finding them a source of distinctive song material, an enterprising independent record label, and a production team. The label was Cadence, run in New York by Archie Bleyer, who came down to Nashville to co-produce the Everly Brothers records with Chet Atkins, who was prepared to moonlight from his job as head of RCA's country division in order to show that it was possible to incorporate concepts from rhythm and blues and rock 'n' roll into country records without completely alienating country radio stations. The crucial ingredients that enabled the plan to work were the songs of Boudleaux and Felice Bryant, a husband-and-wife team who were by now parents with their own teenage children and who showed a remarkable flair for conveying the narcissistic self-preoccupations of adolescents.

Of the first ten singles by the Everly Brothers for Cadence, eight made the national top ten, which put them among the top four or five teen-oriented acts of the period. Their songs have stuck indelibly in the memories of the majority of teenagers who heard them at the time–including not only the kids who turned the radio up and bought their records, but also those who found them embarrassingly cute. The records were definitively well-made, with every line honed to make its point and then rammed home by the high whining voices backed by perfectly-sympathetic rhythm guitar arrangements. "Bye Bye Love" and "Wake Up Little Susie" were both on the charts for six months, propelled by rich acoustic guitar rhythms that suggested Chet Atkins had been listening not only to Les Paul and Mary Ford records (in which multi-tracked guitars sounded almost like an orchestra) but also to Bo Diddley (who played around the two-and-four beat of rock 'n' roll).

"All I Have to do is Dream" joined the short list of teen ballads that never lost their effect for teenagers caught in a particular situation; the song came as close as pop ever dared to the taboo topic of masturbation, as the singer insisted that he did not need his lover because he could fantasize her at any moment. It was not established whether "she" was a particular girl, or just the perfect embodiment of the singer's selfish needs.

"Bird Dog" and "Problems" returned to the more concrete world of the first two hits, and hinted at a humour which was underplayed in the duo's actual delivery. They always sounded very desperate and serious, and their sound became instantly recognizable. As teenagers began to abandon the family radiogram and listen on smaller portable radios in their own bedrooms, it was the high voices of singers like the Everly Brothers which cut through. Among the groups who stuck to those frequencies with great effect during the sixties were the Four Seasons and the Beach Boys in America, and the Beatles, Searchers, Hollies and several more groups in Britain, where the Everly Brothers continued to be popular right through to 1965.

Among the solo singers who also favoured a high register, Roy Orbison was probably the master in the five-year period, 1960–64, when he had nine top ten hits in both America and Britain. After several fruitless years with producers who were successful with other artists (Norman Petty in Clovis, Sam Phillips in Memphis, and Chet Atkins in Nashville), Orbison found a fellow-spirit in Fred Foster, whose Monument label was among the few effective indies based in Nashville. Both fans of a wide range of music, Foster and Orbison fearlessly incorporated a "black"-sounding back-up vocal sound into their arrangements which would inevitably forestall any play on country radio, and Orbison himself made no attempt to sound "country".

The result was "Only the Lonely", one of the most original, and lastingly-effective, pop records of 1960. The opening vocal group chant might have been on a black rhythm and blues record–"dum dum dum dummy doowah, oh yeah yeah yeah yeah"–and it was whispered so softly that Orbison's voice was quite a shock as it soared in, high, clear, and strong. This was another anthem of self-pity, as staked out in the records of the Everly Brothers and Conway Twitty, and Orbison sustained an in-depth survey of every aspect of misery and despair through "Running Scared" (with its "Bolero"-like build-up), "Crying", "Dream Baby" (that escape from reality again), "In Dreams" (and again), and "It's Over". It was quite a change of character for him to switch to out-and-out celebration in the hard-driving "Oh, Pretty Woman", which in 1964 topped the charts in America, Britain, and most other countries which kept score of their best-selling pop records. Yet despite so much unqualified success, Orbison attracted surprisingly few obvious imitators. Bobby Goldsboro, who was guitarist in his band for a while, may have been inspired by Orbison, but he sang with a pinched-nose sound that owed more to the equally melodramatic style of the New York singer Gene Pitney. Apparently defying plagiarists, Roy Orbison remains one of the giant figures of his era, a masterly singer, writer, and arranger who remained admirably impervious to the faddish period he was working in.

Fred Foster's Monument label was nationally distributed by London Records,* the American outpost of British Decca which also acted as distributor for several other independent labels during the early sixties, including Hi of Memphis. Formed in 1959 by Joe Cuoghi, Hi scored a series of hits by the Bill Black Combo; led by Elvis Presley's former bass-player but featuring tenor sax and keyboards in simple groove records like "Smokie" (1960), the Combo strongly influenced the approach of another Memphis-based instrumental group, Booker T. and the M.G.s.

IV

Off the beaten track in Norfolk, Virginia, two notable freelance ventures surfaced. Guitarist Ray Vernon had sung straight country songs on the same shows as Gene Vincent back in the mid-fifties, but turned his name around to become Link Wray and made a series of atmospheric instrumentals of which "Rumble" made the top twenty (licensed to Cadence, 1958). Most of Wray's records (later issued by Epic and then Swan) were too derivative to make their own mark, but that one track had a menacing effect, achieved by maltreating the guitar amp until it distorted: a daring move, in 1958.

The other adventurer in Norfolk was Frank Guida, whose productions for Gary "U.S." Bonds were oblivious of all technical know-how, and sounded as if he had recorded a party going on in the house next door. He stretched the sound through five top ten hits, on his

* LONDON RECORDS. *Formed in 1948 by British Decca.*
Pop: the Tornadoes.

Distributed labels:

MONUMENT. *Formed in Andersonville, Tennessee in 1958 by Fred Foster.*
Country pop: Billy Grammar, Boots Randolph, Charlie McCoy.
Pop: Roy Orbison, the Velvets.

HI. *Formed in Memphis in 1959 by Joe Cuoghi.*
Instrumental groups: the Bill Black Combo, Ace Cannon, Willie Mitchell.
Rock 'n' roll: Gene Simmons, Jerry Jaye.

MONOGRAM. *Formed in Los Angeles in 1962 by Jim Lee.*
Pop: Chris Montez.

own LeGrand* label, 1960–62, riding the crest of the twist craze being hyped by Philadelphia.

Pittsburgh never became a significant recording centre, but nurtured three influential vocal groups, including two with both black and white members–unusual for the times. The Dell Vikings recorded "Come Go With Me" in somebody's basement, and made the top ten with its catchy chant (on Dot, licensed from Fee Bee, 1957), and four years later the Marcels went all the way to the top with a novelty arrangement of "Blue Moon", dominated by a gimmicky bass vocal line (produced in New York by Stu Phillips for Colpix, 1961). In between, the all-white Skyliners made the top twenty in 1959 on the locally-based Calico label with "Since I Don't Have You", featuring a searing falsetto vocal from lead singer Jimmy Beaumont in the "blackest" sounding white vocal group record yet.

In Philadelphia,† the main preoccupation was to identify and exaggerate the elements which had made Elvis Presley so popular. Managers sought out dark-complexioned boys whose pictures would

* LEGRAND. *Founded in 1959 in Newport, Virginia by Frank Guida.*
Pop rhythm and blues: Gary "US" Bonds, Gene Barge.

Subsidiary:

SPQR.
Pop: Jimmy Soul.

† *Philadelphia labels:*

CAMEO RECORDS. *Formed in 1956 by Bernie Lowe and Kal Mann. A&R: Dave Appell.*
Teen pop: Charlie Gracie, Bobby Rydell, Jo Ann Campbell, the Orlons, Dee Dee Sharp, the Rays.
Novelty: John Zacherle.

Subsidiary:

PARKWAY.
Teen pop: Chubby Checker, the Dovells.

SWAN. *Formed in 1957 by Bernie Binnick and Tony Mammarella.*
Teen pop: Billie and Lillie, Freddie Cannon, Dickie Doo and the Don'ts.

Subsidiary:

HUNT. *Partly owned by Dick Clark.*
Teen pop: The Quintones, the Virtues.

JAMIE. *Founded in 1958 by Harold Lipsius with three partners.*
Rock 'n' roll: Duane Eddy, Ray Sharp, Sanford Clark (all produced independently by Lee Hazelwood).
Rhythm and blues: Barbara Lynn.

Subsidiary:

GUYDEN.
Pop: The Sherrys.
Distributed labels:
MONTEL-MICHELE. *Formed in Baton Rouge, La. by Sam Montel.*
Pop duo: Dale and Grace.

look right in the teen fan magazines, and producers harnessed an ever-more blatant beat to their sing-along songs. Song-writers Bernie Lowe and Kal Mann launched their own Cameo Records with a hit version of their song "Butterfly" by Charlie Gracie in 1957, and brought in A&R man Dave Appell to follow through with brash productions for Bobby Rydell. Cameo also picked up distribution rights to a double-sided hit by the Rays, "Silhouettes"/"Daddy Cool", written and produced by Bob Crewe and Frank Slay, who turned out a series of raucous hits by Freddie Cannon for another Philadelphia label, Swan. This was mostly crass stuff, impressive for its single-minded pursuit of the lowest common denominator, but generally lacking any originality which could be traced through to later records as any kind of "influence". Chancellor Records found teen idols Frankie Avalon and Fabian, but Jamie had the best quality of releases because most of them were licensed from outside the city, like the productions by Lee Hazelwood of Duane Eddy, Ray Sharpe ("Linda Lu") and Sanford Clark from Phoenix, Arizona.

The most effective outfit in Detroit in the late fifties was the Talent Artists booking agency of Harry Balk and rving Micahnik, which had represented Little Willie John and the Royaltones before breaking through internationally with Johnny and the Hurricanes and Del Shannon. The hits by the Hurricanes were mostly formula re-arrangements of folk songs in the public domain, arranged by local piano player T. J. Fowler but credited the producers as composers. But Del Shannon was an original, particularly as a writer. His "Runaway" (licensed to Big Top, 1961) featured an unusual organ sound played by co-writer Max Crook, swathed in echo to enhance the desolation of the song's message.

Also in Detroit, and apparently isolated from the influences around him, Canadian Jack Scott made some of the most distinctive rock 'n' roll records of the late fifties, perfecting a studio approach to create hypnotic, almost trance-like moods. No macho postures or extravagant instrumental sound, just repetitive chants over a heavy but acoustic sound dominated by stand-up bass. The ballad "My True Love" (Carlton 1958) was Scott's biggest hit, but the bouncier "The Way I Walk" and "Goodbye Baby" (1959) were more inventive.

Back in pop's headquarters in New York, the music industry never

---

CHANCELLOR RECORDS. *Founded in 1958 by Peter de Angelis. Distributed by ABC-Paramount.*
Teen pop: Frankie Avalon, Fabian.

V-TONE RECORDS. *Formed in 1960 by Lenny Caldwell.*
Rhythm and blues: Bobby Parker, Bobby Peterson.

really rated rock 'n' roll, seeing it as Southern music and part of a culture that was generally patronized and even despised. It took the imported reverence of the Beatles and the Rolling Stones to turn around that kind of attitude, and apart from Jack Scott's experience with Carlton*, rock 'n' roll artists had a hard time finding sympathetic outlets among the New York labels during the late fifties.

Among the established indie label owners, Dave Kapp never did take on a real rocker for his Kapp label,† but his company enjoyed considerable (and often overlooked) success with middle-of-the-road acts including the pianist Roger Williams. Archie Bleyer was music director for the Arthur Godfrey television talent show before deciding to branch out on his own with his Cadence label,‡ and during the late fifties he rivalled Dot and Liberty as one of the most successful new indies. He had the biggest hit with the novelty song "The Ballad of Davy Crockett" in 1955 (by Bill Hayes), as well as several hits by Julias LaRosa and the Chordettes. Although the Chordettes were too old and too early to be classified as a specifically "teen" act, they did achieve an innocence that undoubtedly influenced some of the more obvious teen groups, notably the Teddy Bears and the Fleetwoods. The biggest hit by the Chordettes was "Mr. Sandman" in 1955, but the cool harmonies and fragile perfection of "Born to Be With You" in 1956 set standards which were never improved on by the more amateurish girl groups who followed.

Andy Williams joined Cadence in 1956, and after a top ten hit with "Canadian Sunset" he topped the pop chart with the now-familiar ruse of a cover version, in this case the suggestive "Butterfly". Bleyer probably saw Williams as a crooner for the still substantial section of the youth market which was not entirely convinced about rock 'n' roll. If there was room for a smoothie like Pat Boone, as Randy Wood had established that there was, then why not have a New York-based equivalent? After "Butterfly", Williams wisely stayed clear of rock 'n'

* CARLTON. *Formed in 1959 in New York by Joe Carlton (ex-RCA, ABC).*
Pop: Anita Bryant.
Rock 'n' roll: Jack Scott.

Subsidiary: GUARANTEED
Pop: Paul Evans.

† KAPP. *Formed in 1955 in New York by Dave Kapp (ex-Decca).*
Pop: Roger Williams.
Teen pop: Jerry Keller, Johnny Cymbal.
Black pop: Ruby and the Romantics, Shirley Ellis.

‡ CADENCE. *Formed in 1953 in New York by Archie Bleyer.*
Pop: Julius LaRosa, Bill Hayes, the Chordettes, Andy Williams.
Teen pop: the Everly Brothers, Eddie Hodges, Johnny Tillotson.
Rock 'n' roll: Link Wray.
Black pop: Lenny Welch.

roll, which was not suited to his relaxed delivery, and he duly became a national institution, appealing mainly to a "post-teen" audience.

Impressively coming up with a new major act each year, Bleyer produced the Everly Brothers out of the hat in 1957, and supervised their career with great skill and panache. Compared to most of the new teen idol acts, the Everly Brothers were able to come close to reproducing their recorded sound live on stage every night during the mammoth package tours that reinforced the impact of current teen hits. In collusion with the duo's Nashville-based manager-publisher Wesley Rose, Bleyer kept the group "up there" on the radio, in the charts, and in public view until 1960 when Warner Brothers stepped in with an irresistible offer of $250,000 for their contract.

The departure of the Everly Brothers marked the beginning of the end for Cadence, but Bleyer still found one more hit-maker: Johnny Tillotson had one of the biggest hits of 1960 with the clever and irresistibly catchy "Poetry in Motion", and followed through with several more before Bleyer closed Cadence down in 1964. Ten years was good enough.

Of the New York-based indie labels which were formed more or less specifically to cater for the new teenage market, Roulette and Laurie lasted longest. Roulette* was formed in 1956 by publishers Morris Levy and Phil Kahl as an outlet for the masters they purchased by the Texan pop-rockers Buddy Knox and Jimmy Bowen. The company became a distribution umbrella for a family of labels including George Goldner's Gone, End, and Gee, and maintained a regular output on Roulette itself. Jimmie Rodgers, a folk-pop singer from the Seattle area, had five top twenty hits, and among a slew of one-shot hits and near-misses was a gem from the last of the rock 'n' roll pioneers to get a recording contract, Ronnie Hawkins.

Originally from Arkansas, Ronnie Hawkins made the usual trek to Sun Records in Memphis, failed his audition, and finally wound up in Canada before finding anyone interested in recording him. He was by

* ROULETTE. *Founded in 1956 by Morris Levy, Phil Kahl, and George Goldner.*
A&R: Goldner, Richard Barrett, Henry Glover, Sammy Lowe.
Teen pop: Jimmie Rodgers, Buddy Knox, Jimmy Bowen.
Rock 'n' roll: Ronnie Hawkins.
Sixties pop: Joey Dee and the Starliters.
Novelty: the Royal Teens.

Distributed labels:
GEE, GONE, END, RAMA, RICO (*all owned by George Goldner; see p. 76*).

COED. *Formed in 1958 by George Paxton.*
Teen pop: the Crests, the Duprees, Adam Wade.

HULL
Rhythm and blues group: Shep and the Limelites.

no means a great singer, but he did have a flair for finding good musicians, and he knew how to entertain a crowd with an egocentric display of crude sexual bravado and a repertoire based firmly on the Bo Diddley beat. He managed minor hits for Roulette in 1959 with Chuck Berry's "Forty Days" (for some reason, Ronnie added ten to Chuck's original thirty) and with Young Jessie's "Mary Lou", but his classic recording came later, in 1963, when he had assembled a new band which included drummer Levon Helm from Arkansas and a teenage Canadian guitarist, Robbie Robertson. Together they laid down a breathtaking version of Bo Diddley's "Who Do You Love", to which Robertson contributed a fiery guitar part that broke out into a frenzy in the instrumental break. For once Hawkins sustained a vocal performance to do justice to his musicians, and the entire performance was as exciting as any rock 'n' roll record ever made. But in 1963, this was not what the world was listening out for, and soon afterwards Ronnie's band left him to go out on their own, first as the Hawks, and subsequently as the backing band for John Hammond, Jr., and Bob Dylan, before finally acquiring mythical status as, simply, the Band.

At Laurie,* Dion came as close as any New York singer of the period to a distinctive rock 'n' roll style. Starting out as lead singer with Dion and the Belmonts, Dion ranged from the soft-and-gentle "Teenager in Love" to the wilder "I Wonder Why" without establishing an immediately recognizable identity. But after a couple of inconsequential solo records in 1960, Dion suddenly hit on a new sound in 1961 for "Runaround Sue". The party-time vocal group chant and instrumental arrangement were shamelessly copied off "Quarter to Three", the U.S. Bonds hit which Laurie distributed, but Dion probably arrived at his vocal approach by imitating the demo made by the song's writer, Ernie Maresca. Normally a cultured-sounding singer, Dion adopted a rough-and-ready growl which sounded as if it was sliding out of the corner of his mouth; suddenly the street hoodlums of New York had a voice of their own, and Dion used it again on the equally successful "The Wanderer", The whole stance of brazen confidence anticipated the role of the Fonze presented by actor Henry Winkler in the TV series "Happy Days" during the seventies, and Dion himself could have made more from the sound if he had not

* LAURIE. *Formed in 1958 in New York by Gene Schwartz.*
Teen pop: Dion and the Belmonts, the Mystics, the Jarmels.
Rock 'n' roll: Dion.
Girl group: the Chiffons.

Subsidiary:

RUST
Pop rhythm and blues: Dean and Jean.

become entangled in a self-destructive life-style. He switched from Laurie to Columbia in 1963, and recorded two brilliant revivals of songs that Leiber and Stoller had written for the Drifters back in the mid-fifties, "Ruby Baby" and "Drip Drop", both of which Dion substantially improved with his languorous drawl set against exciting syncopated rhythm tracks.

Most of the other New York labels were backed by large organizations already in the entertainment world and seeking to diversify, notably publishing and movie companies. Hill and Range Publishing set up the Big Top and Dunes subsidiaries,* while Columbia Pictures launched the Colpix label† and bought out Don Kirshner's Aldon Music, setting up Columbia Screen Gems Music. United Artists Pictures set up a New York-based record outlet which mainly issued independently produced records until Don Costa moved from ABC-Paramount to take over its A&R department in 1959.‡ These ventures were all successful from a commercial viewpoint, but there was little worth more than a passing mention in a survey of stylistic innovators and outstanding records. Several of the era's major producers made records for these companies, but apart from the "girl group" records that are discussed in a separate section of this book, the outcome was mostly second-rate.

The most conspicuous exception to that dismissive generalization was Gene Pitney, who made his first mark as writer of "Hello Mary Lou" for Ricky Nelson in 1961 and of "He's a Rebel" for the Crystals

* BIG TOP. *Founded in 1959 in New York by Gene and Julian Aberbach as a division of their Hill and Range publishing corporation.*
Black pop: Sammy Turner, Don and Juan.
Pop rock 'n' roll: Del Shannon, Johnny and the Hurricanes (1960–61).

Subsidiary:

DUNES.
A&R: Stan Shulman, Ray Peterson.
Teen pop: Ray Peterson, Curtis Lee.

† COLPIX. *Founded in 1959 in New York by Columbia Pictures. A&R: Stu Phillips.*
Pop: James Darren, the Marcels, Shelley Fabarers, Paul Peterson, Earl-Jean.

‡ UNITED ARTISTS. *Formed in 1957 in New York. A&R (from 1959): Don Costa (ex-ABC-Paramount).*
Pop rhythm and blues: Marv Johnson, the Exciters, the Clovers.
Rhythm and blues: Garnet Mimms and the Enchanters.
Pop: Jay and the Americans.

Subsidiary:

UNART.
Rhythm and blues: The Falcons.
Distributed label:
MUSICOR. *Formed in 1961 by Art Talmadge and Aaron Schroeder.*
Pop: Gene Pitney, Kenny Dino.
Country and western: George Jones.

in 1962. Both songs were well above average in their lyric content and arrangement ideas, but Pitney wrote surprisingly few of his own hits. He had an extraordinary voice, which somehow managed to combine an over-the-top passion with an extremely precise diction and an overall feeling of complete vulnerability. He recorded for Musicor, a label formed by publisher Aaron Schroeder and supervised by Pitney's manager Art Talmadge, and Pitney's career seemed to be partly designed as a vehicle for songs written by Schroeder's other writers. Burt Bacharach and Hal David contributed the memorable saga, "Twenty Four Hours from Tulsa" and "Only Love Can Break a Heart", and the still-unknown Randy Newman had a couple of minor hits.

In some ways, Gene Pitney was a throw-back to the pre-rock 'n' roll era extravagance of Frankie Laine and Johnnie Ray, but he was seen as picking up the mantle of Paul Anka and Neil Sedaka, and rivalled Roy Orbison as the prince of self-pity during the early sixties. He survived the onslaught of the British Invasion better than most solo singers, and had as many hits in Britain as in America, mostly with different records: of 19 which made the top twenty in one country or the other, only two records made both charts.

Gene Pitney's career was an unusual case where an artist's idiosyncrasies were allowed to dominate the production approach. More often, New York producers and arrangers attempted to dominate their records at the expense of quirks in their material or performers, and in the mid-sixties they all came in for a shock when the world turned away from them in favour of records which had a more spontaneous flavour, most of which owed at least some inspiration to rhythm and blues.

PART II

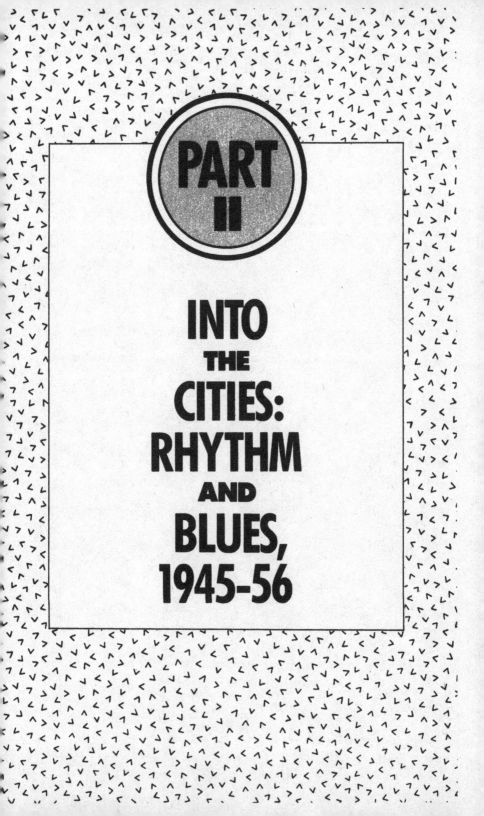

INTO THE CITIES: RHYTHM AND BLUES, 1945-56

6

BLUES-BASED STYLES: DANCEHALL BLUES, CLUB BLUES, BAR BLUES

The roots of rock 'n' roll are mainly to be found in rhythm and blues music, a term which, like the later expression rock 'n' roll, was coined to provide a convenient catch-all description for several distinct musical styles. Some of the styles of rhythm and blues shared musical features; all of them were produced for the Negro market.

Most of the styles contributed at least one singer to rock 'n' roll; all of them served as source material which in different circumstances was either used with care and understanding or simply plundered by singers (black and white) who had no direct experience of the background out of which the styles grew but who needed the music in order to satisfy the demand for rock 'n' roll.

The term rhythm and blues was first coined in the forties. Pre-war record companies had found it convenient to identify their blues product by calling it "race" music, and when *Billboard* began charting the sales of records in the Negro market in 1946, it used this term. By 1948, various companies, particularly the majors, were embarrassed by the expression, and they began using alternatives, including "ebony" (MGM), "sepia" (Decca and Capitol), and "rhythm and blues" (RCA-Victor). In June, 1949, *Billboard,* without any editorial comment, switched its own term to "rhythm and blues", and although as late as 1952, Decca was still advertising its product for the Negro market as "sepia" music, the expression "rhythm and blues" by then had become the generally accepted term to describe music and records for the Negro market.

In general, the expression was a satisfactory name for the music that had developed out of pre-war blues styles, for the most distinctive new element in this music was the addition of a dance rhythm. But "rhythm and blues" was a less satisfactory name for two of the most important later innovations of the period, the various group styles and the gospel-based styles, which were to become increasingly popular as rock 'n' roll began to syphon off the unique spirit of previous rhythm and blues forms. As a market category, however, "rhythm and blues" was simply a signal that the singer was black, recording for the black audience.*

Through the first three decades of the twentieth century the blues extended the difference established by black singers and musicians in New Orleans between the bands that played march and dance rhythms with several instruments and the singers who supplied their own accompaniment, usually on guitar. Of these two modes, the band music gradually subdivided into jazz (developed in most regions of the country by bands emphasizing instrumental improvization and harmony) and band blues (associated from the late twenties mainly with bands in the Southwest–Kansas, Oklahoma, Texas, and parts of Arkansas). At the same time, the self-accompanying blues singers who were first identified with small towns in the rural South began moving into larger towns and cities, and into the North, where they began collecting other musicians to support them, often on piano or harmonica.

Both kinds of blues singing–band- and self-accompanied–were radically affected by the improvements in electrical amplification introduced during the thirties, which enabled singers to be heard without shouting, and guitar-playing techniques to exploit the differences in tone and volume provided by electric amplification. The post-war blues styles of rhythm and blues were different from pre-war styles partly because of this difference in equipment; but they were also different because there were new experiences to be accounted for in music, and new moods that the blues had to accommodate. The singer (or musician) who grew up in the farm community life of Mississippi found a different kind of environment when he moved to Memphis and then to Chicago, different living conditions and different tastes, and his music had to reflect the new conditions. He had moved to the big city. For a time, jazz and band blues had been more or less the same thing, as in the repertoires of Count Basie and Jimmy Lunceford. But once the experiments of the New York "bop" musicians abandoned regular rhythms, jazz and blues became two different kinds of music with different audiences. The most distinctive characteristic of all rhythm and blues styles was the presence of a dance rhythm, and it is primarily this characteristic that distinguished rhythm and blues from post-war jazz, which was

* *Until 1956, there was plenty of justification for classifying the Negro market separately. The black audience was interested almost solely in black singers. Only five records by white singers reached rhythm and blues top ten lists 1950–55, and three of those were rock 'n' roll records–Bill Haley's "Dim Dim the Lights" and "Rock Around the Clock", and Boyd Bennett's "Seventeen".* (*The others were Johnnie Ray's "Cry" and Les Paul and Mary Ford's "How High the Moon".*) *Few white singers had either the interest or the cultural experience to try to appeal to the black audience's taste–until, that is, rock 'n' roll brought a new kind of singer into recording studios.*

rarely recorded as dance music and which could therefore dispense with the convention of maintaining a particular beat throughout a song.

There was a further difference between jazz and the blues in post-war music. In rhythm and blues, the soloists were generally more "selfish", concerned to express their own feelings, depending on the rest of the band to keep the beat going and the volume up while they blew their hearts out and their heads off. In jazz, there was usually more interplay between musicians, more exploration into melody and harmony, less reliance on the emotional force of the musician's tone.

The nature of the blues emphasizes particular qualities of character in its performers: they need to have a strong, consistent character, and a persuasive way of communicating their thoughts and feelings. They may use menace or high-spirited exultation, humour or complete despair, gentleness or rough strength, to set particular moods on an evening's atmosphere. But whatever each man uses, it must be his own, different from anybody else's (unless he intends to do no more than invoke adulation for some revered figure by imitating his style).

Although each man has his own style, there is always a tendency for people with common experience to have comparable styles, and an analysis of the blues can show connections between people from certain regions of the United States, and within those regions distinguish between men who sang with one kind of accompaniment, or in one kind of club, and those who sang with other kinds of accompaniment, or in some other kind of bar.

Accordingly, five main kinds of rhythm and blues can be distinguished in the music of the black culture in the ten years after the Second World War. There were three kinds of blues–dancehall blues, club blues, and bar blues. There were also two kinds of music that developed which were not strictly blues–various kinds of group singing, and gospel-based styles.

The following analysis of rhythm and blues is necessarily based mainly on the evidence of records, backed up with a considerable amount of material collected by researchers and interviewers over the past ten or more years. The discussion pays virtually no attention to pre-war forms of blues, or to jazz, which both have been well described and analysed elsewhere.[1] There has also been some writing on the post-war period, particularly on the Chicago bar blues singers,[2] and to a lesser extent on the dancehall blues musicians.[3] The discussion here takes account of what has already been written, and focuses particularly on the singers and musicians who directly influenced rock 'n' roll. It also endeavours to point out the contemporary significance of certain figures who have had relatively little influence on subsequent music, yet were outstanding exponents of their styles.*

I

Of all the blues styles that were part of rhythm and blues, and from there shaped rock 'n' roll, the dancehall blues are the most various. Three categories are relevant here: big band blues; shout, scream, and cry blues; and combo blues.

i. The big band blues were played by the bands that were closest in stage presentation and musical arrangements to the pre-war Kansas City bands.

The atmosphere at a dance where a big band was playing has been well described by Malcolm X, who recalled working as a shoe-shine boy at the Roseland Ballroom in Boston:

> "*Showtime!*" people would start hollering about the last hour of the dance. Then a couple of dozen really wild couples would stay on the floor, the girls changing to low white sneakers. The band now would really be blasting, and all the other dancers would form a clapping, shouting circle to watch that wild competition as it began, covering only a quarter or so of the ballroom floor. The band, the spectators and the dancers, would be making the Roseland feel like a big rocking ship. The spotlight would be turning, pink, yellow, green, and blue, picking up the couples lindy-hopping as if they had gone mad. "Wail, man, wail!" people would be shouting at the band; and it *would* be wailing, until first one and then another couple just ran out of strength and stumbled off towards the crowd, exhausted and soaked with sweat.[4]

In Newark, New Jersey, LeRoi Jones had similar experiences:

> Lloyd's Manor in Newark, N.J., was a place where they'd have groups, like Illinois Jacquet's, Erskine Hawkins', Earl Bostic's, Tab Smith's, Big Jay McNeely's and all the other wild swingers of the day. There were absolutely no holds barred, musically or

* *There has been a curious tendency–as Charles Keil noted in a witty paragraph in* Urban Blues*–for blues followers of the late fifties and the sixties to devote most of their attention to unsophisticated, "country" forms of blues at the expense of the slicker city blues. Recently, city bluesmen, such as B. B. King and Albert King have been better appreciated, as the audiences's interest has extended to include virtually every rhythm and blues singer who played a guitar. But at the time of this writing, there still is relatively little interest in men who played no instrument but merely sang in front of a band, and little interest too in men, who played the blues on saxophone, both sang and played the saxophone, or whose instrumental accompaniment was supplied by piano and saxophones rather than the currently favoured harmonica and guitar.*

socially, and a band was considered successful if it succeeded in blowing the dancers off their feet. There was also a place called the Graham Auditorium where they used to hold what were called "Teenage Canteens" but a lot of the people must have been teen-agers for 20 or so years. It was a loud blur, climaxed by those shattering saxophone "battles" which featured heavy horns like Jacquet, McNeely and Ammons-Stitt groups and big throated singers like Wynonie Harris, Larry Darnell and Little Esther.[5]

The post-war big band style evolved through several stages out of the music played by Kansas City bands during the late twenties. This music had been inspired by the optimistic feelings of people moving into the wide open spaces of the Southwest and, by all accounts, the wide open nature of Kansas City during the twenties, where crime and good living joined in defiance of Prohibition and the kind of morality it represented. During the thirties big bands were established in most big cities, with a few famous bandleaders–Fletcher Henderson, Duke Ellington, Count Basie, and Jimmy Lunceford–able to recruit the best musicians and arrangers. Towards the end of the thirties, the demand was sufficient to draw some of the bands away from their local audiences: Andy Kirk and Jay McShann left Kansas, and Erskine Hawkins brought his band to New York from Alabama.

During the war, still more important bands formed or became nationally known, including those of Cab Calloway, Milton Larkins, Cootie Williams, Lionel Hampton, and Billy Eckstine. All of them were potentially capable of playing for either jazz or dance audiences, but by the end of the war most of the bandleaders found they had to choose one or the other. Those who chose the rhythm and blues dance music included Lucky Millinder, Tiny Bradshaw, Todd Rhodes, and Buddy Johnson. Compared to the "jazz" orchestras, the rhythm and blues bands used less imaginative arrangements and sometimes less skillful musicians. (The leaders mentioned here, though, were more rigorous than many others in rehearsing their bands and maintaining a varied repertoire.)

During the five years after the war, week after week a succession of magnificent bands followed each other through the towns that had enough black people to support a big dance hall. The bands were judged partly on their ability to generate intense excitement at the end of a dance. For this, they needed at least one saxophonist who could blow hard and long at fast rocking tempos, and at least one singer who could match him, with a clear strong delivery. But to balance these crescendos of sound, a band also had to have soloists who could make the mood soft and mellow, who could bring lovers together and encourage strangers to get to know each other better. A few versatile musicians and singers could be as effective in this role as when they were screaming, but most bands would feature a ballad singer and a shouter, a smooch tenor and a screamer. The instrumental soloists often were excellent, in control of their instruments even when they honked or screeched as if beside themselves with frenzied emotion. The same was true of the singers, who needed strong lungs and a good throat to compete with the roar of the band, but who also needed a sense of timing and the ability to let their voices ride with a rhythm.

Through the forties, the tendency was for increasing attention to be focused on the saxophone solos and decreasing care to be taken with the orchestral backdrop. Arrangements became simpler (which enabled a new man to fit into a band faster, and required less rehearsal time of new material). The bands soon became as well known for their stars as for their leader: Cootie Williams for Willis Jackson, Sil Austin, and Eddie Davis; Milton Larkins for Illinois Jacquet, Eddie Vinson, and Arnett Cobb; Lionel Hampton for Earl Bostic, Clifford Scott, Chu Berry (and, after he took them from Larkins, for Jacquet and Cobb); Billy Eckstine for Dexter Gordon and Gene Ammons (and for a number of musicians known for their jazz abilities).

Apart from the shout blues vocals, many bands also featured songs that were sung by half the band in chorus, and others that were presented in a sing-along style by the ballad or light-voiced singer. Some records by Millinder, Hampton, and Bradshaw featured such light entertainment singing. Jimmy Lunceford introduced one of the most influential vocal groups who used this style, the Treniers (originally a pair of twins but eventually a five-man team). Scat singing, comedy, and a lively stage act were expected of this kind of group.

The exceptional singers tended to use the shouting style, and most of the ballad singing with the big bands was poor, but a few such singers with a good sense of timing were featured, among them Al Hibbler with Duke Ellington and then Jay McShann, Billy Eckstine with Earl Hines and then with his own band, Sarah Vaughan with Eckstine's band, and Arthur Prysock with Buddy Johnson.

Most big bands which recorded for major companies favoured the "jazz" side of their repertoire over the danceable blues, and only Decca regularly encouraged its black big bands to make records which were likely to appeal as much to black record-buyers as to whites. Among the company's impressive roster of black bands in the forties were the bands of Buddy Johnson (often featuring his sister Ella Johnson as vocalist), Jimmy Lunceford, Lucky Millinder and Lionel Hampton, whose recordings were mostly supervised by Milt Gabler. Of the independent companies, King of Cincinatti and Savoy of Newark were the two which had most success with big bands. Millinder (after leaving Decca), Todd Rhodes and Tiny Bradshaw all recorded hits for King in the market which was becoming known as "rhythm and blues", while Johnny Otis brought an extraordinary series of eight huge rhythm and blues hits to Savoy in one year, 1950.

The Johnny Otis Show was one of the last successful big touring bands to be formed. He called his show a "Rhythm and Blues Caravan", and at various times featured a host of fine singers–Little Esther, a big-voiced ballad singer with a style close to Dinah Washington's; Willie Mae Thornton, a rough, almost country-styled singer: Mel Walker, a ballad singer; and Marie Adams, another strong-voiced blues singer. Able to accommodate to the shifting audience tastes in rhythm and blues, Otis's Caravan survived to enjoy success as a rock 'n' roll show.

In order to survive, big bands had to make such shifts, but it became increasingly difficult to do so, and by the mid-fifties almost all the big blues bands had folded. A few fortunate musicians were able to make money as session musicians on rock 'n' roll records.

The bands that played band blues had made an important contribution. At a time when the contemporary white big bands of Glenn Miller, Les Brown, the Dorsey Brothers, and Kay Kyser were tending to impose arrangements on their musicians, the black big bands had opened up and let their musicians run free. The sound of a sax solo breaking loose from a series of driving riffs is one of the most exciting experiences of this century's music. The tension created by the same band, harnessed to a slow tempo and a soft mood, while a singer called the blues in a strong, rich voice, easily took hold of listeners who understood the conventions of the music.

It seemed logical, then, that with the death of the big bands the soloists and the singers should want to achieve these moods by themselves, and for the audience to want the excitement of Illinois Jacquet pure, without having to wait through ensemble playing and solos by less impressive people. So, gradually replacing the big bands, came the featured singers and saxmen, the shouters, screamers, and criers.

ii For rock 'n' roll, the band blues shouters were generally too obviously accomplished (and therefore unable to get the necessary homemade sound in their work) and too adult in their concerns and terms of reference. The open sexual content of their songs needed change–but that could be handled, as Bill Haley showed with his treatment of Joe Turner's "Shake, Rattle and Roll". But it wasn't just the words–the whole character of the shouted blues was adult, in the tone of voice used by the singers, the assumptions behind their songs, and the sophistication of the musical arrangements.

The most celebrated of the blues shouters, Joe Turner, had never been associated with a particular band. He had started singing semi-professionally while still in his teens in Kansas City in the late twenties. His first records were accompanied only by the pianist Pete Johnson; of these "Roll 'Em Pete" (Vocalion, 1938), was a brilliant achievement by both men, the strong vocal and eager boogie achieving the kind of spirit even big bands of the day sometimes failed to get.

Turner's music was infused with the spirit of good-natured optimism which the writer Ralph Ellison has said was characteristic of the Southwestern states during the twenties. Men had come there, out from the deeper South, with hopes for a different kind of life, hopes that experience had not yet disillusioned. The feeling came through even in a musical obituary, one of Turner's best songs and performances, "Old Piney Brown is Gone":

Well he went to California,
Stood on Hollywood and Vine;
Yes, he went to California.
As soon as the news got round,
Yeah the girls all jump and shout,
"Here comes Mister Piney Brown."

The next time I saw Piney
He was standing on 18th and Vine.
The last time I saw Piney
He was standing on 18th and Vine.
Well I tell the world,
Sure was a friend of mine.

Through the forties, while other singers with similar styles were acclaimed as stars, Turner, surprisingly, was a relatively obscure name, moving restlessly from one record company to another without achieving any national hits. In 1950 Turner was contracted to Atlantic Records in New York and belatedly, but in a big way, became known to the black record buyers.

His first record for Atlantic, "Chains of Love" (written by the company's rhythm and blues producer, Ahmet Ertegun) was a major hit in the rhythm and blues market in 1951. Helped by strong sax and piano support, Turner transformed what might have been a trite song into a vehicle for the deep experience-based feelings of the blues. "Chains of Love" was followed by a series of other hits, including "Sweet Sixteen" (1952), "Honey Hush" (1953), and "TV Mama" (1954), the latter having an interesting accompaniment from the Chicago bottleneck guitarist Elmore James.

In 1954, Turner recorded the novelty blues "Shake, Rattle and Roll", whose boogie rhythm and raucous sax breaks attracted the attention of Bill Haley and Decca (looking for rock 'n' roll material). Turner himself later recorded songs by the rock 'n' roll writers Leiber and Stoller, including "Lipstick, Powder and Paint", but his voice betrayed his identity as a blues shouter–he couldn't sound like a rock 'n' roll singer.

The other singers in the style experienced comparable problems. Walter Brown, Eddie "Cleanhead" Vinson, Wynonie Harris, Bullmoose Jackson and Jimmy Witherspoon were probably the best shouters, and all had hits in the rhythm and blues market yet were virtually unknown to the rock 'n' roll audience only a few years later. Their performances were oriented to the kind of situation described in Charles Keil's *Urban Blues*, intimate, relaxed, loaded with sexual references and suggestive plays on words. Bill Haley had been able to clean up "Shake, Rattle and Roll" and still have a song that made some sense. But he could have done nothing at all with Vinson's "I'm Weak But I'm Willing", or "Something Done Stole My Cherry Red", with Wynonie Harris's "Lovin' Machine", or Bullmoose Jackson's "I Want a Bow-Legged Woman". The whole atmosphere of Jimmy Witherspoon's "No Rollin' Blues" (1949) depended on verses such as the following, which appeared in similar forms in several other rhythm and blues songs at the time:

Some people like to love in the parlor,
Others go down lover's lane,
But I like to love in the wee small hours of the morning
When it's pouring down with rain.

Unlike Hank Ballard's "Work With Me, Annie", these songs did not have a strong melody or distinctive rhythm that could be used with entirely different words. The blues shouters often used medium tempos, familiar melodies, even familiar verses, which they sang in such a way that the audience accepted their interpretation as being personal, effectively original.

Wynonie Harris was perhaps an exception, as he did sing with a distinctive melody and strong rhythm, so that structurally his fast records anticipated the northern band style of rock 'n' roll. "Good Rockin' Tonight", "Good Morning, Judge", "Bloodshot Eyes", and "Lovin' Machine" were all fast, memorable, and exciting–and sung with that tone of voice that identified an adult. Rock 'n' roll was supposed to be young people's music.

Among female blues shouters, the pattern was similar. Faye Adams, Little Esther, Varetta Dillard, and Big Maybelle were all committed too firmly to the conventions of the blues to be able to make the transition to rock 'n' roll, despite great reputations as rhythm and blues singers. Big Maybelle's records were particularly good–"Gabbin' Blues" (Okeh, 1952) had fine trumpet and a fascinating arrangement, but a totally adult framework. The two singers who did make an impression as rock 'n' roll performers both recorded for Atlantic–Ruth Brown and LaVern Baker.

Ruth Brown's early records for the company–"Teardrops From My Eyes" (1951, featuring a tenor solo by Budd Johnson), "5-10-15 Hours" (1952, featuring tenor solo by Willis Jackson)–were sophisticated blues-shouting at its finest and much smoother than equivalent records by other performers on King, with a hint of demure suppliance that was associated more with the tones of popular singers than with the blues. Gradually, Atlantic oriented Ruth Brown's records to a wider market, introducing deep vocal group harmonies on "Oh What a Dream" (1954) and a straight pop lyric, by Leiber and Stoller, on "Lucky Lips" (1956). Never a major rock 'n' roll singer, she was one of the few female singers to come close to capturing the feeling of the music.

LaVern Baker succeeded completely. Her records had always been only lightly rooted in the conventions of rhythm and blues, and from 1954 were evidently directed at the popular music market. "Tweedle Dee", with a light tone and a frisky beat, was one of the most charming records of rock 'n' roll, but the singer's biggest success was "Jim Dandy", a novelty song with a heavier beat. Baker proved to be the most adaptable of all the female rhythm and blues singers and she provided almost the only link between this group of singers and the more frequently successful female singers in the early sixties–Mary Wells, Dionne Warwick, and others.

Much more direct contributions to the vocal style of rock 'n' roll were made by singers who cried rather than shouted the blues. Roy Brown pioneered the style, and many followed. Among blues singers, Larry Darnell, B. B. King, Junior Parker, and Johnny "Guitar" Watson adopted styles originally inspired by Brown; James Brown, a gospel-styled singer, Bobby Bland, first a blues singer and later a gospel blues singer, and Little Richard, first a gospel blues singer and then a rock 'n' roll singer, were also influenced by him. Later singers were influenced in turn by these followers of Brown, so that eventually his influence was diffused throughout popular music, taking in the extravagant "Heartbreak Hotel" of Elvis Presley, the heartrending cries of Jackie Wilson, even the twisted shrieks of Chubby Checker.

The most impressive quality of Brown's style was his intense involvement in his singing. Whereas the blues shouters were always evidently in control of the sounds they made, Brown's voice was shaped by the passions of despair or exhilaration. Rocking frantically to a boogie beat, or wracked by desolate doubt, he committed all he was to the song's message.

Based at the start of his career in East Texas and New Orleans, Brown began recording for De Luxe of New Jersey in 1948, with his own composition "Good Rockin' Tonight": "I heard the news, there's good rockin' tonight." This was one of the songs that fired the imaginations of young people bored with white popular music, and several rock 'n' roll singers, including Elvis Presley, Buddy Holly, and Frankie Lymon, testified to its influence by recording their versions.

Brown continued to record contagious dance records, including "Boogie at Midnight" and "Love Don't Love Nobody", and also impassioned slow blues, including "Hard Luck Blues" and "Big Town". "Big Town", recorded with Tiny Bradshaw's band, was a classic expression of a bid for independence foiled by personal insecurity. The singer woke up one morning and decided to leave for the big town:

I packed my old suitcase,
Told my family goodbye,
And my poor little wife,
She broke down. She began to cry,
She said, "Big fine daddy,
Please don't start runnin' wild . . .
And leave me all alone,
Remember, I'm the mother of your child."

But he went, and he spent money on a girl he met in town. When the money ran out so did the girl, leaving the singer to entreat:

I beg for a nickel,
Put in my telephone,
Got to call my baby,
Beg her, please let me come back home.

The impact of the style came from the conviction of Brown's singing, and when Bobby Bland and Little Richard started making records in the early fifties, they sounded like youthful Roy Browns. Bland allowed his voice to rise into tremulous cries in his version of Charles Brown's "Drifting", which Bland recorded for Modern in 1952, as "Drifting from Town to Town". Little Richard recorded several band blues songs for RCA in 1951 (at the age of fifteen) and a couple of records for Peacock in 1953, all in a cry blues style similar to Brown's. Both Bland and Richard gradually became more gospel-influenced in their styles, using deliberately what Brown may have been unaware of. When Richard began recording for Specialty in 1955, his style was gospel blues.

By this time, Roy Brown's records for De Luxe had ceased to sell well, and he shifted to Imperial. Emphasizing the vocal qualities he shared with Little Richard–the "master" apeing the "pupil"–Roy Brown made a good rock 'n' roll record, which didn't sell, "Everybody"/"Saturday Night", and a very poor cover of two rock 'n' roll hits, which didn't sell either, "Party Doll"/"I'm Stickin' With You". Then, remarkably quickly, Brown vanished from the music industry, leaving only the important echoes of his style in the voices of several younger singers.

Apart from those who made a commercially successful rock 'n' roll style out of his high-pitched, intense delivery, there was one performer, B. B. King, who kept some of Brown's feeling alive in a blues style. King, once a Mississippi plantation worker, developed a sophisticated blues style while working as a disc jockey and singer in Memphis during the late forties. His guitar playing owed something to T-Bone Walker, and something to the intense Mississippi style of acoustic guitar playing, and something, too, to the bottleneck techniques of Kokomo Arnold and Robert Johnson. But the diverse influences merged into a style instantly recognizable as King's–economical, glittering, sharp, and very moving. His singing was enlivened by occasional falsetto sighs, reminiscent of Roy Brown but also of gospel singers. He later credited both sources as having been influential.

King was one of the few rhythm and blues singers of his time who made no obvious attempt to reach the white rock 'n' roll audience. His records were often commercial in their arrangements, but the aim was to reach the black people who preferred ballads to hard blues. At their best his records were unrivalled cry blues: "Three O'Clock Blues" and "When My Heart Beats Like a Hammer".

Although the shout and cry singing styles were hard for rock 'n' roll singers–particularly white singers–to imitate, the equivalent instrumental sound, "screaming" saxophone, proved much easier, and the sound endured through various changes in the fashions of musical arrangements and rhythm–rock 'n' roll, twist, soul. During the first period of rock 'n' roll, 1954 to 1956, its most distinctive "trademark" was a break two thirds of the way through the record, in which a saxophone player produced a sound that was liable to tear paper off the walls, a fast screech that emphasized almost every beat for several bars. Rudi Pompilli, the saxophonist of Bill Haley's Comets, was much more exciting in his solos than Haley ever managed to be in his singing, and King Curtis invariably enlivened the records of the Coasters with inspirational jabs during the verses and with stuttering breaks between them.

By far the most successful rock 'n' roll instrumental record was Bill Doggett's "Honky Tonk", in which Clifford Scott took the saxophone solos. The easy medium tempo rhythm was approximately midway between the typical rhythm and blues hits of the previous few years, which had varied from the rich, lyrical tones of Gene Ammons's "My Foolish Heart" (Chess, 1949), Sonny Thompson's "Long Gone" (Miracle, 1948, featuring David Brooks on tenor sax), and Lynn Hope's "Tenderly" (Premium, 1952), to the firmer attack and aggressive rhythm of Paul Williams's "Hucklebuck" (Savoy, 1949), Willis Jackson's "Gator Tail" (King, 1949), and Jimmy Forrest's "Night Train" (United, 1951). Most of these men, along with Sam "The Man" Taylor, Sil Austin, Red Prysock, Maxwell Davis, and King Curtis were responsible for establishing an authentic rock 'n' roll "sound" to accompany both the genuine rock 'n' roll singers (Otis Williams and the Charms, Gene and Eunice, the Coasters) and those who needed to sound as if they were (Bobby Darin, Bobby Rydell, the Diamonds).

In general, the shout and cry singers and the screamer saxophonists supplied rock 'n' roll with inspiration more than with performers who became stars themselves. The shouters' spirit, the criers' style, and the screamers' instrumental support were all made use of, but the blues-styled performers who themselves became stars were invariably jump combo singers and musicians.

iii. Of the various blues-based styles, jump blues, through its boogie rhythm–variously modified as a jump or shuffle rhythm–had the most direct impact on the first singers to become popular with rock 'n' roll: Bill Haley, Chuck Berry, and Fats Domino (who himself had been leader of a jump band).

Typical jump combos featured a strong rhythm section of piano, guitar, bass, and drums, and usually had a singer and a saxophonist up front, with sometimes a second sax man added. Between them, the various instrumentalists emphasized the rhythm that a boogie pianist had achieved alone with his left hand, and in the process of transcribing the effect to several instruments the difference between each beat was either emphasized more–in jump rhythms–or blurred–in shuffle rhythms. Several different regional variations of the style developed, in New York, on the West Coast, in the mid-South (St Louis/Memphis), in New Orleans, in Chicago, and on the Eastern Seaboard.

The pattern for jump combos was set by Louis Jordan's Tympany Five, who in 1942 had one of the first big hits by a black band in the popular market, "Choo Choo Ch'Boogie" (Decca). Singing and playing alto sax, Jordan presented an entertaining stage act, mixing witty lyrics with crisp rhythms to produce a style that appealed equally to black and white audiences. Nobody satisfied both audiences' tastes so effectively until the rock 'n' roll singers Fats Domino, Chuck Berry, and Little Richard.

Most of Jordan's songs concerned the standard topics of the blues–love, drinking, family life, partying–but he sang them without the typical involvement of blues singing. He tended to be detached–amused, perhaps bemused, in any case rarely affected strongly by the events about which he sang. This cool, in some ways corresponding to the attitude of crooners, enabled him to appeal to white audiences. Also, he sang very clearly, in contrast to many blues singers whose regional accents and slurred delivery often made them hard for white people to understand.

Jordan's appeal to black audiences may have derived from the unstated implications of many of his songs, which often seemed to be innocent, joking complaints about women of fate, but which at the same time implied an unjust society. "Saturday Night Fish Fry", a big hit for Jordan in 1951, recalled a night spent by the singer and a friend in New Orleans, where they were invited to a party "where some of the chicks wore expensive frocks,/and some had on bobby socks". Everybody seemed to be having a good time, until the police made a raid. "I didn't know we were breaking the law,/But someone reached up and hit me on the jaw". Arrested and booked on suspicion, the singer was released when "my chick came down and went my bail,/and finally got me out of that rotten jail".*

For more than ten years, Louis Jordan was a major figure in popular culture, inspiring many younger singers with his success. But few singers could assume such a regionless, cosmopolitan style as Jordan's, and most sang both with rougher voices that more firmly identified them with a particular area, and with less sophisticated instrumental accompaniment. Among the first to work out different styles of jump music were three West Coast singers, T-Bone Walker, Roy Milton, and Amos Milburn,

Walker was one of the most sophisticated blues performers, with a vocal style that tended sometimes to be blander that was usual, and a guitar technique that showed an interest in jazz phrasing as much as a need for emotional expression. Walker pioneered the use of electric guitar in jump combos and also developed a dazzling stage act that was reputed to have inspired Bo Diddley and Elvis Presley in its use of the guitar as a stage prop–sometimes for acrobatics, as the singer did the splits and held the instrument behind his head while he continued to play, and sometimes for sexual provocation, as he ground the

** Copyright © 1949 Cherio Corporation. Reprinted by permission.*

guitar against his body or pointed it suggestively out at the audience. (Many other West Coast jump combos blended guitar and vocals in a style similar to Walker's, notably Lowell Fulson and Johnny "Guitar" Watson. Fulson's main contribution was a classic performance of relaxed singing and economical guitar playing in "Reconsider Baby", a song that Presley later recorded.)

A rougher kind of jump blues was pioneered by Roy Milton and Amos Milburn, who were among the first performers to break away almost entirely from the relatively sophisticated arrangements of jazz, and even such jazz-influenced combo leaders as Walker and Louis Jordan. In the music of Milton and Milburn, emphasis was invariably placed first on the rhythm, and instrumental technique or vocal quality was of secondary importance. Roy Milton, who played drums and sang, has one of the strongest claims to be called "the inventor of the rock 'n' roll beat", as his "R.M. Blues", issued in 1945, was among the first records to reorganize the boogie rhythm and present it with an accented offbeat. The novelty and popularity of the sound is confirmed by the record's sales figures: issued on several labels owned by Milton and Art Rupe, and eventually on Rupe's Specialty label, the record accumulated sales of over a million copies, the first to do so in the Negro market.

Milton's style of combo was widely imitated and developed, on Specialty by Jimmy Liggins and Joe Liggins–both of whom had more expressive voices than Milton–and on the rival Aladdin label by Amos Milburn. Milburn's most famous records were a series of songs that concerned the motives, joys, and aftermath of drinking (several of them written by one of the best rhythm and blues songwriters, Rudolph Toombs)–"Bad, Bad Whiskey" (1950), "Thinkin' and Drinkin'" (1952), and others. But although the themes of these songs deprived Milburn of a rock 'n' roll audience, he recorded at least two fast dance records, "Chicken Shack Boogie" (1948) and "Let's Have a Party" (1953), that achieved more excitement than any of the derivative rock 'n' roll hits by Haley, Boyd Bennett, or Larry Williams.

Ironically, the sole rock 'n' roll hit in this West Coast jump combo style was not by Milton, Milburn, or the Liggins brothers, but by a less original singer, Jimmy McCracklin, whose "The Walk" (Chess) was a rather surprising hit in 1958. According to McCracklin, he made the record to prove just how easy it was to meet the simple taste of the rock 'n' roll audience. The success of the exceptionally simple and repetitive record made his point.

There were countless small jump combos playing throughout the country during the forties, but if they were not easily accessible to the studios in Los Angeles, Oakland, or New York, they mostly went unrecorded until the early fifties. In 1950, Joe Bihari of Modern made contact with some of the most popular bands in the Mississippi Delta region, and the following year Henry and Lillian McMurry started Trumpet Records in Jackson, Mississippi. Between them, the two companies recorded some of the best music of the era, ranging from lively, jumping boogies to moody and menacing blues. For many of the performers, music was still a part-time activity, bringing in welcome extra pocket money on top of their regular earnings as farmers or labourers. But one by one they managed to put together enough separate sources of income from music for them to be able to make a living from it, playing residencies in clubs and bars in the small towns along both banks of the Mississippi, and getting their own shows on one of the local radio stations, where they played a couple of live numbers themselves, brought a guest or two in, played a few records, and read out the commercials from their sponsors.

Sonny Boy Williamson was the most famous of these bluesmen, with his own "King Biscuit Show" which he had been hosting on KFFA in West Helena, Arkansas since 1941. Despite his adamant insistence that he thought of the name first, most evidence suggests that Rice Miller should really have called himself Sonny Boy Williamson Number Two, granting priority to the Chicago-based harmonica player who had recorded for RCA's Bluebird label from the thirties until he was killed in 1948. Miller was also a harmonica player, and despite being close to fifty years old by the time he made his first record, he became one of the most influential musicians of the modern era, inspiring many other bluesmen to make use of what was widely regarded as a "toy" instrument; few of them ever managed such an effective combination of rhythmic intensity and atmospheric moods. Sonny Boy's recording debut was the customary rhythm and blues combination of a "jump" side and a "ballad"; "Crazy 'Bout You Baby" had a rollicking boogie piano behind Sonny Boy's urgently energetic vocal and his trademark "wah wah" harmonica riff, while "Eyesight to the Blind" had a funny lyric extolling a girl's attractions–"her daddy must have been a millionaire, 'cause I can tell by the way she walks." He recorded another ten singles for Trumpet in the next three years, most of them sounding as if only one microphone had been used to capture the sound of the whole combo, but all conveying the leader's formidable presence, alternately commanding attention with menace or beguiling it with insidious charm.

A similar combination of moods was represented in the records of another of the Delta's blues stars, Howlin' Wolf, but there was a frightening menace to his records even when he was trying to be friendly. Forty years old by the time he made his first records at Sam Phillips' studio in Memphis, Wolf had an unusual band featuring two harmonica players (himself along with either Junior Parker or James Cotton) but no bass guitar; instead, he used pianist Bill Johnson (known as "Destruction") and an electric guitar (Willie Johnson, Pat Hare or Hubert Sumlin) to play the boogie rhythm, with Willie Steele on drums. This was a powerful band which could swing, rock, and jump at fast tempos, or lay back on a heavy beat on slow numbers. Again, the first record mapped out the essential ingredients: "How Many More Years" bounced along on a relaxed groove, while on the other side "Moaning at Midnight" introduced a heavy reverberating guitar riff from Willie Johnson which was to echo through the next twenty years of popular music. Compared to the delicate, jazz-influenced sound of most guitarists at the time (from T-Bone Walker to Merle Travis), here Willie Johnson sounded as if he was twanging baling wire with a six-inch nail. Undeniably effective as part of the rhythm arrangement, the device was surprisingly melodic too, acting as a kind of counterpoint to Wolf's mournful vocal, which sounded as if he might swallow the microphone and jump out of the juke box speaker at any moment. He had what would now be called "presence", and he became the object of a tussle between Modern Records, who thought they had contracted to release his records, and Chess, who put this one out.

On one of his early visits to the region, Joe Bihari of Modern had run across Ike Turner, already at only twenty the leader of his own band the Kings of Rhythm, and evidently an unusually alert organiser and businessman. Bihari deputed Turner to supervise his recording sessions, contributing arrangements and playing piano himself where appropriate, but somehow some of the tapes were sent up to Chess in Chicago, possibly by engineer Sam Phillips. Wolf subsequently recorded several singles for Modern's RPM subsidiary before Chess made an exclusive contract with him; Wolf moved to Chicago, and in effect bequeathed his band to Junior Parker, who made some intensely exciting boogie blues records for Phillips' new Sun label under the name of Little Junior's Blue Flames. "Love My Baby" in particular featured some blistering guitar playing by Pat Hare, which inspired the rockabilly style discussed elsewhere.

Among the other singers who recorded under Ike Turner's supervision, Jackie Brenston and Rosco Gordon made two of the most influential records in what could be called a Memphis Jump Blues style, although nobody used such a description at the time. Brenston was actually the baritone sax player in Turner's Kings of Rhythm, but he took the vocal on "Rocket 88", a mellow, cruising boogie which featured a tearaway solo from tenor sax player Raymond Hill; top of the rhythm and blues charts for Chess in 1951, the record was one of the first rhythm and blues hits to inspire a cover version, and although

Bill Haley and the Saddlemen's record for Essex did not appear in any national charts, it was a significant signpost for what was to follow.

Rosco Gordon was younger than the country bluesmen like Sonny Boy and Howlin' Wolf, a pianist and singer who lived in Memphis and hung around the clubs and bars, fitting into bands with Johnny Ace, Bobby Bland, B. B. King and the other young hopefuls. In 1952 he recorded "Booted" with Ike Turner, which topped the rhythm and blues chart for Chess, and followed through with an equally successful record later the same year for RPM, "No More Doggin'". Compared to the even beats of boogie, and the more emphatic back-beat of combo records being made in New Orleans at this time, "No More Doggin'" had an unusual emphasis on the first and third beats which never became widespread in American music, but which was picked up more strongly in Jamaica, where Rosco Gordon was particularly popular. During the sixties, that back-to-front beat became a distinctive feature of Jamaican ska, rock steady and reggae music, and it mostly stemmed from this early hit of Rosco Gordon's.

A different version of the jump blues had been developed farther south, in New Orleans and southern Louisiana, and was the source of the phenomenal success of Fats Domino, in the rhythm and blues market first and later as a rock 'n' roll singer. Compared to the other jump singers, the New Orleans performers put more emphasis on vocal expression, sounding either exceptionally exuberant or morosely sad. The rhythm varied accordingly, a lively, bouncing boogie beat on the happy songs, and a more intense, swirling shuffle on the depressed ones. Although Domino was easily the most famous exponent of the style, there were several other exceptional performers in both rhythm and blues and rock 'n' roll styles.

One of them, Roy Byrd, was a powerful influence locally, although his national success in rhythm and blues was confined to one record, "Bald Head" (Mercury, 1950). A long time before it was conventional to assume bizarre names, Byrd recorded as "Professor Longhair and His Shuffling Hungarians", and though he never tried very hard to reach the rock 'n' roll audience, his penchant for witty novelty songs and his "mardi gras" rhythm served as the basis for the successful rock 'n' roll style of Huey Smith and the Clowns.

Apart from Byrd, all of the most successful New Orleans singers made their records for West Coast companies, and were provided with similar styles of accompaniment, invariably supplied by bands led by either Dave Bartholomew or Paul Gayten. The result may have been to make singers sound more similar to one another on record than they might have done in live performance.

Fats Domino, as already noted, was the only rhythm and blues singer to have an extensive series of hits in the rhythm and blues market and then continue having hits as a rock 'n' roll singer. Most rhythm and blues singers were never widely known to the rock 'n' roll audience, and of those that were, most had to make considerable changes in their styles (as Chuck Willis did at Atlantic, Lloyd Price at ABC-Paramount, and Ray Charles first with Atlantic and then with ABC-Paramount), and none had hits as consistently as did Domino.

In his first records, he sang in a high, nasal voice, full of good humour in his fast songs, which he expressed with whoops and scat singing as his records charged along to the beat of his full-chorded piano playing. His first record, "The Fat Man", made in 1949, when he was seventeen, was one of the biggest rhythm and blues hits of the period, and it showed him to be an accomplished pianist as well as a remarkably confident singer. Over the next few years the style was gradually modified, as his voice dropped to a deeper tone, the back-beat of the drummer became more pronounced, and Domino's piano playing lost some of its adventurousness.

Domino's complete transformation into a rock 'n' roll singer was possible because he sang with a plaintive tone which did not seem so adult and alien as did the tone of most of his contemporary rhythm and blues singers. He seemed to be singing about experiences equivalent to those his white listeners knew about, and he was able to take established pop songs like "My Blue Heaven" and "Blueberry Hill" and not sound incongruous while singing them, as say, Amos Milburn or Roy Brown would have done.

Compared to the typical songs of the blues shouters, those of the New Orleans jump band singers in general were less adult and explicit in their implications about relationships with women. In most of his songs, Fats Domino could have been a boy singing about a girl, and it was easy for the youthful white audience of rock 'n' roll fans to identify with him.

For the white audience, Domino maintained his strong Louisiana accent, which took on the charm of a novelty style, but he rarely sang with the high-pitched whoops he used in "The Fat Man". The rough qualities of his sound were eliminated or minimized, leaving a relaxed but infectiously rhythmic beat and a singer who easily communicated his happiness.

Understandably, most New Orleans singers were more impressed by Fats Domino's success than by Professor Longhair's idiosyncracies, and several followed his style quite closely, including Smiley Lewis, Lloyd Price, and Guitar Slim.

Lewis came closest to rock 'n' roll success in 1955, with a performance that was almost identical to Domino's style, "I Hear You Knockin'", but he lost out to Gale Storm's cover for Dot. Usually,

Lewis did not sound quite so much like Domino, singing in a more intense style sometimes reminiscent of Joe Turner's, as in the lively "Bumpity Bump".

Lloyd Price eventually achieved rock 'n' roll success in 1959, with "Personality" and several other big-sounding productions, using arrangements that owed much of their inspiration to those conceived by Dave Bartholomew for Domino and Lewis. But Price had already been a successful rhythm and blues singer, again with a style close to Domino's. His biggest hit was his first record, "Lawdy Miss Clawdy" (1952), which featured a pianist who was either Fats Domino or else sounded exactly like him. Price's voice on the record had a plaintiveness that was slightly more intense than Domino's, and it suggested very gently the kind of influence that gospel styles would come to have in blues singing. Two years later, in 1954, Specialty recorded another New Orleans singer with a slightly more emphatic gospel style, Guitar Slim. The arrangement for Guitar Slim's first record, "The Things That I Used to Do", was conceived and played by the pianist Ray Charles, and somehow emphasized the religious tone in the singer's voice, regretful, but philosophical. Both "Lawdy, Miss Clawdy" and "The Things That I Used to Do" were huge hits in the rhythm and blues market and both had incalculable effects both on rock 'n' roll and on the steadily growing tendency for singers to adopt gospel-influenced styles.

Apart from the "Longhair-shuffle" and "Domino-jump" kinds of New Orleans combo blues, there was a third group of singers whose styles were independent of both of them–the duo Shirley and Lee, and the vocal group the Spiders. The duo had its greatest success as rock 'n' roll singers, using novelty effects and arrangements that drew from the West Coast combo styles of Roy Milton and Jimmy Liggins, but the Spiders were a rhythm and blues group whose lead singer Chuck Carbo used a blues voice rather than the cool style developed by most leads in the North. Although the group often sang fast songs, the accompaniment was not emphatically rhythmic, further isolating their sound from most of their contemporaries (The Clovers, discussed later, were perhaps the most similar.)

Most of the singers who perpetuated the boogie beat in some kind of jump or shuffle rhythm maintained piano in their line ups, even if they spread the responsibility for keeping the rhythm between several instruments. But a few men transferred the rhythm to guitar or guitars: they included T-Bone Walker, already discussed, John Lee Hooker, to be discussed in the section on bar blues singers, and Jimmy Reed.

Although Reed himself never had rock 'n' roll hits, his easy rhythm was one of the few identifiable influences on the generally innovative style of Chuck Berry, and, as already noted, his songs were widely used in the repertoire of other rock 'n' roll singers.

Reed's vocal style had the same slurred, indistinct quality that many of the Mississippi bar blues singers had, but it was much more relaxed and rhythmic than theirs, very rarely imperative or self-confident in its tone but more often gentle, appealing, inquiring. Reed played harmonica and guitar fixed together so that he could play them at the same time, and he was backed by drums and a bass guitarist, Eddie Taylor, who played the equivalent of a pianist's left hand. The jaunty rhythm created by the bass line, and several melodic songs, produced a series of records which amounted to "sing-along blues". Compared to most other blues singers, Reed improvised relatively little, but established a pattern which he repeated each time he played a song. Despite a narrow range of melodic and rhythmic ideas, Reed sustained a long career, and inspired a "school" of imitators, particularly in the South, where Slim Harpo, Lightnin' Slim, and others recorded in a similar style. Reed's songs comprised brief, laconic phrases–as in "Honest I Do" (1955)–which rode easily on the bouncy rhythm:

I told you I love you,
Stop drivin' me mad:
When I woke up this morning,
I never felt so bad.

A relatively minor influence on rock 'n' roll, Reed was one of the most important influences on the rhythm and blues "revival" in the mid-sixties.

Of all the jump combo styles, the most sophisticated was developed on the Eastern Seaboard, chiefly by Chuck Willis and Wilbert Harrison, who both tended to use more sentimental lyrics, lighter accompaniment, less emphatic beats. Willis, from Georgia, started recording for Columbia/OKeh in 1951, and had a series of hits in the rhythm and blues market until 1955, when he shifted to Atlantic and a rather different style. A songwriter with a flair for simple but evocative images comparable to the Arkansas country singer Charlie Rich, Willis's hits for OKeh included the slow ballad "My Story" and the faster "I Feel So Bad", which began typically:

I feel so bad,
Just like a ball-game on a rainy day.

The rhythm dipped and flowed with a Latin feeling, suggesting the effect a bongo player might have achieved if he had tried for a boogie rhythm. Willis's high, wailing voice was sadder and softer than any other combo singer's, but curiously became more conventional when he moved to Atlantic.

Wilbert Harrison recorded, rather unsuccessfully, for Savoy from 1952 to 1956, in a style comparable to Willis's but lacking comparably distinctive material. He had a big hit in 1959, with a relatively even-shuffle rhythm, "Kansas City", and a minor hit–ironically more like his Savoy material–in 1970, with "Let's Work Together".

Between these various performers, the different styles of combo blues suggested an almost infinite range of ways in which a boogie beat could be accommodated by a small band and reshaped to suit individual needs. But when it became necessary to present a national style of music–rock 'n' roll–many of the local interpretations were lost as musicians and their producers merged several styles into one, so that it was difficult to hear the difference in sound between the accompaniment for Larry Williams (in Hollywood) and that for Bobby Darin (in New York).

However, although it seemed that rock 'n' roll had effectively "destroyed" a valuable complex of styles, it could equally be argued that the possibilities for the style had been exhausted–that the music would have changed anyway, even if rock 'n' roll had not drawn off some of the better singers and arrangers, and made others seem old-fashioned and obsolete. As evidence that the styles that were developed during the mid-forties had run their natural course by the mid-fifties was the decline of the club blues style, which was at one time as important as the combo blues and yet declined despite having relatively little contact with the forces of rock 'n' roll.

II

While the jump blues served to express whatever confidence people felt on the West Coast during and after the war, the quieter club blues expressed the more dominant mood there, one tinged with despondency, equivalent to the mood of "helpless frustration" that the critic Robert Bone found in a novel set in wartime Los Angeles, *If He Hollers, Let Him Go* by the black author Chester Himes. Living conditions and earnings in the West Coast cities–mainly Los Angeles and Oakland–were much better than they had been in Texas, but were still much worse for blacks than for the whites working alongside them.

During the war, the migration of blacks into California outpaced the provision of special facilities for them, so that for some years they shared the nightclubs with whites. The unusual integrated audience may have encouraged the black singers to minimize the blues content of their repertoire. In any case, "cocktail" piano playing was common–pretty right-hand tinkling with a light rhythm from bass and brushed drums. The club customers didn't like their conversations to be drowned by the music, so singers and musicians had to develop a style that instilled a mood without requiring that all the words be heard.

One of the originators of the club singing style was Nat "King" Cole, who was never a blues singer but a jazz singer/pianist who gave interpretations–with no particular characteristic mood–of popular songs.

Cole was already well known as a jazz pianist when his vocal abilities were discovered in 1943. He had made records as a pianist for Excelsior and other independent labels which were distributed as jazz to both black and white markets. Cole's popularity as a singer encouraged Capitol to contract him to sing, and his relaxed style was easily accepted by the white audience familiar with the crooning styles of Crosby and Como. That Cole was a Negro was irrelevant to his style and maybe even to his appeal, although possibly he attracted some attention through "exotic" associations.

Because his style had so little to do with Negro musical traditions, Nat "King" Cole was less popular in the Negro market than he was in the white market. Throughout the forties and fifties he was one of the few black singers to be readily acceptable to record company executives, radio programmers, and middle-class record buyers. His success generated a new kind of black singer who was not in any sense a blues, or rhythm and blues singer but a straight popular music ballad singer.

When Cole moved out from the Los Angeles nightclub circuit in 1945, as his popularity grew in the rest of the country, his place as the top West Coast attraction was taken by Johnny Moore's Three Blazers, featuring Charles Brown on piano and vocals. In Brown's style there was none of the self-confidence of the jump combos, the shout singers, or (yet to be discussed) the bar blues singers. Instead, there was extreme sadness, intimately expressed to the gentle accompaniment from guitar, piano, and (sometimes) saxophone. Brown exemplified the fact that to a greater extent than ever before blues singers had become narcissistically preoccupied with the depths of their misery, seemingly unable to find cause for hope or gladness.

Brown's major hit in 1945, "Drifting Blues" (Aladdin), was typical of the club blues songs:

Well, I'm driftin' and driftin'
Like a ship out on the sea. [twice]
Well I ain't got nobody
In this world to care for me.

If my baby
Would only take me back again. [twice]
Well you know I ain't good for nothin' baby,
Well I haven't got no friends.

I'll give you all my money
Tell me what more can I do? [twice]
Well you just ain't no good little girl,
But you just won't be true.

Bye bye baby,
Baby bye bye.
It's gonna be too late,
I'll be so far away.

This was the first of several hits for Brown, who recorded with the Three Blazers and under his own name for Aladdin, Modern, and Exclusive. His style pervaded the West Coast club blues, notably in Floyd Dixon's similar soft dragged-out way of pronouncing words. Cecil Gant, Ivory Joe Hunter, Percy Mayfield, Johnny Ace, Jesse Belvin, and Ray Charles were all influenced to some extent by Brown, although each moved on to something different from the club blues. Gant in particular deserves comment.

Gant was a pioneer in many ways, being among the first post-war singers to mix various blues styles into his repertoire, creating one of the first "cosmopolitan" blues acts. Born in Tennessee, Gant did not begin recording until he was almost thirty-years old, at the end of World War Two. A sleeve note on one of his albums reported how his career began:

> Cecil Gant's magnetic personality and tremendous appeal to any listening audience was first demonstrated at a bond rally conducted from a street platform at the corner of 9th and Broadway in Los Angeles. During an intermission in the entertainment, Private Cecil Gant requested permission from the Treasury representative, acting as master of ceremonies, to come up on the platform and play the piano. The results were electrifying and formal request by the local campaign committee was filed with Private Gant's Commanding Officer to permit him to appear at the local bond-selling campaigns.[6]

At the end of the war, Gant was contracted to the Oakland company Gilt Edge, who billed him as "The G.I. Sing-Sation". His records included light club blues material, popular ballads, and faster jump songs, in an apparent attempt to appeal to the enthusiasts of Charles Brown, Nat Cole, and Louis Jordan.

"I Wonder", released in 1945, was one of the first rhythm and blues/race records to have massive sales, not only reaching across the national Negro market but also selling well in some white districts. (According to George Leanor, who now runs One Derful Records in Chicago but who then owned a record store, it was the success of "I Wonder" that led to the subsequent creation of many of the West Coast record companies.) The song had little connection with previous forms of blues:

I wonder,
My little darlin'
Where can you be
Again tonight
While the moon
Is shinin' bright,
I wonder.

Tinkling piano linked the phrases, and double bass gave a gentle rhythm.

After three good years on the West Coast, Gant returned to Tennessee, where he performed locally and did new versions of his old songs for Bullet in Nashville. In 1950, he signed for Decca, and in New York he recorded several fast boogie piano songs, "We're Gonna Rock", "Shotgun Boogie", and others, which had several qualities of what became known as rock 'n' roll–strong beat, simple words, and an infectiously happy mood.

Ivory Joe Hunter, also influenced by Charles Brown, had a smoother, more melodic voice than Gant, and a knack for writing memorable songs which attracted the white audience and yet stayed near enough to the blues for the Negro audience to care about him. Born in Texas, Hunter made his first records for Exclusive with Johnny Moore's Three Blazers (with whom Brown also recorded), then recorded from 1947 to 50 for King, often with Duke Ellington's sidemen, and in 1950 moved to MGM for whom he cut the million-selling "I Almost Lost My Mind". In 1954 he moved again, to Atlantic, and gave the company its first major pop hit, "Since I Met You, Baby". Compared to Nat Cole, Ivory Joe Hunter did not indulge vocal mannerisms so much, and he had a blues singer's concern for expressing his feelings. But compared to conventional blues, the feelings of Hunter's songs were sentimental, and required a rather self-pitying tone from the singer.

While both Gant and Hunter were sometimes oriented towards the white market, Percy Mayfield almost never was, and he sang blues songs, mostly written by himself, in a soft ballad style. His "Please Send Me Someone To Love" (1950) was one of the most influential songs of the time, widely recorded by other people. In a gentle, modest appeal to heaven, Mayfield expressed his understanding of the wide significance of world conflicts but could not avoid pointing out his own immediate need–for someone to love. With a rare sense of balance that entirely avoided self-conscious irony, Mayfield brilliantly evoked the common dilemma of understanding the significance of others' problems yet being unavoidably bound up in objectively lesser but privately more important personal issues. Happening to coincide with the Korean War, the record sold well over a much longer period than was the normal "lifetime" for a hit–but sold primarily in the rhythm and blues market.

Johnny Ace, Jesse Belvin, and Ray Charles (with Swingtime, 1949 to 1953) all dealt with simpler, more openly sentimental themes than this, and were among the last of the singers who directed a ballad style at the black audience. Their successors invariably adopted a strong gospel influence–as did Ray Charles himself after he moved to Atlantic in 1953.

III

Among the last of the regional rhythm and blues styles to be discovered and widely recorded was the bar blues styles of Mississippi towns, Memphis, and Chicago. Although nobody sang rock 'n' roll in precisely this style, there were echoes of its brash spirit both in Memphis country rock and in the styles of Chuck Berry and Bo Diddley.

Billboard, typically quick to recognize and analyse any new trend, commented in its issue of March 15, 1952:

> Among the important developments that have been taking place in the rhythm and blues field over the past year, one of the most prominent is the increasing importance of the country or southern style blues and country style singer in this market. Another noticeable aspect is the tremendous influence of r & b styles in the pop market.
>
> At one time there was a wide gulf between the sophisticated big city blues and rocking novelties waxed for the northern market, and the country or delta blues that were popular in the southern regions. Gradually, the two forms intermingled and the country blues tune, now dressed up in arrangements palatable to both

northern and southern tastes, have been appearing on disks of all r & b labels. It is true that the largest market for the country blues tune is still in the south and west, especially in places like Dallas, Memphis, Atlanta, New Orleans and Los Angeles, but even the northern cities have felt their influence (i.e. Detroit).

This is not to say that the majority of tunes being waxed for rhythm and blues markets are country, since the sophisticated item is still more important, but that many diskings have the country tinge. Along with this country kick, some exclusively country artists have achieved popularity of late, including Howlin' Wolf, B. B. King, Muddy Waters and other [exponents of the bar blues style]. Modern Records has noted the importance of this southern country market by forming a label called Rhythm and Blues [Modern's label was called Blues and Rhythm] which is recording artists from the Delta area almost exclusively. . . .

The influence of the r & b disks on the pop market both as tunes and artists, has been of great import over the past year. Johnnie Ray, at present a "hot" personality in the pop field, with a singing style close to r & b vocalists, sells just as well in both fields. The same can be said of Kay Starr. In addition to this many r & b ditties have become very important as pops.

Apart from noting a new trend, *Billboard's* comment is particularly interesting for illustrating that the practice of covering rhythm and blues records was common some time before the expression "rock 'n' roll" was coined to describe the cover records, and for identifying a recurrent tendency in the styles of black music–that as some sophisticated styles became popular with the pop music audience, other more basic styles were adopted by the black audience.

In many ways, the bar blues contradicted the qualities of other then recently popular styles. Where Charles Brown and the other club blues singers had been reticent, insecure, and dependent, the bar blues singers were boastful, confident, and self-reliant. Where the combo singers had sung to a quick, light rhythm, the bar blues singers sang to a heavy, often irregular rhythm. Where both club and combo singers had tended to have smooth, round tones, the bar blues voices were rough and apparently careless of melody.

The bar blues was the only major post-war rhythm and blues style whose origins were clearly set in pre-war styles. Several singers who recorded for RCA's Bluebird label–among them John Lee "Sonny Boy" Williamson and Joe Williams–used comparable intense singing styles, dense rhythms, and a similar instrumental line-up, although drums, widely used in bar blues records after 1950, were rare before the war.

Typical versions of the bar blues were developed by a number of performer/singers–harmonica players and guitarists–who moved from Mississippi (or, less often, the Houston area) to Chicago.

With one exception (the relatively lyrical Little Walter), these singers were invariably raucous in their approach to music, immediately establishing their presence through menace, humour, or celebration, and more rarely through despair. The Mississippi singers were strongly influenced by a group of friends who lived and played in the Clarksdale, Mississippi, region before the war–Charlie Patton, Willie Brown, Son House, and Robert Johnson. The rasping, intense vocal styles and the scattered, impatient rhythms, searing guitar sounds, dramatic narratives, and strutting postures had all been heard before. But now the noise was louder, the rhythms more emphatic, though not always more regular, and the accompaniment enhanced by several instruments.

Muddy Waters seems to have been the first of the younger downhome blues singers to get recorded, when he cut some singles for Aristocrat in 1947–48. He had left the South a few years before, and worked as a semi-professional in Chicago until meeting the Chess brothers (who changed their label from Aristocrat to Chess in 1949). Muddy's early records were accompanied, in addition to his own guitar, only by piano and bass. On "Gypsy Woman", "I Can't Be Satisfied", and others, he created a jaunty, aggressive mood through his confident singing and hard, mainly single-string guitar playing.

Muddy Waters rarely "sang", but contented himself with a rough shout, spitting and muttering with a harshness which had few parallels in recorded music. In part, the rawness reflected the spirit of the bars where he formed his style, which were rowdy with the laughter, shouts, and loud conversation of the drinkers, with whose noise the band had to compete. Melody and harmony as conventionally understood were irrelevant here; the Chicago bar blues shot emotion at its audience in heavy loads.

Muddy soon became one of Aristocrat/Chess's best-selling recording artists. Through connections with the Chicago radio and club owners, Chess was able to build him into the city's leading raw blues singer, and as good musicians came North from Mississippi they were either recruited to his band or else had to compete with him. The outstanding musician who joined the Muddy Waters band was the harmonica player Little Walter, whose sharp, melodic tone contrasted brilliantly with the lower pitch of Muddy's voice and guitar. The impact of Little Walter on the band's style can be heard in the comparison between two of Muddy's best records, "Rollin' Stone" (1950) and "Hoochie Coochie Man" (1954). In both songs, Muddy boasted his prowess as a lover, but in the first his tone was relatively casual, with bass and his own guitar setting an intimate mood, whereas in the second the drummer emphasized a much louder beat and the shrill tone of Walter's harmonica, echoing every vocal phrase, made the performance much more dramatic, seeming to encourage the singing to become more aggressive.

For a while, Little Walter was a much more successful recording artist than Muddy himself, adapting to a lighter, more danceable rhythm in his own records for Checker; the all-instrumental "Juke" topped the rhythm and blues cnarts in 1952, and the vocal "My Babe" repeated the trick in 1955. In between, Walter recorded several other successful records, and his fluent improvizations revealed another dimension to the harmonica, which was more often used by bluesmen to repeat rhythmic riffs and provide a dynamic contrast to the other instruments in the band.

But although Little Walter was one of the best-selling recording acts among his contemporary bluesmen, he did not have the organizational ability and charisma to hold together a top-class live group, and the only real contender to Muddy Waters on that front was Howlin' Wolf. Brought north by Chess in 1952, Wolf took several years to come to terms with the different recording conditions at Chess, where bass-player Willie Dixon ruled the roost. Eventually Wolf brought up his former guitarist Hubert Sumlin, and in 1956 they finally recaptured the kind of spirit Wolf had achieved in his Memphis recordings; "Smokestack Lightnin'" revived a guitar riff that Wolf had featured in "Crying at Daybreak", and with the improved recording facilities that sound made much more impact. At the time, it was Wolf's use of harmonica and guitar riffs which influenced his contemporaries in both rhythm and blues and pop fields, but during the sixties various white rock singers began to adopt some of his ferocious vocal mannerisms too, notably the Los Angeles singer Captain Beefheart.

Of the other bluesmen who trekked north as Chicago became the mecca for the bar blues, Sonny Boy Williamson never consistently recaptured the spirit of his best records for Trumpet, but "Don't Start Me Talkin'" was a humorous top ten rhythm and blues hit in 1955, and he settled into some easy-going grooves in the early sixties which owed something to both Booker T. and the M.G.'s and to Jimmy Reed, most effectively on "Help Me" and "Bye Bye Bird".

Elmore James went to Chicago at about the same time as Williamson, but James made his best records while he was still in the South (for Trumpet and Meteor), when his distinctive jangling guitar style was still relatively new to him and to his audience. His style was fairly simple, involving a series of crashing chords, distorted by a bottleneck held across the fret-board, above which the singer declaimed his message. James's vocal range was narrow, but his involvement convincing. His band also had the unusual addition of saxophone, which provided a nominal link with band blues styles. His standard song was "Dust My Blues", a fine hard-driving song with a more regular dance rhythm than most bar singers used, and a slide-guitar sound that was a typical feature of the British blues of the late sixties. (The song was recorded for four or five different labels, but perhaps best for Meteor, 1953.)

Probably the most atypical bar blues singer–but one of the most important–was John Lee Hooker. Hooker's style was midway between the raucous bar blues style and a smoother boogie style (which he had in common with Jimmy Reed), having the former's intensity but the latter's concern with regular rhythm.

For Hooker the blues was a medium of autobiography–as it was for many other singers, but rarely so comprehensively. Yet despite the importance to Hooker of what he was saying, the overall result was often almost unintelligible, since he was always concerned to establish a rhythm even if it meant chopping off words or phrases to get the right cadence, or if it meant drowning the words with a sharper guitar chord. Playing a minimum of chords, Hooker achieved variety through his right hand, constantly shifting pressures and strokes, merging his voice into the melodic line of an upper string. "Moanin' Blues", recorded for King in 1949, exemplified the technique, and only after repeated playing does the message itself come through:

My dear old mother's dead,
My father's turned his back on me.

The words are those of any blues song, and are relegated to a minor role, giving Hooker something to say while he concentrates his and the listener's attention on the mood of despair he is after. From the first play, the desperate sadness is obvious and convincing. The rhythm of the guitar and voice stops and starts, stutters, goes on again, and, through the tensions in mood which it creates, becomes the source of the song's emotional expression.

Nobody at this time was using rhythm this way, and surprisingly few people even tried. Virtually alone in his style, Hooker was the only one who could supply what its audience wanted, and he was under great demand from many record companies. Modern, who released his first record, had a nominal contract with him, which he easily evaded by adopting various pseudonyms:

> I did some as Johnny Williams, I did some as Texas Slim. At that time I was hot as a fire-cracker, and they would give me big money to do some material. Use a different name. Money's pretty exciting y'know, so I was Texas Slim for King, John Lee Booker for Chance and Chess and De Luxe and Johnny Williams for Gotham and Staff.[7]

He was also The Boogie Man for Acorn, Johnny Lee for De Luxe, and Birmingham Sam and His Magic Guitar for Regent.

Hooker's disregard for any semblance of legal niceties reflected the disregard of some company staffs for their musicians. Saul Bihari was interviewed by a *Billboard* reporter and explained.

> We used to bring 'em in, give 'em a bottle of booze and say "Sing me a song about your girl". Or, "Sing me a song about Christmas". They'd pluck around a little on their guitars, then say "O.K." and make up a song as they went along. We'd give them a subject and off they'd go. When it came time to quit, we'd give them a wave that they had ten seconds to finish.[8]

The blues was a product which made money if it was handled right. If singers could be persuaded to create their art for a few dollars and a jug of whiskey, there was more money left for promotion. If the singers didn't know that as composers they were entitled to royalties from sales and public performance of their songs and records, this gave the record company producers an extra source of personal income.

Ironically, as the blues began to loose popularity through the fifties, many of the new singers were as naive about their rights as were the older blues singers they replaced. Young teenagers, just out of school and sometimes still in school, glad enough to sing and live, didn't look too hard at the contracts they signed, and didn't think about the thousands of dollars they might be entitled to if they were handed one hundred in crisp new notes.

7

AFTER THE BLUES: GOSPEL AND THE GROUP SOUNDS

I

The blues had always tended to be a rather disreputable form of music among middle-class and respectable working-class Negroes. It was the music of rough bars, all-night parties, and even brothels. Although there were always some singers who included both blues and religious material in their repertoires, most of them felt a strain in trying to reconcile the two kinds of song and what they implied.

This character of the blues prevented all but the most independent of girls from singing the blues in public, and even restricted the number of men who sang it. But there were still enough men with little enough sense of social status and surface respectability, and perhaps large enough sense of the nature and value of their own experience, that the blues flourished through the South, and when they moved north they took their music with them.

But the people who valued their place in Negro–and American–society wisely chose to sing in church. To the outside world, this seemed to be an admirably conventional thing to do–accepting one of the society's most sturdy institutions, the church of God. And perhaps it seemed too that if everybody believed in God, they would accept the way he had planned the world, which included some uneven distributions of wealth, happiness, and opportunity.

However, the Negro church was not quite so conformist in its role in American society. Because in most areas religious attendance was consistently segregated, often the whole administration of churches was carried out by black people. Economics, politics, welfare, and entertainment came under the control of the ministers and their aides, and attracted some of the most ingenious and ambitious black people to make their profession in the church. Apart from that, in church emotions could be expressed, feelings bared, despair admitted, hope cultivated, and change considered–and white people need never know.

Among those who committed their abilities to religion were the singers, some of whom were amateurs who turned out each Sunday and maybe a couple of evenings in the week to practise. But others were professionals who performed most nights of the week.

There were various kinds of religious singers, including spiritual, gospel, and preaching singers. The spiritual singers emphasized the quality of their voices, impressing their audience with the lyrical beauty of their style; in post-war music, Mahalia Jackson has dominated this kind of singing. Gospel music concentrated more on the interplay between voices, which were often deliberately coarsened to stress the emotional conviction of the singers; Rosetta Tharpe, sometimes in duet with Marie Knight, was among the first successful post-war singers with this style. Preacher singers tended to speak their messages, in an urgent near-shout which often had the phrasing and timing of a singer but had no melody.

During the forties, most of the companies that recorded rhythm and blues music also included some religious records among their releases. There was some criticism of this practice from religious people who objected to God's name being traded across the same counters as the worldly rhythm and blues. Several companies (among them Peacock, Nashboro, Savoy, and Gotham) resolved the problem to some extent by presenting their religious product on different series than their rhythm and blues material, and sometimes on different labels.

In the period 1945–50, a fair amount of religious music was recorded, though, as was the case with rhythm and blues, primarily by companies outside the South. Little was done in the South itself. Columbia and Okeh recorded several spiritual and gospel singers, including the Golden Gate Quartet and Mitchell's Christian Singers; Mercury recorded the Selah Jubilee Singers; and the Decca subsidiary Coral recorded Mahalia Jackson and the Paramount Singers, among many others.

In New York, the independent Apollo became one of the principal gospel labels, with Mahalia Jackson and others (see chapter 2). Another New York company, which successively used the labels Regis, Manor, and Arco, recorded the Dixie Hummingbirds, the Silver Echoes, and the Skylight Singers. Across the river in Newark, New Jersey, Savoy and its Gospel subsidiary recorded James Cleveland, and others. In Philadelphia, Gotham recorded the Dixie Hummingbirds and the Famous Ward Singers of Philadelphia. On the West Coast, the most outstanding roster of gospel singers appeared on Specialty–among them, the Pilgrim Travellers and the Soul Stirrers. (Other West Coast companies, like Modern and Imperial, had relatively infrequent gospel issues.) Not until the early fifties did the South begin to be better represented, as Peacock in Houston and Nashboro in Nashville gathered some of the best singers formerly under contract with the northern companies, and introduced famous but under-recorded groups based in the South. Peacock signed to a regular contract one of the most recorded and most influential groups, the Dixie Hummingbirds, and a second very influential group, the Five Blind Boys of Mississippi. Nashboro recorded the Silvertone Singers, the Skylarks, the Swanee Quintet, Edna Gallmon Cooke, the Consolers, and Professor Harold Boggs.

These spiritual and gospel singers were invariably concerned with emotion in a different way from the focus of the blues. Blues singers tended to be concerned with experience or relationships between people. The abstract nature of the relationship in gospel songs between the singer and God was rare in the blues, but it was close to the unreal ideal conception of love which adolescents often have. Between 1948 and 1952 the potential connection between the emotions of gospel singing and the expectations of adolescent listeners of popular music occurred to various singers, record company executives, and composers. Indirectly and directly, gospel styles and conventions were introduced into rhythm and blues–and constituted the first significant trend away from the blues as such in black popular music.

Retrospectively, it seems that a gospel influence was already present in the styles of one or two band blues singers, for example, in Roy Brown discussed earlier, and in Tommy Brown, an unrelated singer from the Carolinas. In both cases, the singer's voice almost cracked up with the emotional intensity it was trying to express.

But the first deliberate use of gospel-trained singers in "secular" music seems to have been in 1950, when a New York gospel singing instructor, Billy Ward, formed a rhythm and blues group, the Dominoes, with four of his students. A member of the group, Clyde McPhatter, later recalled how worried the group was when aspects of gospel singing were used in popular songs.

> We were very frightened in the studio when we were recording. We had patterned ourselves after the Ink Spots because I had such a high voice, but I just didn't believe in trying to sound like Bill Kenney, and that's how we started the gospel stuff. Billy Ward was teaching us the song, and he'd say, "sing it up", and I said, "well I don't feel it that way", and he said "try it your way". I felt more relaxed if I wasn't confined to the melody. I would take liberties with it, and he'd say, "that's great, do it that way".[1]

The Ink Spots, together with the Mills Brothers, were the major model for imitation among groups of this period–they had made it in the white market, and their success fed the dreams of younger black singers, stuck in ghetto soda fountains with Pepsis, listening to announcements on the radio that the Ink Spots were about to tour Europe. Some of the younger groups based their appeal on a rich bass voice, which the Ink Spots sometimes used.

The Ravens, a New York group, were very successful in the rhythm and blues market in the late forties with a style similar to the Ink Spots, but the change towards gospel influence was emphasized first by the Dominoes, another New York group whose first hit "Sixty Minute Man", featured the group's bass, Bill Brown, boasting about his prowess with a non-gospel-like lyric typical of the time.

If your man ain't treatin' you right,
Come up and see your Dan;
I rock 'em, roll 'em all night long;
I'm a sixty minute man.

The chorus gave some specifics:

There'll be fifteen minutes of kissin',
Then you'll holler, "please don't stop",
There'll be fifteen minutes of teasin'
And fifteen minutes of squeezin'
And fifteen minutes of blowin' my top.

In this song, McPhatter was in the background, sighing "don't stop" at appropriate places in the chorus, but elsewhere whooping in a falsetto cry that other groups also used by this time. A year later, he was featured as lead in "Have Mercy Baby", and in this the gospel influence was much stronger. He sang lead again in "The Bells", at the end of which he seemed to break down in tears, a device often used in gospel performances. Soon after this record he left the Dominoes to form his own group, the Drifters. (His place in the Dominoes was filled by another singer with strong gospel influence, Jackie Wilson.)

The Drifters recorded for Atlantic where McPhatter came under the careful supervision of Ahmet Ertegun. The group's first record was "Money Honey", a song written by a former Kansas City band pianist, Jesse Stone, whose theme was that of many blues songs: lack of finance messes up the singer's life. But the song had a chorus revealing its ambition to satisfy the non-blues popular market, and it was performed by McPhatter with all the intensity expected of a gospel singer. The sadly familiar situation of the song became comic because of the singer's deadpan over-involvement in it.

Well, the landlord rang my front door bell;
I let it ring for a long long spell.
I went to the window and peeked through the blind,

And asked him to tell me what was on his mind.
He said, "money honey; money honey; money honey,
If you want to stay here with me".

Well I was gleaned and cleaned and so hard pressed,
I called the woman that I love best.
I finally got my baby about half past three;
She said, "I'd like to know what you want with me".
I said, "money honey. . . ."

She screamed and said, "what's wrong with you?
From this day on our romance is through".
I said, "tell me baby, face to face,
How could another man take my place"?
She said, "money honey. . . ."

Well I've learned my lesson and now I know,
The sun may shine and the wind may blow,
The women may come and the women may go,
But before I'll say I love them so,
I want money honey. . . .

McPhatter followed up this fine record with other hits as a member of the Drifters. Sometime later, he became a solo singer, always retaining a distinct gospel feeling in his style.

Other groups quickly sought to repeat the success of the Dominoes' gospel-influenced records. One of them, the Five Royales, had begun as a straight gospel group, recording originally as the Royal Sons Quintet (for Apollo). It then switched to rhythm and blues. The group's lead singer Jonny Tanner, had a vocal tone similar to McPhatter's, slightly more hesitant and less melodic, more mature and with a harder drive at fast tempos. Combining a hilarious visual act with a frantic, intense vocal style, the group became immediately popular, and had several hits for Apollo, including "Baby Don't Do It" and "Help Me Somebody". The group's musical accompaniment was closer to band blues than was the rather rudimentary accompaniment of most groups, and when the Five Royales moved to King in 1955, they began to feature their guitarist more and produced the brilliant "Think", which presented an unusual interplay between vocal and guitar. With their witty high spirits and rough harmonies, the Five Royales presented rhythm and blues at its best, keeping the strength of blues lyrics and presenting them with the emotion of gospel singers.

In 1954 a third group capitalized on gospel-influenced rhythm and blues to produce several huge rhythm and blues hits: the Midnighters, who, like McPhatter and the Dominoes earlier, and the Five Royales later, recorded for King. The group's lead singer, Hank Ballard, had a more plaintive tone than did McPhatter or Tanner, and he used it well to express the heartrending events of "Work With Me, Annie", "Sexy Ways", and "Annie Had a Baby", a kind of serialized sad story of long pleading, quick gratification, and inevitable retribution. Ballard's desperate voice betrayed no sign of the humour which others found in his plight. Behind him, one of the roughest rhythms yet recorded was knocked out by guitar, bass, and drums, while the vocal group chanted in sympathetic understanding: "aah-ooh, aah-ooh".

According to one observer (Charles Hobson, who became a disc jockey in New York and host on ABC-TV's "How It Is"), "Work With Me, Annie" was acclaimed as the Negro national anthem for 1954 by its youthful black audience, who were also delighted by the pleasures of "Sexy Ways", "in the hall, on the wall. ..." In "Annie Had a Baby", Ballard came back with a caution:

Annie had a baby,
Can't work no more.
Every time she starts to work,
She has to stop and walk the baby across the floor. ...

Now I know Annie understood–
That's what happens when the getting gets good.

The song was credited to King's producer Henry Glover and "Lois Mann", an alias for King's owner Sydney Nathan, who claimed authorship (and writer royalties) of many of his company's releases. The Midnighters developed the story on this song with a wry follow up, "Henry's Got Flat Feet"–in case Etta James should have thought to present a "straight" version to follow up her response to the first "Annie" song, "Whirl With Me, Henry".

Within the world of black popular music, gospel became increasingly important. James Brown and the Famous Flames cut "Please, Please, Please" (Federal) in a raw preaching style, with minimal instrumental accompaniment and irregular rhythm. The record was a big hit in the rhythm and blues market in 1956, but had no impact in the pop market. For the white audience at this time it was generally necessary to be more melodic, less intense. The uncompromising vocal style of the gospel-oriented harmony groups was unsuited for it, as were the direct lyrics of many of the songs. But the infectious good humour and excitement in their records provided an important model that many rock 'n' roll singers tried to imitate.

The effective transition from black audience to white was made most often with a group style that took account of the latter's taste for more melody, less intensity.

II

With a few exceptions–the entertaining jump blues combo leader Louis Jordan, the "cosmopolitan" Cecil Gant, the club blues pianist-singers–when a black man chose to sing the blues he implicitly made a decision that assumed no white people would listen to him. He sang about his own concerns, for people who shared or knew them.

But increasing numbers of blacks who were born in the North, or who had been in the North from early childhood felt detached from the experiences of blues singers, or at least from the way they chose to express them. In the South, black communities had been close knit, depending on white society for work and services, but self-reliant for entertainment and conversation. In the North, the mass media acted as an agent of disruption of this kind of life. Advertisements, television, movies presented a world of white people, in which a few black faces occasionally appeared in minor roles. Black newspapers and radio stations served black communities, but could not offer the glamour of the colourful visual media. There were other forces working on the northern-born youths. John Lee Hooker explained some of them:

> The average coloured kid, it feels like the blues is embarrassing to them. This is my story. I think they dig it, but they feel like it's embarrassing, because their foreparents and great grandparents were brought up in slavery. They like it, but they feel like in the modern days they shouldn't listen to it. They feel it drags them back. But it don't do that. But that's the way they feel. They're thinking back on slavery, but that's past gone; it ain't anymore.[2]

Reacting to these and other influences, young black people in the North became preoccupied with what they took to be their own styles, with the way they presented themselves to the world, and they developed original patterns of dressing, speaking, walking–and singing. Malcolm X recalled dressing up in "sky-blue pants thirty inches at the knees and angle-narrowed to twelve inches at the bottom, and a long coat that pinched my waist and flared out below my knees". With clothes like that, there had to be new ways to walk, and stand. Malcolm took some pictures of himself, "posed the way hipsters wearing their zoots would 'cool it'–hat dangled, knees drawn close together, feet wide apart, both index fingers jabbed towards the floor. The long coat and swinging chain and the Punjab pants were much more dramatic if you stood that way."

Conversation was equally mannered, as existing words found new meaning and new words were invented. Surprisingly, though, the new singers used words more or less as they had always been used, but identified themselves by their style of pronouncing them and timing their phrases.

Blues styles had been evolved from the interplay of voices with instruments; gospel styles and the new group styles were worked out through vocal harmonies. The band blues, club blues, and bar blues had been developed in dance halls, theatres, clubs, and bars; the new group styles were worked out on the city streets.

The starting point for the new groups, as for the gospel-styled singers, was the style of two black ballad-singing groups who were successful with the popular music audience, the Mills Brothers and the Ink Spots, both of whom had contracts with Decca (who described the Mills Brothers on their records as "five boys and a guitar", with typical disregard of the men's ages). Both groups sang in the close harmony "barbershop" style, accompanied by a light rhythm section. All of the singers had good voices, ranging from alto to baritone and, normally, all the members of the groups sang the words. They were liked because of the ease with which they timed their harmonies, and the purity of their voices.

Some younger groups sought the same impact through similar techniques. The Ravens, for example, featured the rich bass voice of Jimmy Ricks, and the Four Tunes and Four Knights (formerly a gospel group, the Southern Jubilee Singers) sang conventional popular songs with attractive close harmonies. But the groups who wanted to express something about themselves, with less immediate interest in reaching the white audience, moved further from the style of the Mills Brothers.

Whereas almost all the major blues and gospel-styled singers grew up in the southern states, most of the group singers grew up in the North, many of them in the biggest cities, New York, Chicago, Baltimore, or the West, particularly Los Angeles. If the band, club, and bar blues were urban developments of country styles, and gospel-influenced singers used techniques first used in the South, the cool group singers were the first singers to work out a style to express the feelings of people who knew only the life of northern cities. The first successful group to use an original style was the Orioles, who consequently influenced a larger number of others. Managed by the astute Deborah Chessler, the Orioles became full-time professional singers in 1948, when they moved from Baltimore to New York and developed an act, a repertoire (featuring several songs by their manager), and an audience through six months of nightclub appearances. Their first record, "It's Too Soon To Know" (released first on Natural and then reissued by Jubilee), became a national rhythm and blues hit, despite its new sound. A guitar supplied the only accompaniment, played so quietly that its only purpose seemed to be to prevent the group from slowing down so much that they came to a complete stop. In the background the group wailed one wordless melody together, concentrating attention on the voice of lead tenor Sonny Til, who seemed to try to withdraw himself from the situation, refusing to be involved, trying to be cool. Til's voice was the sound of the streets, a strange echo of ghetto-experience. The harsh fast life produced a slow gentle response. The overall impression was of impeccable purity. The lyrics themselves were simple, comparable to some club blues material:

If she don't love me,
Let her tell me so,
I can't hold her
If she wants to go.
Though I'll cry when she's gone,
I won't die, I'll live on,
If it's so,
It's too soon to know.

The Orioles achieved many of the ambitions of the young black people seeking a new style, successfully presenting a new set of standards by which their music was to be judged, closing themselves off from the rest of the world which felt differently, communicating only with those who understood. The group wore the new clothes and worked out an intricate pattern of movements around the microphone–bending, straightening up, turning away from the mike, coming back to it, maybe tugging their shirtcuffs, carefully maintaining movement so that their shiny cufflinks caught the spotlight and reflected back at the audience.

At first such group records had a smaller audience than did the blues records, perhaps primarily because the people interested in the cool group style were young. But as they grew older and successive younger generations maintained interest, the audience grew. By 1954 there were more hits by groups in the rhythm and blues market than there were by blues singers. And throughout the period 1948–54, the Orioles were the major group, their career culminating in the pop market success of their "Crying in the Chapel" in 1953.

After the Orioles had proved that the simple, cool style could be commercially successful, record companies were quick to look for other groups with similar styles, and during the years 1950–52 several cool groups recorded fine records, including the exceptional "My Reverie" by the Larks (Apollo, 1951). The Larks were one of the few groups who kept their sound almost as simple as the Orioles; lead singer Eugene Mumford had a cool voice with charm and detachment comparable to Til's. More typical of the efforts to match the success of the Orioles, though, was "Glory of Love" by the Five Keys (Aladdin, 1951) in which lead singer Rudy West dragged out his voice in a more mannered way than Til or Mumford and was backed up by more complicated harmonies from the rest of the group.

Most record company executives knew very little about the conventions by which the audience judged the cool groups, and few of the executives bothered to find out before they made their records. A group was paid for one record which was tried locally. If it sold well, promotion followed in other districts; if it didn't, the record and the group could be forgotten.

As for the impact of the groups on their audience, boys in school and out of it, in every city in the North, began to see in a professional singing career the chance to escape the economic constraints of their lives, a route to money, a big car, the kind of life suggested by the Coke ads. But sixteen-year-old kids had little more idea about contracts and royalties than did the older blues singers.

The brevity of many groups' careers resulted from both the limited range of themes available to the style and the unpredictable and fiercely discriminating taste of the audience. The buyers of these kind of records were drawn almost entirely from the inner-city adolescents in northern and western cities, at first mainly Negro, but later Jewish, Puerto Rican, Italian, and the rest. These people, who constituted both the performers and the audience, had a much more narrow range of preoccupations than the adult black people who created and listened to the blues.

The blues had involved performer and audience in an autobiographical analysis of their collective experience of life–"*you* know what I'm talking about". When a singer had established contact with an audience, through personal appearances and records, convincing them that he had a particular story to tell which was his own yet meant something to them, he could come to them time and again, repeating himself or adding a new dimension to what they knew of him and his experience. He could borrow old tunes and put his own words to them, or use familiar verses in new contexts. The present was always an extension of the familiar past, while the future remained unconceived.

The group singers dealt with a completely different situation. For them and their audience, the past was, if not rejected and despised, then often ignored. The present was of greatest importance, and the future was looked at with wonder: Does she love me?–it's too soon to know.

The songs were invariably about unfulfilled relationships–the period after acquaintance has been established, before romance has been confirmed. A smaller number of songs concerned the aftermath of a broken relationship.

Limited to a few themes, the group singers were unable to present a very varied repertoire, or to make successive records sound distinct. The easiest way to vary moods was to alternate fast and slow songs, and most groups put a quick song as the 'B' side of their cool songs. To draw attention to themselves, groups had to balance the aspects of their style and character that were similar to other successful groups with those that were different.

Even a group's name became an important source of similarity and differentiation. The Cardinals, under the supervision of Atlantic Records, chose the only other name besides the Orioles' that referred to both a bird and a major league baseball team. The Mellow Moods found a name which accurately evoked the style's sound. Numerous groups took up the connection with birds, including the Larks, the Robins, the Swallows, the Flamingos, the Crows, the Penguins, the Pelicans, the Jayhawks, and the Feathers. The Spiders and the Spaniels were carefully different.

Many of the groups developed variations away from the cool style established by the Orioles. The Spaniels, who recorded first for Chance and then with Vee Jay, exaggerated the cool delivery to achieve the sleepiest, droopiest tone yet, used brilliantly on "Goodnight, Sweetheart, Goodnight" (1954). "Pookie" Hudson, lead singer with the group, wrote the song with Vee Jay's A&R man Calvin Carter; it was one of the first "teen" songs, which quickly grew into a major genre of popular songs.

As the Spaniels sang it, "Goodnight, Sweetheart, Goodnight" was a sad farewell on a girl's porch:

It's four o'clock in the morning,
And we've stayed here far too long;
I hate to leave you but I really must say,
"Goodnight, sweetheart, goodnight".

Despite his regrets, Hudson declined to get involved. He went through the ritual of postponing his departure because that was the convention. But really, he'd just as soon go home to bed. Or that was what he wanted us to believe. The appeal of the cool style was that it was never definite what the singer really felt.

The song was covered for the popular market by the McGuire Sisters, and in the process lost all its enigma. Occasionally, the effect of the cool style–as with the Spaniels–was to make the singers seem effeminate, not only when they went into high wailing sounds, but just through their tone, which seemed much more submissive than a man would be expected to be. Unable to translate this kind of feeling directly, white producers covered one of the most sophisticated black styles with one of the simplest white styles, female vocal groups.

A less drastically different group, who provided the McGuire Sisters with the next song they covered, "Sincerely", was the Moonglows, the protégés of Alan Freed. The group recorded as both the Moonglows (for Chess) and the Moonlighters (Checker), and featured two lead singers, Bobby Lester and Harvey Fuqua. "Sincerely" was released by the Moonglows and featured Harvey singing the lead. His voice was more dramatic than the cool singers of the period, closer in some ways to the established ballad styles in the popular market. "Sincerely" featured some beautiful group noises–"ba-dah-dah" breathed again and again–which gave a soft background to the clear lead.

This dramatic style was used by a second Chicago group, the Flamingos, who featured first Sollie McElroy and later Nate Nelson as lead singers. McElroy's voice seemed a little too strong for the gentle falsetto wails from the group, although "Golden Teardrops" was successful (Chance, 1953). But then the group's lead switched to Nelson, who sang "I'll Be Home" (Checker, 1954) in a cooler style that was still somehow dramatic in its effect. The Flamingos' technique of switching personnel was a successful method of evading the fast decline that befell most groups. With a third singer, Tommy Hunt, as lead, they had hits in a cool/dramatic style for End in the late fifties.

The dramatic lead voice was eventually used to greatest effect by the Platters, for whom Tony Williams sang lead on most of their records. But although the group became major performers in pop music, their records for Federal in 1953 (including their first version of "Only You") were of little significance.

The slow romantic group songs, often more sentimental than most popular music of the time, were effective because the singers, unlike those of the cool groups, seemed deeply involved in their moods. Closing their eyes, listeners could drift into a world of perfect understanding. "Life is But a Dream", sang the Harptones. The same group, in "A Sunday Kind of Love", amid an accompaniment which evoked the awe-inspiring atmosphere of a cathedral expressed the hopes of the time:

Through my Sunday dreamin'
And my Sunday schemin',

I'm hopin' to discover
A certain kind of lover
Who will show me the way.

A few groups adopted some of the characteristics of the cool group style but infused it with a stronger blues emphasis. The first to do so was the Clovers, a Washington, D. C., group who signed for Atlantic in 1951. Atlantic's producer, Ahmet Ertegun, had the group drop their Orioles-based style and emphasize a stronger lead vocal. Ertegun's song "Don't You Know I Love You" was the first of a long series of hits through to 1957 with Atlantic. The harmonies of the group emphasized a rhythm more than most groups of the time did, and on several songs the lead singer sounded like a fugitive from a jump blues combo, as in "One Mint Julep" (1952), yet another composition by Rudolph Toombs on the theme (he did many) of drink's horrific effects.

One early morning, as I was walking,
I met a woman, we started talking;
I took her home to get a few nips,
But all I had was a mint julep–
One mint julep was the start of it all.

The sense of impending doom was confirmed in the last verse:

I don't want to bore you, with my trouble,
But from now on I'll be thinking double,
I'm through with flirting and drinking whiskey–
I got six extra children from getting frisky.

"Your Cash Ain't Nothin' But Trash" contradicted the philosophy of the Drifters' "Money Honey"; "Little Mama", and "Lovey Dovey" (both 1954) were simple novelty songs, but still sung with a blues voice. By 1956 the group yielded much of their blues emphasis, and did well in the rhythm and blues market with the smooth harmony song "Blue Velvet".

While most of the blues styles tended to lose their importance in rhythm and blues as the new access to one popular market affected more recording company policies, most of the group styles endured–or thrived–because from the start they had been developed with an awareness of popular musical forms. The Flamingos, for instance, had been interested even in the early, obscure years of their career in the techniques of the "class" white harmony groups, the Hi-

Los and the Four Freshmen, and tried to duplicate the effects of these groups in some of their earliest material (for Chance), in songs like "Vooit-Vooit" and "Cross Over the Bridge". Other groups, frustrated by the much greater success of the Crew Cuts, Four Lads, and Diamonds, white groups who regularly covered their rhythm and blues hits for Mercury, and of the Ames Brothers, Four Aces, and several "sister" girl groups (McGuire, Fontane, Andrews) with simple harmony styles, tried to achieve the same success with similar techniques. Simple sing-along novelty songs, sung with deadpan voices, were successful for the Crows, the Penguins, and even the Five Keys and the Charms, who both also recorded in genuine group styles for the black market. A few of the novelty groups adopted an obviously "teenaged" lead, notably the Teenagers, for whom Frankie Lymon provided the perfect innocence.

By 1955–56, the general tendency was for companies to record the group style with a regular, identifying pattern, perhaps a particular noise which the group chanted behind the vocal, or an emphatic dance beat. But a few groups maintained more random harmonies and unpredictable rhythms. Examples are the Five Satins and the Charts, two East Coast groups who produced even more extraordinary harmony chants and deliberately cool lead vocals than any previous group had achieved. But the songs–the key to much of the success of the group-style–were still pure innocence. Fred Parris, lead with the Five Satins, sang in "(I'll Remember) In the Still of the Night" (Ember):

In the still of the night
I-I-I held you, held you tight,
'Cause I love you, love you so,
Promise I'll never, let you go,
In the still of the night.

The theme was similar to Clyde McPhatter's frantic "Such a Night", but there was no suggestion in Parris's voice that he did anything but hold his girl in wistful embrace. Behind Parris, the rest of the group droned, chanted, and moaned, to produce one of the strangest records in a period of many bizarre sounds.

"Deserie" by the Charts (Everlast) was weirder yet. This time the words were reduced to elemental simplicity:

My darling you know,
I do love you so.

But the flat tone of the singer seemed careless of tune or key, and the rest of the group had no evident sense of harmony. Yet out of this far from simple, free-form harmony, if it can be called that, came the desired sense of obsessional devotion, with a lonely saxophonist adding to the drone of the vocal group.

What vocal groups brought to rhythm and blues and expressed better than any of its previous types of singer was the desperate loneliness of adolescence. During the following years there would be as many singers trying to recapture the innocence of these groups as there were singers attempting to re-create the excitement of the jump blues.

III

Rhythm and blues gave a lot to American popular music: words, phrases, rhythm, instrumentation, a musical organization, and a verse structure. But more important than all of these, rhythm and blues gave rock 'n' roll a sense of style.

It was a style that suggested adventurousness and discovery ("Rocket 88", "Chicken Shack Boogie"), confrontations with experience and lessons learned from it ("Big Town", "The Things That I Used To Do"), a commitment to back up feeling with action ("Goin' Home", "Boogie Chillen"). Rhythm and blues singers had integrity. At their best, so did rock 'n' roll singers.

Rock 'n' roll narrowed the reference of songs to adolescence and simplified the complicated boogie rhythms to a simple 2/4 with the accent on the back beat. And once these new conventions were established, the rhythm and blues singers were obliged to either adapt to them or resign themselves to obscurity, at best playing for a local audience in some bar, and at worst abandoning music altogether. Wynonie Harris tended bar until he died in 1969, Amos Milburn worked in a Cincinnati hotel, Percy Mayfield became a songwriter, Harvey Fuqua of the Moonglows became a producer at Berry Gordy's Motown Corporation. A few–Joe Turner, Jimmy Witherspoon–became jazz singers, and several–John Lee Hooker, Muddy Waters, Sonny Boy Williamson–played alternately in local bars and as "folk-blues" singers before white audiences in coffee houses and concert halls. A remarkable number died before they were forty, and a handful–Fats Domino, Ray Charles, Sam Cooke–managed to become pop stars.

Meanwhile rock 'n' roll ran its course–inexplicably long to some, and disappointingly brief to others. To those young people in its audience who did not know its source, rock 'n' roll seemed like a necessary, and surely eternal, part of urban life. The industry, with typical sleight of hand, killed off the music but kept the name, so that virtually all popular music (with the exception of what came to be called "easy listening") was branded rock and roll. The abolition of the apostrophes was significant–the term looked more respectable, but sounded the same. Perfect.

Upon a younger generation than that which had discovered and insisted on the original rock 'n' roll was palmed off a softer substitute which carried nearly the same name. And, fittingly, a section of this new music was stuff that still went by the name "rhythm and blues", although much of it had slight connection with the pre-rock 'n' roll styles of the same name.

PART III

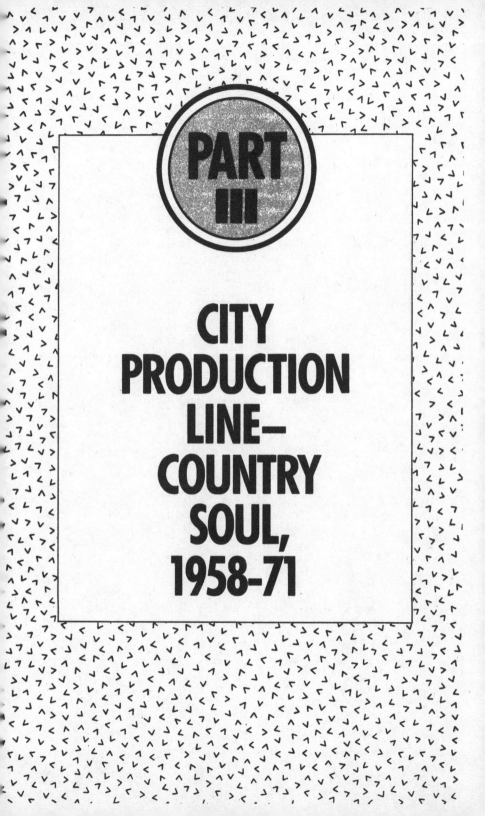

CITY PRODUCTION LINE– COUNTRY SOUL, 1958–71

8

BACK HOME

Throughout the twentieth century, a remarkable proportion of the important stylistic changes in American popular music has stemmed from the southern states. In what has become a predictable pattern, southern singers or musicians work out a style that is quite distinct from any previously available musical style; somebody in the North discovers it, develops it, and becomes famous with it; and then a few of the inventors are "discovered" and earn belated fame. In this sense, rock 'n' roll was just another of a series of examples that could be traced back through jazz to the vaudeville/minstrel singers of the nineteenth century.[1]

Eventually, the sophisticated veneer that northern performers use to cover up the earthy origins of the style saps all its distinctive energies and character, so that the music becomes obsolete, interesting only to collectors and academics who care little for contemporary tastes. Meanwhile, the progenitors of the style are replaced locally by a younger group of southern singers and musicians who have evolved a new, alternative style of expression, reacting to common experiences, events, and environments in new ways.

This pattern is somewhat true of white southerners but to a much smaller degree than it is of black southerners. Bill C. Malone's *Country Music USA* covers the history of the past fifty years of country and western music and shows a tendency for the music to stay very much the same over long periods. This is partly because several white southern styles have never been widely popular with the national American audience, so that singers did not continually have to invent styles that would be special to their local audiences–those invented thirty or forty years ago were still special to a local area, or to the white South.

In contrast, almost every black southern style has proved to have universal qualities that attract national and international audiences, and this situation has placed continual pressure on singers to come up with new styles that are not already widely known and that the local audience can feel to be its own. And invariably, musicians and singers have responded positively to such pressure.

Although white singers have tended to be conservative, and black singers to be inventive, occasionally white singers, working with essentially black styles and forms, have equalled black creativeness by producing distinctive new styles out of a synthesis of previous black and white ones.

From 1957 onward, when rock 'n' roll had momentarily (but with apparent completeness) merged the formerly separate rhythm and blues and popular markets, most black singers were obliged to choose between possible fame as a rock 'n' roll singer or probable obscurity with some existing rhythm and blues style. And while many made their bids for national fame, a few continued to serve mainly local audiences, in a range of styles that included the guitar/cry blues style of Muddy Waters and B. B. King (identified principally with Chicago); the down-home boogie style of Jimmy Reed (identified mainly with southern Louisiana, although Reed himself lived in Chicago); the bayou blues of other southern Louisiana singers, who followed the ballad style of Fats Domino's slow records; the gospel blues of Bobby Bland and Junior Parker, who recorded in Houston, Texas; the novelty dance blues of New Orleans; and "funky" instrumental styles and "soul" singing styles that were developed in Memphis and in cities near Atlanta's Cotton Belt.

Despite superficial similarities in their sound, B. B. King and Muddy Waters offered almost contradictory interpretations of the role of a blues singer. Waters lived and played in Chicago, and rarely left the city. In Chicago his was the band best able to make the intensely exciting and ferociously loud noise that typified the bar blues. But because his music was so specific to the Mississippi/Chicago (black) culture, his records were rarely acceptable even to the national Negro audience, who generally expected something with a lighter beat and more sophisticated, than the brash boasting and harsh sound of the Waters band. After 1955, only one of Waters' records made the rhythm and blues top ten, "Close to You" (1958), which had something like a lilt in it despite the heavy sound.

B. B. King in contrast was not identified with any one place. Once he left Memphis in the early fifties and started touring the country with his band, he just kept going, always listening to what the audience was buying, making some records that sounded close to the Waters sound but doing others with the soft ballad style of the once-popular Percy Mayfield. Where Waters tended to use his voice and guitar as percussive instruments, emphasizing the intense rhythm laid down by the rest of the band, King used both his voice and his guitar to provide melody and harmony. He presented a much wider range of styles and stressed the potential beauty of the blues, sometimes, but not always, at the expense of emotional intensity, and he had a series of varied hits in the rhythm and blues market "Sweet Little Angel" (1956) was sung hard, with a heavy beat; "Please Accept My Love" (1958) was gentle, plaintive, "Sweet Sixteen" (1960) used a strong band riff behind King's voice and guitar and built up into one of the most dramatic blues performances ever recorded, with gospel inflections dominating King's singing at the end of the two-part performance.[2] Because King's style was more sophisticated and modern, even though he had no reputation outside the black culture, he was a more influential figure to younger blues singers and musicians than was Waters, who was rooted more exclusively in traditional conceptions of the blues.

Buddy Guy, a brilliant guitarist with a flair for showmanship that often exceeded his concern for emotional expression; Magic Sam, a singer whose fine control and delicate sense of timing gave him a much wider range of sensitive expression than any other blues singer in Chicago; Junior Wells, a boisterous harmonica-playing singer who matched Guy for showmanship and sang with rough intensity in a style that was able to veer towards soul when that became commercially profitable; these performers and others–Otis Rush, Earl Hooker, James Cotton–continued the blues tradition in Chicago with apparently no awareness of the currently popular styles of Chuck Berry and Bo Diddley. Under the watchful eye of Chess producer and session group leader Willie Dixon, who composed a vast number of classic blues songs, the blues thrived in Chicago long enough for most of these musicians to be able to enjoy the appreciation of a much bigger audience in the years 1965–70, when white musicians, many of them British, established guitar-dominated blues as a popular music style.

Outside Chicago, Albert King in the St. Louis area and Freddy King in Texas played slightly different versions of modern guitar blues, Albert King often using small sax sections to give a punchier sound and Freddy King playing at fast, jump tempos that enabled him to show off his dexterity. Johnny "Guitar" Watson, in Los Angeles, was one of the few people to try to make a rock 'n' roll style out of this kind of blues, and he succeeded quite well in "Gangster of Love" and "Ruben" (for Federal, in the early sixties), but the records were never widely known.

While singers in cities outside the South who wanted to play the blues tended to follow B. B. King and Muddy Waters, most of those who stayed in the South kept closer to established "down-home" styles, first the enduring Texas country blues style and then the comparable rhythm and blues equivalent, the boogie guitar blues of Jimmy Reed.

In the late forties, while the pre-war forms of the Mississippi country blues declined to little-played local entertainment, the Texas country blues was amended by several singers into a form which became a nationally popular rhythm and blues style. Lightnin' Hopkins was the most consistently popular of these singers, but Smokey Hogg, Li'l Son Jackson, Frankie Lee Sims, and others also maintained their popularity into the early fifties. Their main compromise with contemporary taste was the addition of bass and drums, and sometimes a piano, to the singer's own guitar. The rhythm section made the records suitable for juke boxes, and the consequence was that southern blues were supplied to a wide area. (Though Hopkins, Hogg, Jackson, and Sims all made their most commercially successful records for West Coast companies–Hopkins for Aladdin, Hogg for Modern, Jackson for Imperial, and Sims for Specialty–all four singers played chiefly in the Texas area.)

By the mid-fifties, the Texas blues had lost most of its audience and was replaced in popularity by the more emphatic rhythms of the guitar blues of Jimmy Reed (and his bass guitarist, Eddie Taylor). Reed had a long series of rhythm and blues hits for the Chicago company Vee Jay, some of which made the lower reaches of the "Hot 100" in the popular market in the late fifties and early sixties. There was little variation in the overall sound of Reed's records, but they invariably had an infectious rhythm and a memorable chorus. "Ain't That Lovin' You Baby" (1956) and "Baby, What You Want Me to Do?" (1960) were among the best of his hits, supremely relaxed, casual songs, that just kept rolling along.

Of all the Chicago-based blues styles, Jimmy Reed's held up the best against competition from the gospel-derived soul styles in the early sixties, and a couple of other local blues men had hits in his style. Tommy Tucker (easier to remember than his real name, Robert Higginbotham) made the pop top twenty in 1964 with "High Heel Sneakers", an infectious, danceable blues song produced by Herb Abramson, the founder of Atlantic but now out on his own; licensed to Checker, the record did better than any of Jimmy Reed's own releases, to which it owed so much for its basic chord pattern and beat. A year later, G. L. Crockett had a minor rhythm and blues hit with "It's a Man Down There" on the Four Star label of Chicago, but the majority of bluesmen still using this style were based down South.

Both the rhythm and the vocal style of Reed's records were evoked in the records of several men who began recording in southern Louisiana in the mid-fifties. Lightnin' Slim was the first to record and the best. Matching an intimate vocal style to a regular boogie beat, he used the blues to record convincing impressions of his life, culture, and feelings, and of his relationships with women.

Among performers significantly influenced by Reed–Slim Harpo, Lonesome Sundown, Lazy Lester, all of whose records were released through the Nashville company Excello–Harpo was the most successful. His first record for Excello, in 1957, "I'm a King Bee"/"I've Got Love If You Want It", was a big regional hit. Its sound was unusually boastful for post-war country blues. Like Jimmy Reed, Harpo strapped a harmonica to his guitar, and alternated vocal and instrumental passages above a steady boogie beat, "Rainin' in My Heart" (1961) and "Baby Scratch My Back" (1966) sold well, the latter in the pop market where his gravelly voice took on "novelty" appeal.

The French-speaking people of South Louisiana had their own musical style called "cajun" music, which brought fiddles, accordions and traditional two-step and waltz dance beats to a repertoire of mostly public domain folk tunes, sung in French. Despite the buoyant spirit of the music, cajun was considered too obscure for American pop radio, and even country radio gave it only a fleeting chance: the brothers Rusty and Doug (Kershaw) had a couple of minor country hits in 1961 with "Louisiana Man" and "Diggy Liggy Lo" for Acuff-Rose's Hickory label.

Although the cajun singers had a limited market if they stuck to their own music, they evolved for a while an effective commercial formula by adapting a crooning style based on Fats Domino's drawl to an accompaniment that used piano and saxophone instead of accordion and violin; the mournful, almost dirge-like mood provided several pop hits for singers from South Louisiana and East Texas in the period 1959 through 1962, most of which were issued first on local labels and licensed for national distribution by major companies.

The three most consistent indie producers in the region were Floyd Soileau, Huey Meaux, and George Khoury, all of whom were French-speaking cajuns themselves. For Khoury, producing records for his Khoury's label was more or less a hobby which he did as a sideline to other ways of making a living, but in 1959 he did produce the biggest hit to come out of this "swamp pop" era, "Sea of Love" by Phil Phillips and the Twilights. Recorded at the primitive Goldband studio in Lake Charles, Louisiana, "Sea of Love" was a murky, mysterious chant which soon outgrew Khoury's limited distribution network and went all the way to number two on the national chart when Mercury picked up the rights. The Twilights were really a local rhythm and blues band called Cookie and his Cupcakes, who had their own hit the same year on the indie Judd label with "Mathilda", featuring Shelton Dunaway as a soulful lead singer.

Based in Houston, Texas, Huey Meaux had been a barber among

other activities, but went into music full-time after producing two national hits in 1959, "This Should Go On Forever" by Rod Bernard, and "Breaking Up Is Hard to Do" by Jivin' Gene. Both songs were typical of an emerging genre, two-chord ballads which owed equal debts to the intimate style of the late Johnny Ace and to the more intense regret of Guitar Slim's "The Things That I Used to do". Meaux licensed his productions to Jin Records of Ville Platte, Louisiana, whose owner Floyd Soileau in turn licensed them to Argo (in the case of Bernard's record) and Mercury (Jivin' Gene) when demand outstripped his resources. In 1961, the Meaux–Soileau combination worked again, this time with a straight copy of Fats Domino's style by Joe Barry on the old Ted Daffan song, "I'm a Fool to Care". To make sure he got the sound right, Meaux had gone to make the record in New Orleans with as many of the Bartholomew musicians as he could find, and at the same J & M studio where Fats made all his hits. For all its plagiarism, Barry's record had undeniable charm, and made the national top thirty on Mercury's Smash subsidiary.

Huey Meaux's most interesting and original artist in this period was the black, teenage singer-guitarist Barbara Lynn, who topped the rhythm and blues chart and made the pop top ten in 1962 with her first record, "You'll Lose a Good Thing" (licensed to Jamie Records of Philadelphia). At a time when pop music still regarded girl singers as puppets who sang what they were given, this record was a revelation, a quietly confident assertion by the singer that she was worth her partner's "loss of freedom". Although she never wrote another song as good as that first one, Barbara came close with "Oh Baby (We Got a Good Thing Going)", (1964), which attracted a cover version by the Rolling Stones in Britain, and even on more conventional material she retained a sense of serenity and warmth that was rare for the period.

Among the other Texas record men who kept their ears open for an artist, a song, or a record that might have the "magic" to go all the way, were Major Bill Smith and Lelan Rogers, based in Fort Worth and Houston respectively. Smith had his own LeCam label, but he often pressed as few as 200 copies of a release, enough to pass onto a few disc jockeys and local stores to test the reaction. Ideally, a major label came in to offer a national distribution deal outside Texas, letting Smith supply distributors locally.

The most promising artist among Smith's protégés in the early Sixties was Delbert McClinton, a singer, harmonica player and guitarist who recorded with the Straight Jackets (a rousing version of Billy Emerson's "Every Woman I know is Crazy About Automobiles") and the Rondells ("If You Really Want Me to, I'll Go"). But it was another Fort Worth singer, Bruce Channel, who towed the Straight Jackets into the pop charts, with his exuberant yell of delight, "Hey! Baby". Delbert opened the song by blasting a riff on harmonica, and his band settled into a rocking blues shuffle while Bruce wailed the message that kids wished they had the confidence to shout across the street: "Hey! Baby. I want to know, will you be my girl?" Picked up from LeCam by Smash, the record topped the pop chart early in 1962, perfect for parties where they still danced the twist, but with far more spontaneity than any of the records made for that purpose in the North. Bruce Channel had trouble escaping the format of that first hit, but returned to the British charts six years later with a good white soul record, "Keep On". Delbert McClinton had to wait ten years after that before making any kind of impression on the national consciousness, recording an excellent, but overlooked album for ABC, *Victim of Life's Circumstances* in 1975 and belatedly hitting the pop top ten in 1980 with "Giving It Up For Your Love", recorded in Muscle Shoals for Capitol.

Within a year of producing "Hey! Baby", Smith came up with another winner, and by some quirk of fate, this one started with "Hey!" too: "Hey Paula", by Paul and Paula. The song became a teen classic, to stand alongside "Young Love" and "All I Have to do is Dream", and sold several million copies worldwide on the Philips label. Paul was really the song's writer, Ray Hildebrand, who managed just one effective follow-up, "Young Lovers", before the duo faded into obscurity. Smith had one last shot, J. Frank Wilson's "Last Kiss", one of several "death" songs which popped into the charts every year or so; "Last Kiss" made number two in 1964 for Josie of New York.

Lelan Rogers was a less consistent hit-producer than his fellow Texans Huey Meaux and Major Bill Smith, and made some kind of a living as a freelance radio promotion man, representing some of the Northern indie labels like Tamla, Carlton, and Top Rank in the South-West, getting a percentage point off local sales if he managed to spark off substantial sales. Lelan was Kenny Rogers' elder brother, and he occasionally found funds to make a record or two with Kenny, Gene Summers, Mickey Gilley and other young hopefuls in Texas. But his biggest success was Little Esther's "Release Me", which topped the rhythm and blues chart and made the pop top ten on his own Lenox label in 1962; the song had been a regional hit for Jivin' Gene, but Rogers successfully applied the same kind of treatment that Ray Charles had just given to "I Can't Stop Loving You", and brought Esther Phillips back from ten years of obscurity.

Back in Louisiana, the tiny Montel-Michele label wound up this period when unsophisticated productions from the South could filter through the system and reach the top of the charts, with two hits from Dale and Grace: "I'm Leaving It Up to You" (1963) and "Stop and Think It Over" (1964). The duo effectively picked up the boy-and-girl romance story left off by Paul and Paula, adapting Don and Dewey's "Leaving It Up To You" to the Louisiana ballad format, and following through with their own piece of teen philosophizing.

Alongside these pop productions, a few labels continued to release cajun records for the local market, particularly Swallow Records, a subsidiary of Jin whose leading cajun artist was Belton Richard. Swallow also recorded the leading zydeco artist, Clifton Chenier, "zydeco" being the black equivalent of cajun, sung in French and often with a bluesy flavour. Chenier recorded regularly through the sixties, making albums which were licensed for international distribution through Arhoolie Records of California, but the only zydeco record to surface on the pop market was "Sugar Bee" by Cleveland Crochet, which sold enough throughout the South to earn a low placing on *Billboard's* pop chart for Eddie Shuler's Goldband label in 1961.

During the same period that Huey Meaux, Bill Smith and these other "Southern record men" evolved a commercial style out of the ethnic music of the region, producers working at Don Robey's Duke and Peacock labels in Houston shaped a gospel blues style which rarely crossed over to the pop market at the time, but was widely influential ten years later. Two singers in particular were the "fronts" for this style, Bobby Bland and Junior Parker, whose careers were for some years closely linked because they toured as a package, under the banner "Blues Consolidated". Bobby Bland made most of his records with producer-arranger Joe Scott, and Parker often recorded with Bill Harvey, who between them evolved a unique blend of jazz and blues behind the gospel-based styles of the vocalists.

Gospel inflections were slight in Bland's first hit in the rhythm and blues market, "Farther On up the Road" (1957), which had a jaunty band blues accompaniment with riffs and sax solos providing a strong background for the singer's mellow baritone voice. The gospel inflections became more pronounced during the following years, on occasion reaching the intensity of B. B. King, at other times reaching toward the raucous style of Ray Charles. But Bland usually underplayed these devices, establishing conviction through the overall feeling of involvement which came from his tone, rich and pure.

While other companies, like Atlantic, King, and Imperial, allowed the big band blues to degenerate by introducing strings and female groups into their rhythm and blues records, Duke/Peacock kept such techniques to a minimum. Bland's "Cry Cry Cry" (1960), "I Pity the

Fool" (1961), "Stormy Monday" (1962), and later hits were blues of the highest standard, convincingly sung and imaginatively arranged. "Turn on Your Lovelight" (1961), and "Yield Not to Temptation" (1962) had gospel arrangements, with call-and-response structures like that of "Hit the Road, Jack".

Although Bland's records never reached the top ten in the popular music market, many of them sold well, reaching somewhere between forty and twenty on the national lists and much higher in regional lists. Even when he eventually recorded more obviously for the white market, with Latin American rhythms, strings, and girl groups, Bland managed to keep his style, so that "Call on Me" (1963) was one of the finest pop records ever made.

Junior Parker was probably the greatest band blues singer still making records regularly for a national audience during the sixties. Less obviously influenced by gospel styles than Bland, he was almost completely spared the pop arrangements that Bland occasionally sang with. Parker's first rhythm and blues hit was "Next Time You See Me" (1957), which he sang with appropriately relaxed assurance. More firmly based in the blues than Bland, Parker nonetheless had fewer hits in the rhythm and blues as well as the popular market, but in 1961, both "Driving Wheel" and "In the Dark" made the rhythm and blues lists, and the following year the novelty "Annie Get Your Yo Yo" did well in both markets. All three were typical of his style. Some of his nonhits, however, "Mother-in-Law Blues", "Yonders Wall", and "Sweet Home Chicago", were stronger blues, with Parker's harmonica solos, modest, deft, and expressive, giving atmosphere to the already lively arrangements.

The gospel blues style was not restricted to Duke/Peacock Records, although the producers in Houston apparently understood how to record it better than did anyone else. Ted Taylor, with one of the most distinctive voices of his time, was even more obviously influenced by the high intense style of Roy Brown than were B. B. King, Bland, and Parker, but Taylor too had a touch of their gospel flavour. He moved from one company to another without a major hit. After working with various groups (including the Cadets), he sang rock and roll with the West Coast company Ebb ("Keep Walking On", 1958). He was with Okeh for some time during the early sixties, had a minor rhythm and blues hit with the extraordinary "Rambling Rose", in which his voice was almost lost, wailing high and thin in a strong big band arrangement, and also cut "Be Ever Wonderful", a song he had previously recorded during a momentary stay with Peacock. On he went, to Top Rank, Atco, and eventually to Ronn Records of Shreveport, Louisiana, where he had a rhythm and blues hit in 1968, with the exceptionally good "Strangest Feeling".

Among the singers who were influenced by Ted Taylor was a former gospel singer, Little Johnny Taylor, whose "Part Time Love" (Galaxy, 1963) was one of the best gospel blues records; its success in the popular music market, where it made the national top twenty, was one of the first signs that the white audience could again accept direct expressions from the black culture. The song, by Clay Hammond, was a fine blues:

I'm gonna find me,
Lord, I've got to find me a part-time love. [twice]
The next time,
The next time my baby leaves me,
I just got to have me a part-time love.
There's one more thing I've got to say to you right here:

People in the cemetery,
They're not all alone,
Some turn to dust,
And some have bone;
I'd rather be dead,
Six feet in my grave
Than to live lonely
Each and every day.
She came home this morning,
I asked where had she been,
She said "Don't ask me no questions, daddy,
Because I'll be leaving again".

Every, every time my baby leaves me,
I have to suffer the whole time she's gone. [twice]
The next time my baby leaves,
People can't you see I've just got to have me a part-time love.
I'm talking about a love,
One that's gonna stick by me when I get old,
I'm talkin' about a kind of love,
That's gonna wash my dirty clothes,
I'm talking about a love,
I'm talkin' about a part-time love,
I don't think you people know what I'm talkin' about,
I'm talkin' about a part-time love.

The arrangement was close to contemporary B. B. King arrangements, with the guitar (which the singer Bobby Parker has claimed to have played) answering the singer's lines and a gentle sax riff filling in behind, gradually building up the tension towards the end of the song. Little Johnny Taylor's "preaching" style, based in the blues but with strong gospel influence in the way words were dragged out and the voice rose at the end of phrases, confirmed the increasing impact of gospel music on the blues, and the song itself had qualities of a sermon.

Other records of the period also reflected the influence of church songs on blues song writers; Jimmy Johnson's "Don't Answer the Door" was one. His band recorded the song with Hank Alexander singing while organ, tuba, and a far-off vocal group created a dramatic atmosphere:

If your mama want to come visit us,
Tell her I get home about the break of day,
And that's too late to visit anybody,
So tell your mama please stay away,
'Cause I don't want a soul
Hangin' around my house when I'm not at home,
I don't want you to answer the door for your mama
When you know you're home and you're all alone.

B. B. King recorded the song in 1966 (for ABC-Paramount), and it gave him the biggest rhythm and blues hit he had had for some time.

Through 1964, the blues quality of the gospel blues diminished as the gospel emphasis increased, and the relatively sophisticated arrangements were replaced by simpler ones that functioned mainly to supply a rhythm and were less concerned with creating an atmosphere. In all, the songs and style of the gospel blues maintained the Negro culture's musical identity through a period when its close relationship with the white culture seemed likely to drastically change or even destroy this identity.

The destructive element of the interchange between white and black cultures was typified in New Orleans, where the lively sounds of people following Fats Domino, Professor Longhair, and Huey Smith continued to flourish–heavy piano chords, strong saxophone riffs, happy, relaxed singing. But while many interesting records–in terms of their music and their lyrics–were made, the majority of those that were nationally popular were novelty songs such as Ernie K-Doe's "Mother-in-Law" or Joe Jones's "You Talk Too Much".

The most important New Orleans records company, Minit Records, was founded in 1960, with Allen Toussaint as chief songwriter, producer, session bandleader, and pianist. Influenced by the instrumental sound of Ray Charles's gospel blues records for Atlantic, Toussaint was relatively successful. He organized both national hits for Jessie Hill ("Ooh Poo Pah Doo"), Ernie K-Doe ("Mother-in-Law"), and the Showmen ("It Will Stand"/"Country Fool"), and regional hits by Irma Thomas ("Ruler of My Heart"),

Aaron Neville ("Over You"), and several others (all for Minit).

Using the simple "gospel" piano figures Ray Charles had exploited so effectively in "What'd I Say?"–whose echoes were in every Jessie Hill record and several of Ernie K-Doe's–the Showmen's "It Will Stand" was a simple celebration of rock and roll. But "Country Fool", the reverse side, was a fine piece of autobiography, almost hidden in a complicated fast harmony arrangement. Norman Johnson, the Showmen's lead singer and the author of the song, was completely convincing as he sang:

When I left home and came to town,
I thought I was the biggest sport around,
I wore pin-stripe suits and button shoes,
The city boys called me a country dude.
When I got to town, everything had changed,
Everybody lookin' at me so strange.
Horns blowin' at me (beep beep, beep-be-beep)
Dogs barkin' at me (bow-wow, bow-be-bow-wow)
Folks laughin' at me, just laughin' at me (ha-ha, ha-ha)
Sayin' I'm a fool, a country fool.

Yeah, I met this chick, I thought I was hip,
She turned me so fast, she made me flip,
I worked all night, I worked all day,
At the end of the week, I gave her my pay;
Doin' my work, throwin' garbage cans,
I looked up and saw her with another man.

Well I hung my head, begin to feel sad,
Just about then I began to get mad,
I went to the pawnshop, bought me a gun,
I'm goin' back home when this is done,
But now I've found that I wasn't so smart,
I bought my gun to get a brand new start,
I'm a country fool, a country fool.

Toussaint also produced regional hits for the soft-voiced Irma Thomas and Aaron Neville. Thomas had a blues-influenced voice similar to Barbara Lynn's, and under Toussaint's supervision produced the beautiful soft ballad "Ruler of My Heart" (1962). Later, with Eddie Ray as producer, she recorded for Imperial one of the best statements of confident derision, "Time Is on My Side" (1964), which used the massed choir technique of uptown rhythm and blues with brilliant effect. Aaron Neville had a less versatile voice, clear and light, and a particularly unusual ballad style. His voice wavered as if unwilling to choose a specific note, which created a convincing mood of indecision. "Tell It Like It Is", recorded for Parlo under Toussaint's supervision in 1966, provided Neville with an unanticipated national hit, although neither the performance nor the song was any better than records he had made in the previous five years.

In addition to his work with Minit, Toussaint played piano and produced sessions with Lee Dorsey for Fire/Fury, Clarence "Frogman" Henry for Argo (a Chess subsidiary), and many others, creating successful records with the sound that was dominant in New Orleans, always emphasizing its distinctive accent, an accepted part of national popular music since Fats Domino's early rock 'n' roll records. Domino himself continued his string of hits into the early sixties with songs that had the same happy mood, a determination to enjoy life coming out of even the sad songs.

Chris Kenner was one of the few New Orleans singers whose sound and success was more or less independent of Toussaint. He recorded a small rhythm and blues hit, "Sick and Tired", for Imperial, in a style very similar to Fats Domino's. Then, during the early sixties, he had national hits with "I Like It Like That", "Land of a Thousand Dances", and "Something You Got" (Instant)–dance songs whose heavy beat and infectious atmosphere carried on the sound of Huey Smith's Clowns and its featured vocalists, Ford and Bobby Marchan. Marchan had a strange hit in 1960, for Fury, "There Is Something on Your Mind", written by S. Taylor, an adaptation of a song that had been a rhythm and blues hit for Big Jay McNeely the year before. The record opened with a chanted chorus of the song, but after a few seconds, Marchan stopped and proceeded to give the listener some advice:

You know it's so hard to be in love with someone,
So hard to be in love with someone that don't love you,
And it carries a heavy burden on your heart
To know that the someone they love is your very best
friend.
I tell you, when somebody else is rockin' your cradle
Better than you can rock your cradle yourself,
There is only one thing left in this world for you to do:
Pack your clothes,
Turn around,
Walk slowly towards the door,
Look over your shoulder,
And say, [the music begins]

"If you ever think about me,
If I ever cross your mind,
Well you know, you know I'm yours,
I, I know, I know you're mine". [the music stops again]

After you can't stand it no more,
You go down town to the pawnshop
And get yourself a pistol,
And then you make it back up on the scene
Where your loved one and your best friend are now together,
You go right in and bust down the door and shoot him;
You can't shoot her because you know if you shoot her
All of your love in your long life-time will be gone forever;
And just as you make up your mind to forgive her
Here come another of your best friends through the door;
This really makes you blow your top,
And you go right ahead and draw her close to your heart
And shoot her,
And realizin' what you done, you say
"Baby please forgive me, I'm sorry",
And with her last dyin' breath she looks up at you and says
"Do, do, do, whoa, who-oh, [the music returns]
Do, do, do whoah, who-oh. . . ."

Bobby Robinson's Fire/Fury Records was the only company based outside New Orleans to have regular productions in the city. On Fire/Fury he also recorded other local and regional styles in the southern states and on the Eastern Seaboard. The Memphis harmonica player Buster Brown had hits with raw bar blues songs, "Fannie Mae" and "Sugar Babe", two of the least sophisticated records to have wide sales during the sixties. The jump singer-pianist Wilbert Harrison had a million-seller with "Kansas City", a fine relaxed shuffle dance song featuring firm rhythm guitar by Jimmy Spruill in an arrangement close to the original recording of the song, "K. C. Lovin'" by Little Willie Littlefield (Federal 1952).

Brown, Harrison, Bobby Marchan, and several other good but less successful singers (including Tarheel Slim, Elmore James, and Hal Paige and the Whalers), recorded excellent rhythm and blues songs for Fire and Fury through 1961, but the labels also issued records with strong gospel influence. Gladys Knight and the Pips, with "Every Beat of My Heart", and Don Gardner and Dee Dee Ford with "I Need Your Loving", and others, were among the first singers to have hits with a style that obviously depended on church-singing influences.

Once the gospel-styled singing and uptown rhythm and blues productions began to dominate the entire range of black singing styles, the number of blues-influenced singers actively recording declined, and most of the companies that lasted into the early sixties either switched mainly to soul music or folded. In New York, Juggy Murray's Sue* operation had once looked set to bridge the gap between authentic rhythm and blues and commercial pop, with three top forty hits by Ike and Tina Turner, 1960–62, and top ten hits by Barbara George ("I Know", AFO, 1962) and Inez Foxx ("Mockingbird", Symbol, 1963). But the company lay virtually dormant through the rest of the sixties, and surfaced only briefly in 1970 when Wilbert Harrison had a surprising top forty hit with "Let's Work Together", an engagingly simple rearrangement of a song he had previously recorded as "Lets Stick Together" for Bobby Robinson's Fury label. Having had five records top the rhythm and blues charts in 1959–62, Bobby Robinson's labels† were also quiet for almost twenty years, until Enjoy returned with several "rapping" hits in the early eighties.

Minit and Instant‡ followed Sue and Fire/Fury into obscurity,

* SUE. *Formed in 1958 in New York by Juggy Marray.*
Rhythm and blues. Bobby Hendricks, Ike and Tina Turner, Jimmy McGriff, Baby Washington, Wilbert Harrison, the Soul Sisters.

Subsidiary:

SYMBOL
Rhythm and blues: Inez and Charlie Foxx,
Distributed label:
AFO. *Formed in 1961 in New Orleans by Harold Battiste and Mel Lastie.*
Rhythm and blues: Barbara George, Prince La La.

† FIRE. *Formed in 1959 in New York by Bobby Robinson.*
Blues: Buster Brown, Elmore James, Lightnin' Hopkins.
Rhythm and blues: Bobby Marchan, Don Gardner and Dee Dee Ford, Tarheel Slim and Little Ann.

Subsidiaries:

FURY
Rhythm and blues: Lee Dorsey, Wilbert Harrison, Gladys Knight and the Pips.
ENJOY
Rhythm and blues: King Curtis.

‡ MINIT. *Formed in 1960 in New Orleans by Joe Banashak and Larry McKinley. Distributed by Imperial. A&R: Allen Toussaint.*
Rhythm and blues: Jessie Hill, Ernie K-Doe, Aaron Neville, Benny Spellman, Irma Thomas.
Vocal group: the Showmen.

and the decline of these companies left room for other Southern-based companies to meet the enduring demand for blues and basic rhythm and blues. In Shreveport, Louisiana, veteran distributor Stan Lewis set up Jewel Records and a family of subsidiary labels*, and in Nashville Mercury's A&R man Shelby Singleton quit to launch his own SSS International company†, having bought out the Sun catalogue from Sam Phillips. Both men had freak international pop hits, Lewis with John Fred's "Judy in Disguise" (Paula, 1967), and Singleton with Jeannie C. Riley's "Harper Valley PTA" (Plantation, 1968), but their regular sales were in black music.

By the end of the sixties, the market for blues had been given an odd twist, as the emergence of white blues groups in Britain and the States brought belated recognition and demand for black blues-based performers whose own audience had basically disowned them. Records which had long been deleted and unobtainable began to be strung

---

Subsidiary:

INSTANT. *Distributed by Atlantic.*
Rhythm and blues: Chris Kenner.

* JEWEL. *Formed in 1964 in Shreveport, Louisiana by Stan Lewis.*
Blues: the Carter Brothers, Lightnin' Hopkins.

Subsidiaries:

PAULA
Pop: John Fred and His Playboy Band, the Uniques.
RONN
Rhythm and blues: Ted Taylor, Little Johnny Taylor.

† SSS International. *Formed in 1967 in Nashville by Shelby Singleton.*
Rhythm and blues: Peggy Scott and Jo Jo Benson, Johnny Adams.

Subsidiaries:

PLANTATION
Country and western: Jeannie C. Riley.

SILVER FOX. *Formed in 1968 by Lelan Rogers.*
Rhythm and blues: Betty Lavette, Gloria Taylor.
SUN RECORDS. *Bought from Sam Phillips (see p. 90 for roster).*

‡ ALL PLATINUM. *Formed in 1968 in Englewood, New Jersey by Sylvia and Joe Robinson.*
Rhythm and blues: George Kerr.

Subsidiaries:

STANG
Rhythm and blues: the Moments, Whatnauts.
TURBO
Rhythm and blues: Linda Jones.
VIBRATION
Rhythm and blues: Sylvia, Shirley and Co.
CHESS. *Bought from GRT (see p. 79 for rosters).*

together in compilation albums, and catalogue owners enjoyed unexpected income from overseas licensees. While most black music companies were interested in meeting contemporary tastes with "uptown rhythm and blues" and "soul", discussed in the next two chapters. All Platinum Records‡ took the canny step of acquiring the entire catalogue of Chess Records and reissuing for a new audience the works of Muddy, Wolf, Little Walter and the rest.

9

DO THAT AGAIN, THIS WAY: RHYTHM AND BLUES, UPTOWN

Once producers in the North had come to grips with rock 'n' roll they succeeded in re-establishing most of the techniques of popular music and took on any singer that was interested in reaching the teen audience. Almost all of the white singers–now called rock 'n' roll singers–stopped trying to represent personal experience in their records and dutifully sang the material that their producers handed to them, while the studio orchestra played the beat that enabled the company to promote the product as rock 'n' roll. And rock 'n' roll, which had seemed to be a significant expression of the adolescent culture, was revealed to be as transitory as any other pop style, a fashion with no genuine cultural roots. Or that was how it appeared at the time, 1959 to 1963. Events after 1964 suggested that rock 'n' roll, had cultural roots after all–that although the music industry lost interest in it, the audience who had bought the records did not, and kept listening to them.

In contrast to rock 'n' roll, rhythm and blues, which had seemed to be on the verge of extinction as a separate market and set of styles, recovered and flourished, despite the close attention by singers and producers to the tastes of the white audience. The comparative table overleaf shows the extent of the interchange between black and white singers in the two markets.

Black singers had gained unprecedented access to the white market through rock 'n' roll, but they were subject to proportionally greater competition from white singers in their own rhythm and blues market. In 1958, more than half the rhythm and blues hits were by white singers.

These figures, though, may have reflected the change in the policy of former exclusively black-oriented radio stations rather than measuring a real transformation of tastes in the black record-buying market. For a while, hoping to attract white listeners–and the advertisers wishing to reach them–former black-oriented radio stations played a substantial proportion of rock 'n' roll. As a result, the black audience may have known fewer black records and so bought those they heard on their radios. But because not enough

TOP TEN HITS IN THE NEGRO MARKET, 1955 to 1963

	1955	1956	1957	1958	1959	1960	1961	1962	1963
By white singers	3	10	27	45	20	26	9	15	23
Total number	64	81	78	86	71	90	98	92	90

TOP TEN HITS IN THE POP MARKET, 1955 to 1963

	1955	1956	1957	1958	1959	1960	1961	1962	1963
By black singers	9	8	22	16	20	24	37	27	37
Total number	51	55	70	77	89	95	106	88	106

advertisers responded to the opportunities of advertising to a white audience on the former rhythm and blues stations, most of the stations returned to a policy of playing mainly black records.

But, while the black stations could afford to cut down on the number of white records they played without risking the loss of many black listeners, the pop stations could not similarly cut down on black records–or a substantial number of their listeners would join the minority who turned to black stations anyway. Through the late fifties and early sixties, the radio programmers juggled the balance of white and black records, in effect operating a quota system. The aim seemed to be to play as few black records as possible, without actually losing listeners. Kal Rudman, rhythm and blues columnist in the trade paper *Record World*, wrote:

> I have worked at enough pop stations to know where the basic problem is buried. Some pop p.ds [programme directors] (but far from all) would like to be hip and broad-minded by playing these great rhythm songs and great soul ballads. However, the owners and managers are sensitive to criticism from their "high sassiety" cronies at the country club. Some are afraid that their sponsors might be offended, so they rush into the control room and yank out what they usually term "jungle" music. They don't want to hear the lyrics of the ballads or hear about the requests, record hop impact or even the sales of the driving "beat" sounds. If it sounds "too colored", it has to go. Being R&B in form is thus equated with

contaminating the station or the audience. Meanwhile, the R&B stations never had it so good.[1]

Record company producers who worked with black singers had intricate problems–they had somehow to provide the audience with exciting and emotional music yet wrap the sound up in an arrangement that would get by radio station owners who hated "jungle" music. There were plenty of people ready to accept the challenge, young songwriters and producers who had been attracted into popular music by the new opportunities available to enterprising people operating independently of the established record companies and publishers.

With some exceptions (notably the records associated with the twist), records produced in the North and West after 1958 were considerably more sophisticated than those of the rock 'n' roll era. The singers and writers of rock 'n' roll had seemed to become suddenly aware of the noise, violence and excitement of city life–and to be in a hurry to get their feelings on record. But after 1958 the black singers and the writers who worked with them took all that for granted and dealt with their experience in a more sophisticated way. Singers were less blithely confident and allowed for doubts and emotional contradictions, while the writers worked out their themes more thoroughly, often analysing feelings in an allusory way. Instead of the direct celebration of Little Richard's "Long Tall Sally", Ben E. King used the metaphor of a rose in "Spanish Harlem". Compared to the far more complex songs of rock in the late sixties, the attempts at poetry were clumsy but often much better integrated with their musical arrangements.

The best generic term for the music produced in northern studios with black singers as interpreters of other people's songs is "uptown rhythm and blues". The term embraces several distinct kinds of music that were generally worked on by different producers seeking different effects, but they shared an important difference from rock 'n' roll: their intention was to create an effect rather than to express the singer's own experience. Although most of the singers were black, a few–including some of the most successful–were white, notably the Four Seasons and the Righteous Brothers, who used all the effects of uptown rhythm and blues production techniques.

Rock 'n' roll had multidimensional impact–through the strength of the lyrics, the personal relevance of the singing styles, the visual effect of the performers, and the physical force of the music's rhythms. The various kinds of uptown rhythm and blues producers sought to isolate each of these effects and re-create them in a calculated way.

In New York, Jerry Leiber and Mike Stoller pioneered a technique of producing records that attempted to realize an idea conceived by a songwriter who was not himself a singer. The focus of each record was on the lyric, and to showcase it effectively, the musical arrangements and vocal harmony were often stressed more than the lead singer's vocal style–although the lasting quality of the records often depended finally on how well the singer expressed the feelings of the lyric. Because a vocal group tended to have a less fixed vocal image than a solo singer, and so was more flexible and could more easily be shaped by a producer, a large number of New York productions were with groups. From 1961, however, the technique was applied with equal success to solo singers.

The majors handled uptown rhythm and blues with solo singers differently, encouraging the singers to stress the idiosyncrasies of their style to such an extent that they became mannered. The effect contradicted the intention. The companies had been attracted by the singers because of their unusually expressive voices, but by over-emphasizing their distinctive styles rendered their performances unconvincing. Ray Charles at ABC-Paramount and Sam Cooke at RCA were among those to suffer.

In Philadelphia, the producers at Cameo/Parkway used a local nationally networked TV show to promote singers who moved energetically to a mechanically rigid beat, and were depressingly effective in launching the careers of several modestly talented singers.

In Detroit, a team of producers led by Berry Gordy identified the most effective qualities of each technique and reintegrated them in records released by the Motown Corporation's labels, to create what was really the first coherent rock and roll style of the North.

I

Jerry Leiber and Mike Stoller, having established the Coasters as one of the funniest rock 'n' roll acts, started working in 1959 with a new group, the Drifters.* The styles of group singing that were modelled on the pure innocence of the Orioles were still successful through 1958, when excellent recording studios enhanced the clear sound of the Dubs ("Could This Be Magic?", Gone), the Danleers ("One Summer Night", Mercury), and the Flamingos ("I Only Have Eyes

* *The first Drifters has been formed by Clyde McPhatter in 1953, and the group continued to exist after he left them to go solo in 1954. But after a series of relatively unsuccessful records featuring a variety of other lead singers and styles–including the excellent blues-influenced "I Gotta Get Myself A Woman"/"Soldier of Fortune" (1956)–the group disbanded in 1958, leaving manager George Treadwell with several years left in a contract for the Drifters to appear annually at the Apollo Theatre in Harlem. Treadwell persuaded another group, the Five Crowns, to take the name of the Drifters and appear at the Apollo and also arranged for them to continue the recording contract with Atlantic. It was this group that worked with Leiber and Stoller.*

for You", End). But, as usual, Leiber and Stoller showed little enthusiasm for following what had already been successfully tried, and with the Drifters experimented instead with the combination of a high gospel-styled lead voice, a loosely structured song, and an accompaniment that featured a violin section which played rocking riffs as saxophones had done in more conventional records. The sounds fitted each other, and the record made the pop top ten–"There Goes My Baby":

There goes my baby,
Moving on, down the line,
Wonder where
She is bound.
I broke her heart
And made her cry–
Now I'm alone,
So all alone,
What can I do?

The song was virtually free form, almost unique in a time when rhyming lines were mandatory–no matter how tenuous the rhyme, as between such common pairs of words as "time" and "mime", "love" and "of", and "going to" ("gonna") and "want to" ("wanna").

Despite the success of the song, the next records by the Drifters were less revolutionary. As lead singer Ben E. King gradually lowered the register of his voice and cut out the gospel inflections, the songs became more conventional and a Latin rhythm became more pronounced. "Dance with Me" (1959), "This Magic Moment", and "Save the Last Dance for Me" (1960) all made the top ten, after which King left the group to establish a solo career under the supervision of the same producers.

The Drifters' "Dance with Me" was credited to "Elmo Glick and Lewis Lebish" (Leiber and Stoller in jokey disguise), but the next Drifters' hits were written by Jerome "Doc" Pomus and Mort Shuman, pop writers who worked with a variety of styles ("Teenager in Love", a "teen-beat" song by Dion and the Belmonts, was among their hits), invariably producing material that was close to being as sentimental as traditional pop songs were, thereby needing exceptional interpretations by singers to rescue it. Ben E. King's performance on "Save the Last Dance for Me" remarkably raised that song out of its trite setting and made it movingly sad, although King was not helped by the Spanish guitars and lush strings that prevented any kind of improvization by the rest of the Drifters.

When King left the group, his first solo session (for the Atlantic subsidiary Atco) was supervised by a Leiber and Stoller apprentice, Phil Spector, who part-composed (with Leiber) King's first record, "Spanish Harlem":

There is a rose in Spanish Harlem,
A rare rose up in Spanish Harlem,
It is a special one,
It's never seen the sun,
It only comes up when the moon is on the run
And all the stars are gleaming.
It's growing in the street,
Right up through the concrete,
But soft and sweet and dreaming.

King moved from the attempt in this record to capture a city feeling on to more conventional "entertainer" songs, beautiful ballads that he performed with suitable care for the deliberate lyrics–"Stand By Me", "I (Who Have Nothing)", both 1962. Meanwhile the Drifters recruited Rudy Lewis to sing lead in a similar style to King's and had a series of hits that examined life in the city more directly and thoroughly than any previous popular songs had done. "Up on the Roof" (1962), written by Gerry Goffin and Carole King, offered escape:

When this old world starts getting me down
And people are just too much for me to face,
I climb right up to the top of the stairs
And all my cares just drift right into space.

"On Broadway" (1963), written by Barry Mann, Cynthia Weil, Jerry Leiber, and Mike Stoller, accepted the terms of the city's challenge:

They say the neon lights are bright,
On Broadway;
They say there's always magic in the air,
On Broadway;
But when you're walking down that street,
And you ain't had enough to eat,
The glitter all rubs right off

And you're nowhere,
On Broadway.

In amongst the swirling strings was a simple but effective blues guitar solo, which gave the record just the edge to keep it more "rhythm and blues" than "pop". Johnny Moore resumed as lead singer on the group's next big hit, "Under the Boardwalk" (1964), which became one of the definitive summer songs. Bert Berns produced, returning to the baion groove of earlier Drifters' hits.

The Drifters' records became the models for the "production" records of the early sixties, as a generation of sophisticated young adult writers and producers devoted their considerable talents to producing a body of records which detailed with obsessive attention every conceivable moment of teenage lives and fantasies.

Frankie Lymon's "Why Do Fools Fall in Love" had set up the theme and sound for this teen-talk genre back in 1956, and since then Paul Anka, Howie Greenfield (for Neil Sedaka), and Mort Shuman (with Doc Pomus) had shown a consistent feel for expressing teen thoughts in songs. In 1961, the teen world opened up even more, when the first black girl singers came to the centre stage, led by the Shirelles with "Will You Love Me Tomorrow". This was the first hit for Columbia Screen Gems' writers Gerry Goffin and Carole King, the start of a remarkable run for both the publisher and the writers.

Produced for Scepter Records by Luther Dixon, the Shirelles scored seven top twenty hits in three years, featuring lead singer Shirley Owens who achieved a captivating blend of sincerity and suggestiveness as she wondered: "Can I believe the magic of his sighs?" Only four black girl groups had previously made the top twenty before, two having mainly been used to back up male singers like Ray Charles and Lloyd Price, but now they became a permanent element in pop. The Shirelles continued to define the sound and image of vulnerable and suppliant availability that were showcased over and over in the black-girl records. After "Will You Love Me Tomorrow" topped the chart, their previous revival of "Dedicated to the One I Love" gave Scepter a second, simultaneous top ten hit, followed by "Mama Said" (written by Luther Dixon) and "Baby It's You" (by Burt Bacharach and Hal David). As so often, the group's success was inextricably dependant on the direction of producer Dixon, and when he left to form his own Ludix label, sponsored and distributed by Capitol, the Shirelles' career went into decline.

Scepter* had been formed in 1959 by Florence Greenberg specifically as an outlet for the Shirelles, whom she had managed while they had one minor success on Decca ("I Met Him on Sunday", 1958), but rather than pursue other girl groups for the label, she favoured more intense, gospel-based singers including the Isley Brothers and Chuck Jackson, until songwriters Burt Bacharach and Hal David launched Dionne Warwick as the flawless voice for their sophisticated arrangements.

Among the writers and producers who followed the Shirelles more directly, Carole King and Gerry Goffin and the Tokens made the best records, although if Luther Dixon had continued to use Goffin and King's songs with the Shirelles, it is possible that they would not have needed to produce their own outlets. But it was seemingly a natural reflex in the industry, that every producer wanted to monopolize the song-writing on his own projects, which effectively forced other writers to set up in competition if they were to get their material recorded.

Tired of the humilating rounds of plugging his demos to the industry's A&R men, in 1962 Don Kirshner formed Dimension Records as an outlet for Goffin and King. In short order, the duo wrote and produced several classic girl-talk records, along with one of the all-time great dance records, "The Loco-motion" by Little Eva. Compared with most records of the time, this was extremely well recorded, with a very clear sound at the bottom that enabled the solid groove of the rhythm track to have maximum impact. Carole played piano herself, Art Kaplan took the sax part, and the whole record burned with an infectious energy that inspired the new singer to deliver a perfect "come on and have a good time" kind of vocal. The record gave Dimension a number one hit first time out, and in its wake "Keep Your Hands Off My Baby" put Eva back in the top twenty, but she was less convincing where the tough lyric required a more defiant tone, and her second-best performance was in duet with

*SCEPTER RECORDS. *Formed in 1959 in New York by Florence Greenberg. A&R: Luther Dixon, Burt Bacharach and Hal David.*
Girl group: the Shirelles.
Rhythm and blues: Tommy Hunt, Dionne Warwick.
Pop: the Rocky Fellers, B. J. Thomas and the Triumphs.

Subsidiary:

WAND
Rhythm and blues: the Isley Brothers, Chuck Jackson, Maxine Brown.
Pop: the Kingsmen.

†DIMENSION. *Formed in 1962 in New York by Don Kirshner as a division of Aldon Music. A&R: Gerry Goffin and Carole King.*
Girl group: the Cookies.
Girl-talk: Little Eva, Carole King.

Big Dee Irwin on a revival of "Swinging on a Star" for Colpix in 1963.

Dimension's other successes were with the Cookies, a vocal group who had been on various sessions backing up other singers during the early sixties, and lead singer Earl Jean was suitably despondent (in "Chains") and coy (in "Don't Say Nothin' Bad About My Baby") for the records to hit the top twenty. Carole King joined in the fray herself with "It Might As Well Rain Until September", but waited another ten years before committing herself to a real singing career. It was more comfortable writing hits for other people, which she and her husband Gerry Goffin did better than anyone else at the time.

Among all the anonymous and mostly-interchangeable groups who followed up the success of the Shirelles, the most distinctive and consistent was another quartet of black girls, the Chiffons. The group had made its debut in 1960 with a cover of an early Shirelles song, "Tonight's the Night", but effectively started in 1963 with the chart-topping "He's So Fine". Written by a friend of theirs from the South Bronx, Ronnie Mack, the song had an unusual, almost jazzy lilt to it, and lead singer Judy Craig sang it with a mature sophistication that contrasted with the deliberately "little girl" voices of so many of the other girl groups. The record was produced by the Tokens, who had never found a follow-up to their own top-of-the-chart hit for RCA in 1961, a revival of the Weavers' "Wimoweh" (retitled "The Lion Sleeps Tonight"), and they solved the follow-up problem for the Chiffons by adding the group's voices to a track already recorded by Goffin and King of their song, "One Fine Day". There was a lull after that top five hit, but Judy Craig's voice made even mediocre material sound interesting, and in 1965 she created a haunting mood on "Nobody Know What's Going On In My Head But Me" before delivering one last top ten hit for the group with "Sweet Talking Guy".

At the time, most of these girl-talk records passed by in a blur of teen pop music, and no girl group established the kind of identity which Jan and Dean and the Beach Boys built up around themselves on the West Coast. But two men did manage to make careers and lasting reputations out of this genre, Berry Gordy and Phil Spector.

While most producers of the era went for image or a dance beat first, and the song second, Gordy always insisted on the song being the prime focus of every record, and forced his writers to hone their material into distinctive vignettes of teenage experience. Smokey Robinson responded with "Shop Around" for the Miracles (Tamla, 1960), which he sang in so high a voice some listeners thought he was a she, and then with a series of hits for Mary Wells culminating in the classic "My Guy" (Motown, 1964). Meanwhile, Gordy and his team of writer-producers including Mickey Stevenson, Lamont Dozier and

Brian Holland took turns with the Marvelettes, whose "Please Mr Postman" (Tamla, 1961) launched the "mashed potato" dance beat that was widely copied (by Dee Dee Sharp, Little Eva, and even James Brown). With justice, Berry Gordy had "The Sound of Young America" inscribed on his record labels (see pp. 210–219).

Phil Spector's legend was "Tomorrow's Sound Today", and he lived out his promise with a series of painstakingly-produced classics on his own Philles label, formed in partnership with Lester Sill in 1961. Early releases sounded conventional, but Spector hit his stride and the top of the chart in 1962 with the Crystals' "He's a Rebel": "See the way he walks down the street, see the way he shuffles his feet". Gene Pitney's words were effectively delivered by Darlene Love (drafted in from the Blossoms to sing lead), and Spector generated enough income to enable him to indulge his vision of how record production could be transformed. He crammed the Gold Star studio in Hollywood with several pianos, guitarists, and drum kits, and gave arranger Jack Nitzsche and engineer Larry Levine the task of somehow creating enough space for everything to be heard. The thunderous percussive sound of "Da Doo Ron Ron" and "Then He Kissed Me" by the Crystals (with La La Brooks as lead singer) demonstrated Spector's ambitions, while the Ronettes brought a startling visual image to the Spector Sound. Hooded eye make-up, heavy lipstick, grotesquely piled-up hair–the Ronettes exuded a street-toughened sensuality that seemed to say, do you dare? Not everyone who bought their "Be My Baby" could have taken up their challenge.

Spector's reputation as an idiosyncratic loner began to grow, but he was hardly a household name when he made an unusual arrangement with Moonglow Records of Los Angeles to sub-contract the Righteous Brothers in 1964. For the white duo's first session he assembled his biggest studio orchestra yet, and hired Gene Page to arrange the instrumental back-drop to "You've Lost That Lovin' Feelin'" (written with Barry Mann and Cynthia Weil). Alternating between ecstatic crescendos and restful pauses, Bill Medley sang the verses in a warm baritone, and Bobby Hatfield came in with high tenor harmonies on the choruses. Spector was obviously determined to evoke and supercede the emotional records made in the mid-fifties by the Platters and Roy Hamilton, and with this masterful production he brought himself to the attention of those people who had not previously been aware of the role of a record producer. Spector restricted the output of his own label to a few records per year, which he produced with intense concentration and an assumption that if he did his job right they would be hits. In 1966, he made what he justifiably considered to be the masterpiece of his career: "River Deep, Mountain High" by Ike and Tina Turner. Returning to Jeff Barry and Ellie Greenwich, who had written most of his earlier hits,

Spector showed again how he could turn their naïve images and sentimental clichés into what became virtually a philosophy of life for the singer, by generating such a dramatic musical structure that the whole performance was undeniable. Tina sang with an unrelenting passion, and Spector filled every space and every moment with an arresting sound. Inexplicably, American radio programmers ignored the record, but the rest of the world was impressed, particularly Britain, where its success drew attention to Ike and Tina for the first time, and provided the basis for regular tours by their Revue.

The American failure of "River Deep, Mountain High" distressed Spector so much that he temporarily retired from the business, and although he later came back to work on various successful projects, including the last records by the Beatles, he had made his best records in the five years from 1962 to 1966. And just as Leiber and Stoller had introduced the concept of a producer's role into the industry, so now Spector expanded the concept of the role, focusing attention on himself both within the industry, by adopting a confident (some would have said, arrogant) attitude towards his peers, and in the outside world, where "the Spector Sound" became a familiar term. Inevitably, other producers mimicked his sound and spent fortunes on interminable studio sessions with armies of musicians in an attempt to emulate his success, but Spector had effectively achieved most of what could be done to maximize volume in the studio with live music: most of his records were played all in one take, an approach which faded out as multi-track recording equipment allowed musicians to contribute their parts one-by-one. Of the producers who adopted a similar "dominating" role on their projects, directing their singers as "puppet" vehicles for their own ideas, the most effective were those who took the opposite tack to Phil Spector, and stripped down the musical and sound elements of their records to a minimum.

Abner Spector, an unrelated producer from Chicago, made one classic girl-talk record in 1963 with the Jaynetts, a girl group from the Bronx whose "Sally Go 'Round the Roses" (Tuff) owed its eerie menace to the arrangement by pianist Artie Butler. Neither the producer nor the group did anything else of note, but Butler went on to arrange most of the hits on Red Bird Records by the Shangri Las, a quartet of white girls from Queens, New York.

Red Bird* was a venture of writer-producers Jerry Leiber and

*RED BIRD. *Formed in 1964 by Jerry Leiber, Mike Stoller and George Goldner. A&R: Jeff Barry, Ellie Greenwich, George "Shadow" Morton.*
Girl groups: the Shangri Las, the Dixie Cups, Jelly Beans.
Subsidiary:
BLUE CAT
Rhythm and blues: Alvin Robinson.
Mixed group: the Ad Libs.

Mike Stoller to consolidate their future by channelling some of the talented young writers who had worked with them at Atlantic, particularly Jeff Barry and Ellie Greenwich who were signed to Leiber and Stoller's Trio Music (and the only leading New York team not signed to Columbia Screen Gems). George Goldner had been bought out of his own companies by Roulette, and he came in to guide Red Bird's first release, the Dixie Cups' "Chapel of Love," to the top of the American charts in the teeth of the British Invasion in 1964. This was a Spector–Greenwich–Barry song previously recorded by the Ronettes. But where the Dixie Cups were just one more trio of black girls to confuse with all the others, the Shangri Las sounded and looked different; and not just because they were white.

White girls had been moving in on the teen-talk genre for a while: the Angels topped the chart in 1963 with "My Boyfriend's Back" (Smash) written by Feldman–Goldstein–Gottehrer with a sharper edge than was typical for this kind of record, and Lesley Gore scored with a series of hits for Mercury including "It's My Party (And I'll Cry If I Want To)" (1963), which explored every angle of being a teenager. In Britain, Helen Shapiro spoke for everyone when she sang "Don't Treat Me Like a Child" (UK Columbia, 1961).

George "Shadow" Morton, who produced the Shangri Las, took the teen-lament theme to new, epic, extremes, using minimal musical accompaniment, though sometimes elaborated by "documentary" sound effects (shrieking seagulls in "Remember (Walking in the Sand)", squealing tyres in "Leader of the Pack") to enhance the credibility of lead singer Mary Weiss' deadpan voice. The Shangri Las summarized and finalized the girl-talk genre, which more or less ended when Red Bird closed down in 1966.

In all that teen-talk, where were the boys? Mostly out on their own–solo singers Roy Orbison, Gene Pitney, Del Shannon and Dion all worked in this idiom–but one group did fashion a career from a series of songs which could be heard as answers to the girl groups: the Four Seasons.

Bob Crewe, up from Philadelphia, was mainly responsible for bringing the group out of obscurity to become America's best-selling singles act of the sixties, but they did have two major assets: the phenomenal falsetto shriek of lead singer Frankie Valli, who did not just reach high notes but attacked them, and song-writer Bob Gaudio, who had a flair for rhythmic and melodic songs that were crammed with sing-along hooks. Other groups featured falsetto lead vocals had all found great difficulty in avoiding "novelty" status, and were consigned as "one-hit wonders": the Skyliners, Marcels (both from Pittsburgh), Maurice Williams and the Zodiacs, Tokens, and Gene Chandler had all had recent hits without establishing careers when the Four Seasons crashed through to the top of the charts with "Sherry" for Vee Jay in 1962. Bob Crewe marshalled the sound to a stomping beat, adding hand-claps and tambourine to make sure dancers got the point, doubling-up on the dance floor the impact of Valli's voice on transistor radio speakers. Seventeen top twenty hits followed, including two more chart-toppers for Vee Jay, "Big Girls Don't Cry" (1962) and "Walk Like a Man" (1963). Switching to Philips in 1964, Crewe brought in Charles Calello as arranger on more "boy-to-girl talk" ("Dawn", "Rag Doll") and then introduced relief writers Sandy Linzer and Denny Randell; they kept up the flow of hits with the exhilarating "Let's Hang On" (1965) and "Working My Way Back to You" (1966) and also gave Crewe a huge hit for his Dyno-Voice label by the Toys, a semi-classical classic girl-talk hit based on a Bach fugue and called "A Lover's Concerto".

II

The relative diversity and adapability of vocal groups made them particularly attractive to producers who used singers as interpreters of songwriters' material rather than as individuals with their own emotions and ideas to express. Solo singers, on the other hand, usually had a more definite personal style which required particular material to be written for it. Even so, most of the records made by solo black singers between 1958 and 1963 seemed as much determined by market research findings as by personal conviction. The best and most influential solo singers of this period were Clyde McPhatter, Ray Charles, Lloyd Price, Sam Cooke, Jackie Wilson, and Brook Benton, all of whom recorded for major companies.

McPhatter and Ray Charles shared the advantage of having worked for some years with Ahmet Ertegun and Jerry Wexler at Atlantic. McPhatter, one of the first rhythm and blues singers to use a gospel style, with the Dominoes in 1951, had a million seller (for Atlantic) in 1958, with "A Lover's Question". The record used an arrangement very similar to those used by harmony gospel groups (such as the Dixie Hummingbirds), with a bass singer providing a vocal equivalent of a double bass rhythm while McPhatter wailed the melodic, plaintive lyric. Rich guitar chords on an earlier record, "Treasure of Love" (1956), and vibes on the later "Long Lonely Nights" varied the background to McPhatter's voice without intruding on his style, which was widely imitated, most successfully by Dee Clark, Bobby Day, and Jimmy Jones. In 1960 McPhatter's manager had him move to MGM, where conventional string accompaniments jarred with his erratic phrasing, and a year later he went to Mercury, who used him as a novelty/dance song specialist. The individual characteristics of McPhatter largely disappeared in the efforts to accommodate a mass market.

Ray Charles, moving from Atlantic to ABC-Paramount in 1960, experienced, though less immediately, a similar change. For most of his time with Atlantic he was allowed and encouraged, not always to his advantage, to develop his experiments with gospel vocal styles and musical structures, absorbing nursery songs ("Swanee River", "My Bonnie") and pre-war standards ("Come Rain or Come Shine") into his repertoire with varying degrees of success. Working with jazz musicians (including Milt Jackson of the Modern Jazz Quartet), he helped to bring jazz out of the abstract improvizations and random rhythms of bop, back towards what Charlie Mingus, Horace Silver, and Bobby Timmons talked of as "the roots", "funky music", "soul".

Having established Ray Charles as a major figure in both rhythm and blues and jazz, Atlantic attacked popular music in 1959, with "What'd I Say?" Opening with several bars repeating a bass note figure played on the then still novel electric piano, the song developed into a re-creation of a revivalist meeting, with Charles declaring his love for a woman instead of God but screaming, preaching, and haranguing his congregation in an otherwise authentic manner.

Before Atlantic could marshal its resources to follow up the success of "What'd I Say?", ABC-Paramount contracted the singer. Atlantic was able to do no more than repackage all of Charles's previous material, much of which was a revelation to the people who had just discovered him, and was very influential both on the styles of many young white singers and on the taste of their audience. Meanwhile, ABC-Paramount recorded him on a succession of records doing material similar to songs he had done for Atlantic–songs, that is, in sympathy with his style and approach: "Georgia on My Mind", a class song with strings and choir, was like "Come Rain or Come Shine"; "Sticks and Stones" and "Them That Got" were social realist pieces, like "Greenbacks"; "Hit the Road, Jack", was the gospel call-and-response song, after "What'd I Say?". An LP, *Genius Plus Soul Equals Jazz,* arranged by Quincy Jones, allowed the musician/bandleader to run free and produced some fine big band jazz and the bonus of a top ten single, the organ instrumental "One Mint Julep".

The arrangements and material that Charles used in his first two years with ABC-Paramount suggested a considerable change in the company's policy towards rhythm and blues from the one indicated by Lloyd Price's earlier releases. Price had joined ABC-Paramount in 1957, three years before, and was one of the first former rhythm and blues singers to be subjected to a major company's intensive production techniques. The formula was to surround the singer with a barrage of sound and rhythm, amid which he made his presence felt as best he could. Jaunty melodies and catchy choruses were added, and the combination produced some of the biggest hits of 1958 and 1959; "Stagger Lee", "Personality", We're Gonna Get Married". But in all this, there was little evidence of who Lloyd Price was.

With Charles, the company, initially at least, provided a much more open situation. Charles's style was much clearer and more evident in his first records for the company than was Price's. Charles did nothing as silly as "My Bonnie", and his best records, ("Hit The Road, Jack" in particular) were among the best he ever did, intense feeling tinged with humour, economical, imaginative musical arrangements, and strong lyrics.

But in 1962, he recorded "I Can't Stop Loving You", a country and western song in a strong personal style veered towards mannerism. The year before, Atlantic had recorded Solomon Burke with a country and western song, "Just Out of Reach", showing how easily a gospel-trained singer could adjust to the idiom. But whereas when singers raised on (white) country and western music had turned to (black) rhythm and blues, they had combined the strengths of two styles to create a dynamic new one, rock 'n' roll; now when gospel-styled singers used country and western material, they were exploiting the sweet and sentimental aspects of both musical cultures, seeking to entertain and not to express themselves. From 1962, Ray Charles degenerated, a musical decline closely matching that of Elvis Presley. Charles applied his style to anything, inevitably adjusting himself to awkward material, losing contact with the cultural roots that had inspired his style. His flair for sensing a potentially commercial sound, which had led him to experiment with new forms of rhythm and blues and popular music, gave way to a relentless determination to prove that his versatility was literally boundless. But increasingly he revealed the existence of material which could not benefit from his wracked vocals.

Sam Cooke was luckier, or more determined, in his experience with RCA-Victor, whose policy took the opposite direction from ABC-Paramount's, moving from the trivial to the personal. Cooke was contracted to the major company from Keen and, like Jesse Belvin, who was signed to the company two years earlier from Modern/Kent, was initially recorded with production techniques comparable to those which had applied at the Capitol sessions of Nat "King" Cole for the past fifteen years: interpret the material carefully and clearly and tastefully, with as little suggestion as possible of sexual relationships or deep feelings. Belvin was not allowed to establish much sense of himself in his RCA records, and his career was cut short by death.

His voice tended to be rich and deep, Cooke's to be high and pure. The two men were the most popular ballad singers in the black market after the death of Johnny Ace, and curiously, both died violently (as did Ace) within a few years of being contracted to RCA–Belvin in a car crash in 1960, and Cooke in a shooting incident in a Los Angeles hotel in 1964.

Cooke's first RCA records followed the pattern of his Keen hits, trivial sing-along songs which he sang beautifully. "Cupid" (1961) was charming, but "Chain Gang" (1960) was a travesty of the blues. In 1962, he recorded some "twist" songs, a genre that invariably reduced even good singers and composers to formula productions, but Cooke somehow imposed his character on the idiom in such records as "Havin' a Party" and "Twistin' the Night Away".

On the flipside of the first of these, he had a minor hit with a gospel arrangement on "Bring It On Home to Me" (in which he duetted with Lou Rawls, formerly with the Pilgrim Travellers and later a soul-entertainer with Capitol). The song was the first of several that Cooke wrote around a familiar phrase from the black culture, giving it a specific context and yet still implying all the meanings that the phrase was commonly identified with.

Well, if you ever
Change your mind
About leavin',
Leavin' me behind,
Whoa-whoa,
Bring it to me,
Bring your sweet lovin',
Bring it on home to me,
Yeah (yeah), Yeah (yeah), Yeah (yeah).

Rene Hall and Horace Ott provided Cooke's records with more sympathetic accompaniments than many other major company producers came up with. Inevitably they included strings more often than was necessary, but they also used a piano figure, guitar break, or saxophone solo to throw phrases back to the singer and so gave the records an intimate, personal feeling.

Cooke recorded LPs for the "easy listening" market, standards and calypsos, but also continued to make personal statements, most memorably in "A Change Is Gonna Come", which took a phrase out of the black culture and returned it loaded with even more meaning than it had previously implied, so that the song and the expression took on personal, religious, and political suggestions in the mood of growing confidence that had come to the black communities during the sixties:

I was born by the river,
In this little ol' town,
Just like the river,
I've been runnin' ever since.
It's been a long time comin',
But I know a change is gonna come.

"Good Times", "Somebody Ease My Troublin' Mind", and even the dance song "Shake" carried messages to the people who were listening and entertained those who weren't.

Jackie Wilson, another of the most popular singers during this period, also meant different things to white and black audiences, though in this case the source of the double meaning came from his performance, not his lyrics. On ballad songs like "A Woman, a Lover, a Friend", he sang in a soaring, intense melodramatic style, pitched somewhere between the Platters and Mario Lanza; but on other records, including "Doggin' Around", he sang with a more obviously gospel-based style. The conventional orchestral accompaniment on most of his records (for Brunswick) suggested that they were intended principally for the popular market, but in his live performances Wilson re-created the atmosphere of hysteria at revivalist meetings, tearing off half his clothes in frenzy, stirring his audience as Johnnie Ray and Elvis Presley had done, and as James Brown, still virtually unknown to the white audience, was doing.

The last of the most popular solo singers was the baritone Brook Benton. Although (like Wilson, McPhatter, and Cooke) a former gospel singer, Benton recorded with Mercury in a style that was modelled on the earlier crooning styles of Nat "King" Cole and Billy Eckstine. Emphasizing smooth control over his voice, Benton sang pop ballads against better-than-usual orchestrations of strings and made some good duets with Dinah Washington. Baritone singers who could maintain their style through this period, when most styles lost their individuality, were particularly rare. Roy Hamilton, who had been successful with "Unchained Melody" in 1955 (the versions by Les Baxter and Al Hibbler had sold better in the pop market, but Hamilton's had been the hit in the rhythm and blues market), was among the few who did not, like Benton, affect the warbling, crooning style established by Billy Eckstine. Hamilton had further hits in 1958 ("Don't Let Go") and 1961 ("You Can Have Her"), both uptempo songs using a gospel-style call-and-response structure.

During the early sixties, virtually all black baritone singers adopted either the crooning style of Benton or a gospel-tinged entertainer style, such as that used by Ben E. King and Chuck Jackson. From 1963 the emphasis on gospel inflections was to become more obvious, as the more personal "soul" style evolved and the influence of producers apparently decreased.

III

One of the indirect results of the tendency for producers to re-establish their position during the late fifties was the decline in importance of dance rhythms; words and sound became pre-eminent. But the visual and physical aspects of popular singers and music had always been crucial. Further, as films and television assumed major roles as media for communicating music, these aspects gained even greater potential. In 1960 the producers at a small independent in Philadelphia, Cameo-Parkway, recognizing the power of the media, began to promote singers and music whose value was almost entirely visual and physical–the words became immaterial–and gave commercial popular rock and roll a new turn.

After the success in 1956 of the Columbia film *Rock Around the Clock*, various Hollywood companies, including Columbia, went into the production of comparable films. Early reports of the Columbia follow-up said that it would be called *Rhythm and Blues*, but the film was released as *Don't Knock the Rock*, which perhaps can be seen as a defensive evasion representative of the entire entertainment industry's feelings about the domination of the national culture by a creation of the black culture.

Other films by various companies followed–*Rock Rock Rock* and *Mr Rock and Roll, Shake Rattle and Rock*, and *The Girl Can't Help It*. In contrast to the traditional screen musical, in which the songs had at least a formal relevance to the development of the narrative, these films generally were little more than a succession of filmed singing performances, strung together on a tenuous story which involved two or three non-singing characters in situations where they heard rock and roll singers. *The Girl Can't Help It* (directed by Frank Tashlin) was unusual both in its remarkable collection of several of the best rock 'n' roll singers–Gene Vincent, Little Richard, Fats Domino, and Eddie Cochran–and its strong story, witty in the situations involving Jayne Mansfield and Tom Ewell, realistic in its portrayal of the bitter competition between coin machine operators. One scene in the film had Jayne Mansfield swaggering past assorted males of all ages to a soundtrack accompaniment of Little Richard declaring, "The girl can't help it, the girl can't help it." The effect, underscored by the music, was that, seeing Mansfield, people's glasses cracked, milk bottles boiled over, and little boys became transfixed. Moments later the heroine was pictured with a bottle of milk clutched to each breast, leaning dramatically towards a modestly lustful Tom Ewell. In this film at least, the sensuous possibilities of rock and roll, though comically handled, were more directly expressed than they had been, for obvious reasons, on community radio stations.

The international impact of rock and roll owed a great deal to the Hollywood films, which, unlike the more conservative radio stations, introduced the new music in concentrated packages. Many of the films were also fairer to black singers than American radio stations tended to be–singers appeared in the films who had rarely been heard on network radio (Moonglows, Flamingos, Joe Turner)–and the appearances made the policy of covering records by white singers harder to sustain. Chuck Berry, Fats Domino, Little Richard, the Platters, and the Treniers all were in several films, though they were not allowed the extra prestige of speaking parts. They were treated strictly as performers and not as characters or people.

Television complemented the role of films, despite the fact that television producers took longer to devote entire programmes to rock 'n' roll than Hollywood producers did. Most of the shows that included rock 'n' roll singers were all-purpose entertainment shows, among them, Arthur Godfrey's talent-spotting show, Jackie Gleason's show, and the Ed Sullivan and Steve Allen shows. Godfrey played an important role in presenting rock 'n' roll (and rhythm and blues) to an audience that still hadn't heard the music much on the radio. Gleason's show featured rock 'n' roll less often, but made a crucial contribution to the music, and to Elvis Presley's career in particular, by giving Presley a spot for six successive weeks at the time of his first RCA-Victor release, "Heartbreak Hotel". Sullivan allowed Presley on his show provided he wore a dinner suit and the camera was kept above waist level.

The equivalent of the rock 'n' roll film in TV was pioneered by a station in Philadelphia, WFIL-TV, with its "Bandstand" programme. By July, 1956, the show's simple format–one hundred and fifty teenagers dancing to records, with interruptions from commercials and "personal appearances" by singers–attracted a sufficiently large audience to make it the city's top-rated daytime show. At this time, Dick Clark took over as host. A year later, with Clark still as master of ceremonies, the show was broadcast nationally, as "American Bandstand".

Broadcast every Saturday at noon, the programme was watched by enough of the nation's record-buying adolescents so that Philadelphia, always one of the cities to be quickest to pick up a new singer or style, became the nation's opinion leader in popular music. The rule of thumb became that what did well in Philly would probably do well elsewhere; what didn't move in that city was probably not worth pushing anywhere else. Glad to be able to identify a single place as being representative of the national market, the industry focused much of its attention on Philadelphia, and in particular on "American Bandstand".

Clark, as perhaps was to be expected, became subject to payola offers which rivalled those that Alan Freed had been able to consider, and the Philadelphia record companies found themselves exceptionally well placed to promote their product. Among these companies, Cameo-Parkway did well with Charlie Gracie, the Rays, John Zacherle, and Bobby Rydell; Chancellor had hits by Frankie Avalon and Fabian; Swan got Billie and Lillie and Freddy Cannon into the top ten.

A fuller use of television for presenting new performers and songs was still to come.

The pattern set by "American Bandstand" became the model for other local and network shows. Some elaborated on the models by having singers mime their records. (One reason for the miming was that many of the singers could not get close to the sound on their records without the complicated machinery of recording studio echo chambers and the watchful help of their producers).

A result of the audience dance format was that the previous pattern of locally differentiated dancing styles was replaced by a nationally homogenous set of styles derived from the programmes. Whereas previously a dance style might have taken up to a year to move across the country, becoming obsolete in one area as it was picked up in another, the turnover now became much faster. And the increase in turnover of styles modified the meaning of the word "change". Whereas previously the word had meant the substitution of one style for another, or at least a decisive alteration, it now came to mean a relatively minor modification. Since the change itself no longer was so clearcut, the emphasis put on it was increased. The process was most clearly demonstrated in the vast publicity attached to the "twist", acclaimed as an innovation as important as rock 'n' roll. The twist nonetheless was musically almost identical, and many record companies reissued, as twist records, material that had been recorded and issued earlier as rock 'n' roll. (*Do The Twist with Ray Charles*, from Atlantic, made the top forty LP charts.)

The twist was first conceived by Hank Ballard, whose original version of "The Twist" had been the B-side of his rhythm and blues hit "Teardrops on Your Letter", and only a minor hit in its own right (in 1959); a year later, he had much more success with "Finger Poppin' Time", a top ten pop hit which he delivered over a similar robotic beat and which was still on the chart in August 1960 when it was joined by Chubby Checker's cover version of "The Twist", issued on Parkway, a subsidiary of the Philadelphia label Cameo.

The company had been doing well with its "clean" rock and roll singer, Bobby Rydell, but he wasn't much of a dancer, and now that TV had assumed such importance, dancing abilities were something to be exploited. Checker was planned as a visual act by the company, and the plan worked. Aided by plenty of promotion and appearances by Checker on Clark's "American Bandstand", the record did well, and Checker followed up with other dance songs, "The Hucklebuck", "Pony Time". Although he could sing in a middle-range tenor, on the dance songs Checker adopted a high nasal tone, chanting the dance lyrics to the mechanical "twist" beat of the accompanists, and, on the TV programmes, dancing himself all the while. To a greater extent than any previous rock 'n' roll singer, Checker was a puppet who carried out the instructions of his producers.

A couple of other producers saw some of the possibilities opened up by Cameo-Parkway's venture into the twist. Beltone of New York cashed in with Bobby Lewis's "Tossin' and Turnin' ", a strident chant that broke records for the length of its stay in the best sellers, through the summer of 1961. Frank Guida, an East Coast producer, formed Le Grand records and set up Gary Bonds, formerly a member of the vocal group the Turks, as "U.S. Bonds", who sang in an atmosphere of contrived gaiety–but with more conviction than the other twist singers–such records as "New Orleans", "Quarter to Three", and "School Is Out", all of which used the hard beat of the twist to gain an identity. Still, there was not immediately too much to indicate that Cameo-Parkway's promotion was going to have much more impact than that of a minor, temporary fad. With perhaps more hope than confidence, the company had Checker record "Let's Twist Again" for the summer vacation of 1961.

This time the dance was promoted not only to the teenage audience but to the adult discotheque audience in New York. Roulette joined in by having Joey Dee and the Starlighters record "Peppermint Twist" at the end of the year, and, for a second time, in January, 1962, Checker's own "The Twist" again topped the best sellers. With this success dance music was thoroughly established, and a marvellous range of new dance names, though not new rhythms, was concocted to give people something "new" to do. Cameo-Parkway was behind many of the names, including "Mashed Potato Time" and "Ride" (Dee Dee Sharp), "Bristol Stomp" (the Dovells), and "Wah-Watusi" (the Orions)–all hits; Chubby Checker went on to "The Fly", "Slow Twisting", and "Limbo Rock". Occasionally, a relatively authentic dance was introduced, such as the "Pop Eye", first recorded by Huey Smith and the Clowns, the New Orleans group, but then picked up by Parkway for Checker and by Jamie for the Sherrys. Goffin and King invented (for Little Eva) the "Loco-motion", borrowing a musical arrangement previously used by Detroit's Berry Gordy (for the Marvelettes in "Please Mr. Postman") whose work, discussed next, started a whole new sound by itself–the Motown sound.

The isolation of rhythm as the dominant part of popular music distorted the music's character, and none of the successful records had much to recommend them beyond their insistent beat. It was perhaps more than a coincidence that at the same time a series of records that were throwbacks to the pure cool groups, in which the mood was gentle and the style cool, also were popular. Jimmy Charles, with "A Million to One" (Promo), had one of the first big hits of this kind, in August, 1960. During the first months of 1961, the Miracles with "Shop Around" (Tamla), Shep and the Limelites with "Daddy's Home" (Hull), and the Jive Five with "My True Story" (Beltone) deepened nostalgic recollection. In the same period, several companies began issuing compilations of hits from the group rock 'n' roll era. Original Sound's *Oldies But Goodies*, a series of five volumes consisting of hits from 1954–58, made the best selling LP lists. Alan Freed compiled three careful collections of hits (for End) to represent an era he had helped to create.

IV

During the nineteen-sixties, one company, Berry Gordy's in Detroit, seemed to coordinate all the various trends and production techniques that had developed randomly elsewhere, and to apply the conclusions that could be drawn from them.

From 1957 to 1959, Berry Gordy worked as an independent producer, leasing material by Marv Johnson to United Artists and by the Miracles to Chess. In 1959 Gordy's sister Anna formed a label in Detroit–Anna–which had hits by Barrett Strong ("Money"), Joe Tex, and others. A year later, Gordy formed a record company, Tammie, later renamed Tamla.

Gordy had already formed a publishing firm, Jobete, which published all the material written by him (for Johnson, Jackie Wilson, and others) and by Smokey Robinson, lead singer for the Miracles and writer of the group's singles "Got a Job" (Chess) and "Bad Girl" (End).

Despite this experience in the music industry from 1957, Gordy, when he formed his label in 1960, was reported to have given up a job on a Detroit assembly line and to have borrowed six hundred dollars to start his company, said to be the first all-black record company. True or not, this version of Gordy's history had a mythical importance, because Gordy's move represents an apparent realization of the American Dream, given extra romance because the hero was black.

As with other sections of the entertainment industry where black stars were well established–boxing, baseball, football, basketball, jazz–there were very few black people involved in the administration of record companies, either as owners of their own companies or as senior executives of companies owned by white people. The most common administrative position for them was as A&R director of rhythm and blues music. Black owners were exceedingly rare.

Bobby Robinson was one of the first, when he formed Red Robin, later Robin, Records in 1953. During the next ten years, he had a succession of labels, several of which–Everlast, Fire, Fury, Enjoy–produced national hits. His last company folded in 1963. Juggy Murray started Sue Records in New York in 1957, and had rhythm and blues by Ike and Tina Turner and by Charlie and Inez Foxx. Murray also distributed the product of another black-owned label, AFO Records of New Orleans, one of several such companies in the region which were oriented mainly to the local market (although Minit Records had national hits in the early sixties). The singer Sam Cooke and his manager J. W. Alexander formed Sar Records in Hollywood, and had some rhythm and blues hits in 1960-62.

But although there were these few companies with black owners, none were widely known outside the music industry, and the extraordinary success of Gordy's various record labels, and the equally remarkable success of his publishing company, Jobete, appropriately paralleled the transformation of black ideology that took place during the sixties.

Gordy's endurance resulted from his extraordinary understanding of the nation's musical taste, a masterly sense of business administration, and the ability to recognize potential both in singers who had no experience and in those who had been professionals for some time without achieving much success. The experience of the previous five years, 1956-60, had shown him that certain kinds of rhythm and blues had a large market in the popular music market. The success of the contrived productions of rhythm and blues (by Lloyd Price, the Coasters, the Drifters, Jackie Wilson, and Marv Johnson) were evidence that if the producers understood their music, they could provide an acceptable product to the audience.

Gordy's early records by the Marvelettes and the Contours were simple formula products, vocally similar to such groups as the Shirelles and the Isley Brothers, instrumentally like the Cameo-Parkway records. But gradually, Gordy fostered a company image, a set of stylistic characteristics that immediately identified his product with the names of his labels, Tamla, Gordy, Motown, and later Soul and V.I.P. In common with the New York producers, Gordy's dominated the product of his labels, but he took greater care to maintain the separate identity of each singer and group, at least until 1966, after which the company's sound became more homogeneous.

Although Gordy described his product as "the Detroit Sound", there was nothing particularly "Detroit" about it. If Gordy had lived in Pittsburgh he would possibly have been able to develop much the same kind of sound that he evolved in Detroit. On the other hand, Detroit had the fourth largest black population in the States, after New York, Chicago, and Philadelphia, yet did not have an important record company.[3] This meant that whereas performers in the other three cities had outlets for their talent, amateur performers in Detroit tended to stay amateur, unless they were lucky and were "spotted" by somebody who passed on the word to out-of-town record companies. It was in this way that Hank Ballard, Little Willie John, and Jackie Wilson were discovered by Johnny Otis at a talent show in 1951, and recommended to King Records. Other important singers who were discovered in the city included La Vern Baker and Johnnie Ray, both in 1950, and Della Reese in 1956–all of whom made their reputations at the Flame Club–and John Lee Hooker, earlier in 1948. Alto sax player Paul Williams, whose "Hucklebuck" was a major hit in 1949, was also a resident of Detroit.

But perhaps the most significant Detroit performer, in terms of predecessors of the so-called "Detroit Sound", was the Reverend C. L. Franklin, for if there was a common identity in most of the records produced by Berry Gordy, it was their strong church flavour. Franklin was a preacher whose recorded sermons (issued in a series of LPs by Chess) have had steady sales, although recently his daughters, Aretha in particular, but Carolyn and Erma as well, have somewhat overshadowed their father's reputation outside Detroit.

In the company's output from 1960 to 1962, the influence of church singing was stressed on some of Gordy's records, but not in his most successful ones. From 1963 onwards, the emphasis was placed more definitely on the gospel qualities of his singers' voices, and the musical arrangements, accordingly, were closer to the accompaniments that commonly backed up gospel singing. Tambourines, clapping, a steady four-even-beats-to-the-bar rhythm, call-and-response harmony structure, advisory and moralizing songs were all introduced or exaggerated, and by 1965 the sound was fully conceived. More imaginatively than anyone had done before, Gordy and his co-producers had translated the qualities of church music into popular music terms, and yet retained, even enhanced, the excitement and conviction of the religious singers, while satisfying the need for a more sophisticated sound.

Although Gordy showed an outstanding flair for combining good business sense with a seemingly infallible instinct for new, commercial sounds, perhaps his most important ability was his gift for recognizing good performers, writers, producers, and musicians, and for inspiring them to fulfill their potential. Within four years of forming his company, Motown had ten performers capable of making the pop market's top ten, any one of whom could compare with the best singer any other company could offer. Yet none had any kind of reputation before Gordy signed them.

The Temptations, the Miracles, and the Four Tops had all made records before for other companies, without inspiring anybody to sign them to exclusive contracts. Marvin Gaye had been a member of the Moonglows in the years of the group's decline, and Junior Walker recorded for Harvey Fuqua's Harvey label before he moved to Gordy's Soul label. Child prodigy Stevie Wonder, girl singer Mary Wells, and the girl groups the Marvelettes, Martha and the Vandellas, and the Supremes had not made records before they joined Gordy.

Had any other company achieved the unlikely feat of collecting such a roster, and realizing its talent, any hit parade success would probably have been sporadic, as first one act and then another ran out of material to do it justice. Gordy took the precaution of contracting several songwriters to work exclusively for him–usually doubling as producers. Although the pattern does not appear to have been completely rigid, there was a tendency for particular producing teams to work with particular singers, and to do so regularly, so that Gordy could release records in a specific order. Fostering the public image of a tight-knit "family" firm, in which several of his relatives had executive positions, Gordy imposed a rigorous discipline on his staff which occasionally produced publicly declared resentment and resulted in some singers–Mary Wells, Kim Weston–leaving the organization as soon as their first contracts became void, when the singers reached twenty-one. Yet the system enabled the Motown Corporation to have an unparalleled ten-year run in the singles market,[4] with 79 records making the top ten, 72 of them by the 10 performers mentioned above. And although some of the records were essentially pop productions, "processed soul", geared to an audience that liked lush sounds with a strong rhythm behind an emotional voice singing a sad song, a remarkable number of the Motown Corporation's hits were among the best records of their time.

The company's most distinctive performers were the Miracles, who maintained a consistent style through the decade yet consistently evaded imitation despite an apparently simple sound. The group's lead singer, Smokey Robinson, provided its identity as songwriter, producer, and ingenious interpreter of his own lyrics. In a decade that attracted far more accomplished figures into popular music than the fifties had done, Robinson was one of the most outstanding. His voice seemed to be inspired by Sam Cooke, having the same high, pure, controlled swooping sound, and a comparable technique of taking his voice in unexpected directions and risking a miscalculation in pitch (sometimes missing the note he tried for), thereby creating excitement in fast songs such as "Shop Around" (the first top ten hit for Gordy, on the Tamla label, 1960) and "Come On and Do the Jerk" (1964), and intense sadness on slow ones, including "You Really Got a Hold on Me" (1963), "The Tracks of My Tears" (1965), and "More Love" (1967).

Robinson had an unusual consistency in the kind of songs he wrote, regularly hinging them on some curious contradiction in love, whose mystery provided the songs with a distinctive air of innocence, wonder, and discovery: "I got sunshine on a cloudy day" ("My Girl"); "Honey, you do me wrong but still I think about you" ("Ain't That Peculiar"); "People say I'm the life of the party, 'cause I tell a joke or two, but although I may be laughin' loud and hearty, deep inside I'm blue" ("Tracks of My Tears").

Sometimes the images were straight, but they still had a hook that suddenly dragged the listener into the song. In "The Love I Saw in You Was Just a Mirage", Robinson had a line that began like a cliché, then suddenly went further: "All that's left are lipstick traces of kisses you pretended to feel". Yet Robinson never recriminated others, or felt sorry for himself. The sadness was an aura, never a pool he wallowed in as did so many others.

After Robinson, Motown's most expressive interpreters were Marvin Gaye and David Ruffin. Gaye was somewhat less versatile and talented than Smokey Robinson, but nevertheless was a producer, songwriter, and singer of considerable ability. His early records were very close approximations of gospel singing, with a regular rhythm, chanting vocal group support, and lyrics that seemed to be transcriptions of gospel songs–"Can I Get a Witness?", "You're a Wonderful One", "Pride and Joy". Like most of Motown's records before 1964, the rhythm was crudely achieved compared to the more flexible arrangements of 1965, the year when Gaye and several other Motown performers made their most "perfect" records. Gaye's "I'll Be Doggone" and "Ain't That Peculiar" of that year were masterpieces of controlled, flexible, considered uptempo singing, the voice lightly relaxed over a compulsive but varied rhythm. At the end of 1968, Gaye recorded the hit "I Heard It Through the Grapevine", which had much more advanced recording techniques, now available through multitracking for stereo. Although the performance was impeccable and the arrangement brilliantly contrived–thudding bass, virtuoso control of emotional intensity–the earlier records represented the singer's character better.

David Ruffin was the lead for the Temptations until 1968, when he became a solo singer. In 1965, with the group, he made a series of classic call-and-response harmony songs–"Since I Lost My Baby", "It's Growing", "My Girl", and "Get Ready". The group had a deft touch for fast, weaving harmonies that constantly spotlighted Ruffin's phrases, producing interpretations of Smokey Robinson's songs that rivalled his own. Compared to Atlantic's records by the Drifters, 1959 to 1964, these by the Temptations were more intense vocally, had a more assured rhythm, and were considerably more adventurous in their harmonies and lead melody.

When Ruffin left the group, Motown, always ready to meet any perceived change in the audience's taste, and often uncannily able to anticipate and perhaps guide it, let producer Norman Whitfield experiment during 1968 and 1969 with having the Temptations record in what was roughly called "acid-soul", following the style of a San Francisco group, Sly and the Family Stone. The Family Stone had abandoned the gospel call-and-response style of harmony and itself had been experimenting with quick interchanges of scat noises, dialogues between members of the group, and harder vocal tones without the rasp or purity of gospel styles. The Temptations' "Cloud Nine" (1968) and "Runaway Child, Running Wild" (1969), with themes comparable to "Up on the Roof" and "Spanish Harlem", sounded unduly contrived, but served the growing market for more self-conscious forms of music.

Earlier, in 1965, Motown had introduced a third male group, the Four Tops, whose lead singer Levi Stubbs sang even more intensely than Ruffin, higher and more shrilly, and whose harmonies were correspondingly more emphatic. The different character reflected a different conception in production. The records by the Temptations, like those of the Miracles, were produced by Smokey Robinson, while those by the Four Tops were produced, and usually written, by the team of Eddie Holland, Lamont Dozier, and Brian Holland. Where Robinson sought effects through subtlety, Holland-Dozier-Holland went more directly for what they wanted, using less intricate ideas in their songs and a much cruder rhythm. Where Robinson had used orchestral accompaniment sparingly, blended in with voices, Holland-Dozier-Holland used fuller arrangements, with string sections confirming a rhythm already emphasized by hard drumming and a tambourine on every offbeat. The overall effect on the Four Tops records of 1965 was irresistible excitement, particularly in "I Can't Help Myself" and "Without the One You Love". But although the Four Tops continued to have a long succession of hits into 1968, the voice of lead Levi Stubbs had an exceptionally narrow emotional range, and as the overall quality of the records became increasingly melodramatic, the performances lost their earlier convincing spontaneity.

The same criticism could be levelled at most of the records made by Motown from 1966 onwards, yet this was the corporation's most commercially successful period. The earlier distinctions between the production methods of various producers became harder to recognize, and the policy seemed to be to model all the acts on the styles of the particularly successful ones, the Four Tops and the greatest commercial success of all Motown performers, the Supremes.

The appeal of the Supremes was more visual than musical and depended on the increasing acceptability of the idea that a black woman in a public role could be beautiful and exciting. Compared to the little girl appeal in the voices of the Shirelles and the Crystals, and the harder try-me-if-you-dare look of the Ronettes, the Supremes offered themselves as mature young women, respectable but accessible to those who cared truly and deeply. Lead singer Diana Ross had a narrow range, vocally and emotionally, and a whining tone that would have been difficult for a less attractive woman to succeed with. Her sighs and pauses for breath were often more expressive than her words.

With typically thorough promotion, Motown made sure the Supremes were seen, and relied on Holland-Dozier-Holland to produce enough words and a hard enough beat for the records to be reasonably impressive. The group had sixteen records in the national top ten from 1964 to 1969.

Musically, the records of Martha and the Vandellas (1963-66) and Gladys Knight and the Pips (1967-69) were more interesting than those of the Supremes. Martha Reeves had a hard tone that was rarely effective on ballads, but on fast dance songs, such as "Dancing in the Street" (1964) and "Nowhere to Run" (1965), both of which had irresistible driving rhythms, she was persuasively exultant. Gladys Knight and the Pips (who were three men) had been with several labels and had had a couple of top ten hits before they came to Motown, but had never achieved the power of controlled frenzy that they produced in the original "I Heard It Through the Grapevine" (1967), whose arrangement seemed determined to combine the excitement of Phil Spector's arrangement in Ike and Tina Turner's "River Deep, Mountain High" and the more recent Atlantic productions of Aretha Franklin. Dense, tense harmonies by the Pips seemed to box Gladys Knight in, so that her sudden flights up and out were exhilarating and satisfying, while underneath the rhythm tugged and pulled.

Motown defied all the patterns of the industry, consolidating its successes, pushing its teen-oriented singers through to the adult market instead of abandoning them, and concentrating on singers who already had adult appeal. The Supremes began to sound like the Andrews Sisters in their night club act–yet they came out with a couple of singles in 1968 and 1969 that were as close to social comment as popular music had ever reached, "Love Child" and "I'm Living in Shame". Junior Walker, whose 1965 hit "Shotgun" was a throwback to the era of screaming saxophonists, made the top ten in 1969 with a ballad, "What Does It Take?" Stevie Wonder, literally Motown's child wonder in 1963, when as a twelve-year-old he made the top ten with "Fingertips", moved through driving band shouts ("Uptight", 1966), gospel-flavoured cries (probably his best style, as in "I Was Made to Love Her" and "I'm Wondering", 1967), to sing-along ballads.

Gordy had apparently lived out the myth. The Ford machinist now ran the most successful independent company in the industry (the only company that could compare with Motown's success, Atlantic, had been merged with Warner/Reprise and Elektra under the Kinney Corporation's umbrella). In 1965 Gordy claimed that his music expressed the "rats, roaches, and soul" condition of black ghetto life. Part of that condition was the determination to get out of it, which Gordy expressed with infallible accuracy.

In 1970, the whole Motown operation moved to Los Angeles, partly to be closer to the headquarters of the major film and TV studios. Even after proving his judgements to be commercially sound for more than ten years, Berry Gordy was still regarded with scepticism as he cut the umbilical cord with Detroit, but the next decade saw his major artists–Diana Ross, Marvin Gaye, Stevie Wonder, Smokey Robinson–achieve exactly that combination of respect, within the industry, and prestige, outside it, that was normally denied to black performers.*

* DETROIT LABELS

ANNA. *Formed in 1959 in Detroit by Anna Gordy; absorbed into Motown c. 1960.*
A&R: Berry Gordy.
Rhythm and blues: Barrett Strong, Joe Tex.

TAMLA. *Formed in 1960 by Berry Gordy.*
Male vocal group: (Smokey Robinson and) the Miracles, Isley Brothers.
Female vocal group: the Marvelettes.
Male rhythm and blues: Marvin Gaye, Stevie Wonder.
Female rhythm and blues: Brenda Holloway.

MOTOWN. *Formed in 1960 by Berry Gordy.*
Male vocal group: the Four Tops, Spinners, Jackson Five.
Female vocal group: the Supremes.
Male rhythm and blues: Eddie Holland, Michael Jackson.
Female rhythm and blues: Mary Wells, Diana Ross.

The Holland-Dozier-Holland team left the Motown fold, and set up their own Detroit-based companies, Invictus and Hot Wax.* The Chairmen of the Board (featuring former lead singer from the Showmen, Norman Johnson, now known as "General" Johnson) took on the raucous, gritty sound that had been the province of the Four Tops, and made their mark with "Give Me Just a Little More Time" (Invictus, 1970) and Freda Payne pitched into Diana Ross's territory with her poignant delivery of "Band of Gold" (Hot Wax, 1970). The Honey Cone topped the national chart in 1971 with an update on the girl group sound in "Want Ads" (Hot Wax), but, despite that heady start, the company soon floundered, and Detroit reverted to being the backwater it had been before Gordy set up business there.

Meanwhile, Norman Whitfield emerged as Motown's leading producer, showing great versatility as he switched the Temptations from the lyrical purity of "I Wish It Would Rain" (1968) and "Just My Imagination" (1971), both featuring the delicate lead voice of Eddie Kendricks, to the tougher attack of "I Can't Get Next to You" (1969) and the classic story song "Papa Was a Rolling Stone" (1972) featuring Dennis Edwards; Whitfield co-wrote all four songs with Barrett Strong, who was still in the Motown fold all those years after singing the song which had started it all for Gordy's empire, "Money".

TRI-PHI. *Formed in 1961 by Harvey Fuqua; absorbed into Motown, c. 1964.*
Male vocal group: the Spinners.

GORDY. *Formed in 1962 by Berry Gordy.*
Male vocal group: the Temptations, Contours, Bobby Taylor and the Vancouvers.
Female vocal group: Martha and the Vandellas.
Male rhythm and blues: Edwin Starr, David Ruffin.
Female rhythm and blues: Kim Weston.

RIC TIC. *Formed in 1965; absorbed into Motown.*
Male rhythm and blues: Edwin Starr.

SOUL. *Formed in 1965 by Berry Gordy.*
Male vocal group: the Originals.
Mixed vocal group: Gladys Knight and the Pips.
Male rhythm and blues: Junior Walker and the All Stars, Jimmy Ruffin.

V.I.P. *Formed in 1965 by Berry Gordy.*
Male vocal group: the Elgins.

RARE EARTH. *Formed in 1970 by Berry Gordy.*
Rock: Rare Earth.
Pop rhythm and blues: R. Dean Taylor, Stoney and Meatloaf.

* INVICTUS. *Formed in 1970 by Lamont Dozier, Brian and Eddie Holland. Distributed by Capitol.*
Male vocal group: Chairmen of the Board.

Subsidiary:

HOT WAX. *Distributed by Buddah.*
Female vocal group: the Honey Cone.
Female rhythm and blues: Freda Payne.

The Motown policy always depended on a fierce "quality control", sending producers back to re-write, re-record, and re-mix prospective singles until the selection committee was convinced that the record had all the required ingredients; despite a high output, the labels maintained an impressive ratio of hits-per-release. In the early seventies, both Marvin Gaye and Stevie Wonder broke out of this intensive product-oriented approach, defining themselves as "artists" with albums that were expressions of their personal philosophies. Ironically, both turned out albums which were enormously successful; Marvin Gaye's *What's Goin' On* spawned three top ten singles in 1971 whose social comment lyrics floated over lazily sensual rhythms, and Stevie Wonder set a precedent in 1973 by playing almost all the instruments on *Talking Book*, including the powerhouse clavinet on the chart-topping "Superstition".

And still the Motown tradition for crafting rhythmic pop singles prospered, with several new producers moving up alongside Norman Whitfield and Smokey Robinson. Gordy preferred teams of producers, and tried various combinations including "The Clan" and "The Corporation" both of which included himself and Deke Richards, along with Frank Wilson, R. Dean Taylor and Hank Cosby (in the Clan) and Lawrence Mizell and Freddie Perren (in the Corporation), who fashioned three consecutive top-of-the-chart singles to catapult the Jackson Five into the hearts and ears of American teenagers: "I Want You Back" (1969), "ABC", and "The Love You Save" (1970). But even with that kind of success, Gordy still kept everybody on their toes by switching the group to Hal Davis for the more melodic "Never Can Say Goodbye", which proceeded to sell two million copies where the other three had "only" done one million each. And almost every producer on the Motown staff took turns to produce Diana Ross, now split from the Supremes and developing into a genuine institution; Nick Ashford and Valerie Simpson wrote and produced some of her biggest and best hits in the seventies including "Ain't No Mountain High Enough" (1970).

V

Through the sixties, the only city which ever seemed likely to challenge Detroit, as a source of talent and a base for producers to evolve their own sound, was Chicago.* In contrast to the intense, rhythmic

* CHICAGO LABELS
CHESS. *Sold to GRT in 1970 after death of Leonard Chess. A&R, from 1965: Billy Davis.*
Male rhythm and blues: Billy Stewart, Tommy Tucker.
Female rhythm and blues: Fontella Bass.

content of most Detroit records, the sound of Chicago was much cooler, with jazzy horn arrangements and casual guitar licks dominating most productions; where Detroit aimed at the kids, Chicago went for an older, more sophisticated audience. But there were too many production companies competing with each other in Chicago's pool of talent for any one of them to emerge as a serious rival to Motown.

Vee Jay collapsed in 1965 in the midst of all kinds of litigation, and it took their major artist Jerry Butler three years to recover the momentum of his career. Senior producer Calvin Carter never did find a satisfactory base for himself, and neither did Betty Everett, who had been poised for greater success after "You're No Good", "Getting Mighty Crowded" and the top twenty "Shoop Shoop Song (It's in His Kiss)" in 1964.

At Chess Records, Billy Davis came in to run the A&R department after co-writing most of Berry Gordy's pre-Motown hits. Davis produced some of the Chess artists himself, including the fat ballad singer Billy Stewart, whose scat version of "Summertime" made the top ten in 1966; "Rescue Me" by Fontella Bass made the top five the same year, one of the best attempts to capture a Motown kind of sound, produced by veteran St Louis bandleader Oliver Sain. Portents of a more elaborate future for rhythm and blues were heard in four top twenty hits by the Dells, 1968–69, produced by Bobby Miller and arranged by Charles Stepney, who went on to work with Maurice White of Earth, Wind and Fire.

The major figure in Chicago during the sixties was Curtis Mayfield, who came closest to devising a distinctive sound for the city. Originally from the South, Mayfield formed the Impressions in 1957 with himself on guitar and Jerry Butler as lead singer, but took over the singing when Butler went solo following their top ten hit "For Your

---

Subsidiary:
CADET (*formerly ARGO*).
Instrumental: Ramsey Lewis Trio.
Female rhythm and blues: Etta James.
Male vocal group: the Dells.
Distributed label:
TUFF. *Formed in New York in 1963 by Zelma Sanders. A&R: Abner Spector.*
Female vocal group: the Jaynetts (a.k.a. the Hearts).

BRUNSWICK. *Bought from Decca circa 1960 by Nat Tarnopol. A&R, from 1967: Carl Davis.*
Male rhythm and blues: Jackie Wilson.
Female rhythm and blues: Barbara Acklin.
Vocal group: the Chi-Lites.

Subsidiary:
DAKAR (*distributed by Atlantic*): *see page 310.*

Precious Love" (Vee Jay, 1958). Mayfield's specialty was his guitar sound, favouring the lower notes and using a heavy reverb echo that evoked the sound of "Pop" Staples of the Staples Singers, who were also at that time with Vee Jay. Mayfield's arrangement of "He Will Break Your Heart" for Jerry Butler was pure "Pop" Staples, right down to the guitar intro, and, soon after that record made the top ten for Vee Jay in 1960, Mayfield and the Impressions were signed to ABC-Paramount.

Production credits on most of the Impressions' records at ABC were given to arranger Johnny Pate, whose horn lines proved to be the ideal complement for Mayfield's vocal and guitar ideas. The mystical "Gypsy Woman" made the top twenty in 1961, followed by eight more singles through the sixties, most of which expressed a growing solidarity and self-reliance among American black people: "It's All Right" (1963), "Amen", and "People Get Ready" (1965). Mostly adaptations of gospel imagery, the records were delivered with such subtlety and grace that the notoriously conservative white radio programmers let them on the air.

Mayfield and Pate also collaborated on sessions for Major Lance at OKeh Records, recently revived by Columbia as an outlet for soul music under the supervision of Carl Davis, who was credited as producer. Mayfield wrote all four top twenty hits for Lance, including the atmospheric "Um, Um, Um, Um, Um, Um" (1964), and also wrote two top twenty hits for Gene Chandler on Constellation, enabling Chandler finally to shake off the "novelty" tag that had plagued him since his huge hit "Duke of Earl", produced by Carl Davis (Vee Jay, 1962).

In 1966 Carl Davis left OKeh to form his own production company which regenerated Jackie Wilson's career for Brunswick, first with "Whispers" and then with the gospel-tinged dance classic, "(Your Love Keeps Lifting Me) Higher and Higher", which put Wilson back in the top ten for the first time since 1963 (but for the last time, as it turned out). Davis was taken on to run the A&R department at Brunswick, where he built up an outstanding production team including arrangers Willie Henderson, "Tom Tom" Washington and Sonny Sanders, and writers Barbara Acklin and Eugene Record. As an alternative outlet, the Dakar label was formed with distribution by Atlantic, and the new Chicago sound came to maturity on "Can I Change My Mind" by Tyrone Davis in 1968. The balance of horns, guitar and bass worked particularly well, the horns mostly held on long chords in sympathy, while the fluid guitar suggested a more optimistic possibility as Davis expressed his apologies to the girl he had left; the team had benefited equally from both Detroit and Memphis where the Stax session musicians had shown how guitar and bass could emphasize well written story songs.

Playing bass on many of these records, and noticing what worked, was Eugene Record, writer and lead singer of the Chi-Lites, who saw more than ten years of recording finally bring its reward with the international hit "Have You Seen Her?" in 1971. Previous records by the group had veered between the raspy attack of the Temptations and the innocent purity of the Miracles, but with this song Record found his own territory: "situation" songs, presented in fine detail, and sung in a voice that switched from a warm tenor to a soft falsetto. In "Have You Seen Her", Record played all the instruments himself except the drums, generating a convincingly desolate mood; in "Oh Girl", he used country-styled piano and harmonica against a string accompaniment to go all the way to the top of the pop charts in 1972, but later records did better in Britain (four more top ten hits over the next four years) than in the States, where Brunswick faded like the rest of Chicago's labels.

As Chicago's output dropped off, and Motown moved to Los Angeles, "The Sound of Philadelphia" again became a marketable commodity.* But instead of the crass commerciality of the twist era, this time the city became identified with sophisticated arrangements that used most of the instruments of a classical orchestra over danceable grooves, and often behind veteran performers.

Writer-producers Kenny Gamble and Leon Huff came together to capitalize on a decade of varied experience, and achieved a minor breakthrough in 1968 with "Cowboys to Girls" by the Intruders on their own Gamble label. The A&R department at Mercury, struggling to get Jerry Butler back in the charts, shipped him out to "Phillie" and scored five top twenty hits in two years, 1968–69, including "Only the Strong Survive".

Meanwhile producer-arranger Thom Bell had evolved a subtle, melodic approach which landed two big hits for the Delfonics, "La La Means I Love You" (1968) and "Didn't I Blow Your Mind (This Time)" (1970), both for Philly Groove. Apparently realizing the

* PHILADELPHIA LABELS

GAMBLE. *Formed in 1967 by Kenny Gamble and Leon Huff.*
Male vocal group: the Intruders.

PHILLY GROOVE. *Formed in 1967 by Stan Watson and Sam Bell. Distributed by Bell.*
A&R: Thom Bell.
Male vocal group: the Delfonics.

PHILADELPHIA INTERNATIONAL. *Formed in 1971 by Gamble and Huff. Distributed by Columbia.*
Male vocal group: the O'Jays, Harold Melvin and the Bluenotes, the Ebonys, People's Choice.
Female vocal group: the Three Degrees.
Male rhythm and blues: Billy Paul, Teddy Pendergrass.
Instrumental: MFSB.

importance of consolidating the city's achievements, rather than competing with each other, Bell began collaborating on some projects with Gamble and Huff, and in 1972 their Philadelphia International label made a spectacular breakthrough with enormous hits from the O'Jays ("Backstabbers", and six more top twenty hits), Harold Melvin and the Bluenotes, featuring Teddy Pendergrass ("If You Don't Know Me By Now" and others), and Billy Paul ("Me and Mrs. Jones"). Bell continued to work for outside customers, and had impressive strings of hits with both the Stylistics (for Avco-Embassy, run by the veterans Hugo and Luigi) and the Spinners (for Atlantic).

New York, once the centre for uptown rhythm and blues productions, had lost confidence in the idiom during the mid-sixties. Teddy Randazzo, who had failed to become a teen idol in the fifties, had his moment of glory in 1964 with a spectacular production of "Goin' Out of My Head" for Little Anthony and the Imperials (DCP). French horns and tympany filled out a string-oriented arrangement, as Anthony wailed one of pop's most impassioned declarations of devotion.

Burt Bacharach came out of cabaret (arranging for Marlene Dietrich's stage show) through pop (co-writing with Hal David), and brought elements of both to jazz-based harmonic structures in his path-breaking arrangements for Dionne Warwick. A dozen top twenty hits for Scepter Records when the wave of raucous British groups were sweeping across America put Bacharach second only to the Motown producers during the sixties; but where they aimed at the dancing feet of teenagers, Bacharach and lyricist Hal David preferred more adult implications and sparing use of rhythm instruments. Where most female vocalists of the era played for sympathy with hints of out-of-tune vulnerability, Dionne Warwick pitched every note perfectly and achieved her effect with a uniquely sensitive tone, brilliantly showcased by Bacharach's meticulously conceived arrangements. "Anyone Who Had a Heart" and "Walk On By" (both in 1964) provided the link in the chain between the first generation of uptown rhythm and blues productions of the late fifties, and the new breed of the early seventies, whose audience probably constituted the same people, ten and fifteen years older.

10

ARE WE TOGETHER? SOUL MUSIC

Had radio stations begun to operate without regard for particular markets (rhythm and blues vs. popular) from 1957 onwards–when record-buying tastes were generally similar in the two markets–it is possible that the differences in the music of black and white Americans would have been all but eliminated. But the two markets remained separate, and after a time, the music in the rhythm and blues market began to attain a distinctiveness comparable to that of rhythm and blues before rock 'n' roll. But instead of the blues inflection and the blues approach characteristic of music before 1954, now the distinguishing features were qualities of church singing and of songs that resembled revivalist sing-ups or preachers' sermons.

Between 1955 and 1960, the most popular singers in the black market were those who had established themselves in the popular market as rock 'n' roll singers. Among this group was Fats Domino with twenty-four songs on the rhythm and blues top ten lists during the period, Elvis Presley with twenty-two, Little Richard with eleven, Chuck Berry with ten, and LaVern Baker with nine.

The second most consistently successful group of singers in the black market during the same period were gospel-influenced singers. Of these, Ray Charles had fifteen records in the top ten, Jackie Wilson nine, B. B. King and Clyde McPhatter seven each, Sam Cooke six, Little Willie John five, Bobby Bland four, and James Brown three. (Little Richard and LaVern Baker could also be included in this group, since their rock 'n' roll styles relied heavily on inflections borrowed from church singing.) The quality all the singers shared, one they borrowed from church singers, was that their voices gave the impression of being controlled, or strongly affected, by their emotions. At times, the singers seemed to miss the note they were reaching for in their passion, not quite achieving it or sliding past it into a shriek. The listener was deeply moved by the implications of the failure.

There were four fairly distinct periods in the evolution of the soul style–as the use of a gospel singing style in popular music came to be described. The first was from 1955 to 1960, when gospel styles were used randomly. The second period was from 1961 to 1963, when the sources of excitement and intense emotions were tapped more systematically and consistently, but records still used some conventions of popular music in the rhythm and musical accompaniment. The third period was 1964 to 1966, when the style was fully conceived, the musical arrangements complementing the vocal style. It was during this time that a large proportion of the best records in the style were made. The fourth period was from 1967 to 1969, during which the style became stereotyped, subject to the same kind of producer domination that had stifled the individual creativity of uptown rhythm and blues singers.

Conforming with the pattern of stylistic innovation suggested at the start of chapter 8, "Back Home", the first singers who benefited from using the soul style, with its roots in the South, were predominantly northern singers recording for northern record companies.

I: 1955–60

Most of the gospel-styled songs that did well in the popular market before 1960 were conventional popular songs, sentimental, dramatic, or novelty, that happened to be suitably presented by a gospel-styled voice. For example, Bobby Day and Dee Clark, closely following the style of Clyde McPhatter, had hits with, respectively, "Rockin' Robin"/"Over and Over" (Class, 1958) and "Just Keep It Up" (Abner, 1959); Jerry Butler and the Impressions with "For Your Precious Love" (Vee Jay, 1958) and Ed Townsend with "For Your Love" (Capitol, 1958), both following Roy Hamilton's style, had similar hits. Butler's record, however, was good. It had an extraordinary atmosphere of religious devotion, created both by Butler's rich tone and unusual phrasing, and by the deep sounds, somehow evoking the mood of a cathedral, made behind him by the Impressions.

Hamilton, McPhatter, and Sam Cooke also had their own hits, sometimes even with songs that had more obvious structural connections to gospel songs. Hamilton's "Don't Let Go" had a call-and-response structure, and McPhatter's "A Lover's Question" had a vocal bass figure similar to many gospel songs.

Occasionally, these singers used songs whose whole feeling seemed to present a "religious" conception of love, portraying lovers who were dependable, resourceful, worthy of a lifetime's attention–in place of the more usual realism of the blues or the less mature portraits in popular songs, where lovers usually seemed to have great personal charm and physical attractiveness but little character. Ray Charles celebrated women of positive capabilities in several songs, women who brought him breakfast in bed, looked after him if he was desperate, loved him well: "I Got a Woman" (1954) and "Hallelujah I Love Her So". B. B. King, in "Please Accept My Love", James Brown in "Try Me" (1958), and Bobby Bland in "I'll Take Care of You" (1959) presented themselves as comparably reliable sources of security and affection.

Many of these songs were slow, like ballads, and did not have the obvious excitement that the jump blues had had five or ten years before. But the singers themselves were exciting, even singing slow songs, and particularly when seen live. In fact, much of their emotion depended on the relationship between them and their audience, who identified with the singer's image of a closely interdependent couple, each supplying the other's needs. Once the singer had established the fact that he could authentically present familiar scenes of courtship, living together, and breaking up, he could focus on apparently trivial details and still evoke real and important events for the audience. And the best way for him to persuade the audience that he was seriously concerned with the themes of his songs was through the gospel style. The gospel style as Ray Charles, James Brown, and others have said in interviews, was "the natural truth".

Commercial gospel-styled singers who more obviously toned down their styles for the white audience were acceptable to the black audience on the basis of individual records but they could never be sure. Jimmy Jones, Gene McDaniels, and Marv Johnson thus had hits in the black market with versions of Clyde McPhatter's style, but the singers depended on the quality of each song rather than on their own character to interest the audience, and they could not rely on support without a recent hit, as the uncompromised gospel singers could.

Gospel-styled female singers often had the greatest difficulty in sustaining a consistent sound. They generally seemed more subject than male singers to the decisions of producers. LaVern Baker's records from Atlantic ranged from the high, innocent voice of "Tweedle Dee" to the rough voice of the classic blues (in an album of Bessie Smith songs). Most of the female singers had long experience with church singing, but in many cases the aim of hitting the potential supper-club market kept their records soft–Nancy Wilson, Dionne Warwick. A few singers, following Dinah Washington's ballad style, retained the harsh quality of gospel singing. Little Esther, Della Reese, Ruth Brown, and Etta James were among those who used this style successfully in the early sixties.

II: 1961–63

The comparatively haphazard, random production of gospel-styled records ended after the success in 1959 of "Lonely Teardrops" by

Jackie Wilson (Brunswick), "What'd I Say?" by Ray Charles (Atlantic), and "Shout" by the Isley Brothers (RCA). The number of singers recording with some kind of gospel style increased considerably after the popularity of these records, although the full significance of the trend was disguised by the industry's preoccupation with the twist, and by the dominant influence during the same period of the producers emphasizing the uptown rhythm and blues records.

Still, in terms of numbers, gospel-styled singers began to be recorded more often, and when this happened–even though the emphasis in most of these singers was on vocal qualities that were expected to please white tastes–the pioneers of the style became the most popular singers in the black culture. In the years 1961–63, Ray Charles had fifteen records in the rhythm and blues top ten, Sam Cooke had nine, Bobby Bland eight, and James Brown five.

Each of these singers had great influence on the styles of the singers who took up this form of music after 1960, among whom Etta James, with five hits, Ike and Tina Turner, and Solomon Burke, each with four, were the most consistently successful.

After "Lonely Teardrops", "What'd I Say?", and "Shout", several singers made similar "revivalist" songs, with shouted replies from a vocal group. Jessie Hill's "Ooh Poo Pah Doo" in 1960, Etta James's "Something's Got a Hold on Me", and the Isley Brothers' "Twist and Shout" (1962) became progressively more frantic, incorporating aspects of the cry style of James Brown and Jackie Wilson. This frantic style was isolated, with less emphasis on group support, in "I Found a Love" by the Falcons (1962) and "Cry Baby" by Garnet Mimms and the Enchanters (1963).

In these records, the singers committed themselves to creating pure excitement. With few, simple words, but in a dramatic, sympathetic atmosphere created by background singers, the lead singers literally screamed their message. In "I Found a Love", Wilson Pickett, recruited as lead singer of the Detroit-based Falcons, cried and shrieked:

(*Yeah yeah; yeah yeah*)
I found a love; I found a love;
I found a love, that I need.
(*Oh yeah.*)

"Cry Baby" (which cannot be quoted) similarly repeated a simple phrase–the title–allowing Garnet Mimms to vent all the emotional force he could muster.

These records were among the first gospel-styled songs to have accompaniments that were not slightly adapted from some other kind of music. Both songs, unlike most of the records that emphasized a gospel style, had a slow, gentle, lilting rhythm. The uncompromising expressions of ecstasy and intense sympathy they created were unusual among records that did well in the popular market. On other "revivalist" records, the strong rhythms meant that the impact was absorbed physically by the audience and not purely emotionally as in "I Found a Love" and "Cry Baby".

Tina Turner and Etta James also adopted the shrill cry of such gospel singing, but although their vocal style was different from previous ones, their accompaniments were more conventional. Most of the records by Ike and Tina Turner during this period (made for Sue Records of New York) had a shuffle-twist rhythm and, from a girl group, shrill chorus chants which diminished the impact of Tina Turner's harsh, emotional voice. "It's Gonna Work Out Fine", a novelty duet by the Turners (reminiscent of Mickey and Sylvia's rhythm and blues calypso hit "Love Is Strange"), was a minor hit in the popular music market in 1961.

Etta James, after a quiet period with Modern following her 1955 rock 'n' roll hit "The Wallflower", was contracted to Chess in 1961, and had hits in a variety of styles, including ballads and shouting blues, before evolving a gospel blues style–the female equivalent of Bobby Bland's–which gave her five hits in the rhythm and blues market.

Bland's records were among the best gospel-influenced records of this period, with sympathetic arrangements supporting his rich voice. Unlike the more raucous singers (Wilson Pickett, Garnet Mimms), Bland did not sing throughout with cracked tone and unspecific phrasing but melodically and smoothly in some parts and more harshly in others. Sometimes the transition was abrupt and contrived, but in "I Pity the Fool" (1961), "Stormy Monday" (1962), and "Call on Me" (1963) his voice had convincing sadness and sympathetic warmth. A big band maintained an easy swing in "I Pity the Fool", while on "Stormy Monday", one of the finest gospel blues performances of the time, only Wayne Bennett's guitar, played as T-Bone Walker or B. B. King might have done it, gently echoed and reflected the singer's phrases. "Call on Me" placed Bland's voice in a soft setting of Latin beat and smooth sax riffs, but the singer did not yield more than a little, so that the overall effect was an interesting clash of hard and soft tones.

Among the singers who used styles similar to Bland's, Solomon Burke was the first to make an individual impression. Burke's voice suited a more rigid rhythm than Bland's ever did, and adapted more easily to the harder soul dance arrangements of the mid-sixties, but it had a self-satisfied tone which prevented Burke's records from achieving the moods of sympathy or desolation that those of Bland regularly created. Although his live performances created great excitement, both through his ability to win an audience's sympathy and through the steady rhythm of what he called "rock 'n' soul" music, Burke's records lacked the dynamism of some of his contemporaries. His first hit was a slow interpretation of the country and western song "Just out of Reach" (which inspired ABC-Paramount to give Ray Charles the similar "I Can't Stop Loving You"). Like James Brown, Burke often assumed the role of reliable all-round provider, extending the capability to preach on love in general: from "Cry to Me" (1962) through "If You Need Me" (1963) to "Everybody Needs Somebody to Love" (1964). In his exceptionally relaxed tone at any tempo, Burke was the figure in soul who most paralleled Fats Domino's position in rock 'n' roll, but he lacked the humour that distinguished Domino's records from the records of other singers.

Sam Cooke, whose records for RCA-Victor during this period were often shaped to meet popular tastes (though Cooke's phrasing usually ensured a distinctive performance of any song he was interested in), also contributed some good gospel-style records–but as a producer. Cooke produced several records for his company, Sar, some of which showed more clearly than did his own records how fully he understood the potential of gospel styles in popular music. In 1961, the year he recorded the pop song "Cupid" for RCA, he produced "Soothe Me" by the Sims Twins on Sar, and it made the rhythm and blues top ten. As with many records released on Sar–"Lookin' For a Love" by the Valentinos, a rhythm and blues hit in 1962, and "Rome (Wasn't Built In A Day)" by Johnnie Taylor–both the song and the idea were strongly "religious" in feeling.

Matching the increasing importance of producers in the contemporary uptown rhythm and blues productions was the emergence in this evolutionary period of soul of several important parallel figures, among them Jerry Ragavoy, Bert Berns, and Jerry Wexler, producers who were able to bring out the best in singers without imposing themselves too demandingly onto the overall sound.

Wexler had been the producer at the Ray Charles sessions for Atlantic that produced "I Got a Woman" in 1954 and "What'd I Say?" in 1959–the former led to a marked increase in gospel-styled rhythm and blues records, and the latter inspired many popular-oriented gospel-styled records. Wexler also produced Clyde McPhatter's Atlantic records, and worked with Bert Berns on Solomon Burke's sessions.

Compared to Wexler, Berns made his presence more evident on the records, partly because he often wrote material and Wexler rarely did, and partly because he was more impatient to get a particular sound. Nevertheless, in his gospel-styled sessions, Berns allowed singers to keep close to their "natural" styles, and some of his compositions[1] inspired singers to exceed their normal range of expression, as "Cry Baby" did for Garnet Mimms, "Time Is On My Side" did for Irma Thomas, and "Piece of My Heart" did for Erma Franklin (Aretha's sister), all three of which songs were co-written with Jerry Ragavoy.[2]

Ragavoy was an independent producer based in Philadelphia, where he produced the Mimms record for United Artists and later made some interesting records by Howard Tate for Verve, the MGM subsidiary. Like Berns, Ragavoy used production techniques that were recognizably his–generally slow rhythms, with a strong choral chant and heavy beat on the choruses–but again his records served to highlight the distinctive characteristics of the singers he worked with. He rarely used the singers simply as "interpretive vocal instruments" to put his own feelings on the record, as was the tendency for uptown rhythm and blues producers.

But although Wexler, Berns, Ragavoy, and other northern producers of gospel-styled records were more sympathetic to their singers than were many of their contemporaries, they still tended to use the traditional orchestral arrangements of popular music. Less obtrusive arrangements were the invention of musicians in the South, notably of the Mar-Keys, session musicians at a Memphis company formed in 1960, Satellite, renamed Stax in 1961. Following up the bass-led rhythm of the nationally successful local group, the Bill Black Combo, and the tight sax sections and piano-led rhythm of the New Orleans session bands led by Lee Allen, the Mar-Keys laid even greater emphasis on close-knit–tight–sax chords and a more abrupt rhythm, and had a national hit in 1961, with "Last Night".

Curiously, despite the success of this instrumental sound, it was not immediately applied to back up the label's singers. Carla Thomas had a national hit in 1961, with "Gee Whiz", whose accompaniment was principally the piano triplets traditionally associated with soft ballad singing.

The Mar-Keys had a line-up of one or two trumpets, tenor and baritone saxes, plus a rhythm section of organ, guitar, bass, and drums. This rhythm section also recorded separately, as Booker T. and the M.G.'s, and in 1962 had a national hit with the rhythmic mood piece "Green Onions", in which the organist Booker T. Jones played simple melodic riffs with a mellow tone while guitarist Steve Cropper played soft staccato answering chords. In contrast to the then currently dominant twist rhythm, the sound was restrained, reflective, yet in its deeper way just as compulsively rhythmic. The different quality in the sound was the result of a shift in emphasis from drums to bass. When the responsibility for regular rhythm had been with the drummer, his repetitive beats had dominated the entire sound. Now, when the bass player was given the role of keeping the beat, the drummer–and consequently the rest of the group–became more flexible, and, less predictably, more exciting. A drum rhythm hit the head, but a bass rhythm affected the entire body.

In 1962, Stax and its newly formed subsidiary, Volt, made their first gospel-influenced records, "You Don't Miss Your Water" by William Bell (Stax) and "These Arms of Mine" by Otis Redding (Volt). Both singers sang undemonstratively, sadly, and convincingly, in styles midway between the ballad blues style of, for example, Percy Mayfield and the gospel blues style of Bobby Bland. But the accompaniment was still piano triplets. The first time the punchy sound of the Mar-Keys was used behind a singer was in Rufus Thomas's novelty dance songs "The Dog" and "Walking the Dog", in 1963, as tenor and baritone sax riffs alternated behind the strong aggressive singing.

Otis Redding's "Pain in My Heart" (1963) showed producer Steve Cropper closer to working out a suitable arrangement and instrumental sound to back up gospel-styled singing. Repetitive piano chords still linked the song to earlier types of ballads, but Cropper's guitar was now assuming the role of gospel group, answering, echoing, and developing vocal phrases–in much the same way Ray Charles's band had substituted for a gospel group in "I Got a Woman" ten years earlier.

III: 1964–66

In the evolutionary period of soul, there was little correlation between the authenticity of a singer's style (or the quality of his records) and his background experience, a connection that clearly existed among rhythm and blues singers. There was a slight tendency for singers from Georgia and Detroit to adopt gospel styles in contrast, for instance, to main blues styles, which were identified with New Orleans/California, Texas/California, or Mississippi Delta (including Memphis)/Chicago. James Brown and Ray Charles grew up in Georgia, and Little Richard and Wilson Pickett were born there; Jackie Wilson and Little Willie John were born in Detroit, and Pickett grew up there. But Garnet Mimms grew up in Philadelphia, Sam Cooke in Chicago, Roy Hamilton in New Jersey, Clyde McPhatter in New York, and Bobby Bland in Memphis. Despite strong roots in the South, gospel-styled singing evidently could be done by anybody from anywhere. But in the third phase of the style, now known generally as "soul", the most successful singers came predominantly from the south-eastern states of Georgia, Alabama, Florida, and Tennessee, and were recorded either in Memphis, Tennessee, or Muscle Shoals, Alabama.

Memphis, in particular, dominated the years 1964–66, providing the best producers, musicians, and studios, and, repeating the pattern of country rock's evolution ten years before, drawing singers from all over the South to the city. To an even greater extent than with country rock, the Memphis soul style was the product of black and white people working together; almost all of the singers were black, but many of the musicians and some of the songwriters and producers were white.

By December, 1963, tastes in the rhythm and blues and popular music markets had become so consistently similar that *Billboard* ceased to publish a separate list of the best-selling records in the rhythm and blues market. Radio stations aimed towards white audiences seemed prepared to accept even the most extreme gospel-styled records ("Cry Baby") and apparently uncommercial arrangements of gospel blues records ("Stormy Monday", Little Johnny Taylor's "Part-Time Love") as well as more obviously commercial novelty records (Inez and Charlie Foxx's "Mockingbird" and Rufus Thomas's "Walking the Dog"). In the Negro market, pop records, including Paul and Paula's "Hey Paul" and Peter, Paul, and Mary's "Puff, the Magic Dragon", were best sellers according to *Billboard.*

But the situation was not a stable one. Whereas in 1963, thirty-seven of the one hundred and six records that made the popular music top ten were by black singers, in 1964 only twenty-one of one hundred and one were. And whereas in 1963 there were several records in the top ten by black singers expressing strong emotions, in 1964 all of the records by black singers that made the list were uptown rhythm and blues productions, many of them on Gordy's labels and several others produced by Curtis Mayfield and Carl Davis in Chicago. Excitement and emotion, although available in the records of such gospel-styled singers as James Brown, Don Covay, Otis Redding, Joe Tex, and Bobby Bland, were generally preferred in the white market in the forms offered by British interpretations of rhythm and blues. This was a new phenomenon. Although no record by British singers made the pop music top ten in 1963, the very next year there were thirty-one such hits. But the black record buyers did not need second editions of songs they already had, or had rejected when performed by black singers, and they were not interested in the songs composed by British singers using the techniques of rhythm and blues.

With the advent of the British singers, it had become harder for rhythm and blues to make headway in the popular market, but at the same time pressure in the rhythm and blues market from pop records was reduced. A few producers took advantage of the changed conditions, orienting their product more directly to black tastes and interests than they had done for some time. While Motown and Mayfield in Chicago perfected styles which appealed to both markets, producers in Memphis and Muscle Shoals worked out several soul styles. These soon were reflected in productions in Houston, Nashville, Chicago, and Los Angeles, and subsequently even in New York and Detroit, where uptown rhythm and blues came to sound increasingly like "soul". When the novelty impact of British groups had worn off, around 1966–67, soul achieved belated recognition, and most of its best exponents (with the exception of Bobby Bland) had major hits.

The main innovations in the gospel-influenced style from 1964 onwards were a greatly increased emphasis on hard rhythms and a general drift towards the raucous style of James Brown and away from the more lyrical purity of Sam Cooke. The thrilling effects of religious gospel singers' styles were used more and more as singers strove for sheer excitement and audience involvement at the expense of the gradual, cumulative tension they had formerly used. Voices became progressively harsher, with more frequent falsetto shrieks, and the rhythm got more and more abrupt, deep, and insistent.

James Brown was the performer most responsible for the simplification of the style. Almost universally acknowledged as "Soul Brother Number One" by the other major soul singers, Brown was in almost every respect the epitome of what they could hope to be. Bobby Bland was the only other performer among the most successful soul singers who had made his first records in a style that was clearly related to the style Brown presented as soul. But where Bland was an interpreter, using other people's compositions, closely supervised by producers in the recording studio and by his manager in the rest of his career,[3] Brown ran his own musical life.

Brown made his first record in 1956, "Please Please Please" (Federal). This atmospheric, intense song made the rhythm and blues top ten, and sold a million copies over a long period. Like almost all Brown's other records, it was more a reflection of the singer than it was a response to contemporary conventions of what constituted a successful record. Brown was the dominant figure in every record he ever made. In most of his pre-1964 records, he used subdued vocal group support and thin musical accompaniment, which provided sufficient atmosphere to confirm the mood his voice suggested but never relegated him to the role of only presenting words or a sound to the audience. What he sang seemed to matter to him.

On stage, the contrivance of his techniques was obvious, but his impact was even stronger than on record. Each performance had a similar pattern, but he invariably instilled a mood of intense excitement in his audience. After the days of the blues bands, he was one of the first singers to assemble a group of supporting singers and tour the country with his own show. At first the supporting singers were his own vocal group, the Famous Flames, whose individual members often made records under their own names and so could be billed separately on the posters and given their own "spots" in the show. They served to warm up the audience before Brown came on for his section.

Brown's repertoire ranged from slow, pleading ballads, "Try Me" and "Prisoner of Love", to rough dance pieces, "Mashed Potato" and "Night Train". These were among the records that occasionally sold quite well in the white market, though without establishing Brown as a well-known figure. Recording for King (in Cincinnati), he produced his own sessions, made his own financial arrangements, and hired the musicians and assistants who worked for him. A rich man, he lived conspicuously well and was widely reported on in *Ebony*, *Jet*, the *Amsterdam News*, and the rest of the black press. Apparently feeling that King was not the company that would establish him in the national market, Brown ignored his contract in 1964 and recorded a hard dance song, "Out of Sight", for the Mercury subsidiary Smash. The record made the lower reaches of the pop charts, but King re-claimed him, and in 1965 managed to get the pop market radio stations to attend to what he was doing. That year "Papa's Got a Brand New Bag", "I Got You", and other dance songs similar to his Smash record were hits, as was the ballad "It's a Man's Man's Man's World" (1966) as well as most of the records he made afterwards.

Although "Man's World" had the string accompaniment that was the traditional visa for acceptance in the pop market, Brown's vocal style on that and all his other records was his own: harsh, raw, rich. Committing himself totally to the emotion appropriate to each song, Brown whined, begged, pleaded, reassured, declared, preached, exclaimed, cried, and exultantly shouted. The rest of the soul singers rarely had ambitions greater than that of doing some of the same things almost as well; and most of them had to compete on stage with the audience's recollection of Brown's stage performance–on his knees, bent over the mike, with sweat streaming down his face, or leaping high across the stage in a dance whose speed and grace gave reason and meaning to the stuttering rhythm of the band.

Only Bobby Bland made no attempt to compete with the brilliant visual, physical aspect of Brown's act. Bland had been working professionally even longer than Brown, and he had a different technique, more subtle, both intimate and modest. A much bigger man than the lithe Brown, Bland had an almost cumbersome presence on stage, although he too bent on one knee in devoted supplication. But he was much less extreme in his style, and more dependent on good musical arrangements to confirm his mood. He never had a major pop hit, but several of his records sold consistently well, achieving million sales by selling over a long period. "Call on Me"/"That's the Way Love Is" (1963) was his biggest hit, with pop arrangements. But in the following year he returned to stronger blues arrangements in "Ain't Nothin' You Can Do" and "Ain't Doin' Too Bad", which were big hits in the rhythm and blues market and small pop hits. He continued to do well, maintaining his own style of occasionally breaking into a harsh cry in an otherwise relaxed delivery.

In 1964, the relatively harsh sound of Brown and Bland had little impact in the popular market, where uptown rhythm and blues retained a tentative hold in competition with the British records. But the sound was echoed and then developed with increasing confidence and originality in studios in Memphis and nearby Muscle Shoals, Alabama, where the best of the new generation of soul singers–Otis Redding, Joe Tex, Wilson Pickett, Sam and Dave, and Percy Sledge–made their best records in the years 1964 to 1966. Redding was equally expressive with fast or slow songs. The others were less versatile. Pickett and Sam and Dave were invariably better with fast songs, while Tex and Sledge handled slow ones more distinctively. Redding and Sam and Dave made virtually all their records at the Stax studios, where Pickett recorded in 1965. Joe Tex, in 1965, and Wilson Pickett, from 1966 onwards, recorded at the Fame studios of producer Rick Hall in Muscle Shoals, while Percy Sledge recorded all his material in nearby Sheffield, Alabama, at the South Camp studios of Quinn Ivy and Marlin Greene.

Otis Redding worked his way out of a crude Little Richard style, displayed on his first record, "Shout Bamalama" (Bethlehem, 1960) and still evident in "Hey Hey Hey", the "B" side of "These Arms of Mine" (Volt, 1962), to achieve a very distinctive and moving style that was best represented in three successive singles during 1964–65, "Mr Pitiful", "I've Been Loving You Too Long", and "Respect". The first and third of these were fast dance songs which were propelled by looping bass figures from bass guitarist Duck Dunn and by insistent, surging riffs from the Mar-Keys' front line. Able to rely on the band to lay down the rhythm, Redding could afford to stay close to it but without emphasizing every alternate beat, as was the current treatment in fast songs. When he did come in hard with the band, the effect was exhilarating.

Despite the fury of the sound, the words of these songs were important, and Redding used the aggression of the music to make the message clear, particularly in "Respect":

All I want
Is a little respect
When I come home.

In the ballad "I've Been Loving You Too Long", the slow, sawing riffs of the band set up a sad mood that established the reverential mood Redding needed, but the arrangement had progressed beyond simply representing a gospel group's harmonies with instrumental harmonies–a new style had evolved from the experiments with a previous one.

It was ironic that the popular music audience paid so little attention to these records of Redding's, whose riffs and tone and rhythm contributed so much inspiration to the records that were being listened to, particularly those of the British group the Rolling Stones. In an attempt to attract the audience's attention, Redding, at the suggestion of Steve Cropper, recorded the Rolling Stones' song "Satisfaction". He later told an interviewer that he had not wanted to make the record, which was a crude, harsh parody of his earlier performances. But the record achieved the aim set for it. It was played on the pop music stations, and Redding's reputation began to soar. But none of the records he made after 1965 were comparable to those he had already made; in his determination to reach the audience, he took to repeating "gotta, gotta, gotta", and redundant grunts. "I Can't Turn You Loose" had a good fast bass line, but an unjustified hysterical vocal; "Try a Little Tenderness" (1966) began with a searing interpretation that was irresistible, yet it too built up to a frenzy that bore no relation to the words or mood of the song.

Joe Tex was a much less emotional singer, though by coincidence he too had recorded in Little Richard style early in his career, which stretched back to 1954. Tex recorded in a gospel blues style for King, did novelty songs for Ace, and began recording for the Nashville-based Dial Records in 1961, under Buddy Killen's supervision. With Killen, Tex worked out one of the earliest fusions of black gospel singing styles and white country and western material, writing his own songs but in a form similar to the narrative morality plays that were part of the standard fare of country and western music. The arrangements invariably sounded cluttered until late 1964, when Dial, formerly distributed by London, made a new distribution arrangement with Atlantic, and Tex went to Rick Hall's studios in

Muscle Shoals, where he recorded "Hold What You've Got". Although the musicians were the same members of his own band that had been with him for some time, the sound was cleaner, Tex more relaxed, and the rhythm more firmly stated. "Hold What You've Got"–a piece of paternal advice to lovers contemplating the thought of leaving their partners–became the first southern soul song to make the pop top ten, in early 1965.

Subsequently, Tex recorded in New York and Nashville. But he had found the sound he needed and could reproduce it anywhere, and his lyrics became more witty or sermonizing, depending on whether he was celebrating womankind–"I Want To (Do Everything For You)," "A Sweet Woman Like You"–or keeping relationships on an even keel–"The Love You Save (May Be Your Own)". A rumbling piano gave several records a raunchy sound that suggested a sensuality not often present in the lyrics themselves. With a tone midway between Bobby Bland's and Solomon Burke's, Tex had a tendency to sound glib and smug on the sermons, but he seemed truly impressed with the woman who inspired him to gasp, "You got what it takes–to take what I got" (in "You Got What It Takes").

Wilson Pickett was the biggest commercial success of the new generation of soul singers, and had several top ten hits. But like Otis Redding, he made his best records in 1965, when the pop music market was not listening. Having recorded in New York after leaving the Falcons in 1962, he went South to Memphis for the first time in 1965, and with Steve Cropper and the rest of the Stax band cut "In the Midnight Hour" and "Don't Fight It", two of the finest soul dance records, which had a genuinely happy spirit and an easy surging rhythm that contrasted with Pickett's later successes, cut in Muscle Shoals (among others his new versions of "Mustang Sally", "634-5789", and "Land of 1,000 Dances").

Among the few records to rival the excitement of Pickett's 1965 records were "Hold On, I'm A-Comin' ", "You Got Me Hummin' ", and "You Don't Know Like I Know", by Sam and Dave. The use of two voices answering each other in a rapid dialogue at times, echoing each other's phrases at others, and singing harmony in the choruses was a standard device of real–that is, church-based–gospel singing and had been used with less robust rhythmic support by several popular black vocal groups. Marvin and Johnny in the mid-fifties made several fast answer-back records (as well as their more famous slow "Cherry Pie"), Don and Dewey with Specialty had employed similar techniques on several fine duo records, including "Farmer John", and the Sims Twins–and Sam and Dave themselves, for Roulette–had recorded in a more gospel-influenced style during the early sixties. But with Stax, Sam and Dave made records that surpassed the excitement of earlier duo performances because they were answering not only each other but the encouraging riffs of the band. Almost alone of the soul singers who made good records in this period, Sam and Dave were able to maintain their standard into the years when soul became widely popular, from late 1966 onward.

The first soul record to top the best-selling lists in the popular market was "When a Man Loves a Woman" by Percy Sledge, which sought, and achieved, a feeling for sheer beauty that few records could hope for. Sledge had a really good voice, and did not have to lose his control as he reached high, being gently supported by the musicians who had been working with Rick Hall for some time. In contrast to the considerable experience of the other major soul singers, Sledge had never made a record before, and his style was suitably original–and influential. While he managed to come remarkably close to recapturing the delicacy of "When a Man Loves a Woman" with "Take Time to Know Her" and "It Tears Me Up", other singers tried with less success (musically, at least, if not commercially: Procol Harum used surrealist words but almost exactly the same mood on "Whiter Shade of Pale", a huge international hit).

IV: 1966–74

In an attempt to protect its "copyright" on its unique blend of exciting rhythm patterns, expressive singers, and catchy songs, Stax closed its doors to outsiders in 1966. Only artists whose records were released on Stax or Volt could use its house band, staff-writers, and recording studio. The blow was aimed at Atlantic, whose producer Jerry Wexler had fully appreciated the benefits of a studio set-up which did not charge by the hour, but by the completed song.

In New York, where the charges were based on time, most producers hired arrangers to map out the basic parts in advance, and the results were often boringly predictable. But in Memphis, the musicians evolved new rhythm patterns and song structures by playing the songs through over and over, and Wexler had himself made a vital contribution at the session for Wilson Pickett's "Midnight Hour"; the distinctive, "anticipated" beat of that track inspired the Stax sound for the next two or three years, notably on most of Sam and Dave's raunchy, suggestive hits, and Eddie Floyd's "Knock on Wood" (1967).

Ironically, Stax probably suffered more from its own restrictive practice than Atlantic, whose artists Otis Redding and Sam and Dave were able to continue to record there because their records were issued on the Volt and Stax labels. Unable to take his other artists to Stax, Jerry Wexler explored other locations which would give him access to the Southern Groove, and effectively put at least three more studios into America's pop mainstream: Rick Hall's Fame studio in Florence, Alabama; the neighbouring Muscle Shoals Sound studio; and Criteria in Miami. Wexler also captured a close approximation of the Southern sound back at Atlantic's own studio in New York.

Much of this activity was going on virtually unnoticed and unrecognized outside the record industry, because, despite all the musical parallels between soul and rock 'n' roll, soul had no figurehead to compare with Elvis Presley, around whom the marketing men and media commentators could cluster. Otis Redding came close, as he was belatedly "discovered" by the white rock audience in 1967 after coming back from a European tour where he was considered an ambassador of the music which inspired local groups like the Rolling Stones. Otis played the Fillmore in San Francisco and the Monterey Pop Festival, and responded by writing the calm and introspective "(Sitting on the) Dock of the Bay", which he and Steve Cropper recorded with sound effects of seagull cries, lapping waves, and whistling. It was similar to the change of direction that Sam Cooke had made three years earlier with "A Change Is Gonna Come", and by a bizarre coincidence Otis was also killed soon after recording the new style; the single became another of pop's mocking success stories, going all the way to the top of the chart, too late.

Soon afterwards, Stax completed its split from Atlantic by making a new distribution deal with Paramount/Dot, lured by enormous advance payments from their corporate parents Gulf-Western. Al Bell, a black promotion man from Washington, DC, came in to run Stax, which took on an increasingly "black" image in an era when black consciousness was growing fast. Isaac Hayes stepped forward in bare-chest-and-chains, emerging from his role as co-writer of most of Sam and Dave's hits to growl his way through albums of ballads and write the very successful theme tune for the popular *Shaft* movie, using wah-wah guitar to clever effect (top of the chart, 1971).

Johnnie Taylor, a former protégé of Sam Cooke, who had recorded with little success for Stax for a couple of years, suddenly found his form under the supervision of producer Don Davis in "Who's Making Love" (top five in 1968). They followed with other similar dance-oriented songs, fiercely delivered in a Wilson Pickett mode, but Taylor put himself in soul's First Division with a series of slow-tempo, bluesy sermons during the early seventies, including "I Am Somebody" (1970), "I Believe in You" (1973) and "I've Been Born Again" (1974).

Ironically, the most innovative records on Stax in this period were not made in Memphis, but were produced by Al Bell at Muscle Shoals

Sound for the Staple Singers. The veteran gospel group at last found a context to deliver the husky, inviting voice of Mavis Staples to the pop public, with the definitive blend of sexual promise and social togetherness of "I'll Take You There" (top of the chart in 1972) and "If You're Ready (Come Go With Me)" (1973).

The Stax operation closed down in 1974 in a similar debacle to Vee Jay's in Chicago ten years before, leaving Hi Records as the main vehicle for the sounds of Memphis–as it had been at the time Stax started. Willie Mitchell, who had played trumpet on sessions organized by Ike Turner for Modern/RPM in the mid-fifties, and made instrumental records of no particular significance during the sixties, used all his experience to galvanize Al Green into a series of masterly performances in the early 1970s.

At last, soul found itself a true star, as Al Green crooned, beseeched, and insinuated his way into real acceptance by pop radio and its listeners, without losing the black fans of rhythm and blues music. Mitchell produced and engineered, while a band of new names followed every subtle inflection of Green's voice with an always appropriate instrumental touch; three Hodges brothers–Tennie on guitar, Charles on keyboards, and Leroy on bass–rivalled the best that Booker T. and his Memphis Group had achieved back in the heydays of Stax, alongside the drummer from those days, Al Jackson. Possibly the greatest drummer of his time, Jackson was shot dead at his home in Memphis, and was deputized by another outstandingly tasteful time-keeper, Howard Grimes.

Al Green's first big hit "Tired of Being Alone" (in 1971), was followed by "Let's Stay Together" and "I'm Still in Love With You" (1972), all classics of understated passion. While Green kept his place for seven more top twenty hits, Willie Mitchell and the Hi rhythm section worked their spell for other singers. Ann Peebles put her foot in the doorway of pop fame with the moody "I Can't Stand The Rain" for Hi in 1973 and Syl Johnson seemed poised for bigger success with "Take Me to the River" in 1975, but by then the nation's dancers were tuned to a different kind of groove. Denise LaSalle, although signed to Westbound of Detroit, used the Hi set-up on "Trapped By a Thing Called Love" (top of the rhythm and blues chart, 1971) and the humorous "Man-Sized Job" (1972). After a decade when most female singers were obliged to sing songs written by men and delivered in a demure, accessible manner, Denise LaSalle exuded a tougher challenge which recalled the styles of Willie Mae Thornton and LaVern Baker. In the vanguard of this new role for women, was Aretha Franklin.

The daughter of Detroit church minister C. L. Franklin, Aretha had spent five almost fruitless years at Columbia, recording with orchestras, jazz trios, and everything in between, without ever capturing the combination of charismatic personality and vocal power which her admirers had witnessed in live performances. She switched to Atlantic in 1967, and for her first session went with Jerry Wexler down to Rick Hall's studio in Florence, Alabama, home of recent hits by Joe Tex and Wilson Pickett.

Aretha Franklin's first record for Atlantic was "I've Never Loved a Man (The Way That I Love You)", a classic performance that opened with a quiet but dramatic organ figure in some kind of soul-waltz time, and built into a hammering, screaming, but always controlled, yell of delight. The brilliantly organized band arrangement fed one instrument after another into the cauldron being stirred by the singer's emotion: a swaying sax riff, shimmering guitar licks, surging bass. Where so many soul records found one solid groove and stuck unwaveringly to it, this one had dynamic variations that turned it into a real pop record, and it deserved better than to just scrape into the top ten.

If that first record caught the world by surprise, everyone was ready from then on, and Aretha had an unparalleled series of hits–eight in the top ten, followed by ten more in the top forty, and then five more top ten hits by 1974. But although this run had been started in the Muscle Shoals, Aretha would not go back there. Instead, Wexler had to piece together a session team in New York which learned to play with the flexibility and rhythmic passion that distinguished the Southern teams. At first, he shipped Southern musicians to the north, but gradually, and with the help of veteran saxman King Curtis, Aretha and Wexler assembled a local team who fitted the bill: Richard Tee on keyboards, Cornell Dupree on guitar, Chuck Rainey on bass, and Bernard Purdie on drums. Other players came in around this nucleus, and soon New York had its own soul source.

Aretha Franklin was not much of a writer, but like Ray Charles before her she had a gift for turning songs inside out, redefining their feel, mood and meaning, and often establishing the definitive approach to them. She delivered Otis Redding's "Respect", Don Covay's "Chain of Fools" and Bacharach and David's "Say a Little Prayer" with sass, passion, and class, while Wexler commissioned Goffin and King to write a song specially for her called "A Natural Woman",which inspired one of Aretha's best performances. The all-stops-out approach began to get wearing, but in 1971 Aretha slowed down her pace in a masterly reading of Paul Simon's "Bridge Over Troubled Water", and then topped even that with a complete transformation of "Spanish Harlem", recorded in Miami with some deliciously deft touches on organ from Mac Rebennack. By then, engineer Tom Dowd and arranger Arif Mardin were being credited with Wexler as co-producers, and in effect this team managed to merge the previously distinct streams of "soul" and "uptown rhythm and blues". The days of the spontaneous jam session led by the vocalist were numbered (Al Green was probably the last of this kind of soul singer), and producers of black music would increasingly impose the shape and feel of recording sessions.

While independently-produced soul records continued to surface from Southern studios, Atlantic* was one of the first to offer some kind of licensing or distribution deal. Jackie Moore's old-fashioned soul ballad "Precious Precious", produced in Atlanta by Dave Crawford in 1971, was signed direct to Atlantic, and King Floyd's sparse "Groove Me" was picked up for national distribution from Chimneyville records of Jackson, Mississippi the same year; the bass-player on "Groove Me" had obviously been listening to recent reggae records from Jamaica, and his odd timing gave the record a hypnotic fascination. In turn, the Muscle Shoals bass player on "I'll Take You

* ATLANTIC. *Directed by owners Ahmet Ertegun, Nesuhi Ertegun, and Jerry Wexler. Rhythm and blues: the Drifters, Solomon Burke, Don Covay, Clarence Carter, Wilson Pickett, Percy Sledge, Barbara Lewis.*

Subsidiary:

ATCO
Pop: Sonny and Cher.
Rock: Buffalo Springfield.
Rhythm and blues: Ben E. King, Otis Redding (also on Volt, see below), Arthur Conley.

Distribution labels:

STAX. *Formed in 1960 in Memphis as Satellite Records by Jim Stewart and Estelle Axton, who changed the name to Stax in 1961. Distributed by Atlantic until 1968; by Paramount/Dot from 1968 to 1971; by Columbia from 1972. A&R: Jim Stewart, plus assorted in-house musicians and writers: Steve Cropper (guitar), Booker T. Jones (keyboards), Al Jackson (drums), Isaac Hayes (keyboards) and David Porter, Don Davis, Al Bell.*
Male rhythm and blues: Rufus Thomas, William Bell, Eddie Floyd, Johnnie Taylor, Isaac Hayes, Frederick Knight.
Female rhythm and blues: Carla Thomas, Mabel John, Shirley Brown, Jean Knight.
Vocal group: the Staples Singers.
Blues: Albert King.
Instrumental: the Mar-Keys, Booker T. and the M.G.'s, the Bar-Kays.

Subsidiary:

VOLT:
Male rhythm and blues: Otis Redding.

DIAL. *Formed in 1962 in Nashville by Buddy Killen. Distributed by London 1962 to 1963 and by Atlantic from 1964.*
Male rhythm and blues: Joe Tex, Paul Kelly.

FAME. *Formed in 1962 in Florence, Alabama, by Rick Hall. Distributed by Vee Jay, 1962 to 1964; by Atlantic from 1965 to 1968; by Capitol from 1968 to 1972; and by United Artists from 1973.*
Rhythm and blues: Jimmy Hughes, Clarence Carter, Candi Staton.

There", by the Staple Singers, heard "Groove Me", and added more notes to the same basic rhythm line.

Miami had already begun to emerge as a source of soul productions before Jerry Wexler took Aretha down to record there, but in the wake of her success the area seemed to explode. Betty Wright's "Clean Up Woman" was the first local production to make the national top ten, and one of the last soul records whose guitar riff was a more important rhythmic feature than bass and drums. Atlantic distributed that hit on Alston, but the label owner Henry Stone subsequently went through independent distributors with several huge hits on Glades (Timmy Thomas) and TK (George McCrae, KC and the Sunshine Band), which opened up the "Disco" boom of the mid-seventies.

The only New York company to challenge Atlantic's dominance in the South during the late sixties was Larry Utall's Bell Records*, which distributed Goldwax and Rising Sons, and licensed product from AGP of Memphis, Papa Don of Florida, and Sansu of New Orleans. Sansu was one of the companies owned by Marshall Sehorn and Allen Toussaint, whose productions always stood apart from contemporary Southern records, rhythmically distinct and lyrically quirky.

* BELL. *Formed circa 1964 in New York by Larry Utall after a merger between his own Madison label and Al Massler's Amy-Mala. Bell was bought by Columbia Pictures in the late sixties, with Utall still as president until he sold out in 1974 to form his own Private Stock label, while Clive Davis was brought in to run Bell, now renamed Arista and sold to Ariola of Germany in 1980.*

AMY. *Formed by Al Massler in 1960.*
Pop: Al Brown's Tunetoppers, Tico and the Triumphs.
Rhythm and blues: Lee Dorsey.

MADISON. *Formed in 1960 by Larry Utall.*
Pop: Dante and the Evergreens.

MALA. *Formed in 1961.*
Rhythm and blues: Bunker Hill.
Pop: the Box Tops.

BELL. *Formed in 1964.*
Pop: Merrilee Rush, Dawn, the Partridge Family featuring David Cassidy, the Syndicate of Sound.
Rhythm and blues: James and Boby Purify, Oscar Toney Jr (both leased from Papa Don Enterprises, run by Don Schroeder in Pensacola, Florida).
From UK: Gary Glitter, the Bay City Rollers.

Distribution labels:

DIMENSION. (*see previous roster*).

DYNOVOICE/NEW VOICE. *Formed in 1966 in New York by Bob Crewe.*
Pop: The Toys, Mitch Ryder & the Detroit Wheels.

GOLDWAX. *Formed in 1966 in Memphis by Quinton Claunch and Doc Russell.*
Rhythm and blues: James Carr, the Ovations.

Allen Toussaint's career as a hit producer had been interrupted when he was drafted in 1963, and by the time he came back in 1965 most of the musicians he had worked with at Minit had gone west to California. But Toussaint built a new studio team around keyboard player Art Neville, and continued his explorations of the peculiar New Orleans rhythms known as "the second line". There were probably better singers in the city than Lee Dorsey, but his rough-and-ready but always friendly tone seemed best-suited to Toussaint's songs. "Ride Your Pony" (1965) and "Get Out My Life, Woman" (1966) put the team back in the rhythm and blues charts, and was followed by two international pop hits in 1966 with "Working in a Coalmine" and "Holy Cow", all for Amy Records. Dorsey's career tailed off, but his last hit for Amy in 1969 turned out to be an accurate prediction of the direction black music took in the seventies: "Everything I Do Gonh Be Funky (From Now On)".

"Funk" had been used as one of those euphemistic black expressions for years: it suggested the smells of sex, a simple lifestyle, and a particular kind of raunchy rhythm which mimicked the grind of love-makers. In New Orleans, pianists played around with the beats of their left hand in a way that was sometimes called "funky", and bass-players began to mess about with the timing between their beats and the drummers'. For musicians bored with the same old two-and-four off-beat, funk was fun to play, and the man who pursued it most fanatically was James Brown.

Acknowledged by most other soul performers as "Soul Brother Number One", James Brown rarely returned to the conventional structures of "Papa's Got a Brand New Bag", "I Got You" and "It's a Man's World" that had given him the biggest pop hits of his career in 1965 and 1966. Instead he turned all his attention to the function of funk for dancers, reducing the verbal content of his records to repeated phrases and exhortations. The rare exception was "Say It Loud, I'm Black and I'm Proud", which gave him his last top ten pop hit (King, 1968) with a recognizable chorus and a clear message. Otherwise, he settled for sales to juke boxes and to dancers, leaving others to borrow the guitar licks, bass lines and drum patterns from his records and put them into more accessible contexts: Dyke and the Blazers ("Funky Broadway", Original Sound, 1967), the Fat Back Band, and Funkadelic were among the bands whose careers were closely based on Brown's rhythmic innovations. Sly and the Family Stone, David Bowie, and many more made occasional use of them.

Rock 'n' roll's first singing songwriter: **Roy Brown** (New Orleans)
(photo by James Kreigsman)

Louis Jordan's Tympany Five
(Louis, from Brinkley, Arkansas, third left, with alto sax)

Hank Williams
(Birmingham, Alabama; seated left)

Amos Milburn
(Houston, Texas)

Aladdin 78 sleeve

Joe Turner
(Kansas City, Missouri)

Atlantic 78 sleeve

The Clovers
(from Baltimore; lead vocalist Buddy Bailey, second right)

The Five Royales
(from South Carolina; lead vocalist Johnny Tanner, front left; guitarist-writer Lowman Pauling, center)
(photo by James Kreigsman)

New Orleans Pioneers

Shirley and Lee
(photo by James Kreigsman)

Fats Domino
(*The Big Beat* [UPI])

From Georgia

Ray Charles
(Albany)

Little Richard
(Macon)

From Mississippi

Howlin' Wolf
(West Point)

Muddy Waters
(Rolling Fork)

The Rock 'n' Roll Prophets

Cleveland-based disc jockey **Alan Freed**
(From *Rock Rock Rock* [Directors Corporation of America])

Bill Haley & His Comets
(Pennsylvania; Haley, top right, with kiss-curl)

The New Exuberants

Elvis Presley
(Tupelo, Mississippi)

LaVern Baker
(Chicago) (*Rock Rock Rock* [Directors Corporation of America])

Pop Goes the Guitar

Chuck Berry
(St. Louis) in *Mr Rock 'n' Roll* (Paramount Pictures)

Lonnie Donegan
(Glasgow, Scotland)

Gene Vincent and the Bluecaps
(Norfolk, Virginia: Gene in striped shirt) in *The Girl Can't Help It*
(20th Century Fox)

Buddy Holly
(guitar; Lubbock, West Texas) with fellow Crickets, Jerry Allison (drums) and Joe Mauldin (bass), on TV in Britain (*Off The Road* [BBC])

Rock 'n' Roll Entertainers

From Sugarhill in Harlem to top of the bill in England:
Frankie Lymon and the Teenagers
(photo by Al Ferdman)

The Coasters
(Los Angeles)

Jerry Lee Lewis
(Ferriday, Louisiana)
in *High School Confidential*
(Loews incorporated)

Sam and Barbara Cooke
(*Jet* [Johnson Publications)]

Sam Cooke
(Chicago) (AP)

The Everly Brothers
(Kentucky)

Dion and the Belmonts
(The Bronx)

The Shirelles
(New Jersey; lead singer Shirley Owens, right)

Early Sixties Hardcore R & B

Junior Parker
(Clarksdale, Mississippi)

Bobby Bland
(Rosemont, Tennessee)

Ike
(Clarksdale) and
Tina Turner
(Nutbush, Tennessee)

Little Willie John
(Camden, Arkanasas)

The Changing Faces of Sixties Pop

The Springfields
(Dusty, center; London, England)
(*It's All Over Town* [British Lion Pictures])

The Beach Boys
(Los Angeles, California)

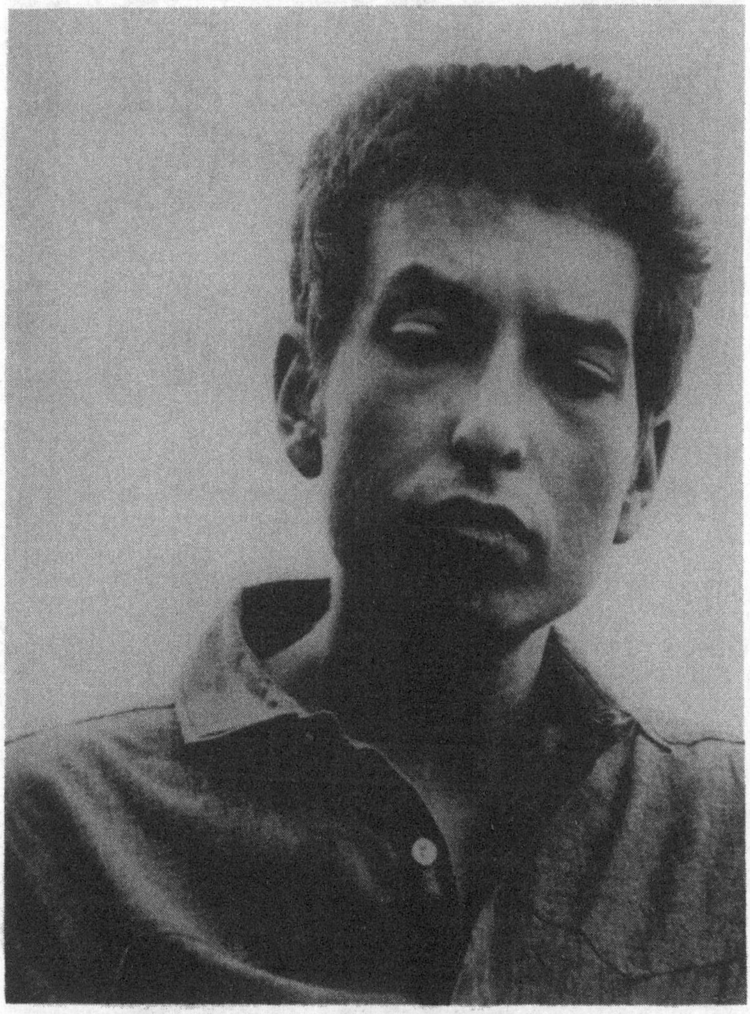

Bob Dylan
(Minnesota)

Detroit's Motown Teams, Part One

The Miracles (bottom), whose lead singer **Smokey Robinson** (seated) also wrote hits for **Marvin Gaye** (following page) and the **Temptations** (top; lead singers Eddie Kendricks [own mike, right] and David Ruffin [glasses])

Detroit's Motown Teams, Part Two

Lamont Dozier (at piano) with Brian and Eddie Holland, writer-producers for the **Supremes** (opposite page, top; Diana Ross on left) and the **Four Tops** (bottom; Levi Stubbs on right)

Mobbed in America

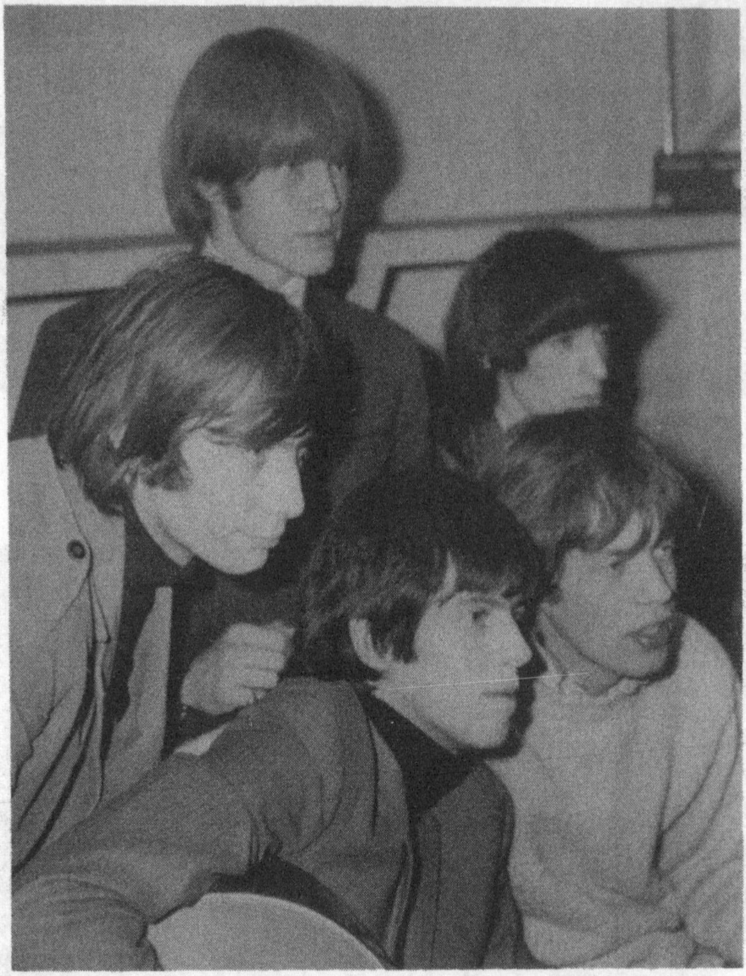

The Rolling Stones (from London, England) with Mick Jagger (right), Keith Richard (front), Brian Jones (standing), Charlie Watts (left) and bass-man Bill Wyman.

The Beatles
(from Liverpool, England) with vocalists John Lennon, Paul McCartney (bass) and George Harrison (guitar) and drummer Ringo Starr on British TV — *Thank Your Lucky Stars* (ITV)

Harbingers of the video age: picture bags for singles.

Revered in Britain

James Brown
(Augusta, Georgia)

J.B. in London with British singers **Georgie Fame** (Liverpool; left) and **Eric Burdon** of the Animals (Newcastle)

Jimmy Reed
(Leland, Mississippi)

John Lee Hooker
(Clarksdale, Mississippi)

Mid-Sixties New York

The Upside: **The Lovin Spoonful** (John Sebastian, bottom right)

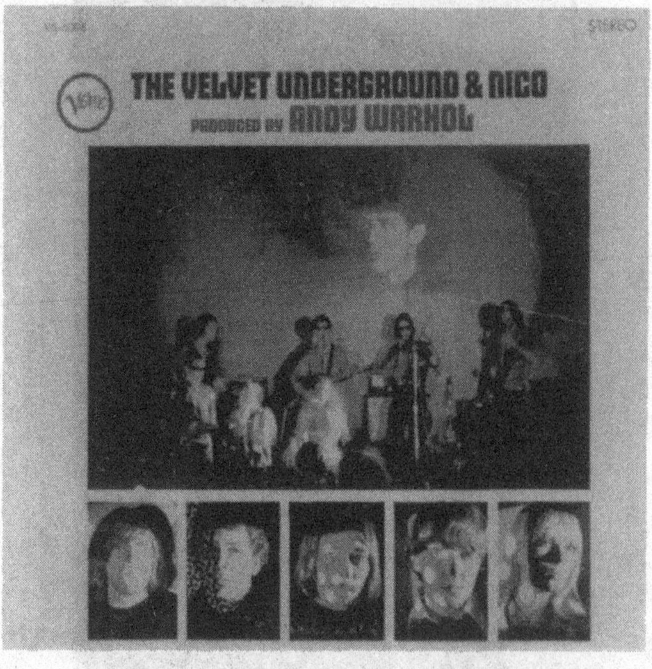

The Downside: **The Velvet Underground** (Lou Reed, second left)

Producer Tom Wilson (right) with Eric Burdon (*Ebony* Magazine [Johnson Publications])

Simon & Garfunkel
(New York) (Monterey Pop [Pennebaker Films])

Memphis, 1967

Sam & Dave
(from Florida and Georgia)

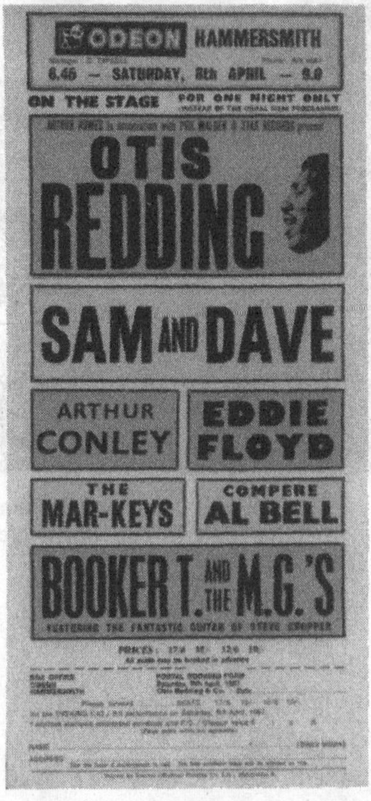

Handbill from UK Tour

Steve Cropper
(Missouri), guitarist with
Booker T. & the MGs
and cowriter/coproducer

Otis Redding
(Macon, Georgia)
(*Monterey Pop*,
Pennebaker Films)

British Guitarists

Eric Clapton
(reading the *Beano*)

Jeff Beck, front left, with the **Yardbirds**

Jimmy Page
of Led Zeppelin

Pete Townshed
(airborn) with the **Who**

Buffalo Springfield
(Stephen Stills far right, next to Neil Young)

The Doors
(Jim Morrison, right)

Janis Joplin
(Port Authur, Texas) in *Monterey Pop* (Pennebaker Films)

Jimi Hendrix
(Seattle, Washington)

Aretha Franklin
(Memphis-born, Detroit-raised)

The Staples Singers,
led by guitarist Roebuck "Pops" Staples (Winona, Mississippi) and featuring his vocalist daughter Mavis (Chicago; right)

Creedence Clearwater Revival
(Northern California; John Fogerty, left)

The Band
(mostly from Canada, except Arkansas-born Levon Helm, center)
(photo by Eliot Landy)

Sly & the Family Stone
(San Francisco; Sly Stone, front right)

The Wailers
(Jamaica, West Indies; Bob Marley, center)

Curtis Mayfield
(Chicago)

Al Green
(Arkansas-born, Michigan-raised; recorded in Memphis)

Van Morrison
(Belfast, Northern Ireland)

PART IV

ECHOES FROM THE CITY CENTRES, 1962–71

11

TRANSATLANTIC ECHOES

Rock 'n' roll took so many people by surprise in 1956 because it was based on a conception of popular music different from the one previously held by audiences, performers, and people working in the industry. Popular music, it had been assumed, was entertainment, and entertainment was escape, which necessarily meant the substitution of sentimental pleasantries, or sensational effects, for a more authentic consideration of relationships and experience.

But rock 'n' roll singers treated popular music as a medium for self-expression, and rock 'n' roll composers directed their lyrics to specific situations instead of amorphous generalities. Without much conscious determination to be artists, the singers and composers created a music that altered the way attentive people in the audience subsequently reacted to their own experience. Audiences of jazz and classical music had always included people who assumed that such an alteration of consciousness was the role of music and who, accordingly, expected to enjoy music intellectually as well as (sometimes instead of) emotionally. Few people in the rock 'n' roll audience deliberately or consciously considered music in the same light. Rock 'n' roll gave them pleasure, in a way no other music had or could. Compared to the forms the popular music audience had known, rock 'n' roll had not compromised itself nor had it resorted to contrived effects in order to be commercial. Rock 'n' roll records did not get boring, and did not seem to date, as did other kinds of popular music. So people listened to their rock 'n' roll records more often and over a longer period than they listened to other kinds of music–and absorbed, without necessarily intending to, an intuitive understanding of the people who had performed the music on the records.

It was not the business of people working in the music industry to consider the artistic possibilities of rock 'n' roll. Radio programmers and most record producers believed in any case that the potential audience for rock 'n' roll was not a sufficient proportion of the total popular music market to justify any special provision. So, after its period of popularity, the music was plundered for anything that could be used in some other mode with wider appeal, and it otherwise was more or less ignored. Occasionally, odd circumstances led to the production of a good rock 'n' roll record during the sixties, as in the session of Ronnie Hawkins and the Hawks that produced "Who Do You Love" at the Roulette studios in New York in 1963, or the session by the Indiana guitarist Lonnie Mack that produced the instrumental "Memphis" (Fraternity) in Nashville the same year. By coincidence "Memphis" sounded sufficiently similar to the current West Coast "surfing music" which was a fad at the time for the record to make the national top ten, though it was immeasurably better than the surfing music–a development of rock 'n' roll that used several modestly amplified guitars to generate an emphatic but quietly played rhythm, while Mack improvized variations to the melody of Chuck Berry's "Memphis, Tennessee". Mostly this was a period of crude dance records, image singers, and uptown rhythm and blues productions.

Meanwhile, the audience that had been excited by rock 'n' roll went on living, finishing school, going to work or college. Many of them continued to buy records and a few of them played music. What they bought and heard and played was to some extent determined by their experience of rock 'n' roll. Chasing the vivid images of the lyrics or the implied protest of its mood, the excitement of its rhythms or the techniques of its musicians, the audience discovered the blues, folk music, rhythm and blues, and jazz. Those who knew which station to tune to, which club to go to on which night, which magazine or paper to read, which friend to visit, managed also to keep in touch with the few contemporary records that retained contact with the culture that had originally inspired rock 'n' roll.

Then, in 1962, a new music began to emerge, played by people who both delved back and yet also kept familiar with present styles. In homage to its source of inspiration the music was generically called "rock", although as usual there were many distinct musical strains disguised under the single, simple category. A major source of the new music was Britain, which had made no previous significant contribution to popular music in the twentieth century. But in the years around 1962, Britain served the useful function of re-establishing popular music as a medium for personal expression rather than as the raw material for mass-produced entertainment, which it once again had become.

The reaction to rock 'n' roll in Britain had been slightly different from the reaction in the States, where it had evolved gradually out of relationships between audiences and performers, which had expressed themselves through secondary channels of communication, the specialist radio stations and maverick disc jockeys. In Britain, there was no comparable network of secondary media. There was an establishment, and virtually nothing else: four major record companies and two radio networks, one owned by the government and the other effectively controlled by the record companies. There were no specialist radio stations in Britain and no maverick disc jockeys. This situation meant that if audiences and performers were to communicate with each other they had to do so in live performances, and if, in this process, they managed to create a form of music with a sufficiently wide interest, the record companies and radio stations would then recognize it, record and broadcast it. The companies and stations did not appear to conceive of innovation as part of their roles.

I

Britain had had little sense, in the twentieth century, of its own popular culture, either regionally or nationally. A few folk styles survive from the nineteenth century and earlier. In music, a few people have attempted to extend the lyric ballads of folk song into the twentieth century, to record their reactions to contemporary experience with a style of melody and harmony drawn from an earlier period, but these singers have never had consistently wide appeal.

Culture, in Britain, has been identified mainly with a middle and upper class which has few regional roots–except perhaps in London, where the head offices of all the national press, the headquarters of the national radio and television company (the BBC), and the film companies, publishing houses, and major theatres are all based.

Although all of these entertainment industries have produced commercially successful material, much of it has been either derivative of American material or else stunted by the narrow conceptions of its producers. The culture/entertainment industry has become one of the few possible careers that give ambitious arts graduates both the salary and social status they want; it is much less accessible to the unqualified but talented and/or imaginative man who, in the United States, might become the equivalent of Sam Phillips, Alan Freed, or Berry Gordy.

Theatre, painting, poetry, classical music, and fiction are the preferred art forms. But because of their small audiences they do not provide many people with a living, and the majority of people working in the culture/entertainment industry have to take music, radio, TV, and film as the more accessible alternatives of earning a livelihood. Even through these media, the other forms are perpetuated, so that plays, poetry, and classical music take up large sections of time on radio, while TV and film often adapt stage plays or novels. The emphasis has tended to be on the higher arts, which has meant on cultural forms that rarely express the concerns of more than a small proportion of the nation's people and that are inaccessible to the rest. (This description is less accurate than it would have been three or four years ago, largely because of the extraordinary impact on British culture of the musical changes described here–and their associated social changes.)

As an alternative to all of this, there was American culture, readily available and easily enjoyed. In comic books, western and gangster films, and detective fiction, the confrontations between characters were direct (rarely tangled in the conventions of class, accent, and status that pervaded British equivalents), experience was recorded simply, feelings were open, ambition was (it seemed) unlimited, success was (so we understood) real.

In music, as with the rest of popular culture, the British institutions distributed the American product, reproduced their own versions of American records, and made a few halfhearted attempts to create some kind of "British" popular music.

Four record companies dominated the market during the mid-fifties–EMI, Decca, Philips, and Pye. Controlling the market even more effectively than did the six big American companies, they had virtually all the hit records, both through their contracts with American companies for releasing the latters' product, and through their own English records.

Of these companies, EMI and Decca were the strongest, particularly after rock 'n' roll records began to appear among the music sent from America for British release. The two companies between them had access to virtually all the important sources of American hits.*

Among the few small British companies that had any impact on

* *From 1956 to 1960, the four British majors handled the following labels:*

EMI: HMV (included product from RCA-Victor until 1957): Parlophone; Columbia; Capitol (from 1956, when EMI took over ownership of the American company, whose records had previously been released by Decca); MGM; and Mercury (from 1958, when rights were acquired from Pye).

American companies whose records were released on these labels: ABC-Paramount (on HMV); Atlantic and Chess (1957, on Columbia); King (1957 to 1960, on Parlophone); Roulette; Gee.

DECCA: Decca (limited to British-produced records); Brunswick (restricted to material from US Decca); Vogue-Coral, later Coral (released material from US Brunswick and US Coral); London (see below); RCA.

American companies whose records were released on London: Specialty, Sun, Imperial, Atlantic, Modern, Keen, Dot, Liberty, Cadence, Atlantic, Chess.

American companies released through Vogue (a semi-independent company owned by Decca but administered from separate offices): Aladdin: King (until 1957); Duke/Peacock. Vogue's records were oriented primarily to jazz audiences or to Britain's West Indian audience.

PHILIPS: Distributed product from American Columbia.

PYE: Pye, Pye-Nixa, Mercury (1956 to 1958).

this period were Oriole, Ember, and Top Rank, each of which had occasional hits. Top Rank, formed in 1958, obtained the rights to Scepter/Wand, Fire/Fury, and Vee Jay, but despite the interesting material it thereby released still could not maintain independent status and was taken over by EMI in 1960. Two other companies, Melodisc and Starlite (the latter a subsidiary of a jazz label, Esquire), were oriented to the West Indian market, which was concentrated in London and Birmingham.

The only two ways the independents could reach the public was through the two radio networks. The BBC was government-owned; it had two national channels (one of "light entertainment" and one of specialist high culture material) plus a third channel which was regional in orientation and had very little music. By an arrangement with the British Musicians' Union, the BBC had a limited allocation of time allowed for playing recorded music as such. Most of its airtime was devoted to a varied selection of new radio dramas, comedy shows, opinion panels, and live music shows, the latter of which ranged from cinema organ sessions through palm court trios to jazz and popular music. During the period of rock 'n' roll, most of the music shows were family-oriented request programmes, which invariably concluded with a presumably educative extract from a classical music composition. The exception was a two-hour programme every Saturday morning which began in 1958. Called "Saturday Club" and hosted by Brian Matthew, the programme developed a distinctive, coherent format, mixing live singers and records with interviews and an informed commentary from Matthew.

The alternative radio outlet was Radio Luxembourg, a commercial station based on the continent which had an English language programme for five or six hours every evening. Some of the station's shows were request programmes, a few were light entertainment shows, but the largest part of the station's income came from several nightly programmes that featured the product of a record company. Able to finance several such shows each week, the big companies consolidated their advantage over the small ones, which necessarily had to depend on a few plays on request shows for their exposure.

Apart from various foreign language stations which could be heard in Britain, and the American Forces Network and Voice of America shows, to which a minority tuned in, there was no alternative to the BBC and Luxembourg shows. People who developed specialist taste had to find out about their music from friends, and from the pop music press.

Unlike the United States, which had "serious" magazines devoted to jazz (*Down Beat, Metronome*) but only trade papers (*Billboard, Cash Box*), fan magazines (*Hep Cats*), and lyric magazines (*Hit*

Parader) dealing with pop music, Britain in this period had two weekly papers devoted to pop music. *Melody Maker* was devoted mainly to jazz, but it increased its coverage of popular music as its interviewers and reviewers discovered that some singers were interesting, even intelligent. The *New Musical Express* was concerned mostly with popular music, and instigated Britain's first official hit parade in 1952.

During 1952–62, the songs and sounds were the same as or similar to those listed in *Billboard*. Compared to the American public, British audiences liked dramatic ballads more and instrumental mood music less, and occasionally substituted a home-grown star for an American one. But the differences were nominal.

II

Lacking any regular access to the sounds of Hank Ballard, Amos Milburn, Wynonie Harris, and Muddy Waters during the early fifties, most people were taken by surprise when Bill Haley's "Shake, Rattle and Roll" and "Rock Around the Clock" were issued in late 1954. "Shake" was for many people the first record of its kind that they had heard, and it was in the top ten for the first eight weeks of 1955; "Rock", which did not appear in the American lists until later in the year, was a minor hit in Britain in January and a major hit at the end of the year. It appeared that the lively atmosphere and insistent beat meant as much to people in Britain as they did to Americans. The history of rock 'n' roll in Britain after this was similar to its history in America–though a few specifics were modified: Little Richard's records were not released until 1957 because Specialty did not negotiate an English outlet before then; Chuck Berry's "Maybellene" could not be played on the BBC because his reference to Cadillacs and V-8 Fords would have been construed as advertising, which the BBC could not permit (later records with similar references were sometimes amended specially for the British market: Johnny Bond's "Hot Rod Lincoln" became "Hot Rod Jalopy" and the Playmates rerecorded "Beep Beep", substituting "bubble car" for "Nash Convertible"); Gene Vincent's "Woman Love" was banned by the BBC because it was thought to be too suggestive.

Rock 'n' roll's emergence in Britain also coincided with a gathering problem of juvenile delinquency and became identified as an inspiration for violent behaviour, a thesis presumably confirmed when the film *Rock Around the Clock*, after a successful, quiet opening in London's West End, provoked audiences in some working class areas to rip out the movie seats in order to give themselves room to jive. But although there was undoubtedly some relationship–a sort of emotional affinity if nothing else–between rock 'n' roll and violence, there was never anything like conclusive evidence to prove that the first created the second.

Delinquency had been a growing problem before the appearance of rock 'n' roll, as youths throughout the country grew increasingly dissatisfied with, for one thing, the facilities for entertainment and expression available to them. Dance halls played "strict tempo" ballroom dancing music, and youth clubs tended to be run by religious groups, or watched under close supervision. Their usual clientele was sedate and orderly. But rock 'n' roll brought sounds to the dance halls and youth clubs that attracted from the streets the people who had been breaking shop windows and telephone boxes and prowling round in gangs on the lookout for other gangs (and occasionally beating up old people). Sometimes the gangs reassembled at the end of the dances, or made menacing groups in cafes, which seemed to point to rock 'n' roll as an evil inspiration for hoodlums. Such was the kind of evidence on which the association was based.*

Of the American singers who had hits in the United States with rock 'n' roll songs, those with the most impact in Britain were Presley, Little Richard, Jerry Lee Lewis, Buddy Holly and the Crickets, Duane Eddy, the Everly Brothers, and Eddie Cochran. Buddy Knox, Rick Nelson, and other image singers were less successful because Britain produced its own local versions of them more easily than it could reproduce the effect of the real rock 'n' roll singers. But almost all of the British rock 'n' roll records through to 1962 were shoddy, partly because most of them had accompaniments from musicians who, accustomed to supporting crooners, had no feeling for the rhythms of rock 'n' roll, and partly because the singers themselves could find no style of their own to accommodate the rock 'n' roll idiom but sang instead in mock-American accents.

The most accomplished and successful British singer was Cliff Richard, with a style and image originally modelled on Presley but subsequently located somewhere between Rick Nelson and Paul Anka. Compared to the other British rock and roll singers, Richard had good vocal control, access to writers who provided competent and suitable material (similar to Rick Nelson's), and an unusually capable and disciplined rhythm group, the Shadows, who also had their own instrumental hits and pioneered a jaunty, disciplined sound that provided the basis for Britain's "beat" music in the early sixties.

* *The only piece of research which has been done on the relationship between violence and rock and roll–by Colin Fletcher–suggests that the music had a tendency to absorb violence, and to redirect violent energies into making music or into partisan but essentially non-violent support for particular groups and singers. Most of Fletcher's article, which originally appeared in* New Society, *has been reprinted in* The Pop Process, *Richard Mabey, ed.*

Having failed to rival any of the first generation of American rock 'n' roll stars, the British music industry recovered its ground as the Americans replaced the originals with a new generation of more conventional entertainers, under the canny guidance of publishers who were keen to supply the right kind of teen-romance material. Once the focus was back to songs, rather than mysteriously indefinable concepts such as rhythmic feel and authenticity, the British industry was able to deliver the goods again: singers with the appropriate qualities of vulnerability (to their audience) and malleability (to their managers). Impresario Larry Parnes learned the ropes by managing Tommy Steele, an entertainer with show business instincts who was briefly foisted on Britain as a rock 'n' roll singer before veering to a more convincing role in stage shows; Parnes followed up with a host of singers with cartoon names, among whom Marty Wilde, Joe Brown, Billy Fury, and Georgie Fame turned out to have some musical depth. Most of Marty Wilde's hits were cover versions of American ones, but Billy Fury set a precedent by writing most of his 19 top twenty hits himself; but both of them, like virtually every other British pop singer of the time, did their best to sound American without actually going beyond the forms laid out in the arrangements of Roy Orbison, the Everly Brothers, the Drifters, and the other current American hit "machines".

Among the singers from outside Parnes' "stable", Adam Faith evolved a distinctive sound in a series of records written by Johnny Worth (under the name "Les Vandyke") and arranged by John Barry; inspired by the sound of Buddy Holly's posthumous hit, "It Doesn't Matter Anymore", the team confected a persuasive character who managed to be simultaneously "hip" and accessible, and Faith had eleven top ten hits, 1960–3. The only female singer to make an individual impression in this period was the teenaged Helen Shapiro, whose astonishingly mature and accomplished singing was unfortunately offset by some of the most crass vocal group arrangements in an era which specialized in them. "Don't Treat Me Like a Child", written by John Schroeder, was one of the best statements of teenage defiance of the time, but after four more top ten hits Helen disappeared under the avalanche of groups who swept through Britain from 1963 onwards.

In retrospect, the most notable British act of the early sixties may have been Johnny Kidd and the Pirates, whose "Shakin' All Over" topped the charts during 1960. Altogether tougher and more abrasive than Cliff Richard and the Shadows, the group anticipated the emergence of a distinct "rock" strain of pop music, in which the rhythm–and particularly the guitar part–was integral to the construction of the whole song. From start to finish, the guitar led the way, with the vocal flitting around it and making way for its vibrating, penetrating solo. But as there was no media structure of radio, press and live venues to support a group with this kind of approach, Kidd and the Pirates were obliged to follow conventional pop formulas in search of hit singles, and so lost the originality of their biggest hit.

But although the transformation of rock 'n' roll into pop music–which the producers of Cliff Richard and the other British singers accomplished as thoroughly as did their American counterparts–was of little musical significance, it created in the late fifties a situation similar to the one created in the States in the early fifties: a popular musical culture so unsatisfactory to large numbers of participants and consumers alike that audiences and performers worked independently of the official media of communications to produce a more lively and personal style. Moreover, whereas the first British singers who tried rock 'n' roll seemed to have little awareness of any music other than the records that had been million sellers in the United States, the second group of singers had had time to discover the musical background of rock 'n' roll. Rhythm and blues, which was virtually unknown in Britain in 1956 was by 1962 dominant in a subculture which was located in basement clubs throughout the country, whose audience included students at school, college and university and an unusual cross section of young working people. The channels for national communication between these people were *Melody Maker*, with its focus on jazz, and a new paper, the *Record Mirror*, which had been formed since rock 'n' roll and reported particularly on contemporary rhythm and blues music.

III

There had been a tradition in Britain since the twenties, maintained by a substantial minority of people, of being interested in declining forms of Negro popular music. As a succession of stylistic trends in the United States rendered various styles virtually obsolete, a group of enthusiasts in Europe devoted themselves to perpetuating the music by collecting records, by importing, if possible, the original performers to Europe to make a tour or even take up residence, and by playing the music themselves. New Orleans jazz, Dixieland, Chicago jazz, swing, boogie woogie, big band jazz, bop, hard bop, cool jazz, and their many variants all developed enough adherents in Britain and several other European countries for record companies to make a steady income by compiling albums from rare 78s in each of the various styles and, perhaps more importantly, for bands to be able to earn enough to survive by playing several nights a week across the country, mainly in clubs and occasionally in public dance halls.

In addition to the jazz enthusiasts, there was a similar group of people interested in American folk music, which in their view included the "pure" folk music of Kentucky and the more contemporary forms developed by such itinerant white singers as Jimmie Rodgers and Woody Guthrie and their more sophisticated, city-raised followers, such as Pete Seeger and the Weavers. For this group, folk music also included what they knew of the country blues as sung by Big Bill Broonzy, Josh White, Leadbelly, Sonny Terry, and Brownie McGhee.

Relatively few people were interested in post-war forms of the blues, particularly if it had a strong jump beat or heavy electrical amplification. Humphrey Lyttelton, who led one of the best British bands to be modelled on New Orleans jazz bands, expressed the general attitude of the British enthusiasts towards rhythm and blues in his weekly column in the *New Musical Express*.

> Of all the contemporary jazz sounds which qualify for the title of Tomorrow's Corn, "boot" tenor playing is hottest favourite with me. I mean the sort of rabble-rousing stuff which relies for its effect on single-note honking and frenetic riffs, relieved by an occasional rude noise from one or other of the instrument's extremities.
>
> Illinois Jacquet can claim distinction as the father of this style, although it is really in effect a debasement of several earlier styles, notably those of Coleman Hawkins, Lester Young, and Ben Webster.
>
> In recent years there has been something of a vogue for "boot" tenor playing, until now, a position has been reached where a player of very little improvisational talent can achieve instant success with the mob by playing three or four successive choruses on one note. Provided, of course, that he heightens the impression of inspirational fervour by blowing himself blue in the face and marking time like an epileptic sergeant major.
>
> I am prepared to prophesy that our jazz-loving descendants will regard these noises with the same amused indulgence which we nowadays bestow upon the slap-tonguing and tricky 'mute' effects of some early jazz.
>
> The Rhythm and Blues lists are a breeding ground for the "boot" style, and in many people's minds the two are closely associated.[1]

This kind of puritanism–or purism–was typical. In his own playing, Lyttelton was sufficiently eclectic to outrage many purist followers of New Orleans jazz, for whom another British band, Ken Colyer's, epitomized the *truth*. Colyer stayed religiously close to the sound of late nineteenth and early twentieth century New Orleans bands–or rather to what he imagined they would have sounded like–even going so far at one recording session as to put a biscuit tin over the microphone in order to get the echoing effect of a club which the listener could imagine was in New Orleans.

Colyer's conviction, and a devoted if fairly small following, attracted good musicians to his band, but his extreme purist policy usually frustrated the more imaginative, who left to form their own bands or to join others. Among those who once played with Colyer was the leader of the best and most influential British "traditional jazzband", Chris Barber, once a trombonist with Colyer. Barber formed his own band in 1953, together with Monty Sunshine and Tony Donnegan, who, respectively, had been the clarinet and banjo players with Colyer. Augmented with trumpet, bass, and drummer, Barber's band became the most successful of its kind throughout the fifties, gradually extending its repertoire and stylistic range to include Duke Ellington compositions, Memphis jug-band songs, classic blues, and "folk blues".

In 1954 Barber cut an album for British Decca which included two songs by Donnegan, now calling himself Lonnie Donegan (in homage to the pre-war blues singer/guitarist Lonnie Johnson), playing guitar and accompanied by Barber on bass and by the band's classic blues singer, Beryl Bryden, playing washboard. In response to audience interest Decca released the songs on a single, "Rock Island Line"/"John Henry" by "Lonnie Donegan and his Skiffle Group", which became a hit not only in Britain but in the United States, where it made the top ten in May, 1956.

The simple instrumental accompaniment of the skiffle group–guitar, bass, and washboard (or, in sophisticated groups, drums)–attracted countless young people who lacked the musical ability to be jazz musicians or even effective popular musicians, but who could easily learn three or four chords, and strum and sing the skiffle repertoire, which Donegan, now on his own, quickly developed. His sources were the entire folk heritage of the United States, but particularly the repertoires of Leadbelly and Woody Guthrie. Donegan performed their songs with a quick dance beat, in a high, nasal, fake American voice. Despite being almost completely derivative in his material and style, he was much better at what he did than were any of the British contemporary rock 'n' roll singers at representing American rock 'n' roll, and from 1956 to 1959, he was the most consistent hitmaker in Britain. Donegan's songs dealt with real events unsentimentally and unromantically–or so it seemed to his audience, who saw nothing romantic in a young man from Glasgow beginning a song, "Well, I gambled up in Washington, and I gambled down in Maine . . .", or, "Well, the new sheriff, sent me a letter. . . .", in "Gamblin' Man" and "Dead or Alive".

Eventually, Donegan's audience discovered the sources of his material and began buying the original versions, as albums of Broonzy, Leadbelly, and Guthrie became available in Britain. Donegan then turned to British folk culture, and was equally successful with "Does Your Chewing Gum Lose Its Flavour?" and "My Old Man's a Dustman", which inspired a short run of similar hits by other singers who emphasized regional British accents–but usually with modern novelty pop songs–Mike Sarne, Joe Brown, and Tommy Steele. But these songs were "instant" folk culture with no authentic cultural background to give them a coherent feeling, and their rhythms had little connection with the verse structure.

Meanwhile, Chris Barber continued playing jazz and educating his audience in a more direct way, by featuring on his tours various blues singers, including Broonzy, Rosetta Tharpe, Sonny Terry and Brownie McGhee, Muddy Waters, and Louis Jordan. Through long interviews, biographies, and record reviews in the *Melody Maker*, and with this firsthand experience of legendary singers, a substantial British audience developed a sophisticated knowledge of the blues. And at first its members were as purist as Ken Colyer's devotees and could hardly bear it when Muddy Waters played electric guitar on his tour with Barber in 1957. Electric guitar was commercial rock 'n' roll, the kind of thing tasteless people like Chuck Berry and Bo Diddley played.

These specialist audiences rarely understood or paid much attention to contemporary forms of black music and often distorted the nature of the music they did like. Big Bill Broonzy had played for years in Chicago with small groups–piano, harmonica, bass and drums–but in England was encouraged to play acoustic guitar with no other accompaniment, which he obligingly did. Although the blues had covered a wide range of topics but particularly relationships with women, the British folk audience was interested primarily in the songs that expressed some kind of protest or criticism against the American social system. (Broonzy's "Get Back" was a favourite.)

By the early sixties, people up and down the country were singing songs like this, sometimes fitting them into a consciously political context, as on antinuclear defence marches, other times singing them as folk entertainment. Even in the latter instance, the folk singers usually sang about, and on behalf of, some person or group of people other than themselves–the working class, black people, poor people, hobos, union leaders: the images, places, and phrases of the songs were American.

The repertoire of the folk singers overlapped with that of the skiffle singers, but the former mostly used only acoustic guitar (and occasionally harmonica) whereas the latter used enough instruments to make a dance rhythm. But during the early sixties, various groups, beginning to acknowledge post-war styles of rhythm and blues, started playing blues with a strong accompaniment. In the years 1960–62, their presence was hardly noticed outside the few clubs they sang in, because the dominant minority cult, traditional jazz, had temporarily become a major part of British popular music, as "trad" jazz. During those years not only clubs but radio and TV featured the "trad" bands of Chris Barber, Kenny Ball, Acker Bilk, and many others, until finally dancers grew bored with the rigid banjo rhythm, predictable harmonies, and gruff singing (based on Louis Armstrong's style), and the "trad" phase petered out.

The clubs then began featuring as main attractions some of the "rhythm and blues" groups which had been playing in the intervals.

In London, the dominant influence was Alexis Korner, whose tastes in blues were as eclectic as Chris Barber's tastes in pre-war jazz, and who played a comparable role in educating the taste of both the musicians who played and sang with him and the people who listened to his band, Alexis Korner's Blues Incorporated. Most of his protégés formed groups of their own. Cyril Davis, Graham Bond, John Mayall, and some of the Rolling Stones were among those who played with him and learned about rhythm and blues from him. The sounds of Howlin' Wolf, Muddy Waters, Jimmy Reed, Slim Harpo, Sonny Boy Williamson, and John Lee Hooker, with which they had first become acquainted through Korner, were echoed in the intense guitar, shrill harmonica, and raw singing of these performers.

By 1963, "rhythm and blues" was a familiar expression in the *Melody Maker* and *Record Mirror*, and had become the dominant style in London clubs. By the end of the year it was in the hit parade and was one of Britain's national styles of popular music, carried in on the wave of the "beat music" of various Lancashire groups which swept through the charts during 1963.

IV

Beat music was much less "academic" than was British rhythm and blues. It was always conceived as "popular" music, essentially as a local dance club alternative to the national forms of pop music distributed by the music industry and played on the BBC. Many of the groups were former skiffle groups who kept playing after the skiffle phase faded, and most of them were strongly influenced by Cliff Richard's rhythm group, the Shadows. Some abandoned vocals altogether, and other featured vocals on a few songs and instrumentals the rest of the time. Very few sang any kind of harmony until 1962, when the success in Britain of the American group the Four Seasons and the Liverpool group the Beatles altered the musical approach of many of them.

Until the Beatles made their first record in the fall of 1962, it had been very difficult for any group based outside London to gain access to the record companies. It had almost always been necessary for ambitious musicians, singers, and groups to move to London and hope to attract the attention of somebody who mattered.

Without the reputations that came through records, groups outside London had to depend on the support of people who knew them through direct hearing, which meant that a group famous in Newcastle could be unknown thirty miles away on Tees-side, and that groups in south Lancashire had little demand in Yorkshire. Accordingly, Bristol, Birmingham, Glasgow, and other cities each had its own local groups.

The equivalent situation in the United States would have meant that each city's groups had their own distinctive styles and that enterprising local businessmen in some of the cities would have formed record companies to exploit the inflexibility of the majors (the London-based companies), who usually rejected the few groups they did agree to audition, on the grounds that they were too noisy and lacked the control and technical proficiency expected of singers and musicians who made records. But in Britain there was little opportunity for such enterprise because there were no local radio stations to reach the local audiences. So with few exceptions, the groups remained unrecorded until the Beatles' manager, Brian Epstein, with more persistence than most, and a better group to promote, finally persuaded EMI to record the group in the fall of 1962.

The success of "Love Me Do", which made the lower reaches of the top twenty, and "Please Please Me", which made second place, enabled Epstein to place several other south Lancashire groups he represented on EMI's roster, and a large proportion of them were successful. But apart from the Beatles, the south Lancashire groups had much less ability or individuality than their success suggested. Their important quality was a freshness which contrasted with the relatively characterless singers that audiences were accustomed to. But as singers, musicians, arrangers, and composers they were not only amateurs compared with the Americans they copied, but had little to say or express about their experience and feelings. They were pop music singers who lacked the kind of assurance that, for example, would allow one of them to improvise from an agreed arrangement without panicking the others.

The Beatles were different in several respects from the other groups with whom they were bracketed as part of "the Mersey Sound", both as musicians with a thorough understanding of the culture from which they drew their style, and as people who were unlike entertainers previously familiar to audiences and journalists.

The group's vocal style was a derivative of two American styles which had not previously been put together, the hard rock 'n' roll style of singers like Little Richard and Larry Williams, and the soft gospel call-and-response style of the Shirelles, the Drifters, and the rest of the singers produced by Leiber and Stoller, Luther Dixon, and Berry Gordy. Instrumentally the Beatles were at first less inventive, producing a harsh rhythm and shrill sound comparable to some of the better American "twist" records, including Bruce Channel's "Hey! Baby" and Buster Brown's "Fannie Mae".

Although the twist had been fairly successful (without the impact it had in America), the gospel-harmony groups had very little success in Britain, and the result for the British audience was a sound with a familiar rhythm and a novel vocal style. The way the Beatles echoed one another's phrases, dragged out words across several beats, shouted "yeah", and went into falsetto cries, was received in Britain as their own invention; it seemed that Britain had finally discovered an original, indigenous rock and roll style.

The Beatles made no pretence that this was so and stressed how much they owed to Chuck Berry, the Miracles, and Buddy Holly and the Crickets. In an interview with the *New Musical Express* (February, 1963) during the first flush of their popularity, they listed as their favourite singers Chuck Jackson and Ben E. King (given by both Lennon and McCartney), the Shirelles and Miracles (Lennon), Larry Williams (McCartney), and Little Richard (McCartney and Harrison). Harrison also mentioned Eartha Kitt, who was not evidently much of an inspiration to the sounds he made; Ringo Starr's choice of Brook Benton and Lightnin' Hopkins similarly had little bearing on his style (which more likely drew on Carl Perkins).

On their singles and albums through 1963, the Beatles continued to draw from their American influences, trying to realize their ambition to record a great raving dance song but invariably sounding better when they sang at a medium tempo, hitting the harmonies Lennon was interested in and doing so with precisely the confidence in themselves that the other British groups lacked, a confidence that enabled them to take risks, be unorthodox, and shrug off disasters.

Some of the records they made in this period were good. Their LP tracks "You Really Got a Hold on Me" and "Baby It's You" transformed the innocence of the interpretations by the Miracles and the Shirelles into much stronger songs and created a sense of greater resilience behind the tender messages. In contrast to the expressiveness of these and other LP songs, the group's singles were more obviously concerned with effect, "Please Please Me", "From Me To You", and "She Loves You" successively using more devices calculated to excite and offering less complexity in their arrangements.

But for the audience at the time, it was the simplicity of the Beatles' arrangements that endeared them to their listeners. The first LP sleeve notes mentioned that only one track had any kind of double-tracking or other such studio tricks. The British audience valued authenticity, and despised the lush contrivances of contemporary American records. The Beatles re-established the singer's autonomy in the studio. They were able to do so because they played their own instruments, and were therefore less subject to their producer than a studio group would have been. They came to their recording sessions with their own songs, many of which they had tried before live audiences on their tours. They listened attentively to the records that sold well in the United States and borrowed anything that seemed to fit what they were already doing. The Four Seasons, the Beach Boys, Phil Spector's sound were all saluted in their sounds, and the early rock 'n' roll singers continued to provide inspiration, though their performances were never transcended by the Beatles' versions of the songs.

Musically, the Beatles were exciting, inventive, and competent; lyrically, they were brilliant, able to work in precisely the right kind of simple images and memorable phrases that distinguished rhythm and blues from other kinds of popular music. They were also facile, so that some songs were words to sing and did not represent feelings the singers wanted to express–for example, "It Won't Be Long" and "All I've Got To Do" on their second LP (called *With the Beatles* in England and *Meet the Beatles* in the United States). They had enough ability to endure as institutional hitmakers alongside Cliff Richard and the Shadows. But there was something else about them, and it was this that transformed the nature of the world's popular music as decisively as rock 'n' roll had done nine years before–their character as people.

The Beatles provided in meat and bone and a sharp glance across a room the spirit that several authors and playwrights had been trying to depict in fictional characters and the film industry subsequently tried to represent with actors. John Osborne drew Jimmy Porter in *Look Back in Anger*, and Richard Burton played Porter in the film. Alan Sillitoe created Arthur Seaton in *Saturday Night and Sunday Morning* and Colin Smith in *The Loneliness of the Long Distance Runner*, who were played by Albert Finney and Tom Courtenay with much more authenticity than Burton had brought to Porter. But the characters as such still carried too much structured statement to be convincing. The authors had social messages to get across, and the characters inevitably came second, functioning as conduits for the writers' ideologies. In themselves, though, the films seemed much more real than the traditional product of British studios. They presented life in the working class as being more real, interesting, and honest than in the middle class, a belief that middle-class socialists had had for some time but a novel theme for films.

The Beatles unwittingly exploded this image of working-class youth. In their first two years of fame, they did not make long structured criticisms of established society, but spoke briefly, obscurely, epigrammatically, in the same spirit that they wrote their best songs. Their social message was rarely expressed, but hung about their heads as an aura of impatience with convention and evident satisfaction with wealth and fame, and was expressed in their carefully chosen styles of bizarre clothes. Where authors had shown working-class youth as caged within a harsh physical world, resentful towards those they believed had made it that way, but resigned to their place in such a world, the Beatles presented working-class youth loose and free, glad to be out, unafraid to snub pretension, easily able to settle in comfortably where a rest could be found.

This image also turned out to be illusory, or at best only temporarily true. The Beatles ultimately settled for what they first pulled faces at, the luxuries of the wealthy, but not before they had significantly shifted the taste of audiences throughout the world. In contrast to the pained narcissism of most singers, the Beatles lightly mocked themselves as they sang, amused at the frenzy they aroused in their audiences. They were one of the few popular music acts to have more or less equal support from male and female admirers, and one of the few who were as interesting musically as they were visually.

In the United States, their success was not immediate. Their first four records were released in 1963 with little promotion or reaction. Capitol, who had first option for the American release of EMI's product, allowed other companies, including Vee Jay and Swan, to take up the group's records. The rest of the world took the British group more seriously, and at the end of 1963 Capitol conceded to the pressure of EMI, the Beatles' manager, and, in effect, world opinion, and itself put heavy promotion behind the next Beatle record, "I Want to Hold Your Hand". It went quickly to the top of the national charts, followed by several earlier Vee Jay releases and Swan's "She Loves You", so that in one week in March the Beatles had the top five records in the country, an unprecedented phenomenon. As in Britain, the extent of the group's impact was more visual and social than musical, and depended on the intensive coverage in the press and on television. America was no more accustomed than Britain had been to singers who were witty and intelligent and derisive of social conventions, who built out of this character a new kind of sex appeal, and who attracted the attention of both music critics and social critics.

And among the people who were most surprised by all the fuss were the Beatles themselves. For, as they kept telling anyone who would listen, there was nothing particularly new or startling in any of their records. For reasons that defied discovery, a large proportion of the Western world was determined to imbue the Beatles with all the qualities that could possibly be ascribed to any and all kinds of popular music. With stamina and versatility that were themselves worthy of admiration, the Beatles did their best to keep up with expectations. They listened to a vast number of current releases, read newspapers, looked at photographs, remembered bits of slang from their youth. And from it all they produced a commentary of their times, picking up ideas so fast that it sometimes seemed they had thought of them first ("Help", in 1965, borrowed ideas from a new Bob Dylan LP; "I Feel Fine" used feedback that the Yardbirds had developed in their live performance but not yet put on record; "Norwegian Wood" used sitar, again following the Yardbirds).

Following their discovery by the American audience, the Beatles rapidly improved as musicians, and Lennon and McCartney became more fluent songwriters. But with the greater ease came glibness, words strung together because they scanned and rhymed, regardless of what they meant. So "Yesterday" was a tritely sentimental ballad, and "Nowhere Man" kicked the corpse of some poor suburbanite without showing any of the sympathy that the singer's tone half-indicated.

Blessed with the talent of being able to throw out songs as they needed to–for a new single, a new LP–they seemed to lose contact with their own emotions. Their songs began to seem like finely produced but unfeeling pieces. One of their most celebrated songs, "Eleanor Rigby", was sung in a strangely deadpan manner, and owed much of its formal beauty to the strong accompaniment orchestrated by George Martin, their arranger and producer, who seemed to have a particularly strong influence on the Beatles' records in the period 1966 to 1968. The emotionally expressive rock and roll singers of "Love Me Do" had given way to people apparently ready to try any style known to man, contemporary eastern, nineteenth century vaudeville. And while it seemed that McCartney would be happy seeing how many different things he could do well, John Lennon moved with determination back to music that expressed feelings, simple, repetitive, but personal–"All You Need Is Love", "Revolution", "Come Together".

Whatever the Beatles did, or drew attention to, inspired a legion of followers. Their impact reached its peak following the release of *Sergeant Pepper's Lonely Hearts Club Band* in 1967, which presented a suite of songs in a specific order, in contrast to the traditional concept of an album as a convenient way of packaging twelve randomly collected tracks. Many of the songs were obscurely surreal and seemed, as Lennon insisted, rather too casually put together to justify the intensely philosophical interpretations that were read into them. The record showed the group at its most removed from its material, and the singers subsequently returned to more intense vocal styles and, in "Lady Madonna" and "Get Back", to instrumental patterns close to Fats Domino and Chuck Berry, respectively.

After the Beatles broke up in 1969, none of them, on their own, came close to recapturing the extraordinary spirit they had achieved together–and neither could anyone else. The Beatles had transformed many of the attitudes, approaches, and relationships in the recording industry, but they had surprisingly little stylistic influence on other innovators.

Much fuss was made in the mid-sixties about the "Mersey Sound", but by the time groups had been shipped down from Liverpool and Manchester to record in London, there was little to distinguish them from the rest of the country's pop groups. Most of the Mersey groups fitted neatly into existing patterns of production and marketing, recording cover versions of American records or new songs supplied by established British publishers, and smiling at the cameras. The Searchers, produced by Tony Hatch, did evolve an interesting "folk-rock" sound featuring twelve string guitars, but even that was based on the sound of Jackie de Shannon's original American versions of their hits "Needles and Pins" and "When You Walk In the Room". The Hollies and the rest presented themselves as traditional show business entertainers, more anxious to meet audience expectations than to challenge them.

By contrast, the groups which emerged out of the rhythm and blues scene exuded a more defiant spirit, expressed in snarling vocals, raucous guitars, and baleful glares at photographers. Among the groups which pioneered a rough-and-ready, take-me-as-I-am approach were the Rolling Stones, the Animals, Manfred Mann, the Yardbirds, Them, the Kinks, the Who, and the Spencer Davis Group. And in the case of these groups, the challenge to "the system" went further than simply their own sound and image; the producers and managers who worked with them contributed to a fundamental change in the structure of the British record industry. And unlike the American reaction to a similar challenge in the rock 'n' roll era, these groups and their business partners really did institute a permanent shift in the balance of power in the British record industry.

V

Although the members of the rhythm and blues groups did not all have exactly the same background, there were common threads. The most conspicuous shared experience was art school. The traditional British pop singers and musicians had left school at the earliest possible moment, and saw pop as a way out of the routine jobs that were the most likely future for them; the popular British press often featured "where-are-they-now" reports on briefly-famous pop singers who had gone back to jobs on the milk round or the factory floor. But in the early sixties, an increasing number of school-leavers looked for ways to delay the decision of what job to take, and many opted for art school courses in printing, graphics, commercial design, and photography–as well as the traditional painting and sculpture courses. Kids who had been regarded at school as eccentrics in their musical taste found kindred spirits at art colleges who shared a devotion for Ray Charles, Howlin' Wolf and other still-obscure black Americans, and ad-hoc bands formed out of casual jam sessions.

The archetypal band with this kind of background was the Rolling Stones, although lead singer Mick Jagger was actually at a conventional university college (the London School of Economics) when he got together with guitarist Keith Richard.

Throughout their career, the Rolling Stones were a conspicuous (and often deliberate) contrast to the Beatles, going against the grain of conventional behaviour expected both within the music industry and outside in the world at large. And as the world reacted with outrage and alarm to the long hair and surly derision of the Stones, the group learned the truth of the show business adage, "any publicity is good publicity". The more the establishment expressed its disapproval, the larger became the army of the group's ardent supporters. Of all the British groups who had reason to thank the Beatles for opening up the world as a market, the Rolling Stones made the most of the opportunities; step-by-step, blow-by-blow, they followed each move of the Beatles with a complementary response: hard, heavy, and dark, where the Beatles were soft and light. The Rolling Stones gave a savage twist to the blues and soul music that provided their musical inspiration. Selfish, spiteful, and sexually threatening, they stirred subliminal feelings that popular music normally preferred to leave alone, but which in black music had always been closer to the surface.

By the time Decca released the first single by the Rolling Stones, their version of Chuck Berry's "Come On" in June 1963, EMI was already dominating the charts with the new "Mersey Sound" of the

Beatles, Gerry and the Pacemakers, and the rest, and it was not immediately obvious that the Rolling Stones would be a serious rival. Like most of the rhythm and blues groups, they were determined to be faithful both to the "pure" character of their material, and to the "authentic" sound of their own live performances on stage. Virtually all of the art college rhythm and blues groups began their recording careers with conscientious versions of a couple of American rhythm and blues songs which had proved the most exciting numbers in their live sets; invariably, the records were duly bought by the group's faithful fans but failed to attract the attention of many people who had never heard of them before. The groups who succeeded were those who realized that making hit records was a different activity from playing live, requiring an attention to structuring arrangements and highlighting melodies which had not been necessary to excite a club audience. In most cases, the rhythm and blues songs which had made such good live numbers would not easily adapt to the new requirements, and the groups had to look elsewhere for material; the Animals and Manfred Mann resorted to the traditional ruse of digging up obscure American songs, and the Spencer Davis Group found an unknown writer from Jamaica, Jackie Edwards, while the Yardbirds found an unknown in Britain, Graham Gouldman. The Kinks, the Who, and, eventually, the Rolling Stones, wrote their own.

But while these British groups forsook their rhythm and blues material they still hankered after the attack which had made rhythm and blues records so exciting. John Lennon of the Beatles shared many of the attitudes of the rhythm and blues musicians, and later recalled his frustration with British engineers who would not allow their volume meters to go into the red. He was sure that the harsh crack on the off-beat on so many Motown records was achieved by ignoring such rules. The Beatles made all their records with producer George Martin at EMI's Abbey Road Studios, and had to nag the engineers into experimenting. The Rolling Stones, along with most of the rhythm and blues groups, were independently produced, and their manager Andrew Oldham took the earliest opportunity to get them across to America; fittingly, they booked into the Chess studios in Chicago, where they recorded their first British number one (a version of the Valentinos' "It's All Over Now") and their first American top ten hit (a version of Irma Thomas' "Time is on My Side").

Compared to the tinny sound of their earlier records, these had more weight and "bottom", but the group did not achieve its full potential until they shifted locations in 1965 to the RCA studio in Hollywood, where engineer Dave Hassinger achieved a perfect balance between Keith Richard's menacing guitar riff and Mick Jagger's arrogant vocal on their own composition, "(I Can't Get No) Satisfaction".

With "Satisfaction", the Stones at last found a way to express, on record, the threat and derision which they had put across in person, and they followed through with several more classic singles whose chorus titles summed up the message of each song: "(Hey You) Get Off Of My Cloud", "(Here Comes Your) 19th Nervous Breakdown", "Paint It Black", "Jumping Jack Flash", and "Honky Tonk Women". By the end of the sixties, the Rolling Stones had virtually created a new category for themselves; having moved on from the Chuck Berry/Bo Diddley/Muddy Waters boogie blues, through the soul influence of Solomon Burke and Don Covay, which represented the entire panorama of the past fifteen years of black dance music, they welded it all to lyrics which enabled a young white audience to identify themselves with the messages. And all this, while continuing to ignore "the rules" by which popular entertainers traditionally found acceptance in the media. So far as anyone could tell from the outside, the Rolling Stones did not care what anyone thought about them, and this insolence gave them great strength.

The wheel turned full circle, and hardly anyone argued when the Rolling Stones were called "the greatest Rock 'n' Roll Band in the world". Mick Jagger exuded a sensuality which recalled early photos of Elvis Presley, and although his stage movements hardly compared with the grace and dexterity of James Brown or Sam and Dave, somehow he defined a set of criteria which eliminated them from the competition. The Stones carved their own niche, and sat tight in it.

Of the British rhythm and blues groups who hit the charts in the wake of the Rolling Stones, neither Manfred Mann nor the Animals managed to establish such an interesting repertoire of self-written songs; they both "compromised" themselves in pursuit of the obvious hit single, and never achieved the same awed respect. Both groups were with EMI, but while Manfred Mann's records were produced by senior A&R man John Burgess, the Animals were independently produced by Mickie Most.

Manfred Mann's singer Paul Jones was one of the best British singers of the era, confident and distinctive, and the group's records were generally good-natured, memorably melodic cover versions of American records; "Do Wah Diddy Diddy" topped both British and American charts in 1964, and "Pretty Flamingo" repeated the trick in Britain in 1966, while in between the group did an effective job on a previously unrecorded Bob Dylan song "If You Gotta Go, Go Now". Musicians with the highest pedigree passed through the band, but it never received the kind of committed affection that several contemporary bands won from their audiences.

The Animals looked likely to become a major British institution after scoring six top ten hits in eighteen months, 1964–65. But lead singer Eric Burdon was never able to write songs that were as suited to his own sound and image as the material chosen for him by producer Mickie Most. It was Most's idea to record a "rock" version of "The House of The Rising Sun", a traditional folk song which Bob Dylan had recently revived on his first album for American Columbia in 1962. An almost Bach-like organ part, arranged and played by Alan Price, set a suitably haunting mood, and Burdon delivered the song with an authentically rough-hewn, experience-stained voice. Despite its sombre mood and unusual length (over four minutes), the record topped the chart in Britain and then in America, where it inspired other producers to experiment with similar combinations in what became known as "folk-rock".

Among the later Animals singles, "We've Gotta Get Out of this Place" was outstanding, sung with a gritty conviction by Burdon which belied his resistance to doing the song in the first place–he felt the group should be seen to be recording its own material. Ironically, the writers of the song, Barry Mann and Cynthia Weil, were also reported to be unhappy with the record; they had intended it to be sung with more subtlety, as the Drifters might have done it. The writers might have been thinking about Harlem when they wrote the song, but it worked just as well as Burdon placed it on Tyneside:

In this dirty old part of the city
Where the sun refuse to shine
Don't you know people tell me
It ain't no use in tryin'.

In 1966 the group began disintegrating, leaving EMI and Mickie Most for Decca, and working with a different producer (Alan Price left to pursue a solo career). Eric Burdon eventually moved to America, and although he enjoyed some success, he never recaptured the spirit of those early hits. An interview he gave in *Ebony* Magazine revealed attitudes typical among rhythm and blues musicians at the time:

> I grew up in Newcastle, England, a typical ship-building, coal-mining area. I was a typical northern, ship-building, coal-mining school-leaver with a few years of college in between. I was in Newcastle when I heard my first "soul record". I lived in a flat and

downstairs in another flat was a merchant seaman who frequently visited the U.S. He used to bring back records with him, ranging from Bill Haley (this was before the rock craze) to Dave Brubeck. In between were some strong-sounding sides by people with strange-sounding names like Fats Domino, Robert Johnson, Big Maybelle. The first records to really knock me out were "Don't Roll Those Blood Shot Eyes at Me" by Wynonie Harris and "Sam Jones Done Snagged his Braces" by Louis Jordan. I knew from then that someday I just had to try and sing like that. . . .

I started collecting things–photographs, newspaper articles, magazine clippings–to find out why Negroes were being mistreated, often brutally so. When I was around 17 I fell madly in love with an African girl and had often thought about taking her to America. But after I got here and saw the relationship between the races, I said forget it.

I think because I am white and from another country I often learn a lot more about prejudice in some ways than a lot of Negroes.

When I was in Mississippi I spoke to the mayor of Laurel and other government officials. Whatever they may say in the newspapers, I found out where they are really, because they talked to me as a fellow white person. I taped one interview and brought it back to New York. I listened to it time and again and thought, "Jesus Christ, you know, those guys are running a state!"

Another time I was in Mobile, Ala. A young white girl came up to me and asked for an autograph. I signed one and we began chatting. During the conversation I mentioned that Otis Redding had played there the night before. She said, "Yeh man, he's too much, isn't he? I think his recording of *My Girl* is fantastic". I told her, "Yeh, it's my favourite record too." Then I asked her if she had seen him perform. She said, "Did I see him? You got to be joking, man, the place was full of niggers."[2]

It was with this kind of affection and conviction that a generation of British singers and musicians brought black music styles into the mainstream of British pop–and, taking coals to Newcastle–of American pop too. And as well as the group lead vocalists like Jagger, Paul Jones, and Burdon, there were solo singers in Britain who championed black music, notably Dusty Springfield, Georgie Fame, and Tom Jones.

Dusty Springfield was probably the best British studio singer of the mid-sixties, and had already made her mark in America before the success of the Beatles made it easier for British acts to get recognition there. "Silver Threads and Golden Needles" was an American top twenty hit in 1962 for the Springfields, for whom Dusty sang lead until she went solo in 1963. Compared with most other solo singers of the time, Dusty Springfield had an unusual degree of influence in the choice of material and the arrangements of her recordings, whose sophisticated arrangements bore comparison with the best American "uptown rhythm and blues" records. Connoisseurs could detect echoes of records by Dionne Warwick and Baby Washington in Dusty's vocal inflections and arrangement ideas, but her sympathetic tone and faultless sense of time invariably brought the ultimate meaning from every song she recorded. "I Only Want to Be With You" provided a jaunty launch to her solo career in 1963, and among several outstanding records the spectacular ballad "You Don't Have to Say You Love Me" was a huge international hit in 1966 Dusty later tried several more fashionable producers, but Philips Records' A&R man Johnny Franz turned out to have provided the best context for her.

Georgie Fame and the Blue Flames were among the handful of rhythm and blues bands which could be guaranteed to draw a good crowd to the West End clubs in the early sixties, but their repertoire and approach was distinct; instead of a guitar-based band playing Chicago-styled rhythm and blues, the Blue Flames were geared to Fame's own organ-based arrangements, and brought a jazzy touch to a wide range of material which included some Jamaican and African songs as well as a clutch of Mose Allison and King Pleasure songs. After a couple of so-so rhythm and blues covers in 1964, Fame recorded the much jazzier "Yeh Yeh" and hit the top of the chart; he repeated this success two years later with his own song "Get Away", produced by freelance Ian Samwell, whose previous claim to fame was to have written "Move It" for Cliff Richard back in 1958. Georgie Fame's later career was disappointingly oriented to cabaret and family TV shows, sometimes in partnership with ex-Animal, Alan Price.

This cabaret world claimed Tom Jones virtually from the start of his recording career, after years of singing rock 'n' roll and rhythm and blues songs in clubs throughout South Wales. His writer-producer-manager Gordon Mills guided Jones towards the Las Vegas spotlights, and achieved the dubious distinction of establishing him as second only to Elvis as an interpreter of over-blown ballads with country or Italian influences.

On the edge of this British rhythm and blues scene, drawing their inspiration from the same sources as the rest and yet never quite seeming to be in the mainstream, stood Van Morrison of Them, and Stevie Winwood of the Spencer Davis Group. During the seventies, they both emerged as major artists who evolved their own pastoral rock styles, drawing jazz and folk into their atmospheric arrangements, and even back in the mid-sixties they radiated an almost aloof sense of never quite surrendering to the excitement of their music.

Van Morrison brought his group Them to London from Ireland, and after one unsuccessful single was assigned to Bert Berns, the American producer-writer whose "Twist and Shout" had become a staple of practically every British group of the period. Having produced the Drifters and Solomon Burke for Atlantic, Berns watched the onslaught on the American charts by one British act after another during the first months of 1964. In an unusual "exchange," Decca's arranger Mike Leander went to work in New York with Atlantic, and Berns crossed over to work in London with Decca, Atlantic's British licensee. Berns was assigned to produce Lulu, a young Scottish singer whose "Shout" had given her a hit first time out, but her version of Berns "Here Comes the Night" was unconvincing; Lulu switched labels to EMI's Columbia, where Mickie Most waved his magic wand and took her to the top of the American charts with "To Sir With Love" in 1967. Meanwhile, Berns had formed a more effective alliance with Them, producing the group's only hits, "Baby Please Don't Go" (with blistering guitar-work by session-man Jimmy Page) and, second time lucky, "Here Comes the Night".

The personnel of Them tended to change by the day, with lead singer and writer Van Morrison the only constant factor. He seemed to be trying to find a gap between Mick Jagger and Eric Burdon, and his phrasing sometimes seemed forced and unnatural. But he was stuck in an era where groups were the acceptable format for an artist trying to determine his own style and repertoire, and the fifty tracks Them recorded for Decca amounted to sketches for the music that Van Morrison eventually succeeded in developing after he went to live in America in 1967. Bert Berns was the catalyst for the move, sending Van the plane ticket, and recording his first solo material for Bang! Although Them had never achieved more than cult success in America, Van Morrison's "Brown Eyed Girl" made the top ten while being virtually unnoticed at the time in Britain.

In stark contrast to the mismanaged career of Them, the Spencer Davis Group looked in retrospect as if it had been planned in advance. Based in Birmingham, the group was discovered in 1964 by Chris Blackwell, the owner of Island Records which specialized in releasing Jamaican records for the West Indian immigrants living in Britain, with an offshoot called Sue which leased rhythm and blues records from independent American labels. Blackwell had just produced an international hit, "My Boy Lollipop" by Millie which he licensed to Philips, and when he found the Spencer Davis Group he placed them with Philips too.

Confusingly, the main figure in the group was not Davis, a student at Birmingham University who played rhythm guitar, but the sixteen-year-old singer and organist Stevie Winwood. His high, emotional voice sounded for all the world like a young black American, and he played the organ with the flair, taste and drive of Ray Charles. As usual, the only stutter in the group's progress came as they tried to translate their live impact directly into chart success by recording covers of American rhythm and blues songs, but late in 1965 they changed tack by recording "Keep on Running", written by Island's Jamaican singer Jackie Edwards. Stevie's brother Muff Winwood played a pounding riff on bass guitar which may have been inspired by Keith Richard's guitar line in the recent "Satisfaction" hit by the Stones; Steve played a simple, infectious lead guitar figure while Davis hammered a manic rhythm guitar on every beat (the main lift from Edwards' own version). "Somebody Help Me" repeated the formula and also went to the top of the British chart, but when Stevie switched back to organ and the group started writing its own material, they came dangerously close to sounding like a white parody of the Stax soul records of Sam and Dave and Otis Redding. For their last hit, "I'm a Man" (1967), Chris Blackwell brought Jimmy Miller from New York to produce the record in London, and Miller stayed to work with other British acts including the Rolling Stones, who used him as producer on their best albums: *Beggars Banquet* (1968), *Let It Bleed* (1969), *Exile on Main Street* (1972) and *Goat's Head Soup* (1973). Meanwhile, Stevie Winwood went off to concoct a fusion of jazz and folk as part of Traffic, with Miller as producer.

VI

Alongside those former rhythm and blues singers who either stuck fairly closely to the musical ingredients of rhythm and blues (the Stones, Animals) or else reverted to conventional pop (Manfred Mann, Tom Jones), were a few groups who evolved variations of a new style which became known as "British rock". The distinction from Pop was partly cosmetic: the British music press began to point out distinctions between groups whose records seem to be planned or contrived by business-minded managers and producers, and those which were the "artistic" expression of the musicians themselves, who wrote their own songs, played their own instruments, and sounded pretty much the same on record as they did at their live appearances. The distinction was sometimes hard to sustain, when so-called "rock" records were discovered to have been played by session musicians while the members of the band sat in the control room, and there were rumours that session guitarist Jimmy Page had been present at early sessions by both the Kinks and the Who; he did play bass on a couple of singles by the Yardbirds, and guitar on Them's "Baby Please Don't Go".

As time passed, the reality was less important than the impression; where the Mersey pop groups never managed to build up a repertoire that presented any kind of consistent musical or personal character, these British rock groups did make records which stood the test of repeated playing. The act of recording was always partly an illusion, contriving an impression of spontaneity, and it scarcely mattered if a professional musician could convey that impression better than the inexperienced member of the group. Apart from the writers who came up with the songs for these groups, the crucial participants were the independent producers who acted as catalysts for the recording sessions: Mickie Most was in a class of his own, equally happy to produce would-be credible rock acts like the Animals, the Nashville Teens (whose "Tobacco Road" was a minor classic rhythm and blues hit for Decca), Donovan, and Jeff Beck, or out-and-out pop records for Herman's Hermits and Lulu. Some way behind Most, but still very important to the evolution of autonomous British pop music, were Shel Talmy (the Kinks and the Who), and Paul Samwell-Smith (the Yardbirds).

Shel Talmy had been a very minor freelance producer in Los Angeles before he decided to chance his arm and come to Britain, where he persuaded Decca to let him produce their new Irish cabaret vocal group the Bachelors in 1963. With their big hits under his belt, he moved on to produce the Kinks for Pye Records, and played an important part in enabling the group's writer and singer, Ray Davies, to achieve the sounds that enhanced his songs. After two flops imitating the pretty harmonies of the Mersey Sound, they harnessed guitar, bass guitar, and drums to a very simple beat which hammered home the chorus of "You Really Got Me": one two-and-three-four. A graceless vocal and anarchic guitar solo contributed to the macho mood, and the record topped the British chart and made the top ten in America.

After an almost identical follow-up with "All Day and All of the Night", they slowed down the riff and laid a much more relaxed vocal over it in "Tired of Waiting for You", which showed a more reflective and in-depth side to the group; the well-constructed song gave them another number one in Britain, and set the precedent for eight more top ten hits which began to present cleverly drawn cartoon portraits of contemporary British life. Where necessary, extra instruments discreetly embellished the basic two guitar-bass-and-drums line-up of the group: piano rolled along in the mocking lament of an aristocratic dilettante, "Sunny Afternoon", and a trombone played out over the end of "Dead End Street", which went to the other end of the social scale to portray the working class. Davies mocked the desperate-to-be-hip consumers of Carnaby Street in "Dedicated Follower of Fashion", but was at his best covering a soporific mood in "Waterloo Sunset", which he sang with such indolence, it sounded as if he could hardly be bothered to open his eyes to describe what he could see. Many of these songs were delivered by the group dressed in pink hunting clothes, which tended to undermine their impact at the time, but the records stood the test of time and served to inspire and influence other British writers to deal with the British way of life, sung and played in an English manner.

Either by coincidence, or because he was an outstanding judge of potential talent, Talmy also played a major role in the early records by the group built around Britain's other great "social comment" writer of the period, Pete Townshend of the Who. In contrast to the Kinks, where Ray Davies was the dominant and only important element, the Who was a much more volatile combination, in which each member vied to attract attention. From the start of his career, vocalist Roger Daltrey sounded travel-torn, and his "I've-seen-it-all-before" tone was the perfect vehicle for Pete Townshend's double-edged lyrics. Townshend's guitar seemed to strain at the leash, ready to burst into an uncontrolled din if given half a chance, and drummer Keith Moon preferred to crash around his tom-toms rather than keep steady time on snare and bass drum; only bass-player John Entwistle gave an impression of recognizing a traditional role for himself.

The group's managers Kit Lambert and Chris Stamp saw how greedily the press jumped upon any "anti-social" behaviour accidentally exhibited by the Rolling Stones, and set about contriving a comparably rebellious and controversial image for the Who. Shel Talmy's task was to give an impression of equivalent mayhem in the studio, but the first single "I Can't Explain" sounded fairly tame, using a cleaner version of the riff from "You Really Got Me", but sounding more reminiscent of some of the records made by the Crickets back in 1957. "Anyway Anyhow Anywhere" was more lively, and "My Generation" at the end of the year achieved a real fury; Daltrey seemed to be on the verge of swearing, and the three musicians took turns to make themselves heard.

After that anthem of youthful defiance ("I hope I die before I get old"), Townshend turned to more whimsical topics. "Substitute" made a play with contradictory images, aided by a Motown-styled use of bass guitar and tambourine; "I'm a Boy" told a bizarre tale of a kid whose mother treated him as if he were a girl; "Happy Jack" celebrated a down-and-out, typical of the eccentrics seen around most English country towns; and "Pictures of Lily" confessed to fetishism. These records were all top ten British hits, but despite doing tours in America the Who did not make the top ten there until 1967 when "I Can See for Miles", a more conventional pop topic and a much cleaner recording, belatedly established them. Originally affiliated with the "mod" era of pill-popping, obsessively fashion-conscious British teenagers, the Who were subsequently weighed down with an image which was more gimmicky and contrived than their music, and it was not until Pete Townshend put together the material for the first "Rock Opera", *Tommy* (1969), that the Who achieved the status and prestige already accorded to the Beatles and the Rolling Stones. But, as so often, the recognition came after the event; the best ideas had surfaced in the sequence of hits from 1965 to 1967.

After helping to launch the Who, Shel Talmy was displaced as producer by their managers Lambert and Stamp, who supervised their records through the rest of the sixties, often using engineer Glyn Johns, who had worked with Talmy on all the Kinks and Who sessions. Johns went on to become a major producer in his own right, in the vanguard as British studio techniques caught up with and even overtook the Americans, and as British artists finally escaped the cul-de-sac of working in essentially American musical idioms. Probably the most influential of all the British groups in this period were the Yardbirds, whose hits were produced by their bass-player Paul Samwell-Smith.

The early part of the Yardbirds' career was dogged by expectations that they would somehow be an equivalent to the Rolling Stones, whom they had replaced as resident band at first the Crawdaddy in Richmond (a suburb of London), and then the Marquee in the West End. Giorgio Gomelsky, manager of the Crawdaddy, became the group's manager and negotiated with EMI one of the first contracts which gave substantial control and ownership of an artist's recordings to the artist's manager. Gomelsky produced the early records, but after a couple of failures he passed production responsibilities on to Paul Samwell-Smith.

The Yardbirds were famous primarily as a vehicle for one of Britain's first "guitar heroes", Eric Clapton, but Samwell-Smith ignored that reputation and instead constructed an elaborate, dramatic arrangement around "For Your Love", written by Graham Gouldman, a young song-writer from Manchester. Pattering bongos were the most prominent instrument, framed by chiming guitars meshed with a harpsichord played by sessionman Brian Auger. Clapton left the group in disgust at the brazen commerciality of it all, but, undeterred, Samwell-Smith repeated the formula with equal success on "Heart Full of Soul". Jeff Beck came in to play guitar, and his flair for weird, distorted sounds was showcased in three songs written by members of the group, "Still I'm Sad", "Shapes of Things", and "Over, Under, Sideways, Down". These five records all made the top ten in Britain in 1965 and 1966, pioneering an adventurous approach to recording which the Beatles responded to with *Revolver*, and inspiring a generation of so-called "Progressive Rock" musicians including the Pink Floyd in Britain and the Buffalo Springfield and Todd Rundgren in America. The Yardbirds did not survive to capitalize on their own reputation; Samwell-Smith dropped out of the band in 1966, making way for Jimmy Page to come in, first as bass-player and subsequently as guitarist (featured in Antonioni's film, *Blow-Up*) until the whole band split up in 1967.

From some points of view, the peak years of British Rock were still to come, as British groups made evermore extensive tours of the States and sold millions of albums with support from FM radio stations and journalists who championed their music as "Art". Studio techniques improved, and artists became more autonomous, controlling more aspects of their recording and packaging through powerful managements with expert legal and accountancy advice.

But there was a spirit of spontaneous adventure in the best British recordings made in the years 1964 to 1966 which became harder to achieve as groups became more conscious of the pressures to meet the expectations of their "markets", particularly in America. In these years a generation of musicians who had been raised on skiffle and rock 'n' roll explored the roots of those forms, and came up with a wide range of derivations, culminating in the distinctly British records of the Beatles, the Who, the Kinks and the Yardbirds.

In most of their autobiographical recollections, the members of the groups have generally expressed various forms of discontent with their relationships with their record companies, ranging from being paid low royalties (royalties of one and two per cent were not uncommon, compared with ten or more per cent which became standard practice during the seventies), to interference from unsympathetic A&R departments who chose the wrong material, released the wrong singles, failed to promote artists, and any number of other complaints. And yet, by accident or design, the four British major labels between them recorded and released the vast majority of the hit records of the period, and responded far more swiftly to the changing market than their American counterparts had done during the equivalent period of rock 'n' roll back in the mid-fifties.

EMI* was consistently the most effective major in the period,

* EMI. *A&R: Norman Newell, assisted by John Burgess.*
Roster split into three labels; produced by own head of A&R except: † *by Norman Newell;* ‡ *by John Burgess;* ^ *for Columbia by George Martin;* * *independently produced for Columbia by Mickie Most;* ° *independently produced.* (*US licensees added in parentheses.*)

making a virtue of its vast size ("The Largest Recording Organization in the World" was the proud boast of its advertisements) by splitting its roster between three semi-autonomous labels, each with their own A&R head. George Martin at Parlophone was the company's "star" of the period, contributing incalculably to the Beatles' recording with a combination of suave diplomacy and astute musical arrangements.

In the States, Capitol had first option on EMI's roster, but by the time the company was prevailed upon to reconsider the Beatles at the end of 1963, Capitol had already declined its option on the bulk of EMI's artists, who were gleefully snapped up by the rest of the American record business. As the roster breakdown below shows, MGM, Imperial, and Epic reaped a substantial harvest.

Having generally outrun EMI during the fifties, Decca* had to settle for second place through the sixties, particularly as so many of

---

HMV. *A&R: Wally Ridley, assisted by Peter Sullivan.*
Groups: Johnny Kidd & The Pirates, Mike Berry & the Outlaws, Manfred Mann (1964–66, licensed to Ascot in US), Swinging Blue Jeans (Imperial).

COLUMBIA. *A&R: Norrie Paramor, assisted by John Schroeder & Bob Barrett.*
Solo Pop: Cliff Richard, Rolf Harris^, Lulu (1967–69) (all Epic), Helen Shapiro (Capitol), Frank Ifield (Vee Jay), Shirley Bassey (1960–63)†, Ken Dodd†.*
Instrumental: Russ Conway†, the Shadows.
Groups: Georgie Fame & the Blue Flames° (Imperial), the Animals, Herman's Hermits* (both MGM), the Seekers, Peter & Gordon† (both Capitol), Freddie & the Dreamers‡ (Tower), the Dave Clark Five°, the Yardbirds°, the Jeff Beck Group*(all Epic), Gerry & the Pacemakers^ (Laurie).*

PARLOPHONE. *A&R: George Martin, assisted by Ron Richards.*
Solo Pop: Adam Faith† (Amy), Cilla Black (Capitol), Peter Sellers.
Instrumental: the John Barry Seven†, the Temperance Seven.
Groups: Cliff Bennett & the Rebel Rousers‡, the Beatles (Vee Jay, 63, Swan, 63, Capitol from 64), Billy J. Kramer & the Dakotas (Imperial), the Hollies (Imperial 1964–67, Epic from 67).

Licensed labels from the United States:

CAPITOL. *Released virtually every substantial artist on the label (see p. 58 for roster).*

STATESIDE. *An outlet for material from various companies, including ABC, Ace, Bell, Fire-Fury, Tamla-Motown-Gordy, several of which acquired their own British label identity from 1965 alongside Liberty and United Artists, still licensed through EMI.*

* DECCA. *Still administered by founder-owner Edward Lewis. A&R: Dick Rowe, Peter Sullivan; "blues producer": Mike Vernon.*
Solo pop: Billy Fury, Tom Jones, Eden Kane, Val Doonican, Dave Berry, Marianne Faithful, P. J. Proby (1964), Lulu (1964–65), Billie Davis, Chris Andrews.
Instrumental group: the Tornadoes.
Vocal groups: Brian Poole and the Tremeloes, the Rolling Stones, the Small Faces (1965–66), the Zombies, the Moody Blues, Them, the Fortunes, the Nashville Teens, Unit Four Plus Two, the Alan Price Set, the Animals (1966).
Blues groups: Alexis Korner's Blues Incorporated, John Mayall's Bluesbreakers.

Licensed American labels:

BRUNSWICK. *Outlet for American Decca.*
UK group: the Who (1965 only).

LONDON. *Outlet for material licensed from various American labels including Hi, Monument, Tribe, Philles.*

the independent American companies which had supplied its London label with British hits in the fifties had now closed down or drastically reduced their output. There was no equivalent to George Martin at Decca, an A&R man who could enhance his projects with discrete advice, and the label's most successful band of the sixties, the Rolling Stones, conspicuously avoided using Decca's own studio or staff. A substantial proportion of Decca's artists achieved American success, and most of them "stayed in the family", being licensed to London or its Parrot subsidiary.

Among Decca's hits in the mid-sixties were two from 1965 which deserve special, ironic "honourable mentions" for managing to beat the Americans at their own game, just as the Americans were themselves abandoning it: both "Concrete and Clay" by Unit Four Plus Two and "You've Got Your Troubles" by the Fortunes were pop songs in the tradition of the material that Pomus and Shuman, Goffin and King, and the rest had written for the Drifters five years earlier. "Concrete and Clay" bounced on a Latin rhythm, and featured impeccable Spanish guitar as well as an effective "Ben E. King" type of vocal from co-writer and singer Tommy Moeller; surprisingly, the producer John L. Barker never repeated his success, whereas Roger Cook and Roger Greenaway, the writer-producers of "You've Got Your Troubles", went on to become one of the most successful teams in British pop for the next five years, although they never surpassed the combination of message and melody in this hit.

Pye Records* held on to third place in the UK label rankings, although it was generally a company without much of an "image", dedicated to selling records in the most straightforward way and not particularly responsive to the peculiar needs of the new kind of "artist" who considered personal integrity above commercial success. The Kinks had some famous confrontations at Pye, but the company's A&R man Tony Hatch was probably the most able writer-arranger working for a major British company at the time, and in addition to his sympathetic productions for the Searchers, he wrote and produced Petula Clark's big hits, "Downtown" and "I Know a

* PYE. *Head of A&R: Tony Hatch.*
Solo pop: Lonnie Donegan; Pet Clark, Sandie Shaw (both Reprise); Joe Brown; Donovan (Hickory, 1965; Epic, from 1966).
Vocal groups: the Searchers (Kapp); the Kinks (Reprise).

Subsidiary:

PICCADILLY
Soul: Geno Washington and the Ram Jam Band, the Rockin' Berries, the Ivy League.

Licensed American Labels (some released on Pye International).
Cameo-Parkway, A&M, Sceptre-Wand, Reprise, Colpix, Hickory, Red Bird, Dot, Chess, Warner Brothers, Kama Sutra and Buddah.

A&M, REPRISE, VANGUARD

Place", which confounded the singer's previous show biz image with their rousing arrangements and effective moods.

Pye's other leading artists of the period were Sandie Shaw, pure British pop at its most captivating, written and produced by freelance Chris Andrews, and Donovan, who switched from trying to sound like American folk singer Bob Dylan in "Catch the Wind" to some of the earliest hippie sing-alongs, "Sunshine Superman" and "Mellow Yellow", both produced by Mickie Most and hugely successful in America in 1966.

Pye was quicker than the other British major labels to realize that American labels preferred to release their product in Britain on their own labels, and captured Reprise, A&M, and Vanguard among others; Reprise took up options to release Pet Clark and the Kinks in the States, and had hits with both, but Donovan somehow slipped out on the Nashville country label Hickory before Epic picked him up in time to top the charts with "Sunshine Superman".

Philips* trailed as the fourth British major through the early sixties, often slow to move on the latest fads and apparently content to stick to the middle-of-the-road artists who had been the company's traditional strength in the fifties when it was the British licensee for American Columbia. CBS formed its own British outlet in 1962, leaving Philips A&R man Johnny Franz to piece together a British-based roster. Apart from the Springfields and Dusty Springfield, the most successful teen-oriented act on the Philips label was the Walker Brothers, a canny collusion of three previously unconnected American singers who moved to Britain to present themselves as a locally accessible alternative to the Righteous Brothers. The device worked to plan, and Johnny Franz arranged several effective epic productions including the chart-topping "Make It Easy on Yourself" (a cover of Jerry Butler's American hit) and "The Sun Ain't Gonna Shine Any More" (1966) (written by the Four Seasons team of Bob Crewe and Bob Gaudio).

Most of the teen-oriented signings were issued on the Fontana label, and apart from Millie and the Spencer Davis Group they

* PHILIPS. *Owned by Philips of Holland; licensed to American affiliates Philips, Fontana, Mercury and Smash. A&R: Johnny Franz, Jack Baverstock.*
Solo pop: Dusty Springfield.
Groups: the Springfields, the Walker Brothers.

Subsidiary:

FONTANA
Solo pop: Millie (Small).
Groups: Wayne Fontana and the Mindbenders, the Merseybeats, the Merseys, the Spencer Davis Group (United Artists in America), the Troggs (records by the Troggs were subject to some confusion in the States, where the first three singles came out on both Atco and Fontana).

included some of the better Mersey groups (Wayne Fontana and the Mindbenders, and the Merseybeats) and the Troggs, who defied comparisons. Where most groups of the time made some attempts to boast their instrumental prowess, the Troggs seemed to revel in their lack of musical graces, and under the direction of independent producer-manager Larry Page, declared undisguised sexual preoccupations: "Wild Thing", "With a Girl Like You", "I Can't Control Myself". Written by an American, Chip Taylor, "Wild Thing" had been recorded before, but it was this version which turned the song into a standard of sleazy suggestiveness.

This four way carve-up of the British market was soon to be challenged by a host of new companies, including the German-based Polydor, several independent labels started by managers of successful British groups, and most of the major American companies who wanted direct access to British talent instead of having to license it from British companies. But first, these American companies had to come to grips with the invasion of their own market by British artists.

The table below shows the sudden change in America between 1963, when only one British-made record reached the American top ten, and 1964, when 32 got there; in the same period, American-produced hits dropped by almost forty per cent, from 113 to 68. As usual, indie labels were faster than the majors to spot the new trend, but by 1967 the majors had managed to exercise options on most of the successful British acts, and improved on the share of the market which they had been struggling to hold before the British Invasion.

US TOP TEN HITS, 1962–69, BY TYPE OF COMPANY AND NATIONAL SOURCE

Year:	1962	1963	1964	1965	1966	1967	1968	1969
UK productions	2	1	32	36	30	22	16	11
leased to US majors	1	–	20	30	23	22	15	11
leased to US indies	1	1	12	6	7	–	1	–
US productions	96	113	68	74	97	90	93	96
issued by US majors	40	51	26	24	34	45	55	55
issued by US indies	56	62	42	36	60	45	38	41
Total US hits	98	114	100	110	124	112	109	107

In many ways, the American record business in the mid-sixties went through a crash revision course of the lessons that had been learned in the mid-fifties. But this time round, the major labels managed to move faster and get a firmer grip on the artists who had caused all the trouble, and even used them to outpoint the larger rhythm and blues indies, who were poised to make a clean sweep of the nation's dance music. Once again, the majors discovered a market they had not known was there, a market which preferred its music to be played by artists with an identity; this time, the majors took the point.

12

COAST TO COAST

During the mid-sixties, the American record industry was given a new impetus from three sources: from the brilliant pop dance records being turned out by Berry Gordy's empire in Detroit; from the more passionate soul records from the southern studios in Memphis and Muscle Shoals; and from the mass invasion of pop and rock records from Britain. 1964 was the year of greatest upheaval, as one generation of independent companies virtually abandoned the industry, and the few survivors adopted most of the strategies and structures of major labels. Imperceptibly, the "centre of gravity" of the industry drifted away from New York towards Los Angeles. Several of the largest companies maintained headquarters in New York, but most of them opened West Coast offices, and were obliged to scour the entire country in search of the kind of artists whose music could live on the radio alongside the new contenders.

There were three broad categories of white American artists whose records "stood up": singers who had been based in the folk scene, and who adapted their material to suit a heavier accompaniment after the Animals showed that the combination could work in "The House of the Rising Sun"; groups whose rough-and-ready approach to singing and playing their instruments had previously been considered OK for a local bar band, but not professional enough for radio fare; and industry professionals who, seeing how effective these two types of artist were becoming, put together studio-based equivalents, some of whom were subsequently marketed as "real" groups if the records attracted enough attention to make the exercise worthwhile.

Apart from reawakening American interest in some of the "source" idioms of pop music, the British groups–and particularly the Beatles and the Rolling Stones–aroused a more intense interest in pop music itself. The most obvious result was that more people started buying more records, effectively expanding the basic pop music market to reclaim an audience which thought it had "grown out of" pop music. The increasing popularity of folk-based performers was a by-product of this new kind of pop fan, but although there was a streak of dissent and social comment running through the folk material, and there were several independent labels specializing in recording folk artists, the merger of folk and pop consolidated the position of the major labels, and helped them to recover some of the ground that had been lost in the rock 'n' roll era.

The few threats from independent labels mostly came from companies which picked up the so called "garage-band" groups who had no obvious political consciousness, but were simply ambitious to make music like the Beatles and Stones, earn some of the money that was flying around, and attract the attention of the millions of American teenage girls who were apparently besotted by the images of the British boys. But there were no new independent companies to compare with the rhythm and blues pioneers, and only Bang! Records in New York managed to build a small roster of significant artists. Most of the rest tended to fade away after a couple of hits, or tie themselves in with existing companies for promotion and distribution.

For companies based on the West Coast, this was the period when all those years of erratic success began to pay dividends for the more persistent writers and producers, firstly with music that was loosely categorized as "surf music", and then with various combinations of "folk", "pop", and "rock" catalysed by several refugees from the New York folk scene.

I

The modern American folk movement dates back to the strong unionization activities of the thirties reinforced during the war years when Leadbelly and Woody Guthrie emerged as leading club entertainers; it flowered in national pop hits of their material in 1950–51 by the Weavers, with "Goodnight Irene", "This Land is Your Land", and others. But the McCarthy era of red-baiting and witch-hunting drove independent expression underground, leaving the innocuous calypsos of Harry Belafonte, The Tarriers, the Easy Riders, and others to represent "folk music" on pop radio.

Throughout the fifties, it seemed that the creators and audiences of pop music accepted the limitations of pop's role, circling around the same situations of unrequited fantasy, agonized courtship, narcissistic fulfilment, and suicidal loss, relieved only by trivial novelties and abstract instrumentals. In fact, there were writers and singers who presented unorthodox situations in their songs, and expressed attitudes of defiance, rejection, and independence which were not simply petulant outbursts of adolescence, but lively alternatives to the passive status quo. Chuck Berry, Buddy Holly, Leiber and Stoller, and Carl Perkins all wrote songs whose social content would have been quickly acknowledged by folk fans if they had been delivered with acoustic accompaniment by an "authentic" folk singer. Broadcast on pop radio, they escaped attention, and it took the Beatles and the Stones to rescue their songs from the trash-can into which America threw its old hits. Meanwhile, folk existed in a world of its own until Bob Dylan dragged it, screaming, into pop in the mid-sixties.

"Folk Music" conjured up two particular images: a seated singer, crouched over an acoustic guitar; or, a group of three or four singers, ranged around one microphone and playing a variety of acoustic stringed instruments (permed from guitar, banjo, mandolin, fiddle and double bass). In either case, no drums or electrically-amplified guitars intruded to break the spell of timelessness.

The solo singers carried on the tradition of the itinerant street entertainers whose repertoire had been extensively recorded during the twenties and thirties. Black singer-guitarists were recorded for the so-called "race" market until their audience began to prefer records featuring electric guitars and a more emphatic dance beat, at which stage most of the country-blues musicians retired from a professional career in music. But a few took a new tack, adapting their repertoire and delivery to the tastes of a mostly white, college educated, and often politically left-wing audience, who responded to the realistic subject matter and authentic delivery of the black "folk blues". Among the favourites in this new context were Josh White from South Carolina, and the duo of Brownie McGhee and harmonica player Sonny Terry, who had been minor figures in the race market; but most popular of all was Leadbelly, who was even more obscure.

Leadbelly's story was a classic "rags-to-riches romance": he was discovered while serving time in the Louisiana State Penitentiary at Angola in 1933 by the folk archivists John and Alan Lomax on one of their field research trips through the Southern States. Managing to secure Leadbelly's release from jail, the Lomax father-and-son took their discovery north to New York, where his gravel voice, intense delivery, and extensive repertoire made a great impression on the tastes and styles of everyone who heard him. Through his live performances and his recordings (on many different labels including specialist collector labels and several of the majors), Leadbelly introduced a slew of folk songs which became well-known during the next thirty years on both sides of the Atlantic, including those he wrote himself and others which he pieced together from songs he heard during his childhood: "Rock Island Line", which later launched the career of British skiffle singer Lonnie Donegan; "Midnight Special", which was recently adopted as the title of a live music series on American TV, after countless recordings; "Goodnight Irene", and many more.

Parallel with the black folk singers, an equivalent tribe of white folk singers wandered through the Southern States performing a similar repertoire, but it did not occur to the recording industry that they might constitute a source of commercial music. Many of the street singers, black and white, were more or less forced to play guitar because of some infirmity that made it difficult to obtain any other kind of job. Crippled, blind, they were seen as little better than beggars. Jimmie Rodgers helped to redefine the image of such men, following the surprising success of his first records for Victor, made in 1927.

Known as "The Singing Brakeman", Jimmie Rodgers was very similar to the black blues singers in both his repertoire and his instrumentation, but his records soon achieved sales comparable to the most commercial singers of the day, and actually held up better than most through the Depression years of the thirties. Virtually every substantial white Southern singer who emerged in the next twenty years cited Rodgers as their major influence, including Roy Acuff, Ernest Tubb, and Hank Williams, who himself became the next major influence for a new generation of Southern singers in the fifties, by now classified as "country and western".

Like the blues singers who augmented their accompaniment with saxophones, pianos and drums, these country and western performers added band accompaniment to their own guitars during the forties, and adapted their style and repertoire to conform to the requirements of rowdy honky tonk clubs and to the expectations of "country and western" radio stations. But there was another way to take the Jimmie Rodgers approach, as Woody Guthrie showed.

Originally from Oklahoma, which was on the edge of the territory associated with country and western music, Woody Guthrie never attempted to cater for that market, but instead moved west, north, and eventually east, continually writing songs about the Depression-wracked world he saw around him. In 1940, Woody joined forces with three New York folk singers, Pete Seeger, Lee Hays, and Millard Lampbell, and together they formed the Almanac Singers whose repertoire and stage delivery were designed to galvanize the working people of America to recognize their common links and heritage. With a national tour and regular New York concerts, the Almanac Singers established the urban folk group as an effective format. There had been previous country folk groups with a similar line-up, notably the Carter Family, who had coincidentally made their first recordings at the same Victor session as Jimmie Rodgers. But the Carter Family was more concerned to document and revive the "pure" folk tradition which stretched back into the nineteenth century and across the Atlantic to Britain for its sources. Folk performers from this camp sometimes disapproved of the propagandist approach of the Almanac Singers and their successors.

The Almanac Singers disbanded in 1942, but the folk scene flourished in a low key way through the forties, with Woody Guthrie and Leadbelly as the major figures. Among the Guthrie songs which passed into the standard folk repertoire were "This Land is Your Land", "So Long, It's Been Good to Know You", and "This Train is Bound for Glory", while his "Talkin' Blues" format has been adopted and adapted by countless singers. Like most of the folk singers, he did not have an exclusive recording contract, and recorded for several companies including Folkways and Victor, but few people heard his own versions of his songs, compared to the millions who heard them performed by other artists, notably the Weavers.

The original Weavers comprised two ex-Almanac Singers, Pete Seeger and Lee Hays, along with Ronnie Gilbert and Fred Hellerman, and it was this group which brought folk music out of the side streets and into full public prominence. The record industry was still sceptical when the group was formed in 1949, and the only way they could record was when Decca's Music Director Gordon Jenkins offered to credit them as "featured vocalists" on a session booked for his own Orchestra. Their version of Leadbelly's "Goodnight Irene" was immediately a huge hit in 1950, going all the way to the top of the charts, and sticking on the lists for six months; too late for Leadbelly to benefit–he had died in December 1949. Subsequently signed to Decca in their own right, the Weavers had a run of hits, including Woody Guthrie's "So Long", and an adaptation of an African folk song, "Wimoweh (The Lion Sleeps Tonight)", but the Weavers' ethic of self-reliance and self-expression was making some people uncomfortable.

This was the height of the McCarthy era, when right-wing Americans lined up behind Senator Joe McCarthy in a witch-hunt to expose and expunge all public and media figures with "left-wing leanings", whatever they were. Insidious pressures were put on friends of friends to secure "confessions" of "Communist sympathies", and the American entertainment industry, inextricably tied into the advertising industry through the system of sponsored TV and radio shows, in general yielded to the blackmail and turned a cold shoulder on anyone with a hint of left-wing associations. Pete Seeger had a well-documented career of encouraging people to stand up for their rights, and the Weavers were obliged to disband at the end of 1952, rather than endure more humiliations of being turned down by various engagements with no satisfactory explanation.

For a few years, folk music was regarded with some mistrust by the major record companies, even after the McCarthy furore had died down, which enabled some of the specialist independent labels* to record most of the leading folk performers and build themselves into substantial operations. Folkways, formed in the forties by Moe Asch, never showed any ambition to break out of its collector market, nor did the similar Tradition label, but both Vanguard and Elektra made inroads into the commercial market.

Elektra was formed in 1950 by Jac Holzman, who ran the label virtually as a hobby during the fifties, although the growing demand for records by Josh White and Theodore Bikel forced the company to expand. Vanguard owners Seymour and Maynard Solomon formed the label primarily to record classical music, but developed an extensive catalogue of jazz and folk artist during the fifties, recruiting the Weavers when they reformed in 1956.

But in contrast to the rock 'n' roll era, when the major labels allowed the indies to get a headstart which lasted for several years, folk was never ignored to the same extent. As albums became an increasingly important factor in the record industry, folk was clearly an attractive proposition, provided artists could be found who were not as politically suspect as the Weavers. In the event, many folkies turned out to be even more political, but many of them signed to the larger companies on the rationalization that their message would reach more people than if they recorded for an independent company. Whatever their motive, the folk performers played an important role in enabling the major companies to recover their position in the pop market, and some of them became the cornerstones of their companies' rosters during the sixties.

The next commercial phase for folk music was sparked off in 1957 from a new angle, by two versions of a calypso-styled song called "The Banana Boat Song" by the Tarriers (for Glory Records) and by Harry Belafonte (for RCA-Victor). Belafonte had pursued parallel

*INDEPENDENT FOLK LABELS:

FOLKWAYS. *Formed in 1948 in New York by Moe Asch and Marion Distler.*
Folk: Leadbelly, Woody Guthrie, Pete Seeger, Burl Ives, Josh White.
Blues: Brownie McGhee and Sonny Terry.

VANGUARD. *Formed circa 1948 in New York by Maynard and Seymour Solomon.*
A&R: in mid fifties: John Hammond; in late fifties and early sixties: Sam Charters.
Folk: the Weavers, Joan Baez, Odetta, the Rooftop Singers.
Rock: Country Joe and the Fish.

ELEKTRA. *Formed in 1950 in New York by Jac Holzman. Bought by Kinney Corporation in 1968; merged with Asylum in 1973 under corporate umbrella of Warner Communications Inc.*
Folk: Theodore Bikel, Josh White, Tom Paxton, Phil Ochs, Judy Collins.
Blues: the Paul Butterfield Blues Band.
Rock: the Doors, Love.

and equally successful careers as an actor and a singer, and after starring (but not singing) in the film *Carmen Jones*, he was signed to RCA, for whom he recorded an album of calypso songs, including "The Banana Boat Song". RCA had scored with two singles, "Jamaica Farewell" and "Mary's Boy Child", when a substantially different version of "The Banana Boat Song" was issued on Glory by the Tarriers, a fairly straight harmony folk group led by banjo-player Erik Darling and also including Alan Arkin (who subsequently left to pursue a successful career as an actor). RCA rushed out the Belafonte version of "Banana Boat" (subtitled "Day-O" because of the distinctive cry in the chorus), and both songs made the national top ten, reaffirming a place for folk music in the scheme of things.

Over the next couple of years the majors all made sure they had at least one folk act on their books. They saw how many albums Belafonte was selling and could see that he did not seem to be causing any consternation behind the scenes, where advertisers and board directors compared notes. Ironically, Belafonte became very active in the Civil Rights Movement during the sixties, and virtually retired from show business. But that was later; now, he followed up his hits with relentless live work, and helped to introduce his audience to several young folk acts, notably Odetta, who joined him at RCA after recording albums for Tradition and Vanguard. Decca signed Burl Ives, whose career stretched back to the war years, and his avuncular appeal was successfully oriented both to nursery-level kids and the pop charts; Capitol picked up the Kingston Trio, whose college-boy manner took them into the pop mainstream, with several hit singles (including the chart-topping "Tom Dooley" in 1958) and some of the best-selling albums of the period; Columbia signed the similar Brothers Four, and much more daringly took on Pete Seeger, now a solo performer and always a vital catalyst for the whole folk movement. UA picked up the Highwaymen, RCA the Limeliters, and Warner Brothers got Peter, Paul and Mary, who lifted folk up another notch on the scale of pop acceptability with a female lead singer whose onstage vivacity matched her flawless voice.

Vanguard did well to hold out against the marketing and distribution strength of the majors, and even managed to improve its own share of the pop market. The big coup for the label was when Joan Baez chose Vanguard against competition from several larger companies, after she had made a show-stopping debut at the Newport Folk Festival in 1959. From the beginning of her career, Joan Baez struck a very different image from the normal female stereotype that pop music was used to; instead of make-up, turned-on "vulnerable" smiles, and figure-conscious poses, she exuded a serene self-confidence, wearing comfortable clothes and speaking her mind on all kinds of normally unspeakable subjects like the American government's oppressive policies towards native Indians, the Far East, Latin America, southern blacks. She chose her own material, played guitar, and sang like a bird, or an angel, or whatever analogy conveys purity and clarity. Her albums, recorded both "live" in concert, and in the studio, all made the best-selling charts, but pop radio programmers virtually boycotted her records, appalled by this agent of dissent in their midst. Not until Joan took the tried-and-true route of recording in Nashville did she crack their defences, belatedly making the top three in 1971 with "The Night They Drove Old Dixie Down".

Vanguard's first really big hit was "Walk Right In" by the Rooftop Singers in 1963; in effect, this was a delayed follow-up to "The Banana Boat Song" for Erik Darling, who had formed the Rooftop Singers after a stint as Pete Seeger's replacement in the Weavers. But that was one of the last pure folk hits; a couple of months later, Peter, Paul and Mary hit with "Puff The Magic Dragon", a charming fable for kids, but then got down to the heavier stuff with "Blowin' in the Wind", and from then on most "folk" hits were either political, or else much fuller instrumentally.

II

By 1962 the folk movement had spread to most large cities, enabling the leading performers to make a living by touring the country, with the annual highlight of the Newport Folk Festival, inaugurated in 1959, where reputations could be made and enhanced. Magazines including *Sing Out* reviewed albums and concerts, printed song lyrics, and debated with rising intensity what was and what was not acceptably defined as "folk music". Much of the discussion focussed on modes of accompaniment–whether or not electrically amplified instruments were acceptable–and whether songs could be personal and contemporary, or should be "third person", historical, and traditional. The modernists had blues singers on their side.

After Leadbelly died in 1949 the leading black folk singers were Josh White, Big Bill Broonzy, and the harmonica-and-guitar duo, Sonny Terry and Brownie McGhee. Singing with a clear light voice, typical of North Carolina bluesmen, Josh White not only embraced appropriate traditional songs from black folklore, notably "House of The Rising Sun", but also included songs with a white, even European heritage. Much more intense, originally from Mississippi, and more recently based in Chicago, Big Bill Broonzy also extended his repertoire beyond the conventional blues framework, to include songs which were easy to sing along with and had some inherent social message like the moving "Get Back". Brownie McGhee (from Tennessee) and Sonny Terry (raised in North Carolina) maintained an unusual double career, recording with band accompaniment for the black audience and acoustically for the whites.

During the late fifties, these pioneer black folk blues singers were joined by many of their contemporaries who had either given up performing or were playing to the dwindling black audience for acoustic blues in their home towns. Following the trails left by John and Alan Lomax, several researchers made trips to record, interview, and photograph surviving bluesmen during the fifties. Frederick Ramsey, Harold Courlander, Sam Charters and Paul Oliver made several Southern field trips, leasing many of their tapes to Folkways; Charters' book *The Country Blues*, Ramsey's *Been Here and Gone*, Courlander's *Negro Folk Music, USA* and Oliver's *Blues Fell This Morning* sparked off widespread interest in the blues, and particularly in the blues artists they recorded, many of whom were subsequently invited to appear in folk clubs and college theatres around the country.

Lightnin' Hopkins proved to be the most adaptable to the new white audience, apparently able to invent intriguing narrative blues for anybody who paid him to sing a song into a microphone. After recording prolifically for many rhythm and blues labels during the late forties and early fifties, Hopkins had been inactive since 1953, and re-emerged with an album recorded by Charters for Folkways in 1959, the year that brought several other blues artists to the white audience for the first time, including Robert Pete Williams, and slide guitarists Fred McDowell and Furry Lewis. In 1960 the New York street singer Reverend Gary Davis recorded an album for the jazz label Prestige, whose special blues subsidiary Bluesville could, by 1962, boast an impressive roster: Lonnie Johnson, an enormously popular commercial blues singer-guitarist who had recorded regularly from the late twenties to the early fifties; the New Orleans guitarist Snooks Eaglin, whose repertoire included contemporary rhythm and blues hits transposed to the folk-blues idiom of acoustic guitar; and several blues pianists including Memphis Slim, Roosevelt Sykes, Victoria Spivey, Little Brother Montgomery, and Sunnyland Slim. In Chicago, record store owner Bob Koester ran Delmark Records as a lively sideline, recording many local blues artists and the nine-string guitarist Big Joe Williams; on the West Coast, one-man band Jesse Fuller recorded for Good Time Jazz.

Apart from introducing their new audiences to unorthodox styles of tuning and playing guitar, achieving thrilling effects impossible for conventional folk technicians, the bluesmen also unwittingly gave evidence on behalf of those who argued that folk music could be personal music, and did not have to adhere to the traditional ballad form of third person narratives. The world of blues opened up as more researchers and collectors unearthed and reissued more records, and rediscovered more authentic exponents of the art, men who had recorded during the twenties and thirties, and who had long since abandoned music as a career. Skip James, Bukka White, Son House, Sleepy John Estes, the Reverend Robert Wilkins, and Mississippi John Hurt were discovered alive and still able to play the music of their younger days, returning to the recording studio after up to thirty years absence, while reissue companies including Yazoo, Arhoolie's Blues Classics and Biograph made their original recordings available on albums for the first time.

Although these blues singers were never heard by more than a tiny proportion of the popular music audience, their indirect impact was enormous, through their influence on the audience and especially on the performers in folk clubs during the early sixties, both in the States and in Europe, where those still fit enough to travel made extensive tours. The power and beauty of the blues singers' delivery and material was a vital inspiration to frustrated performers and audiences looking for more personal expression than was available in either mainstream pop or orthodox folk music.

Once the acoustic guitarists had introduced the folk club audiences to the blues, more contemporary singers became acceptable too, including most of the leading Chicago bluesmen. John Lee Hooker, Bo Diddley, Jimmy Reed (who had a device for holding a harmonica above his guitar so he could play both at the same time), Howlin' Wolf, Muddy Waters and Sonny Boy Williamson all played in the folk houses of Boston and Greenwich Village and at campus folk concerts during the early sixties.

While the blues styles were rediscovered and revitalized, so were acoustic forms of white Southern country music which had been rendered obsolete as pop music by the stereotyped "Nashville" sound. The mandolin-banjo-and-fiddle line-up of Kentucky Bluegrass music was specially favoured, played by Bill Monroe and many of his former side-men including Lester Flatt and Earl Scruggs, prime exponents of a style which laid emphasis more on instrumental virtuosity than on rhythm or emotional vocals. Among younger, Northern-based groups in this style, the New Lost City Ramblers were the most versatile and popular.

Survivors of the famous Carter Family became favourites on the folk circuit too, with their repertoire of traditional and sacred mountain songs, as gospel music from all sources became more widespread in response to the need for emotionally-charged sing-along songs for the protest movements of America and Britain.

III

The folk movement had flourished during the fifties in Britain, where there was no equivalent to the suppressive McCarthy period suffered in the States. While Lonnie Donegan presented many essentially folk songs by Leadbelly and Woody Guthrie to the national pop audience by putting a rhythm section behind them, there was, however, a strong, defiantly non-commercial, movement of musicians who sustained traditional forms of Irish, Scottish, Welsh and English country music, alongside ballads written during the industrial revolution of the nineteenth century, and bolstered by contemporary songs composed in traditional idioms. Ewan MacColl was the acknowledged leader of the folk singers and used traditional forms to comment, critically, on current society, enjoying support from BBC radio producer Charles Parker for the series "Radio Ballads" which would have been inconceivable in the States.

At Easter, 1958, the Campaign for Nuclear Disarmament (CND) inaugurated an annual protest against the manufacture of nuclear weapons in Britain by marching from the armaments factory at Aldermaston fifty miles to Trafalgar Square in London, taking four days to complete it. The event brought dissenting people of all ages together from all over the country, and stimulated the development of a repertoire of radical songs which carried over into club performances during the intervening years, inspiring new compositions and leading to an increasing appreciation of American blues and folk material, introduced by Americans including Peggy Seeger and Alan Lomax (resident in Britain during the fifties) and regular visitors like Ramblin' Jack Elliott.

A parallel peace movement eventually emerged in the States, using the British CND symbol as its emblem (☮), but the first political movement of the era in America focussed on Civil Rights demonstrations enforcing the Desegregation Laws in the South. The main tools of civil nghts protests were sit-ins and marches, both tests of physical endurance which passed more easily with communal singing. Many of the early anthems were songs written or associated with Pete Seeger, who helped to inaugurate the Newport Folk Festival in 1959, and pioneered folk "hootenannies", concerts where the audience participated in the singing. When ABC-TV networked a show called *Hootenanny* to capitalize on the folk boom which followed the Kingston Trio hits, they refused to allow Seeger onto the show because of his political associations, but John Hammond defiantly signed Seeger to Columbia Records as a solo artist after he left the Weavers.

A brave and irreproachable spokesman for the freedom of thought and speech during the period when American media treated even moderate liberals with paranoid suspicion, Seeger played an incalculable role in keeping the spirit of conspicuous individualism and political protest alive. A champion of other folk singers who lacked his propagandist flair, he laid the groundwork upon which the sixties folk boom was based, and had enormous influence on the repertoire of songs adopted by the protest movements; his own compositions included "If I Had a Hammer", "Where Have All The Flowers Gone", "Turn Turn Turn", and "We Shall Overcome".

Music had a relatively minor role in the first civil rights event, a bus boycott in Montgomery, Alabama, which followed a spontaneous refusal in December 1955 by black housewife Rosa Parks to give up her seat to a white passenger on a bus, as was the local custom.* Although it had no direct musical side-effects of its own, the passive non-violence of the Montgomery bus boycott became the model for future civil rights demonstrations, including a sit-in at a coffee shop in Greensboro, North Carolina by four black students in 1960. While they waited to be served, a sympathy sit-in at the Fisk University in Nashville turned into a long-term demonstration where among the songs chanted was an adaptation of Little Willie John's "Leave My Kitten Alone", sung as "you'd better leave desegregation alone". Following the Fisk sit-in, Guy Carawan, an associate of Pete Seeger, began to assemble a repertoire of songs which would serve at such events in the future.

In support of the traditional black rights organizations, NAACP (National Association for the Advancement of Coloured People) and CORE (Congress of Racial Equality), various student-based organizations were formed, notably SNCC (Student Non-violent Co-ordinating Committee) and SDS (Students for A Democratic Society), with a particular focus on assisting black people in the South to register their right to vote, and organizing tenants in Northern ghettoes where neglectful private landlords and city councils had contributed to appalling living conditions. Coinciding with a growing awareness and abhorrence of American intervention and military activity in the Far East which grew into a fully-fledged Peace Movement, the Civil Rights Movement was supported by many folk singers, writers, and musicians, some of whom became national stars even for the non-political mainstream pop audience.

Peter, Paul and Mary were the first openly political artists since the

* *To protest against her arrest and fine for this "offence", a few black people suggested a boycott of the Montgomery bus service by the blacks who constituted the majority of its passengers. Reported in the local papers, and supported by local black church groups, the boycott became a topic of national interest as it stretched over several months, making, in the process, two local ministers the Reverend Martin Luther King and the Reverend Ralph Abernathy into national leaders of black independence.*

Weavers to be accepted by the major institutions of America's mass media. Brought together by Albert Grossman, manager of Chicago's leading folk club, the Gate of Horn, Peter, Paul and Mary were signed by Warner Brothers in 1961 and made the top ten the following year with Pete Seeger's anthem of peace, "If I Had a Hammer" and again in 1963 with "Blowin' in the Wind", written by the then obscure Bob Dylan. Paradoxically, despite their genuine political beliefs which they expressed by singing free at political rallies around the country, the sound of Peter, Paul and Mary (produced by Milt Okun) was soft and easy-on-the-ear, unlikely to stir activity in the passive pop audience, a large proportion of whom may not even have registered the political implications of the delightfully melodic "Blowin' In the Wind". Nevertheless, Peter, Paul and Mary played an invaluable role on behalf of the writers whose songs they recorded on their best-selling albums. They opened the doors through which Bob Dylan and others walked, out of the coffee houses and into the limelight.

Bob Dylan's career represents the growth of folk music in general, although he was actually part of the scene for a relatively short period. Having shared his generation's teenage enthusiasm for the stars of rock 'n' roll, Dylan was dismayed with the way the music business seemed to absorb their spirit while casting aside their individualism, and saw in folk music a better framework for self-expression. Ambitious, doggedly-determined, and uncommonly quick to absorb new influences and experiences, Dylan more than compensated for whatever he lacked in the basic techniques of singing and playing guitar (by all accounts, he had trouble singing in tune, or keeping to set chord-change patterns). One other important quality: Dylan attracted the attention of important people; within a year of arriving in New York in 1961, Dylan received glowing reviews in the *New York Times* from Robert Shelton, was signed to Columbia by John Hammond, and was managed by Albert Grossman.

In folk circles, however, several singer-songwriters would have been ranked higher than Dylan in terms of proven ability and likely potential, notably Dave Van Ronk. An eclectic and adventurous musician, Van Ronk was championed by the "modernist" folkies, not as an outstanding technician or singer, but as an arranger who was widely imitated. But the easy-going Van Ronk had no particular ambition to reach beyond the already converted folk audience, which is probably why one of the other leading folk singers of the day, Ramblin' Jack Elliott, never achieved more than a cult following.

A New Yorker whose real name was Elliott Adnopoz, Ramblin' Jack buried his identity beneath a reincarnation of Woody Guthrie, who during the nineteen forties had almost single-handedly invented a new style of contemporary folk music, "talking blues"–social commentaries about politics, living off his wits on the road, and idealizing the rural way of life in the face of encroaching urbanization. Singing Guthrie's songs, and composing his own in a similar style, Elliott was a familiar figure in folk clubs throughout the States and in Britain too, where he made several extended visits.

When Dylan recorded his first album for Columbia in 1961, he was still strongly under the influence of Elliott, Van Ronk, and a blues-inflected folk singer from Cambridge, Massachusettes, Rik Von Schmidt. Most of the songs were standards on the folk circuit, as the liner notes elaborated in considerable detail, and only two were Dylan originals, both in the Guthrie/Elliott talking blues style. Apart from the startling confidence with which the singer attacked his material, the record was unremarkable, and hardly justified the apparently wayward decision of John Hammond to append him to Columbia's middle-of-the-road roster.

A crucial stage in Dylan's development came in 1962, when Pete Seeger returned from a trip to Britain very impressed by the contemporary song-writing of Britain's folk singers. In association with two other leading figures on the folk scene, Sis Cunningham and Gil Turner, Seeger founded the magazine *Broadside*, which would publish the lyrics of the best newly-composed folk songs. With this forum as an outlet, Dylan seemed galvanized into action, and during the following year he wrote a succession of thrilling songs, sometimes stringing images and phrases together in stream-of-consciousness inspiration, and in other songs crafting choruses with the aplomb of a Brill Building professional. Responding to the mood of the times like a seismograph, Dylan became the expression of all that the folk and protest movements collectively represented. Following Peter, Paul and Mary's recordings of two of his songs from this period, "Blowin' In The Wind" and "Don't Think Twice, It's All Right", Dylan recorded his second album, *The Freewheelin' Bob Dylan*, which astounded everyone who heard it.

Not since the great days of Elvis, Buddy Holly, and Jerry Lee Lewis had a white American pop singer sounded so defiantly *real* and uncompromising; here was a new voice for youth to recognize, identify with, and follow. Some of the songs were directly political–"A Hard Rain's A-Gonna Fall" and "Masters of War". Others were anarchic–"Bob Dylan's Dream". But others were love songs with a twist or two in their tails–"Girl From the North Country" and "Don't Think Twice, It's All Right". This was no dry ideologist, but a vulnerable fighter with a wicked grin.

In 1964 Dylan's third album was released, *The Times They Are A-Changing*, whose themes and style were similar to *Freewheelin'* although at Albert Grossman's insistence John Hammond had been withdrawn as producer, deputized by a junior member of Columbia's A&R staff, Tom Wilson. Following the release of the album, Dylan went to perform in Britain, where *Freewheelin'* had topped the album charts and stirred a lot of excitement among the emerging generation of groups, most of whom were still limited to rehashing rhythm and blues numbers. Inspired by Dylan's ability to express protest and defiance in a modern and widely accessible style, the British writers began to put more "content" into their songs.

Dylan was equally impressed with what British musicians could achieve with a style based on the music of his adolescence. In particular, he was struck by the Animals' treatment of "House of the Rising Sun", a song first introduced to modern folk repertoire by Josh White, but sung by Dylan on his first album in an arrangement devised by Dave Van Ronk. Now bolstered by Alan Price's percussive organ and a rhythm section, the song had more power than ever before, and Dylan returned to the States determined to record his next album with musicians.

Another Side of Bob Dylan was a musically cautious step towards "folk-rock", with rhythm support kept tactfully in the background, but a much clearer indication of the new direction came in 1965 with the single "Subterranean Homesick Blues". A bluesy, amplified rhythm section blasted away while Dylan shouted the lyric almost too fast to catch, sounding for all the world like Chuck Berry singing "Too Much Monkey Business" back in 1956. The next album confirmed the new direction, with electric guitarist Bruce Langhorne fronting a unit of session musicians on all the songs on the first side of *Bringing It All Back Home*.

At the 1965 Newport Folk Festival, Dylan sang part of his set with members of Paul Butterfield's Blues Band, and later the same year toured Britain with the musicians who had previously been Ronnie Hawkins' Hawks, and more recently played with John Hammond Jr (the son of the Columbia A&R man). The audiences included disappointed purists who preferred the acoustic protest singer, but Dylan had made his move towards the larger pop music audience, and he reached it with some remarkable songs on the three albums released in 1965 and 1966, *Bringing It All Back Home*, *Highway 61 Revisited*, and *Blonde on Blonde*. Not only Dylan's own career, but the entire folk-rock movement reached its peak with those records.

Dylan more or less abandoned overt political protest after *Times They Are A-Changing*, turning his critical attention to more personal relationships, although in "Maggie's Farm" on *Home* he took a stand against authority and routine, delivered with humour to a socking beat. "She Belongs to Me" on the same album was a rare statement of unashamed admiration and devotion, full of brilliantly ingenious and irresistibly moving couplets which established, beyond any doubt, Dylan's place among America's great popular song-writers.

The best-known song from *Bringing It All Back Home* became "Mr. Tambourine Man", recorded on the West Coast by the Byrds: a classic melody and a lyric packed with intriguing images provided a perfect anthem for an audience which was in the process of discovering "soft" drugs for the first time, and which recognized allusions to "trips" in the song. Having abandoned the instrumentation and subject matter of traditional folk music, Bob Dylan created a new body of contemporary folk songs for an audience which had never been interested in "authentic" music. Despite his very personal imagery and phrasing, many of the songs held up in versions by other singers: "All I Really Want to Do" from *Another Side* was a hit for both the Byrds and Cher, while "It Ain't Me Babe" from the same album was a hit in the States for the Turtles and in Britain for Johnny Cash; "If You Gotta Go, Go Now" was a British hit twice, first by Manfred Mann and then in French translation by Fairport Convention. Also in Britain, folk singer Donovan craftily reconstructed Dylan's persona for local consumption, and hit the charts with his own song "Catch the Wind", a fair approximation of Dylan's style but altogether more wistful than Dylan would ever allow himself to sound.

In the summer of 1965, almost exactly a year after hearing the Animals' "House of the Rising Sun", Dylan finally achieved his ultimate goal of a top-of-the-charts hit single with the six-minute epic "Like a Rolling Stone" (split into two halves on the radio station version). The musical sound was the fullest Dylan had yet used, with Al Kooper's organ riffs spreading out behind the vocal, and a prominent bass guitar playing a simple "Louie Louie" pattern throughout the dirge-like song. Even more conspicuous was the change in Dylan's tone; where he had sounded defiant and outraged, vulnerable or amused, here he sounded smug and cynical, as if he was singing with a sneer. He had climbed to the top and now he was gloating. The next single, "Positively Fourth Street", continued the theme of relentlessly mocking a former friend in vicious detail and at almost unbearable length; but the new stance was not permanent, just another mood that Dylan needed to work out of his system.

Highway 61 Revisited extended the musical and thematic approach of *Home*, crammed with astonishing impressions and observations, much of it probably written while Dylan was stoned, but still holding up equally well under close scrutiny or as casual background listening. After "Like a Rolling Stone", Dylan refused to work anymore with Tom Wilson, who had contributed invaluably to Dylan's evolution into folk-rock, sifting through the available musicians in search of people who could adapt to Dylan's primitive musical technique without either smothering him or exposing his limitations. Bob Johnston, from Columbia's Nashville division, produced the balance of *Highway 61* using the same musicians that Wilson had introduced, but took Dylan to Nashville for the next album, *Blonde on Blonde*, where they worked with some of the city's best young session men including pianist "Pig" Robbins, bass player Wayne Moss, drummer Norbert Putnam and guitarist Jerry Kennedy, supplemented by Robbie Robertson and Al Kooper from earlier associations, and Joe South from Atlanta.

"Rainy Day Women # 12 & 35" was the single which gave advance warning of what was to follow, a crazy zonked-out invitation–or maybe command is more like it–to get stoned, with a trombone filling out the harmonica line, a polka bass and tambourine bashing out the beat. "I Want You" came next, another lively number with an improbably straight title and direct chorus for a Dylan song, but with verses as weird as ever. Most of the rest of the double album comprised long slow numbers including one which lasted a whole side, "Sad Eyed Lady of the Lowlands", and another love song destined to be a "standard", "Just Like A Woman". The tension of the New York sessions was replaced by stoned relaxation.

By the time *Blonde on Blonde* came out, folk-rock was a meaningless term, but nobody came up with a better one. Just as the Beatles defied categorization, so did Dylan. There was no precedent for the way he used pop music as a kind of public diary for his beliefs and opinions, his thoughts and memories, his dreams and fantasies. Record companies were not used to being outlets for political propaganda (Columbia refused to issue two of his songs on *Freewheelin'*, but those that came out were stronger and more direct than anything pop music had known before), and radio was not normally an open-line, one-way phone between a writer and his friends and enemies, who could not hang up when every radio in the city was blasting those messages of scorn in "Like A Rolling Stone" and "Positively Fourth Street".

Dylan achieved all that any of the folk singers of Greenwich Village had dreamed of, and far more. He never did become more than a rudimentary technician, which tended to limit the accompaniment to basic twelve-bar forms, but he more than compensated for musical deficiencies with a torrent of words sung with supreme confidence. None of the other poets and propagandists on Bleecker Street could ever take the same way out, and all the other singer-writers to emerge from that New York folk scene were fully-fledged musicians who conformed to commercial conventions, notably Paul Simon and John Sebastian.

Paul Simon, far from being in the right place at the right time, was not even in America when Simon and Garfunkel's "Sounds of Silence" was adapted to fit the new folk-rock idiom in 1965. Simon was an ambitious song-writer from the beginning and wrote a minor national hit while still in high school–"Hey Schoolgirl" (Big, 1957), recorded with his friend Art Garfunkel under the pseudonym Tom and Jerry at a time when they were strongly influenced by the Everly Brothers. Still pursuing a straight pop hit as late as 1962, Simon anticipated the hot rod type of record with "Motorcycle" by Tico and the Triumphs, an enterprising and accomplished rocker. Three years later he had adapted to changing trends, reuniting with Garfunkel to record an album of acoustic folk songs for Columbia, much too "soft" for the prevailing pop market.

The catalyst in Simon and Garfunkel's career was the producer Tom Wilson, whose personal taste and musical background favoured jazz, but who was assigned by Columbia to produce most of their "non-pop" artists, while Andy Williams, Dion and the rest were safely cared for by the arranger Bob Mersey. Fascinated by the problems of adapting Bob Dylan's songs to rhythm section accompaniment, Wilson was impressed first by the Animals' treatment of "House of the Rising Sun" and then by Terry Melcher's production of "Mr. Tambourine Man" for the Byrds, whose drum-and-bass arrangement took Dylan's song to the teen audience. Confident that Paul Simon's "meaningful" lyrics in the right musical setting could impress the same audience, Wilson experimentally overdubbed a rhythm section on to the title track of Simon and Garfunkel's album, *The Sounds of Silence*. Paul Simon, still pursuing an acoustic folk style in London where he recorded *The Paul Simon Songbook* album for the local CBS division of Columbia, and knowing nothing about Wilson's experiment was astonished to read in *Billboard* that Simon and Garfunkel had a hit in the American "Hot 100".

Simon and Garfunkel reconvened in New York to follow up the success of "Sounds of Silence" with an album of folk songs with a rhythm section, produced by Bob Johnston. They wore college scarves for the album cover photos session, making sure to attract attention in the properly educated section of the market. In contrast to the raw "reaction" lyrics of Dylan, Paul Simon's were measured, carefully crafted, perfectly suited to the new middle-class audience which had discovered pop music through the Beatles and wanted some substantial songs to relate to. Reflective (to the point of outright nostalgia) and philosophical (to the verge of pretension), "Homeward Bound" and "I Am a Rock" followed "Sounds of Silence" to the top ten, still mainly folk with only a token flavour of rock.

After a relatively fallow period in 1967, Simon and Garfunkel returned in 1968 with a much more satisfactory fusion of words and rhythm in "Mrs. Robinson", a hit single featured both on *Bookends*, their *tour-de-force* concept album, and on the soundtrack of *The Graduate*, whose directionless hero (played by Dustin Hoffman) was universally identified with by the middle-class of the time. Absorbing a widening range of musical influences, Simon and Garfunkel included Latin, reggae, and gospel tracks on their final album in 1970, *Bridge Over Troubled Water*. A highly disciplined master craftsman, Paul Simon harnessed the essential elements of almost every major pop style, commendably avoiding any trace of parody and often stimulating investigation by his audience of his sources. For all his deft way with words and adaptability to a variety of idioms, Simon's voice lacked emotional depth, which was exposed after he split from Garfunkel, whose pure high tenor was definitively showcased on the gospel-styled "Bridge Over Troubled Water".

John Sebastian was in almost every way the opposite of Paul Simon, despite comparable background experience. Son of a professional musician and himself formerly a member of the Even Dozen Jug Band, Sebastian was one of the few New York folk singers to work in a genuine group framework where the other musicians were not merely background accompanists but contributed to the unit's identity. Flippant, light-hearted, self-revealing, mischievous and always very warm, Sebastian's engaging songs invariably stayed close to the traditional subject of pop, usually approaching them from an odd angle.

"Do You Believe in Magic?", the Lovin' Spoonful's first hit (Kama Sutra, 1965), was an unabashed tribute to rock 'n' roll, the best evocation of its power since Chuck Berry's "Rock and Roll Music", with an unmistakable mid-sixties flavour:

Do you believe in magic
In a young girl's heart
How the music can free her
Whenever it starts
And it's magic
If the music is groovy.

Inspired by hearing the Beatles (and seeing *A Hard Day's Night*), the Lovin' Spoonful formed and were to become a popular attraction at the Night Owl coffee house in Greenwich Village, but inexplicably they were not signed up by any of the New York record companies. Months after producer Erik Jacobsen had recorded "Do You Believe in Magic?", a new label, Kama Sutra, was formed to release the record, which led to an incomparable series of nine top twenty hits through 1967 which represented the innocent pop spirit better than any other records of the time, achieving the elusive combination of commercial appeal and an unmistakably real identity.

Apparently oblivious of the social and political ferment around him, John Sebastian wrote two kinds of song, wistful love ballads and atmospheric impressions. Of the love songs, "You Didn't Have to Be So Nice", and "Darlin' Be Home Soon" were soft and straight, but "Did You Ever Have to Make Up Your Mind" and "Younger Girls" (a Lovin' Spoonful album track covered on singles by the Critters and the Hondells) were desperately familiar fantasies; how to choose between two equally desirable girls, and how to resist the aching temptation offered by young admirers.

Alternating with the "love" songs came evocative "atmosphere" songs, conjuring a time and a place with a disarmingly casual, almost off-hand delivery in "Daydream", and with surprising power and intensity in "Summer in the City". Behind Sebastian's instantly recognizable, husky voice the musicians played simple, relaxed but lively rhythms with a minimum of arrangement and production. Although the members of the Lovin' Spoonful (guitarist Zal Yanofsky, bass player Steve Boone, and drummer Joe Butler) shared tastes in blues (evident in several album tracks) and country music (subject to a tribute in the single "Nashville Cats"), the overall style of the Lovin' Spoonful was a beguiling blend which, like much of the best pop music, defied easy categorization. The evasive tag "good-time music" will do.

The New York record industry never did come to terms with the folk club movement which sprouted up and briefly bloomed in Greenwich Village, a district which the New York media regarded as a seedy neighbourhood for down-and-out buskers and out-of-town tourists. Since redevelopment had closed down most of the jazz clubs on 52nd Street, jazz had moved down to various clubs in and around the Village (including the Village Gate, the Half Note, the Village Vanguard, and, further east, Slugs). Most of the coffee houses which featured folk singers were smaller and less comfortable than the jazz clubs. Although performers at Gerde's Folk City and The Bitter End were sometimes reviewed in the press, the best that most of the folk singers could hope for in the way of publicity was a box in the entertainments section of the classified ads in the *Village Voice*, or more likely a handwritten sign outside one of the clubs, The Gaslight, the Cafe Wha? or Cousins.

Through the mid-sixties, the pioneering Elektra label continued to record a substantial roster of the coffee house folk singers without ever achieving mass sales, while owner Jac Holzman explored the outer reaches of music styles related to folk by signing the Chicago-based Butterfield Blues Band, and by sponsoring a "concept" album of blues material by a loose collection of New York-based musicians which was released under the title *The Blues Project*.

Within the folk world, the all-electric Butterfield Blues Band were regarded with high suspicion, and it was the group's guitarist Mike Bloomfield who caused such consternation at the 1965 Newport Folk Festival when he played "too loud" as part of Bob Dylan's backing group. But from a pop point of view, there were obvious parallels between the Butterfield approach and the folk revivalists. Butterfield had grown up in Chicago listening to Muddy Waters, Little Walter and the rest of the city's resident blues legends, and his band was dedicated to playing their material as faithfully as possible. In contrast to the more adventurous, less respectful approach of the Rolling Stones, the Butterfield group never made any obvious attempts to commercialize the blues, and Butterfield himself had neither the irreverent panache nor the sexual allure that made Jagger so compelling. Never a major recording band, the Butterfield group did play a notable role in helping to introduce young white Americans to the material and approach of blues singers whose own records had never been played on pop radio. And for a growing section of that audience which appreciated pure instrumental virtuosity, the interplay of guitarists Mike Bloomfield and Elvin Bishop was rapturously received.

In New York Steve Katz, Al Kooper and some other musicians who had been involved in Elektra's *Blues Project* decided to keep that name for a real group. A couple of national college tours helped to sell their albums for Verve, but neither the Blues Project nor the Butterfield Blues Band were in the same league as the imported blues groups from Britain, the Cream and the Jimi Hendrix Experience. Most other American bands which played the blues were less self-conscious about their repertoire and approach, simply throwing in the odd blues song in with other rhythm and blues, soul, and rock 'n' roll standards.

The most successful of the American blues groups in this period was Canned Heat, led by blues-collector Bob Hite, but notable for the delicate singing and harmonica playing of Al Wilson. "On The Road Again" and "Going Up the Country" gave the group (and Liberty Records) a couple of top twenty hits in 1968, both charming and disarmingly simple sing-along songs which managed to stay true to the spirit of the pre-war country blues while absorbing a steady, danceable rhythm from kit-drums and electric bass. But Wilson was more or less unique among white blues singers in being able to maintain a vulnerability and sensitivity in the midst of electrical amplification; when he died in 1970, Canned Heat fell to the cruder devices of the other blues revivalists.

IV

By the middle of 1966, it seemed that there was hardly anybody left in Greenwich Village to entertain the faithful and the tourists. The ambitious folk singers had either become famous, or left for the West Coast frustrated at being ignored: Jim "Roger" McGuinn, Barry McGuire, John Phillips, and Stephen Stills all managed to find the kindred spirits and context in Los Angeles to make their talents effective. Among the few who stuck it out to provide some kind of entertainment in the Village was a bunch of former beat poets and anarchists who assembled at the Cafe Wha? as the Fugs, but their records (for ESP, and later Reprise) were not conceived as serious musical propositions.

A few blocks east, an equally motley collection of performance artists, actors and musicians occasionally performed in a converted Polish restaurant above the Dom Discotheque as part of Andy Warhol's Exploding Plastic Inevitable, calling themselves the Velvet Underground after the name given to the suburban parties where husbands and wives swapped partners for the night. Andy Warhol was at that time as famous as most pop stars could ever hope to be, a so-called "pop-art" painter who chose mass-produced images as the subjects of his paintings and prints (baked beans labels, Marilyn Monroe's face). This art world was belatedly recognizing pop music's role as a soundtrack to modern city life, and the Velvet Underground took part in Warhol's "happenings", along with mime artists, flashing lights, and screenings of Warhol's notoriously uneventful films, *Empire State*, *Sleep*, *Kiss*. It was a sign of the changing times that a major label, MGM, rather than an indie, offered to release a record by the Velvet Underground, who showed no obvious signs of conventional commerciality.

Columbia and MGM were the only two major record companies to make effective contact with the New York club scene. At Columbia*, Bob Dylan and Simon and Garfunkel became the cornerstones of the

* COLUMBIA. *A&R: Bob Mersey, John Hammond, Tom Wilson (to 1965), Clive Davis (from 1967).*
Adult-pop: Andy Williams, Barbra Streisand, O. C. Smith, Tony Bennett.
Writer-singers: Bob Dylan, Simon and Garfunkel, Leonard Cohen, Laura Nyro.
Folk: Pete Seeger, the Brothers Four, the New Christy Minstrels.
Rock: Big Brother and the Holding Company featuring Janis Joplin, Johnny Winter, Electric Flag, Moby Grape, the Byrds, the Buckinghams, Blood, Sweat and Tears, Dr Hook and the Medicine Show.
Pop: Gary Puckett and the Union Gap, Paul Revere and the Raiders, Dion.
Country: Lynn Anderson, Billy Joe Royal, Johnny Cash, Marty Robbins.

company's re-emergence as a major force, enabling the A&R men to persuade other new artists to sign to the label, and finally recovering some of the market share which Mitch Miller had gained during the early fifties but lost at the height of the rock 'n' roll era. Out on the West Coast, Terry Melcher maintained an impressive run of hits with both Paul Revere and the Raiders and the Byrds while the Epic label reinforced this home-grown strength with astute pickings from Britain, including the Dave Clark Five, the Yardbirds, and Donovan.

RCA*, Decca†, and ABC's New York office‡ never made contact with the new breed of artists who wrote their own material and insisted on participating in how they were marketed, and MGM¶

EPIC
Head of A&R: Dave Kaprilik (pop), Billy Sherrill (country).
Soul: Sly and the Family Stone.
Country: Tammy Wynette, David Houston, Charlie Rich.
From UK: Marmalade, the Tremeloes (from UK CBS), Lulu, Chad and Jeremy, the Hollies, the Jeff Beck Group (from UK EMI), Donovan (from UK Pye).

DATE
Soul: Peaches and Herb.
From UK: the Zombies (from UK CBS).

* RCA-VICTOR
Pop: Elvis Presley, Neil Sedaka, Paul Anka, the Tokens.
Country: Porter Wagoner, Don Gibson, John D. Loudermilk, Eddy Arnold, Bobby Bare, Skeeter Davis, Waylon Jennings, Dolly Parton.
Rhythm and blues: Sam Cooke.
Folk: the Limeliters.

† DECCA
Pop: Rick Nelson (from 1963), Brenda Lee, Len Barry.
From UK: the Who.
Country: Bill Anderson, Webb Pierce, Kitty Wells, Loretta Lynn, Warner Mack.

‡ ABC
Pop: Tommy Roe, Ray Charles.
Rhythm and blues: B. B. King, the Tams, the Impressions.
Subsidiary:

DUNHILL. *Based on West Coast; see p. 335 for roster.*

¶ MGM. *A&R: Jerry Shoenbaum, Tom Wilson (from 1966).*
From UK: the Animals, Herman's Hermits.
Pop group: Sam the Sham and the Pharaohs.
Subsidiary:

VERVE. *Formed in 1949 in Hollywood by Norman Granz; bought by MGM in 1958.*
Pre-1958 roster: Ella Fitzgerald, Oscar Peterson, Johnny Hodges.
Post-1958: jazz: Jimmy Smith, Wes Montgomery.
Pop: the Righteous Brothers (from 1966).
Rhythm and blues: Howard Tate.
Rock groups: the Velvet Underground, the Mothers of Invention, the Blues Project.

VERVE FOLKWAYS (*later VERVE FORECAST*).
Solo: Tim Hardin, Laura Nyro, Janis Ian, Ritchie Havens.
Groups: the Hombres, Friend and Lover.

was able to take its pick from what they ignored. Jerry Shoenbaum joined the company to supervise the Verve label, which had been formed back in the late forties as a jazz label by Norman Granz, who sold his entire interest to MGM in 1958. For a while, Verve continued to be known primarily as a jazz label (surfacing on the pop charts with organist Jimmy Smith's "Walk on the Wild Side" in 1962), but under Shoenbaum Verve turned to the emergent rock artists, evidently designed to be a rival to the independent Elektra label. He recruited producer Tom Wilson from Columbia in 1966, and signed singer-songwriters Tim Hardin, Laura Nyro, and Janis Ian, as well as two of the most controversial new groups of the time, the Velvet Underground and the Mothers of Invention. MGM's promotion and distribution lamentably failed to do justice to this enterprisingly selected roster, and only the Righteous Brothers managed to sell as many records on Verve as the MGM parent label achieved for the Animals and Herman's Hermits, and for the Texas-based pop group, Sam the Sham and the Pharaohs.

Tim Hardin, in particular, deserved a better fate. His fragile love songs achieved the elusive balance between personal miseries and universal sufferings, notably in "Don't Make Promises", "Reason to Believe" and "Hang on to a Dream" on his first album, and "If I Were a Carpenter", "Black Sheep Boy", and "Lady Came from Baltimore" on his second. Not really a folk singer, but a song-writer who accompanied himself on guitar, Hardin's distinctive effect was to seem to be on the brink of tears, apparently stumbling on a phrase with a sob. Sympathetically produced by Erik Jacobsen (for the first album) and Koppelman and Rubin (for the second), the haunting moods were enhanced by strings arranged by Artie Butler, but it was left to other people to make Hardin's songs well-known (including Bobby Darin, who made his comeback in 1966 with "If I Were a Carpenter" for Atlantic).

Sales of Verve's releases by the Velvet Underground were even worse than Tim Hardin's, but the reasons were easier to see. Lead singer and writer Lou Reed had once been among the young hopefuls trying to place songs with Brill Building publishers, but by 1966 he had drifted into a pattern of desultory and self-destructive performances which were not designed to endear him to anyone. Not that he cared; provided he could get his drugs, nothing else mattered.

For various reasons, drugs were a permanent feature of the music scene, but while a few jazz musicians were known to have been "busted" at various times in their careers, the world of pop music generally kept such stories out of the papers. Lou Reed took the opposite tack, eulogizing the whole experience of a fix in "Heroin", track one on side two of the album *The Velvet Underground and Nico*. The inclusion of that track made the record virtually untouchable for American radio in 1966, despite several other eminently-playable songs including "There She Goes Again", "Run Run Run", and "I'm Waiting for My Man"; the last of these was a wry description of waiting in Harlem for his fixer, but the references were sufficiently veiled that the song could have slipped onto the airwaves, if it had not been for the presence of "Heroin" on the album.

There were echoes of Chuck Berry in the way Lou Reed strung evocative visual images together to comment on his friends and foes, but the deliberately primitive musical accompaniment seemed to have filtered all the black influences out of rock 'n' roll, leaving an amateurish, clumsy, but undeniably atmospheric background to Reed's acidic commentary.

Tom Wilson remixed and edited that first album, and he took a shot at producing the second, *White Heat/White Light*. But he lost the fight to discipline Reed and John Cale, the other musical mind in the group, who had trained as an avant garde violinist and here played guitar and electric violin in "subversive" ways that made listening difficult. Cale left, and with Doug Yule as a replacement the group produced their third album themselves; *The Velvet Underground* was relatively uncontroversial and accessible, featuring a classic love song in "Pale Blue Eyes", but the group's media image was still "negative". A switch of labels to Atlantic resulted in the most polished record yet, *Loaded*, but Reed left as the album came out. By then the accepted means of promotion was live work; without a band acting as travelling salesmen for their product, the company had no alternative strategy, and the Velvet Underground were consigned to being a "cult" group. In their case, the status had some meaning; despite the low sales of their records, they were exceptionally influential, particularly in Britain where David Bowie and Roxy Music both drew heavily from the self-consciously decadent image and musical approach of the Velvet Underground. It was entirely fitting that it should be David Bowie who rescued Lou Reed from apparently inevitable obscurity by producing his only top twenty hit, "Walk on the Wild Side" (for RCA in 1973); an entirely different song from Jimmy Smith's hit mentioned earlier, this one was a laconic checklist of the characters who had hung around the Warhol clique back in those earlier Velvet days.

The British Invasion of 1964 had a traumatic effect on the New York record industry, and particularly on the independent labels. Many of the indies which had sprung up during the rock 'n' roll and teen-pop eras closed down, and very few new ones tried to take their place. Atlantic* survived, but mostly with out-of-town talent. Jerry Wexler's southern connections kept a flow of soul hits going through the distribution and promotion structures, while Ahmet Ertegun made productive contacts (and contracts) with producers in Los Angeles. The only notable local act signed to Atlantic in this period was the Young Rascals, a Long Island bar band who played current rhythm and blues hits with a proficiency and excitement that made them likely rivals to the equivalent sounds being shipped in from Britain. Assigned to the production team of engineer Tom Dowd and arranger Arif Mardin, the Young Rascals' first hit "Good Lovin'" was one of the best American records of 1966, with a sophisticated but unfussy arrangement setting up a lively song, leaving space for percussion and organ to make themselves heard.

Among the few New York-based labels which managed to start up and get through to the national top ten in this period, two were formed by ex-Atlantic producers: Leiber and Stoller's Red Bird (discussed earlier), and Bert Berns' Bang†. Before joining Robert Mellin's publishing firm in the late fifties, Berns had worked in night clubs in the Caribbean, reinforcing a passion for Latin American

* ATLANTIC. *Directed by Ahmet Ertegun, Nesuhi Ertegun, and Jerry Wexler, who sold company to Kinney (later renamed Warner Communicatins Inc.) in 1967.*
A&R: Jerry Wexler, Tom Dowd, Arif Mardin, Joel Dorn, Dave Crawford.
Pop: Bobby Darin (1966–67), the Young Rascals, Roberta Flack.
Singer-writers: Jerry Jeff Walker, Loudon Wainwright III.
Rock: Crosby, Stills, Nash and Young, Vanilla Fudge, Velvet Underground.
Soul: Aretha Franklin, Percy Sledge, Jackie Moore, the Spinners, Archie Bell and the Drells, Wilson Pickett.
From UK: Led Zeppelin, Yes (*signed direct*), *King Crimson* (*from UK Island*).

ATCO
Pop: Sonny and Cher.
Rock: Iron Butterfly, Dr John, Delaney and Bonnie, Derek and the Dominoes.
Soul: Donny Hathaway, King Curtis.
From UK: the Bee Gess, Cream, Eric Clapton (*from Robert Stigwood/Polydor*).

COTILLION
Soundtrack: the Woodstock *album.*

Distributed labels:

† BANG. *Formed in 1965 in New York by Bert Berns ("B"), in partnership with Ahmet ("A") and Nesuhi ("N") Ertegun and Gerald ("G") Wexler.*
Pop: the McCoys, Neil Diamond, the Strangeloves.

Subsidiary:

SHOUT
Rhythm and blues: Freddie Scott, Erma Franklin.

ALSTON. *Formed in 1968 in Miami, Florida by Henry Stone. A&R: Steve Alaimo, Brad Shapiro, Howard Casey, Clarence Reid.*
Female rhythm and blues: Betty Wright.

DAKAR. *Formed in 1968 in Chicago by Carl Davis.*
Male rhythm and blues: Tyrone Davis, Otis Leaville.

music which had been sparked off by hearing Puerto Rican salsa music in New York, and which inspired the musical arrangements of many of the pop records he wrote and produced during the sixties.

Before Berns made Latin rhythms and chord-changes a consistent feature of his songs, Spanish-based music had been an erratic influence in American pop music, surfacing in the "baion" rhythms of the Drifters and Jay and the Americans, in the Mexican epic ballads of Marty Robbins, and also in a distinctive Latin chord sequence which recurred at least once a year after Bobby Freeman introduced it in his "Do You Wanna Dance" in 1958. Ritchie Valens claimed it back for Mexican Americans in "La Bamba" in 1959, and from then on the industry tended to refer to "those 'La Bamba' changes". Bert Berns and Wes Farrell used the pattern in "Twist and Shout", a hit for the Isley Brothers in 1962, and again in "My Girl Sloopy" by the Vibrations in 1964. The changes were slowed down by the Kingsmen in "Louie Louie" in 1963, were elaborated by Phil Spector in "You've Lost That Lovin' Feelin'" in 1964, and by Bob Dylan's group in "Like a Rollin' Stone" in 1966; but the best and most blatant use of the pattern was probably in "Hang on Sloopy" (a rewrite of "My Girl Sloopy"), produced by Berns for the McCoys and released on his own Bang label in 1965. The Four Seasons could have done the song (they coincidentally had a hit three months later with a similar title, "Let's Hang On"), but Berns made do with the McCoys, a group from Union City, Indiana, with a conveniently English sounding name, and a guitarist Rick Derringer who was able to play a lively solo in the instrumental break.

Bang's major artist was Neil Diamond, who shared some of Berns' enthusiasm for Latin rhythms, and who used those familiar changes on his first big hit, "Cherry Cherry" in 1966. A pop singer-songwriter in the tradition started by Paul Anka and Neil Sedaka, Neil Diamond had a much deeper, more adult sounding voice; where they had cultivated a narcissistic whine, he sounded almost macho as he confidently crooned "Girl, You'll be a Woman Soon".

Among Bang's other hits was "I Want Candy" by the Strangeloves (in 1965), an undisguised shout of lust, chanted over an old-fashioned Bo Diddley beat. The British Invasion had reached such proportions that there was mileage in pretending that the group was from Australia, but the culprits were actually the song-writing team which

---

CAPRICORN. *Formed in 1970 in Macon, Georgia, by Phil Walden.*
Rock: the Allman Brothers Band, Wet Willie (distribution later switched to Warner Brothers label).

CHIMNEYVILLE. *Formed in 1970 in Jackson, Mississippi by Wardell Quezerque.*
Male rhythm and blues: King Floyd.
Female rhythm and blues: Jean Knight (licensed to Stax).

had recently been responsible for the chart-topping "My Boyfriend's Back" by the Angels–Richard Gottehrer, Jerry Goldstein, and Bob Feldman. But what these guys faked, dozens of bands were doing for real all round the country: bashing out old rhythm and blues and rock 'n' roll beats, and evolving a new genre of American pop that has become known as "garage-band music".

V

The American record industry had a two-stage reaction to the success of the British group records. First, the major labels took steps to acquire licensing rights to the British records, which sometimes involved biding time while an independent company benefited from being faster off the mark; and second, they took steps to nurture some home-grown equivalents. But, just as with rock 'n' roll eight or nine years earlier, it was virtually impossible to distinguish a one-hit wonder (which major labels were generally not interested in), from a group with a talent that could be sustained.

For thousands of young American musicians, the impact of the Beatles and the Rolling Stones and the other British groups was more far-reaching than Elvis Presley's impact had been to the previous generation of would-be pop stars. Although it has since emerged that Elvis had considerable autonomy in choosing his material and determining the musical arrangements, the general impression in the industry was that he was a teen idol, and that was the marketing approach applied to most of his contemporaries. But the whole marketing emphasis on the Beatles and Stones was that they were autonomous: they wrote their own songs, and played their own arrangements on their own instruments. The ethic was: do-it-yourself.

There was already a long-established tradition in America of local bar bands who acted as "living juke-boxes", playing songs from the current best-selling charts alongside a selection of oldies, at high school dances, college parties, and all kinds of clubs. And in practically every town there was some little recording studio where the band could document its sound; the hard part was finding somebody who thought the recording was worth pressing up as an actual record, but this stage became a lot easier in the wake of the British Invasion. More often than not, the record was never known outside the town the band played in, but during the mid-sixties, the American charts began to be peppered with odd "regional break-outs", which worked their way round the radio stations and every now and then showed signs of going "all the way". To make that last step, they usually needed co-ordinated distribution from a larger company, and most of the "garage-band" hits were licensed or distributed by one of the more alert indie survivors: Atlantic, Bell, Liberty, or Roulette.

"Garage-band" is the evocative term used to describe the records which were mostly made in unsophisticated studios (very rarely actual garages!), and is less misleading than the other term which has retrospectively been applied to them: "punk". The problem with applying "punk" to most of the records is that it implies some kind of self-conscious rebelliousness which was very rarely applicable. In the fifties, "punk" was used as a derogatory description of city teenagers, implying a badly educated and probably unemployed semi-hoodlum, who spoke out of the corner of his mouth with a sneering drawl, settled arguments with his fists or even a knife, and showed no awareness of any responsibilities or self-discipline. Whether such a person really existed was not the point: he became the stereotype for discussions about juvenile delinquency, and was regularly featured in Hollywood movies and Broadway melodramas like *West Side Story*.

Looking back at the images presented by some of the previous generations of rock 'n' rollers, Eddie Cochran's "Summertime Blues" and "Somethin' Else" had that punk edge, and Dion's "The Wanderer" and "Runaround Sue" were deliberate vehicles for a punk attitude. The whole aura of the Rolling Stones was an embodiment of this anti-social stance, but, although many of the American groups imitated the sound of the Stones, few of them were deliberately rebellious. What they did all share with each other was a hard-to-read dumbness, which came out as an inarticulate grunt, slammed across with a primeval beat. As their playing improved, and the singing became better defined, the music became more obviously straightforward pop; very often, a supposed "punk" record had simply been so badly recorded that the singer had been irretrievably buried in a cacophony of distorted drums and guitar.

Compared to the British groups, for whom the guitar was invariably the dominant instrument (Manfred Mann and the Animals were honourable exceptions), the majority of the American answer-groups used a portable organ as mass-produced by Vox, Farfisa, and Hohner.

The garage-band groups split into two fairly distinct categories: some of them had been playing for several years before the British Invasion, and evolved a repertoire of old rhythm and blues and rock 'n' roll songs which still held up more than five years later, mixed together with more recent rhythm and blues hits like "Shotgun", "Money", "Do You Love Me", and "Ooh Poo Pah Doo". Coming on to the scene more recently were the groups formed by people who had only been inspired to learn an instrument after hearing the British records (or seeing the groups on TV), and had much less knowledge about the body of black records which had inspired most of the British groups in the first place.

The former was the first to surface on the charts, and most of the groups came from the following three areas: the Pacific North West (the Kingsmen, Paul Revere and the Raiders); Texas (the Sir Douglas Quintet, Sam The Sham and the Pharaohs, and ? and the Mysterians); and the Mid-West (the McCoys, Mitch Ryder and the Detroit Wheels, the Shondells, and the Shadows of Knight). The second category amounted to a national epidemic, but the majority of groups who managed to make the upper reaches of the national chart were based on the West Coast, either around the San Francisco Bay, or in the Los Angeles area.

In Seattle, Washington, although the rest of the country seemed to have more or less forgotten about rock 'n' roll, there were several groups who kept playing some of Little Richard's old hits, along with their own mostly instrumental tunes and whatever oldies somebody could remember all the words to. One song was in practically everybody's repertoire: "Louie Louie", first recorded by its author Richard Berry in 1956 as a kind of calypso-rhythm and blues chant, but never a national hit for him. A Seattle group called the Frantics was the first group to play the song live, but although they had three minor national hits for Dolton in 1959, they never recorded "Louie Louie"; seven years later, three ex-members appeared on the new San Francisco scene as part of Moby Grape. Dolton meanwhile had international success with "Walk Don't Run" by the Ventures, an all-instrumental group led by guitarist Don Wilson, who went on to record a series of best-selling albums, augmented by Los Angeles sessionmen. When the Ventures moved on, the most famous group left in Seattle was the Wailers, whose "Tall Cool One" made the top forty for Golden Crest in 1959, but it was not enough to make them national stars; their set was mostly instrumental, but they did record a couple of raving rockers, "Mau Mau" and "Dirty Robber", and to meet the demand for a recording of "Louie Louie", they also put that out. But still nobody outside the north-west was interested in the song until the Kingsmen, and Paul Revere and the Raiders recorded it on successive days in 1963, for the local Jerden and Sande labels, respectively. The Raiders version sold well enough for Columbia to license the record, but nothing happened east of the Rockies until six months later when a disc jockey in Boston, Massachussetts began to play the version by the Kingsmen.

This time, the thing caught hold. Wand Records of New York licensed the record, and it eventually went all the way to number two on *Billboard*, right in the thick of the first wave of hits by the Beatles.

The record hardly stands up to attention out of context, as it had been recorded with a vocal so muffled that suspicious minds thought they could detect obscene suggestions in the lyric. But it did have those "La Bamba" chord changes rumbling along the bottom, and a dumb chorus that was undeniably catchy. The Kingsmen duly cleaned up their sound and became the straight pop group they had probably always wanted to be, but ironically it was Paul Revere and the Raiders who became the biggest group to emerge out of the North West.

Originally from Indiana, where they recorded a minor instrumental hit in 1959 for the local Gardena label, "Like Long Hair", Revere and the Raiders moved to Portland, Oregon in 1962, and stayed there until Columbia picked up the rights to their version of "Louie Louie" in 1964. The Raiders went on to fame and fortune under the guidance of producer Terry Melcher, but back in Seattle the Wailers were never able to find a song to take them into the national consciousness. However, the Electric Prunes responded to the intriguing experiments with guitar sounds on the Yardbirds' records, and Reprise Records put them in a studio with Dave Hassinger, who had recently engineered a series of hits for the Rolling Stones in Los Angeles. In many ways, the Electric Prunes wound up sounding like a British "progressive rock" group on their first and biggest hit, "I Had Too Much Dream Last Night", with wildly-echoed and distorted guitar spinning around the petulant vocals. The unspoken inference of the song was that the singer had taken too many drugs, probably LSD, and this record made a bridge between the self-pitying, victim-of-society, stance of "punk", and psychedelic music, which represented the inner torments-of-the-soul. A similar merger was recorded at about the same time (the end of 1966) by another refugee from Seattle's club scene, Jimi Hendrix, who recorded "Hey Joe" as his first single with the Experience in London, and later celebrated one of those Seattle clubs in "Spanish Castle Magic".

Down the Coast from Seattle, around San Francisco's Bay Area, a few groups sprang into the charts in 1966, but they did not have the same kind of in-depth background as the bands from the North-West. From San Jose, the Syndicate of Sound came up with a distinctive sound on "Little Girl", confidingly sung by Hawaiian-born Don Baskin and recorded with a home-made simplicity; issued first on the local Hush label, the record made the national top ten after Bell licensed the rights. Three months later in 1966, the Count Five took a San Jose label, Double Shot, all the way to the national top ten with "Psychotic Reaction", which was based half on the Stones (in the vocals) and half on the Yardbirds (in the instrumental sections, particularly on the manic solo). Neither group repeated its success, but Double Shot lasted long enough to get back into the top ten a year later with the catchy pop-soul song "Gimme Little Sign" by Brenton Wood.

While the rest of the country became increasingly studio-oriented during the early sixties, live music continued in the South to be the main activity for young musicians. There was not as yet a breakdown of roles into "writers" and "producers", but simply a self-sufficient unit which was often led by a main figure who played guitar, wrote (or chose) the songs, and then sang them. There were a few people who scratched a living as "producers", notably Huey Meaux in Houston and Major Bill Smith in Fort Worth (already encountered earlier in this book), but their prime role was to document a self-contained live band.

Most of the qualities of rhythm and blues and rock 'n' roll survived in Texas throughout the early sixties, upheld equally by surviving pioneers from the late forties and fifties and by young white musicians who caught the spirit from them. The guitarists T-Bone Walker, Lightnin' Hopkins, Johnny "Guitar" Watson, and B. B. King were firm favourites and major inspirations, along with the pianists Amos Milburn and Charles Brown, inseparable friends who toured and recorded together. Among the young white Texans who were paid for playing in clubs while they were still well below the legal age limit for even walking through the door, were Doug Sahm from San Antonio, the brothers Johnny and Edgar Winter from Beaumont, Domingo "Sam" Samudio and Steve Miller in Dallas, Delbert McClinton in Fort Worth, and Tony Joe White in Corpus Christi.

While the mass media was filtering and separating, refining and homogenizing the elements which had made rock 'n' roll such a heady mixture in the mid-fifties, these musicians were still exposed to the original elements in their raw form, and more besides. Alongside those blues pioneers were current rhythm and blues stars Bobby Bland and Junior Parker, and some maverick country-oriented rock 'n' rollers for whom the spirit of Jerry Lee Lewis was as important as that of Hank Williams (notably Jerry Lee's cousin, Mickey Gilley, who sounded just like him and played constantly around Houston). The warm sax-and-piano rock 'n' roll of Fats Domino's band was still a major influence, alongside the peculiar local ethnic styles of cajun music from South Louisiana and the polka-based "conjunto" music of the Texas-based Mexicans. Throw into the pot the current soul hits, then stir in the British contributions from the Beatles, Stones, and the rest, and then stand back to see what happens.

Some reacted faster than others. Steve Miller took off for Chicago, where he put together a blues band to rival Paul Butterfield, before moving to San Francisco where, with fellow-Texan Boz Scaggs, he evolved a rock style which eventually became very successful for both of them. Tony Joe White moved to Nashville, but never forgot Lightnin' Hopkins. The Winter brothers had their turn in the spotlight when virtuoso blues musicians became the rage, but neither of them ever surpassed the records they had made as teenagers for every tiny local label that would pay for them to go in a recording studio. Their version of the Amos Milburn/Charles Brown song "Please Come Home For Christmas" was delivered with a charm and sensitivity which they later forsook in favour of harsh pyrotechnics.

By coincidence, both Doug Sahm and Sam Samudio hit the national pop charts in the same week in April 1965, having simultaneously, but independently discovered how effectively a simple "Tex-Mex" organ pattern could be fitted into a novelty pop song.

Doug Sahm recorded regularly through his teens, mostly for the Harlem label of San Antonio, and his problem was deciding what to choose of all the things he could do so well; equally happy playing T-Bone Walker-style blues, singing Jimmie Rodgers' songs, or messing about with pop, Doug finally found his direction under the supervision of Huey Meaux, who recognized a "Tex-Mex" feel in the Beatles' "She's A Woman" (officially a B-side, but played almost as intensively on the radio as the A-side, "I Feel Fine"). Organist Augie Meyer came up with a repetitive riff that fitted a Ray Charles-style song by Sahm called "She's About a Mover", and Meaux put the record out on his own Tribe label under the jokey fake-British disguise, the Sir Douglas Quintet. Most of the disc jockeys who played the record assumed that it was British, but fast-talking Doug blew the disguise the moment he opened his mouth to answer a TV interviewer. By then, the record was established, but the Sir Douglas Quintet lost momentum when they achieved the dubious distinction of becoming America's first pop group to be busted for taking dope.

On release, Sahm left Texas in search of the more tolerant ambience of San Francisco, but although he scored a minor hit in 1969 with "Mendocino" and made several of the most interesting American albums of the late sixties (for Mercury), he never achieved either the commercial or cult recognition he deserved. It was small consolation to be credited as an obvious inspiration for several much more successful groups who adopted a similar merger of blues, country, and rock 'n' roll, including Creedence Clearwater Revival, the Band, and Commander Cody and the Lost Planet Airmen. But none of them had a singer who was as expressive and relaxed as Doug Sahm.

Sam Samudio was never able to find anybody in Texas who would record his group, Sam the Sham and the Pharaohs; he had to trek to

Memphis, where Stan Kesler took a chance, paying for the session which resulted in "Wooly Bully" and then releasing it on his XYZ label. From the opening count-down in Spanish, through all the near-gibberish verses, non-stop organ triplets, and King Curtis-like sax solo, the record maintained a delirious excitement which the band was able to sustain both in its live performances and on its first album for MGM (which had picked up the band's contract). The songs on that first album gave a good indication of the musical sources and inspiration of a Southern bar band at that time: alongside five of their own songs, they did Junior Walker's "Shotgun", the Falcons' "I Found a Love", Johnny "Guitar" Watson's "Gangster of Love", Little Richard's "Long Tall Sally", and a hilarious version of Billy Emerson's "Ev'ry Woman I Know is Crazy 'Bout Automobiles". Among the few American groups of the time who matched the best British groups both vocally and instrumentally, Sam the Sham and the Pharaohs presented themselves as a novelty act (wearing turbans, and arriving at gigs in a hearse), but they never acquired that elusive "credibility" which enabled a group to sustain a career without necessarily having a hit single in the charts all the time.

Both the Sir Douglas Quintet and Sam The Sham and the Pharaohs have sometimes been classified as "punk" by retrospective chroniclers, because their hits had the straight-ahead simplicity of other garage-band records of the era, but there were other Texas groups which fitted the category more naturally. The Thirteenth Floor Elevators in Fort Worth were led by a zany character called Rocky Erikson, whose antics under the influence of who-knew-what generated a cult reputation beyond the audience which put the group's "You're Gonna Miss Me" into the lower reaches of the singles chart in 1966.

Texas was always a home for maverick musicians who ignored the conventions of their time, but after that flurry of garage-band music, most of the successful musical performers from the state tended to be more obviously country-based. Roy Head had a hit in 1965 with a frantic white soul record called "Treat Her Right" for Duke's Back Beat subsidiary, but after him the most popular white artist from Texas was B. J. Thomas, who had a big pop hit in 1966 with his version of Hank Williams' "I'm So Lonesome I Could Cry", which he followed with several more big hits, all for Scepter of New York.

Producer Huey Meaux finally hit the jackpot in the early seventies with several hits by Freddy Fender, a Mexican-American who had made several local hits in the South Louisiana style in the early sixties. But all this was a far cry from garage-band music, which found a more permanent home in the mid-west.

*

Among the flurry of groups which flooded the recording studios of America in the wake of the British invasion, a few from the mid-west lasted more than just the first six months, suggesting that they were more than pure opportunists cashing in on a new fad. Inevitably, Chicago and Detroit were the principal recording centres, but against the odds two of the biggest records were from tiny towns, made by ? and the Mysterians and the Shondells.

? and the Mysterians was the inscrutable alias for a group of Mexican-Americans who had to wait for two years and travel all the way to Flint, Michigan, before finding a time and a place to record "96 Tears", written by the group's lead singer Rudy Martinez. Originally released on Pa-Go-Go, the record was picked up for national distribution by Cameo of Philadelphia, where promotion man Neil Bogart had moved after a stint at MGM which had coincided with the success of "Wooly Bully". Bogart knew the potential for a record with a socking beat and a catchy organ riff, and this time there was a good song, delivered with convincing desperation by Martinez. "96 Tears" topped the chart in October 1966, the last pure punk record to do so, if there could be such a thing as a pure punk record.

The Shondells were still at high school when they recorded a version of "Hanky Panky" for the local Snap label in Niles, Michigan in 1964. The song had been recorded the year before by writers Jeff Barry and Ellie Greenwich under their recording alias of the Raindrops, as the B-side of "That Boy John" on Jubilee, and there was little obvious reason for anyone to rescue the nonsense novelty from oblivion. Apart from the disc jockey who financed their recording, nobody played the Shondells version for two years, until some disc jockey in Pittsburgh dug it out of a pile of discards and found that the phones "lit up" with enquiries when he played it. By the time the group discovered that their record had an audience, pirates in Pittsburgh had bootlegged thousands of copies (between 20,000 and 80,000, according to different reports). This was par-for-the-course for a punk record: it was virtually a prerequisite that the original label be so small that pirates could fearlessly supply a local demand, knowing that the original company would be powerless. Roulette Records managed to contact the group, still in Niles, and took the record all the way to the top of the charts in July 1966. Remarkably, considering what a basic and unmusical record "Hanky Panky" was, the group–renamed Tommy James and the Shondells–not only had eight more top twenty hits, but came up with some of the best pop records of the period. "I Think We're Alone Now", co-written by producer Ritchie Cordell and Bo Gentry, was a charming, gently suggestive teen love song, while "Crimson and Clover" was an adventurous, hypnotic chant that put the group back at the top of the chart in 1968. Almost imperceptibly, they took over the mantle as the top East Coast vocal group from the Four Seasons.

Meanwhile, the Four Seasons' producer Bob Crewe found a new protégé to challenge these new punk upstarts, in Mitch Ryder and the Detroit Wheels. Crewe had consistently found projects which placed sing-along material in a ruthlessly danceable context, most blatantly with Freddie Cannon, then much more imaginatively with the Four Seasons, and with Mitch Ryder he effectively showed how all this new music was basically a rehash of what had gone before by merging two rock 'n' roll standards into one frantic chant. Mitch Ryder had a raw, expressive voice, and he soared over the raucous accompaniment like a gospel singer at a revivalist meeting. His first and best hit was "Jenny Take a Ride" (issued on Crewe's own New Voice label, distributed by Bell, 1965), a medley of Little Richard's "Jenny Jenny" and Chuck Willis' arrangement of "C. C. Rider", taken at a breathless tempo and sounding like a wild Motown record–suitably enough, for a Detroit singer. The distinctive features were percussive organ chords and a tambourine on the off-beat, but the formula did not hold up to repetition, and Crewe proved unable to come up with a lasting structure. Ryder continued to be an effective live performer, and his records were a major influence on the larger than life productions adopted ten years later by Bruce Springsteen and Meatloaf.

Apart from Mitch Ryder, the other popular white singer from Detroit in the mid-sixties was Bob Seger, who moved to Capitol Records in 1968 after Cameo had failed to translate several local hits into "national breakouts". A hard working journeyman, Seger was a prototype for the typical American rock artists of the seventies, delivering reliable entertainment as a live performer and gradually building up a following whose tastes were less whimsical than the traditional pop audience.

In Chicago, there was a moment when it seemed that a couple of these do-it-yourself groups might lead to a resurgence for independent labels in the city. In March 1966, Dunwich Records made the top ten with a cover version of Them's "Gloria" by the Shadows of Knight, but it was soon apparent that the song had been greater than the group. At the end of the year, the indie USA* label did even better with "Kind of a Drag" for the Buckinghams, which made the top of the chart.

* *USA had been going for some time, recording several of the best Chicago bluesmen who for one reason or another were not with Chess-Checker or Vee Jay, including Willie Mabon, Junior Wells, and Billy Emerson. Among USA's best releases before the Buckinghams joined the label was "Look Out, Mabel" by G. L. Crockett, an extraordinary out-of-time record for 1965 when there was no known market for what sounded like a black rockabilly record, complete with blistering electric guitar solo. The record attracted enough interest for Checker to license it, but with no better luck.*

The Buckinghams stuck around with USA for one more record (a revival of "Lawdy Miss Clawdy"), but then switched to Columbia, where Jim Guercio took over their production and guided them towards an attractive blend of harmonies and powerful rhythms which gave them four more hits (including the beguiling "Susan" in 1967). And this was the typical pattern: indie labels were seen as temporary stepping stones for groups which preferred the apparent security of a major company's national distribution system and more powerful promotion. Interviewers who dug up some of the group members ten years later invariably found them ruefully wishing that they had not been so quick to jump out of the situation which had been the catalyst for their first success, but by then they were reduced to rehashing old hits in cabaret clubs, and it was usually too late to go back and make amends. In any case, because so few groups supported the indie labels in the sixties, ten years later there were hardly any left, not even in Los Angeles.

The dominant sound of Los Angeles in the mid-sixties was guitars and vocal harmonies, which contributed to the "folk-rock" style of the next chapter. But lurking in the shadows were a few groups who either used an organ in their line-up, or else hammered their instruments so chaotically that their "rock" elements drowned out the "folk" quotient.

The first of the Los Angeles garage-bands to hit the pop charts were the Stondells, whose best material was written by their producer Ed Cobb; with impressive adaptability, the former Four Prep and writer of Brenda Holloway's "Every Little Bit Hurts" came up with a very passable imitation of the Rolling Stones' sound and stance in "Dirty Water", which the Stondells delivered with exactly the right tone of derision. But the same combination of producer and group could not repeat the trick on later releases (for Capitol's subsidiary label, Tower).

The Rolling Stones were also the prime influence on the early records by Love, one of the era's cult bands whose records never sounded as good as the group's live performances and song material had promised. Love's first hit was a version of a song whose unlikely source was a movie soundtrack written by Burt Bacharach and Hal David, "My Little Red Book". But the group's own writer, the black guitarist and singer Arthur Lee, never managed to organize his ambitious concepts into coherent arrangements, and Elektra Records never recovered their investment.

One of the songs in Love's repertoire was "Hey Joe", which had been written by a San Franciscan folk singer (exactly which one, was the subject of expensive legal debate), and another Los Angeles group, the Leaves, had two shots at turning it into a hit record for the indie Mira label; their second try more or less worked, but their anarchic mixture of muttered vocals and a guitar line borrowed from Jackie De Shannon's "When You Walk in the Room" failed to deliver the song's inherent menace. The Seattle guitarist Jimi Hendrix picked up "Hey Joe" while jamming with Arthur Lee, and incorporated it into his live act, first in New York and then in London, where he finally captured its qualities in a record produced by Chas Chandler.

Among the best punk records made in Los Angeles was "Talk Talk" by the Music Machine, which made the national top twenty on the Original Sound label at the end of 1966. A blast of almost incoherent anguish, hammered out by rhythmic riffs and interrupted by a wild "Yardbirds" styled guitar break, "Talk Talk" was an archetypal punk record, where the sound counted for more than the group's image or identity. Whoever the Music Machine were, the world never heard from them again after that one shout of outrage. Original Sound survived primarily by repackaging the rock 'n' roll era's hits in the best series of *Oldies but Goodies* albums on the West Coast, and owner Art Laboe managed to pick up the street-funk group Dyke and the Blazers, who had four hits between 1967 and 1969.

Virtually by definition, a punk group or a garage-band did not ingratiate itself into the pop music establishments by having regular hits or making a musically coherent album. A garage-band had to be a one-hit wonder, and those groups who managed to follow through almost always metamorphosed into a more conventional kind of pop group, like Tommy James and the Shondells. The natural album format for these records was a compilation of the various artists and chronicler Lenny Kaye retrospectively did justice to the idiom by bringing many of the favourites together on the double-album released by Elektra in 1972 under the title *Nuggets: Original Artyfacts From the First Psychedelic Era, 1965–1968*. This was more or less the last gasp by performers and record men representing the "indie" spirit that had been integral to the rock 'n' roll uprising of the mid-fifties. But no substantial record company emerged out of association with the punk movement; the closest was Buddah, which marketed a derivative genre that came to be called "bubblegum".

Buddah Records* was set up during 1967 by Neil Bogart, the radio promotion man who had been actively involved in persuading radio stations to play first "Wooly Bully" by Sam The Sham and the

* BUDDAH RECORDS. *Formed in 1966 in New York by Neil Bogart.*
Bubblegum: the Ohio Express, the 1910 Fruitgum Company.
Writer-singer: Melanie.
Soul: Gladys Knight and the Pips.
Rock: Captain Beefheart.

Pharaohs for MGM, and then "96 Tears" by ? and the Mysterians for Cameo. It was indicative of how the industry had changed, that where indie record labels had previously tended to be formed by people involved in either the manufacturing, distributing and selling side of the business, or else in recording, engineering and supervision, now the critical expertise was achieving radio play. It took Bogart a while to find a satisfactory source of material to promote, but during 1968 and 1969 he struck up a liaison with producers Jerry Kasenetz and Jeff Katz who placed most of their Super-K productions with Buddah.

Where punk had been accidental, erratic, and disconnected, the Super-K records were planned, predictable, and consistent. The musical ingredients were basically the same, but now they were deliberately arranged so that every note and every beat made its point effectively. As sing-along dance songs, the records were irresistible, and the world found itself chanting "Simon Says" along with the 1910 Fruitgum Company, and mumbling "Yummy Yummy Yummy" with the Ohio Express. No menace, no mystery, no magic; a travesty of what the garage-bands had tried to be, the bubblegum records used the same kind of percussive organ, and effectively wiped that sound out of American pop. No self-respecting group wanted to be mistaken for a bubblegum confection.

Alongside the Super-K productions was one other hugely successful bubblegum campaign called the Archies. This time the ever present Don Kirshner was involved, as backer for writer-producer Jeff Barry. Most of the groups whose bubblegum records were released by Buddah did actually exist in some form, and went out to play live gigs even if they might not have played all the parts on their records. But the Archies was a pure studio project, designed to provide music for a TV cartoon series. Jeff Barry was a particularly apt choice, since among the string of hits he wrote with Ellie Greenwich during the sixties were several with nonsense titles: "Da Doo Ron Ron", "Do Wah Diddy Diddy", and "Hanky Panky". Clearly a man with a gift for the inane, Barry conspired with Andy Kim to write "Sugar Sugar", which session singer Ron Dante delivered with commendable desperation. Compared to the crude Super-K productions,

---

KAMA SUTRA. *Formed in 1965 by Charles Koppelman and Norm Rubin.*
Folk-rock: the Lovin' Spoonful.

Distributed labels:

PAVILION
Gospel: the Edwin Hawkins Singers.

CURTOM. *Formed in Chicago by Curtis Mayfield.*
Soul: Curtis Mayfield, the Impressions, the Five Stairsteps.

HOT WAX. *Formed in Detroit by Holland-Dozier-Holland.*
Soul: the Honey Cone, the Flaming Ember.

"Sugar Sugar" had a groove and a flow, and the classy pop record became one of the best-selling records of all time, issued in the States on Kirshner's Calendar label with distribution by RCA.

Despite the huge success of the Archies' record, the days of this kind of pop production were numbered, as the American record industry became increasingly preoccupied with ways to sell albums. Nobody was going to persuade millions of people to buy bubblegum albums. Bob Dylan had shown how to sell them, and the West Coast division of the record industry set out to turn his idiosyncracies into a formula. It might be harder than making bubblegum out of punk, but it could be done.

VI

While most New York-based producers and artists seemed to go into a state of shock as the British Invasion gathered force during 1964, there was the opposite reaction on the other side of the country in Los Angeles. Many of the producers, writers, musicians and singers who had been achieving only erratic success with their gimmicky, novelty-oriented productions during the early sixties now suddenly grasped the nettle of straightforward commercial pop music, and produced a complete range of West Coast alternatives to the British groups. In many cases, the comparisons were unashamedly blatant, and for each popular British act there was at least one West Coast equivalent, or "answer", to use the music business euphemism for a copy: the Beau Brummels and Monkees (stand-ins for the Beatles), Paul Revere and the Raiders and the Stondells (for the Rolling Stones), Gary Lewis and the Playboys (for the Hollies), the Byrds (a mixture of the Searchers, Beatles, and Bob Dylan), the Count Five and the Electric Prunes (for the Yardbirds). And whoever didn't copy a British group, took their lead from Bob Dylan's so-called folk-rock style.

A crude index of this turnaround could be taken from the geographical location of the records which topped the American charts: in 1963, records made in New York had been top of the charts for half the year (26 out of 52 weeks), while Los Angeles had three, and London none; of the rest, Texas was ahead with ten; in 1964, London-produced records held the top slot for 23 weeks, while New York slipped to 12, and Los Angeles had three weeks again (Detroit meanwhile picking up from three in 1963 to ten in 1964); in 1965, London still held the top position for 23 weeks, but Los Angeles producers jumped up to take 20 weeks, and only one New York record made the top of the chart ("Hang On Sloopy" by the McCoys, for one week).

This resurgence of the Los Angeles recording scene was partly attributable to the alacrity with which a few astute producers jumped on to the beat-group and folk-rock bandwagons, and partly to the emergence of an elite pool of versatile and rhythmically exciting session musicians. But just as the previous era of successful Los Angeles records had been tied into the proximity of the film studios where Elvis Presley, Pat Boone, Tab Hunter, Ricky Nelson and the rest had churned out their teen-oriented movies, now the crucial factor was the return of the TV pop music show. Very appropriately, the catalyst was the British producer Jack Good, who had orchestrated and prolonged the British appreciation and interpretation of rock 'n' roll with his choreographed presentations of Gene Vincent, Eddie Cochran and native rockers Marty Wilde and Cliff Richard. Moving to the States in 1965 Good persuaded ABC to back a networked music show called *Shindig* with basically the same formula he had honed in England, using a regular back-up group (the Shindogs, whose alumni turned into some of the most celebrated musicians of the late sixties–guitarists James Burton and Delaney Bramlett, pianist Leon Russell) and an array of girl go-go dancers. NBC responded with *Hullabaloo*, and Dick Clark shook off the taints of payola that had hung around his head since the *Bandstand* days, and presented *Where the Action Is* for CBS. These three leading shows, along with countless local derivatives, showcased any and all available British visiting groups, but the audiences who tuned in to see them could not avoid exposure to all the supporting acts, most of whom were based in Los Angeles.

In many ways, this was a repeat of the process that had seen Philadelphia producers take the image of Elvis Presley and repackage it as Frankie Avalon, Fabian, Freddie Cannon, and the rest; but this time, there was a much more even balance in the relationship between the participants in the recordings, at least on some of the records. There had not been much that the real rock 'n' roll singers from the South could learn from listening to Bobby Rydell records made in Philadelphia, but the British groups did listen with interest to some of the records made in Los Angeles in response to their own records; this was, after all, the home of the records produced by Phil Spector, which they admired so much, and as already noted the Rolling Stones made their outstanding series of hits between 1965 and 1966 in Hollywood.

Not quite all of the West Coast records of this period were made as "answer" records; there was a lively teen "leisure" scene, which had already spawned its own musical idiom before the British groups stormed onto the national airwaves: surf music.

*

The musical style which came to be called "surfing" music started out as a random collection of records which happened to have the right kind of beat for the kids to dance to at the beach parties along the Pacific Coast near Los Angeles. There was a similar scene on the Carolina Coast, but there was no recording industry in the Carolinas.

Until about 1962, the California beach parties made do with what they could find, and provided a reliable demand for all the instrumental records made by Sandy Nelson (including "Teen Beat" for Original Sound, 1959, and "Let There Be Drums", Imperial, 1961) and the Ventures ("Walk Don't Run" for Dolton, 1960, and a series of albums during the sixties). Other instrumentals adopted by the *après-surf* dancers included the old Bill Doggett shuffle, "Honky Tonk", still going strong ever since its original release in 1956; a remake of Arthur Smith's "Guitar Boogie Shuffle" by the Virtues (issued by Hunt of Philadelphia, 1959); "Stick Shift" by the Duals, complete with the sounds of a revving car engine (Sue, 1961); "Hideaway" by blues guitar virtuoso Freddie King (Federal, 1961); and "Memphis", a surging instrumental version of the Chuck Berry song by Cincinatti guitarist Lonnie Mack (Fraternity, 1963).

The consistent success of these records at parties inevitably led local musicians to begin to tailor their records specifically for this scene; Dick Dale and the Deltones were probably the first to build an entire repertoire of songs whose lyrics were geared exclusively to the slang and activities of surfers: "Let's Go Tripping" was a minor hit in 1962 on Dale's own Deltone label.

The references were widened to take in the parallel scene of hot-rodding, and a bunch of musicians formed a double identity outfit which recorded surf numbers as the Marketts (two hits for Liberty, "Surfers' Stomp" and "Bilbao Blue" in 1962, and one for Warner Brothers, "Out of Limits" in 1963) and hot-rod numbers as the Routers (two hits for Warner Brothers, "Let's Go" and "Sting Ray" in 1963). Other national hits included "Pipeline" by the Chantays and "Wipe Out" by the Surfaris, semi-novelty instrumentals with surfing connotations, both recorded for minor independent labels and picked up for national distribution by Dot during 1963.

Although the titles of these custom-made surf numbers were slang expressions from the surf lexicon, they sounded good enough on the radio to qualify as straightforward pop records, and many of them were hits far beyond the coastal resorts; few of the people who bought "Wipe Out" in Britain were aware that the title meant to fall off a surf board. But this surf scene provided an invaluable base for any artist who could make a connection with it, offering the possibility of building a name and selling enough records to get into the national charts.

As usual, the established companies were slow to appreciate the potential of a grass-roots musical scene, but several of the larger West Coast labels did eventually respond. Despite picking up those hits by the Chantays and the Surfaris, Dot never found a substantial teen-oriented artist during the early sixties, but Capitol, Liberty, and Imperial each found at least one consistent hit maker by opening their doors to the producers, writers, and musicians who had committed themselves to representing the surfers and hot-rodders.

The principal players in this scene included: the duo Jan and Dean; freelance producers Lou Adler, Steve Barri, Terry Melcher, Bruce Johnston, and Gary Usher; the Beach Boys' songwriters Brian Wilson and Mike Love; and the disc jockey Roger Christian. For Wilson and Love, the surf scene was a genuine interest, probably the only subject they could have written songs about with any conviction. For most of the others, it was a convenient focus for careers which had previously been directionless.

For Jan and Dean and their producer-manager Lou Adler, surf-music in effect redefined the pattern of their careers, giving a sense of inevitable destiny to what had at the time been simply a series of opportunist jumps. Jan and Dean were still part-time performers working their way through college when Adler managed to secure a contract for them with Liberty in 1962. For the first year, they continued to make rough-and-ready variations on East Coast black vocal group records, having fun with the interplay between a falsetto lead and a deep-voiced counterpoint without finding any focus for a unique sound or identity. But in 1963 Jan Berry collaborated with Brian Wilson of the Beach Boys to write a song which eulogized life on the California beaches: "Surf City". With its two-girls-for-every-boy chorus, this was the definitive fantasy for every teenage boy going on vacation, and the record went to the top of the national charts.

The success of "Surf City" was a watershed for the whole California music industry, proving that the rest of the States was prepared to share in vicarious enjoyment of the "layabout" lifestyle. Jan and Dean had five more top twenty hits, all encyclopaedic portraits of life in Los Angeles, mostly crammed with obsessive detail and sung in a dead-pan monotone; but there was genuine tension and drama in "Dead Man's Curve" (1964), and ironic humour in the minor hit on its B-side, "New Girl in School". The career of Jan and Dean was abruptly ended in 1966 when Jan Berry was involved in a serious car accident, which left the Beach Boys to continue as unopposed standard-bearers for the sun-sand-and-surf scene.

The personnel of the Beach Boys shifted through the years, but the main creative input always came from Brian Wilson, whose father

Murry had been a professional song-writer himself. Murry put up the money to issue the first Beach Boys single on the Candix label in 1962, and respectable sales for that record, "Surfin' ", led to a contract with Capitol where the group stayed throughout the decade. Early records by the group were no more imaginative than their titles: "Surfin' Safari", "Surfin' USA", "Surfer Girl". The records would have been effective advertising jingles for mail order catalogues for surf-board hire companies or for travel agencies looking to attract the nation's youth to Santa Monica. Musically, they borrowed freely from rock 'n' roll, particularly from Chuck Berry, whose "Sweet Little Sixteen" was the basis of "Surfin' USA". The playing on these records was at best enthusiastically amateur–tinny-sounding rhythm guitars, and erratic organ–and the success of these Beach Boys' hits provided advance warning of the message that was to be hammered home so forcefully by the British groups: that a large section of the pop music audience was ready to identify with a do-it-yourself sound in preference to the processed formula records being turned out by the American music industry.

During 1964, as the British records began to flood the American charts, the quality of the Beach Boys' records improved, as Brian Wilson began to showcase catchy melodies and increasingly elaborate harmonies. The whoops on the fade-out of "Fun Fun Fun" were particularly thrilling, and the whole energetic drive of "I Get Around" showed that Wilson had responded to the challenges of current records by the Beatles and the Four Seasons. In the following year, Wilson finally escaped the basic rock 'n' roll boogie shuffles that had tended to give an old-fashioned feel to his records, and in "Help Me Rhonda" and "California Girls" he evolved a jaunty, authoritative sound with invaluable assistance of session players including Carole Kaye on bass and Hal Blaine on drums, whose contributions were not widely advertised at the time–this was meant to be a "real" group.

By 1965, the Beach Boys had become an American pop institution, but although they continued to cultivate a visual image in line with their name and early repertoire, there was a limit to how many different ways Wilson could celebrate the wonders of living in Southern California. Waiting for inspiration, he filled the gap with oldies, duetting on "Barbara Ann" with Dean Torrence from Jan and Dean, and sounding more like the Kingston Trio in "Sloop John B.".

Originally dismissed by serious pop fans as a trashy pop group for kids, the Beach Boys began to attract awed admiration just as Brian Wilson found the strain of public adulation more than he had bargained for; retreating from live performances (where Glen Campbell and then Bruce Johnston deputised for him), Wilson spent most of his time in the recording studio, constructing the songs which were eventually issued as the album *Pet Sounds* in the summer of 1966. Much less successful in the States than earlier, simpler albums, the elaborate arrangements and haunting moods of *Pet Sounds* kept the album in Britain's top ten for six months, and inspired several British groups to make more experimental use of recording studio techniques.

The naïve innocence of the Beach Boys' records was a stark contrast to the contemporary records by Dylan, the Beatles and Rolling Stones, which were all heavy with cynicism, sceptism, and sarcasm. If Brian Wilson heard their stuff on the radio, or ever read a newspaper, he gave no clue; instead, at the end of 1966 he delivered his definitive record, "Good Vibrations". Technically immaculate, "Good Vibrations" was one of the first records to flaunt studio production as a quality in its own right, rather than as a means of presenting a performance. The sound of each instrument, the hypnotic effect of the new Moog synthesizer, and the subtle shifts of mood all contributed to an impression of absolute perfection, and the record was an enormous international hit. For the rest of the sixties, countless musicians and groups attempted to represent an equivalently blissful state, but none of them ever applied the intense discipline and concentration that Wilson had devoted to the recording.

The Beach Boys continued to record and perform for another fifteen years, managing eventually to shake off the early associations of being a disposable pop group, but their records never matched the peaks of 1965 and 1966. And the surf scene dropped out of sight, confirming that none of the other writers and producers had been as serious about their role in it as Brian Wilson had been. Most of them shifted to more conventional pop forms, which at this time in California mostly meant matching the sounds coming from Britain, or devising some combination of folk and pop.

If the most interesting pop hits out of California in this period were those with a folk base of some kind, the most successful outfits were the groups which mirrored British beat: Gary Lewis and the Playboys had eight straight top ten hits in the 18 months 1965–66; Paul Revere and the Raiders had ten top twenty hits, 1965–69, and one last-fling chart-topper in 1971; and the Monkees had nine top twenty hits (including three number ones) between 1966 and 1968. They all proved how efficient the system could be, and were all closely tied into TV shows.

Gary Lewis and the Playboys was the last in an impressive string of projects produced by Snuff Garrett for Liberty before he left the company to form his own Viva label in partnership with another

Texan, Jimmy Bowen from Reprise. Liberty* merged with Imperial in 1965, and between them the two companies represented a cross-section of the best West Coast pop music at the time, but the combined labels never succeeded in finding one of the major rock acts which emerged in the late sixties. Son of the comedian Jerry Lewis, Gary Lewis had an unremarkable voice, and his records were notable mainly as a stage in the career of pianist Leon Russell, who arranged many of the sessions and acquired experience which he put to his own advantage later.

Paul Revere and the Raiders were by contrast a "real" group, which had been together for five years when they signed to Columbia in 1964. Under the production supervision of Terry Melcher, who formed a good-humoured partnership with lead singer Mark Lindsay, the Raiders made some of the best, uninhibited American rock records of the mid-sixties. Obviously impressed by contemporary records by the Rolling Stones and the Animals, Melcher and Lindsay did not simply ape them, but either wrote or found songs which enabled a similar air of defiance to be conveyed. "Just Like Me", the group's first big hit, included some wild guitar playing, and after a couple of vehicles for pent-up expression from the ubiquitous Mann and Weil ("Kicks" and "Hungry") Melcher and Lindsay wrote a string of hits themselves, of which "Him or Me–What's It Gonna Be?" was outstanding. Chosen to be the resident group on Dick Clark's *Where the Action Is*, the group undermined their musical strengths by appearing in all kinds of novelty uniforms which played on their name. They won a young audience, but were never taken seriously by the older fans of the Rolling Stones, and never captured that increasingly important album market. Yet their *Greatest Hits* compilation holds up better than most other collections from the period, a tribute to the production skills of Terry Melcher and to the infectiously good-natured delivery of vocalist Mark Lindsay.

Don Kirshner, now head of Columbia Screen Gems, witnessed the events of the mid-sixties with mixed feelings. Just when he had

* LIBERTY
Pop: Gary Lewis and the Playboys.
Rock: Canned Heat.

in 1963 took over IMPERIAL.
Pop: Cher, Johnny Rivers, Jackie De Shannon, the Classics IV.
UK groups: the Hollies (1964–66), Georgie Fame, Billy J. Kramer and the Dakotas (all licensed from EMI).

merged in 1968 with UNITED ARTISTS.
Pop: Bobby Goldsboro.
Folk: Don McLean.
UK groups: the Spencer Davis Group, Traffic.
Rhythm and blues: War.

seemed to have a stranglehold on the process of supplying America with hit pop records, along came Berry Gordy's Detroit-based productions and all those British records to upset his applecart; and then Los Angeles reacted faster than New York in coming up with acceptable alternatives. Yet scattered through both the British and the Los Angeles productions were recordings of songs by Columbia Screen Gems writers, including covers of existing recordings and new versions of tailor-made compositions. Kirshner took the logical step of switching his headquarters from New York to Los Angeles. He already had very good "ins" with West Coast producers including Phil Spector (who regularly used songs from Mann and Weil), Snuff Garrett (who favoured Goffin and King), and Terry Melcher. Just as he had once made it a principle to work only with writers who were signed to him exclusively, Kirshner was now preoccupied with setting up a production outlet which was exclusively committed to using songs published by Screen Gems; if it proved expedient to use songs from writers who were not tied into Screen Gems, they must assign their rights in the particular songs used by the Screen Gems production unit. Towards the end of 1966, Screen Gems backed the most spectacularly successful marketing campaign in American pop history: America's Answer to the Beatles: the Monkees.

The invention, launch, and inevitable break-up of the Monkees epitomized the state of American pop in the mid-sixties. The scam was to make a TV series in which four young men sang songs and played the fool, just as the Beatles had done in *A Hard Day's Night*. It seemed that every young musician in Los Angeles answered the audition ads, but the chosen four found that they were not allowed to play on their own records; like the test pilots who were expected to do nothing on their remote-control flights into space as astronauts, the Monkees were required to pretend to be musicians while experienced session men actually made the records. Monkeys, indeed!

The whole concept of the Monkees ran against the grain of what was going on in America, but the impact of the Beatles had been so great that this transparently obvious imitation was gratefully accepted. Even more impressive than six top three singles in two years was their take-over of the top position on the album charts for 31 consecutive weeks from November 1966 until June 1967, 13 weeks with *The Monkees* and 18 with *More of the Monkees*. The extent of this success could only partly be explained by the intensity of the marketing campaign; the crucial extra factor was that the records were, considering the circumstances, surprisingly good. Well chosen songs were produced with brash confidence by Tommy Boyce and Bobby Hart, using the elite Los Angeles session-men including Hal Blaine, Larry Knechtal, Don Wilson of the Ventures, *et al.* Boyce and

Hart's own "Last Train to Clarksville" was a blatant copy of the Beatles sound of ensemble singing and melodic guitars, but the arrangement of Neil Diamond's "I'm a Believer" was more "American", with a catchy organ riff managing to disguise the weak lead vocal of Davy Jones. The ever-adaptable team of Goffin and King supplied "Pleasant Valley Sunday", and ex-Kingston Trio leader John Stewart came up with "Daydream Believer". There seemed to be no reason why the project could not go on indefinitely, providing an outlet for all those song-writers who had begun to feel obsolete as the trend moved to self-contained groups who wrote their own material. But the Monkees were themselves uncomfortably aware of that trend, and that they were seen to be a contrived anachronism. For Mike Nesmith, the strain was unbearable; he had proved he could write a hit by providing "Different Drum" for the Stone Poneys, a charming song whose message of spirited independence carried more weight because it was sung by a woman, Linda Ronstadt. A hit for Capitol in 1967, the record gave Nesmith the confidence to take a stand and demand that the Monkees be allowed to write their own material and play on their own sessions. Screen Gems conceded, but although their albums continued to sell well to the fans who had bought the earlier records, the Monkees never converted the sceptical "rock" audience, who preferred to retain their prejudice that the Monkees represented the despicable world of teenybop pop.

The Monkees' records were released by Colgems, a label owned by Columbia Screen Gems but marketed and distributed by the New York-based major, RCA. It was a paradox of the period that while the creative impetus shifted from the East Coast to the West, several of the biggest Los Angeles-based artists recorded for New York-based companies. Columbia had the Byrds and Paul Revere, Atco had Sonny and Cher and the Buffalo Springfield, Elektra signed the Doors. Of the West Coast labels, only Liberty, Imperial and Dunhill showed more than average initiative. Capitol, Warner-Reprise and A & M missed much of what was going on around them, although they inevitably picked up a few winners.

At Capitol*, Nick Venet was the "youngster" on the A&R staff

*CAPITOL. *A&R: Voyle Gilmore, Nick Venet, Ken Nelson (country division).*
Pop: Nat "King" Cole, Nancy Wilson.
Vocal groups: the Lettermen, the Beach Boys.
Country: Buck Owens, Merle Haggard, Sonny James.
UK pop: the Beatles, Peter and Gordon, Cilla Black (all from EMI).
Subsidiary:
TOWER
Rock: the Standells.
UK pop: Freddie and the Dreamers, Ian Whitcomb.

who kept the company in touch with the hustling world of independent productions, and he was mainly responsible for nurturing the Beach Boys in their early days. But the company's image of itself as a bastion of discreet taste would probably have held out, if it had not been for the determination of the Beatles' manager, Brian Epstein, to get his group's records out in America on the label which had the first option on product from its British parent company, EMI. The Beatles carried Capitol to the top of the league of American record companies, but the A&R staff seemed shell-shocked by the extraordinary success, and did not manage to make the most of the opening the Beatles made for them. As has been already noted, Capitol turned down the options on most of the other British acts available from EMI, and hardly made the most inspired choices in holding on to Peter and Gordon, Cilla Black, and Freddie and the Dreamers. And no major American acts were signed, to back up the two groups who chased each other up the charts with each release (a race which the Beatles won easily, with 20 number one hits to the Beach Boys' three).

Warner–Reprise* also missed most of the action in teenage pop music in the mid-sixties, and focussed its attentions on the middle-of-the-road market which was still regarded as the main outlet for albums. In 1963, Warner Brothers made the first in what became a long series of moves to merge with other companies, gradually building up a catalogue which eventually enabled the combined labels to set up their own distribution centres across the country, and to rival Columbia/Epic as one of the two largest major companies in the industry. The first move was to join with Reprise Records, which had been formed three years earlier by Frank Sinatra as a vehicle for himself and his Las Vegas cabaret and Hollywood movie associates, Dean Martin, Sammy Davis Jr, Louis Prima, *et al.*

Although the two labels were jointly owned after the merger, they retained separate A&R divisions for a while, and Jimmy Bowen at Reprise showed more flair with pop than his counterpart Joe Smith at Warners, who only came into his own in the next "post-Monterey Pop" phase. Among the neat completions of a cycle that pop occasionally allows were the productions of records by Frank Sinatra's

* WARNER BROTHERS. *A&R: Joe Smith, Ted Templeman, Lenny Waronker.*
Pop: the Everly Brothers, Routers.
Folk: Peter, Paul and Mary.
UK pop: Pet Clark

REPRISE. *A&R: Jimmy Bowen.*
Adult pop: Frank Sinatra, Dean Martin.
Teen pop: Nancy Sinatra.
Rock: Electric Prunes.
UK rock: the Kinks.

daughter Nancy by Lee Hazelwood. The whole concept had a jokey edge to it: make some hits by the boss' daughter. And the challenge was particularly daunting because Nancy's voice had a narrow range and little apparent charm. But the musicians, who had been picked up out of obscurity by Hazelwood back in 1958 for his Duane Eddy sessions, were now among the best-paid players in Hollywood and they evidently had a lot of fun inventing arrangements for novelty songs which made a virtue of Nancy's tuneless drone. "These Boots Are Made For Walkin'" was a tough song–to the point where it had sado-masochistic implications–and the gimmick which took the record right to the top of the charts was a bass-line played by Carole Kaye which descended in quarter-notes on the intro to each verse. This turned out to be Lee Hazelwood's last successful project, but he made a lot of mileage from it, producing three more top twenty hits by Nancy on her own, a chart-topping duet with her dad ("Something Stupid") and even two duets with himself, which made the top twenty–a country-tinged answer to Sonny and Cher.

A&M Records* was one of the biggest success stories of the American record business in the mid-sixties, and perhaps significantly achieved a secure place in the industry without exploiting any of the dominant trends of the period. During its first three or four years, A & M dabbled with some of the most interesting artists on the West coast, recording Waylon Jennings, Captain Beefheart, Dr John (in the Zu Zu Blues Band), Leon Russell and Toni Basil years before they became well-known. But it was Herb Alpert himself who put the label on the charts: his first ten albums all made the top twenty, including five which went to the top, all following a simple formula of playing catchy melodies with Spanish flavoured arrangements in the style of his first hit single "Lonely Bull" in 1962. If the terms "middle-of-the-road" and "easy listening" did not already exist, they would have been coined to describe the sound of Herb Alpert and the Tijuana Brass, and some of the other artists who continued in this field for A&M: Chris Montez, the Sandpipers, and Sergio Mendes.

Alpert's partner Jerry Moss (the "M" of A&M) made several astute moves to widen the stylistic base of the label's roster, and persuaded two independent British producers to place their artists

* A&M Records. *Formed in 1962 in Los Angeles by Herb Alpert and Jerry Moss.*
Latin pop: Herb Alpert and the Tijuana Brass, Sergio Mendes, the Sandpipers, Chris Montez.
Folk-pop: We Five.
From the UK: Procol Harum, the Move, Joe Cocker, Jimmy Cliff, Cat Stevens, Fairport Convention.
Country rock: the Flying Burrito Brothers.
Rhythm and blues: Sonny Charles and the Checkmates.

with A&M for America. A deal with Denny Cordell brought Procol Harum, the Move and, most important of all, Joe Cocker to A&M, while a similar arrangement with Chris Blackwell of Island Records secured Jimmy Cliff and Cat Stevens. Among the artists based closer to home, We Five had a top three hit with "You Were on My Mind" in 1965, but in general A&M missed the folk-rock boat.

The experience of Herb Alpert's former partner Lou Adler could hardly have been more different; his Dunhill* label thrived on the folk-rock boom, as we'll see in the next section, but Adler eventually sold the label to its distributor (ABC) and started again with a new label, Ode and a new distributor (CBS). Even this combination was not satisfactory, and the tidy conclusion was that A&M wound up as the distributors for Ode, just in time to be involved in the biggest record of Adler's very successful career, Carole King's *Tapestry* in 1971.

Apart from A&M, independent labels had a hard time surviving on the West Coast, despite the apparent advantages of being close to the TV and recording studios, and a very substantial local market for records. A couple of ex-Liberty salesmen started White Whale Records, and sustained the Turtles' career as a West Coast "answer" to the Lovin' Spoonful, notably with four big hits written by previously unknown New York writers Gary Bonner and Alan Gordon, and produced by newcomer Joe Wissert: "Happy Together" in particular conveyed a buoyant joyfulness which was becoming rare in American pop by 1967.

Valiant Records scored a teen-pop classic in 1963 with "Rhythm of the Rain" by the Cascades, and then came back in 1966 with "Along Comes Mary" and "Cherish" by the Association, which made them attractive enough for Warner Brothers to buy up the whole label. But in general, and in sharp contrast to the manic, ant-like scurry of little labels which had flourished in Los Angeles a few years earlier, the era of indie labels was over. A&M and Dunhill were exceptions to the rule that only the strong survived, even when the content was the potentially radical, if not revolutionary, force of folk-rock.

*DUNHILL RECORDS. *Formed in 1965 in Los Angeles by Lou Adler. A&R: Steve Barri and P. F. Sloan.*
Folk-rock: Barry McGuire, the Mamas and the Papas.
Pop: the Grass Roots, Three Dog Night.
Rock: Steppenwolf.
Sound-track: Easy Rider.
Distributed by ABC, who bought the company in 1966.

Apart from the people involved in surf music, and the obvious "answers" for the British groups, almost everybody who emerged out of the Los Angeles recording scene into the national charts in the mid-sixties played some kind of "folk-rock". The term embraced so many different sounds and styles, it almost became meaningless, but it did have a value: there was a difference between the records being made in 1965 and 1966, compared to the typical pop record five years earlier. Where it had previously been necessary to search hard for songs with social connotations, the majority now had a specific context for the lyrics; and where most records had obviously been put together in the traditional manner, with an A&R man, an arranger, and session musicians determining the framework for the singers, now there was a spontaneity about the sound in many of them. Subsequent investigation often revealed the differences to be illusory: many of the "meaningful" songs were written by the same writers who had been working earlier as commercial professionals, and many of the records were still played by session musicians and not by "real" groups. But the illusion was important, because both the audience and other younger musicians took it as being real, and the next generation of groups really did do it themselves.

In New York, the effective definition of "folk-rock" had been a merger between songs with a "message" (typified by Bob Dylan) and a so-called "rock 'n' roll" accompaniment including electric guitar and kit drums. In Los Angeles, "folk-rock" tended to relate to the sound more than to the content; Bob Dylan's own songs were a useful reference point, but West Coast groups generally preferred to adapt his love songs, rather than represent his political stance. Eventually, and ironically, the California version of folk-rock returned to the pretty harmonies of pre-Dylan folk music; the Mamas and the Papas picked up where Peter, Paul and Mary had left off, and the vaguely subversive associations of "folk-rock" were safely buried in a return to easy-on-the-ear-and-mind "folk-pop".

The genealogy of California's folk-rock and folk-pop is an intricate and sometimes incestuous family tree which starts out, inevitably, from Phil Spector's sessions. The success of Phil Spector's expensive and obsessive productions had enormous influence on all the musicians and arrangers who made up the massed forces assembled at Gold Star studios for the Crystals, Ronettes, and Righteous Brothers' dates. To many of the participants, Spector's entire performance was a con-job which they could see through and hope to emulate: if what the world wanted was a vast wall-of-sound noise behind little-girl-lost vocals, give it to them. But they underestimated the crucial element of Spector's own methodical selection process; it may have seemed arbitrary, but there was a consistent vision which filtered out the superfluous elements.

Two of the men who made the most of their apprenticeship under Spector were arranger Jack Nitzsche and jack-of-all-trades Sonny Bono. They had scuffled with little success for several years before coming together in 1963 to write "Needles and Pins" for Jackie De Shannon, whose recording was arranged by Nitzsche for Liberty. The use of dramatic tympany in the background behind the singer's plaintive vocal recalled Spector's approach, but a distinctive counter-melody played on guitar set a precedent which was used more emphatically in Jackie's next recording of her own song "When You Walk in the Room". The two records passed virtually unnoticed, but were covered in Britain by the Searchers, whose producer Tony Hatch exaggerated the role of the guitars even more, filling the sound out by using twelve-string instruments. Most British groups used guitars in a harsher way, more concerned with rhythm than melody, and the main follow-through to those Searchers hits was made back in Los Angeles, by Sonny Bono on records featuring himself and Cher, and by Roger McGuinn with the Byrds. Jackie De Shannon meanwhile switched labels from Liberty to Imperial when the two companies merged in 1965, and belatedly had her first top ten hit with "What The World Needs Now is Love". The song was written by Bacharach and David, which was ironic for a woman who had already written several hits herself for Brenda Lee ("Dum Dum", "Heart in Hand", and others) and the Fleetwoods ("The Great Imposter"), with co-writer Sharon Sheeley. A versatile singer and writer who did not fit into any of the available categories of "little-girl-lost", "folk-pop", or "sexy image", Jackie De Shannon seemed destined to remain a music industry favourite who would never attract public attention, and it was not until many years later, as writer of "Bette Davis Eyes" for Kim Carnes in 1981 that she had her biggest hit; a long way from folk-rock. But, back to the chronology, where we find Terry Melcher linking up with Roger McGuinn.

Terry Melcher was the son of Doris Day and he had made his first records as Terry Day for Columbia in 1963, at sessions arranged by Jack Nitzsche. He messed around with surf and hot-rod numbers in partnership with Bruce Johnston, producing a top ten hit for the Rip Chords ("Hey Little Cobra", 1964) and some flops as Bruce and Terry. In 1965, Terry Melcher found his stride as house producer for Columbia, embarking on a long series of hits with Paul Revere and the Raiders, and launching the career of the Byrds with the "folk-rock" sound of "Mr Tambourine Man".

The Byrds represented a watershed in America's pop history. Although they recorded in the traditional manner under the supervision of a staff A&R man, with session musicians standing in for members of the group on the first single, they managed to exude an image of self-determination. The group's leader Roger McGuinn had a solid background of regular work on the borderlines between pop and folk, working as an opening act for Bobby Darin and as a spare-change busker at the Greenwich Village folk clubs. In Los Angeles he found kindred spirits in the guitarist David Crosby and bass-player Chris Hillman and, after recording demos for World Pacific Records, managed to land a contract with Columbia. The group were already playing "Mr. Tambourine Man" in their live set, but producer Terry Melcher had doubts that they could hold the steady time-pulse needed for a danceable radio single. The necessary professional feel was supplied by three of Los Angeles's top sessionmen, whose experience included most of Phil Spector's sessions: Larry Knechtal played the elegant and captivating bass-line, while Hal Blaine kept time on drums; Leon Russell's first instrument was piano, but here he played guitar, blending in with the distorted clang of McGuinn's twelve-string guitar which was to become the trademark of the Byrds's sound. The rest of the group stood around shaking tambourines and singing along on the chorus.

Compared with the pure and clean sound of Peter, Paul and Mary's "Blowin' In The Wind", the Byrds' "Mr. Tambourine Man" had a rough and ready feel which aroused public curiosity about the song's writer, and the record effectively launched Bob Dylan's career, as well as that of the Byrds. It topped the singles' chart and triggered the folk-rock explosion which led to most of the major companies taking on at least one equivalent act and several artists covering Bob Dylan's songs. But while America's airwaves were overloaded with mournful lead voices backed up by harmonies and accompanied by droning guitars, the Byrds themselves never made the most of their early lead. Instead, after one more chart-topper with Pete Seeger's arrangement of "Turn Turn Turn", the group lost its momentum as America's "answer to the Beatles", which is what they had been touted as. Instead, the group splintered and regrouped several times, as McGuinn first pursued a semi-mystical direction (represented on the hit "Eight Miles High" in 1966) and then moved towards country music at a time when pop and rock fans still found it "hick" and un-hip. Terry Melcher dropped out as producer after the first two albums, since the group had begun to use the studio as a place to experiment and follow the music predilections of the particular musicians who were there at the time; the hits had put the band in credit with Columbia, so they were recording at their own expense, taking as long as it took to find the right sounds, the right groove, the right atmosphere.

The Byrds became one of the first "cult" groups, breaking off a piece of the rock market and holding on to it through their various personnel and stylistic changes, while some of the leaving members went on to establish careers elsewhere—Chris Hillman in the Flying Burrito Brothers, and David Crosby with Crosby Stills and Nash. Meanwhile, the flames of folk-rock were fanned by other Los Angeles producers who found it easier to keep their focus on the ingredients which made records into hits, particularly Sonny Bono and Lou Adler.

In the summer of 1965, as "Mr. Tambourine Man" started to fall from the top of the chart, it seemed as if every second record on American top forty radio was by Bob Dylan. He did have his own epic-length hit, "Like a Rollin' Stone", but the effect was compounded by three other hits which sounded very similar: two simultaneous covers of his song "All I Really Want to Do" by Cher and by the Byrds, alongside "I Got You Babe" by Sonny and Cher.

Sonny Bono had been on to some kind of folk-rock sound back in 1963 when he wrote "Needles and Pins" with Jack Nitzsche for Jackie De Shannon. Throughout 1964 he struggled to pull something out of the fire in the various records he made with his wife Cher, whom he had met in the perfect place–at a Phil Spector recording session. Sonny himself had a limited voice, to put it kindly; but when he heard the nasal whines that Bob Dylan and Roger McGuinn were getting away with, he figured he could do as well. He plotted his course with care: where Phil Spector had been a shadowy presence, pulling the strings of his puppet vocal groups without ever being seen, Sonny would play the role up front, writing, producing *and* singing with his wife. But compared with Spector's wayward genius, Sonny Bono was merely a journeyman, and his scheme only took shape when he recruited Harold Battiste as the arranger. A trained jazz and classical musician from New Orleans, Battiste provided the elegant frameworks which put the project into the top ten eight times in three years.

Compared with most of the stereotyped girl singers in short skirts and tight sweaters, Cher exuded a calm serenity which lent a touch of class to everything she did, although she was hard put to retain her cool through this period when she and Sonny became fashion models for whatever outlandish garb Hollywood's designers could throw onto them. But Sonny did make one point very strongly: he, as producer-artist, conceived and promoted the vehicle for his own success, and the record companies involved were merely distributors of his records.

One of the two companies was Atco, the subsidiary label of the pioneer New York indie, Atlantic. The connection with the West Coast had been made in the early sixties, when Atco's Bobby Darin had moved to Hollywood in order to be near the film studios where he planned to base his career. While working with Darin on sessions in Los Angeles, Atlantic's owner Ahmet Ertegun had established the contacts with local musicians which brought him a number one hit in 1963 with "Deep Purple" by Nino Tempo and April Stevens, two more from the cast of thousands who worked with Phil Spector. Tempo recommended Atco to Sonny Bono, who duly made a deal for Sonny and Cher without telling the New York company that he had also made a separate deal for Cher as a solo singer with Imperial. There was no obvious difference in the sound of the two records which launched these two parallel arrangements; Sonny's voice was just as apparent on the record credited to Cher as it was on Sonny and Cher's "I Got You Babe". Both records were much more effective follow-ups to "Mr. Tambourine Man" than anything the Byrds came up with themselves; Cher's version of "All I Really Want to Do" trounced the Byrds' version of the same song, but it was Sonny's own song "I Got You Babe" which most clearly defined the sound of Los Angeles folk-rock. The guitar opening hinted at the sound of the Byrds, but then the record shifted into a merry-go-round atmosphere, with guitar and organ playing a melodic riff behind the treacle-heavy sentiments of the lovers' duet. The anthem of young love was number one in the nation for three weeks in August 1965, and gave the duo a lifetime's career in show business; that first sweep of the charts ran dry when Harold Battiste was dropped as the arranger, but they had a strong come-back in the early seventies under Snuff Garrett's production for Kapp records, when Cher topped the chart again with "Gypsies, Tramps and Thieves".

Although the Beach Boys, Phil Spector and Sonny Bono were better known to the general public, the archetypal West Coast musicman of the sixties was Lou Adler. The early part of his career has already been noted, as a partner in management and song-writing with Herb Alpert in the late fifties, and as the West Coast agent for Columbia Screen Gems in the early sixties, who placed songs with Snuff Garrett at Liberty and secured a contract with the label for Jan and Dean. Lou Adler's career effectively took off when he left Screen Gems in 1964 and formed the Dunhill production company which recorded a live album, *Johnny Rivers at the Whiskey A Go Go*. At the age of 22, Rivers was already a veteran who had made 16 records for 11 different companies, mostly on the East Coast, but he had never been close to the national charts when Adler signed him to Imperial in 1964. At any other time, Rivers would have been regarded as just another bar-band singer whose repertoire was a bunch of old rock 'n' roll songs. But the British groups were reawakening Americans to those songs, and here was an easy-going album of well recorded versions, with the added novelty value of a "live" background ambience of an audience. Three top twenty singles were spun off the album, including another version of Chuck Berry's "Memphis", and revivals of his "Maybellene" and Harold Dorman's "Mountain of Love". The cheaply recorded album finally established both Adler and Rivers, both of whom built up substantial publishing and production companies over the following years. Rivers signed songwriter Jim Webb, who became one of the most successful non-performing writers of the late sixties, and Rivers also formed the Soul City label, which had seven top twenty hits by the Fifth Dimension, between 1967 and 1969. Meanwhile, Lou Adler formed the Dunhill label.

Dunhill was the last substantially successful American label set up by an active record producer to be more than just an outlet for his own productions. Increasingly, the trend was for labels to be formed by radio promotion men (like Neil Bogart's Buddah) or by lawyers and accountants who hired A&R men to front their companies. Dunhill reversed the pattern, as Lou Adler brought in Jay Lasker to administer promotion, marketing and distribution. Lasker's immediate decision was to place Dunhill's distribution with ABC, and for a couple of years it appeared to be an effective partnership; within six months, Dunhill topped the national chart with Barry McGuire's "Eve of Destruction", and within another six months had one of the best-selling acts in the country when the Mamas and the Papas hit the top five with six records in two years.

Inevitably influenced by his previous experience at Columbia Screen Gems, Lou Adler structured Dunhill around his protégé producer-writers, particularly Steve Barri, Phil "P.F." Sloan, and John Phillips. All three had made unsuccessful records on their own before joining Adler–Barri and Sloan in Los Angeles, and Phillips back East in New York–but they seemed to find it much easier to channel their energies under Adler's unerringly commercial direction.

For Phil Sloan, as for so many others, Bob Dylan showed the way with his songs that catalogued the world's troubles, such as "Masters of War" and "A Hard Rain's Gonna Fall". Sloan 19 years old at the time, made out his own shopping list of likely causes of imminent disaster in "Eve of Destruction", which ex-New Christy Minstrel Barry McGuire delivered with exactly the right tone of growling indignation. This was a far tougher song than any of Bob Dylan's own singles, but, despite receiving much less airplay than most pop hits, it hit the top of the charts within five weeks of its release. The musical arrangement was disarmingly simple, just harmonica, acoustic guitar, bass and drums; but what drums. It was the fourth number one hit in the year to feature the exciting, dramatic style of Hal Blaine, a graduate of the Phil Spector sessions who had learned to pace himself through a song with a simple, sympathetic support on the verses so that any flourish he made on the tom-toms came through with maximum impact. Most recording was still being done on simple equipment: the musicians all played together and had to get everything right in the same "take". For the casual listener, Blaine's drums were not the most noticeable feature of "Help Me Rhonda", "Mr. Tambourine Man", "I Got You Babe", or "Eve of Destruction", but for the singers and for the other musicians on the sessions his patterns provided exactly the right combination of relaxation and urgency that made the whole performance sound so convincing. On "Eve of Destruction", he began with a couple of crashes on some kind of tympany, and then allowed the vocal to dominate, until the last verse and chorus where Blaine picked up a marching-band drum roll to convey the declamatory, preaching mood of the song.

For Barry McGuire, the record proved a mixed blessing; he had built his career steadily and systematically to this point, writing one hit in 1963 for the Kingston Trio ("Greenback Dollar") and singing the lead on another later in the year with the New Christy Minstrels ("Green Green"), but after "Eve of Destruction" his voice was irretrievably associated with that one song, and he had no more hits. But for Lou Adler, this was another turning point; at the sessions convened to record a follow-up album for McGuire, Adler met the singers who had been hired to sing back-up vocals, and a new career was set into motion: the Mamas and the Papas.

Vocal groups which combined male and female voices were surprisingly rare in American pop music; in between the folk-based Weavers (three men, one woman) in the early fifties and Peter, Paul and Mary in the early sixties, there were just a few one-or-two-hit wonders: the Teddy Bears (one girl, two boys), the Fleetwoods (one boy, two girls), the Essex (one woman, three men), and the Springfields (Dusty Springfield, her brother Tom, and one other man). The international success of the Springfields (who had an American hit in 1962, before such things were common for British groups) was probably the main inspiration behind the formation of the Australian folk group, the Seekers, who moved to Britain where they recorded three international hits in 1965, all written by Tom Springfield and including "I'll Never Find Another You". The sweetness-and-light sound of Judith Durham's lead vocal against three male back-up singers was the most obvious antecedent for the Mamas and the Papas, together with the similar balance in Peter, Paul and Mary of Mary Travers' voice against the two men. But leading Papa John Phillips favoured a more melancholy, almost gloomy atmosphere, and used his own unremarkable voice as a counterpoint to the soaring sound of Mama Cass and Michele Gilliam.

Lyrically the Mamas and the Papas stayed clear of the social and political protest messages which were usually part of the folk-rock repertoire, and mostly covered the traditional pop topics of love laments and celebrations. But their first two hits were unorthodox: "California Dreamin'" effectively carried on the West-is-Best ethic cultivated by the Beach Boys, and "Monday Monday" went back to a favourite topic of the blues. Alongside their own love songs, they revived the Five Royales' "Dedicated to the One I Love" for the second time (it had been a hit for the Shirelles in 1961), and their last hit, "Creeque Alley" in 1967, showed how introverted the pop culture had become, describing in witty detail the story of the group's own genesis alongside the Byrds and the Lovin' Spoonful out of the Greenwich Village folk scene. Larry Williams had used the characters and titles from other rock 'n' roll songs in "Short Fat Fannie" in 1958, but now the names of members of groups became part of the pop mythology: "McGuinn and McGuire were just a-gettin' higher in L.A., you know where that's at".

For one week in 1966, *If You Can Believe Your Eyes and Ears* by the Mamas and the Papas topped the American album chart, only the second album by an American group to challenge the virtual monopoly of that market by the Beatles, sound-track albums, and trumpeter Herb Alpert. *The Beach Boys' Concert* had held the top slot for three weeks in 1964, but in general American groups had not managed to present the kind of sound and image to attract older, album-buying pop fans. The Mamas and the Papas came up with two more best-selling albums before "personal and musical differences" undermined their momentum. The group did however play an important role in shifting the focus of the American record industry towards a substantially older pop audience than it had previously acknowledged. It had always assumed that when pop fans grew up, they would settle down to listen to cabaret crooners, but here were adults buying the same albums as teenagers.

To emphasize the point, Lou Adler, John Phillips and a few other hip young businessmen organized the Monterey Pop Festival in the summer of 1967, which fulfilled, for this new world of adult-pop, the same function that Alan Freed's Cleveland concerts had achieved for rock 'n' roll back in 1953, by showing what this new audience looked like and how extensive it was. Representatives from all the major record companies, TV networks and national magazines came, saw, and were conquered. The nucleus of the Monterey bill were groups from nearby San Francisco, but among the others there were the three big "folk-rock" groups from Los Angeles: the Byrds, the Mamas and the Papas, and the Buffalo Springfield.

At the time, the Buffalo Springfield were seen as the latest in the on-going genealogy of folk-rock, partly because their line-up included two more exiles from the Greenwich Village coffee house scene, Stephen Stills and Ritchie Furay. But, along with the Doors, the Buffalo Springfield were actually the start of a new era, which brought together all the strands of American music–folk, country, blues, and soul–and fashioned an idiom that was loosely known simply as "rock". And as usual, the first were the best.

Conveniently for the historians, the new "rock" era was launched in January 1967 with the first Buffalo Springfield single, "For What It's Worth". Stills and Furay had found a third guitarist, the Canadian Neil Young, to complete the range of sounds and styles they wanted to combine, and with that first single they established a new mood: "For What It's Worth" was written by Steve Stills after he watched a TV news report from Los Angeles's Sunset Strip, where police violently cleared the pavements of demonstrators who were staging a sit-down strike against local tradesmen who had refused to serve long-haired "hippie" customers. There was a chilling air of menace to the song, as Richie Furay slowly unfolded the lyric:

There's something happening here
What it is ain't exactly clear
There's a man with a gun over there
Telling me I've got to beware

I think it's time we stopped, children
What's that sound?
Everybody look what's going down

There's battle lines being drawn
Nobody's right if everybody's wrong
Young people speaking their minds
Getting so much resistance from behind

What a field day for the heat
A thousand people in the street
Singing songs and carrying signs
Mostly say "hooray for our side"

Paranoia strikes deep
Into your life it will creep
It starts when you're always afraid
Step out of line and the man
will come and take you away

As "Blue Suede Shoes" had been for rock 'n' roll fans ten years before, "For What It's Worth" became an anthem for the new rock audience. Instead of Bob Dylan's highly personal diatribes like "Like a Rolling Stone", this song allowed each listener to assume the "first person" position that Stills had put into it. It was unusual for a pop song to have such a specific event for its inspiration, and this one retained its relevance throughout the rest of the sixties as American students confronted their college administrations all across the country.

Despite that heady start, the Buffalo Springfield never managed to capture their essential ingredients so effectively in any other one song, and their albums were mostly tantalizing hints of what the group might have been, if they had been better-disciplined and perhaps if they had liked each other more. They were managed and produced by Charles Greene and Brian Stone, who signed the group to Atlantic's Atco label, which had proved such an effective outlet for Greene and Stone's other protégés Sonny and Cher. For the still independent Atlantic, the Buffalo Springfield represented a major coup, but an expensive one; the group managed to dissipate its advances in an extravagant life-style of high rents and an indulgent use of drugs, and never really concentrated on making a first-class album. Instead, there were a few hints of what the individual members would move towards later: Steve Stills had grown up in the South and spent some time in Cuba, and there were distinct soul influences in his "Rock & Roll Woman"; Richie Furay had a background in country music, and although he contributed a small proportion of the group's recorded output, his "Kind Woman" was a classic country soul song; Neil Young was the most enigmatic of the three, coming across as an abstracted loner with strange preoccupations, which he delivered in a whining voice that was an acquired taste. There were rumours of dissension long before the group's break-up was finally announced, and some interesting horse-trading followed as new formations were announced. Neil Young had gone to Reprise as a solo singer, but Stills wanted to form a group with Dave Crosby of the Byrds and Graham Nash from the Hollies, both of whom were with Columbia/Epic; this new line-up was signed to Atlantic, who in return allowed Richie Furay to go to Epic to form Poco. Whatever Atlantic had lost on the Buffalo Springfield, the company made up through the substantial success of Crosby, Stills and Nash, who then persuaded Neil Young to come back to record the aptly titled *Déjà Vu* album with them, which topped the chart in 1970.

While the Buffalo Springfield dissipated the position they had achieved for themselves with a top ten hit at the start of 1967, the Doors followed through with a much more impressive and sustained assault on the charts which they kept up right to the end of the decade. By coincidence, this group also signed to a New York indie label, in this case Elektra; having failed to reap direct benefit from the folk-rock movement, despite its fifteen-year history of recording folk singers, it was ironic that Elektra should scoop the most successful American rock band of the late sixties from under the nose of the major companies. But there may have been a direct connection between Elektra's tradition and the Doors' decision to sign with the company: Elektra had a reputation for not interfering with its artists' recording processes or dictating their careers. At a time when the new rock artists were more concerned with controlling the quality and concepts of their albums than with scoring hit singles, Elektra's approach looked very attractive to the Doors.

Where the Buffalo Springfield had a background in folk and country, into which they grafted vocal and guitar styles from soul music, the Doors worked in the opposite direction: there was a basic blues feeling to their repetitive chord sequences, over which they laid jazzy instrumental improvizations and a folk-styled vocal approach from Jim Morrison. Elektra's staff engineer-producer Paul Rothchild supervised the recordings, and helped to achieve a simple, coherent framework for the group's songs which ranged from fairly conventional "come-on" songs like "Light My Fire" through quirky pop tunes like "Break On Through", to the much more moody atmosphere they experimented with in "The End". Those three were all on the first album, *The Doors*, and each subsequent record tended to include all three types of song, of which the "come-on" items resulted in the biggest hit singles. In his live shows, Jim Morrison exaggerated the macho pose implied in "Light My Fire", "Hello I Love You" and "Touch Me", and he became increasingly extreme and unpleasant as he reached for ever more provocative poses. The downward spiral resulted eventually in a sordid suicide in 1972, leaving an impression of violence and disgust which was liable to overshadow the musical contributions of the rest of the group, particularly on the early albums. Organist Ray Manzarek had been classically trained, but he played with admirable restraint and sympathy, creating hypnotic moods which were enhanced by his bass-lines (recorded separately, thanks to the miracles of multi-track recording).

Jim Morrison had a background in the performing arts–theatre and film–and there were echoes of the German musicals of Kurt Weill and Berthold Brecht in both his verbal imagery (allusive, mysterious) and his phrasing (full of self-conscious pauses). While *Sergeant Pepper's Lonely Hearts Club Band* by the Beatles held the top of the album charts for fifteen weeks during the summer and fall of 1967, *The Doors* album spent most of the period just below it in second place; an edited version of "Light My Fire" topped the singles chart, and the song became a standard number in the repertoire of countless bands. Along with the Velvet Underground, the Doors became a major influence on the groups of the seventies who were loosely bracketed as "New Wave" (while the majority played safe and hammered out blues guitar chords in the ever lengthening wake of the Rolling Stones).

Most of the musical acts working in Los Angeles during the mid-sixties found it convenient to be included in the catch-all categories of "folk-rock" and "pop" that were applied by the media at the time. But three of the most interesting artists defied all attempts to link them with their contemporaries: Frank Zappa, Captain Beefheart, and Dr John simply did what they wanted, and it was up to the marketing and promotion men to figure out what to do next. In each case, what happened was that the marketing and promotion men didn't know what to do with them, and so none of them sold many records. Yet in the years since, each has become acknowledged as a true original who deserved a better fate.

All three artists were steeped in black music. Frank Zappa and Don Van Vliet both grew up in Southern California, and as school friends shared an obsession with obscure rhythm and blues vocal group and blues records. Taking on the identity of "Captain Beefheart", Van Vliet recorded a couple of singles in 1965 for A&M which attracted no attention, and two years later made the album *Safe as Milk* for the New York indie, Buddah. Produced by Richard Perry, and including slide guitarist Ry Cooder from Taj Mahal's group the Rising Sons, this album was the most coherent and potentially the most commercial of all Captain Beefheart's records. Most of the tracks had a powerful boogie blues rhythm, over which Beefheart declaimed his eccentric lyrics in a voice that obviously owed a lot to Howlin' Wolf. But although Beefheart had evidently done his best to adapt to the conventional structures that Perry had built for his songs, it soon became apparent that this was not Beefheart's destiny. He assembled his own group, gave them all pseudonyms, tagged the assemblage his Magic Band, and proceeded to jump from one company to another in search of understanding. In 1969, he joined Frank Zappa's Bizarre Records, and made the legendary *Trout Mask Replica*, a double-album recorded in a straight eight-hour session one night; this would have been considered par-for-the-course for a jazz group, but pop and rock records were not made this way. Beefheart eventually became an indulgence, tolerated but never tamed by the record industry, devotedly admired by many musicians.

While Captain Beefheart gave the impression of living in a world of his own in which the record industry's occasional intrusions were a perpetual surprise, Frank Zappa waged an unceasing war against the entire structure of the industry, making provocative attacks through his songs and through public statements against record companies, radio programmers, the audience, and their collective social habits. An accomplished musician, Zappa was an obsessional workaholic whose chief failing was an inability to distinguish his inspirational moments from childish and mundanely obvious bad jokes. The result was a prolific series of albums, several of them issued two-at-a-time, whose quality was extremely inconsistent.

MGM's Verve label was the first company to take on the Mothers of Invention, and house producer Tom Wilson managed to impose some semblance of order and selectivity into the recording and sequencing processes. The second album, *Absolutely Free*, sold respectably, and the third, *We're Only In It For The Money* actually made the top thirty (in 1968). Complete with a spoof cover which parodied the Beatles' *Sergeant Pepper*, this record was a fairly coherent assault on the self-satisfied hippie movement based in San Francisco, but from then on Zappa tended to become more random in his choice of targets and subjects, while substantially raising the quality of the musicians in his outfits. Several outstanding figures received an invaluable boost to their careers through a temporary association with the Mothers, notably the jazz pianist George Duke, violinists Jean Luc Ponty and Don "Sugarcane" Harris (yes, the same Don who once sang with Dewey for Specialty), and guitarist Lowell George, who went on to form Little Feat. After releasing five albums through Verve, Zappa licensed his own Bizarre label to Warner–Reprise, and over the years built up his constituency of followers who indulged his lack of self-critical faculties and appreciated the moments of true wit and instrumental inspiration.

Dr John was the persona adopted by Mac Rebennack, a keyboard and guitar player from New Orleans who moved to Los Angeles in the mid-sixties. Several producers and arrangers were still using some kind of Southern feel, which had been part of the "sound of Los Angeles" since the forties, and Rebennack played on countless sessions for Phil Spector, Sonny Bono, H. B. Barnum, and Harold Battiste. It was Battiste who helped him evolve a career of his own, initially in partnership with another exile from New Orleans, Jessie Hill, who joined him in the Zu Zu Blues Band. A single for A&M in 1965, "Zu Zu Man" featured some of the elements of what were to follow: a growled, gravelly vocal almost buried in a murky, mysterious mush of piano, guitar, bass, and drums–like Booker T. and the M.G.'s having a nightmare.

As drugs spread through the white culture during the mid-sixties, and the Byrds, Doors, Buffalo Springfield and the rest evolved suitable music as soundtracks for their stoned audiences, Mac Rebennack developed a spectacular congregation of dancers, singers and musicians who played "Gris Gris" music under the direction of Dr John the Night Tripper. Manager-producers Greene and Stone, who had successfully placed Sonny and Cher and the Buffalo Springfield with Atco, now landed Dr John's album *Gris Gris* on the label, but the music was too "far out" even for an audience that favoured the weird and way out. Instead of virtuoso solos, Dr John presented textures, moods, atmospheres: choral backing vocals, swampy percussion sounds, meandering contributions from guitar and bass, all emphasizing Dr John's intimate, confiding vocals. "Mama Roux" had a conventional song structure, presenting a model that Sly Stone followed more successfully four years later with "Family Affair", but most of the other tracks were pure mood-pieces. Later albums followed similar patterns, but with less evident direction, until Atlantic's Jerry Wexler stepped in to guide Dr John towards a more accessible style in the album *Gumbo*.

Of all the performers caught up in "rock" music of the late sixties, Dr John had perhaps the most thorough grounding in the source music of the fifties, and Wexler encouraged him to bring this out with celebrations of songs by Professor Longhair, Huey "Piano" Smith and other New Orleans originals. That album was too obviously a revival record to have any commercial potential, but it served the important function of reconnecting Dr John to conventionally structured popular songs. He followed with an album of his own songs produced in New Orleans by Allen Toussaint, aptly titled *In the Right Place*; he finally achieved a top ten hit with "Right Time, Wrong Place", which showed off a witty, perceptive view of life that had been hard to detect in the mumbo jumbo of the earlier albums. Despite that success, Dr John was unable to sustain the kind of touring schedules that were necessary to reinforce the impact of a hit single, and instead sold many of his best performances as a session player on other people's records, notably in "Small Town Talk" by Bobby Charles (another drug casualty from Louisiana) and "Spanish Harlem" by Aretha Franklin. Meanwhile, another Los Angeles session pianist, Leon Russell, pulled together a live show based on Dr John's and made several best-selling albums and singles in a similar style.

VII

Every time the record industry thought it had come to grips with rock 'n' roll's elusive spirit, the thing evaporated and went to play in some other obscure place out of public view. From those first moments back in the fifties when it had danced in Memphis and New Orleans, in Newport, Virginia and Clovis, New Mexico, the spirit of rock 'n' roll defied every attempt to analyse and reproduce its basic formula for more than a few months. And so through the sixties, it sprang to life in Detroit and then in London, teased the industry by coming as close to home as Greenwich Village and then jumped across the country to Hollywood. And finally, or so it seemed at the time, the rock 'n' roll spirit made a mockery of the entire industry by shifting its base to San Francisco, where everything the music business had been based on was turned upside down.

In San Francisco, groups recorded and sold albums without having made singles first, and other groups acquired national reputations without having recorded at all. In San Francisco, radio stations abandoned the strict rotation-of-hits policy which had become the standard formula across the country, and instead let disc jockeys play whatever came into their heads and hands–album tracks, unreleased tapes, obscure B-sides. In San Francisco, the distinction between musical groups and their audience blurred into a confusing mass of people who sometimes had clear roles–guitarist, lighting man, sound engineer–but more often just hung around as friend, lover, drug supplier, dancer, or simply supporter.

For a while, San Francisco-based groups seemed to embody something closer to the original carefree spirit of rock 'n' roll than had been represented in the records made by the professional careerists in Los Angeles. A new generation of journalists, led by the staff of the San Francisco-based *Rolling Stone* magazine, cultivated this impression, acclaiming the new musicians as visionaries with a spiritual purity that could permanently alter art, politics, and society. For the first time, the national media acknowledged the concept of a "Sound of a City", and reported almost every day on the latest developments of the Sound of San Francisco, embellished with sensationalist accounts of a new so-called counter-culture which not only tolerated but actually championed "free sex", drugs as an alternative to alcohol, and barter-trade instead of a money-based economy.

A small city by American standards (less than a million inhabitants), San Francisco had been long established as a home for avant garde artists, especially during the mid-fifties when specialist bookshops and publishers encouraged local Beat poets and writers including Allen Ginsberg and Lawrence Ferlinghetti. Jack Kerouac's celebrated "odyssey" novel of the fifties, *On The Road*, recounted an adventurous drive across America, with San Francisco as the goal.

During the sixties, the Berkeley campus of the University of California (across the bay from San Francisco) became a centre for radical students and teachers, while the black neighbourhoods of nearby

Oakland spawned some of America's strongest black power groups and leaders. This combination of avant garde artists and radical activists generated a lively scene which fostered jazz and folk music in clubs like the hungry i, where the Kingston Trio had first attracted attention, and where "alternative" comedians Lord Buckley and Lenny Bruce made regular appearances.

With this tradition of supporting the unorthodox, the eccentric, and the unwanted-by-the-rest-of-America, San Francisco was the natural home for singers and musicians experimenting with different forms of popular music in the wake of Dylan and the Beatles, especially as the city had a reputation for tolerating drugs more than most places. There never was a substantial record company based in San Francisco, but two men helped to provide a sufficiently reliable structure for music to be heard, to enable the experiments to evolve into viable commercial shapes which attracted the attention of the national record industry: radio programmer Tom Donahue, and promoter Bill Graham.

Tom Donahue had been a disc jockey since the late forties, and played rhythm and blues records on Philadelphia stations throughout the fifties before moving west to KYA in San Francisco in the early sixties. KYA was a "top forty" station, and in 1964 Donahue took a shot at running his own pop music label, launching Autumn Records with a top five hit, "C'Mon and Swim" by Bobby Freeman, produced by a black disc jockey, Sylvester Stewart. The following year, Stewart produced a couple of sounds-like-the-Beatles hits by the Beau Brummels, "Laugh Laugh" and "Just a Little", and made some unsuccessful records on his own as Sly; it took him a couple of years to figure out a more original format for his talents, as Sly and the Family Stone.

Donahue sold Autumn Records to Warner Brothers (whose hopes of turning the Beau Brummels into a major act never materialized) and during 1967 inaugurated 24-hours-a-day free-form rock music programmes on the FM station, KMPX. FM radio had been in existence for years, but had been used as a parallel, high quality output for the same programmes being broadcast on medium-wave AM stations. In the mid-sixties, the Federal Commission for Communications (FCC) decreed that FM wavelengths must be used for entirely different programmes from AM radio, and so for a while FM became a backwater of specialized minority and ethnic programmes whose music content was restricted mainly to classical music and jazz.

The widespread assumption in radio was that effective pop music programming had to be based on the principle of repeating current hits as often as possible; the only question was, should the list of "hits" be as long as forty different records, or as short as fifteen? This format may have suited the tightly packed hooks-and-back-beat records aimed at young teenagers, but it was no kind of vehicle for the emerging "folk-rock" acts whose album tracks explored different ways of presenting moods and ideas. During 1966, a new generation of groups were formed in San Francisco who made no attempt to shape their repertoire and approach to the requirements of top forty radio, and with perfect timing Donahue and Larry Miller provided an outlet for them in 1967 on KMPX.

The basic principle of this new "rock" format was that the individual presenters used their own discretion and taste to determine what they played. To a far greater extent than was normal on AM top forty radio, the FM presenters championed the local music community, announcing forthcoming live appearances by relatively unknown bands whose names began to become familiar even though they had not yet recorded: the Jefferson Airplane, the Great Society, Quicksilver Messenger Service, the Grateful Dead. Pausing to take a drag on a joint between words, the announcers made it clear that they were part of the new subculture, and they helped to exaggerate some of the divisions in popular music between artists who were seen as being part of the traditional "show-business" sector of the music industry, and the hip alternative groups who were building a new future. The Beatles generally defied such categorization, and among the other successful groups who were regarded as being "all right" were Bob Dylan, the Rolling Stones, the Byrds, and the Lovin' Spoonful. But contemporary black artists were mostly ignored by the FM disc jockeys, although it was apparent that many of the groups they did play were still recycling the bass and drum patterns of current Motown and Stax records.

During 1967, KMPX fanned the flames of the thriving San Francisco scene, which expanded as musicians and entire groups flocked from all over the country to join in all this sex, drugs and rock and roll. Early in 1968, Tom Donahue left after disagreements with the management, and with most of the KMPX staff set up a rival rock format on another FM station, KSAN. Between them, KMPX and KSAN substantially redefined the framework for the entire American music industry, inspiring similar stations to be set up throughout the country. Very soon, the free-form approach was abandoned, and playlists were inaugurated to give a sense of structure for the audience and a reliable promotional format for the record industry. But the shift to albums from singles was decisive and permanent, and henceforth every self-respecting new act expected to record an album within months of signing a record contract, whereas before an album had only been deemed to be marketable when an artist had scored at least one substantial hit single. The distinction had devastating repercussions for independent companies, because now a new artist represented a substantial investment, which only the larger companies could afford.

By the time KMPX committed itself to "rock around the clock", the San Franciscan music scene was already thriving. Local bands reopened ballrooms which had not been in regular use since the heyday of the big bands in the thirties and forties; playing benefits for local stores and magazines, or to raise bail for somebody busted on a drugs charge, these bands and their managers revealed the existence of an enormous audience hungry for regular live music. And the figure who emerged to co-ordinate events in this potentially chaotic situation was Bill Graham, a former mimetroupe manager who promoted regular events at the Avalon, Carousel, and Fillmore Ballrooms.

Throughout 1966, a few bands emerged as having the combination of a musical identity and business structure to be able to entertain a live audience on a regular basis, and in January 1967 they were collected together for a gigantic open-air festival in Golden Gate Park, billed as the Human Be-In: the Jefferson Airplane, the Grateful Dead, Moby Grape, the Quicksilver Messenger Service, the Steve Miller Band, Country Joe and the Fish, and Big Brother and the Holding Company. The event attracted 20,000 people, and shocked the American record business into realizing that these groups with long hair, silly names, and no obvious hit singles in their repertoire had to be taken seriously.

For the next three years, the major American record companies spent a fortune on signing up, recording, and publicizing those groups and many more who sounded like them, and although commercially they may only have broken even, they established a once-and-for-all hold on the American record industry which was not shaken loose in the next fifteen years. Although these San Franciscan bands purported to stand for an alternative to the traditional structures of the entertainment industry and were better placed than any of their predecessors to record for independent companies, only two of the leading seven chose indies, and one of those jumped ship to a major after one album. Country Joe and the Fish recorded for Vanguard, and the group's first album *Electric Music for the Mind and Body* was an influential blend of strong lyrics from singer Country Joe McDonald and searing electric guitar solos by Barry Melton. Big Brother and the Holding Company, featuring lead singer Janis Joplin, made one album for Bob Shad's Mainstream label, but switched to Columbia after being "discovered" at the Monterey Pop Festival in June 1967.

Monterey Pop was a deliberate attempt by organizers Lou Adler and Alan Pariser to recreate the Be-In for the benefit of the people in the record industry and the national media who had missed it the first time around. In the intervening six months, the Jefferson Airplane had released their first album for RCA (*Takes Off*), recruited a new lead singer (Grace Slick), and hit top forty radio with a single, "Somebody to Love". This hippie music had distinct commercial possibilities, and here were the leading contenders up for auction. To broaden the base, extra bands were featured: from Los Angeles, the Byrds, the Mamas and the Papas, and the Buffalo Springfield; from Britain, the Who and the Jimi Hendrix Experience; plus the Electric Flag, recently formed by members of various blues groups; soul singer Otis Redding; and Indian sitar-player Ravi Shankar.

At Monterey, the record industry abandoned virtually all the principles by which it had operated for more than fifty years, and openly surrendered its autonomy to the artists. Throwing caution and control to the winds, the A&R men brought out their cheque books and bid frantically with each other to grab anything with long hair and a guitar: Clive Davis, recently promoted out of Columbia's accounts department to run the company's A&R office, signed the Electric Flag, Moby Grape, and–for $250,000–Big Brother and the Holding Company, featuring Janis Joplin; since Big Brother was already signed to Mainstream, the deal involved paying a transfer fee. Warner Brothers had already signed the Grateful Dead, and at Monterey added the Jimi Hendrix Experience to their roster. Steve Miller and the Quicksilver Messenger Service played hard to get, but afterwards both signed to Capitol for substantial advance payments. Mercury, coming in a little late, grabbed what they could find at whatever price had to be paid, and never recouped the money they doled out for Mother Earth and the Sir Douglas Quintet, two bands who had come up from Texas in search of money that would never have come to them if they had stayed at home.

The most extreme symptom of the lemming-like panic of the major record companies to get in on this scene was the attempt by MGM to foster an alternative base to San Francisco for the new music, by signing up several bands from Boston and marketing them as the "Boss-town Sound". The campaign was an expensive disaster: a group had to boast the tag "from San Francisco", which from December 1967 onwards ensured the support of *Rolling Stone* Magazine. Formed by Jann Wenner with help from veteran jazz chronicler Ralph Gleason, *Rolling Stone* became the first regular popular music publication in America to feature in-depth interviews and critical reviews, along with gossipy columns and photographs which helped to sort out which musicians had adopted the counter-culture uniform of long-hair, roach-clips, and robes.

The role of drugs in all this was hard to define; at the simplest level, drugs simply replaced alcohol as the relaxing agent for this culture, just as they had done for some years in the jazz world. The whole rigmarole of rolling a joint and passing it around was a genuinely sociable activity which brought strangers into contact with each other at a live concert, but there were other drugs apart from marijuana. This was the period when lysergic acid first surfaced on a mass scale, and while there were persuasive arguments that under controlled conditions this LSD could have medical and psychological uses, it was not the wisest move for an insecure teenager to take it without supervision. And then there were the more malevolent drugs–depressant "downers" and stimulant "uppers" alongside addictive powders like heroin and cocaine.

Musicians and their audiences experimented with these drugs, and the music which resulted did not always travel as far or as effectively as the record industry anticipated. The most fundamental effect was that conventional standards of singing in tune were abandoned, along with any sense of self-discipline when taking a guitar solo. The potential weaknesses of the situation were showcased in the albums that the Grateful Dead recorded for Warner Brothers. Lead guitarist Jerry Garcia was a fluent musician with a thorough grounding in the "root" forms of country, bluegrass, and rhythm and blues music, and in live concerts he could galvanize the other musicians into entrancing, hypnotic grooves that enraptured an audience already high on whatever they had taken that night.

For their first album with Warner Brothers, the Grateful Dead enlisted Dave Hassinger as producer, but there was not much he could do to disguise the essentially amateur approach of the band, and the record sounded more like a rehearsal than a finished master. The basic musical reference points were the Rolling Stones and the Byrds, but the Grateful Dead never managed to come up with original songs distinctive enough to attract an audience beyond the fans who wanted a souvenir of the live gigs. Despite these musical weaknesses, the Grateful Dead became a symbol of the new "underground" music scene, and bestowed a "credibility" upon Warner Brothers that enabled the company to convince other album-oriented acts to sign for them; all those years as a "middle-of-the-road" label were hastily buried and hopefully forgotten, as the Warner staff put their suits in their wardrobes and came out wearing beads, saying "hi, man", and taking a toke on a roach.

The Jefferson Airplane was a much more substantial commercial success, scoring top ten hits for RCA in 1967 with the catchy love song "Somebody to Love" and the thinly-disguised drug song "White Rabbit". Their album *Surrealistic Pillow* was on the top ten album chart for most of the summer, and the group toured the country as a headline act. The term "progressive rock" began to be applied to these groups who played long guitar solos, but the Jefferson Airplane was essentially a folk-rock group whose antecedents were the British folk singer Donovan and the female American singers like Joan Baez and Judy Collins. Grace Slick's voice was reminiscent of Joan Baez, and many of the songs by the group's leader and other main singer Marty Balin were optimistic anthems for an idealistic future. In interviews, the group expressed admiration for the songs and music of the Kinks, Yardbirds, and the Who, but their own songs showed little understanding of the need to hone and craft their ideas into a shape that would make them attractive and accessible to listeners not already converted to the belief that bands from San Francisco were "special". While continuing to be the most consistently successful of the San Francisco groups, the Jefferson Airplane had no more hit singles and settled for being a "cult" group until they disbanded in the early seventies.

The most spectacular success among the San Francisco groups was Big Brother and the Holding Company, whose first album for Columbia, *Cheap Thrills*, topped the album charts for eight weeks in 1968. This was a triumph of a marketing campaign to make the group's lead singer Janis Joplin a national star, capitalizing on her uninhibited, beguiling and unselfconscious sexuality. A genuine enthusiast of the blues singer Bessie Smith and the jazz singer Billie Holiday, Janis threw herself into a desperate, self-destructive lifestyle which might give some authenticity to the tortured sound of her wracked voice.

Despite pop's obsession with songs about love, and by implication about sex, the private lives of popular musicians were in general presented in a surprisingly prudish manner. *Rolling Stone* broke down the taboo with a long piece about "groupies", the name given to girls who slept with whichever musicians counted in their particular pantheon of stars; some of them kept score, others kept diaries, and a couple made plaster casts of musicians' cocks. Janis Joplin was the first female pop singer who made no bones about the connection between the messages of the songs she sang, and her own personal needs; or perhaps she was the first woman whose needs were reported in the press. Some of the female singers of the twenties had made no attempt to hide their sexual appetites, but there were no photographers and journalists on hand to report their every indiscretion. In Hollywood, press agents were sometimes run ragged trying to keep some sense of decorum in the reports about the after-dark exploits of their moviestar clients, but this was new and scurrilous stuff for pop fans after those years of discrete silence. Janis Joplin lived out the fantasies for a voyeuristic industry, achieved enormous success, and buckled under the pressure. After her suicide in 1970, "Me and Bobby McGhee" and *Pearl* topped the singles and album charts–an ironic and enigmatic epitaph for the most successful white blues singer of her era.

When the dust had settled after the record industry had swept through San Francisco and signed virtually every group of musicians who could put together enough songs to fill an album, there was surprisingly little musical content to justify all the fuss. Of the indigenous San Franciscan groups, neither the Grateful Dead nor Quicksilver Messenger Service fulfilled their promise, and a strong case could be made to support the thesis that the essence of the successful sound of San Francisco originated in Texas. Janis Joplin grew up in Port Arthur, and Steve Miller in Fort Worth before moving to Chicago and then to San Francisco where his first band included another Texan, Boz Scaggs. Other Texas-derived groups included Mother Earth, whose lead singer Tracy Nelson never fulfilled her potential of becoming a rival to Janis Joplin as a soulful singer with more taste; and the Sir Douglas Quintet, whose leader Doug Sahm continued to draw from blues, soul, and country music in the albums he made in San Francisco for Mercury.

But if there was not really a Sound of San Francisco, there was certainly an ambience, and it filtered through the record industry to the rest of the world, particularly to London where a few artists made more of it than the San Francisco-based groups had managed to do themselves: the Cream, the Jimi Hendrix Experience, the Pink Floyd, Traffic and Procol Harum were all imbued with those mysterious vibes.

The biggest hit to cash in on the city's name and aura was Scott McKenzie's "San Francisco", written by John Phillips and produced by Lou Adler for his own Ode label, distributed at the time by CBS. The record made number four in the States, but around the world it was an enormous best-seller, one of the biggest hits of all time; made in Los Angeles, of course.

For people caught up in all the excitement in San Francisco, it was sometimes hard not to lose perspective, but Bill Graham seemed to understand that beneath all the hair and behind the clouds of smoke the musicians were mostly playing the same old rhythm and blues grooves, and consistently promoted some of the active blues pioneers as support acts to the local heroes. The three Kings of the guitar blues all regularly played the Fillmore, and Albert responded particularly well, recording an exciting live album at the Fillmore for Stax, *Live Wire/Blues Power*. B.B. and Freddy began their move away from the "chittlin' circuit" too, along with Buddy Guy and Otis Rush, and also Chuck Berry and Bo Diddley, rock 'n' rollers who were temporarily redefined as bluesmen. Rock 'n' roll was still an outcast idiom, part of the unacceptable body of pop music.

There were two odd postscripts to the San Francisco saga, two artists whose music seemed only marginally, if at all, related to the rest of what was going in the Bay Area: Sly and the Family Stone, and Creedence Clearwater Revival. But these were two of the most successful and influential acts of the late sixties.

Sly and the Family Stone was the unorthodox collection of black and white men and women convened by Sylvester Stewart early in 1967 to sing and play his music. Since his successful productions of Bobby Freeman and the Beau Brummels for Autumn, Sly had recorded a few straight soul dance numbers in a style based roughly on James Brown and Otis Redding, but Sly and the Family Stone emerged as a more radical format for arrangements which interchanget instruments and voices. Yet another exile from Texas, Sly Stone had never stuck to the market distinctions that tried to isolate "soul" music from "pop" or "rock", and when he signed with Epic Records it was on the understanding that he was not to be marketed as a "black" artist. On the first album, *A Whole New Thing*, Sly turned the gospel call-and-response structure into a theatrical device in which his lead vocals and backing singers built up a commentary on life, music, and love. The world hardly noticed the record, but in 1968 Sly pulled his ideas into shape in "Dance to the Music". Within two weeks of hitting the rhythm and blues chart, the single was on the pop chart too, and eventually made both top tens, sowing seeds which were to sprout up regularly over the next fifteen years as one group after another used similar devices as the basis of their style.

The immediate, and lasting, impression of "Dance to the Music" was of a boundless energy, sustained by having instruments and voices continually pick up the melody from each other in an endless relay. After a six-month lull, Sly came back at the end of 1968 with a more serious anthem of togetherness called "Everyday People"; over a slower beat, the song again used a chorus chant, and Sly sounded genuinely upset as he implored his audience to accept differences between themselves. The record topped the singles chart, and set Sly and the Family Stone up to be one of the major acts of the era, but impenetrable perversities caused Sly to confound his admirers and supporters. He maintained an irregular output of releases, mostly alternating between the good-time celebrations along the lines of "Dance to the Music" and more sombre analytical commentaries on society in general and his own plight in particular. "Thank You (Falettinme Be Mice Elf Again)" was, despite the silly spelling of the title, an ironic and brilliantly evocative description of life in a ghetto, and put him back on top of the singles chart in 1970. Bass-player Larry

Graham, who had been in the group since the start, came to the front of the sound on this record, playing a pop-pop-popping line which hypnotized dancers and inspired an entire generation of bass-players to adopt a similar slapping, percussive approach to the instrument. The track was included on the album *There's a Riot Goin' On* in 1971, which topped the chart along with another single, "Family Affair", a moody, introspective shuffle in which Sly pioneered the use of a mechanical rhythm machine as the basic core of his track.

Unlike many contemporary black artists, whose stage presentation was locked into traditional conventions of cabaret with uniforms and precisely choreographed movements, Sly and the Family Stone had a suitably "hip" image, in which Sly himself was a charismatic figure with his hair fluffed out like a black halo. The white world was ready to pay homage to his genius, but Sly spurned its attentions and sank from view, leaving lesser talents to carry on his musical concepts without sharing his social vision.

Creedence Clearwater Revival was also dominated by one person, in this case guitarist-writer-singer John Fogerty, who stuck doggedly to the concept of making short, sharp singles while the rest of the musicians in San Francisco yearned to stretch one song across the whole side of an album. It may have made a difference that Fogerty had his base across the Bay in Berkeley, where the group recorded for Fantasy, the local independent label which had recorded modern jazz since the early fifties. With no evident ambition to be acclaimed as a visionary or virtuoso, Fogerty set out to recapture the rhythmic attack and infectious melodies of Southern dance records.

To listeners unaware that Fogerty and the rest of Creedence all lived in northern California, the records sounded as if they had been made in Memphis or New Orleans. Whereas fifteen years before, producers outside the South had never quite recaptured the essential qualities of Southern rock 'n' roll, Creedence managed to make remarkably convincing and effective "clone" versions of the Sound of the South.

VIII

During the sixties, country music virtually isolated itself from the world of pop, and most of the time it seemed that the artists and their record companies were equally happy to keep the worlds apart. The major labels each had Nashville offices with A&R chiefs looking after the country artist rosters, and little attempt was made to push even the biggest country stars onto pop radio.

Capitol Records were typical. Once frustrated by his brief to keep country artists in the country market, Ken Nelson now accepted his role and unerringly delivered the goods by cultivating three of the biggest country stars of the sixties: Sonny James (20 number one hits between 1956 and 1971, 16 of them with consecutive releases): Buck Owens (19 number ones, 1963–71, 15 of them consecutive); and Merle Haggard (11 number ones, 1966–71). Yet the pop audience hardly knew that these singers existed. Sonny James had had one huge pop hit with "Young Love" in 1957, but although most of his country hits of the sixties were revivals of well-known pop or sometimes rhythm and blues songs, they made only token appearances at the bottom of *Billboard*'s Hot 100. Tailored to suit the conservative requirements of country radio, the records had none of the flair, personality, or rhythmic drive to challenge current pop records.

Buck Owens and Merle Haggard both recorded in Bakersfield, California, which was successfully established as an effective West Coast outpost of Nashville values and techniques, despite using some of the same session musicians who were currently featured on pop hits made in Los Angeles. Although his records were rarely played on pop radio, Buck Owens did manage to get his face known outside the strict country market through TV appearances, and a couple of his songs were picked up by outsiders: Ringo Starr did a good-humoured version of "Act Naturally" on an early Beatles album, and Ray Charles had the last top ten hit of his career in 1965 with a langorous treatment of Owens' "Crying Time". Owens underscored some of the confusions and contradictions encountered in trying to define a pure country record by topping the country charts in 1969 with a version of Chuck Berry's song "Johnny B. Goode". Like many of the leading country performers, Owens was frustrated at being straight-jacketed, but like most of them he generally played safe and did not rock the boat.

Merle Haggard was among the most original singer-writers to emerge in the country market during the sixties, and his sequence of hits amounted to one of the most vivid and sympathetic portraits of white working class Americans since Jimmie Rodgers' songs back in the late twenties. But where Rodgers, Hank Williams, and Elvis Presley had forced country music to accept and adopt new musical approaches with strong blues elements, Merle Haggard tended to play musically safe. James Burton played some scintillating guitar on a few hits (notably, "Working Man Blues" in 1969) and Haggard's regular sideman Roy Nicholls added memorable licks to many of the others, but overall the impression tended to be that Haggard was sticking to established musical rules, and the pop world knew him only, if at all, for his red-neck anthem, "Okie From Muskogee". In this song and its follow-up "The Fightin' Side of Me" Haggard took a stand against the new life style of San Francisco (marijuana, sandals), encouraging the American government to call up its youth to fight in Vietnam. Reinforcing a general impression that country music somehow embodied the conservative right-wing, Haggard subsequently drifted into the same repertoire of songs about drinking and infidelity that preoccupied most of the other male country singers, especially George Jones.

Originally from Texas, where he flirted briefly with rock 'n' roll in the mid-fifties, George Jones was the archetypal country singer of the sixties, exaggerating his Southern drawl to a sometimes ludicrous extent, and invariably using the accompaniment of steel guitar and fiddle to enhance the loneliness which dominated most of his records. Of 60 country hits recorded for Mercury, United Artists and Musicor in the period from 1955 to 1971, only four appeared on the pop chart, and all very low down.

Mercury was the one major label which did not adhere to the strict divisions between pop and country that the others were content to maintain. Shelby Singleton moved in to run the Nashville office in 1961, bringing Shreveport guitarist Jerry Kennedy to help run his sessions, and he resolved to push his artists into the pop market as much as they would let him. He made his point almost immediately, chasing Leroy Van Dyke's "Walk On By" into the pop top five after it had topped the country chart; the record was a classic lament about a married man's affair, with a lively piano-based arrangement untypical of current country records, and it became an international pop hit in territories where conventional country records were often not released at all.

Sales in the country market were relatively low–100,000 copies represented a very big hit, and the main reward for the artists came in the higher fees they could charge for their live performances in the wake of intensive airplay for their latest release. Singleton was more interested in looking for million-selling pop records, and always had his ear to the ground for records which might spring out of the South West. He found Bruce Channel's "Hey! Baby" in January 1962 and Paul and Paula's "Hey Paula" at the end of the year. After both records topped the pop chart, the industry joke was that Shelby would take any record that started with "Hey", even if the rest of the song was a string of obscenities. Meanwhile, he brought some of Mercury's pop acts to record in Nashville, including the black singers Brook Benton and Clyde McPhatter; and he nurtured the wayward talent of Ray Stevens, a jack-of-all-trades from Atlanta who could play every instrument in the band and imitate every style from redneck country, through cabaret pop and novelty rock 'n' roll, to gospel and rhythm and blues. "Ahab the Arab" gave Stevens a top five hit in

1962 (including a reference to a camel called Clyde who was named after McPhatter!); but, apart from the Coasters, no pop act has ever managed to build a consistent recording career out of novelty records, and so after a modest success with a couple of genuinely funny follow-ups, "Harry the Hairy Ape" and "Speed Ball", Stevens retreated to session work for a few years.

Roger Miller joined Mercury's Smash subsidiary in 1964, and became the first singer of the sixties to figure out a way to bridge the chasm between country and pop: all but two of his 16 country hits were also pop hits, including five which made the pop top ten. Producer Jerry Kennedy was the catalyst for this "miracle", allowing Miller to sound as relaxed and spontaneous as if he were sitting in a front room, and providing a bluesy accompaniment on acoustic guitar which hardly sounded "country" at all. "Dang Me" and "Chug-A-Lug" in 1964 were childishly simple plays on words and sounds, but "King of the Road" in 1965 was a classic autobiography of a down-and-out hitch-hiker. In contrast to so many country singers, Miller made no attempt to exaggerate his Southern accent, and he sounded more like the actor Jack Lemmon, jamming with a jazz combo in some side-street night club. But Roger Miller had "paid his dues" in Nashville, and country radio stayed faithful to him, even when he came back from his travels promoting "King of the Road" to write a song called "England Swings"; another top ten hit, country and pop. That turned out to be his last big pop hit, but as his own song-writing inspiration slowed down, he picked a couple of winners by other people, recording the first versions (and first country hits) of Bobby Russell's "Little Green Apples" and Kris Kristofferson's "Me and Bobbie McGhee". For Kristofferson, this was the recording which launched his career, but Miller had had enough, and in the seventies he settled for being the proprietor of one of the best-loved night clubs in Nashville, appropriately called the King of the Road.

Two other artists on Mercury's Nashville roster were also noticed by the pop world, although neither achieved the success of Ray Stevens and Roger Miller. Jerry Lee Lewis was one of the rock 'n' roll singers who had to switch to country after finding it increasingly hard to get noticed as a pop artist, and Tom T. Hall wrote songs which crossed over, even though his own recordings were stuck with a "country" tag.

Jerry Lee's career was the archetypal example of the struggle for a Southern rock 'n' roll singer to achieve due recognition from whoever it was that took decisions about whose records could qualify as "pop", and which performers should be invited onto TV. Always a galvanizing live performer, Jerry Lee Lewis was a "natural" musician who liked to busk and bluff his way through a song, dragging his musicians in his wake, and when pop productions began to be more carefully crafted in the late fifties, Jerry Lee's sounded too much like spontaneous jam sessions–which is what most of them were. Like Ray Charles, he tended to take well-known material and reshape it to suit his own instincts, but he had none of the disciplined approach to arrangements with which Ray Charles transformed his best recordings. After four or five fruitless years with Smash, in 1968 Jerry Lee surrendered to producer Jerry Kennedy's advice on material, direction, and arrangements, and delivered a succession of honky-tonk ballads that George Jones would have been pleased to sing so well: "What's Made Milwaukee Famous (Has Made a Loser Out of Me)", "She Even Woke Me Up to Say Goodbye", and "There Must Be More to Love Than This" were all big country hits. This was pure country, which Jerry Lee delivered with even more conviction in his live performances, captured on the album *Live at the International, Las Vegas*.

Tom T. Hall was one of the most sophisticated writers who ever chose to make a living from writing country songs, and he continually came up with odd subjects and situations as a basis for his material. His voice was a limited instrument, technically and emotionally, and it took the extraordinary success of Jeannie C. Riley's version of his "Harper Valley P.T.A." in 1967 to bring attention to his own recordings. Producer Jerry Kennedy was by now head of Mercury's A&R office in Nashville, as Shelby Singleton had left to form his own independent operation in the city, triumphantly proving just how far a Nashville recording could go by selling almost four million copies worldwide of "Harper Valley" on his Plantation label. Tom T. Hall continued with country hits celebrating diverse subjects in "Ballad of Forty Dollars", "A Week in a Country Jail", and "Salute to a Switchblade". But his *tour-de-force* was the semi-concept album *In Search of a Song*, which spawned several hit singles including the country chart-topper "The Year That Clayton Delaney Died"; the album presented a challenging portrait of the South, but went unnoticed outside the country market because the pop world was still–in 1971–suspicious of straight country accompaniment.

Of the other major labels, RCA was still a dominant force in the country market under the prestigous direction of Chet Atkins, but after the limited pop success of Don Gibson few RCA country records managed to cross over. Among the artists who left the company in frustration were Roy Orbison and Roger Miller, and among those who stayed, but were probably less successful in the pop field than they should have been, were Jerry Reed and Dolly Parton.

Jerry Reed was a fireball of a guitar player from Atlanta, Georgia, who must have missed being a rock 'n' roll star in the fifties by a hair; he had recorded for Capitol and had a song or two recorded by Gene Vincent before switching to Columbia in the early sixties. Chet Atkins took him onto RCA's roster and told anyone who would listen what a remarkable guitarist he was, but Jerry never had a country hit until "Guitar Man" made the lower rungs in 1967. The theme was like "Johnny B. Goode", but the song had its own clever twist in the story-line, and a breath-taking guitar riff that carried the song along like a truck on a freeway. "Tupelo Mississippi Flash" followed, another funny tale of a man whose story has certain parallels with another boy from Tupelo, Elvis Presley. Justice was done when Elvis picked up "Guitar Man" for himself and made the pop top fifty with it, followed by a slightly bigger hit with another of Reed's songs, "U.S. Male". These were two of the best records that Elvis had made for at least seven years, but Reed had to wait until 1970 before he finally made the record which captured both his own demonic energy and public attention: "Amos Moses". Another song with a strong plot, this was all about a preacher in the Louisiana swamps who had trouble with alligators and the law, but what carried it into the pop top ten was a relentless, aggressive electric guitar riff which would have probably passed as a top-class dance record in a rhythm and blues club, if it had been released as an instrumental record with no vocals. Rock 'n' roll was back, and with the blessing of Chet Atkins; during the seventies, a few other blatant rock 'n' roll records sneaked into the country charts in the wake of "Amos Moses", and Jerry Reed himself had regular hits, although he tempered the rockers with a few sentimental ballads as corny as anything a Nashville crooner might have come up with.

Dolly Parton was one of the few successful country singers who did not adopt the nasal whine that characterized country singing after Hank Williams. Instead, her pure, clear-as-a-bell voice recalled the folk tradition upheld during the thirties by the Carter Family, reflecting her upbringing in the Blue Ridge region of East Tennessee. In contrast to the often tragic and always exhausting lives of so many female country singers, Dolly Parton somehow always retained an impression of being mistress of her own destiny, adapting, but never compromising, her style and material to suit the demands made of her. Throughout the late sixties, she partnered veteran country star Porter Wagoner on his TV show and in duets for RCA, and alongside their eight top ten hits together from 1967 she made some inroads with her own records, switching to RCA from Monument in 1968 and hitting the top of the country chart for the first time in 1970 with "Joshua". Projecting herself as a caricature busty blonde, Dolly Parton justly emerged through the seventies as not only the major female country star of the era, but the main inspiration for successful "country-rock" singers Emmy Lou Harris and Linda Ronstadt. But through this early period of her career, Dolly Parton had no pop hits at all.

Meanwhile at Columbia Records, the traditional division between country and pop came under more pressure as a result of an interesting interchange between Johnny Cash, his producer Bob Johnston, and the "folk-rock" singer Bob Dylan. Johnny Cash was among the few singers who refused to recognize the difference between country and pop, and maintained a maverick attitude to material, venues, musicians, and associates which continually upset the country establishment. He was a law unto himself, as he always had been even back in the Sun days when his ballads-with-a-beat had little connection with the boogie-and-blues based material of the label's other artists. For casual outsiders, Johnny Cash was often the only "country" artist they could think of, and of the 71 records which hit the country charts between 1955 and 1971, 40 also made the pop charts. The two biggest pop hits were "Ring of Fire" in 1963 and a good-humoured live recording of Shel Silverstein's "A Boy Named Sue" in 1969. But from the point of view of the relationship between country and pop music, his recording of Bob Dylan's "It Ain't Me Babe" in 1964 was probably more important, even though it was only a minor pop hit.

For the country music establishment, Bob Dylan represented everything that was anathema to God-fearing Americans, an upstart Jewish kid whose songs threatened to undermine the very foundations of American society. At the time, Dylan himself was still insecure about his relationship with the music industry, his audience, and other performers, and it was a great reassurance when Johnny Cash gave his seal of approval by recording "It Ain't Me Babe" and inviting Dylan to be a guest on his TV show. Dylan formed a connection with Bob Johnston, Columbia's Nashville-based producer who took over production of Dylan in New York and then brought him down to make the double album *Blonde on Blonde* in Nashville.

For many of Dylan's followers, it was a revelation that country musicians could sound so stoned and bluesy, but there on the sleeve was the unmistakable credit, "Recorded at CBS Studios, Nashville", along with the names of mostly unfamiliar musicians. Dylan went back to record his next two albums there, *John Wesley Hardin* and *Nashville Skyline,* in both of which he adopted a singing style which was more obviously "country" and evidently influenced by the recently adopted straight country style of Jerry Lee Lewis. At the time of making this move towards country music, Dylan was still the single most influential performer in the world of rock, and his every move was watched with avid interest by other performers who were inclined to transform his whims into major new trends in pop music. Producer Bob Johnston was catapulted into prominence as one of the most famous producers in the entire industry through his association with Dylan, although he never found another comparably successful artist after he left Columbia to pursue a freelance career. Countless other singer-songwriters trekked down to Nashville to see if some of the magic would rub off on them, but it was generally more advisable for a non-Southern artist to make country records outside Nashville, preferably on the West Coast where "country rock" became the most prominent new style of the early seventies.

By coincidence, just as Dylan was confusing the well-established divisions between country, pop, and rock, Columbia's Nashville division underwent a dramatic revival of fortunes with a string of straight country hits produced by Billy Sherrill and Glen Sutton for both Columbia and its Epic subsidiary. Sherrill became particularly successful as writer and producer of hits for David Houston, Tammy Wynette, and Charlie Rich which managed to "cross-over" (to use the industry expression that emerged at the time) from country to pop without any evident compromise being made in the arrangements.

Originally from Alabama, Sherrill had played rhythm and blues music in his youth, and worked in the early sixties at the studio Sam Phillips had set up in Nashville in an attempt to infiltrate the country establishment. But by 1966, Sherrill had adopted the conventions of straight country music, in which steel guitar (often played by Pete Drake) was the trademark. Billy Sherrill's songs were sometimes like caricatures of the attitudes implicit in country music, but they came out sounding convincingly sincere when Tammy Wynette sang them. Among six consecutive country chart-toppers (1967–69), "D–I–V–O–R–C–E" was a minor pop hit and "Stand By Your Man" made the pop top twenty; along with other Tammy Wynette material, they were used very effectively by director Bob Rafelson in *Five Easy Pieces*, in which Karen Black sang along with Tammy in the vain hope that the words might mean something to Jack Nicholson. The majority of the movie's audience never gave country music any attention, and for some it was a revelation that country songs could be heard as ironic commentaries, rather than as simple, sentimental slush.

The only independent record company which managed to survive in Nashville during the sixties was Fred Foster's Monument, despite losing its major artist Roy Orbison to MGM in 1965 just after scoring his biggest ever international hit with "Oh Pretty Woman". Dolly Parton recorded for the label with little success before going to RCA, and Ray Stevens revived his career with "Mr Businessman" (1968) and "Gitarzan" (1969). But the winners came through Foster's publishing arm, Combine Music, which was one of several independent publishing firms that served to feed fresh blood into the Nashville music industry; in Tony Joe White and Kris Kristofferson, Foster found two evocative story tellers with a gift for memorable titles and phrases but little obvious ambition to become recording stars themselves.

Tony Joe White did have one top ten hit with his own version of "Polk Salad Annie", an amusing recollection of a tough girl from the Louisiana swamps; producer Billy Swan devised an interesting concoction of rock (wah-wah guitar) and soul (horns, and the overall dance feel) which anticipated–and may even have influenced–the style favoured by the Rolling Stones in their "Honky Tonk Women" and "Brown Sugar". But after Brook Benton turned White's "Rainy Night in Georgia" into a standard with his hit version for Atlantic in 1970, Tony Joe never found the necessary motivation to make a recording career for himself.

Kris Kristofferson was more of a craftsman than White, and although he looked like a refugee hippie from San Francisco (which did not endear him to the collar-and-tie brigade in Nashville), his ambition was to write country songs. His break came in 1969 with recordings of "Me and Bobby McGhee" by Roger Miller and "Sunday Morning Coming Down" by Ray Stevens, and although his own album for Monument in 1970 served mainly to prove what a limited singer he was, it did introduce the world to "Help Me Make It Through the Night". Sammi Smith recorded the first hit version of the sensual song, and scored a number one country hit and a place in the pop top ten early in 1971 (produced by Jim Malloy for the independent Mega Label). Unlike Tony Joe White, Kristofferson kept going, carving a niche for himself as one of the new breed of Nashville "outlaws", and then moving into the mainstream of American entertainment by becoming a major Hollywood movie star.

Inch-by-inch, a few writers, musicians, and singers chipped out an alternative to the straight-down-the-line productions that typified Nashville's output during the sixties. The musicians who had played on Bob Dylan's records formed a recording unit on their own as Area Code 615 (the Nashville telephone code), and in the early seventies the Oklahoma guitarist J. J. Cale dropped by to use some of them on his own rhythm and blues-derived grooves, but none of them could resist the lure of playing on the straight sessions as well. To make truly distinct, idiosyncratic music, it was necessary to get out of Nashville altogether, but there were remarkably few alternative recording centres in the South. There was only Memphis, with Muscle Shoals and Atlanta as possible, but less-than-ideal, choices.

*

IX

Having been the prime source of white rock 'n' roll in the mid-fifties, Memphis was associated primarily with rhythm and blues music throughout the sixties. But just below the surface, the connections were stronger than they seemed: in the rhythm section at Stax, guitarist Steve Cropper and bass-player Duck Dunn were white, alongside the black keyboard player Booker T. Jones and drummer Al Jackson; and all of the Mar Keys horn-players were white. After Al Bell joined Stax, first as promotion man but soon becoming a major directing force, the company presented an increasingly "black" front, which left the white musicians, writers and artists of the Memphis area to look for a different outlet. In 1967, Chips Moman, Dan Penn and Spooner Oldham, all writers and musicians who had worked more in Muscle Shoals with Rick Hall than in Memphis itself, formed a new production company, AGP, and almost immediately hit the jack-pot with "The Letter", a number one hit for the Box Tops on Bell's Mala subsidiary.

The Box Tops were primarily a vehicle for sixteen-year-old singer Alex Chilton, whose voice sounded as if he had already lived the hard life of a forty-year-old blues singer. In many ways parallel to the British singer Stevie Winwood, Chilton shared a more-than-casual interest in the more progressive music associated with the contemporary psychedelic movement, and while Winwood left the Spencer Davis Group to form the more experimental Traffic, Chilton tried to pull the Box Tops into music that had less drive but more atmosphere. Hardly a purist disciplinarian himself, producer Dan Penn did well to pull two more top twenty hits out of the situation, both straightforward white rhythm and blues songs that Chilton delivered with a rare balance of intensity and relaxation: "Cry Like a Baby" and "Soul Deep".

In 1968 AGP produced another hit for Bell, with Merrilee Rush's version of the Chip Taylor song, "Angel of the Morning". In 1969, Elvis came "back home" to make an album in Memphis, and Atlantic brought the British singer Dusty Springfield to make the critically acclaimed (but commercially-disappointing) *Dusty In Memphis* album. King Curtis showcased the musicians in his entertaining and galvanizing "Memphis Soul Stew", and Chips Moman produced three pop top twenty hits for MGM Nashville secretary Martha Sharp under the *nom-de-disque* of Sandy Posey; "Born a Woman" and "Single Girl" had the flavour of the girl-talk records of the early sixties, innocent and submissive at a time when some of the folk-based female singers were beginning to present a more assertive image of womanhood.

Despite these projects, there was not enough regular and lucrative work to keep AGP going, and one by one most of the musicians moved to Nashville, where Chips Moman became one of the most successful producers of the seventies (notably with the self-described "Outlaws" Waylon Jennings and Willie Nelson).

Georgia was home to a whole host of major rhythm and blues artists who had a major influence on American pop music, but because there was no real recording scene in Atlanta, the state's musical importance always tended to be overlooked. The common thread that linked most of them was an intense, raucous vocal delivery inspired by country gospel singers; although Chuck Willis (born in Atlanta in 1928) was relatively gentle, the other four major singers delivered their songs with an unprecedented but widely influential attack: James Brown (also born in Atlanta in 1928), Little Richard (Macon, 1932), Wilson Pickett (Pratville, 1941), and Otis Redding (Dawson, 1941). Atlanta disc jockey Zenas Sears was a useful agent for the New York based record companies, but apart from Otis Redding, all these artists had to leave the state to find the studios, managers, and promoters who helped launch their careers.

For white artists, it was a different story, thanks to Bill Lowery's efforts to prove that a substantial music company could have a base in Atlanta and still be an effective force in the national industry. Lowery was a disc jockey until the mid-fifties when he launched his publishing company by representing Gene Vincent's hit "Be-Bop-A-Lula", which led to a fruitful relationship with Capitol's A&R man Ken Nelson. In 1957 Nelson produced the Sonny James version of "Young Love", which had previously been recorded by co-writer Ric Cartey as the B-side of an obscure single for RCA. After Tab Hunter had made a second cover version for Dot which outsold the James version, Lowery wound up representing one of the best-selling songs of the decade, and he ploughed the income into his own independent record label, optimistically called the National Record Company.

Launched in 1958 with a minor novelty hit by eighteen-year-old Joe South ("The Purple People Eater Meets the Witch Doctor"), NRC put out records by the cream of Atlanta's young pop and rock 'n' roll singers, several of whom went on to become major international artists; but Lowery had to close down the label and its Fairlane subsidiary within three years, on the verge of bankruptcy. Among the other now famous names whose records were issued in this period were Jerry Reed, David Houston, Ray Stevens, Clarence and Calvin (Clarence Carter), and Billy Joe Royal. The only real hit was the sing-along novelty, "Robbin' the Cradle" by Tony Bellus, which stayed on the pop chart for six months in 1959, but Bellus himself was among the company's few artists who was never heard from again.

Just as Lowery was forced to close his record operation, his luck turned. Leroy Van Dyke's recording of a Lowery copyright "Walk On By" took off on Mercury, where Ray Stevens coincidentally and simultaneously had his first hit with "Ahab the Arab". But both those records were Nashville recordings, and Lowery was determined to avoid the risk of losing his writers to Nashville publishers, and he was anxious to keep clear of the limited country market. In 1962, he made contact with Rick Hall, who had produced a national pop hit for Dot by a local bell-hop, Arthur Alexander; the rhythm and arrangement of "You Better Move On" were superficially similar to the hits by Ben E. King since he left the Drifters, but there was an edge of menace and forboding in Alexander's song and delivery which gave it a special character. The Rolling Stones were inspired to cover the song, and Bill Lowery was inspired to get in touch with producer Rick Hall to find out more about his studio, ambitions, and approach. The two men shared a common mistrust of the closed-door attitudes in Nashville, and Lowery put several of his writers in Hall's hands.

The first successful project to come out of this new Muscle Shoals/Atlanta liaison was a black vocal group, the Tams, who had a minor hit with Joe South's "Untie Me" on the independent Arlen label in 1962, and then made the pop top ten the next year with "What Kind of Fool" on ABC-Paramount, written by another Lowery protégé, Ray Whitley. The connection with ABC had been made the year before, when they picked up Tommy Roe, an Atlanta pop singer whose "Sheila" had been a minor local hit on the indie Judd label in 1960. Roe's re-recording of the song for ABC topped the pop chart in 1962, and he was back up in the top three the following year with another nursery rhyme kind of song, "Everybody". One of the first solo singers to recover from the shock of the British Invasion, Roe came back with two more top ten hits in 1966, and actually topped the chart again as late as 1969 with "Dizzy", yet another hit which used the "La Bamba" chord progression. Hardly a memorable innovator in the annals of pop, Tommy Roe did prove Bill Lowery's belief that a Southern boy could be a consistent pop hit-maker.

By far the most interesting and original writer in Lowery's stable was Joe South, who for most of the sixties was better known in the industry as a session guitarist than as the singing writer he wanted to be. A guitarist with a distinctive "low" sound reminiscent of Pop Staples and Curtis Mayfield, Joe played on countless sessions in Muscle Shoals (for Rick Hall), New York (on sessions produced by

Jerry Wexler for Aretha Franklin, and by Bob Johnson for Simon and Garfunkel), and Nashville (including Dylan's *Blonde on Blonde* sessions produced by Bob Johnston). Although Joe South was defiantly not a country artist and had little patience with Nashville attitudes, his first consistent success as a writer came from a series of pop hits he wrote for Billy Joe Royal, another Atlanta artist who recorded for Columbia in Nashville and whose versions of "Down In The Boondocks" (top ten in 1965) and "Hush" established two standards for South; the British group Deep Purple revived "Hush" in 1968 and made the American top five, which may have provided the leverage that secured Joe South a recording contract with Capitol.

A versatile musician and an adept recording engineer, Joe South was among the first performers to use multi-track facilities as a means of singing and playing virtually all the vocal and instrumental parts of his records himself, and what he lost in technical quality he made up for in "feel". His sombre, soul-searching songs were collected into an album appropriately called *Introspect*, but the psychedelic artwork failed to lure the desired "rock" audience to a singer who was unmistakably Southern and not at all fashionable. South's passionate, preaching delivery was undeniably sincere as he railed against prejudice and hypocrisy in "Birds of a Feather", "Redneck", "These Are Not My People" and "Games People Play", the last of which became a top twenty hit as a single in 1969. The title of that hit was taken from a popular psychology paperback by Eric Berne, but the ideas were clearly South's own beliefs, spat out with vengeance and backed up with heavily-distorted guitar; ironically, the song's melody was so strong that it was soon absorbed into every cabaret singer's repertoire, where it lost most of its rebellious character.

Yet another Atlanta singer, Freddy Weller took "Games People Play" and "These Are Not My People" into the country charts (for Columbia) in 1969, and the following year Lynn Anderson had a world-wide hit with her version of another song from *Introspect*, "(I Never Promised You a) Rose Garden". Freddy Weller's career took a strange turn when he joined Paul Revere's Raiders in 1969; he wrote a couple of minor hits for them, and sang lead on the group's first ever number one hit, "Indian Reservation" by John D. Loudermilk (1971). He managed to do justice to Joe South's "Bird of a Feather" with a version that gave the Raiders their last top thirty hit the same year, while simultaneously sustaining a career under his own name as a straight country singer with a country hit version of Chuck Berry's "Promised Land", and with several songs of his own which treated sex more openly and honestly than was usual on country radio.

For Bill Lowery, the widespread pop success of Tommy Roe, Joe South and Freddy Weller was vindication of his long campaign to establish an Atlanta-based equivalent of the publishing/production operations which Don Kirshner had set up, so successfully, in New York and Los Angeles. Some of Lowery's earlier artists such as Ray Stevens and Jerry Reed had signed to Nashville-based publishers, but among the more recent recruits to Lowery Music were the writers Buddy Buie and Jim Cobb who wrote and produced several moody pop hits with a jazz-cum-folk flavour for the Florida-based group the Classics IV, including "Spooky" (1967), "Stormy" (1968) and "Traces" (1969), all for Imperial. Cobb and Buie were later involved in the moderately successful rock group the Atlanta Rhythm Section, but the late sixties had seen the pinnacle of Atlanta's contributions to American pop music.

Although it was possible to dig into the pop charts and find proof that Southern studios, writers, producers and performers could still overcome the odds stacked against them and make hits, the overriding impression during the late sixties was that for every hit made in the South, there were several made elsewhere with ingredients that were unmistakably Southern. Those same elements of blues, country, and gospel music were still at the core of many of the era's best-selling acts, just as they had been in the hey-day of rock 'n' roll; and they were most obviously–and deliberately–the ingredients of Creedence Clearwater Revival.

The series of hits by Creedence Clearwater Revival–nine top ten hits in the years 1969 to 1971–managed to embody the essence of what had always made Southern records unique. The words and melody of each song were simply stated, so that it was impossible to think of the words or the tune without intuitively feeling the rhythmic drive. With each record, the writer John Fogerty seemed to set himself a slightly different model: "Proud Mary" conjured the smooth glide of the Stax rhythm section of the mid-sixties, whereas the follow-up, "Bad Moon Rising", went back ten years to the Sun sound of Scotty Moore or Carl Perkins, with a guitar lick weaving through the song. "Green River" had a tougher feel, closer to the bluesy funk of Dale Hawkins' "Susie Q", a cover version of which had actually given Creedence its first top twenty hit in 1968.

All of these hits were for Fantasy, and it was somehow very appropriate that these tributes to the sound of the south should be recorded for an independent label at a time when so many artists were selling out to majors at the first opportunity. "Down on the Corner" in 1969 went back to the sound of Booker T. and the M.G.'s, adapting the figure from "Soul Limbo" to accompany an evocative song about kids playing out in the street, but "Travellin' Band" was too close for comfort to the feel of Little Richard's "Good Golly Miss

Molly". There were more hits to come, but they served mainly to showcase Fogerty's increasing versatility; he did use a rhythm section of drummer Doug Clifford and bass player Stu Cook, but it was apparent that Fogerty could have played everything himself, as he proved later with the Blue Ridge Rangers.

Tough and assertive, without being macho and mindless like so many white blues records, the Creedence singles were timely reminders of how effective rock 'n' roll could be if it stayed simple and did not try to be too clever; but there was an unavoidable sense that Creedence achieved success by default, because the Box Tops and Joe South lost concentration. And what distracted them, apart from what was going on across the bay from Berkeley in San Francisco, were the games people were playing with Southern music across the Atlantic in Britain.

13

ELECTRIC WHITE ORCHESTRAS: BRITISH ROCK PROGRESSES

While America reeled in shock under the impact of the first British Invasion, back in Britain another generation of musicians gathered their resources for a second wave assault. But whereas the Beatles and their cohorts had in effect revitalized American pop and its associated sources of rock 'n' roll and black dance music, this second wave went further and deeper into America's root forms, into blues and gospel. The distinction was between "pop" and "rock", which led to important distinctions between radio and live music, and between singles acts and album acts.

These two different worlds were reminiscent of the divisions which had opened up in the mid-fifties, when rock 'n' roll attracted fans who despised most of the conventional, contemporary pop; but at that time, the industry had not been interested in restructuring itself to maintain those distinctions, and had instead absorbed into the mainstream the more adaptable rock 'n' rollers while leaving the others to fade into obscurity. This time there was a new breed of manager and producer in the British music industry who recognized the opportunities there would be for themselves and their protégés if they maintained and exaggerated the distinctions between "pop" and "rock".

One of the fundamental differences between pop and rock was that a pop act was essentially unknown until it had a radio hit. From a radio producer's point of view, it did not matter whether a record had been made by a group which had "paid its dues" for years in obscure clubs, or if the entire project had been confected in a studio by a producer who wrote the song, hired the musicians and singers, and made up a name to go on the label. What counted in a pop record was, is it catchy, melodic, entertaining?

During 1967, the British Labour Government finally closed down the off-shore pirate radio stations which had provided most of Britain with all day pop music for the first time, making a mockery of the old fashioned fare still being served up by the BBC's Light Programme. To forestall national outrage at losing the pirate stations, the BBC was obliged to concede, at last, that there was a real demand for a pure pop station; Radio One was inaugurated, modelled closely on the pirate stations and using many of the disc jockeys they had brought to fame.

Either by coincidence, or as a result of an unofficial, but effective policy, there was a sharp reduction in the "black" content of Radio One compared with the pirates, both literally in the sense of records made by black Americans, and indirectly in records made by British groups with black influences. But while pop on the radio was getting whiter and lighter, British live music took the opposite direction, absorbing more blues influence than ever and, for the first time, coming to grips with gospel forms as well.

When pop groups performed live, they normally attracted an audience which expected to see them play their well-known songs as near as possible to the way they had recorded them. But the definition of a rock group was that it included some element of improvisation in its live performance, and that its ability to attract a substantial audience to its gigs was not completely dependent on having just had a hit single. In practice, these distinctions were not absolute: there were "pop" groups who did dare to improvise, and there were rock groups which played basically the same set in the same manner night after night. But for a large section of the audience, the difference between "pop" and "rock" was of vital importance, and the music press encouraged its readers to regard rock performers as "artists" whose every thought on any subject deserved serious attention.

For the groups who were classified as "pop"–either by choice or by the pigeon-holing chroniclers of the day–the daunting prospect of shaking off comparisons with the Beatles was more than they could cope with, and much of their output was second-rate. In contrast to the flock of British pop groups which had enjoyed substantial American success in the mid-sixties, only one British pop group of the late sixties had more than an isolated hit–significantly, the Bee Gees' manager Robert Stigwood also looked after Cream, one of a bevy of rock groups who were rapturously received in the States.

Stylistically, this new British "rock" drew from three musical idioms. Blues was the obvious inspiration for Cream, the Jeff Beck Group, the Jimi Hendrix Experience, Led Zeppelin, and Fleetwood Mac, while gospel was an important influence for Traffic, Procol Harum, and Joe Cocker, and folk was part of the basis for the Pink Floyd and David Bowie.

Most of these bands and musicians started out in a similar way, through the archetypal "rock" route of playing live, attracting an increasingly strong following which translated directly into album sales; there were important exceptions to the basic pattern, and in some cases there was even a conscious attempt to pretend that this pattern applied when in fact a more "pop" method had really been used. Not only were some of the acts launched with records made with session musicians, but several of them were more dependent on the impetus given by a hit single than their supporters cared to admit.

The exact truth is not always what counts. The music press built up a mythical world of "rock" in which music was "progressing" at unimagined rates, leaving all its predecessors behind like prehistoric curiosities. Championed in Britain by the *Melody Maker*, the groups made pilgrimages to America where *Rolling Stone*, FM Radio, and audiences at live concerts welcomed them even more enthusiastically. Hearing the "far-out" lyrics and "spaced-out" solos of the Doors, the Jefferson Airplane, and The Grateful Dead, the British musicians returned to Britain fired with the enthusiasm to be even more experimental and adventurous.

Although there were many parallels between the development of music in Britain and in America in this period, there was one fundamental difference which had repercussions that lasted for at least the next fifteen years. In America, the leading underground bands all signed direct to major record companies, enabling those companies to reinforce their hold on the American record industry and effectively drive out virtually all the indie companies. The result was a drift into conformity, sterility and repetition that destroyed much of the momentum of the previous fifteen years.

In Britain, the reverse happened. Most of the adventurous British musicians were managed by men who used their power to drive a wedge into the British record industry, forming production companies or independent labels which licensed product to the majors without sacrificing autonomy or losing all ownership rights. Directly and indirectly, the British progressive rock groups financed and inspired a generation of new independent record labels which provided the platform for the inventive British musicians of the seventies.

The late sixties turned into a fascinating three-way struggle for power and control, in which the four major companies who had traditionally dominated the British industry–Decca, EMI, Philips, and Pye–were challenged by new competitors from abroad, notably CBS and Polydor, but at the same time all of them were being undermined from below by the independent managers and producers.

Most of the indie operators already had at least one foot in the door of the British record industry before they started their own labels or production companies, either as managers of successful groups or as producers who had recorded hits on a freelance basis. Their story is a tangled web which defies a straightforward linear narrative, and is prefaced with a reference to a couple of labels which predated them, Oriole and Melodisc.

Oriole Records* was a well organized, full-blown independent label which scored international hits in the mid-fifties with Russ Hamilton and Chas McDevitt's Skiffle Group. During the early sixties, Oriole was licensee for Berry Gordy's family of labels, but just at the moment when the balance of power was about to shift in favour of independent labels, in 1965 Oriole's owner Maurice Levy sold his entire operation–recording studio, pressing plant, and catalogue–to the American Columbia company (who thereby got a headstart for its British CBS label which its American competitors never recovered). Oriole's distribution was handled by a network of independent wholesalers based in each of the major conurbations–London, Manchester, Glasgow, Birmingham, and Belfast–which otherwise dealt mainly in slow moving items in specialist categories like folk, jazz, and classical music; and one other category: West Indian music, which was Melodisc's line.

Melodisc† had been started in the early fifties, when calypso music from Trinidad was the best known West Indian idiom, and in 1961 owner Emil Sharrock launched a subsidiary label, Blue Beat, to cater for an emergent new style from Jamaica, known there as "ska". Pronounced as a Russian might say it, with a silent "y", "sky'a, sky'a sky'a" was the sound that the guitar made on every first and third beat. This was a back-to-front reversal of the familiar second-and-fourth back-beat of rock 'n' roll, but it had an infectious danceability that reached not only the immigrant Jamaican community in Britain, but also attracted native British kids who began to discover these records by Prince Buster, Laurel Aitken, Derrick Morgan and others.

* ORIOLE RECORDS. *Owned by Maurice Levy; sold to CBS in 1965. A&R: Jack Baverstock, John Schroeder.*
Pop: Russ Hamilton (licensed to Kapp in U.S.), Chas McDevitt's Skiffle Group with Nancey Whiskey (licensed to Chic), Maureen Evans.
Licensed from US: Mercury (mid-fifties), Motown (early-sixties).

Subsidiaries:

EMBASSY. *Budget-line cover versions of current hits, sold exclusively through Woolworths. Several well-known artists are reputed to have made their first professional recordings for Embassy, whose best-known singer was Johnny Worth; as Les Vandyke, Johnny wrote most of Adam Faith's and Eden Kane's hits.*

REALM. *A jazz and blues budget label which licensed material from Savoy, Shad, and other American labels.*

† MELODISC. *Formed in 1952 by Emil Sharrock.*
Calypso: Lord Kitchener.

Subsidiary:

BLUE BEAT.
Ska: Prince Buster, Laurel Aitken, Derrick Morgan.

As mentioned earlier, British bands including Georgie Fame and His Blue Flames began to include the "ska" beat and songs in their jazz and rhythm-and-blues repertoire, which helped to spread an appreciation for the originals made in Jamaica.

The Jamaican industry was chaotic by British or American standards, because singers very rarely signed exclusive contracts with one record label. Prince Buster was in that respect unusual: he was a club disc jockey who not only wrote, sang, and ran his own band, but owned his own shop and record label; he did not sing for other producers, and so his contracts with Blue Beat were effectively exclusive. But the other producers were not also singers; they hired a vocalist on a song-by-song basis, paying a flat session fee, and then making whatever profit they could by selling the rights. So if one producer had a hit with a singer, all the other producers quickly recorded something by the same singer, or released something they had previously recorded with him. Concerned only with selling a few thousand records, the producers did not show any interest in the concept of nurturing a singer's career by restricting his availability and output.

Prince Buster became particularly popular, especially through a series of records which presented a cartoon-like parody of a Jamaican judge called Judge Dread, who handed out ferocious sentences lasting five hundred or a thousand years to young men who wept in a vain appeal to his better nature. Behind the banter and village-hall overacting, the band played a steady rhythm (known in Britain as "blue beat", after the name of the label which issued Prince Buster's records) and a group chanted a sing-along chorus. These records were too bizarre and ethnic to qualify as straight pop records on British radio, and their influence did not really show until more than ten years later when the "Two-Tone" bands swept through the British charts: the Specials launched this movement with "Gangsters" in 1979, which was closely based on Prince Buster's only British top-twenty hit, "Al Capone" (Blue Beat, 1967): Madness took their name from one of Buster's songs, and launched their career with a single dedicated to him ("The Prince") and an album named after another of his songs (*One Step Beyond*, Stiff, 1979). The belated success of groups with the sax-organ-and-guitar line-up of ska bands confirmed the impression that with better distribution, ska might have gained earlier acceptance into the mainstream of British pop music. But Melodisc never showed signs of such ambitions, and it was left to Island Records to break down the barriers and infiltrate the labyrinths of the British entertainment industry, where prejudice against black music, and particularly against colonial immigrants, was so easily disguised by terms like "ethnic minority interest".

Once Blue Beat established a steady flow of releases from Jamaica to Britain, there were soon more records being made in Jamaica than Blue Beat could handle, and in 1962 Island Records* was formed as a rival alternative by Chris Blackwell. A young white Jamaican who had been educated in Britain, Blackwell was a music fan for whom running a record company sometimes seemed like a hobby, but in partnership with David Betteridge he gradually applied a more systematic approach and eventually established an operation which became an inspiration and model for a new generation of British record companies.

Island licensed productions from the leading producers of the period, notably Coxone Dodd at Studio One, Duke Reid at Channel One, Lee Perry and Leslie Kong, but it became clear that the only way to achieve exclusive rights was to sign singers direct and record them in Britain. Jackie Edwards, Jimmy Cliff and others were duly flown to Britain, but it proved surprisingly difficult to recreate the atmosphere of a Jamaican studio which would bring out the best from these singers. And there was a second problem: most of the Jamaican singers regarded their own music as a poor cousin of American soul music; what they really wished for was to be able to make records like Otis Redding, Sam Cooke, the Impressions–Curtis Mayfield of the Impressions was a particularly big influence. So once the singers had a chance to find different musicians from the Jamaican session-players, they tried to make soul records.

Undoubtedly frustrated by all this, Blackwell pulled off one coup with Millie's "My Boy Lollipop" in 1964. He convened a bunch of British session musicians (including Rod Stewart on harmonica), and had them play a Jamaican "blue beat" accompaniment for an old rhythm and blues song from 1956; Millie was a young Jamaican singer who sounded very much like Shirley from Shirley and Lee, the New Orleans duo who had been enormously popular in the West Indies in the mid-sixties. Blackwell could hardly have anticipated the extraordinary success of his production, which topped the British charts, and went to number two in the USA. But he must have expected something unusual to happen, because instead of putting the record out on his own Island label, he licensed the production to Philips.

* ISLAND RECORDS. *Formed in 1962 by Chris Blackwell.*
Reggae (1962–66): Jackie Edwards, Jimmy Cliff, the Blues Busters, Owen Gray, the Wailers, the Vikings, the Skatalites.

Subsidiary:

SUE. *Manager by Guy Stevens.*
Rhythm and blues (licensed from America): Inez and Charlie Foxx (licensed from US Sue), Bob and Earl (licensed from Marc), various blues and soul records from Ace, Fire-Fury, etc.

As noted earlier, Blackwell subsequently licensed the Spencer Davis Group to Philips for Britain, and achieved two British chart-toppers with versions of soul songs written by Jackie Edwards, "Keep On Running" and "Somebody Help Me". Significantly, Blackwell retained the right to license the group's material in the States, which became an increasingly relevant factor for British independent producers. Previously, British majors had signed artists for the world, and made substantial income from foreign earnings; now they had to settle for British rights, paying higher royalties than they had been accustomed to.

From 1965 to 1969, the major British labels–Decca, EMI, and Pye–found themselves being squeezed out of the British market which they had taken for granted since the mid-fifties, together with the Dutch Philips company. At their own level, these majors were challenged by British-based subsidiaries set up by most of the American majors companies and several indies: after CBS set up its UK office in 1965, RCA, MGM, and MCA followed suit (with much less success), along with Liberty-United Artists, Atlantic, and Bell, while the German Deutsche Grammophon company set up its Polydor subsidiary in Britain in 1966.

All this activity would not have made sense if selling records in Britain had been the only aim; the lure was the possibility of selling records around the world with British artists. But such masterplans were thrown into confusion by independent producers who beat all the record companies to the post, signing artists on world-wide contracts and then licensing territory-by-territory as Chris Blackwell had done with the Spencer Davis Group.

Compared with most independent producers at this time, Chris Blackwell had two distinct advantages: he had considerable independent means, which enabled him to finance his own recordings and therefore negotiate from a position of strength; and he had the background experience of running Island records, which meant he knew what he was looking for from a distributor. Most of his contemporary independent label owners had more limited experience when they started their companies, usually as managers, sometimes as producers.

Of the independent labels which recorded influential artists in this period, Immediate was the first to be founded. Andrew Oldham had become well known in the British music industry as manager of the Rolling Stones, and was able to persuade EMI to offer his Immediate label what was called a "P&D deal" in 1965. "P&D" stood for pressing and distribution: under this arrangement, the label owned all rights to the material and was responsible for marketing and promotion; the distributor pressed the records and sold them to the shops. A crucial detail was subject to negotiation–who paid for the overstocks if too many records were pressed up; in this case, EMI took what was called "the stock risk".

The first release on Immediate was "Hang On Sloopy" by the McCoys, licensed from Bert Berns' Bang label, which duly made the British top five and set Immediate up as a credible alternative to the majors. Oldham and his partner Tony Calder were able to persuade managers to move their protégés from other labels (the Small Faces and Amen Corner left Decca, Fleetwood Mac left Blue Horizon), and it did not hurt to be able to bring in a Rolling Stone or two to write or produce a record: Mick Jagger did a spectacular job for Chris Farlowe on "Out of Time", achieving one of the best balances of a rock rhythm section against a string arrangement, and pulling a vocal out of Farlowe which he was never able to repeat.

Immediate* looked set to become a major force in the British record industry, with the Small Faces as its premier act. Early records with Decca had suggested that the Small Faces were nothing more than a second division imitation-soul group, but with "Itchycoo Park" (1967) and "Lazy Sunday" (1968) for Immediate, the group's main songwriters Steve Marriott and Ronnie Lane temporarily closed the gap between pop and rock, coming up with records that were full of both melody and character. Aided and abetted by engineer Glyn Johns, the Small Faces experimented with studio tricks while bringing out a much more "British" sound than their earlier releases: "Itchycoo Park" was a straight forward celebration of being stoned; "Lazy Sunday" was sung in a cockney accent, and followed in the line of Ray Davies' songs for the Kinks, a portrait of London life which brimmed over with infectious humour.

Ironically, Immediate never quite managed to spread the impact of its British success abroad, and despite getting in on the early days of another major act, the Nice, the label closed down in 1970; symbolically, the American Warner Brothers label took over its offices.

The second important British indie of this period was formed by Robert Stigwood, an Australian who had managed actor-singer John Leyton and now represented the Bee Gees and Cream, who would at the time have been classified as archetypal representatives of the distinct "pop" and "rock" camps. In 1966, Stigwood placed the Bee Gees directly with the newly formed Polydor label, while

* IMMEDIATE. *Formed in 1965 by Andrew Oldham and Tony Calder.*
Pop: Chris Farlowe and the Thunderbirds, Small Faces (from 1967), Amen Corner, P. P. Arnold.
Rock: Fleetwood Mac (1969), the Nice, Humble Pie.
From US: the McCoys (licensed from Bang).
Distributed by EMI (1965–66), Philips (1967–69).

licensing his own Reaction label to the same company.*

The Bee Gees were the best of the contemporary groups who sounded–intentionally or by accident–like the Beatles, and they had a long series of hits both in Britain and America, almost all dirge-like ballads featuring Barry Gibb's sobbing vocals. Cream represented a new concept in pop music, an all-star line-up of poll-winning musicians from three different groups who came together to display their virtuosity and pursue a policy of musical adventure and exploration together. Bass-player Jack Bruce and drummer Ginger Baker were both highly respected among other musicians, but the popular hero of the trio was undoubtedly the guitarist Eric Clapton, who had achieved his fame by the most indirect method, dropping out of two groups just at the moment they each became commercially successful.

Clapton's defection from the Yardbirds has already been noted; he joined John Mayall's Bluesbreakers, a purist blues group dedicated to recreating as accurately as possible the sound and style of contemporary Chicago blues players, including Otis Rush, Buddy Guy, and Magic Sam; a couple of Texan guitarists qualified as inspirations too, Freddy King and Albert Collins. None of the American musicians were in any way widely known in Britain, where even B. B. King was still so obscure that hardly any of his records were issued in Britain. Clapton invariably insisted that his own playing fell short of their masterly control and emotional effect, but for the British fans who flocked to see the Bluesbreakers playing live, Clapton was the best. John Mayall was by comparison a journeyman singer and instrumentalist, but to his credit he retained a genuine commitment to the blues while encouraging a succession of British blues musicians to develop their skills. His group recorded for Decca, who deputed teenage blues fan Mike Vernon to produce them, aided by engineer Gus Dudgeon. With the emphasis on authenticity–no overdubs, no studio effects–the Bluesbreakers recorded an album featuring Clapton, who left the group before it was issued. To the surprise of all

* POLYDOR. *British division of Deutsche Grammophon set up in 1966.*
Pop: the Bee Gees.
Licensed labels:

REACTION. *Formed in 1966 by Robert Stigwood.*
Rock groups: Cream (1966–67), the Who (1966).
(Label absorbed by Polydor in 1968 and reconstituted as RSO in 1974).

TRACK. *Formed in 1967 by Kit Lambert and Chris Stamp.*
Rock: the Who (from 1967), the Jimi Hendrix Experience, the Crazy World of Arthur Brown, Thunderclap Newman.

MARMALADE. *Formed in 1968 by Giorgio Gomelsky.*
Rock: the Brian Auger Trinity with Julie Driscoll.

ATLANTIC. *British division of American Atlantic.*
Rock: Led Zeppelin, Yes.

concerned, the record hit the British album charts, and while Mayall recruited a new guitarist Peter Green, Clapton responded to Robert Stigwood's encouragement to form Cream.

In retrospect, there was an air of inevitability about the success of Cream in Britain, where rock 'n' roll was primarily a guitar-based music. While Americans were twisting it into a vehicle for teen idols who did not play their own instruments, Britain favoured the guitar heroes: Buddy Holly, Eddie Cochran, Gene Vincent, and the Everly Brothers. The huge success of the Shadows depended on an army of followers who identified with the three young men wielding guitars, and most of the British pop groups of the mid-sixties featured guitars both in their sound and their visual images. Few British guitarists dared to be as bold and sexually suggestive with their instruments as Chuck Berry, Bo Diddley, Johnny "Guitar" Watson and other black Americans, but Keith Richard of the Rolling Stones became increasingly aggressive, pointing his guitar more like a gun than a sexual organ. And along with a more assertive visual use of guitar, the musicians were turning their sound up and finding that the audiences liked it.

So when Cream came on stage and bombarded their audience with an onslaught of virtuosity and power, word got out and people lined up around the block to get in. A residency at London's Marquee club and a college tour turned out to be all that was necessary to launch a legend, and that combination was soon institutionalized for every would-be blues-rock group.

Cream duly hit not only the British album charts but also the singles charts with surprisingly commercial songs: "I Feel Free" had a haunting melody and a beguiling lyric, as well as some searing guitar-work from Clapton. But the group's real breakthrough was in America, where they found an audience which encouraged them to improvise and extend far longer than they had ever dared in Britain. During 1968, Cream became one of the best-selling acts of the year, topping the album charts with *Wheels of Fire* and filling every hall and stadium they played in. The group broke up a year later, but by then the seeds had been sown in thousands of young American musicians, and the blues was belatedly recognized as the basis for most of what was now called "rock music".

Back in Britain, Polydor followed up the successful liaison with Robert Stigwood by making a similar arrangement to license Track Records, formed by the Who's managers Kit Lambert and Chris Stamp. The Who's first three singles had been released on Brunswick, the British arm of American Decca who retained American rights to the group while British rights switched to Stigwood's Reaction for three singles and then to Track from mid-1967. For a while, Track looked set to become a substantial force in the British industry, achieving top-of-the-chart singles with the Crazy World of Arthur Brown ("Fire", 1968) and Thunderclap Newman ("Something in the Air", 1969), and six top ten albums by the Jimi Hendrix Experience. Throughout the late sixties, Hendrix rivalled Eric Clapton as rock's number one guitar hero, and it was an index of how times had changed that the American had to go to Britain to establish his reputation.

Born in Seattle, Washington, in 1942, Jimi Hendrix personified almost the entire story of rock 'n' roll in a career that included playing with two of the real stars of the era, Little Richard and the Isley Brothers. Although his own tastes ranged across most of current rock 'n' roll, Hendrix was always likely to be classified as a blues, rhythm and blues or soul musician while he stayed in America, and his break was to be seen at a club in Greenwich Village by Chas Chandler, the bass-player with the Animals, who paid his fare to London and acted as his manager and producer in partnership with the Animals' manager Mike Jeffreys.

In Britain, Jimi Hendrix was encouraged to live out a life of extravagant, exotic flamboyance. Flanked by bass-player Noel Redding and drummer Mitch Mitchell, two previously unknown British musicians who roamed restlessly around the rhythms and melodies of his guitar improvisations, Hendrix recorded as his first single the song "Hey Joe" which he had heard by the Leaves in Los Angeles earlier in the year. Mysterious, menacing, and dynamically very well paced, the record in effect picked up on the blues where the Rolling Stones had left the idiom after topping the British charts with "Little Red Rooster" in 1964, and "Hey Joe" by the Jimi Hendrix Experience made the British top ten early in 1967. Just as Britain was beginning to feel the reverberations of the drug culture of San Francisco, here was a young black man from the West Coast with frizzy hair, outrageously colourful clothes, and no inhibitions about using the guitar as a sexual symbol.

Vocally, Hendrix was no great shakes, but when he found a song that suited his more-or-less conversational delivery, he filled in all the meaning and emotions with flickering guitar work. Where Clapton played with attack and tension, Hendrix tended to take his time and stay relaxed; who was "better" was a matter of personal taste, but the rivalry helped to focus attention on blues guitar-playing in general, and even led to some attention for the originators. The two guitarists who seemed to have impressed Hendrix most were John Lee Hooker and Albert King, the one moody and menacing, the other casual and dextrous.

Having taken Britain by storm, Hendrix returned to the States triumphantly, on his own terms. At the Monterey Pop Festival in June 1967 he displayed all the tricks of his stage show, seeming, at one point, to play the guitar with his teeth (an old trick adapted from T-Bone Walker's gimmick of playing it behind his head–the fret-board fingers do the playing), and finally setting fire to the guitar itself. Reprise Records signed him for America, and Hendrix joined Sly Stone as one of the two black musicians who defied all the normal stereotypes that the music industry liked to pin on its black artists. They both experimented with "wah-wah" guitar effects, spent an eternity in the recording studio, and delivered erratic but sometimes brilliant live performances. The commercial pinnacle was the double-LP *Electric Ladyland*, which topped the American album charts a few weeks after Cream in 1968, but the lifestyle attendant on being the music industry's favour black hippie guitar hero was too much; Hendrix's name was added to the roll call of rock's casualties in 1970 after a drug overdose.

Of all the other guitarists who sprang to prominence during the late sixties, Jeff Beck and Jimmy Page bore comparison with Clapton and Hendrix. Jeff Beck had replaced Clapton in the Yardbirds, and played an important role in introducing improvised guitar solos into pop music through his brief instrumental breaks in their hit singles. After leaving the group, he recorded two albums for British EMI under Mickie Most's studio supervision, but although they both made the American top twenty album charts, and the group (featuring Rod Stewart on vocals) toured the States, Beck never became a "first division" name.

Jimmy Page was probably the most accomplished rock guitarist of his generation, and was still in his early twenties when he played vital roles on several seminal records by the Who, Them and Joe Cocker, among countless other sessions. But payments for session work were normally flat fees, and it became increasingly apparent that the name of the game was to be on a royalty share of a successful record; the only way to qualify for that was to be prepared to form a self-contained group which would back up its recordings with live work. By a circuitous route, Page arrived at the logical solution: he had played some live dates with the Yardbirds in their last year or so, and when they finally disbanded altogether, Page undertook to fulfil a contract for a short Scandinavian tour under the name of the New Yardbirds, with three hastily-recruited allies. Changing the group's name to Led Zeppelin, managed by former Yardbirds roadie Peter Grant, the new group signed direct to American Atlantic (whose co-director Jerry Wexler had heard about Page's prowess from Dusty Springfield and producer Bert Berns). And by another circuitous route, Led Zeppelin's records were released in Britain through Polydor.

Back in the fifties, Atlantic licensed its records to Decca's London label, along with most of the other American indies. As Atlantic outlasted the others into the sixties, the company became more concerned with its own label's identity, but the only concession that Decca would make was to adapt its label to read "London-Atlantic". This still frustrated Atlantic, who found a more flexible licensee in Polydor. Anxious to acquire the rights to Atlantic's substantial catalogue and wide-ranging roster, Polydor not only offered Atlantic its own label identity in Britain, but offered Atlantic first option on the American rights to the artists on its own roster. Atlantic were thus able to pick up the American rights to the Bee Gees and Cream, and so struck up a fruitful relationship with Robert Stigwood which led to the formation of his RSO label in the States. Meanwhile, the timing of the deal gave Polydor a hit with Percy Sledge's "When a Man Loves a Woman", the gospel-laced soul hit which turned out to be a hugely influential record in Britain. Among the other Atlantic artists who came out in Britain through this Polydor tie-up was Led Zeppelin.

The first album by Led Zeppelin was fairly subdued, compared both to other rock blues records of its time (1969) and to the subsequent releases by the group. Obviously modelled on the sound and format of the Jeff Beck Group, Led Zeppelin's record was altogether more disciplined and better-paced. In addition to the experienced Jimmy Page, bass-player John Paul Jones was a proficient arranger who had worked on many pop hits, and between them they evolved effective structures for the intense attack of Robert Plant's vocals and the thunderous drumming of John Bonham, who had previously played together in the obscure Band of Joy.

Where Cream had tended to veer away from the straight blues format, Led Zeppelin stuck more faithfully to predictable patterns, and became the world's best-selling group during the early seventies. The crunching attack of Muddy Waters' "You Shook Me" and Bo Diddley's "I'm a Man" were harnessed by these four young Britons and unleashed in live concerts at unimagined volume levels, battering audiences into blissful submission. What had once been a communal music now came dangerously close to being a tool of authoritarian control.

The only major British blues group which generally avoided this overbearing approach was Fleetwood Mac, and it was perhaps not a coincidence that this was the one which fared least well in the United States in this period. The group was formed in 1967 as a break-away from John Mayall's Bluesbreakers, featuring Peter Green, the guitarist who had replaced Clapton a year earlier, along with bass-player John McVie and drummer Mick Fleetwood, plus newcomer Jeremy Spencer on slide guitar. While Spencer was a rudimentary player with plenty of bravado, Peter Green was in a class of his own as a writer, singer, and guitarist of unusual sensitivity and imagination, and his songs held up very well as classy pop records.

Fleetwood Mac's first three albums were recorded for Blue Horizon, a new label formed by producer Mike Vernon, licensed to the British division of CBS.* The first album sold remarkably well for a new group with no hit single to its name yet, and stayed on the album top ten for 17 weeks in 1968; at the end of the year, the shimmering instrumental "Albatross" was boosted by being used as background music to a TV programme and went to the top of the charts early the following year. The group switched to Immediate for one single, the laconic vocal "Oh Well", and then moved on to the newly formed British division of Reprise for two more sombre hits, "Man of the World" and "Green Manalishi". Throughout the seventies the group's personnel kept shifting after Green dropped out, and eventually moved to America where its success paid for the entire cost of setting up the British office of Warner-Reprise.†

In 1967, the year that Track Records was formed, and the year when Cream and Hendrix began the "second wave" assault on America from Britain, two important independent ventures were launched which carried a more pastoral kind of music across the Atlantic, Island Records and Straight Ahead. In the case of Island, the term should probably be "significantly expanded", rather than "launched", since, as we have seen, the label had already been going for five years. The turning point came when Stevie Winwood left the Spencer Davis Group and, after a lull, formed Traffic; his manager Chris Blackwell had to decide whether to license the recordings to another company, or branch out into the world of pop with Island Records. Choosing the latter course, he made a distribution deal with Philips.‡

* CBS. *Formed in 1965 as the British division of American Columbia.*
Pop: the Tremeloes, Marmalade, Love Affair.

Subsidiary:

DIRECTION
Pop soul: Johnny Johnson and the Bandwagon.
Licensed label:
BLUE HORIZON. *Formed in 1967 by Mike Vernon.*
Blues rock: Fleetwood Mac, Chicken Shack.

† WARNER-REPRISE. *Formed in 1969 as British division of Warner-Reprise.*
Rock: Fleetwood Mac, Family.

‡ PHILIPS. *Subsidiary of Dutch Philips. A&R: Johnny Franz, Jack Baverstock.*
Solo pop: Dusty Springfield, Scott Walker.
Progressive rock: David Bowie.

Subsidiary labels:

FONTANA
Pop: Dave Dee, Dozy, Beaky, Mick and Tich; the Herd, the New Vaudeville Band.

Although Stevie Winwood's voice was still the instant "trademark" of Traffic, there were several major distinctions from the Spencer Davis Group, which had been caught in the familiar blind alley of trying to sound as if it comprised black musicians from Memphis. Traffic was a catch-all for virtually every current style and influence, embracing "Hendrix" style guitar from Dave Mason, jazzy flute and sax playing from Chris Wood, and loose, almost free-form drumming and "poetic" lyrics from Jim Capaldi. An ambience of good-natured vibes hung over the group, sustained by live appearances at festivals, the artwork of their album covers, and a distinct lack of egocentricity on the part of Stevie Winwood.

Traffic picked up where the Spencer Davis Group left off, in the sense of continuing to have three hit singles during 1967, but from 1968 the group stuck principally to albums and became one of the favourite "cult" bands of the period, making the album charts both in Britain and America (on United Artists) without needing the constant stimulus of a new hit single. The group was widely admired by other musicians, and, although at the time its laid-back approach yielded centre stage to the more flamboyant blues groups, in the long run Traffic had a more permanent influence. A month before its first single "Paper Sun" hit the British chart, Procol Harum appeared with "A Whiter Shade of Pale"; a month later, Van Morrison hit the American chart with "Brown Eyed Girl". Between them, these three

---

VERTIGO
Rock: Rod Stewart.

MERCURY
(*American-originated material.*)

Distributed labels:
PAGE ONE. *Formed in 1967 by Larry Page.*
Pop: the Troggs.

ISLAND. *Jointly-owned by Chris Blackwell and David Betteridge; switched from independent distribution to Philips in 1967.*
Rock (Island-managed artists): Traffic, Spooky Tooth, Free, Mott the Hoople, Cat Stevens.
(Witchseason Productions by Joe Boyd): Fairport Convention, John and Beverly Martyn, Nick Drake.
(Chrysalis-managed artist): Jethro Tull.
(EG Management artists): King Crimson, Emerson Lake and Palmer, Roxy Music.
Reggae: Jimmy Cliff, Bob Marley and the Wailers.

Associated Island labels distributed independently of Philips:
PYRAMID. *Formed in 1967 by Graham Goodall and Lee Gopthal in partnership with Island to release productions from Leslie Kong.*
Reggae: Desmond Dekker and the Aces, Toots and the Maytals.

TROJAN. *Formed in 1968 as partnership between Lee Gopthal and Island, with distribution by B&C. Island sold interest in 1972.*
Reggae: the Pioneers, the Harry J. Allstars, the Upsetters, Bob and Marcia, Toots and the Maytals, Dave and Ansell Collins.

hits of summer 1967 echoed through the next fifteen years, most obviously in the sound of the Band, but also in the hands of Eric Clapton, who formed a temporary liaison with Winwood in 1969 as Blind Faith. Although that group lasted long enough to make just one album, Clapton's career in the seventies was geared much more towards the "integrated" approach of Traffic than towards the selfish, virtuoso stance of Cream.

And as Traffic became a favourite among musicians, the group's evidently harmonious relationship with its record company became a model and inspiration for other bands and managers. Not only were groups glad to benefit from Island's civilized attitude to its artists, but substantial independent production and management firms made exclusive arrangements with Island too. By the early seventies, Island was in a class of its own as the leading British independent company, matching the transatlantic achievements of Atlantic, Elektra, and A&M. Ironically, the price that Chris Blackwell paid to achieve this position was to drop Island's role as a vehicle for Jamaican music. In fact the break was not quite as extreme as it appeared, but appearances were important: after all those years as a "specialist minority music" label, Island had to be seen to shake off its associations in order to be taken seriously as a "pop" and "rock" label by the British media; Atlantic and Elektra had both experienced the same problems, the one having been a rhythm and blues label, the other a folk label. Prejudices die hard, and the simplest way was for Island to drop all West Indian names from its roster.

Many of the artists who had been released through Island until 1967 were shifted first to Pyramid and then to Trojan, whose distribution was entirely separate from Island's arrangement with Philips. And just as this switch took place, Jamaican music finally broke through the barriers and into the British charts.

First to hit the top twenty was Prince Buster with "Al Capone" for Blue Beat in February 1967, a mostly instrumental dance number with novelty spoken passages and a gimmicky "tickety-tickety" sound chanted along with the rhythm guitar. Next up was "007 (Shanty Town)" by Desmond Dekker and the Aces for Pyramid, sung with such a heavy Jamaican patois that most British people couldn't understand anything except the title in the chorus. It took six months for the record to surface through the dance clubs, where its lilting guitar set it apart from and above most current rivals, and after repeated plays the storyline of the song cut through–it was a gentle celebration of the tough street kids of Kingston, known as "rude boys", and if the words had been any clearer the record would probably have been banned for inciting violence. Paradoxically, it came across as an invitation to live in peaceful coexistence, and for the remainder of the sixties Jamaican music–now known as "reggae"–provided most of the period's best dance records. Rhythmically original, lyrically ingenious, and emotionally delivered, reggae became more professionally produced and more widely accessible just as the Southern Groove soul records of Stax began to repeat their formulas. But British radio was still leery of opening up to the music and during 1968 very little surfaced.

The notable reggae success of 1968 was "Hold Me Tight" by Johnny Nash, an American singer who had previously failed to establish a distinctive niche between Sam Cooke and Johnny Mathis. In 1967 he went to record in Jamaica with local session musicians, and after proving that he had captured an authentic feel by scoring a hit locally on his own JAD label, he leased "Hold Me Tight" to EMI in Britain. The combination of his flawless vocal, a catchy pop song and the immaculate rhythm track overcame radio resistance to reggae, and the record not only made the British top five but repeated the trick in the States, where no Jamaican-made record had ever done so well.

In 1969, Desmond Dekker came back with a second, even bigger hit for Pyramid, "The Israelites", which topped the British chart and made the American top ten for UNI; the lyric was again virtually undecipherable and appealed primarily as an irresistibly danceable novelty record. Like the previous Desmond Dekker hit, "The Israelites" was produced by Leslie Kong, who became the catalyst for the belated breakthrough for Jamaican artists later on in 1969. Where most of the other Jamaican producers still thought first of all about satisfying the relatively specialist needs of the dance clubs in Kingston, Leslie Kong was alert to the higher production standards outside Jamaica, and without compromising his singers or their material, he made sure that the instruments were in tune and clearly recorded, and he even managed to secure some semblance of exclusivity with his singers.

"Long Shot Kick The Bucket" by the Pioneers put the Trojan label just outside the British top twenty, and "Wonderful World, Beautiful People" by Jimmy Cliff made the top ten. For Cliff and Kong, this was a particularly sweet success, as the two had entered the recording business together nine years earlier, but had parted company after achieving only minor local hits. Jimmy Cliff had struggled in vain to be accepted in Britain as a soul singer, but his voice lacked the power of his American rivals, and it was some kind of desperate last measure to reunite in Kingston with Leslie Kong. The record, "Wonderful World", was an infectious anthem of togetherness which also made the top thirty in the States on A&M, but despite a starring role in the successful cult film *The Harder They Come*, he never did fulfil his potential to become Jamaica's first genuine international star. Of the other likely contenders for that role, the Maytals never had a major British hit despite several catchy songs delivered in a raspy, Otis Redding style by lead singer Toots Hibbert, and the Pioneers became too slick after they moved to Britain to capitalize on their hit. It was a delicate balance, retaining the authentic feel that was hard to recapture outside Kingston, while broadening personal horizons and audience support by appearing live in Britain and the United States. Having failed to guide Jimmy Cliff down the narrow path, Chris Blackwell turned his attentions to the Wailers, a trio whose records had been popular in Jamaica without causing much impression in Britain. After a long period of nurturing the group, Blackwell's policy was vindicated as the group's leader, Bob Marley, emerged in the mid-seventies as one of pop music's major figures, not simply the biggest reggae star but one of the ten "superstars" of the decade.

There were numerous other notable Jamaican performers during the late sixties, vocal groups, session groups, solo singers and producers, whose story has not yet been systematically documented, but they did not rise to the surface of international pop music in a way that influenced other artists at the time. The sound of Kingston, Jamaica, was recorded, but its impact was delayed, mostly beyond the time limits of this book.

Parallel with the emergence of Island Records as a strong, rock-oriented label, Denny Cordell established Straight Ahead Productions within the bosom of the surviving British majors. The success of Immediate and Reaction had made the majors insecure about the old fashioned associations of their own long-established labels, and during 1967 Decca formed a subsidiary called Deram and EMI formed Harvest; Pye subsequently followed suit with Dawn, and Philips with Vertigo. All four were designed as modern labels with their own logos, art style, and label managers.

Considering its impressive roster of only a couple of years before, Decca* went through a particularly abrupt decline, and survived

* DECCA. *Still administered by founder-owner Edward Lewis. A&R: Dick Rowe, Peter Sullivan.*
Solo pop: Tom Jones, Engelbert Humperdinck.
Rock groups: John Mayall's Bluesbreakers, Rolling Stones.
Pop group: the Alan Price Set.

Subsidiary:

DERAM.
Pop: Amen Corner (1967–68), Cat Stevens, the Move, Procol Harum (and Straight Ahead Productions).
Rock groups: the Moody Blues, Ten Years After.
Licensed labels:
MAM. *Division of the MAM Agency owned by Gordon Mills.*
Pop: Dave Edmunds, Gilbert O'Sullivan.
LONDON. *Outlet for licensed American product, mainly Hi of Memphis.*

through the late sixties and early seventies mainly through the "cabaret pop" roster of artists managed by Gordon Mills: Tom Jones, Engelbert Humperdinck , and Gilbert O'Sullivan. The company's attempt to achieve credibility with up-and-coming rock acts by forming Deram seemed to have worked when Denny Cordell placed some of his Straight Ahead Productions with the new label in 1967.

Denny Cordell had made his first mark in 1964 as producer of "Go Now" for the Birmingham group, the Moody Blues. One of the few groups who managed to switch from "pop" to "rock" in this period, the Moody Blues were also one of the few to stick with Decca; supervised by producer Tony Clarke, they scraped into the top twenty with "Nights in White Satin" on Deram in 1968, and then formed their own Threshold label which they licensed worldwide to Decca in 1970. Their serious, elaborately arranged music was popular with the growing college audience, but they did occasionally make accessible pop singles including "Question" and "Nights . . ." which made the American top three as a reissue in 1972.

Meanwhile Denny Cordell solved every independent producer's quandary of how to finance his productions by forming an alliance with the Essex Music publishing company, who acquired the publishing rights and copyright ownership of his recordings in return for financing his studio time. During 1967 and 1968, Straight Ahead Productions introduced several of the major British acts of the next few years: the Move, Procol Harum, Joe Cocker, David Bowie, and Tyrannosaurus Rex (later shorted to T. Rex). Cordell produced the early records by the first three, and recruited a young American musician and arranger Tony Visconti who looked after Marc Bolan's Tyrannosaurus Rex (and, later on, Bowie).

For the first six months of 1967, Straight Ahead Productions were licensed to Deram, but in September Cordell switched to EMI,* who

* EMI. *Maintained several distinct label rosters.*

COLUMBIA
Pop: Cliff Richard, Ken Dodd, Rolf Harris, Lulu (1967–69), Des O'Connor.

PARLOPHONE
Pop: the Hollies, Cilla Black.

HARVEST
Rock: Pink Floyd, Deep Purple.

REGAL ZONOPHONE. *Exclusive outlet for Straight Ahead Productions.*
Rock: Procol Harum, Joe Cocker, Tyrannosaurus Rex.
Pop: the Move.
Reggae: Johnny Nash.

APPLE. *Formed by the Beatles in 1968.*
Pop: the Beatles, Mary Hopkin.
Rock: John Lennon and the Plastic Ono Band.

reactivated the long defunct Regal Zonophone label in order to give Cordell an exclusive outlet for his productions. Where many British records of the period still betrayed a parochial, too obviously commercial intention, Cordell managed to instil some of the authority, confidence, and grandeur that exuded from the Beatles' records with George Martin.

In the case of the Move, the comparison with the Beatles was all too apt; the group's leader, singer, and writer Roy Wood went for a similar combination of nostalgic recollection and studio trickery that the Beatles had introduced in *Rubber Soul* and *Revolver* and brought to near perfection in *Sergeant Pepper*; but Wood's voice had neither the power of John Lennon nor the charm of Paul McCartney, and despite many catchy tunes none of the Move's ten British hits made any mark in America.

Denny Cordell's early productions for Procol Harum and Joe Cocker, on the other hand, dared to go into the one territory which the Beatles had been shy to try, white soul. British singers and musicians were generally in awe of the passionate gospel-styled black Americans like Ray Charles and Sam Cooke, but the record which seemed to galvanize them into having a go was "When a Man Loves a Woman" by Percy Sledge. The combination of Percy's searing vocal and the solemn, almost fugue-like organ pattern was the catalyst for both Traffic and Procol Harum to evolve a pastoral style which evoked the atmosphere of a cathedral with its doors open: reverential, but accessible.

Cordell has openly acknowledged that "When a Man Loves a Woman" was the vital inspiration behind the arrangement that worked so well for Procol Harum in "A Whiter Shade of Pale". Top of the British singles chart for six weeks during the dizzy summer of 1967, the record symbolized the new age that so many people thought had begun that year, but despite endless interpretation and analysis the lyrics defied all attempts to pin down any real meaning. Like an abstract painting, they fitted together in an attractive pattern, but it was the singing (by Gary Brooker) and the hypnotic organ part (played by Matthew Fisher) which made the record so effective. For Brooker, this was the belated reward for four fruitless years playing

---

CAPITOL
(*Outlet for American Capitol.*)

Licensed labels:
LIBERTY-UNITED ARTISTS
Pop: P. J. Proby, Peter Sarstedt, the Bonzo Dog Band.
BELL (*primarily as outlet for US material from Amy-Mala-Bell*).
TAMLA MOTOWN (*primarily as outlet for Gody's Detroit labels*).
STATESIDE. (*The catch-all outlet for other US material, including ABC-Dunhill.*)

with a Southend-based rhythm and blues band called the Paramounts, whose records for Parlophone had been ignored; one by one, he recruited the members of that group into Procol Harum, while tending to favour the "classical" and "rock" elements at the expense of the original gospel inspiration. Meanwhile, producer Denny Cordell carried gospel to its logical extreme with Joe Crocker, producing an "over-the-top" version of a song from *Sergeant Pepper*, "With a Little Help From My Friends".

Like "A Whiter Shade of Pale", "With a Little Help From My Friends" was essentially a studio record, played by hand-picked musicians rather than by an existing live group; the British music press was still highly suspicious of such ventures, which smacked of "pop" techniques rather than "rock" authenticity, but in both cases the moods required highly skilled professionals to put them across. For Cocker's record, Cordell used bass-player Chris Stainton from Cocker's own Grease Band, alongside drummer, B. J. Wilson, once of the Paramounts, now in Procol Harum (but not at the time of their first single!), and guitarist Jimmy Page–this was 1968, before the formation of Led Zeppelin.

On *Sergeant Pepper*, Ringo Starr had sung "With a Little Help From My Friends" in a deadpan manner–casual, off-hand–and the first impression of Cocker's version was that it was entirely unsuitable. But in much the same way as Ray Charles had redefined "Georgia On My Mind" and Otis Redding had transformed "Try a Little Tenderness", now Cocker made his approach work. Helped by searing guitar from Page and backed up by what sounded like a cast of thousands on the chorus, Cocker screamed and cried his way through the song, and right to the top of the charts.

In live performance, Cocker managed to live up to the extravagant expectations raised by the record; a desperately tense figure in a dishevelled T-shirt and wild "acid" hair, he mimicked every instrument in the band as he retched his way through the set. Cordell made a blanket licensing deal with A&M in America for his Straight Ahead Productions after the shift from Decca to EMI in Britain, and A&M undertook to pay the tour support for Cordell to bring Cocker and his Grease Band to America. Once over there, Cordell decided to stay and work with Leon Russell who masterminded a huge cavalcade of singers and musicians to back up Cocker on a second nationwide tour under the banner "Mad Dogs and Englishmen". Carrying coals back to Newcastle, Cordell and Cocker had helped to launch a kind of "rock-gospel" genre in the States, where Delaney and Bonnie, Ike and Tina Turner, the Rolling Stones, and Leon Russell himself all used back-up vocal groups and churchy chord progressions to galvanize their audiences into feeling part of the event rather than submissive observers of it. And back in Britain, Rod Stewart–with, and then without, the Faces–and Elton John adopted and adapted some of these same elements to become major international stars of the seventies.

Where pop music had once offered a short-term interlude of fame and (occasionally) fortune, during the late sixties it began to offer the possibilities of a real career, with the prospects of earning a life-time's income to musicians who accepted how the system worked.

The recording process itself had become much more sophisticated, with more advanced equipment enabling engineers to record more volume, particularly in the lower frequencies of bass drum and bass guitar, and allowing the producers to delay decisions about balancing the instruments against each other by recording them on to separate tracks: the recording machines jumped from two track to four track to eight, sixteen and eventually twenty-four track. Every part of the drum kit could be isolated, and the solo musicians and vocalists could record several alternative performances before deciding which was the best one to use. The recording process became more self-conscious and less spontaneous, and the physical location of a studio hardly mattered at all: musicians disappeared into studios for weeks on end, and could transfer their tapes to another part of the world if they wanted to use a particular soloist, or mixing engineer.

By the end of the sixties, British musicians were as capable as their American counterparts of representing what rock 'n' roll had become. Compared with the clean sweep of the first stage of the British Invasion of America, when so many different British groups had topped the American singles charts, this second phase was not so obvious. No British artists, apart from the still-popular Rolling Stones and Beatles, topped the American singles chart during the years 1967–70, and only four new British acts topped the album charts in that period: Cream, the Jimi Hendrix Experience (two-thirds British!), Blind Faith and Led Zeppelin. But as British groups and individual musicians visited America on nation-wide tours, they began to see what would be entailed if they were to succeed in "the American market", and they regrouped and revamped until they got it right.

The roster of groups on Island's books during the sixties turned out to be a particularly fecund source of talent with "America-appeal". The blues-rock group Free not only had substantial success in its original line-up, but lead singer Paul Rodgers subsequently formed the even more popular Bad Company, in partnership with guitarist Mick Ralphs, who had been in another Island group, Mott the Hoople. This stadium-oriented music reduced the blues formula to ever more basic elements, delivering macho lyrics with crude posturing and ear-splitting volume. Members of Spooky Tooth achieved success in other incarnations, notably bass-player Mick Jones with Foreigner, whose guitarist Ian Macdonald had been in yet another Island act, King Crimson.

Although the original managers and producers of these musicians were not always still involved by the time they achieved their success in America, it was certainly not a coincidence that such a high proportion of the most successful British musicians were products from the "stables" of Chris Blackwell, Robert Stigwood, and Denny Cordell, all three of whom had themselves spent a substantial part of each year in America. A&M and Atlantic were the two American labels who were most receptive to these ambassadors of British rock, and both hauled themselves into the front-line of the American record industry as a result.

Back in Britain, another collection of British musicians pursued alternatives to the retreads of American blues and gospel forms. Folk and classical music were the traditional European idioms, and were a more natural starting point for many of the middle class musicians who had only lately noticed pop music's existence. Before the Beatles, the vast majority of both the musician-performers and the industry's management had been from Britain's working class, but now a college-educated generation had become involved. Less concerned with the repetitive chords of American dance music than with finding musical structures for free-form poetry and melodic improvisations, these artists included the Pink Floyd, the Nice, and David Bowie, none of whom made much impact in the States during the sixties.

The Pink Floyd emerged from a new underworld of basement cellars which sprang up during 1966 and 1967 as an alternative to the beer-and-cigarettes world of pubs and clubs that spawned the British blues groups. At the Middle Earth and UFO in London's West End, the audience took acid or smoked dope in the gloom, while a grandly-titled "lights show" projectionist lit up the wall at the back of the stage with oil-slides that stirred under the heat of his lamp. The erratic rhythms of the musicians threw the audience into spasm-dance movements, while the guitarists carried themselves off into space. This was the spirit of San Francisco, 6,000 miles East.

Miraculously, the Pink Floyd managed to recapture some semblance of order when they recorded at EMI's Abbey Road studios. Norman Smith, engineer for the Beatles, was promoted to producer, and the group had two hits in 1967 for EMI's Harvest label, "See Emily Play" and "Arnold Layne". Cute, quirky, and very English, these records carried on the "portrait" approach of the Kinks and the Who, but the Pink Floyd's chief songwriter Syd Barrett could not cope with the pressures and discipline of being in a regular working group, and after his departure the Pink Floyd became known primarily as a "musical" band whose lyrics were less important than their studio effects and their musical arrangements. An impressively self-contained unit, they were among the first British rock groups to establish a balanced relationship with a major company, and they remained with EMI throughout the seventies.

Alongside the Pink Floyd, the British underground scene launched countless new bands, attracting already established musicians like Stevie Winwood and Gary Brooker to branch out into more adventurous forms, and bringing others in from jazz, folk, and wherever else they had been lurking. Keyboard player Keith Emerson had been part of the backing group for P. P. Arnold, a black American gospel singer who recorded for Immediate, before forming the Nice as a showcase for his pyrotechnics. As Immediate began to experience "difficulties", the Nice's manager Tony Stratton-Smith formed his own Charisma label* which scored several album hits by the group before Emerson left to form Emerson Lake and Palmer whose EG management placed them with Island. Charisma meanwhile became home for several of the new "middle class" rock groups including Genesis.

Along with everything else, Island Records also nurtured a British version of folk-rock, primarily through an association with American producer Joe Boyd, but also through a separate arrangement with the Chrysalis management team. Boyd had been present at the famous 1965 Newport Folk Festival when Dylan "went electric", and he was a leading promoter of underground concerts in London during 1966 and 1967. He produced the British folk group Fairport Convention for Island, but although the group attracted a devoted following in Britain, they never achieved the American sales that were necessary to make a rock group truly self-sufficient.

Chrysalis was formed by two ex-university social secretaries Chris Wright and Terry Ellis, who placed Jethro Tull with Island on an arrangement that would give them their own licensed label if the group achieved a certain sales target. To the surprise of all concerned, Jethro Tull achieved the target within a year, scoring two top ten hits in Britain in 1969 and going on to become one of the most successful British acts in America during the seventies, with several best-selling albums on Reprise.

Two other "graduates" from this underground school made their maximum impact during the seventies after making several false

* CHARISMA. *Formed in 1970 by Tony Stratton-Smith.*
Rock: Nice, Genesis, Van Der Graaf Generator, Rare Bird.
Folk-rock: Lindisfarne.

starts during the sixties: Marc Bolan and David Bowie. They were both intensely ambitious and had no particular affinity or loyalty to a specific musical genre, and they roamed from one style and label to another during the sixties in search of an approach that worked. Denny Cordell signed them to his production company, and his assistant Tony Visconti turned out to be the catalyst who brought the best out of both of them. As Tyrannosaurus Rex, Bolan had a couple of minor hits in 1968 for Regal Zonophone, "Deborah" and "One Inch Rock", but he really hit his stride in 1970 with "Ride a White Swan", a top two hit which was followed by nine consecutive top five hits by T. Rex in Britain, all produced by Visconti with a basic boogie rhythm under Bolan's very "English" voice. Folk-rock, of a sort.

Although most of Bowie's hits in the seventies were also produced by Visconti, his one hit of the sixties was produced by Gus Dudgeon, who had been the engineer for producer Mike Vernon, when Bowie had recorded several unsuccessful singles and an album for Deram in 1967. The lone hit was "Space Oddity" for Philips in 1969, an odd monologue as spoken by a space traveller trying to make contact with home base back on earth. Received at the time more or less as a novelty record, "Space Oddity" turned out to be a diversion in Bowie's career, which recovered its momentum only after he joined RCA in 1972.

Between them, Bolan and Bowie rekindled the spirit of teenage pop music through astute combinations of accessible "pop" songs and coherent "rock" identities. Presenting themselves with gaudy images decorated in lipstick, powder and paint, they laid the foundation for a lively music scene in Britain, where most of the international innovators of the seventies were based. Back in America, the industry finally won its battle to stabilize the elusive ingredients of popular music, and more or less abandoned the young teenagers who had supported most of the best music of the previous fifteen years.

14

GOODNIGHT, AMERICA

By the end of the sixties, pop and rock had completely reversed the positions they had held when rock 'n' roll first appeared in the mid-fifties. Then, pop was a catch-all category embracing virtually all currently popular music styles, and when rock 'n' roll first appeared, the industry wavered between hoping it would go away and trying to absorb it into pop. For the major label A&R men, among whom Mitch Miller at Columbia was the most successful and influential, the inherent problem with rock 'n' roll was that because it was evidently aimed at young teenagers, it would primarily be sold on 45 rpm singles and its artists would have a short career of mass popularity. Then, the aim of an A&R man was to secure a long career for his artists, enabling them to ride the crests of one fad or fashion after the other. Looking back twenty years later, Mitch Miller had no reason to regret his policies: many of the singers he had helped to launch had not only had ten-year spans as hit-making artists at the height of their popularity, but were still maintaining lucrative careers as TV, film, and cabaret entertainers as they approached the age of conventional retirement: Doris Day, Rosemary Clooney, Johnnie Ray, Frankie Laine, and Guy Mitchell were still meaningful names, and of course Johnny Mathis had outlasted all the rock 'n' roll singers who sprang into the spotlight alongside him.

For a while, it seemed that Mitch Miller's attitudes were vindicated, as a three-year cycle began to emerge in this new teen stratum of pop music. The taste-making section of a particular age-group would latch on to a certain kind of artist and music, obsessively buy the related records, and then fade away as a younger group came through to exert its distinct taste and support a new clutch of singers and sounds.

But during the mid-sixties, the original audience for rock 'n' roll reappeared as the performers of a new kind of pop, originally dubbed "folk-rock" and eventually renamed simply "rock". Instead of growing out of rock 'n' roll, these performers and their contemporaries had grown up with it, and this time around they fulfilled many of the criteria that Mitch Miller would have prescribed for the artists he was prepared to work with: they made albums, and they saw themselves as career-artists, not simply as opportunists looking for a brief moment of fame.

And so the companies which had been undermined by misjudging the extent and intensity of rock 'n' roll's appeal were able to recover their share of the market by taking on the majority of popular rock artists during the mid-sixties. Columbia, Capitol, and the newly combined Warner-Elektra-Atlantic had picked up the cream of the crop by the end of the sixties, and they followed the natural instincts of major organizations to try to stabilize their market, to lengthen the careers and spread the appeal of their artists. And, to forestall a repeat of the fifties situation, when indie labels specializing in black music had sprung a surprise on the majors, the majors began picking off the available black artists too. They could not stop Motown, at the peak of its popularity in 1970 with 18 records at the top of the American singles chart, but they could try to sweep up the rest with licensing and distribution deals where they could not get the artists direct.

For independent companies, the prospects were dim. The formation of Warner-Elektra-Atlantic into one company with its own warehouses and distribution system had robbed the independent network of a substantial catalogue, and most of the companies who stuck with independent distribution were primarily singles-oriented, where the profit margins were slim and getting worse: Bell, Buddah, Roulette, and Scepter upheld what was left of the New York indie label tradition, but it was fading fast. Once the all-inclusive genre of popular music, pop was now whittled down to describe the music aimed at young teenagers, the exact equivalent of the audience which ten years earlier had cultivated rock 'n' roll. Now they took what they were given, which in the late sixties was bubblegum (thanks to Kasenetz-Katz, Buddah Records, and Don Kirshner's Screen Gems plots behind the Monkees and Archies) and in the early seventies teenybop (courtesy of Bell Records in collusion with Kirshner again, this time on behalf of David Cassidy and the Partridge Family, and joined by MGM, a major label which, in its dying throes, gave the world Donny and the Osmonds before being gobbled up by Polydor).

With "pop" now reduced to being a synonym for the most cynical music that the American record industry could throw at an audience it had no feeling for, "rock" was elevated to something close to "art", which it could rarely live up to. The functions of pop music were always fairly basic, and very often secondary: music gives a beat for dancing, a soundtrack for reading, working, or travelling, a background for talking, embracing and making love. The words of songs caricature messages and feelings which people are inhibited from saying to each other, and the music sometimes generates the mood in which they can say those things to each other.

But during the sixties, the audience began to turn more attention towards the music, reaching beyond the records to identify the writers, musicians and singers, and going out to see them perform live. Not just, as in the days of the package tours, to be able to say "I've seen him or her", but to make a connection, to understand the technique, to surrender to a charismatic leader.

The audience for rock began to see itself as a tribe, and adopted any number of visual ornaments and personal habits to make sure its associations were clear for all to see: not only to establish a togetherness with others of similar tastes, but to declare a distinction from the rest of the world. In 1968 the movie *Easy Rider* symbolized the new generation gap, as *Blackboard Jungle* had done in 1955; and once again, there was a musical soundtrack to emphasize the point, this time with Hendrix, Steppenwolf, the Byrds and songs by Bob Dylan and the Band to make the connections. The story was simple: two "long-hairs" make a trek through the South on Harley Davidson motorbikes with elongated handlebars, and predictably enough encounter prejudice and rejection most of the way. Directed by Dennis Hopper, starring himself along with Peter Fonda and memorable mainly for a cameo role played by Jack Nicholson, the film attracted the "counter-culture" audience into cinemas. A couple of years later they returned in their millions to watch the movie version of the Woodstock Festival.

The Woodstock Festival was one of those "milestone" events which occasionally occur to make it simpler for chroniclers to define the beginnings and ends of eras. Woodstock was both at the same time, bringing together many of the leading rock artists of the previous two or three years, and launching several more, taking them from the minor leagues and making them major attractions in their own right.

The organizers had no background in the industry, but pulled off a major coup by convening yet again most of the San Francisco veterans of the Be-In and Monterey Pop, along with representatives from Los Angeles, New York, and Britain. For one reason or another, the really big names were not there: no Beatles or Rolling Stones, no Dylan or Simon and Garfunkel, no Doors or Led Zeppelin. And, conspicuously, no soul acts–no Aretha Franklin, Stevie Wonder, Marvin Gaye or the Temptations. But 250,000 people showed up to see who was there, and their word of mouth reports along with media coverage (a triple album on Atlantic's Cotillion label, along with a movie and of course acres of press reports) gave a huge boost to the extravagant performers whose crowd-pleasing antics suited the huge venue: Janis Joplin, Joe Cocker, Jimi Hendrix, and the Who all leaped into "first division" status as a direct result of the exposure from the Festival, whose success inspired several other attempts to recapture its ambience.

There were enormous logistical problems in organizing festivals, not the least of which was making sure everybody paid to get in, but the principle of playing rock music to huge audiences was established. All the major companies signed up groups who could tour the country, gradually building up loyal audiences as they raised their status on the bills, starting out as opening acts which had to endure disinterested or even resentful audiences, and working their way to the top of the bill. These kinds of groups dominated American popular music during the seventies, but although their music could be traced to roots in the blues, as filtered through the rock groups of the late sixties, they had eliminated the elements of "spiritualness" that made the late sixties potentially attractive.

Ironically, one outfit in the Woodstock cast which really had contributed to pop's ongoing evolution was virtually overlooked in all the hype that surrounded and followed the event: the Band. Earlier incarnations as Ronnie Hawkins' backing group and as Bob Dylan's electric band have already been noted, but the group's own recording career effectively began in 1968 with the release by Capitol of their album *Music From Big Pink*, with a cover picture by Dylan.

First impressions of that album were confused; there were obvious associations with familiar styles, but this group played softly where contemporary blues musicians would have been loud, was restrained where psychedelic groups were indulgent, immaculate where punk was lazy, austere where pop was immature. Intensity and passion, mystery and despair were infused in every track, including "The Weight", which was a minor hit but a major influence towards the end of 1968. Ironically, in view of what was to come, the group recorded their album in Woodstock, at a studio owned by Bob Dylan's manager Albert Grossman, who also looked after their affairs.

Released six months after Dylan's *John Wesley Hardin* album, *Music From Big Pink* was a modest but not remarkable commercial success (making the top thirty albums), but the follow-up, released late in 1969 and simply called *The Band*, was not only a musical milestone but made the top ten too. As if they had shaken off the "deep" influences of Dylan, this time the Band sounded good-natured and mischievous, throwing in some uptempo songs (notably the British hit, "Rag Mama Rag") into the pot. Drummer Levon Helm came to the fore, singing lead on several songs, playing mandolin, and laying out a new style of syncopated drumming that was to sweep through half of American music during the seventies.

The unofficial leader of the Band was guitarist and main songwriter Robbie Robertson, but he studiously avoided using the group as a vehicle for his own undisputed virtuosity, and instead favoured the gothic organ arrangements that centred on keyboard player Garth Hudson. The group made connections between the desolate gospel music of America's South and the evocative experiments of the British groups Traffic and Procol Harum, and in many ways *The Band* was a definitive summary of where rock 'n' roll had got to, at the end of the sixties.

The Band recorded for Capitol Records,* and although by now most of the major labels were so big and impersonal that it was impossible to detect any kind of "house taste", there was a consistent thread which connected at least some of Capitol's acts to each other, the flavour of Southern music which was represented directly by Joe South, and at one remove by records made in Los Angeles by Glen Campbell (originally from Oklahoma), Linda Ronstadt (from Arizona) and Bobbie Gentry (from Mississippi).

Glen Campbell and Linda Ronstadt were "traditional" pop singers in the sense that they recorded songs written by other people; Campbell was yet another graduate of the Los Angeles session musician scene, who made his way through hard, professional graft. His version of Jim Webb's "By the Time I Get to Phoenix" was a minor hit in 1967, followed by bigger "geographical" hits, "Wichita Lineman" (1968) and "Galveston" (1969). Linda Ronstadt had her first hit in 1967 as lead singer with the Stone Poneys on "Different Drum", written by Mike Nesmith of the Monkees; the tough, live-my-own-life lyric was beguilingly set off by an unusual arrangement that featured a harpsichord, and although Linda later became one of the best-selling acts of the seventies, her solo records were never so interesting as this early production by Nick Venet.

Bobbie Gentry's "Ode to Billie Joe" was in a class all of its own, essentially just a hypnotic, bluesy guitar lick weaving around Bobbie's story of something that had happened one day in June back in Mississippi. She wrote, sang, and played the song herself, and the only embellishment was a dramatic arrangement of cellos by Jimmie Haskell. Brilliantly evocative, with deft instrumental and vocal inflec-

* CAPITAL RECORDS. *A&R: Nick Venet, Al de Lory.*
Pop: Glen Campbell, Nancy Wilson, Linda Ronstadt.
Singer-writers: Fred Neil, Joe South, Bobbie Gentry.
Rock: the Band, Quicksilver Messenger Service, Steve Miller Band.
Country: Buck Owens, Merle Haggard.

HARVEST
UK rock: Pink Floyd.

APPLE
UK pop: the Beatles, Mary Hopkin.

tions enhancing the narrative, the record topped the American singles chart in 1967, and it was a great disappointment to witness the rapid absorption of Bobbie Gentry into the show business world of cabaret and family TV shows. There were still very few women in the vanguard of American pop music, and it was wasteful to squander such talent when it finally surfaced.

The Band persevered with several more albums for Capitol through the early seventies, but had nothing more to add to the suite of songs and range of music on *The Band*. The group's "heritage" oriented approach to music spread to other performers, among whom Ry Cooder faithfully celebrated the same roots, while remodelling old songs to suit the electric guitar and kit-drum format of a rock group; bringing contemporary reggae, calypso and soul rhythms to songs with strong story-lines, Cooder stuck to a low-key, small hall context for his live performances and never surrendered his music to the stadiums which claimed most other rock-blues stars. Lowell George, who left the Mothers of Invention to form Little Feat, took a different tack from Cooder, applying a mumbled vocal, slide guitar, and funky drum approach to his own songs about life on and off the working musician's road.

Both Cooder and Little Feat recorded for Reprise, which kept its own identity although now fully incorporated into Warner Brothers Records. For the large major labels, any concept of "label identity" was difficult to sustain in the pursuit of several parallel commercial styles, but Warner-Reprise managed better than most to retain a credible image of a company whose staff still cared about what kind of music it was involved in. In particular, the company signed several performers who began to be bracketed together as "singer-songwriters", although they often had little in common with each other beyond recording under their own name, rather than under a group name. Among the artists signed by Warner-Reprise* during

* WARNER BROTHERS. *Directed by Mo Austin and Joe Smith. A&R: Ted Templeman, Leeny Waronker.*
Folk-pop: Peter, Paul and Mary, the Association.
Writer-singers: Van Morrison, James Taylor.
From UK: Petula Clark (from Pye).
Soul: Charles Wright and Watts 103rd Street Band, Lorraine Ellison.

REPRISE
Pop: Kenny Rogers and the First Edition, Frank Sinatra, Norman Greenbaum.
Writer-singers: Joni Mitchell, Randy Newman, Neil Young, Arlo Guthrie.
Rock: Ry Cooder, Little Feat, Ides of March.
From UK: the Jimi Hendrix Experience (from Track), the Kinks (from Pye), Jethro Tull (from Chrysalis), Fleetwood Mac (from UK Warner-Reprise).

Distributed label:

BIZARRE. *Formed in 1969 by Frank Zappa.*
Rock: the Mothers of Invention, Frank Zappa, Captain Beefheart, Tim Buckley.

the late sixties were Randy Newman, Joni Mitchell, Neil Young, Van Morrison and James Taylor, probably all of whom owed a debt to Bob Dylan for the freedom which their record company gave them to record more or less what they pleased. The success of Dylan had virtually reversed the balance between the record company and artist to the point where lawyers and managers now dictated many of the terms by which their protégés signed to companies, and the artist subsequently recorded apparently by whim rather than according to release schedules. This freedom was actually less apparent at Dylan's label, Columbia, than at Warner-Reprise, which really did seem like an artist-oriented label.

Randy Newman was among the more enigmatic recording artists of the new era, appearing to have more in common with pre-rock writers like Hoagy Carmichael than with his more up-front contemporaries such as Dylan and Paul Simon. He was a song-craftsman who had been a staff writer in the early sixties at Liberty's publishing company, Metric Music, alongside Sharon Sheeley and Jackie De Shannon; signed by Aaron Schroeder in 1964, Newman contributed songs for Gene Pitney, but he was scarcely an established writer even in 1968 when Warner Brothers signed him to make his own records. His reluctance to record became legendary, but although it soon became clear that he was not made of the stuff from which international stars are fashioned, Warners continued to indulge him: his first album was made with vast orchestras, his second with a small group including Ry Cooder, and his third was a live recording of just himself at a piano. It was all too subtle and sophisticated, but here and there another artist picked out some gems for themselves: Alan Price had a British hit in 1967 with "Simon Smith and His Amazing Dancing Bear", and Three Dog Night topped the American chart with "Mama Told Me Not to Come" in 1970. But other artists rarely caught the irony of Newman's own recordings, in which he somehow stood outside the characters whose stories he sang. Pop and rock were both almost always autobiographical, and the audience found it hard to relate to a singer who detached himself from his material and sang weird songs about lechers and hookers, racists and arsonists.

Joni Mitchell was a sophisticated lyricist, too, but delivered her songs with one of those "angel" voices that Joan Baez and Judy Collins had made familiar in the early sixties. Judy Collins actually gave Joni her "break", when her version of Joni's song "Both Sides Now" made the top ten in 1968 (for Elektra). Originally from Canada, Joni moved to Los Angeles where she became part of a new "aristocracy" of singer-writers whose private and professional lives became fare for gossip columnists in the rock press. Joni was particularly associated with Crosby, Stills, Nash and Young, and wrote the song which gave them their first hit single, a from-the-heart celebration of "Woodstock" (Atlantic, 1970). There were other, better songs including "Chelsea Morning" and "Big Yellow Taxi" (a British hit for Joni herself in 1970), and during the seventies Joni emerged as one of the most idiosyncratic women in rock, proving she could play the game straight with the album *Court and Spark* in 1974, but more often exploring whether and how folk and jazz phrasing could be balanced against rock rhythms.

Neil Young was also a Canadian with a background in folk music, but his phrasing merged more easily into the instruments and rhythms of rock. Overcoming a whining, nasal voice with plaintive melodies, Young typified a new kind of anti-star whose songs were mostly morose and morbid, carrying to absurd lengths the sorry-for-himself role that had been central to many of the early sixties hits by Roy Orbison and Gene Pitney. Flirting with the Crosby Stills and Nash axis for a while, Young eventually branched off into a separate career, and survived the effects of bad habits to become a best-selling recording artist in the seventies.

Of all the attempts to deliver fairly complicated lyrics within some kind of rock format, Van Morrison came closest to a genuine new fusion of folk, jazz, and rock. Since moving to the States after the break-up of his British-based group, Them, Van had made a top ten hit with Bert Berns' Bang label, "Brown Eyed Girl", whose back-up group included such unlikely participants as Berns and Jeff Barry. A true folk-rock record at a time when the term had generally become a euphemism for any commercial rock record, "Brown Eyed Girl" was a classic song of nostalgic recollection, and bubbled with a feeling of joyous spontaneity that Van Morrison was to pursue obsessively for the rest of his career.

By the time Van Morrison was signed to Warner Brothers in 1969, recording studios were full of engineers and producers who studied every sound and every beat to make sure that no mistake could possibly occur, systematically wiping out the elements of surprise and risk that had originally been the essence of rock 'n' roll. But while virtually every performer of the period surrendered to these technicians, Van Morrison stood firm.

For his first album, Van more or less abandoned conventional rock forms, and instead used the "jazz" accompaniment of stand-up bass (played by Richard Davis) and brushed drums (Connie Kay) to follow his apparently improvised vocals, supported by a back drop of flute, saxophone, and strings. *Astral Weeks* fell outside the known categories of the day, and failed to make much mark either on the radio or in any charts. But over the years, the album began to be recognized as a brave step in a new direction, looking for new ways to evoke memories and situations while staying within the loose definitions of rock and pop. A genuine explorer, whose occasional meandering into pretentious and meaningless lyrics were an inevitable by-product of his fearless experiments, Van Morrison led the way into a kind of "head-soul" music, at a time when Isaac Hayes, Curtis Mayfield and Marvin Gaye were using similar devices to conjure a sensual ambience.

Morrison's second album for Warner Brothers, *Moondance*, was more conventional without being at all derivative; in addition to spawning a minor hit, "Come Running" which had some of the same mood that "Brown Eyed Girl" had presented, the album roamed into folk, jazz, and soul in well structured songs that culminated in the haunting atmosphere of "Into the Mystic". This time the record made the American top thirty album chart, and could have provided a platform for Morrison to become one of the major acts of the seventies. But to achieve such a position, he would have been obliged to take his songs out on the road and play them night after night, a process which would have defied his determination that his music should always be spontaneous. Refusing to surrender to the role of being a travelling salesman for his albums, Van Morrison settled for a career as a cult artist, while several others marched into the space he left: Elton John, Bob Seger, and Bruce Springsteen all pursued nostalgic recollection with a similar combination of country, soul, and rock 'n' roll, although with conspicuously less jazz.

Nostalgia seemed to be the central focus for many singer-writers, and it certainly attracted a huge audience. The pinnacle for the movement came in the early seventies, signalled by the success of James Taylor in 1970, and carried further by Carole King, Carly Simon, and Don McLean the following year. In each case, the producer was crucially important, in helping the writer to go further than simply laying out personal preoccupations, by crafting catchy choruses which would indelibly implant themselves on their audience. Just when it seemed that the live world of rock had been about to break away from many of the traditional criteria for making popular music, these singer-writers brought them back into contention. For the entire industry, the popularity of Taylor, and even better, Carole King, provided a reassurance that after all the fuss about freedom and revolution, what the world loved to sing was a love song.

James Taylor had made one album before he joined Warner Brothers, but was still basically unknown when his song "Fire and Rain" began to get radio play; the almost "poetic" imagery was nicely timed for an audience which had retreated from the intensities of the mid-to-late sixties, comforting proof that rock 'n' roll had grown up.

Producer Peter Asher had learned the basic rules of the pop game with eight American top twenty hits as half of the duo Peter and Gordon in the original British Invasion, and he framed Taylor's songs with disarmingly simple accompaniment–piano, bass, and drums alongside Taylor's uncluttered guitar. The second album, *Mudslide Slim & the Blue Horizon* was more of much the same, boosted by a number one single version of Carole King's song, "You've Got a Friend".

Carole King finally broke through to mass popularity herself that year with *Tapestry*, using basically the same team of musicians that Asher had convened around James Taylor, but with Lou Adler as producer for his own Ode label, licensed through A&M. For all involved, the success was a rare case of patience being amply rewarded, although none of the participants had exactly been starving while they waited.

As writer of more than twenty-five top twenty hits during the sixties, Carole King and her lyric-writing collaborator Gerry Goffin were among the top five songwriting teams of their era, but their run seemed to be over when they separated after writing "Pleasant Valley Sunday" (for the Monkees) and "Natural Woman" (for Aretha Franklin) in 1967. Lou Adler had formed Ode after selling Dunhill to ABC that year, and recorded an album by the City, with Carole King as featured singer and main writer. Switching his label's distribution from CBS to A&M, he tried again with an album titled *Carole King: Writer*, before hitting the jackpot with *Tapestry*.

Since the end of the pre-Beatles "teen idol" era when Connie Francis and Brenda Lee had rivalled the most popular male singers, there had been no major white female artist in popular music. The change was very abrupt: where there had been dozens of girl singers and groups all over the radio, with Lesley Gore, the Shangri Las, and the Singing Nun among those who topped the charts in 1963 and 1964, suddenly it all got much harder, and only Petula Clark and Lulu (riding the crest of the British wave), Nancy Sinatra, Bobbie Gentry, and Jeannie C. Riley managed the trick in the next seven years. A couple of others sneaked through as part of groups, but essentially the sound of pop music in America through the second half of the sixties was predominantly male, and the only regular challenge was from black singers, notably Diana Ross, with and then without the Supremes, and Aretha Franklin.

Rock singer Janis Joplin upended some of the stereotypes of female singers, but in some ways it seemed that she was parodying the approach of the macho male singers who dominated the "objects" of their songs. Carole King's *Tapestry* offered the other extreme, comfort and wistful regret being the dominant themes typified in "You've

Got a Friend" and "It's Too Late". In many ways, this was a return to the conventions of pop music before rock 'n' roll presented alternative ways to approach the world, and more than ten million people declared their allegiance to such values by buying the record.

Carole King was a reserved public performer, and in many ways Carly Simon presented a more accessible persona, prepared to smile more engagingly at cameras and to sing more openly about the physical aspects of her friendships. Produced by Richard Perry, Carly's "You're So Vain" had a vengeful streak which took the song all the way to number one in 1972, but most of her songs shared a kind of wistfulness that characterized most of the singing writers and which was typified in Don McLean's "American Pie".

Released right at the end of 1971 by a previously unknown singer whose producer Ed Freeman had no special track record, "American Pie" came to be the epitaph for the fifteen-year era just ended. Starting out with a recollection of crying when Buddy Holly died, the song alluded to the heroes of the sixties one by one in a neat allegory that was carried to the top of the chart by a brilliant chorus that rhymed "Chevy" with "Levee" and was impossible not to sing along with. For an audience which found itself offended by the bubblegum trivia being passed off as pop music, and which found the sheer volume of the stadium-based rock-blues groups hard to handle, here was the perfect embodiment of their mounting nostalgia for the irretrievably lost era.

These singing writers were the final "maturity" of rock 'n' roll, which had been born out of a union between rhythm and blues and country and western music, which had gone to primary school with Bill Haley, to high school with Chuck Berry and Buddy Holly, and to college with Bob Dylan. The Beatles and Stones had shown up to prove that music for kids could still be fun for grown-ups, and the first rock groups had shown what the musicians had learned from those high school records. But now here was pop music and its audience settling down at home with a mortgage to pay, and kids to put to bed. Goodnight, America.

PLAY LIST

These are the records which moved rock 'n' roll another inch or two forward. The reasons for including each record vary, but each of them became a part of the background for anyone making records thereafter. Some are here because they brought a new musical idea into the framework of "rock 'n' roll"–piano boogie, guitar boogie, bass boogie; others redefined the use of an instrument–electric guitar, back-beat drums, electric bass, electric piano. And each new way of using a voice is represented by the person who thought of it first, usually with their first hit.

The list is biased against the real giants of the era–Elvis Presley, the Beatles, Bob Dylan–whose every record tended to be a trigger for a host of imitators; for them, and for the Motown artists, a few representative records are listed, trying to catch most facets of what they did. It is easier to represent contributions by the majority of performers who only had one basic idea.

Most of the records in the list were best-sellers, and they are listed in the chronological order in which they first surfaced on a national chart in the USA (pop, rhythm & blues, or country and western) or Britain. In addition to the artist, title, and record label, the recording location and producer are listed, to give an idea of the geographical shifts during the period, which saw records made in most regions of the United States and then, increasingly important through the sixties, in Britain.

A few records are listed which were not hits, mostly to represent the first recording of a song which became part of the rock 'n' roll repertoire, but occasionally to acknowledge a record whose value was recognized too late to affect its chance of making the charts.

The term "producer" did not come into common use in the music industry until around 1957, so for prior recordings the terms "arranger" and "supervisor" have been used. The letters "p", "a" and "s" are used in the following pages. Ideally, the name of the recording studio and the recording engineer would be provided too, but as such information is still largely undocumented, I have not attempted to find it.

The labels listed sometimes include the original label in parentheses before the name of the label which licensed the record for national distribution; and sometimes add in parentheses the name of a parent company where the record was a hit on a subsidiary label.

YEAR and Sequence Number	ARTIST Recording Location	TITLE Producer (p) Supervisor (s) Arranger (a)	RECORD LABEL
1946: 1	CECIL GANT Oakland	I WONDER Bob Geddins (s)	Gilt Edge
2	ROY MILTON Hollywood	R.M. BLUES Art Rupe (s) Roy Milton (a)	Juke Box (Specialty)
3	ELLA MAE MORSE (with FREDDIE SLACK) Los Angeles	HOUSE OF BLUE LIGHTS Dave Cavanaugh (s)	Capitol
4	JOHNNY MOORE'S THREE BLAZERS (with CHARLES BROWN) Los Angeles	DRIFTING BLUES Eddie Mesner (s)	Philo (Aladdin)
5	LOUIS JORDAN & HIS TYMPANY FIVE New York	CHOO CHOO CH'BOOGIE Louis Jordan (a) Milt Gabler (s)	Decca
6	THE DELMORE BROTHERS Cincinatti	FREIGHT TRAIN BOOGIE Louie Innes (s)	King
1948: 1	THE RAVENS New York	WRITE ME A LETTER Herb Abramson (s) Howard Biggs (a)	National

YEAR and Sequence Number	ARTIST Recording Location	TITLE Producer (p) Supervisor (s) Arranger (a)	RECORD LABEL
1948: 2	WYNONIE HARRIS Cincinatti	GOOD ROCKIN' TONIGHT Hal "Cornbread" Singer (a)	King
3	SONNY THOMPSON Chicago	LONG GONE, Parts 1 and 2 Sonny Thompson (a)	Miracle
4	THE ORIOLES New York	IT'S TOO SOON TO KNOW Deborah Chessler (s)	Natural (Jubilee)
5	AMOS MILBURN Los Angeles	CHICKEN SHACK BOOGIE Maxwell Davis (s, a)	Aladdin
1949: 1	JOHN LEE HOOKER Detroit	BOOGIE CHILLEN Bernard Bessman (s)	Modern
2	STICK McGHEE New York	DRINKIN' WINE SPO-DE-O-DEE Herb Abramson and Ahmet Ertegun (s)	Atlantic
3	DINAH WASHINGTON New York	BABY GET LOST Leonard Feather (s)	Mercury
4	ROY "BALDHEAD" BYRD (PROFESSOR LONGHAIR) New Orleans	MARDI GRAS IN NEW ORLEANS Herb Abramson and Ahmet Ertegun (s)	Atlantic
1950: 1	IVORY JOE HUNTER New York	I ALMOST LOST MY MIND (unknown)	MGM

2	FATS DOMINO New Orleans	THE FAT MAN Dave Bartholomew (s, a)	Imperial
3	HANK WILLIAMS Nashville	LONG GONE LONESOME BLUES Fred Rose (s)	MGM
4	JOE LIGGINS Los Angeles	PINK CHAMPAGNE Art Rupe (s)	Specialty
5	ROY BROWN Cincinatti	HARD LUCK BLUES Henry Glover (s)	DeLuxe (King)
6	RUTH BROWN New York	TEARDROPS FROM MY EYES Herb Abramson and Ahmet Ertegun (s) Budd Johnson (a)	Atlantic
7	PERCY MAYFIELD Los Angeles	PLEASE SEND ME SOMEONE TO LOVE Art Rupe (s)	Specialty
8	FIVE BLIND BOYS Houston	OUR FATHER (unknown)	Peacock
1951: 1	JAMES WAYNE Houson	TEND TO YOUR BUSINESS Bob Shad (s)	Sittin' In With
2	JACKIE BRENSTON Memphis	ROCKET 88 Ike Turner (s, a)	Chess
3	THE DOMINOES Cincinatti	SIXTY MINUTE MAN Ralph Bass (s) Billy Ward (a)	Federal
4	THE CLOVERS New York	DON'T YOU KNOW I LOVE YOU Herb Abramson and Ahmet Ertegun (s) Frank Slay (a)	Atlantic

YEAR and Sequence Number	ARTIST Recording Location	TITLE Producer (p) Supervisor (s) Arranger (a)	RECORD LABEL
1951: 5	SONNY BOY WILLIAMSON Jackson, Mississippi	EYESIGHT TO THE BLIND Lillian McMurray (s)	Trumpet
6	JOHNNIE RAY & THE FOUR LADS New York	CRY Mitch Miller (s)	OKeh/Columbia
7	B. B. KING Memphis	THREE O'CLOCK BLUES Joe Bihari (s) Ike Turner (a)	RPM
1952: 1	JIMMY FORREST Chicago	NIGHT TRAIN (unknown)	United
2	ELMORE JAMES Jackson, Mississippi	DUST MY BROOM Lillian McMurray (s)	Trumpet
3	ROSCO GORDON Memphis	NO MORE DOGGIN' Joe Bihari (s) Ike Turner (a)	RPM
4	LLOYD PRICE New Orleans	LAWDY MISS CLAWDY Dave Bartholomew (a) Art Rupe (s)	Specialty
5	LITTLE WALTER Chicago	JUKE Leonard Chess (s) Willie Dixon (a)	Checker (Chess)

6	WILLIE MABON Chicago	I DON'T KNOW Leonard Chess (s)	Chess
1953: 1	THE FIVE ROYALES New York	BABY DON'T DO IT Lowman Pauling (a) Bess Berman (s)	Apollo
2	HANK WILLIAMS Nashville	YOUR CHEATING HEART/ KAW LIGA Fred Rose (s)	MGM
3	WILLIE MAE THORNTON Houston	HOUND DOG Johnny Otis (s, a)	Peacock
4	FAYE ADAMS New York	SHAKE A HAND Al Silver (s) Joe Morris (a)	Herald
5	CLYDE McPHATTER & THE DRIFTERS New York	MONEY HONEY Ahmet Ertegun and Jerry Wexler (s) Jesse Stone (a)	Atlantic
6	THE HARPTONES New York	A SUNDAY KIND OF LOVE Raoul Cita (a)	Bruce
1954: 1	GUITAR SLIM New Orleans	THE THINGS I USED TO DO Ray Charles (a) Johnny Vincent (s)	Specialty
2	THE CROWS New York	GEE George Goldner (s)	Rama

YEAR and Sequence Number	ARTIST Recording Location	TITLE Producer (p) Supervisor (s) Arranger (a)	RECORD LABEL
1954: 3	MUDDY WATERS Chicago	HOOTCHIE COOTCHIE MAN Leonard Chess (s) Willie Dixon (a)	Chess
4	THE MIDNIGHTERS Cincinatti	WORK WITH ME ANNIE Henry Glover (a) Ralph Bass (s)	Federal
5	THE SPANIELS Chicago	GOODNIGHT SWEETHEART GOODNIGHT Calvin Carter (s)	Vee Jay
6	JOE TURNER New York	SHAKE RATTLE AND ROLL Ahmet Ertegun and Jerry Wexler (s) Jesse Stone (a)	Atlantic
7	ELVIS PRESLEY Memphis	THAT'S ALL RIGHT Sam Phillips (s)	Sun
8	CHORDS New York	SH-BOOM Ahmet Ertegun and Jerry Wexler (s) Jesse Stone (a)	Cat (Atlantic)
9	CHUCK WILLIS New York	I FEEL SO BAD Leroy Kirkland (a)	OKeh (CBS)
10	MARVIN & JOHNNY Los Angeles	TICK TOCK/CHERRY PIE Maxwell Davis (s, a)	Modern

11	LOWELL FULSON Dallas	RECONSIDER BABY Lowell Fulson (a) Stan Lewis (s)	Checker (Chess)
12	THE MOONGLOWS Chicago	SINCERELY Leonard Chess (s) Harvey Fuqua (a)	Chess
13	THE PENGUINS Los Angeles	EARTH ANGEL Dootsie Williams (s)	Dootone
1955: 1	LaVERN BAKER New York	TWEEDLE DEE Ahmet Ertegun and Jerry Wexler (s) Jesse Stone (a)	Atlantic
2	JOHNNY ACE Houston	PLEDGING MY LOVE Johnny Otis (s, a)	Duke
3	RAY CHARLES Atlanta, Georgia	I GOT A WOMAN Ray Charles (a) Ahmet Ertegun and Jerry Wexler (s)	Atlantic
4	ETTA JAMES Los Angeles	THE WALLFLOWER (ROLL WITH ME HENRY) Johnny Otis (s, a)	Modern
5	JIMMY REED Chicago	YOU DON'T HAVE TO GO Al Smith (s)	Vee Jay
6	BO DIDDLEY Chicago	BO DIDDLEY/I'M A MAN Leonard Chess (s) Willie Dixon (a)	Checker (Chess)

YEAR and Sequence Number	ARTIST Recording Location	TITLE Producer (p) Supervisor (s) Arranger (a)	RECORD LABEL
1955: 7	FATS DOMINO New Orleans	AIN'T IT A SHAME Dave Bartholomew (s, a)	Imperial
8	BILL HALEY & HIS COMETS New York	ROCK AROUND THE CLOCK Milt Gabler (s)	Decca
9	THE NUTMEGS New York	STORY UNTOLD Leroy Kirkland (s, a)	Herald
10	ELVIS PRESLEY Memphis	BABY LET'S PLAY HOUSE Sam Phillips (s)	Sun
11	THE PLATTERS Chicago	ONLY YOU Bobby Shad (s) Buck Ram (a)	Mercury
12	CHUCK BERRY Chicago	MAYBELLENE Leonard Chess (s) Willie Dixon (a)	Chess
13	ELVIS PRESLEY Memphis	MYSTERY TRAIN/I FORGOT TO REMEMBER TO FORGET Sam Phillips (s)	Sun
14	THE EL-DORADOS Chicago	AT MY FRONT DOOR Calvin Carter (s)	Vee Jay
15	LITTLE RICHARD New Orleans	TUTTI FRUTTI Bumps Blackwell	Specialty

16	THE CADILLACS New York	SPEEDOO Jesse Powell (a)	Josie (Jubilee)
17	THE TURBANS New York	WHEN YOU DANCE Leroy Kirkland (s, a)	Herald
1956: 1	LONNIE DONEGAN London	ROCK ISLAND LINE Dennis Preston (s)	Decca
2	FRANKIE LYMON & THE TEENAGERS New York	WHY DO FOOLS FALL IN LOVE? George Goldner (s) Richard Barrett (a)	Gee (Roulette)
3	CARL PERKINS Memphis	BLUE SUEDE SHOES Sam Phillips (s)	Sun
4	ELVIS PRESLEY Nashville	HEARTBREAK HOTEL Chet Atkins (s)	RCA-Victor
5	HOWLIN' WOLF Chicago	SMOKESTACK LIGHTNIN' Leonard Chess (s) Willie Dixon (a)	Chess
6	JAMES BROWN & THE FAMOUS FLAMES Cincinatti	PLEASE PLEASE PLEASE Ralph Bass (s)	Federal
7	LITTLE WILLIE JOHN Cincinatti	FEVER Henry Glover (s)	King
8	JOHNNY CASH Memphis	I WALK THE LINE Sam Phillips (s)	Sun
9	GENE VINCENT Nashville	BE-BOP-A-LULA/WOMAN LOVE Ken Nelson (s)	Capitol

YEAR and Sequence Number	ARTIST Recording Location	TITLE Producer (p) Supervisor (s) Arranger (a)	RECORD LABEL
1956: 10	SHIRLEY & LEE New Orleans	LET THE GOOD TIMES ROLL Dave Bartholomew (s, a)	Aladdin
11	ELVIS PRESLEY New York	HOUND DOG/DON'T BE CRUEL Steve Sholes and Chet Atkins (s)	RCA-Victor
12	BILL DOGGETT Cincinatti	HONKY TONK, Part II Henry Glover (s)	King
13	THE FIVE SATINS New Haven, Connecticut	(I'LL REMEMBER) IN THE STILL OF THE NIGHT Fred Parris (a)	(Standord) Herald
14	FATS DOMINO New Orleans	BLUEBERRY HILL Dave Bartholomew (s, a)	Imperial
15	BOOGALOO & HIS GALLANT CREW Hollywood	COPS & ROBBERS/CLOTHES LINE Kent Harris (a)	Crest
16	MICKEY & SYLVIA New York	LOVE IS STRANGE King Curtis (s)	Groove (RCA)
17	YOUNG JESSIE Los Angeles	MARY LOU Maxwell Davis (s, a)	Modern
18	RICHARD BERRY Los Angeles	LOUIE LOUIE (Unknown)	Flip
1957: 1	THE DEL VIKINGS Pittsburg, Pennsylvania	COME GO WITH ME Barry Kaye (s)	(Fee Bee) Dot

2	THE DIAMONDS Chicago	LITTLE DARLIN' Clyde Otis (s)	Mercury
3	JUNIOR PARKER Houston	NEXT TIME YOU SEE ME Bill Harvey (s, a)	Duke
4	ELVIS PRESLEY Hollywood	ALL SHOOK UP Elvis Presley (a)	RCA-Victor
5	THE COASTERS Hollywood	SEARCHIN'/YOUNG BLOOD Jerry Leiber and Mike Stoller (p)	Atco (Atlantic)
6	THE EVERLY BROTHERS Nashville	BYE BYE LOVE Archie Bleyer and Wesley Rose (s)	Cadence
7	DALE HAWKINS Shreveport	SUSIE-Q Stan Lewis (s)	Checker (Chess)
8	JERRY LEE LEWIS Memphis	WHOLE LOTTA SHAKIN' GOIN' ON Jack Clement (s)	Sun
9	HUEY SMITH & THE CLOWNS New Orleans	ROCKIN' PNEUMONIA & THE BOOGIE WOOGIE FLU Johnny Vincent (s)	Ace
10	THE CRICKETS Clovis, New Mexico	THAT'LL BE THE DAY Norman Petty (s)	Brunswick
11	ELVIS PRESLEY Hollywood	JAILHOUSE ROCK Elvis Presley (a)	RCA-Victor
12	SAM COOKE Hollywood	YOU SEND ME/SUMMERTIME Bumps Blackwell (s) Rene Hall (a)	Keen
13	THURSTON HARRIS & THE SHARPS Hollywood	LITTLE BITTY PRETTY ONE Earl Palmer (s)	Aladdin

YEAR and Sequence Number	ARTIST Recording Location	TITLE Producer (p) Supervisor (s) Arranger (a)	RECORD LABEL
1957: 14	BUDDY HOLLY Clovis, New Mexico	PEGGY SUE Norman Petty (s)	Coral
15	DANNY & THE JUNIORS Philadelphia, Pennsylvania	AT THE HOP Artie Singer (s)	(Singular) ABC-Paramount
16	JOHNNY "GUITAR" WATSON Hollywood	GANGSTER OF LOVE Bumps Blackwell (a, s)	Keen
1958: 1	THE SILHOUETTES Philadelphia, Pennsylvania	GET A JOB Kae Williams (s)	(Junior) Ember
2	THE CHANTELS New York	MAYBE Richard Barrett (p)	End
3	CHUCK BERRY Chicago	SWEET LITTLE SIXTEEN Leonard Chess (p)	Chess
4	DON GIBSON Nashville	OH LONESOME ME/I CAN'T STOP LOVING YOU Chet Atkins (p)	RCA-Victor
5	CHUCK BERRY Chicago	JOHNNY B. GOODE Leonard Chess (p)	Chess
6	LINK WRAY Norfolk, Virginia	RUMBLE Ray Vernon (p)	Cadence
7	BOBBY DARIN New York	DREAM LOVER Ahmet Ertegun (s)	Atco (Atlantic)

8	BOBBY FREEMAN New York	DO YOU WANNA DANCE? (unknown)	Josie (Jubilee)
9	THE COASTERS New York	YAKETY YAK Jerry Leiber and Mike Stoller (p)	Atco (Atlantic)
10	JACK SCOTT Detroit	LEROY/MY TRUE LOVE Jack Scott (p)	Carlton
11	JERRY BUTLER & THE IMPRESSIONS Chicago	FOR YOUR PRECIOUS LOVE Curtis Mayfield (a)	(Falcon) Abner (Vee Jay)
12	DUANE EDDY Phoenix, Arizona	REBEL ROUSER Lee Hazelwood (p)	Jamie
13	EDDIE COCHRAN Los Angeles	SUMMERTIME BLUES Jerry Capehart (s)	Liberty
14	CLIFF RICHARD London	MOVE IT Norrie Paramor (p)	Columbia
15	CONWAY TWITTY Nashville	IT'S ONLY MAKE BELIEVE Jim Vienneau (p)	MGM
16	THE TEDDY BEARS Hollywood	TO KNOW HIM IS TO LOVE HIM Phil Spector (p)	Dore
17	CLYDE McPHATTER New York	A LOVER'S QUESTION Ahmet Ertegun and Jerry Wexler (p)	Atlantic
18	JAMES BROWN Cincinatti	TRY ME James Brown (p)	Federal
19	JACKIE WILSON New York	LONELY TEARDROPS Dick Jacobs (p, a)	Brunswick
20	THE PLATTERS New York (?)	SMOKE GETS IN YOUR EYES Clyde Otis (p)	Mercury

YEAR and Sequence Number	ARTIST Recording Location	TITLE Producer (p) Supervisor (s) Arranger (a)	RECORD LABEL
1958: 21	RITCHIE VALENS Los Angeles	DONNA/LA BAMBA Rene Hall (a)	Del-Fi (Keen)
1959: 1	THE SKYLINERS Pittsburgh	SINCE I DON'T HAVE YOU Joe Rock (s)	Calico
2	WILBERT HARRISON New York	KANSAS CITY Bobby Robinson (p)	Fury
3	DION & THE BELMONTS New York	A TEENAGER IN LOVE Bob and Gene Schwartz (s)	Laurie
4	THE DRIFTERS New York	THERE GOES MY BABY Jerry Leiber and Mike Stoller (p) Stan Appelbaum (a)	Atlantic
5	THE FLAMINGOS New York	I ONLY HAVE EYES FOR YOU Sammy Lowe (a)	End (Roulette)
6	RAY CHARLES New York	WHAT'D I SAY? Jerry Wexler and Ahmet Ertegun (s) Ray Charles (a)	Atlantic
7	JOHNNY & THE HURRICANES Detroit	RED RIVER ROCK Irving Micahnik (s)	Warwick
8	MARTY ROBBINS Nashville	EL PASO Don Law (s)	Columbia

9	ADAM FAITH London	WHAT DO YOU WANT? Norrie Paramor (s) John Barry (a)	Parlophone (EMI)
10	BUSTER BROWN New York	FANNIE MAE Bobby Robinson (s)	Fire
11	BILL BLACK'S COMBO Memphis	SMOKIE, Part 2 Joe Cuoghi (s)	Hi
12	BRENDA LEE Nashville	SWEET NOTHIN'S Owen Bradley (s)	Decca
1960: 1	JIMMY JONES New York	HANDY MAN Bob Mersey and Leroy Kirkland (a, s)	Cub (MGM)
2	BARRETT STRONG Detroit	MONEY Berry Gordy (p)	Anna (Gordy)
3	EDITH PIAF Paris, France	MILORD Robert Chauvigny (a)	Pathe Marconi
4	ROY ORBISON Nashville	ONLY THE LONELY Fred Foster (p)	Monument
5	JOHNNY KIDD & THE PIRATES London	SHAKIN' ALL OVER Wally Ridley (s)	HMV (EMI)
6	THE EVERLY BROTHERS Nashville	CATHY'S CLOWN Wesley Rose (s)	Warner Brothers
7	THE SHADOWS London	APACHE Norrie Paramor (s)	Columbia (EMI)

YEAR and Sequence Number	ARTIST Recording Location	TITLE Producer (p) Supervisor (s) Arranger (a)	RECORD LABEL
1960: 8	IKE & TINA TURNER New York	A FOOL IN LOVE Ike Turner (p)	Sue
9	THE DRIFTERS New York	SAVE THE LAST DANCE FOR ME Jerry Leiber and Mike Stoller (p)	Atlantic
10	RAY CHARLES Los Angeles	GEORGIA ON MY MIND Ray Charles (p)	ABC-Paramount
11	GARY "U.S." BONDS Norfolk, Virginia	NEW ORLEANS Frank Guida (p)	LeGrand
12	THE SHIRELLES New York	WILL YOU STILL LOVE ME TOMORROW Luther Dixon (p)	Scepter
1961: 1	BEN E. KING New York	SPANISH HARLEM Jerry Leiber and Mike Stoller (p)	Atco (Atlantic)
2	BOBBY BLAND Houston	I PITY THE FOOL Joe Scott (p, a)	Duke
3	DEL SHANNON Detroit	RUNAWAY Irving Micahnik (s) Max Crook (a)	Big Top
4	THE MARCELS New York	BLUE MOON Stu Phillips (p)	Colpix

5	HELEN SHAPIRO London	DON'T TREAT ME LIKE A CHILD Norrie Paramor (s)	Columbia (EMI)
6	ERNIE K-DOE New Orleans	MOTHER-IN-LAW Allen Toussaint (p, a)	Minit (Imperial)
7	BILLY FURY London	HALFWAY TO PARADISE Ivor Raymonde (a)	Decca (UK)
8	CHRIS KENNER New Orleans	I LIKE IT LIKE THAT Allen Toussaint (p, a)	Instant (Atlantic)
9	BOBBY PARKER Philadelphia	WATCH YOUR STEP Bobby Caldwell (s)	V-Tone
10	THE MAR KEYS Memphis	LAST NIGHT Jim Stewart (s)	Satellite (Stax)
11	MARVELETTES Detroit	PLEASE MR POSTMAN Berry Gordy (p)	Tamla (Gordy)
12	RAY CHARLES Los Angeles	HIT THE ROAD JACK Ray Charles (p)	ABC-Paramount
13	DION New York	RUNAROUND SUE Gene Schwartz (s)	Laurie
14	THE SHOWMEN New Orleans	IT WILL STAND/COUNTRY FOOL Allen Toussaint (s)	Minit (Imperial)
15	JAMES RAY New York	IF YOU GOTTA MAKE A FOOL OF SOMEBODY Hutch Davie (a)	Caprice
16	THE MIRACLES Detroit	SHOP AROUND Berry Gordy (s)	Tamla (Gordy)

YEAR and Sequence Number	ARTIST Recording Location	TITLE Producer (p) Supervisor (s) Arranger (a)	RECORD LABEL
1962: 1	GENE CHANDLER Chicago	DUKE OF EARL Carl Davis (p)	Vee Jay
2	BRUCE CHANNEL Fort Worth	HEY! BABY Bill Hall (p)	Smash (Mercury)
3	SAM COOKE New York	TWISTING THE NIGHT AWAY Hugo and Luigi (s)	RCA-Victor
4	ARTHUR ALEXANDER Muscle Shoals, Alabama	YOU BETTER MOVE ON Rick Hall (p)	Dot
5	KETTY LESTER Los Angeles	LOVE LETTERS Lincoln Mayorga (p, a)	Era
6	WILBERT HARRISON New York	LETS STICK TOGETHER Bobby Robinson (s)	Fury
7	CHUCK JACKSON New York	ANY DAY NOW Burt Bacharach (s, a)	Wand (Scepter)
8	RAY CHARLES Los Angeles	I CAN'T STOP LOVING YOU Ray Charles (p)	ABC-Paramount
9	THE ISLEY BROTHERS New York	TWIST AND SHOUT Bert Berns (p)	Wand (Scepter)
10	BARBARA LYNN Houston, Texas	YOU'LL LOSE A GOOD THING Huey Meaux (p)	Jamie
11	SAM COOKE New York	BRING IT ON HOME TO ME/ HAVING A PARTY Hugo and Luigi (s)	RCA-Victor

12	LITTLE EVA New York	THE LOCOMOTION Gerry Goffin (p, a)	Dimension
13	BOOKER T. & THE M.G.'S Memphis	GREEN ONIONS Jim Stewart (s)	Stax
14	THE FOUR SEASONS Philadelphia	SHERRY Bob Crewe and Frank Slay (p)	Vee Jay
15	THE CRYSTALS New York	HE'S A REBEL Phil Spector (p)	Philles
16	THE BEATLES London	LOVE ME DO George Martin (p)	Parlophone (EMI)
17	THE MIRACLES Detroit	YOU'VE REALLY GOT A HOLD ON ME Smokey Robinson (p)	Tamla (Gordy)
1963: 1	THE CHIFFONS New York	HE'S SO FINE Gerry Goffin (p)	Laurie
2	OTIS REDDING Memphis	THESE ARMS OF MINE Jim Stewart (s)	Volt (Atlantic)
3	THE DRIFTERS New York	ON BROADWAY Jerry Leiber and Mike Stoller (p)	Atlantic
4	THE CRYSTALS Los Angeles	DA DOO RON RON Phil Spector (p)	Philles
5	LESLEY GORE New York	IT'S MY PARTY Claus Ogerman (a)	Mercury
6	LONNIE MACK Cincinatti	MEMPHIS Harry Carlson (p)	Fraternity

YEAR and Sequence Number	ARTIST Recording Location	TITLE Producer (p) Supervisor (s) Arranger (a)	RECORD LABEL
1963: 7	INEZ FOXX New York	MOCKINGBIRD Juggy Murray (p)	Symbol (Sue)
8	GARNET MIMMS Philadelphia	CRY BABY Jerry Ragavoy (p)	United Artists
9	THE RONETTES Los Angeles	BE MY BABY Phil Spector (p)	Philles
10	THE BEATLES London	SHE LOVES YOU George Martin (s)	Parlophone (EMI)
11	THE JAYNETTS New York	SALLY GO 'ROUND THE ROSES Abner Spector (p) Artie Butler (a)	Tuff (Chess)
12	THE IMPRESSIONS Chicago	IT'S ALL RIGHT Curtis Mayfield (p) Johnny Pate (a)	ABC-Paramount
13	DUSTY SPRINGFIELD London	I ONLY WANT TO BE WITH YOU Johnny Franz (p)	Philips
14	THE DAVE CLARK FIVE London	GLAD ALL OVER Dave Clark (p)	Columbia (EMI)
15	DIONNE WARWICK New York	ANYONE WHO HAD A HEART Burt Bacharach (p, a)	Scepter
16	THE BEATLES London	I WANNA HOLD YOUR HAND George Martin (s)	Parlophone (EMI)

17	RONNIE HAWKINS New York	WHO DO YOU LOVE? Henry Glover (p)	Roulette
1964: 1	THE SEARCHERS London	NEEDLES AND PINS Tony Hatch (p)	Pye
2	MILLIE London	MY BOY LOLLIPOP Chris Blackwell (p)	Fontana (Philips)
3	THE BEACH BOYS Hollywood	I GET AROUND Brian Wilson (p, a)	Capitol
4	MANFRED MANN London	DO WAH DIDDY DIDDY John Burgess (s) Manfred Mann (a)	HMV (EMI)
5	THE DRIFTERS New York	UNDER THE BOARDWALK Bert Berns (p) Mike Leander (a)	Atlantic
6	THE ANIMALS London	THE HOUSE OF THE RISING SUN Mickie Most (p) Alan Price (a)	Columbia (EMI)
7	THE SUPREMES Detroit	WHERE DID OUR LOVE GO? Brian Holland and Lamont Dozier (p, a)	Motown (Gordy)
8	THE BEATLES London	A HARD DAY'S NIGHT George Martin (s)	Parlophone (EMI)
9	THE KINKS London	YOU REALLY GOT ME Shel Talmy (p)	Pye
10	MARTHA & THE VANDELLAS Detroit	DANCING IN THE STREET William "Mickey" Stevenson (p)	Gordy

YEAR and Sequence Number	ARTIST Recording Location	TITLE Producer (p) Supervisor (s) Arranger (a)	RECORD LABEL
1964 11	THE SHANGRI LA'S New York	REMEMBER (WALKING IN THE SAND) George "Shadow" Morton (p) Artie Butler (a)	Red Bird
12	DON COVAY & THE GOODTIMERS New York	MERCY MERCY Horace Ott (s)	Rosemart (Atlantic)
13	ROY ORBISON Nashville	OH PRETTY WOMAN Fred Foster (p)	Monument
14	LITTLE ANTHONY & THE IMPERIALS New York	GOIN' OUT OF MY HEAD Teddy Randazzo (p)	DCP
15	PETULA CLARK London	DOWNTOWN Tony Hatch (p, a)	Pye
16	SANDIE SHAW London	(THERE'S) ALWAYS SOMETHING THERE TO REMIND ME Chris Andrews (p)	Pye
17	THE RIGHTEOUS BROTHERS Los Angeles	YOU'VE LOST THAT LOVIN' FEELIN' Phil Spector (p) Gene Page (a)	Philles

18	GEORGIE FAME London	YEH YEH Tony Palmer (p)	Columbia (EMI)
1965: 1	THEM London	BABY PLEASE DON'T GO*/ GLORIA† * Bert Berns (p)/†Dick Rowe (p)	Decca
2	SAM COOKE Los Angeles (?)	SHAKE/A CHANGE IS GONNA COME Hugo and Luigi (s)	RCA-Victor
3	THE TEMPTATIONS Detroit	MY GIRL Smokey Robinson (p)	Gordy
4	OTIS REDDING Memphis	MR PITIFUL Steve Cropper and Otis Redding (p)	Volt (Stax)
5	JOE TEX Muscle Shoals, Alabama	HOLD WHAT YOU'VE GOT Buddy Killen (s) Rick Hall (a)	Dial
6	JUNIOR WALKER Detroit	SHOTGUN Berry Gordy and Lawrence Horn (p)	Soul (Gordy)
7	WILLIE TEE New Orleans	TEASIN' YOU Wardell Quezerque (p)	Atlantic
8	SOLOMON BURKE New York	GOT TO GET YOU OFF OF MY MIND Jerry Wexler (p)	Atlantic
9	THE YARDBIRDS London	FOR YOUR LOVE Paul Samwell-Smith (p)	Columbia (EMI)
10	BOB DYLAN New York	THE TIMES THEY ARE A-CHANGIN' Tom Wilson (p)	Columbia

YEAR and Sequence Number	ARTIST Recording Location	TITLE Producer (p) Supervisor (s) Arranger (a)	RECORD LABEL
1965: 11	SAM THE SHAM & THE PHARAOHS Memphis	WOOLY BULLY Stan Kesler (s)	MGM
12	THE DIXIE CUPS New York	IKO IKO Jeff Barry and Ellie Greenwich (p)	Red Bird
13	THE SIR DOUGLAS QUINTET Houston, Texas	SHE'S ABOUT A MOVER Huey Meaux (p)	Tribe
14	THE FOUR TOPS Detroit	I CAN'T HELP MYSELF Brian Holland and Lamont Dozier (p)	Motown (Gordy)
15	THE BYRDS Hollywood	MR. TAMBOURINE MAN Terry Melcher (p)	Columbia
16	SONNY & CHER Hollywood	I GOT YOU BABE Sonny Bono (p) Harold Battiste (a)	Atco (Atlantic)
17	WILSON PICKETT Memphis	IN THE MIDNIGHT HOUR Jerry Wexler (p)	Atlantic
18	JAMES BROWN Cincinatti	PAPA'S GOT A BRAND NEW BAG James Brown (p)	King
19	THE MIRACLES Detroit	THE TRACKS OF MY TEARS Smokey Robinson (p)	Tamla (Gordy)

20	THE ANIMALS London	WE GOTTA GET OUT OF THIS PLACE Mickie Most (p)	Columbia (EMI)
21	BOB DYLAN New York	LIKE A ROLLIN' STONE Tom Wilson (p)	Columbia
22	THE McCOYS New York	HANG ON SLOOPY Bert Berns (p)	Bang
23	BARRY McGUIRE Los Angeles	EVE OF DESTRUCTION Lou Adler (p)	Dunhill (ABC)
24	THE LOVIN' SPOONFUL New York	DO YOU BELIEVE IN MAGIC? Erik Jacobsen (p)	Kama Sutra
25	THE ROLLING STONES London	(I CAN'T GET NO) SATISFACTION Mick Jagger and Keith Richard (p)	Decca
26	FONTELLA BASS Chicago	RESCUE ME Oliver Sain (p)	Chess
27	MARVIN GAYE Detroit	AIN'T THAT PECULIAR Smokey Robinson (p)	Tamla (Gordy)
28	THE WHO London	MY GENERATION Shel Talmy (p)	Brunswick
29	SIMON & GARFUNKEL New York	THE SOUNDS OF SILENCE Tom Wilson (p)	Columbia
30	THE SPENCER DAVIS GROUP London	KEEP ON RUNNING Chris Blackwell (p)	Fontana
31	MITCH RYDER & THE DETROIT WHEELS Detroit	JENNY TAKE A RIDE Bob Crewe (p)	New Voice (Bell)

YEAR and Sequence Number	ARTIST Recording Location	TITLE Producer (p) Supervisor (s) Arranger (a)	RECORD LABEL
1965: 32	THE BEATLES London	WE CAN WORK IT OUT/ DAYTRIPPER George Martin (p)	Parlophone (EMI)
33	STEVIE WONDER Detroit	UPTIGHT (EVERYTHING IS ALL RIGHT) Hank Cosby and Mickey Stevenson (p)	Tamla (Gordy)
1966: 1	THE MAMAS AND THE PAPAS Hollywood	CALIFORNIA DREAMIN' Lou Adler (p)	Dunhill
2	NANCY SINATRA Hollywood	THESE BOOTS ARE MADE FOR WALKING Lee Hazelwood (p)	Reprise
3	THE BOBBY FULLER FOUR Hollywood	I FOUGHT THE LAW Bob Keene (s)	Mustang (Keen)
4	THE ISLEY BROTHERS Detroit	THIS OLD HEART OF MINE Brian Holland and Lamont Dozier (p)	Tamla (Gordy)
5	THE YARDBIRDS London	SHAPES OF THINGS Paul Samwell-Smith (p)	Columbia
6	THE YOUNG RASCALS New York	GOOD LOVIN' Tom Dowd and Arif Mardin (p)	Atlantic
7	CHER Hollywood	BANG BANG Sonny Bono (p) Harold Battiste (a)	Imperial

8	DUSTY SPRINGFIELD London	YOU DON'T HAVE TO SAY YOU LOVE ME Johnny Franz (p)	Philips
9	PERCY SLEDGE Muscle Shoals, Alabama	WHEN A MAN LOVES A WOMAN Quin Ivy (p)	Atlantic
10	SAM & DAVE Memphis	HOLD ON, I'M COMIN' Isaac Hayes and Dave Porter (p)	Stax
11	THE TROGGS London	WILD THING Larry Page (p)	Fontana
12	THE TEMPTATIONS Detroit	AIN'T TOO PROUD TO BEG Norman Whitfield (p)	Gordy
13	IKE & TINA TURNER Hollywood	RIVER DEEP, MOUNTAIN HIGH Phil Spector (p)	Philles
14	THE LOVIN' SPOONFUL New York	SUMMER IN THE CITY Erik Jacobsen (p)	Kama Sutra
15	LEE DORSEY New Orleans	WORKING IN A COAL MINE Allen Toussaint (p)	Amy (Bell)
16	THE BEATLES London	ELEANOR RIGBY George Martin (p)	Parlophone (EMI)
17	THE SUPREMES Detroit	YOU CAN'T HURRY LOVE Brian Holland and Lamont Dozier (p)	Motown (Gordy)
18	NEIL DIAMOND New York	CHERRY CHERRY Bert Berns (p)	Bang
19	THE FOUR TOPS Detroit	REACH OUT (I'LL BE THERE) Brian Holland and Lamont Dozier (p)	Motown (Gordy)
20	? & THE MYSTERIANS Flint, Michigan	96 TEARS Rudy Martinez (a)	(Pa Go Go) Cameo

YEAR and Sequence Number	ARTIST Recording Location	TITLE Producer (p) Supervisor (s) Arranger (a)	RECORD LABEL
1966: 21	THE BEACH BOYS Los Angeles	GOOD VIBRATIONS Brian Wilson (p)	Capitol
22	THE SUPREMES Detroit	YOU KEEP ME HANGIN' ON Brian Holland and Lamont Dozier (p)	Motown (Gordy)
23	AARON NEVILLE New Orleans	TELL IT LIKE IT IS Allen Toussaint (p)	Parlo
24	THE MONKEES Los Angeles	I'M A BELIEVER Tommy Boyce and Bobby Hart (p)	Colgems
25	THE ELECTRIC PRUNES Los Angeles	I HAD TOO MUCH TO DREAM LAST NIGHT Dave Hassinger (p)	Reprise
26	CREAM London	I FEEL FREE Robert Stigwood (p)	Reaction
1967: 1	THE JIMI HENDRIX EXPERIENCE London	HEY JOE Chas Chandler (p)	Polydor
2	MARVIN GAYE & KIM WESTON Detroit	IT TAKES TWO Mickey Stevenson (p)	Tamla (Gordy)
3	BUFFALO SPRINGFIELD Los Angeles	FOR WHAT IT'S WORTH Charles Greene and Brian Stone (p)	Atco (Atlantic)

4	THE TURTLES Los Angeles	HAPPY TOGETHER Joe Wissert (p)	White Whale
5	DYKE & THE BLAZERS Los Angeles	FUNKY BROADWAY Coleman and Barrett for Desert Sound (p)	Original Sound
6	PRINCE BUSTER Kingston, Jamaica	AL CAPONE Prince Buster (p)	Blue Beat
7	ARETHA FRANKLIN Muscle Shoals, Alabama	I NEVER LOVED A MAN Jerry Wexler (p)	Atlantic
8	THE JEFFERSON AIRPLANE San Francisco	SOMEBODY TO LOVE Rick Jarrard (p)	RCA-Victor
9	THE RASCALS New York	GROOVIN' The Rascals (p)	Atlantic
10	PAUL REVERE & THE RAIDERS Los Angeles	HIM OR ME, WHAT'S IT GONNA BE Terry Melcher (p)	Columbia
11	THE KINKS London	WATERLOO SUNSET Ray Davies (p)	Pye
12	PROCOL HARUM London	A WHITER SHADE OF PALE Denny Cordell (p)	Deram
13	THE DOORS Los Angeles	LIGHT MY FIRE Paul Rothschild (p)	Elektra
14	STEVIE WONDER Detroit	I WAS MADE TO LOVE HER Hank Cosby (p)	Tamla (Gordy)
15	TRAFFIC London	PAPER SUN Jimmy Miller (p)	Island

YEAR and Sequence Number	ARTIST Recording Location	TITLE Producer (p) Supervisor (s) Arranger (a)	RECORD LABEL
1967:16	DESMOND DEKKER & THE ACES Kingston, Jamaica	007 (SHANTY TOWN) Leslie Kong (p)	Pyramid
17	VAN MORRISON New York	BROWN EYED GIRL Bert Berns (p)	Bang
18	BOBBIE GENTRY Los Angeles	ODE TO BILLIE JOE Kelly Gordon (p) Jimmie Haskell (a)	Capitol
19	PINK FLOYD London	SEE EMILY PLAY Norman Smith (p)	Harvest (EMI)
20	THE BOX TOPS Memphis	THE LETTER Dan Penn (p)	Mala (Bell)
21	THE SMALL FACES London	ITCHYCOO PARK Ronnie Lane and Stevie Marriott (p)	Immediate
22	JACKIE WILSON Chicago	(YOUR LOVE KEEPS LIFTING ME) HIGHER AND HIGHER Carl Davis (p)	Brunswick
23	HUGO MONTENEGRO Hollywood	THE GOOD, THE BAD AND THE UGLY Hugo Montenegro (p)	RCA-Victor
24	GLEN CAMPBELL Hollywood	BY THE TIME I GET TO PHOENIX Al De Lory (p)	Capitol

25	GLADYS KNIGHT & THE PIPS Detroit	I HEARD IT THROUGH THE GRAPEVINE Norman Whitfield (p)	Soul (Gordy)
1968: 1	OTIS REDDING Memphis	(SITTIN' ON) THE DOCK OF THE BAY Otis Redding and Steve Cropper (p)	Volt (Stax)
2	THE DELFONICS Philadelphia	LA LA MEANS I LOVE YOU Thom Bell (p)	Philly Groove (Bell)
3	SLY & THE FAMILY STONE San Francisco	DANCE TO THE MUSIC Sylvester Stewart (p)	Epic (CBS)
4	THE SMALL FACES London	LAZY SUNDAY Steve Marriott and Ronnie Lane (p)	Immediate
5	MERILEE RUSH & THE TURNABOUTS Memphis	ANGEL OF THE MORNING Tommy Cogbill and Chips Moman (p)	Bell
6	STEPPENWOLF Los Angeles	BORN TO BE WILD Gabriel Mekler (p)	Dunhill
7	CREAM New York	SUNSHINE OF YOUR LOVE Felix Pappalardi (p)	Atco (Atlantic)
8	THE BAND Woodstock, New York	THE WEIGHT John Simon (p)	Capitol
9	THE BEATLES London	HEY JUDE George Martin (p)	Apple
10	JAMES BROWN Cincinatti	SAY IT LOUD, I'M BLACK & I'M PROUD James Brown (p)	King

YEAR and Sequence Number	ARTIST Recording Location	TITLE Producer (p) Supervisor (s) Arranger (a)	RECORD LABEL
1968: 11	JOHNNIE TAYLOR Memphis	WHO'S MAKING LOVE Don Davis (p)	Stax
12	TAMMY WYNETTE Nashville	STAND BY YOUR MAN Billy Sherrill (p)	Columbia
13	DIANA ROSS & THE SUPREMES Detroit	LOVE CHILD The Corporation (p)	Motown (Gordy)
14	MARVIN GAYE Detroit	I HEARD IT THROUGH THE GRAPEVINE Norman Whitfield (p)	Tamla (Gordy)
15	FLEETWOOD MAC London	ALBATROSS Mike Vernon (p)	Blue Horizon
16	TYRONE DAVIS Chicago	CAN I CHANGE MY MIND Carl Davis (p)	Dakar (Atlantic)
1969: 1	JOE SOUTH Atlanta, Georgia	GAMES PEOPLE PLAY Joe South (p, a)	Capitol
2	CREEDENCE CLEARWATER REVIVAL San Francisco	PROUD MARY John Fogerty (p, a)	Fantasy
3	PETER SARSTEDT London	WHERE DO YOU GO TO MY LOVELY Ray Singer (p)	United Artists

4	THE EDWIN HAWKINS SINGERS San Francisco	OH HAPPY DAY Edwin Hawkins (p, a)	Pavilion (Buddah)
5	DESMOND DEKKER Kingston, Jamaica	THE ISRAELITES Leslie Kong (p)	Pyramid
6	FLEETWOOD MAC London	MAN OF THE WORLD Fleetwood Mac (p)	Immediate
7	TONY JOE WHITE Nashville	POLK SALAD ANNIE Billy Swan (p)	Monument
8	THE ROLLING STONES	HONKY TONK WOMEN Mick Jagger and Keith Richard (p) ("The Glimmer Twins")	Decca
9	THE ARCHIES New York	SUGAR SUGAR Jeff Barry (p)	Calendar
10	DAVID BOWIE London	SPACE ODDITY Gus Dudgeon (p, a)	Philips
11	CROSBY, STILLS & NASH Los Angeles	SUITE: JUDY BLUE EYES Crosby, Stills and Nash (p)	Atlantic
12	MERLE HAGGARD Bakersfield, California	OKIE FROM MUSKOGEE Ken Nelson (p)	Capitol
13	THE PIONEERS Kingston, Jamaica	LONG SHOT KICK THE BUCKET Leslie Kong (p)	Trojan
14	HARRY J ALLSTARS Kingston, Jamaica	THE LIQUIDATOR Harry Johnson (p)	Trojan
15	JIMMY CLIFF Kingston, Jamaica	WONDERFUL WORLD, BEAUTIFUL PEOPLE Leslie Kong (p)	Trojan

YEAR and Sequence Number	ARTIST Recording Location	TITLE Producer (p) Supervisor (s) Arranger (a)	RECORD LABEL
1969: 16	THE JACKSON FIVE Detroit	I WANT YOU BACK The Corporation (p)	Motown
1970: 1	SLY & THE FAMILY STONE San Francisco	THANK YOU (FALETTINME BEMICELF AGAIN)/ EVERYBODY IS A STAR Sly Stone (p)	Epic (Columbia)
2	SIMON & GARFUNKEL New York	BRIDGE OVER TROUBLED WATER Phil Ramone and Paul Simon (p)	Columbia
3	THE MAYTALS Kingston, Jamaica	MONKEY MAN Leslie Kong and Warrick Lynn (p)	Trojan
4	FREDA PAYNE Detroit	BAND OF GOLD Greg Perry (p)	Invictus
5	FREE London	ALL RIGHT NOW Free (p)	Island
6	PAUL KELLY Nashville	STANDING IN THE NAME OF THE LORD Buddy Killen (p)	Happy Tiger
7	EDWIN STARR Detroit	WAR Norman Whitfield (p)	Gordy
8	NEIL DIAMOND New York	CRACKLIN' ROSIE Tom Catalano (p)	UNI

	9	JAMES TAYLOR Hollywood	FIRE AND RAIN Peter Asher (p)	Warner Brothers
	10	KING FLOYD Jackson, Mississippi	GROOVE ME Wardell Quezerque (p)	Chimneyville (Atlantic)
	11	T. REX London	RIDE A WHITE SWAN Tony Visconti (p)	Fly
	12	JERRY REED Nashville	AMOS MOSES Chet Atkins (p)	RCA
	13	DOLLY PARTON Nashville	JOSHUA Bob Ferguson (p)	RCA
1971:	1	SAMMI SMITH Nashville	HELP ME MAKE IT THROUGH THE NIGHT Jim Malloy (p)	Mega
	2	THE STYLISTICS Philadelphia, Pennsylvania	YOU'RE A BIG GIRL NOW Thom Bell (p, a)	Avco-Embassy
	3	THE TEMPTATIONS Detroit	JUST MY IMAGINATION Norman Whitfield (p)	Gordy
	4	MARVIN GAYE Detroit	WHAT'S GOIN' ON Marvin Gaye (p)	Tamla (Gordy)
	5	DEREK & THE DOMINOES Miami, Florida	LAYLA Tom Dowd (p)	Atco (Atlantic)
	6	CAROLE KING Los Angeles	IT'S TOO LATE Lou Adler (p)	Ode (A&M)
	7	FREDA PAYNE Detroit	BRING THE BOYS HOME Greg Perry (p)	Invictus

YEAR and Sequence Number	ARTIST Recording Location	TITLE Producer (p) Supervisor (s) Arranger (a)	RECORD LABEL
1971: 8	AL GREEN Memphis	TIRED OF BEING ALONE Willie Mitchell (p)	Hi
9	DENISE LASALLE Memphis	TRAPPED BY A THING CALLED LOVE Willie Mitchell (p)	Westbound
10	ROD STEWART London	MAGGIE MAY Rod Stewart (p)	Mercury
11	ISAAC HAYES Memphis	SHAFT Isaac Hayes (p)	Stax
12	THE CHI-LITES Chicago	HAVE YOU SEEN HER Eugene Record (p)	Brunswick
13	SLADE London	COZ I LUV YOU Chas Chandler (p)	Polydor
14	BETTY WRIGHT Miami, Florida	CLEAN UP WOMAN Willie Clarke and Clarence Reid (p) "Little Beaver" (a)	Alston (Atlantic)
15	DON McLEAN New York	AMERICAN PIE Ed Freeman (p, a)	United Artists

RECOMMENDED RECORDS

In the past, any list of recommended records has risked being hijacked by the inconsistent reissue policies at most companies, where changes of staff often result in the deletion of releases painstakingly compiled by a previous dynasty. But times are changing, led in the United States by the Los Angeles-based reissue label Rhino Records. Employing technical staff who go to inordinate lengths to trace the original studio masters for all their releases, hiring experts to select and annotate the compilations, and presenting the results in attractive packaging, Rhino and a couple of European counterparts have set standards which other companies have felt obliged to meet. Atlantic, which has always maintained a consistent policy of keeping its back catalog available, entered a joint venture relationship with Rhino, providing funds to enable buyouts of masters and even entire catalogs from some of the smaller labels. In Berkeley, Fantasy Records added the Specialty and Stax catalogs to its huge jazz archives, and released many marvellous compilations and boxed sets in conjunction with its licensees around the world.

Meanwhile some of the major companies have belatedly set out to make sense of their catalogs and acquisitions. MCA, having added Chess to its own Decca, ABC, and Duke/Peacock catalogs, has embarked on a thorough trawl through its archives; and a start has been made at EMI/Capitol, owners of Aladdin, Imperial, Liberty, Roulette, and Sue. Polygram has initiated a coherent series of reissues under the *Chronicles* banner, while Time-Life, in partnership with Warner Special Products, has licensed material from many sources and released several series; the problem with many "Special Products" divisions of major labels has been staff with a marketing-based rather than music-based orientation, with a consequently cavalier attitude towards the quality of tapes they use. But in the past two or three years, there has been a dramatic improvement in attitudes and practices.

In Europe, the majors have mostly ignored the collector market, leaving the way clear for several enterprising independents to take up the slack and meet the growing demand. Ace in Britain and Bear

Family in Germany, diligent in pursuing original master tapes and hiring experts to compile and annotate their releases, both celebrated their twentieth anniversary in 1995.

A note of warning: although compilations on CD provide a convenient way for the armchair listener to hear music from another era, it's important to bear in mind that not all of them manage to recapture the true experience of how the music sounded at the time. The deep and wide grooves of 78 rpm singles generated a big, warm sound which progressively disappeared with each successive format—45 rpm singles, 33 rpm albums, and digitally-mastered CDs all tended to favour higher frequencies, at the expense of the "bottom end." Played through the huge speakers of jukeboxes, 78s delivered a massive sound which can only be vaguely approximated by CDs on a domestic hi-fi or portable system. Owners of Elvis's 78 rpm singles on Sun justifiably believe that no other format has come close to reproducing their impact. It may help to turn up the bass on your amp, but you'll never quite get there.

When 45 rpm singles became the standard format for pop music, and the focus of mastering engineers shifted from jukeboxes to radio, it became common practice to vari-speed tapes to raise the tempo, add compression to make records seem louder, and boost treble frequencies to enable them to cut through on poor quality transistor radios. Sometimes records which sounded terrific on the radio could be hard to bear on a good home system, where their harsh, brittle power seemed inappropriate. So now, when mastering compilations of these old records, engineers have to strike a balance between acknowledging their original function while seeking to meet a new generation's expectations of a clean, clear sound from CDs. In general, there's a tendency for most recordings to sound more "polite" on CD, and sometimes it can be hard to understand why some tracks were ever regarded as being exciting. There's no absolute rule—sometimes the CD version delivers a presence and warmth that had never been caught on vinyl; but often, CDs fail to recapture the hard-to-describe "earthy" qualities present on the microgroove pressings.

The selection below is devised with the aim of representing all the records on this book's Playlist in the version that was a hit at the time, in a range of various artist compilations; with a minimum of track duplication between records; and favoring companies which have shown a commitment to keeping records in their catalogs. The guide is by no means definitive, and all kinds of pitfalls lie in store for the inexperienced buyer: not only were there often alternative takes and mixes of the original versions of many hits (stereo, mono, and longer album versions), but many artists recorded their famous songs more than once, as they hopped from one label to another in their declining years. The list below sticks to companies whose policy is to use only the originals (although Rhino, frustrated by lack of access to the original version of Chubby Checker's "The Twist," substitutes a later recording instead of taking the opportunity to pretend it never existed in the first place). For more information on each compilation, including identification of mono and stereo tracks and assessment of sound quality on each CD reissue, see Mike Callahan's *Oldies on CD* referred to in the bibliography.

Unless otherwise indicated, compilations are single CDs issued in the United States; R2 prefix indicates a Rhino release.

Many thanks to Roger Armstrong and Gary Stewart for their help.

Key to the rating system:

***	essential for a general beginner;
**	highly recommended;
*	recommended.
no star	for diehard fans only!

1. Location-based compilations

Chicago

***The Chess Blues Box*. (4 x CD. MCA/Chess CHD4-9340.)
Chess/Checker was the greatest in-depth postwar blues company, and here is the evidence—101 tracks from Muddy, Wolf, Sonny Boy Williamson, J. B. Lenoir, Little Walter *et al.*

**Chess Rhythm and Roll*. (4 x CD. MCA/Chess CHD4-9352.)
The commercial side of the Chess catalog, from the rock 'n' roll of Chuck Berry and Bo Diddley, vocal groups including the Moonglows and Flamingos, to the soul of Fontella Bass & Bobby McClure, Little Milton, and Sugar Pie De Santo.

****Post-War Chicago (Blues Masters, Vol 2)*. (R2 71122.)
Faultless selection of the city's finest, from Muddy Waters and Howlin Wolf to Otis Rush and Buddy Guy.

***The Vee Jay Story*. (4 x CD. Vee Jay NVS 2—3 400.)
John Lee Hooker, Jimmy Reed, Betty Everett, Jerry Butler and many more, from the only substantial black-owned label to pre-date Berry Gordy's Detroit-based company. [This box was deleted just as we went to press, but may remain in some stores until the catalog's current owners establish a new licensee.]

Cincinatti

****The King R&B Box Set.* (4 x CD. King KBFCD 7002.)

Three of the four CD's include relevant tracks by most of the artists missing from Rhino's otherwise definitive *R&B Box* (see **Rhythm and Blues**, below): Earl Bostic, Roy Brown, Wynonie Harris, the Dominoes, the Five Royales, Little Willie John and Bill Doggett; the fourth has material of documentary interest, including words from the company's irascible founder, the late Syd Nathan.

Detroit

****Hitsville USA: The Motown Singles Collection, 1959-1971.* (4 x CD. Motown 372463 6312 2.) No other label ever had such a high percentage of hits-per-release over such a long period. This box has 104 tracks, and every one's a winner, from "Money" by Barrett Strong and "Shop Around" by the Miracles, through the Supremes and the Temptations, to Marvin Gaye, Junior Walker, and the Jackson Five.

Georgia: Atlanta/Macon

Nothing available, although there is scope for a four-part series of CDs, starting with the remarkable roster of black singers born in the state (Ray Charles, Chuck Willis, James Brown, Little Richard, Otis Redding), working through sixties pop of Ray Stevens and Joe South and seventies boogie bands like the Allman Brothers, and coming up-to-date with the B-52s and REM. Maybe Atlanta's 1996 Olympics will be the spur.

Houston/Texas

***Duke-Peacock's Greatest Hits.* (1 x CD. MCA MCAD-10666.) Bobby Bland, Junior Parker, and others, mostly recorded with the bands of Joe Scott and Bill Harvey.

**Texas Blues (Blues Masters, Vol 3).* (R2 71123). T-Bone Walker's "Stormy Monday Blues" through Percy Mayfield and Willie Mae Thornton.

Texas Music Rhino series which covers several bases:

**Vol 1: Postwar Blues Combos*. (R2 71781.)
Parallel with *Texas Blues,* above with no duplications. Charles Brown, Amos Milburn, Freddie King, Frankie Lee Sims.

**Vol 2: Western Swing & Honky Tonk.* (R2 71782.)
Many big names of the forties, including Bob Wills ("Take Me Back to Tulsa") and Hank Thompson ("Wild Side of Life").

**Vol 3: Garage Bands and Psychedelia.* (R2 71783.)
Mid-to-late sixties stuff from a hotbed of vibrant American music: Sir Douglas Quintet, Sam the Sham, The Ron-Dels (with Delbert McClinton).

Kingston, Jamaica

***The Trojan Story.* (2 x CD. UK: Trojan CDTRD 402.)
Most of the reggae hits which made the UK pop charts during the sixties and early seventies—Desmond Dekker, Pioneers, Jimmy Cliff.

****The Harder They Come.* (Mango RRCD 11.)
The film soundtrack which helped to establish reggae in the United States—astute collection of the best Jamaican music of the time, from Jimmy Cliff, the Maytals and others.

**Tougher Than Tough: The Story of Jamaican Music.* (4 x CD. Mango 1BXCD 1/518 401-2.) The first two volumes are from the years 1958-74 and demonstrate the evolution of Jamaican music from New Orleans-style R&B to the distinctive rhythms of reggae: Prince Buster, early Bob Marley, Maytals.

Los Angeles

***The Aladdin Records Story.* (2 x CD. EMI 7-24383 08822 5.)
From Illinois Jacquet's "Flying Home" in 1945 to Thurston Harris' "Little Bitty Pretty One," by way of Helen Humes, Amos Milburn, Shirley & Lee, and Gene & Eunice. Consistently good, often great.

***Back to Mono, 1958-1969 (The Phil Spector Box Set).* (4 x CD. ABKCO 7118-2.) All the hits and many obscurities from the Ronettes and Crystals and many more, including the masterpiece that American radio refused to play because Spector didn't offer enough payola, "River Deep, Mountain High" by Ike and Tina Turner.

The Birth of a Dream: Capitol's Early Days. (Capitol CDP 7-98664.) Includes Ella Mae Morse & Freddie Slack 1942 version of Don Raye's marvellous "Cow Cow Boogie."

The Del-Fi & Donna Story. (UK: Ace CDCHD 313.) Starring "La Bamba" by Ritchie Valens, alongside mostly second-division artists, including another chicano singer, Chan Romero, whose "Hippy Hippy Shake" was covered by a few Liverpool groups.

Dot's Cover-to-Cover... Hit Upon Hit. (UK: Ace CDCHD 609.) Musically indigestible—30 of Dot's white pop cover versions of R&B hits; Pat Boone, Gale Storm, the Fontane Sisters among the guilty parties.

Imperial. No label compilation currently available.

***The Modern/RPM Story.* (4 x CD. UK: ABOXCD 6, scheduled for UK release Spring '96, and in US through Virgin soon afterwards.) From Hadda Brooks and John Lee Hooker, through B. B. King and Johnny "Guitar" Watson, to Marvin & Johnny and Etta James.

Sam Cooke's Sar Records Story, 1959-65. (2 x CD. ABKCO 2231-2.) Parallel with his own, often commercialized recordings, Sam Cooke encouraged a more authentic sound when producing other artists for his label, including Bobby Womack (in the Valentinos) and Johnny Taylor.

***The Specialty Story.* (5 x CD. Fantasy/Specialty 5SPCD 4412-2.) Hours of entertainment, featuring Little Richard's master-blasters alongside the combo blues of Roy Milton, through Lloyd Price, Percy Mayfield, and the Soul Stirrers with Sam Cooke, to the proto-punk of Don & Dewey.

**The Surf Set.* (3 x CD. UK: Sequel NXTCD 249.) There's no U.S. equivalent to this definitive 72-track collection, with virtually every hit and many misses from the surf & hot rod era of the early sixties—Dick Dale, Jan & Dean, Beach Boys, Surfaris and many more.

Minor LA-based label compilations available on Ace Records (UK): Challenge (*More Hollywood Rock 'n' Roll*), Class/Rendezvous, Dig, Dootone, Ebb, and Era.

Memphis

***Blue Flames: A Sun Blues Collection.* (R2 70962.)
Jack Brenston, Howlin' Wolf, and the wonderful original version of "Mystery Train" by Little Junior's Blue Flames.

**The Hi Records Story.* (UK: Hi CD 101.)
Mostly mellow grooves, from Bill Black's Combo and Ace Cannon's "Tuff" to Willie Mitchell's productions of Al Green and Ann Peebles.

**Memphis Blues (Blues Classics, Vol 12).* (R2 71129.)
From the pre-war Beale Street Sheiks to Bobby "Blue" Bland and the Beale Streeters, via John Estes and Rosco Gordon.

The Complete Stax Singles, 1959-1968.* (9 x CD. Atlantic/Stax 7 82218-2.) The sound of Memphis as it evolved from rock 'n' roll derivations and flowered into soul innovations—literally every single released by Stax and its various subsidiaries, until termination of its distribution deal with Atlantic. Inevitably uneven, as all the misses are here as well as the hits, most of which are also found on *The Atlantic Rhythm & Blues* box (see **New York, below).

**The Complete Stax Singles, Volume Two: 1968-71.* (9 x CD. Fantasy/Stax 9SCD-4411-2.) From the period after Stax broke away from Atlantic, when the company's output was more consistent in both its sound and its success. Many thrilling moments, particularly from Johnnie Taylor and the Staple Singers.

***The Sun Records Collection.* (3 x CD. Rhino R2 71780.)
For the first time the pathbreaking Sun recordings of Elvis Presley are compiled in chronological order with tracks by other artists made in the same studio, 1950 through 1963. From the inspirational original versions of "Just Walking in the Rain" by the Prisonaires and "Mystery Train" by Little Junior's Blue Flames, through the hillbilly rock of Carl Perkins and the country skiffle of Johnny Cash, to the wild piano boogies of Jerry Lee Lewis.

Muscle Shoals, Alabama

***The Muscle Shoals Sound* (R2 71517)

Deep soul from the South: Arthur Alexander to the Staple Singers, via Percy Sledge and Aretha Franklin.

Nashville, Tennessee

**Excello Records.* (2 x CD. Excello CD 3001.)
Much of this material was recorded in Crowley, Louisiana and licensed to Excello of Nashville; when released in Britain on EMI's Stateside label in 1963, the swampy blues became a major influence on young British R&B groups of the time, among whom the Rolling Stones, Kinks, and Yardbirds recorded covers of songs by Slim Harpo, Lazy Lester, and Lightnin' Slim.

Hillbilly Fever, Vol 3: Legends of Nashville. (R2 71902.)
Pre-Elvis country, from Red Foley, Kitty Wells, etc.

Monument Records—no compilation of Fred Foster's label available.

New Orleans

The Best of Ace Records: The R&B Hits. (Scotti Brothers 72392 75406-2.) Huey Smith & the Clowns, Earl King, Bobby Marchan. [Rumored to have been deleted as we go to press.]

**The Minit Records Story.* (2 x CD. EMI/Minit 7-24383 08792 1.)
Allen Toussaint's productions in the early sixties of Ernie K-Doe, the Showmen, and Aaron Neville.

***The Rock 'n' Roll Era: The New Orleans Sound.* (Time-Life 2RNR-39/Warner Special Products OPCD=2597.) Imaginative 24-track selection drawn from several sources—Irma Thomas, Professor Longhair, and Chris Kenner, as well as Fats Domino, Smiley Lewis, and Shirley & Lee.

NB: *The Specialty Story* contains many of the city's finest recorded moments (see **Los Angeles**, above); *The Sue Story* has a few more (see **New York**, below); and *The Imperial Story,* if it is ever compiled, will provide many of the rest (see **Los Angeles**).

New York

*** *Atlantic Rhythm & Blues.* (7 x CD. Atlantic 82305.)

From the label's 1949 breakthrough with "Drinkin' Wine Spo-De-O-Dee" by Stick McGhee, through Ruth Brown and Joe Turner, the Clovers and Ray Charles, various formations of the Drifters, on to the soul era of Otis, Percy, and Aretha; with hits on various distributed labels, notably Stax. Includes 35 tracks on the Playlist. Incomparable.

The Brill Building Sound. (4 x CD. Era 5025-2.)
Enterprising concept, gathering together from nay sources the hit versions of songs written by Goffin & King, Pomus & Shuman, Mann & Weil, Sedaka & Greenfield and the rest, for whom writing a song was just another day at the office. Reportedly has uneven sound quality.

The Cadence Story. (1 x CD. UK: Ace CDCHD 550.)
Clean-cut pop from the Everly Brothers, Johnny Tillotson, etc.

Jubilee. Although there have been a number of very CD-specialized compilations by the label's individual artists, including comprehensive boxed sets from Bear Family documenting the entire output of the Orioles (6 x CD) and Cadillacs (4 x CD), there is no various artists compilation of the label's hits.

**New York City Blues (Blues Classics, Vol 13).* (R2 71131.)
Nice collection by the jazzy big bands which immediately predated the sawn-off combos of rock 'n' roll: dance hits from orchestras led by Lionel Hampton, Duke Ellington, Lucky Millinder, Count Basie.

**The Scepter Story.* (3 x CD. Capricorn 9-42003-2.)
Impressive in-depth collection, including Dionne Warwick, the Shirelles, Chuck Jackson.

** *The Sue Records Story.* (4 x CD. EMI/Sue 7-24382 80932 6.)
Most of the output from the pioneering New York-based label owned by Juggy Murray, including the first Ike & Tina Turner hits (recorded in St Louis) and several tracks from the AFO label of New Orleans (including "I Know" by Barbara George).

Phoenix, Arizona

No compilation dedicated solely to Lee Hazelwood's productions (see **Philadelphia**: *The Jamie-Guyden Story* below).

Philadelphia

Cameo-Parkway. Controlled by ABKCO, who report no plans for any label compilation as we go to press; "96 Tears" by ? & the Mysterians remains elusive.

The Jamie-Guyden Story. (2 x CD. Bear Family BCD 15874-BH.) Most of the company's output was commissioned from independent producers around the country, notably Lee Hazlewood, based in Phoenix, Arizona (Duane Eddy, Ray Sharpe) and including Houston-based Huey Meaux (Barbara Lynn's "You'll Lose a Good Thing," recorded in New Orleans).

San Francisco

San Franciscan Nights. (R2 70536.)
The poppier side of the city's productions—Youngbloods, Sly & the Family Stone, Beau Brummels; includes the Great Society (featuring Grace Slick on an early version of "Somebody to Love"), but no Jefferson Airplane (see **Sixties**: *Classic Rock: 1967* and *Monterey* below).

Seattle

Despite belated recognition of the area's active music scene, which produced major figures from Jimi Hendrix to Nirvana, there's no compilation of seminal groups of the early sixties like the Wailers and Frantics.

St Louis

Never a major recording centre, the city was home base for Ike & Tina Turner for many years (see **New York**: *The Sue Story*).

United Kingdom

The British music industry is so London-dominated, there has been no comprehensive effort to present British music through compilation CDs on a city-by-city or region-by-region basis. Rhino's *British Invasion* series is disappointingly indiscriminate, not only putting the genuinely innovative ("You Really Got Me" by the Kinks) alongside the crass and the inferior (Freddie & the Dreamers and pre-EMI Beatles) but confounding geography by including Australia's Easybeats and Spain's Los Bravos. The crucial stuff by The Big Two—the recordings by the Beatles for EMI and the Rolling Stones for UK Decca (US London)—are not available for license to various artist compilations.

***The Ultimate Sixties Collection.* (2 x CD. UK: Castle Communications CTVCD 305.) At last the wheat has been separated from the chaff, and this really is the Best of British, alongside a few gems from across the Atlantic. Dusty Springfield, Searchers, Animals, Manfred Mann, Byrds, Beach Boys, Small Faces, Who, Joe Cocker, David Bowie.

2. Genre-Based Compilations.

Blues

***Electric Blues, Vol 1 (Legends of Guitar).* (R2 70716.) Wonderful set which draws belated attention to some of the musicians whose uncredited contributions have long been admired: Wayne Bennett, formerly with Amos Milburn, is acknowledged for his role on Bobby Bland's "Stormy Monday Blues" and Floyd Murphy gets the credit for the blistering electric guitar on Junior Parker's "Love My Baby," previously attributed to another Memphis guitarist, Pat Hare.

***Electric Blues, Vol 1 (Legends of Guitar).* (R2 70564.) John Lee Hooker's "Boogie Chillen" takes pride-of-place, but Lowell Fulson's "Reconsider Baby" and Elmore James' "Dust My Blues" are show-stoppers too.

***Jump Blues Classics (Blues Masters, Vol 4)* (R2 71125.) Among the few compilations with tracks licensed from King, this includes Wynonie Harris' "Good Rockin' Tonight" and Roy Brown's "Rockin' at Midnight," alongside Joe Turner's "Shake Rattle and Roll" and Ann Cole's original version of "Got My Mojo Working."

**More Jump Blues (Blues Classics, Vol 14)* (R2 71133.) Hits by Louis Jordan, Joe Turner, and Faye Adams, plus intriguing obscurities from Professor Longhair ("Ball the

Wall") and Little Richard ("Little Richard's Boogie," recorded for Peacock in '53).

***Urban Blues (Blues Masters, Vol 1.)* (R2 711121.)
Impeccable selection of band blues (piano and sax as well as guitar): Guitar Slim, Chuck Willis ("Feel So Bad"), T-Bone Walker, Junior Parker.

**Urban Blues (Soul Shots, Vol 4)* (R275758.)
Overlaps the preceding compilation with one track, Junior Parker's "Driving Wheel," and takes the style forward to the sixties, with two tracks each by Bobby Bland ("Stormy Monday Blues" and "I Pity the Fool"), Little Milton (including his version of "Feel So Bad"), and B. B. King.

Country

From the Vaults: Decca Country Classics, 1934—1973 (3 x CD. MCA MCAD3-11069.) Produced by the Country Music Federation, the collection demonstrates how country music at first resisted but then absorbed the "black" influences of full kit drums and electric guitars, winding up with the clean white sound of seventies Nashville.

Hillbilly Fever. Excellent surveys, for the non-specialist who wants to hear original versions of well-known songs and a track or two by all the famous names of country music, most recorded before country music began to adapt itself to meet the conservative criteria of Nashville's Grand Ol' Opry.

Vol 1: Legends of Western Swing. (R2 71900.) Southwest bands from the forties—Bob Wills, his brother Johnnie Lee, etc.

**Vol 2: Legends of Honky Tonk.* (R2 71901.) "Honky Tonkin'" by Hank Williams sounds like rock 'n' roll seven years too soon, and Red Foley's "Tennessee Saturday Night" also shows how country musicians were listening to black music long before Elvis.

Vol 3: Legends of Nashville. (R2 71902.) Eighteen tracks, ranging from the original "Tennessee Waltz" by Pee Wee King to teen-oriented hits by Sonny James and Marty Robbins.

**Vol 4: Legends of the West Coast.* (R2 71903.) The "western" of country and western; music made for the movies in the forties and early fifties, intended to conjure wide open spaces and life on the range: "High Noon," "Cool Water," "Mule Train"; and a couple of tracks made in the sixties by country singers who happened to be based on California, Buck Owens and the great Merle Haggard.

Gospel

***Greatest Gospel Gems*. (Specialty CDCHD 344.)
Aptly-titled collection from Specialty's incomparable roster: Soul Stirrers (featuring Sam Cooke), Swan Silvertones, Pilgrim Travellers, Alex Bradford, Five Blind Boys of Alabama.

Jubilation. Astute, near-definitive collections from Rhino.

**Vol 1: Black Gospel.* (R2 70288.) From Mahalia Jackson to the Edwin Hawkins Singers, by way of the Swan Silvertones and the Dixie Hummingbirds.

***Vol 2: More Black Gospel.* (R2 70289.) Stronger than *Vol 1* to these ears, with The Caravans, Sensational Nightingales, Five Blind Boys of Mississippi ("Our Father") and Staple Singers in their early days ("Uncloudy Day").

Vol 3: Country Gospel. (R2 70290.) For "country," read "white": Hank Williams, Martha Carson, Roy Acuff.

Rhythm & Blues

****The R&B Box: 30 Years of Rhythm & Blues (1943-72).* (6 x CD. Rhino R2 71806.) If you want just one record as the soundtrack for reading *Sound of the City*, this collection of 108 tracks must be it. Almost fifty of its tracks are in the Playlist, as well as more than thirty alternative tracks by artists on the list; many of the rest could be added to it. From the early days—Helen Humes, Roy Milton, Amos Milburn, Sticks McGhee; from the rock 'n' roll era—Shirley & Lee, Fats Domino, the Cadillacs; from the soul era—Mary Wells, Joe Tex, James Carr, and Johnnie Taylor. Licensing restrictions blocked the inclusion of Sam Cooke, Phil Spector productions (which may not have qualified on generic grounds), and any King artists (see note under Cincinatti, above); but otherwise it is remarkably comprehensive.

Billboard Top R&B Hits. Straightforward year-by-year compilations by Rhino of R&B hits which also 'went pop'; there's a lot of duplication with other compilations, including Rhino's own *Top Rock 'n' Roll Hits* (see below).

1955. (R2 70641.) Five tracks from the Playlist including "Pledging My Love" by Johnny Ace and "When You Dance" by the Turbans.

1956. (R2 70642.) Five more from the Playlist, including Little Richard and Fats Domino.

***Rock Instrumental Classics, Vol 4: Soul.* (R2 71604.) Misleading title for a marvellous compilation of sixties club classics: three by Booker T & the MGs and two by the Young Holt Trio more or less meet the "soul" billing, but the balance comprises hits with a strong Latin or African flavour, by Mongo Santamaria, Ray Barretto, Hugh Masekela, Manu Dibango, and El Chicano.

*** *Rock 'n' Roll Era—The Roots of Rock, 1945-56.* (Time-Life 2RNR-30/Warner Special Products OPCD 2570.) The best one-CD collection from the pre-rock 'n' roll era, with twelve from the Playlist, including Wynonie Harris's "Good Rockin' Tonight," Amos Milburn's "Chicken Shack Boogie," and Muddy Waters's "Hootchie Cootchie Man."

***Rock 'n' Roll Era—The Roots of Rock: Vol 2.* (Time-Life 2RNR-43/Warner 2627.) Another flawless collection, with a rare chance to get Jimmy Forrest's marvellous "Night Train," as well as "Baby Don't Do it" by the Five Royales.

Rock 'n' Roll

There is no satisfactory rock 'n' roll multi-CD compilation with full annotation to set alongside Rhino's *Doo Wop* and *R&B Box* collections, so it's a matter of hunting around, hoping not to wind up with the same tracks on too many different records; Time-Life's *Rock 'n' Roll Era* series could be the best bet, although Callahan warns about uneven sound in the series—some CDs are mastered from original tapes, but tapes used on others have hiss, dropout, and distortion.

** *American Graffiti.* (2 x CD. MCA MCAD2-8001.) The soundtrack album of the film which helped to launch the nation back into the past—completely remastered for CD release from original studio tapes. Some tracks have Wolfman Jack talking over them, and a couple more are by a seventies revival group, but the album works as a "listening experience," with a good balance between rock 'n' roll (Bill

Haley, the Crickets, Fats, Chuck) and vocal groups (Orioles, Crests, Clovers, Platters).

45s on CD, Vol 1. ('56—59) (Mercury 832 041-2)
Polygram starts to trawl through its rapidly expanding archives, with reportedly excellent sound. "Sea of Love" by Phil Phillips, "Handy Man" by Jimmy Jones, "Lonely Blue Boy" by Conway Twitty.

*****Max Weinberg Presents: Let There Be Drums, Vol 1: The 50s.* (R2 71547). Not just an interesting concept which draws attention to the crucial role of drummers in rock 'n' roll, but a flawless 17-track selection: Fats Domino's "The Fat Man," Bill Haley's "Rock Around the Clock," Little Richard's "Long Tall Sally," Gene Vincent's "Be-Bop-A-Lula," Buddy Holly's "Peggy Sue," and Ray Charles' "What'd I Say?"

**Rock Instrumental Classics, Vol 1: The 50s.* (R2 71601.)
The selection lives up to the billing—eighteen tracks, including the ones we want to hear from Duane Eddy, Link Wray, Santo & Johnny, and the Champs.

The Rock 'n' Roll Era. Time-Life series of over forty compilations on a variety of themes, from the straight year-by-year selections to imaginative concepts; sound quality meets Callahan's approval on the following:

*****1954-55.* (2RNR-08/OPCD 2535.) Seventeen of the 22 tracks are on the Playlist, and we're not arguing with the other five.

**1956.* (2RNR-14/OPCD 2544.) Ten more from the Playlist, and the rest are fine too; but Callahan questions the sound quality.

**Rock Classics: The Originals.* (2RNR-39/OPCD 2597.) Richard Berry's original "Louie Louie," Dr Feelgood's "Mr Moonlight," and Arthur Alexander's "Anna."

Top Rock 'n' Roll Hits. Disarmingly simple concept—year-by-year single CD compilations on Rhino, each with ten big hits, 1955 through 1974.

*****1955.* (R2 70598.) Eight of the ten tracks are on the Playlist, including Chuck Berry's "Maybellene" and Bill Haley's "Rock Around the Clock."

****1956.* (R2 70599.) Seven from the Playlist—Gene Vincent's "Be-Bop-A-Lula" and both sides of Elvis's "Hound Dog"/"Don't Be Cruel" single, "I'm in Love Again" by Fats Domino and "The Fool" by Sanford Clark.

*__1957__. (R2 70618.) Five more from the Playlist, with two by Buddy Holly, "Peggy Sue" and the Crickets' "That'll Be The Day," and Jerry Lee's "Whole Lotta Shakin'."

The Golden Age of American Rock 'n' Roll, 1954-63. Adventurous thirty-track selections, each including a few big U.S. hits alongside middling and minor hits which have previously been hard to find, annotated for the UK-based Ace label by Rob Finnis, whose fascinating notes are based on interviews not only with most of the relevant producers, but bass-players who missed the sessions.

*_Volume 1._ (UK: Ace CDCHD 289.) "Mule Skinner Blues" by the Fendermen, "Eddie My Love" by the Teen Queens.

*_Volume 2._ (UK: Ace CDCHD 445.) "Memphis" by Lonnie Mack, "Stay" by Maurice Williams & the Zodiacs, "Get A Job" by the Silhouettes, "Rumble" by Link Wray.

*_Volume 3._ (UK: Ace CDCHD 497.) "Endless Sleep" by Jody Reynolds, "Western Movies" by the Olympics, "There is Something On Your Mind" by Big Jay McNeely.

*_Volume 4._ (UK: Ace CDCHD 500.) "Drip Drop" by Dion, "Don't Let Go" by Roy Hamilton, "You'll Lose a Good Thing" by Barbara Lynn.

*_Volume 5._ (UK: Ace CDCHD 600.) "Just a Little Bit" by Rosco Gordon, "Sleep Walk" by Santo and Johnny.

Sixties

Classic Rock. Excellent series from Time Life/Warner Special Products.

**_Shakin' All Over: 1964._ (2CLR-16/2585.) Interesting selection of some less obvious but still-classic tracks: Dionne Warwick's "Walk On By," Brenda Holloway's "Every Little Bit Hurts," the Searchers' "Don't Throw Your Love Away."

**_1965._ (2CLR-01/OPCD 2556.) Strong 22-track selection includes 13 from the Playlist—good balance of American pop, soul and British, including "Mr Tambourine Man" by the Byrds, "In the Midnight Hour" by Wilson Pickett, and "For Your Love" by the Yardbirds.

**_The Beat Goes On: 1965._ (2CLR-08/OPCD 20581.) More from modern pop's golden year: "She's About a Mover" by the Sir Douglas Quintet and "Rescue Me" by Fontella Bass.

***Shakin' All Over: 1965.* (2CLR-14/2580.) And even more: James Brown's "Papa's Got a Brand New Bag," Marvin Gaye's "Ain't That Peculiar," Cannibal and the Headhunters. Shame about Freddie & the Dreamers.

Classic Rock: 1966. (2CLR-02/OPCD 2557.) Another ten from the Playlist, including Aaron Neville's "Tell It Like It Is" and the Bobby Fuller Four's "I Fought The Law."

***Shakin' All Over: 1966.* (2CLR-16/2585.) Lee Dorsey's "Working in the Coal Mine," "Ain't Too Proud to Beg" by the Temptations, "Bang Bang" by Cher, "These Boots Are Made For Walkin!"

Classic Rock: 1967. (2CLR-01/OPCD 2558.) Nine from the Playlist, including "Somebody to Love" by the Jefferson Airplane, "Whiter Shade of Pale" by Procol Harum, and "The Letter" by the Box Tops.

Frat Rock Assembled by Rhino from some of the tougher black and white dance records of the mid-sixties; party time!

***Vol 1.* (R2 75778.) Songs you'd hope for from Sam the Sham, the Kingsmen, Barrett Strong and the Contours.

**Vol 2: Son of Frat Rock* (R2 75772.) "You Really Got Me" by the Kinks finds appropriate company.

***Vol 3: Grandson of Frat Rock.* (R2 70732.) "Shout, Parts 1 & 2" and "Twist & Shout" by the Isley Brothers, "Johnny B Goode" by Chuck Berry, "Hang on Sloopy" by the McCoys.

**Rock 'n' Roll Era: 1962.* (Time-Warner 2RNR-02/WSP OPCD 2534.) Pretty good selection, with Sam Cooke's "Twistin' the Night Away" and Bruce Channel's "Hey! Baby."

****Max Weinberg Presents: Let There Be Drums, Vol 2: The 60s.* (R2 71548.) Another genre-busting, cream-of-the-crop compilation (see also **Rock 'n' Roll**, above). Sometimes the role of drums was obvious, like on "I Want Candy" by the Strangeloves and "In the Midnight Hour" by Wilson Pickett, but Max also picks out tracks where the drummers were more subtle—Roy Orbison's "Running Scared" and Percy Sledge's "When a Man Loves a Woman."

***Monterey Pop.* (4 x CD. Rhino/MIPF R 70596.)
Remarkable document of a remarkable event. Substantial sets from The Byrds, Jefferson Airplane, Who, Jimi Hendrix, and Otis Redding, and selections from fifteen more acts.

NB: Bob Dylan's material is virtually never licensed for use on various artists compilations; the notable exception is the 7 x CD box set, *The Rolling Stone Collection: 25 Years of Essential Rock, 1967–1992* (Time-Life R102-34), which goes far beyond the period covered in *Sound of the City.* Apart from including several Dylan tracks including "Like a Rolling Stone," the entire selection is well-judged and recommended.

Soul/Funk

Most soul compilations tend to be thrown together casually, their marketing appeal being based on well-known songs and singers rather than conceptual elegance; the cream of the soul crop is among some of the recommendations in other categories—*Hitsville USA* (see **Detroit**), *The Complete Stax Singles, 1959-68 & 1969-72* (**Memphis**), *Muscle Shoals Sound* (**Muscle Shoals**), *Atlantic Rhythm & Blues* (**New York**), and *The R&B Box* (**Rhythm and Blues**). The following two are also recommended.

***Billboard Top R&B Hits: 1971.* (R2 70659.)
Five from the end of the Playlist, including King Floyd's "Groove Me," Marvin Gaye's "What's Goin' On," and Chi-Lites' "Have You Seen Her"; plus Aretha's brilliant reworking of "Spanish Harlem."

*** *In Yo' Face: The History of Funk, Vol 1.* (R2 71431.)
Near flawless selection from one of the most radical turning points in black dance music: pivotal tracks by James Brown ("Sex Machine"), Sly Stone ("Thank You . . ."), Parliament, Charles Wright, and King Floyd.

Vocal Groups

***The Doo Wop Box: 101 Vocal Group Gems From the Golden Age of Rock 'n' Roll.* (4 x CD. Rhino R2 71463.) From the Orioles to Shep & the Limelites, via the Cadillacs, Skyliners, and Marcels. May be a bit dense for the non-specialist to take in at one sitting, but all the gems are here.

BIBLIOGRAPHY

Details refer to the most recent publication in the United States, favoring paperbacks.

Chet Atkins (with Bill Neely). *Country Gentleman.* (Chicago: Henry Regnery, 1977.) Evocative recollections of struggling up the low rungs of the ladder on the country and western scene in the forties.

Tony Bacon. *Rock Hardware.* (Poole, Dorset, UK: Blandford, 1981.) Useful discussion of how electric amplification and technological invention affected the evolution of musical instruments and thereby influenced the resultant music.

Lester Bangs. *Psychotic Reactions & Carburetor Dung.* (NY: Vintage, 1988.) Of all the writers whose reaction to music was personal, rather than historical, musicological, or social, Lester was the most consistently inspired, funny, and readable. He died far too soon, at the age of 31.

Amiri Baraka (LeRoi Jones). *Blues People*. (NY: Quill, 1971.) Powerful writing from a man who witnessed many of the R&B stars at their peak in the 40s.

Chuck Berry. *Chuck Berry: The Autobiography*. (NY: Harmony, 1987.) The only one of the great rock 'n' rollers to write his own story without assistance from a "ghost" writer; predictably quirky.

Alan Betrock. *Girl Groups.* (NY: Delilah, 1982.) Probably the best of several similar books on the same theme.

Stanley Booth. *Rythm Oil.* (NY: Vintage, 1993.) The trouble with reality, it keeps slipping through our fingers like mercury. Memphis-based writer Stanley Booth takes snapshots in words, catching life on the road and in the backs of bars and cars, and gets closer than most to capturing those moments in time when music slides into the unconscious and sticks there like a limpet.

Viv Broughton. *Black Gospel: An Illustrated History of the Gospel Sound.* (Dorset, England: Blandford, 1985.) Extends the range of Tony Heilbut's earlier *Gospel Sound.*

John Broven. *Walking to New Orleans.* (Bexhill-on-Sea, Sussex, UK: Blues Unlimited, 1974.) Blow-by-blow account of the city's rhythm-and-blues scene.

James Brown (with Bruce Tucker). *James Brown.* (NY: Thunder's Mouth, 1990.) Does justice to one of the most remarkable stories in modern popular music.

Mike Callahan. *Oldies on CD.* (2nd ed. Virginia: Both Sides Now, 1994.) Thorough survey of compact disc reissues, including both sole artist and various artist compilations; the latter are listed under album title and cross-indexed to the indivudal artists and tracks. Thorough reports on particular takes and mixes used, with comments on sound quality for every track. Exhaustive and invaluable.

Ray Charles (with David Ritz). *Brother Ray.* (NY: Da Capo, 1992.) Another astonishing story, evocatively rendered in what is possibly the best artist biography for the period covered in *Sound of the City.*

Sam Charters. *The Country Blues.* (NY: Da Capo, 1975.) The first of its kind, this seminal book still conveys an infectious sense of wonder.

Sam Charters. *The Blues Makers.* (NY: Da Capo, 1991.) Filled-out and corrected parts of *The Country Blues.*

Nik Cohn. *Awopbopaloobop Alopbamboom: Pop From The Beginning.* (London: Paladin, 1973.) Amusing, impressionistic pop history, from a British perspective.

James Lincoln Collier. *Jazz.* (NY: Dell, 1978.) Widely-acknowledged as the best survey of jazz by a writer who appreciates all its aspects; accessible even to a pop fan.

Ken Cree. *Stack-O-Wax.* (Philadelphia: Stack-O-Wax, 1981.) Mammoth four-volume log of every record released by every label with a substantial proportion of pop or rock 'n' roll releases. Available from Goldmine Bookshelf, Box 187, Fraser, Michigan 48026, USA.

Tony Cummings. *The Sound of Philadelphia.* (London: Methuen, 1975.) Well-researched survey, tracking the city's emergence as a soul capital in the early seventies, and going back thirty years.

Frederick Dannan. *The Hit Men.* (NY: Random House, 1991.) No-holds-barred investigation of the music industry, by a newspaper journalist who not only exposes mafia links, which had been a taboo subject for many years, but paints unflattering portraits of many of the industry's leading figures. Leaves a nasty taste in the mouth.

Miles Davis. *Miles Davis*. (NY: Simon & Schuster, 1989.) Confirmation that sublime music can come from a flawed source; Davis makes no attempt to present himself in a flattering light, and his story is all the more compelling.

Jim Dawson and Steve Propes. *What Was the First Rock 'n' Roll Record?* (Winchester, Mass: Faber & Faber, 1992.) Ingenious idea, entertainingly presented: the detailed story behind each of fifty contenders for the title.

Fred Dellar. *The NME Guide to Rock Cinema*. (London: Hamlyn, 1981.) Who sang what, in which film.

Dr John (with Jack Rummel). *Under The Hoodoo Moon*. (NY: St Martin's, 1994.) Considering what Mac Rebennack has put himself through, his brain and memory remain surprisingly intact, and this is as accurate and evocative an account of a musician's life in New Orleans as we are ever likely to get.

Bob Dylan. *Writings and Drawings*. (London: Panther, 1974.) Usually song lyrics need music to make them work, but the rhythms to the words of Dylan's best songs evoke their melodies.

Brian Epstein. *A Cellarfull of Noise*. (London: Souvenir, 1964.) Convincing account of the early part of the Beatles' career from their manager's point-of-view, ghostwritten by Beatles publicist Derek Taylor before everybody got wise after the event.

Colin Escott and Martin Hawkins. *Good Rockin' Tonight: Sun Records and the Birth of Rock 'n' Roll*. (NY: Rev. ed., St Martin's, 1991.) How a backwater became the source of some of the century's best popular music.

Pete Frame. *The Complete Rock Family Trees*. (NY: Rev. ed., Omnibus, 1995.) Unique and apt approach to the bewildering kaleidoscope that lies just below the surface of rock. Frame maps every move by each musician in most of the major British and American white rock groups of the past thirty years—who played with whom, for how long, and where they went next.

Vic Fredericks (Ed). *Who's Who in Rock 'n' Roll*. (NY: Fell, 1958.) Published as an exploitation quickie—publicity photos and thumb-nail biographical notes convey the unprecedented emergence of fifty black artists into the pop spotlight.

Michael Freedland. *Al Jolson*. (NY: Stein & Day, 1972.) An early instance of black music providing the basis of a successful career for a white singer, providing many insights into how the industry operated in its early years.

Simon Frith. *Sound Effects*. (NY: Pantheon, 1981.) One of the best analytical surveys of pop, by a rare academic who, as a fan himself, understands why people like pop.

Roland Gelatt. *The Fabulous Phonograph*. (NY: Collier, 1977.) Reissue of the standard history of the record industry pioneers.

Linnel Gentry. *Encyclopaedia of Country, Western and Gospel Music.* (Murfreesboro: Tennessee University, 1964.) Possibly the best of several similar works.

Nelson George. *The Death of Rhythm and Blues.* (NY: Pantheon, 1989.) Nice balance of analysis and information from a man who knows.

Charlie Gillett. *Making Tracks: The Story of Atlantic Records.* (London: Souvenir, 1986.) The first history of a postwar independent label, based on interviews with principal and secondary protagonists.

Ralph Gleason. *The Jefferson Aeroplane and the San Francisco Sound.* (NY: Ballantine, 1969.) Enthusiastic, on-the-spot report by the former jazz writer.

Isaac Goldberg. *Tin Pan Alley.* (NY: Ungar, 1961.) Evocative account of the New York music business, best on the nineteen twenties and thirties.

Burt Goldblatt and Robert Shelton. *The Country Music Story.* (NY: Bobbs Merrill, 1966.) Picture book with a good commentary.

John Goldrosen and John Beecher. *Remembering Buddy: The Definitive Biography of Buddy Holly.* (NY: Penguin, 1986.) Strong on the musical, social and personal background of the idiosyncratic, engaging rock 'n' roller.

Robert Gordon. *Came from of Memphis.* (Winchester, MA: Faber & Faber, 1995.) In effect, a companion to Stanley Booth's *Rythm Oil,* equally well-written.

John Grissim. *Country Music: White Man's Blues.* (NY: Paperback Library, 1970.) Journalistic report on the Nashville scene of the late sixties, based on illuminating interviews with producers Jerry Kennedy, Billy Sherrill, and Shelby Singleton as well as the mavericks, Johnny Cash and Waylon Jennings.

Peter Guralnick. *Feel Like Going Home.* (NY: Penguin, 1995.) First published in 1971: from-the-heart, interview-based portraits of blues and rock 'n' roll masters, including Howlin' Wolf and Charlie Rich.

Peter Guralnick. *Sweet Soul Music.* (NY: Harper & Row, 1986.) Encounters with men who worked behind-the-scenes in Memphis and Muscle Shoals, and with the singers who sang their songs.

Peter Guralnick. *Last Train to Memphis*. (NY: Little Brown, 1995.) Intensively-researched documentation of the early Elvis years—retracing his steps not only through every recording session he attended and every gig he played, but to every girl he kissed.

John Hammond (with Irving Townsend). *Hammond on Record.* (NY: Penguin, 1981.) Unique story by the man who discovered Count Basie and Bob Dylan, Billie Holiday and Aretha Franklin, Joe Turner and Bruce Springsteen.

W. C.Handy. *Father of the Blues.* (NY: Da Capo, 1985.) Improbable but true, a success story from the early years of the century, of the man from Memphis who wrote or arranged several jazz-blues standards including "St Louis Blues."

Phil Hardy & Dave Laing. *The Faber Encyclopaedia of Rock.* (London: Faber, 1991.) Periodically updated since its first publication in 1974, the best one-volume reference work.

Tony Heilbut. *The Gospel Sound.* (NY: Simon & Schuster, 1985.) Reissue of the thorough survey of the century's black American religious music, first published 1975.

Gerri Hershey. *Nowhere to Run: The Story of Soul Music.* (NY: Da Capo, 1994.) Excellent survey of black music of the sixties.

Jerry Hopkins. *Elvis.* (NY: Simon and Schuster, 1971.) Non-sensationalist and thorough biography, written while Elvis was still alive; but disappointingly thin on details about the recording sessions.

Dorothy Horstman. *Sing Your Heart Out, Country Boy.* (Rev. ed. Nashville: Country Music Foundation, 1986.) Simple idea, well-executed: the author makes a selection of classic country songs, and invites the applicable songwriters to recall how and why they wrote them.

Barney Hoskyns. *Say It One Time for the Broken Hearted.* (London: Fontana, 1987.) Sometimes overlaps *Making Tracks, Nowhere to Run,* and *Sweet Soul Music.* This British author brings a sharp eye and a keen ear to the milieu where music was made by black singers with mostly white producers and musicians in Memphis and Muscle Shoals during the sixties.

LeRoi Jones. *see* Amiri Baraka.

Charles Keil. *Urban Blues.* (Chicago: University Press, 1966.) Unusual and influential blend of firsthand observation, interviews (notably with B. B. King and Bobby Bland), and sociological research.

William Knoedelseder. *Stiffed: The True Story of MCA, the Music Business and the Mafia.* (NY: HarperCollins, 1994.) Follows Fred Dannan's *The Hit Men* with more revelations about the devious deceptions of high ranking executives; but nothing about music.

Colin Larkin (ed). *The Guinness Encyclopaedia of Popular Music.* (London: Guinness, 1995.) Over three million words in six volumes; safe to say, it's comprehensive!

Mike Leadbitter, Neil Slaven. *Blues Records, 1942–1970, A to K.* (London: Record Information Services, 1994.)

Mike Leadbitter, Les Fancourt, Paul Pelletier. *Blues Records, 1943–1970, L to Z.* (Milford, NH: Big Nickel, 1995.) Great improvement on the first one-volume 1968 edition, extending its range to include most R&B and many black rock 'n' roll artists.

Alan Lomax. *Mister Jelly Roll.* (NY: Pantheon, 1993.) Excellent biography of the seminal jazz composer from New Orleans.

Colin McInnes. *Sweet Saturday Night: Pop Song, 1840-1920.* (London: MacGibbon & Kee, 1967.) Survey of British music hall performers, many of whom crossed the Atlantic well before the 1964 "British Invasion."

Bill Malone. *Country Music USA.* (Austin: University of Texas, 1968.) The standard work, with special attention to the sources of modern country music—bluegrass, western swing, and honky-tonk.

Bill Malone and Judith McCulloch. *Stars of Country Music.* (NY: Da Capo, 1991.) Handy paperback reference.

Greil Marcus. *Mystery Train.* 3rd Revised Edition. (NY: Dutton, 1990.) Provocative arguments positing the greatness of the author's pantheon of twentieth-century music masters: the Band, Sly Stone, Robert Johnson, Randy Newman, and Elvis Presley.

Ian McDonald. *Revolution in the Head.* (London, Fourth Estate, 1994.) Track-by-track analysis of every song released by the Beatles—entertaining, illuminating, and inevitably contentious.

George Melly. *Revolt into Style.* (NY: Anchor Doubleday, 1971.) Witty observations on the eruption of British pop culture in the sixties.

Bill Millar. *The Drifters.* (NY: Collier, 1971.) Valiant attempt to keep track of personnel changes by a group whose records reflected the industry's evolution as R&B turned into first rock 'n' roll and then soul.

Jim Miller (editor). *The Rolling Stone Illustrated History of Rock & Roll.* (NY: Random House, 1976.) Not so much a history, more a collection of separate articles on all rock 'n' roll's major figures and genres, many of them outstanding.

Charles Shaar Murray. *Crosstown Traffic.* (NY: St Martins, 1991.) The best book on Jimi Hendrix, placing him in his pivotal role between the blues and rock.

Joseph Murrells. *The Book of Golden Discs.* (London: Barrie & Jenkins, 1974.) From a pre-rock 'n' roll background, Murrells brings a quaint approach to his subject, and he seems to have been gullible in accepting some claims of "million sellers."

Paul Oliver. *The Story of The Blues.* (London: Barrie and Rockcliff, 1967.) The definitive account, with many wonderful photographs.

Robert Palmer. *Deep Blues.* (NY: Penguin, 1982.) One of the best accounts of the blues roots that led to rock 'n' roll, by a "second generation" blues writer who likes the music at both ends of the process.

Mike Paris & Chris Comber. *Jimmie The Kid.* (NY: Da Capo, 1981.) The story of Jimmie Rodgers, the original "poor Southern boy who becomes world famous and dies early." In many ways, Hank Williams and Elvis Presley were parts two and three in the same series.

Guy Paellaert. *Rock Dreams.* (London: Pan, 1973.) Nik Cohn added captions, but the Belgian artists's paintings spoke for themselves, articulating and graphically illustrating for the first time the seedier sides of rock 'n' roll life—lust, often perverted; addiction, to drugs and alcohol; ambition, ruthless and relentless.

Jo & Tim Rice, Paul Gambaccini, Mike Read. *The Guinness Book of British Hit Singles.* (London: Guinness, 1995.) Regularly updated.

David Ritz. *Divided Soul.* (NY: Da Capo, 1991.) Biography of the enigmatic Marvin Gaye, which provides insights into the elusive workings of Berry Gordy's Motown empire.

David Ritz. *see also*: Ray Charles, Jerry Wexler

John Storm Roberts. *The Latin Tinge: The Impact of Latin American Music on the United States.* (NY: Oxford University, 1979.) The constant influence of Latin rhythms in American pop is widely overlooked (not least in *The Sound of the City*) and this book is an important reminder of how strong the impact has been, and who made it.

Johnny Rogan. *Starmakers and Svengalis.* (London: Futura, 1988.) Portraits of leading British managers, from the fifties up to the present. Illuminating.

Ross Russell. *Bird Lives.* (NY: Da Capo, 1996.) The story of Charlie Parker, by a man who released some of his records (on

Dial). Alongside Miles Davis, Parker was the most influential jazz musician of his generation, and there is much relevant material for a rock 'n' roll fan here.

Tony Russell. *Blacks Whites & Blues.* (London: Studio Vista, 1972.) One of the confusing aspects of Southern segregation was that it did not prevent a regular two-way flow of lyrics, melodies and rhythms between the black and white cultures; the author reveals the surprising origins of many songs long assumed to have started out "white"' or "black."

Linda J. Sandahl. *Rock Music on Film.* (Dorset, England: Blandford, 1987.) Strictly a reference book.

Russell Sanjek and David Sanjek. *American Popular Music Business in the 20th Century.* (NY: Oxford University, 1991.) Long-time BMI employee Russ Sanjek helped many independent labels to form publishing companies, and was well-placed to write with an insider's perspective.

Anthony Scaduto. *Bob Dylan.* (London: Abacus, 1972.) Scaduto was ahead of the avalanche of Dylanology books that followed, and his may still be the best.

Arnold Shaw. *The Rockin' Fifties.* (NY: Da Capo, 1987.) The author was actively involved in the New York record business of the era.

Arnold Shaw. *Honkers and Shouters.* (NY: Macmillan, 1978.) Expanding on his earlier book with reminiscences from other protagonists, Shaw gives a good flavour of the period.

Joseph Smith. *The Day The Music Died.* (NY: Evergreen, 1981.) The title is not the best signal for the contents of the only novel in this list, which catches the spirit of the David-and-Goliath battles between small and major labels. The author had hits as a songwriter and singer under the name Sonny Knight, including the extraordinary "But Officer."

David Toop. *Rap Attack: African Rap to Global Hip Hop.* (NY: Serpent's Tail, 1984.). Sharp insights by one of Britain's leading music journalists, who is also an active musician.

Nick Tosches. *Unsung Heroes of Rock 'n' Roll.* (Rev ed. NY: Harmony 1991.) Despite its title, most of the book's entertaining portraits are of stars and "great unknowns" who *preceded* rock 'n' roll—Ella Mae Morse, Wynonie Harris, etc.

Jerry Wexler (with David Ritz). *The Rhythm and the Blues.* (London: Jonathan Cape, 1994.) The most literate and erudite record man of his era chose a high-class collaborator to help organize his memoirs. Among the book's most poignant passages are the weekly humiliation of handing payola money in a brown paper bag to an Alan Freed acolyte, and coming to terms with the death of his daughter, who had been introduced to heroin by one of Wexler's musician protegees.

Joel Whitburn. *Top Pop Records, 1955-93. Top Country and Western Records, 1944-88. Top Rhythm & Blues Records, 1942-88.* (Menomenee Falls, Wis: Record Research; regularly updated.) Every entry to *Billboard's* national charts of hits, with helpful notes and cross-references. Until recently, uneven patterns in radio-play and sales across the country meant that chart positions in a particular week in *Billboard* did not reflect the exposure during the entire run of many records, particularly first hits by artists with no history, where radio programmers and distributors could be slow to be convinced of a newcomer's appeal; by the time "major markets" finally picked up on a regional hit, faster-reacting stations had already dropped it from their playlists. Many local chart-toppers never made *Billboard's* national chart, while other heavily-promoted records achieved high positions despite low sales. These are the only available logs of the marketing impact of singles over the entire period, meticulously researched and well-presented.

Charles White. *The Life and Times of Little Richard.* (NY: Da Capo, 1994.) Suitably flamboyant narrative for the wildest of the rock 'n' roll legends.

Timothy White. *Catch A Fire: The Life of Bob Marley.* (NY: Holt Rev. ed. 1989.) Admirably thorough account, balanced between Marley's social background, his emerging religious beliefs, and the processes of writing, recording and promoting his music. It is a good sign of changing times that since writing the first edition, the author has become editor of *Billboard.*

Paul Williams. *Outlaw Blues.* (NY: Dutton, 1969.) Instant reactions from the editor of the first of the new rock magazines of the sixties, *Crawdaddy.*

Richard Williams: *Out of His Head: The Sound of Phil Spector.* (NY: Outerbridge & Lazard, 1972.) Britain's best music writer takes the measure of America's studio genius.

Roger Williams. *Sing a Sad Song: The Life of Hank Williams.* (NY: Bantam, 1973.) No-holds-barred account of the great country writer and singer's desolate life.

Daniel Wolff. *You Send Me: The Life and Times of Sam Cooke.* (NY: Morrow, 1995.) Admirably thorough account, from a writer whose musical taste enables him to distinguish the sublime from the mundane.

ACKNOWLEDGEMENTS

The idea of attempting to investigate the development of rock and roll came to me in January, 1966, when I was looking for a subject for a masters' thesis. I'm grateful to Teachers' College, Columbia University, New York, and particularly to Dr. Herbert Gans for having the flexibility to accommodate a subject that seemed odd at the time.

Much of the raw material for the thesis came from microfilmed back copies of *Billboard* stored in the library at the Lincoln Center for the Performing Arts, New York, where I encountered strange names I'd never known before–the Five Royales, Sonny Til, and the Orioles. I was at this point given invaluable help by Charles Hobson, now in charge of "How It Is" at ABC-TV, but at that time a part-time disc jockey with WBAI-Radio, New York. Charles spent several hours playing to me the music of his youth, which enabled my thesis to carry some authority.

Back in Britain, I decided to try to reshape the material of the thesis into something more accessible to a non-academic audience, and I soon discovered that there were several people in Britain with astonishing stores of information and huge collections of records, and some of them have spent hours filling in the gaps left open in the thesis. For their help on various chapters and sections of the book, I am very grateful to the following people: John Anderson (country rock, rock 'n' roll), Art Ardolino (groups), Tony Cummings (groups, soul), Errol Dixon (shouters), Mike Leadbitter (Texas blues), Dave McAleer (soul), Bill Millar (rock 'n' roll), Rod Patton (shouters, New Orleans rhythm and blues), Gary Richards (shouters, rock 'n' roll). To the many other people who have informed me of errors and given me other useful pieces of information and advice, I must say a more general thank you and apologize for not listing them all by name.

For giving me the chance to clarify my thinking on specific singers and theories by writing about them, I am grateful to the following editors: Nelson Aldrich, Jr., of *The Urban Review*, Paul Barker of *New Society*, Tony Cummings of *Soul Music* and *Shout*, Colin Ward of *Anarchy*, Michael Locke of *Education*, and Peter Jones of the *Record Mirror*.

Thanks also to my editor, Harris Dienstfrey. I would not have set myself to finishing this project without his tactful prods.

Every effort has been made to locate the copyright owners of the material quoted in the text. Omissions brought to our attention will be credited in subsequent printings. Grateful acknowledgement is made to those publishers who asked that their ownership be noted either below or in the text.

Mind", Despenza/Wolfolk, Copyright 1969 Dakar Productions, Inc.; Edwin H. Morris & Company, Inc. for "It's Too Soon To Know", Deborah Chessler, Copyright © 1947 & 1948 Edwin H. Morris & Company, Inc.; and Marielle Music Co. for "It's Only Make Believe", Conway Twitty & Jack Nance.

ACKNOWLEDGEMENTS TO THE SECOND EDITION

Since the publication of the first edition of *Sound of the City*, I have moved from the fringes of the music industry to being in the thick of it, and I cannot give proper credit to all the people who have unwittingly enlightened my understanding of how the pop process works. But I would like to thank a few friends whose decisions to give me things to do had the effect of putting me face to face with the realities of the pop life.

While still at school, one of my fantasies was to play records on the radio, to subject listeners to my choices and hope that I could attract interest in the records I liked. In 1972, I achieved my ambition when David Carter at BBC Radio London let me loose on the airwaves with a show called *Honky Tonk*, named after the rough music joints in America's southern States and featuring Bill Doggett's record as its theme tune.

Every Sunday for seven years I played an arbitrary mixture of obscure oldies and current favourites, mostly records but sometimes demonstration tapes, and used any opportunity to bring to the studio people whose experience, taste and comments would go beyond the limitations of my own. In a real sense, *Sound of the City* came alive. Artists whose records I had made futile efforts to describe in print now sat at the microphone and talked about the circumstances in which they had made those records. These words lie too neatly on the page to convey my continual astonishment and appreciation that so many performers were prepared to get out of bed early on a Sunday morning, often after a late gig on a Saturday night, and come into the studio for the mid-day start.

B. B. King and Muddy Waters, whose parallel careers had taken such different courses, the one touring constantly while the other made his base in Chicago, both came in on separate occasions and talked with serene self-confidence but also with humility about their way of life. For them, and many others, records were probably a less relevant factor in their careers than the day to day live work, and this book unavoidably overstates the role of best-selling records as a yardstick for measuring an artist's importance, whereas for them the crucial factor was the size of the crowd they could draw.

One way or another, each of the visitors helped to dispel at least one more misconception that I had held while writing the first edition of *Sound of the City*, and in particular they eroded some of the hard lines I had drawn between the market categories of music. Although *Billboard* logged "Rhythm and Blues" records separately from "Pop" back in the forties and fifties, the black artists were often more aware of pop than I allowed for. They listened to pop, and hoped to play night clubs!

One of the greatest pleasures was to have a visit from Roy Brown, to whom I had given credit for virtually inventing the gospel-blues style that was to permeate right through rhythm and blues in the fifties. Roy himself, gracious and appreciative about such credit, could only insist that his favourite singer was Bing Crosby, and his greatest disappointment was that nobody seemed to think much of his own crooning. Roy's vivacious recollections of life as a rhythm and blues star were peppered with sad tales of the kind of cheating that went on in some of the pioneer indie companies celebrated in this book, but it would have doubled the length of even this enlarged edition to have gone into proper detail of who screwed who and how. Soon after visiting Britain, Roy died back home in Los Angeles; but we won't forget you, Roy.

Among the other visitors to the *Honky Tonk* studio were several musicians from New Orleans who confirmed my impressions that the city's music was the most fundamental source of what we know as rock 'n' roll. Piano players Professor Longhair, Art Neville and Dr. John came in to talk, and so did Earl Palmer, the drummer who helped to spread the unique syncopations of New Orleans through the Los Angeles record industry from the mid-fifties to the mid-sixties when local boy Hal Blaine took over the seat as number one kit-man. It is beyond me to put down in print the complexities of Earl's playing, but I can only insist that it is as fundamental to rock 'n' roll as the electrical amplification of the guitar, and to recommend that you listen to the records he played on, by Fats Domino, Eddie Cochran, and many more.

An unexpected by-product of presenting *Honky Tonk* came from those listeners who were active in the record business themselves, as musicians, singers, and writers, and as promoters, managers, and record company decision-makers. To my surprise and delight, I discovered that people with similar tastes and attitudes to mine were going into London pubs and presenting musical entertainment which generated the kind of atmosphere I had been hoping to evoke with *Honky Tonk*. I began to receive demo tapes from some of these "active" listeners, and I was able to give the first radio "exposure" to

Graham Parker, Elvis Costello and Dire Straits. Watching what happened to them next, I saw the process in action from the front row.

The Graham Parker tape was actually sent in by the man who had recorded it, Dave Robinson, who at that time was juggling at least three roles, as manager of several bands, promoter of gigs in the basement of a pub in Islington called the Hope and Anchor, and engineer-producer in his own studio on the first floor. Practically on his own, Dave created an active scene for up-and-coming bands in London, and he subsequently went on to form Stiff Records, which has brought the world Elvis Costello, Ian Dury, Lene Lovich, and Madness. For bringing that indie pioneer spirit to London, thanks Dave.

After the first edition of *Sound of the City* received a favourable critical reaction, my American publishers invited me to do a follow-up on a subject of my choice, and what I chose was Atlantic Records, whose rags-to-riches story seemed like a fairy-tale from a distance. With encouragement from Jerry Wexler, I spent a month in various parts of the States interviewing the various participants in the story, and wrote *Making Tracks* which was intended to be a kind of "live" companion to *Sound of the City*, making maximum use of first-person accounts of the events which I had reported in the third person. Thoroughly inspired by Jerry's example, I returned to Britain with a resolve to form my own label, which has been realized in Oval Records in collusion with friend and partner Gordon Nelki.

We served our apprenticeship in the music industry by managing Kilburn and the High Roads during the early years of the London "pub rock" era, 1973–74. Led by Ian Dury, the Kilburns were the one band on the circuit who went beyond straightforward celebration of American root music: not only did Ian write some of the funniest and cleverest lyrics I had ever heard, but saxman Davey Payne seemed like a man possessed by demons, and pianist Russell Hardy was miraculously oblivious of fashions and trends, conjuring melodies and rhythms which suggested a Broadway musical one moment, a New Orleans bar the next. Hearing that band play its set night after night probably had a more profound influence on my musical appreciation than anything I had heard since the first early rush of rock 'n' roll records on the American Forces Network back in 1955 and 1956, when Gene Vincent, Fats Domino, and Little Richard records had sounded like something from another planet, compared to the soft stuff on the BBC's Light Programme. Now, at last, the Kilburns obliged me to shake off my prejudices about the innate inferiority of British music and face the fact that there was nothing coming out of America as exciting as this band of odd-balls who threw in bits of

Alma Cogan and (heaven forbid) Freddie Cannon alongside Roland Kirk and Albert Ayler, all based on rhythms which ranged from Calypso and reggae to flat out rock 'n' roll, with interludes of uncategorizable anarchy as everybody got lost.

Kilburn and the High Roads never came close to capturing in a studio the magic of their best live performances, and after a vain effort to make an album, we parted company; four years later, Ian achieved his destiny with a British number one hit on Stiff, "Hit Me With Your Rhythm Stick". Thanks, Ian, for the education.

Oval has continued to work with the people who have walked in with their songs, guitars, and hopes, trying to set up effective contexts for each person's talents and ambitions. Towards the end of 1977, we assembled a group called the Exiles to play and record the songs of two of our writers, Bobby Henry and Jimmy O'Neill, recruiting the then unknown Lene Lovich to play saxophone and sing back-up vocals.

With Lene, we learned at first hand what people mean when they use words like "charisma", "star quality" and "presence". We watched with fascinated delight as Lene would switch into another dimension when it was her turn to perform: a person of great charm, she delivered her songs with an electric intensity that seemed impervious to the context, whether it was a rehearsal room, a small club, or a concert stage.

Where our experience with Kilburn and the High Roads had been an uphill struggle with no final resolution from Oval's point of view, progress with Lene was much more swift. We found songs that suited her unusual, vulnerable voice, and recorded demos which we took to Dave Robinson at Stiff; he allocated a place to Lene for the forthcoming Second Stiff Tour, and commissioned an album for which Lene wrote some intriguing new songs. Less than a year later, we were all rewarded with a top three hit, "Lucky Number", and Lene was a national star whose quirky style and eccentric costumes inspired a host of imitators. For faith and inspiration, thanks Lene.

With all this going on, writing has receded into the background, and I am grateful to the friends who have encouraged me to complete what I had started with the first edition of this book. Ernest Hecht, my British publisher, has exercised diplomacy to achieve the desired effect, and Simon Frith and Tony Russell made helpful comments about early drafts. Tim Blackmore hired me for two projects which not only provided a living while they lasted, but brought me in contact with people I could not otherwise have met: we planned and wrote *The Story of Pop* together for BBC Radio One in 1974, and more recently Tim hired me to present a weekly show at Capital Radio, where I now play more new records than old ones, and look out for people trying to achieve some new combination of rhythm and emotion. As one wave of musicians explore the sounds and effects of synthesised keyboards and drums, another is emerging from Africa, reminding us how satisfying a melody played on guitar can still be. Today, these records sound "foreign" and "new". Tomorrow, they become oldies, take on nostalgic associations, and we want to know more about them: who wrote and produced the records, where, and what was the name of the bass-player?

To all you addicts out there who have got hooked on music and can't let it out of your lives, this book is for you. I'll look forward to your comments.

Charlie Gillett
London, 1983

I am very grateful to the readers of the British publication of this new edition for the painstaking care with which they noted errors of fact and presentation, particularly Chris Gillard, Neil Holliday, and Laurence Purcell.

CG, London, 1984

NOTES

1. THE SOUND BEGINS

1. The twenty-nine included nine by Artie Shaw, seven by Glenn Miller, four by Jimmy Dorsey, and three by Harry James.
2. Joe Murrels, comp. *Daily Mail Book of Golden Records* (London: McWhirter, 1966).
3. For a full account of the styles, songs, and business organization of country and western music, see the entertaining and informative book *Country Music Story* by Robert Shelton and Bert Goldblatt (New York: Bobbs-Merrill, 1966).
4. David Riesman, "Listening to Popular Music", *American Quarterly* 2 (1950): 359–71.
5. The history of films oriented to the adolescent market or featuring "teenagers" in the main roles is related with suitable humour but diligent detail in Richard Staehling, "The Truth about Teen Movies", *Rolling Stone*, 16 January, 1970.
6. Billy Rose's statement is quoted in Vic Fredericks, ed., *Who's Who in Rock 'n' Roll* (New York: Frederick Fell, 1958).
7. *Rock and Roll Personality Parade* (London: *New Musical Express*, 1957), p. 5.

2. FIVE STYLES OF ROCK 'N' ROLL

1. American Forces Network, September, 1962.
2. *New Musical Express*, 21 September, 1956.
3. *Haley News*, 1966.
4. *Hit Parade* (Britain), January, 1957.

3. HOW TO MAKE A ROCK 'N' ROLL RECORD

1. Record sales, 1945–60 in millions

1945	1946	1947	1948	1949	1950	1951	1952
109	218	224	189	173	189	199	214

1953	1954	1955	1956	1957	1958	1959	1960
219	213	277	377	460	511	603	600

Figures from *Billboard.*

2. Breakdown of *Billboard*'s top ten hits, 1955–59, by type of company and style of music

YEAR	1955	1956	1957	1958	1959
Number of records in the top ten	51	55	70	77	89
Records by majors	40	36	30	38	30
Rock 'n' roll	3	9	14	11	9
Pop records	37	27	16	27	21
Records by independents	11	19	40	39	59
Rock 'n' roll	5	10	29	28	29
Pop records	6	9	11	11	30
All rock 'n' roll records	8	19	43	39	38
Pop cover versions of rhythm and blues hits	7	4	–	3	–

4. THE MAJORS

1. In the comparable period in the Beatles' career, from January, 1964, to January, 1966, the group had the best-selling record in the United States in only thirty-one of one hundred and four weeks.
2. *Melody Maker*, 19 July, 1952.
3. Rock 'n' roll singers with most records in the top ten, 1955–59: Elvis Presley, RCA, fifteen; Fats Domino, Imperial, eight; Rick Nelson, Imperial (and Verve), eight; the Everly Brothers, Cadence, six; Pat Boone, Dot, five; the Coasters, Atco, five; Chuck Berry, Chess, four; Jerry Lee Lewis, Sun, three; Little Richard, Specialty, three; Lloyd Price, ABC-Paramount, three.

5. THE INDEPENDENTS

1. Number of records on Atlantic/Atco in the rhythm and blues top ten, as listed in *Billboard*, 1950–59.

1950	1951	1952	1953	1954	1955	1956	1957	1958	1959
3	8	9	6	15	16	17	10	6	11

2. For the full introductory chant, see Richard Goldstein, *The Poetry of Rock* (New York: Bantam Books, 1969).
3. For instance, Lillian Roxon, *Rock Encyclopedia* (New York: Grosset & Dunlap, 1969).

6. THE BLUES-BASED STYLES

1. See bibliography, but particularly the following: Paul Oliver, *The Story of the Blues* (London: Barrie & Rockcliff, 1969); Francis Newton, *The Jazz Scene* (London, Penguin, 1961).
2. See Paul Oliver, *The Story of the Blues*; Charles Keil, "Blues Unlimited", *Urban Blues* (University of Chicago Press, 1966).
3. See various writings of LeRoi Jones, including *Blues People* (New York: William Morrow & Co., Inc., 1963) and *Black Music* (New York: William Morrow & Co., Inc., 1968).
4. Malcolm X, *Autobiography* (New York: Grove Press, 1965).
5. LeRoi Jones, from notes to Willis Jackson's album *Thunderbird* (Prestige).
6. Notes from the LP *The Incomparable Cecil Gant* (Sound 601).
7. Interview with Pete Welding, *Collector's Classics*, 2 (a *Blues Unlimited* publication, 1964).
8. "World of Soul", *Billboard*, 1966.

7. AFTER THE BLUES

1. Interview with the author, *Record Mirror*, 7 June, 1969.
2. Interview with Welding, *Collector's Classics*, 2, 1964.

8. BACK HOME

1. See Constance Rourke, *American Humor* (New York: Doubleday & Company, Anchor Books, 1953).

2. For a fuller and fascinating discussion of King, see Charles Keil, *Urban Blues*.

9. DO THAT AGAIN, THIS WAY

1. *Record World*, 12 March, 1966.
2. The girl group hits had been the Teen Queens' "Eddie My Love" (RPM, 1956), the Bobettes' "Mr. Lee" (Atlantic, 1957), the Chantels' "Maybe" (Gone, 1958), and the Quintones' "Down the Aisle of Love" (Hunt, 1958).
3. Among the Detroit labels were Fortune, Sensation, and JVB. The French magazine *Rhythm and Blues* (no. 36) devoted its entire issue to the history and discography of Detroit music.
4. Top ten hits by the Motown Corporation, 1960–69

1960	1961	1962	1963	1964	1965	1966	1967	1968	1969
1	1	4	6	5	10	12	14	13	13

10. ARE WE TOGETHER?

1. Berns used the name "Bert Russell" on his compositions, made some soul records as a singer, for Sue, using the name Russell Byrd, and even recorded as a country and western singer.
2. Ragavoy used the name "Norman Meade" on his compositions.
3. For an observation of how Bobby Bland's career and music is planned by his record company, see Charles Keil, *Urban Blues*.

11. TRANSATLANTIC ECHOES

1. *New Musical Express*, 23 October, 1953.
2. "Englishman Who Sings the Blues", *Ebony*, August, 1966.

INDEX OF NAMES

INDEX OF SONGS

INDEX OF ALBUMS

INDEX OF FILMS

INDEX OF LABEL ROSTERS

Copyright Owners and Sources of Photographs

Every effort has been made to trace photographers and owners to ensure proper credits; any inadvertent errors will be corrected in future editions upon appropriate notification, c/o the publisher. Photos are reproduced with kind permission of the following copyright owners and archivists. Special thanks to Bo Sandell, Bill Millar and John Beecher for their generous and speedy responses to my requests for help.

Copyright Owners (where not shown with caption)	*Page Number*
ABKCO	25 (bottom left)
Ace Records	15 (bottom left)
Atlantic Records	5 (top & bottom), 6 (top left), 7 (top left), 13, 30 (top), 31 (left), 33 (top), 36 (top)
Cadence Records	15 (top)
Castle Communications	10 (bottom)
Curtom Records	39 (bottom left)
Demon Records	32 (bottom), 39 (bottom right)
Elektra Records	34 (bottom)
EMI Records	4 (top & bottom), 6 (bottom left & right), 12, 23 (top), 18 (bottom), 25 (bottom right), 37 (bottom)
Fantasy Records	7 (bottom right), 31 (left), 36 (bottom), 37 (top)
Island Records	39 (top)
Kama Sutra Records	28 (top)
King Records	1, 6 (top right), 17 (bottom)
MCA Records	2, 7 (bottom left & right), 8 (bottom), 16 (top & bottom)
Polygram Records	3, 20 (top & bottom), 21, 22 (top & bottom), 24, 26 (top & bottom), 28 (bottom), 32 (top), 33 (bottom), 35 (bottom)
RCA Records	9 (top)
Scepter Records	15 (bottom right)
Sony Records	19, 29 (top), 38
Vee Jay Records	27 (top & bottom)
Warner Music	40

Sources

Bo Sandell Collection	1, 2, 3, 4 (top & bottom), 5 (bottom), 6 (bottom left), 7 (top left), 14 (inset)
Charlie Gillett collection	3, 5 (top), 6 (top left & right), 7 (top right), 8 (bottom), 10 (bottom), 11 (bottom) 13 (top), 15 (top; bottom left), 16 (top & bottom), 17 (top & bottom), 18 (bottom), 19 through 30; 31 (right), 32 (top), 33 (top), 34, 35 (bottom), 37 (top), 39 (top; and bottom left), 40
BFI Stills Library, London	6 (bottom right), 8 (top), 9 (bottom), 10 (top), 11 (top), 18 (top), 29 (top), 35 (top)
MCA Records	7 (bottom left & right)
Malcolm Jones Collection, by arrangement with John Beecher	9 (top), 31 (left) 33 (bottom), 36 (top & bottom)
Bill Millar Collection	12, 14 (main picture), 15 (bottom right), 38, 39 (bottom right)
BMI Archives	22
Demon Records	32 (bottom)
EMI Records	37 (bottom)

ABOUT THE AUTHOR

CHARLIE GILLETT's other books include five volumes of *Rock Files*, *Making Tracks*, and *Rock Almanac*, and he has written for *Rolling Stone* and *New Musical Express*. He was instrumental in launching such names as Elvis Costello, Graham Parker, and Dire Straits. He is at present a disc jockey in London, where he makes his home, and runs Oval, an independent record label and publishing company.

CPSIA information can be obtained
at www.ICGtesting.com
Printed in the USA
LVHW092009140522
718767LV00002B/3

9 780306 806834